IN THE BEGINNINGS
Early Man and His Gods

IN THE BEGINNINGS

Early Man and His Gods

H. R. HAYS

G. P. Putnam's Sons   New York

MANUFACTURED IN THE UNITED STATES OF AMERICA

VAN REES PRESS • NEW YORK

To ALFRED KROEBER

a great scholar in both the fields of archaeology and anthropology

Acknowledgments

Thanks are due to the University of Chicago Press for permission to quote from the *Gilgamesh Epic* and *The Babylonian Genesis,* translated by Alexander Heidel; to Doubleday & Company for material from *Thespis,* by Theodor Gaster; to Harper & Row for material from the Torchbook edition of *Sumerian Mythology,* by Noah Kramer; to the University of Texas Press for permission to quote Lee M. Hollander's translation of *The Poetic Edda;* to David Neiman, lecturer in comparative religion at the New School, for a critical reading of the entire manuscript; and to Walter Minton without whose encouragement the book would not have been written.

i

Contents

7

ASIA

AFRICA

45. What Happened in Early Religion 527

Summary and conclusions—hunting magic—animal identification—trickster and shaman develop into earliest deity—shaman and creator god—head taking, warrior ethos—fertility goddess and bull as male potency symbol—sacral king and blood sacrifices—priesthoods and political power—growth of pantheons—religion and the unconscious.

The illustrations appear in sections following pages 64, 160, 320, and 448.

MAPS

Paleolithic Europe

CHAPTER I

What Is Religion?

*Need for sociological criteria—distinction between religion and science—con-
cept of mana—consolatory role of religion and myth—art provides religious
symbols—primitive religion creates social cohesion—geographical plan of
book.*

THIS book covers the beginnings and early growth of religion
throughout the world, from the first traces of spiritual activity
deduced from the heritage of the cave dwellers to, and including, the ancient
city civilizations of Eurasia and the Americas. In the modern era it covers
the beliefs and practices of contemporary preliterates in Africa, Asia,
Oceania, and North and South America, in many ways allied to those of the
past. We are here, therefore, dealing with religion as a folk institution before it was transformed by an individual founder or prophet. Of course, in
the ancient world and in the primitive present, there were many individual
contributions by imaginative shamans or priests but these were absorbed
into tradition and the imprint of a single mind is less important than the
over-all shaping of group acceptance.

In the course of the story we shall become familiar with the curious relation which arises between men and animals as the ancient hunter invents
magical recipes that he believes will ensure an abundance of game. We shall
also see that this relationship to animals is not easily forgotten and persists all over the world in later stages of culture. We shall examine the
practices arising in relation to burial of the dead, rites which develop from
the placing of a few artifacts in the grave to the building of great stone
tombs or pyramids, equipped with all the luxury of this life and intended to
maintain the status of the deceased in the house of death or in another world.

We shall see that as man made the great transition from hunting and
gathering to a settled existence dependent upon agriculture and domestic
animals the form of his religious imagination also changed. In some areas
woman's ability to bear children was symbolically associated with the fertility of the fields and even with animal increase, giving rise to the poetic

concept of the earth mother or fertility goddess. Likewise the potency of the bull became a symbol of male strength and warlike prowess.

It will also become clear that the increasing complexity of man's social organization shaped his beliefs concerning his dead ancestors. Dramatized sometimes by fantastic images, sometimes represented by musical instruments, these disembodied spirits were placated or urged to fulfill their duties as members of the tribe.

Above all we shall find that man has always danced before his gods, danced to attract their attention or danced in their shapes, believing himself possessed by supernatural power. And thus, from the animal mimicry of the shaman to the barbaric ceremonials, bright with feathers and jewels, which preceded the bloody rites carried out on the pyramids of Middle America, music and song have accompanied the rhythmic pattern of prayer or invocation.

Before embarking on this journey into the past and into remote areas of desert and jungle, where an astonishing variety of strange, violent, and often brutal practices will be encountered, it is necessary to clarify the basic unity of the subject. What is religion? There have been various definitions.

The modern sophisticate will think of numerous answers—from going to church on Sunday to private mysticism. When we try to define the religious area in nontechnological stages of society we also encounter a wide range of human activities from spells which make use of a dried frog to elaborate and poetic rituals chanted by a state-supported priesthood. Are we going to rule out the dried frog in favor of only those aspects of ceremonial which we find aesthetically pleasing? Obviously this method will not work. We must search for some characteristic which really helps to define our subject.

One method is to decide arbitrarily that there is a special emotion, commonly called awe, with which religious activity is infused, which divides it from the secular. In the first place, it is next to impossible to decide whether an ancient or primitive people really felt or feels awe. If we must depend upon archaeological facts they may tell us little. If we are dealing with modern primitives they may be enigmatic or unable to describe their own feelings accurately. Furthermore, in some parts of the world, such as Africa or China, dead ancestors are treated like members of the family and scolded or praised according to whether they seem harmful or helpful. No trace of awe can be found, yet it is certainly wrong to rule ancestor cults out of religion. Awe, then, is a subjective test which will not do.

The trouble with such approaches is that religion is a sensitive, personal affair. The scholar or historian has tended to concentrate on activities which have some relation to his own beliefs or which he can at least interpret in terms of his own beliefs. If we are to understand cultural history, however, of which religion is an important part, a sociological and psychological approach is necessary.

Let us start then from a simple statement. Most people, no matter whether they are hunters, fishermen, lawyers or bank clerks, want certain things out of life. They want enough to eat, they want to live as long as possible and keep well, they want sexual satisfaction, they want to avoid being afraid or anxious, they want to have children and to provide their children with these same benefits, and finally they want to be successful as success is defined in their group, in other words they want social approval.

There are two ways of attaining these aims; in modern times one has come to be called scientific. When Pasteur took bottles containing nutritious jelly up to high altitudes, exposed them and stoppered them, nothing grew in the jelly. Others, equally sterile, he exposed to the ordinary air in his home town. In the latter, molds and tiny organisms grew in the jelly. He repeated this experiment many times. Since the same result always recurred under the same conditions, it was quantitative proof that there were organisms in the air about him. He felt it reasonable to believe that a specific action was related to a specific result. Thus the scientific method assumes a certain attitude toward cause and effect. In performing this experiment, Pasteur, although he wished to prove something, was ready to accept whatever result repetition seemed to show. He was searching for an abstract law, a law which had nothing to do with human feelings or desires. We all know how further experiments of the same sort led to the formulation of the germ theory of disease which, in turn, affected medical practice and eventually helped people to keep well.

What does this have to do with religion? As a matter of fact, among ancient and primitive peoples the warding off and curing of disease is always the job of the religious specialist. His method is quite different from that of the scientist. It never occurs to him to perform experiments to find out what causes the disease or what may cure it. Very often, instead, he has a dream or he throws himself into a trance during which he has a vision telling him that an ancestor or spirit is making trouble. Then a spell or an offering is used to make the spirit behave and cure the patient.

In contrast to the scientist, therefore, the religious specialist operates on an emotional plane. He does what his feelings and imagination tell him to do in order to obtain the gift of health. He does not check his remedy to make sure it really works. If the patient dies he has an emotional way out. His magic was not strong enough or the spirit perversely refused the offering. In any case both the patient and doctor feel happier, whether the disease is actually cured or not.

This distinction between religion and science applies all along the line in man's efforts to get what he wants. On the one hand emotion, human will and imagination dictate what is to be done to obtain happiness and success, on the other repeated experiment and logical analysis are used to search for basic relationships in the world. When discovered, these relationships can often be applied practically and by so doing we get penicillin, television sets and rockets. Such benefits are by-products, however, for the original research must be done with the attitude that man is an atomic pattern among the inconceivably vast atomic patterns of the universe.

How far has all this brought us in our search for a definition of religion? One thing has emerged and that is a difference in method by which man tries to get what he wants and tries to understand the world. By elimination, the whole area of thinking and feeling, willing and doing which disregards experiment tends to be religious. As a result magic formulas, traditional stories of the supernatural, chanted rituals, sacred objects, pictures, idols, temples, sacrifices, ceremonial sexual intercourse, are all a part of religious expression, including the dried frog with which we began.

Since primitive people never make a clear-cut distinction between religion and science in their own minds, although they do possess simple scientific knowledge, their religious attitude tends to infiltrate all of their social behavior. For instance, the Trobriand Islander knows a great deal about the qualities of the soil; he also knows that he must plant and cultivate in order to grow a successful yam crop. Yet all this is not enough, because he must also have rain if the plants are to sprout. His practical experimental knowledge does not help him here but religion does or he thinks it does. As a result he chants a magic spell.

It is not only in practical matters that religion is important to ancient and primitive peoples. In the list of benefits that most men wish for from life, the desire to avoid anxiety or fear bulks very large. The scientific approach tends to explain and make acceptable to modern man much that happens in the world. Man is not fond of novelty. Educational psychologists have shown that disruption of habit causes distress to human beings and even animals. The primitive, therefore, who does not easily search for logical cause and effect, reacts with real anguish to the strange or unusual. Evidence from all over the earth shows that he does not investigate each new or disturbing event with the aim of understanding it but instead develops a generalized feeling about it. He tends to believe that there is an underlying power, unseen and above or beyond the norms of his daily habits, which must be dealt with. This power has been given the name of *mana* in anthropological literature.

Mana infuses things or events which cause concern to primitive peoples almost like an electric current. It is felt concretely in such occurrences as birth, sexual maturity, and death. Since early religion is shaped by men, the other sex, and particularly female procreative power, is imbued with mana. Likewise the unusual person, the shaman who sees visions, the priest or king is full of mana, as is the successful warrior. Mana is not, however, limited to human beings. Comets, strange animals, unusual weather conditions, too much or too little success, even weapons used in warfare are connected with mana.

Mana is often thought of as dangerous, contagious (hence rituals of purification) and frightening, but imagination and the human will dictate ways to control it and eventually to use it. Since it is outside the normal course of events it becomes the means by which man challenges the determinism of what, in modern times, we call scientific law, and a way of asserting his will. The magician or priest is a specialist in mana. In dealing with this dangerous stuff he may lose the benefits of the ordered world and become a kind of outlaw or even a hero who willingly or unwillingly dies a sacrificial death in order to obtain benefits for his fellows.

From this it follows that ancient and primitive religion involves nearly all of man's psychic life. Religion is not only a technique for obtaining practical benefits, it becomes a solace for the deepest anxieties. Impersonal scientific investigation satisfies only a part of man's basic needs. Something must be done to shape his emotions and make them bearable when a relative or friend dies. Thus he creates techniques for protecting himself from and propitiating the dead and sometimes he pictures an afterworld in which the deceased enjoys eternal bliss. When an eclipse of the sun threatens to darken the earth forever, he shapes a story to explain it and beats drums to drive away the jaguar which is eating his source of light. Everything must have a beginning, or at least man demands such a pattern. The primitive therefore invents various stories about the beginning of the world, his own race, or various tribal habits. These stories often justify or explain rites or ceremonies.

Which came first, the myth or the rite? There is probably no general rule. In some cases myth arose after the action. The personification of the sacrificial fire in Vedic religion is evidently secondary. On the other hand, among the plains Indians of America, the regalia and proper performance of dances originated dreams and fantasies. In fact, dreams and waking fantasies stemming from the unconscious play an important role in determining the forms of religious expression.

Having come this far, it will be clear that art, being nonexperimental, intuitive and emotional, falls into the area of religion. Although, in the historical era, art has achieved autonomy, in ancient times and among primitives it is practiced either by the religious specialist or by a specialist who serves him. Man is the only symbol-using animal. One of the curious characteristics of civilization is the fact that various images are accepted as standing for feelings, ideas, people, events or other images. The connection is quite arbitrary but it produces pleasure and emotional satisfaction. The power of mana, therefore, is everywhere made concrete in terms of symbols which are contributed by the artist. It is for this reason that so much of our study of early religion must concern itself with pictures, idols, stories, song, architectural monuments, and dances.

But, it may be objected, if religion is all fantasy and irrationality, concerned with nothing which can be described by science, what real purpose does it serve? We have already indicated its consolatory function which helps man to contain the disturbing elements in his world. The sociologist sees an important extension of this function. When human beings decide to live together in groups, they are obliged to inhibit many of their appetites and desires in order to remain in harmony with their fellows. Here, of course, religion performs a most important function in justifying and symbolizing the rules and restrictions. Taboos, developed to avoid the dangers of mana, are religious; also they justify police regulations. Primitive ethics are based upon them and upon general group approval or disapproval. Moreover, as restrictions and obligations become symbolized in more and more aesthetic form, as they are embodied in myth and ritual, they become important group experiences; they are woven into the texture of communal living, giving it color and individuality. It is this basic shared experience and this general acceptance of certain symbols which create the conscious character of the tribe.

In the ancient and primitive world, therefore, religion unites the social unit, channelizes human anxiety into aesthetic forms and lends poetry and meaning to man's conception of the universe and himself.

Throughout the present account of ancient and primitive religions an attempt has been made to assemble the available facts in context. In many early treatises on this subject isolated bits of evidence were plucked from all over the world and fitted into some preconceived scheme. In the writer's view, discussion of religious phenomena apart from their background inevitably results in distortion. Only when we have some notion of the relation between psychic and material life do we see the former in any sort of perspective.

Then, too, the nature of religion cannot be grasped by merely listing gods, cults and ceremonial details. The emphasis, feeling tone, sincerity and dynamism of belief are also important; so is the atmosphere evoked in ritual activity. Ideally anthropology should be total. In actual practice (especially in the case of older reports), often all that is available is a catalogue of facts. Religions known only through archaeological investigation are, of course, even more skeletally recorded. Whenever possible, however, the writer has attempted to sketch a configuration of culture. Such a program requires a good deal of space but it has the advantage of stressing the fact that every religion is innately related to the special human situation of its adherents.

The geographical plan of the present book makes clear the movements of peoples and the flow of culture throughout the habitable world. A secondary historical linkage has also been attempted, although the over-all pattern has necessitated moving backward and forward in time.

Value judgments are not supposed to enter into anthropology but even the driest monograph exhibits them; they influence the author in his choice and emphasis and very often tip the balance when it comes to the acceptance of explanations or theories. The writer confesses to a prejudice against bloodshed and violence. The reader will therefore discover that non-neutral language is employed in describing these aspects of human behavior.

CHAPTER 2

Skulls and Bear Cult

Lower Paleolithic—evidence suggesting headhunting or secondary burial—analogical material from the Papuans and Jívaro—treatment of bear skulls as proof of hunting magic—Ainu bear ceremony as analogy.

THE story of religion doubtless begins when man first acquired language, the ability to manipulate symbols and to communicate with his fellows. There is no record of these developments and what hints we do obtain from archaeology concerning the early Stone Age are tantalizingly fragmentary. Later on, more data come to light but throughout prehistory scholarship must depend entirely on material objects which have survived the eroding forces of nature. Thus it comes about that whatever can be said about prehistoric man's spiritual and intellectual attainments results from a kind of skilled detective work. The relationships between artifacts, bones of animals, a study of weather conditions, together with the skeletal remains of primitive man himself, provide certain clues. When man reaches the point of making pictures of living things, a kind of language emerges which scholars can attempt to decipher.

The study of prehistory, therefore, when it goes beyond description, classification and dating of objects, necessarily involves a good deal of speculation. Data from the cultures of living preliterates can be used with caution to supplement what is unearthed by the excavator's spade. It must always be remembered, however, that speculation and argument by analogy must be accepted provisionally. New facts are continually coming to light which change the picture to such an extent that the historical detective must be always ready to modify his theories.

At the same time it must also be remembered that speculation, backed by critical examination of all sorts of evidence, constitutes the creative side of scholarship. Classification and dating are not ends in themselves. Some attempt must be made to interpret what is being classified or the study of ancient culture becomes sterile and lacking in meaning. Archaeology is a young science which has spent its first hundred years on the pedestrian task of assembling evidence. It is only recently that some work has been done to clarify geographical relationships and we can begin to trace the interplay between ancient cultures with something like certainty.

It is convenient to begin with the religion of the Stone Age in Europe, not because this area is believed to be the point of origin of Homo sapiens but because European scholars have understandably dug in their own backyards. It is here that the best detective work has been done. Although we know something of Pithecanthropus, who made the all-purpose hand axes and managed to survive by migrating during the middle periods of glaciation, it is only when we come to the Neanderthal man and peoples like him that we begin to get a hint of psychic activities. From his habit of occupying caves which became available during the next to the last glacial period, we obtain more data concerning his activities, since his detritus has been preserved on the floors of these rock shelters.

Neanderthal man has been publicized as a low-browed, hairy, projecting-jawed brute. The specimens which have been excavated in Europe conform to this image but finds in more temperate climates such as the Near East suggest men somewhat less shaggy and more modern-looking. Exclusively a hunter and fisherman by trade, Neanderthal man made small hand axes, awls, and used wooden spears with points hardened by charring. Modern Pygmies use such spears in hunting such large animals as elephants. Since chipped scrapers have been recovered, the Neanderthaler probably dressed skins and wore them but he had not advanced to the point of using bone or antler for tools. He was not yet an artist, if we can trust the negative evidence, since not a single carving or engraving or painting has been identified with his culture and absolutely no personal ornaments have been discovered.

The first guess we can make concerning religion in the culture involves human skulls. A skull found at Monte Circeo, Italy, was broken open at the base as if for the purpose of extracting the brain. The skull was surrounded by stones and near it other groups of stone surrounded animal bones. Other skulls found at Steinheim and Weimar, Germany, and at Pech de l'Aze, France, had been treated in the same way. A large number of skulls found at Krapina in Yugoslavia exhibited the same operation, as did the still earlier skulls at Chou-k'ou-tien in China. In the case of the Chou-k'ou-tien man, the long bones of the skeleton were also found split open as if the marrow had been extracted.

What is the significance of these emptied skulls? Three suggestions have been put forward: headhunting, ritual cannibalism, and secondary burial.

Evidence from contemporary preliterate cultures of the fishing and hunting stage indicates that the head is often an object of special significance. The head of a Polynesian chief was so sacred that it could not be touched by another person. If the chief touched his own head with his finger he was obliged to bring his finger immediately to his nose to breathe in the sanctity the finger acquired from the head. Captain Cook recorded a ceremony involving decapitation on his third voyage to Tahiti. In an emergency, he wrote, when the chief considered human sacrifice to be necessary, the victim (said to be generally a criminal) was killed with clubs or stones. Cook counted forty-nine skulls lying on a sort of stone platform. Actual headhunting ceremonies have been described among the Kiwai Papuans of British New Guinea. In this group, if a man had not brought back a head of an enemy, he was not supposed to begin regular sexual inter-course with his wife. When he did obtain a trophy head, he decorated himself with red paint, and if he begot a son about that time the son was sure to become a strong fighting man. In actual battle the adolescent boys were brought forward when a wounded enemy was about to be killed. A boy was made to swallow a medicine which had been touched to the head of the enemy. He was then told to cut off the head. Sometimes the arms, legs, or penis were also cut off. Dried blood was kept and administered to the boys to make them warriors. After the battle the heads were placed in a row while the great fighters of the tribe went and stood over them with their legs wide apart and stone-headed clubs on their shoulders. They stood facing the direction of the enemies' home. The young men were ordered to crawl between the lines of legs. Ginger was rubbed on the heads and given to the boys to swallow so that they would never be afraid. During the crawling operation the boy had to bite the forehead of one head, lift the trophy in his teeth, and put it down. Then from the same head the medicine man cut a bit of flesh, chewed it with an herb and made the boy swallow it. The in-formant remembered that when he was forced to crawl over the bloody heads as a boy it had made him very sick—"Smell belong heads too bad." Despite his squeamishness the older men sternly held him to his duty, in-sisting it would make him a great warrior. After the ceremony the heads were stored under the house platform.

Other Papuans removed the brains from the enemy's skull, ate them, and deposited the skull in the family sanctuary. The Jívaro of Ecuador were accustomed to carry out a ceremony after the shrinking of the captured heads had been completed. The heads were dipped in tobacco water, chicha (maize beer) and pure water. The liquids were then poured into the mouth of the headhunter.

It has been argued, in disproof of the theory that the Stone Age man was a ritual headhunter, that when heads are cut off and preserved for ceremonial purposes one or two neck vertebrae still adhere. This is not true of the Lower Paleolithic skulls. If, however, brain cannibalism were practiced the vertebrae would be absent. Likewise trophy heads are sometimes emptied of their contents before preservation. At Ofnet, Bavaria, some skulls dating from a later period (Mesolithic) were found arranged in two nests of concentric circles, one containing twenty-seven skulls, and the second six. Some of these did have the cervical vertebrae attached and many had the marks of lethal hatchet blows. Powdered red ochre surrounded them and, in the case of the women's skulls, deer teeth and snail shells were present, all indications of burial ritual.

The case for headhunting in the Lower Paleolithic, therefore, is fairly strong. The alternate theory, proposed by Henri Breuil, that of secondary burial or cult of skulls, presupposes a different psychological attitude. If the headhunter regarded the skull of his victim as a magical, strength-giving trophy, an object which was to be both feared and placated, in secondary burial the head of a beloved relative became a kind of household amulet.

The Kiwai headhunters also practiced this rite. When a relative was buried, the grave was filled up to the head and its flesh was cut through to help it decay. Each day the relatives came and poured water over the head, slowly pushing the flesh off the skull. The men who carried out this ritual meanwhile painted themselves black, beginning with their feet and carrying the mourning color a little higher up the body each day. When the skull was finally taken from the body, it was decorated; lips, ears and nose were modeled from beeswax, eyes and nostrils were indicated with pieces of shell. The whole was surmounted with a feather headdress. It was placed in a shrine around which a dance was held. One of the songs went as follows:

> My friend is now a spirit;
> That man he sits inside the shrine.
> I try to wake him up.
> He is my friend no more.
> My throat is no good now [an expression of mourning].

The relatives then walked around the shrine waving branches. This was done to make the spirit belonging to the head fly away. Afterward the skull was kept for some time in the house.

The Negritos of Ceylon and the Andaman Islanders used to carry the skulls of their dead with them as magical mementoes. The Andaman Islanders, after burying their dead, went through a period of mourning during which several taboos were observed and the corpse had time to decay. It was then dug up, the soft tissues removed by washing, and the bones brought back to the settlement where they were again mourned. The skull and lower jaw were decorated with red and white earth colors and hung about the neck of the survivor from a plaited cord. Parents wore the skulls of their children, women wore the skulls of husbands, children, or brothers and sisters.

The skull found at Monte Circeo showed that the owner had been killed by a blow on the temple; it had originally been elevated on a stake and surrounded by a ring of stone. Since it was also associated with animals' bones surrounded by stones, some ritual practice is indicated. Certain skulls from the Upper Paleolithic in the Grotte des Hommes, France, were found carefully arranged on a rock slab and in the Placard cave a female skull was surrounded by shell ornaments. The weight of the evidence "leaves no doubt at all as to the existence of rites involving a cult of skull," writes Henri Breuil.

If Stone Age man practiced some type of skull cult, we cannot be sure of its precise nature. Evidently the head was felt to possess a magical character. If something in the nature of secondary burial went on, the chances are that kinship relationships were strong and probably tinged with religious significance. Whether the spirits of the dead were actually worshiped we have no way of knowing.

Another proof that the Paleolithic man's dead were of significance to him can be derived from certain burials. So far no interments earlier than the period of the Neanderthaler have been found. This may be accounted for by the fact that since Pithecanthropus did not live in caves, bodies which he buried in the open would have washed away. At any rate, the oldest indications of concern for the welfare of the dead occur in such Neanderthal burials as those at Spy, Belgium, and Le Moustier, France. The latter revealed a young man's skeleton lying on its right side, the legs slightly bent, the head resting on the right arm, the right hand close to the back of the head. There was a pillow of flint flakes under the head, a hand ax and a flint scraper near the left hand. Other tools and animal bones were scattered about the skeleton. At Spy charcoal indicated that a fire had been lit above the grave. At La Ferrassie, France, a whole cemetery was found. The skeletons were accompanied by food offerings placed a little distance away; one man had a flat stone at his head and one on each shoulder. He was also covered with chipped flint tools and bones. Burials of Neanderthal peoples have been found in other areas, such as Mount Carmel, Palestine, where the skeletons were buried in a tightly flexed position. In central Asia a child's skeleton was found surrounded by a circle of ibex horns.

What can be inferred from these facts? It is evident from the presence of grave goods such as flint artifacts and animal bones that death was considered a kind of continuation of life and that the dead needed to be provided for. This is the first indication of what has been called the living corpse concept. The flexed position of some of the skeletons mentioned above has been cited as an indication that the survivors feared the dead and perhaps bound the bodies to prevent their harming the living. The layer of charcoal above the Spy burial suggests that a fire had been lit to warm the chilled body. The presence of animal bones in large numbers in at least one site has been used as an argument that funeral feasts were held. Such a practice might suggest a cult of the dead, endowing them with unusual powers for good or evil, or at least enabling them to exercise some magical influence over the living.

Again data from contemporary hunting and fishing culture is suggestive. Maurice Leenhardt discusses the psychic attitudes of the Kanakas of New Caledonia (who also incidentally conserve ancestral skulls). This people's religious belief is almost exclusively concerned with ancestor worship. To them death is merely a negative aspect of life; the dead can always return. In fact, an informant who had been to Australia explained that the great crowds walking about in the cities were proof that many dead were present among the living. To the Kanakas, ancestors were gods to the extent that they were supermen who helped their descendants in war, in artistic activities, in housebuilding and in other social matters. The ancestors were thought of as having insubstantial bodies but real heads, hence the preservation of skulls. The continuity between life and death presents a contrast to modern man's historical sense. "The Kanaka sees perennialness. No division is possible, no end, no death, no past or future. The Kanaka lives in the present and also lives in the era of myth."

If Neanderthal man was concerned with one of the great mysteries, that of death, he was also a practical person. Living as he did the precarious life of a hunter, he was bound to be concerned with the problem of plenty of game. A series of spectacular discoveries in Switzerland, France, Austria and Germany tells us something concerning his attitude toward one of his most important game animals. The caves of the Alps during the last glacial period were inhabited by great shaggy cave bears, one of the most dangerous beasts which early man dared to track down and kill. In one cave in Austria the deposits of bear bones were so immense that phosphates were extracted from them for industrial purposes. It has been estimated that during a period of about 10,000 years, 30,000 to 50,000 of these ancient animals must have died there.

In 1917 Emil Bächler, a Swiss archaeologist, discovered in a cave 8,000 feet up in the mountains of Switzerland, the Drachenloch (or Dragon's Hole), a series of bear skulls which showed that the early hunters had practiced some sort of ceremonial dealing with this formidable animal. A large antechamber led to a second room which had served as a human habitation, since two fireplaces were found. Within this living room there was a sort of bin with a limestone wall full of cave-bear bones, among them many skulls, arranged in groups. There were traces of blows which showed that the bears had been killed. The investigators also found a stone chest about three feet square with a limestone lid containing seven bear skulls and a number of long bones. The third portion of the cave revealed six bear skulls set in niches, some with other bones, all lying on flat stones bordered by other flat stones. In one case a skull had the femur of a smaller bear thrust through the arch of the cheekbone. At the back wall of room three, there were nine more skulls behind stone slabs leaning against the rock. The same archaeologist found a skull behind a slab and five others, together with long bones, within another cave in eastern Switzerland appropriately named Wildenmannlisloch (Wild Man's Hole). Other discoveries of a similar nature occurred in Yugoslavia and in the cave of Petershöhle in the South German Alps. In the latter cave countless skulls were set in niches both on and three feet above the floor, and others were set on stone slabs. As recently as 1946 five skulls in a circle, three on stone slabs, were found in a cave in Cluny, France, and in 1950 in the Salzofen cave in the Austrian Alps five more skulls were found in nichelike hollows. They were placed on rocks, surrounded by other rocks and covered with a film of charcoal. Other cave-bear bones lay near them.

As always, ingenious minds have come up with several explanations. A simple theory is that the skulls were stored as a spare meat supply, the brain being a delicacy. This has been dismissed because meat would not keep long and also it seems unlikely that so many caches should have been forgotten. Moreover meat is normally stored by hunting peoples after some process of drying or smoking so that it will not spoil.

The careful preservation of the skulls, the impressive manner in which they were set on stone slabs as if on altars, and in some cases the patterns in which they were arranged, all point to a hunting ritual, some more than casual relationship between man and the animal upon which he subsists.

Research among contemporary primitives reveals certain practices which by analogy help us to picture the Neanderthal ritual. The two constant factors in these finds are the emphasis upon the bear as game and a special treatment of the animal's head. A. Irving Hallowell makes some interesting observations concerning the relation between animals and hunting peoples. "Animals are believed to have essentially the same sort of animating agency which man possesses. They have a language of their own, can understand what human beings say and do, have forms of social or tribal organization, and live a life which is parallel in other respects to that of human societies." Some species of animals are thought to have magical powers; they may turn themselves into other creatures or even into human beings (as evidenced in fairy tales and folklore). Some use their special powers to help man in his pursuits and others may be hostile to him. They sometimes communicate with man through dreams; they may be guardian spirits, messengers of the

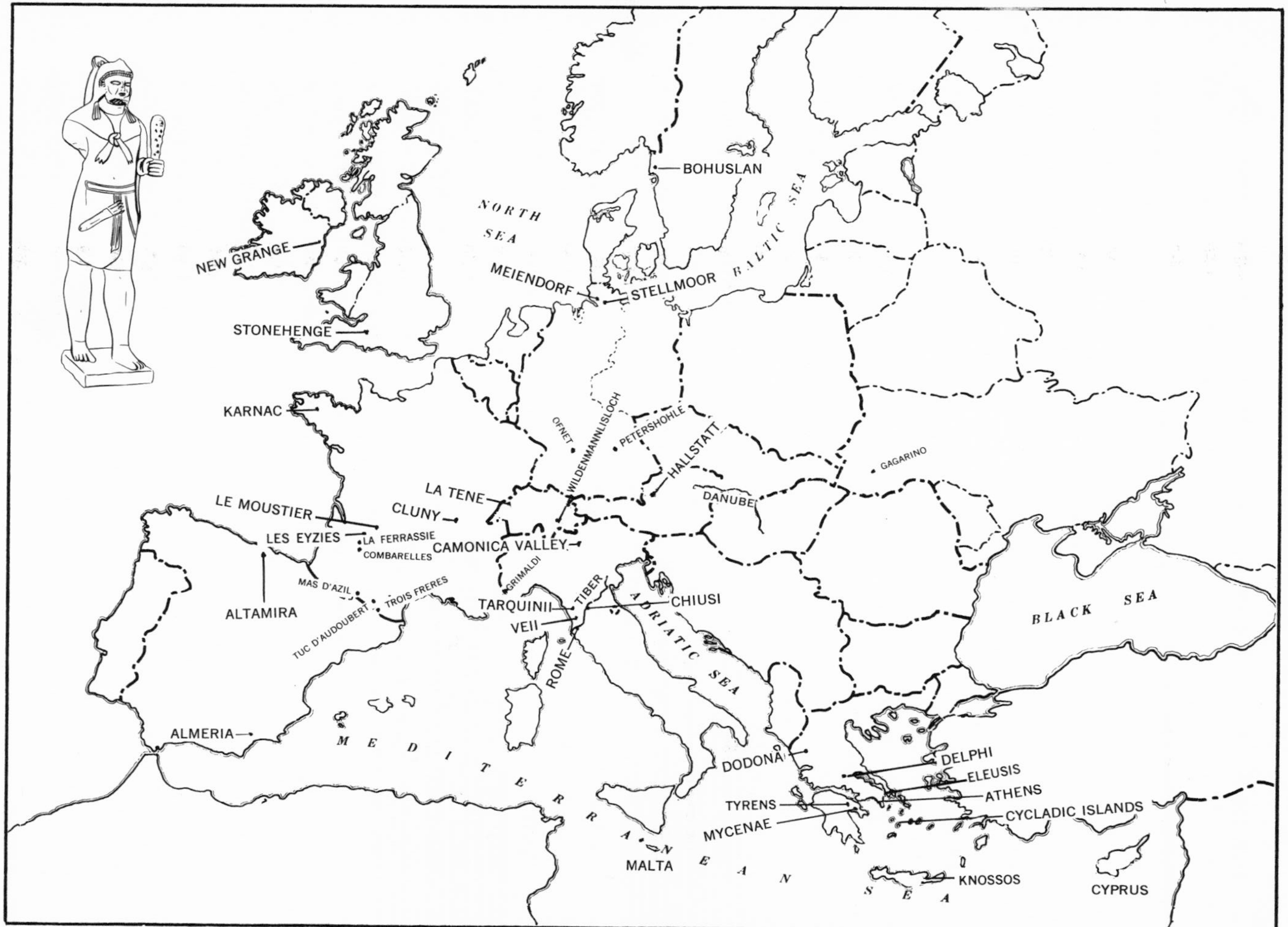

EUROPE

BLACK SEA

BALTIC SEA

NORTH SEA

ADRIATIC SEA

MEDITERRANEAN SEA

AEGEAN SEA

CYPRUS
KNOSSOS
CYCLADIC ISLANDS
ATHENS
ELEUSIS
DELPHI
DODONA
TYRENS
MYCENAE
MALTA
CHIUSI
TIBER
ROME
VEII
TARQUINII
GRIMALDI
DANUBE
HALLSTATT
PETERSHÖHLE
WILDENMANNLISLOCH
GARGANO
OFNET
LA TENE
CLUNY
CAMONICA VALLEY
LA FERRASSIE
COMBARELLES
LES EYZIES
TROIS FRÈRES
MAS D'AZIL
LE MOUSTIER
TUC D'AUDOUBERT
ALTAMIRA
ALMERIA
KARNAC
STONEHENGE
NEW GRANGE
BOHUSLAN
STELLMOOR
MEIENDORF

gods, or temporary or permanent abodes of gods themselves. When men die their souls are sometimes thought to enter into animals, and animals are often considered to be human ancestors. In all this complicated psychical network of relationships it is not surprising that hunting strategy comprises much more than mere skill in capturing game; it often involves propitiation, flattery, cajoling, or even a reverential attitude.

Throughout the northern region of Asia, Europe, and America, the bear received special treatment among the hunting peoples of similar ethnic strains. Apparently these primitives were much impressed by the bear's sagacity, his habit of hibernating during the winter and requiring no food. Oddly enough, the folk belief that he obtained nourishment by sucking some sort of secretion from his paws was nearly coextensive with the rituals which Hallowell studied.

All these people believed that it took particular courage to hunt the bear, they carried out an elaborate ritual when killing it, treated the bear almost like a human being and preserved the head after the beast was killed. In many cases the bear was addressed as Old Man, Grandfather, or Older Brother, or other kinship terms were used before killing it. Speeches were made to it apologizing for killing it, urging it to cooperate, and thanking it for becoming a victim.

Of particular interest is the Ainu bear festival, which we shall describe in some detail. The Ainu are a Siberian people who, having migrated to Japan, now live on reservations comparable to the Indian reservations in the United States. Bear hunting among them is or was considered an especially manly activity. It was considered proper to kill the bear with knives or spears in single combat. If the hunter happened to be killed, they decapitated the bear and buried the head. The actual festival, however, dealt with a bear cub, captured by these people and carefully reared in a cage until it was two or three years old, the wife of its captor sometimes even giving her breast to the cub. At the feast the villagers were dressed in their best, the men wore crowns with images of animals, and fetish sticks (willow sticks shaved so that their tops were curly) were set up at the hearth and worshiped. The speaker then approached the bear, asked its pardon for what he was about to do, hoped it would not be angry, and told it what an honor was about to be conferred upon it. He continued, "O you divine one, you were sent into the world for us to hunt. O precious little divinity, we worship you, hear our prayers. We have fed you and brought you up with great care and trouble all because we love you so. Now that you have grown big we are about to send you to your father and mother. When you get to them please speak well of us and tell them how kind we have been. Please come to us again and we will sacrifice you."

The bear was then taken out of the cage, roped, and shot at with blunt arrows to anger it. When it was tired out, it was seized by several people, two poles were placed above and below the neck partly strangling it, and an arrow was shot into its heart. No blood was allowed to fall to the ground. Later its blood was drunk sometimes by the hunters to absorb its courage.

The bear was then skinned and its head cut off with the skin on. This was taken to the east window of the hut and placed on a special mat ornamented with fetish shavings. A piece of its own flesh was cut off and placed under its snout along with dried fish, millet dumplings and (evidently borrowed from the Japanese) saké. The speaker then said to the head, "O cub, we give you these cakes and dried fish. Take them to your parents and say 'I have been brought up for a long time by an Ainu father and mother and have been kept from all trouble and harm. Now that I am big I have come to you. I have also brought cakes and dried fish. Please rejoice.' Say this to them and they will be glad."

The old men then danced; a cup of boiled flesh of the bear was set before its snout; the rest of the bear was cut up and eaten. The head of the bear was then skinned and set upon a pole among the fetish sticks outside the house of the hunter. Libations of food continued to be offered to such skulls.

All this was done, Hallowell comments, because "the bear was believed to represent, or was under the spiritual control of some supernatural power which governed either the potential supply of certain game animals or the bear species alone. It is the propitiation of this supernatural agent which is actually desired and not the animal itself."

It seems reasonable to suppose, therefore, that the Neanderthal bear hunter practiced some kind of ritual involving the head of the bear. The presence of other bear bones and sometimes charcoal in the caves suggests the possibility of ritual feasting. Whatever rites were carried out were certainly intended to ensure an increase of the game supply. Whether the entity to which respect was paid was the bear itself or, as in the case of the Ainu, a more powerful being, or master of beasts, depends upon the imaginative development of early Stone Age man. Since his symbolical sense had not developed sufficiently for him to contrive pictures or ornaments, it seems unlikely that his powers of abstraction or generalization were very high.

In any case, in the thinking of our most remote ancestors we can already detect the themes which we shall find woven in and out of all primitive religious imagination; hunting magic and a psychic relation to animals.

CHAPTER 3

Hunting Magic
and Venus Statuettes

Upper Paleolithic—evidence of ceremonial burial—stones placed on corpses suggest fear of the dead—cave art as hunting magic—masked figures suggest shaman—modern American Indian buffalo dance as analogy—female figurines considered to be cult objects, possibly a deity.

D URING the final interglacial period the climate of Europe changed. The ice sheets began to return and covered large areas of land while the thick forests turned to bare, cold steppes. Some species of animals became extinct, others migrated south. Fantastic new beasts such as the mammoth, a shaggy elephant, and the woolly rhinoceros ranged the tundras. All of a sudden a type of humanity that was essentially modern appeared. Apparently a series of population movements took place; waves of new arrivals came from western Asia and spread over eastern Europe while other migrants moved into North Africa and eventually into Spain. These new peoples were taller, lighter and slenderer than the indigenous population and stood fully erect, while the Neanderthaler was probably somewhat hunched. The brain cavity was as large or somewhat larger than that of contemporary man and the faces could well have been very handsome by our standards. The existing ethnic strains of man are probably descended from this one species, Homo sapiens. What happened to the Neanderthaler we do not know. As his culture ceases abruptly in Europe, he may have been exterminated or absorbed by the newcomers. In more southern areas his form of life persisted. Whether the contemporary strains of man were already differentiated at this time is debatable. It has been suggested that the diversification of skin pigment, for example, was a gradual adaptation following the colonization of new territories. Ethnic differences cannot be proved on the basis of existing remains and the art of the peoples who drew the human figure is not sufficiently detailed to furnish real clues.

It was during the Upper Paleolithic period that men spread over the greater part of the earth. Their predecessors had confined their colonization to Africa, south and middle Europe, southwest Asia, India and China. Now that man's culture was developing and his techniques for wresting a living from the earth improved, he marched on into northern Eurasia, into Australia and the islands of the Pacific and into the continents of the New World. This diffusion took place between forty and fifty thousand years ago.

The culture of the Upper Paleolithic peoples of Europe differed slightly in various areas (where they have been given specific names), but they all exhibited remarkable new material and intellectual advances. Their stone industries indicate new skills, for they made knife blades, delicate projectile points with evenly fluted flake scars, burins for engraving, and they added bone and antler and ivory implements, fashioning lance heads, harpoon heads, perforated batons and leatherworking tools such as awls and eyed needles. Greater specialization and greater material progress had begun to go hand in hand. Although the new people were also hunters, fishermen and gatherers of fruit, nuts and perhaps wild grain, and lived a nomadic life in the summer, in winter they retired to the caves. They may have made skin tents or some sort of dome-shaped huts. In eastern Asia where the glacial dust settled in great fields of what is now called loess, sometimes twenty-five feet thick, remains of the culture of the mammoth hunters of this period have been found. These people, having no caves, dug oval houses in the ground, ringing them with boulders and probably roofing them with skins. All in all, they had reached a stage of culture not unlike that of the Eskimo or some tribes of North American Indians.

Above all, suddenly the new peoples had become artists. The cave walls which they covered with amazingly vivid portrayals of animals are now famous; their carvings are treasured in modern museums, and eventually, in Spain, they developed several styles of treatment of the human figure which are full of action and vitality. Within their particular areas of interest the artists of the Upper Paleolithic have not been surpassed, and indeed contemporary painters have studied their work with profit.

Along with these technical and material advances, it is clear that man's conceptual world must have become tremendously enriched. Although his art was probably not produced from purely aesthetic motivations, it showed that he had attained a whole new area of sensitivity. The fact that he indulged in a variety of personal ornament suggests new ceremonial development, and his ability to create visual symbols indicates that he may well have achieved the verbal symbolization of poetry.

In Upper Paleolithic burials evidence of much more elaborate ceremony appears in the variety of grave goods and the adornment of the bodies. At Galles du Sud, France, a skeleton was found covered with red ochre, a mammoth skull behind the head. At Les Eyzies, in France, five skeletons were accompanied by many small shells and pierced teeth. In the Grimaldi grotto in Italy an ochre-covered skeleton was found, a bonnet sewn with shells on the skull and a crown of pierced reindeer teeth. In a nearby grotto two children's skeletons were found, one covered from navel to upper thighs with a skirt sewn with shells. Again in Dordogne, France, an ochre-covered skeleton was found with a stone at its head and two at its feet, several capstones supported on upright stones creating a kind of dolmen. There were flint tools and necklaces of shells and stag teeth. A fire had evidently been built on top of the stone dolmen and not far off were the remains of a food offering.

The regular appearance of flint knives and chipped points in most of the Upper Paleolithic graves shows that the conception of the living corpse continued to exist. Henri Breuil points out that a grave is not only a shelter but also a prison. Stones placed upon the head or shoulders may well be to keep the dead from walking and injuring the living. If so, this indicates an ambivalent attitude. The living must both provide for the dead and protect themselves from them. The custom of sprinkling red ochre upon the bodies which is widespread in this period has interesting anthropological connotations. It has been suggested that red was meant to simulate blood and thus enable the corpse to maintain its supposed vitality. Carl Clemen adds, "Also among [modern] primitives the dead were provided with . . . not only color to paint the body, put into their hands so they might gleam red in the land of the soul, but they themselves were also painted or at least wrapped in a red covering, laid in a red coffin and in a red-painted grave."

Whatever the symbolism of the color, its use already implies a step forward in the imaginative development of the Paleolithic mind. The decorative objects and amulets must also have had some magical significance; cowrie shells, for instance, may possibly have suggested fertility.

Most striking of all Upper Stone Age developments is the animal art which, it is generally agreed, is connected with hunting magic. The skeptical reception with which the discovery of the frescoed caves of Altamira was received is one of the ironies of archaeology. Civilized man from his pinnacle of technology was unwilling to admit that his Stone Age ancestor was capable of such achievements. Eventually the caves of Lascaux and many other painted grottoes in France, Switzerland and Spain displayed their treasures, a sobering experience for modern man, who is forced to admit that material progress is no guarantee of progress in artistic sensitivity.

Why did the Upper Paleolithic hunters cover the walls of their shelters with herds of reindeer, galloping wild horses, grazing bison, ponderous mammoths? In Les Combarelles, in France, for instance, one gallery alone contains pictures of eighty bison, forty horses, twenty-three mammoths, seventeen reindeer, eight wild cattle, four antelopes, two woolly rhinoceroses, a bear, a wolf, and a lioness. Careful examination showed that the pictures were not correlated with the habitable portions of the caves. They were generally placed deep in the interior, in alcoves thousands of feet under the earth, in inaccessible dark chambers where they could only be seen with the aid of artificial light, on high rock bosses that could only be reached by climbing and, in the case of Montespan, a subterranean stream intervened between the mouth of the cave and the decorated area. Sometimes the pictures were drawn on the ceiling, sometimes on walls with so little space between them that it was very difficult to get a good view of them. Finally, in many cases one set of pictures had another group superimposed upon them, creating a palimpsest which was not easy to make out. Sometimes, too, a drawing was retouched, one animal being transformed into another. In other cases the lines of the drawings followed the contour of the wall, disappearing around corners, or wandering over protrusions in such a way that the whole work of art could not be perceived until it was carefully mapped and reproduced.

It is clear that the function of cave art was not that of mere decoration. Two facts provide some clue to its meaning. A large number of animals were shown pierced by spears or arrows. Many, too, were depicted as pregnant. The symbolical principle of sympathetic magic seems to be behind the animal representation. By dramatizing an event primitives feel they can bring it about.

An interesting sculptured parallel occurs in the Montespan cave in France. Here the explorer found a clay figure of a bear almost four feet long and two feet high. The body was pierced by holes. There was no sculptured head; instead there were traces of a wooden stick and on the floor between the forepaws lay a bear skull. The figure had evidently once been completed with a real bear's head and perhaps its skin. It had then been pierced with arrows or spears in order to dramatize a successful hunt.

On the other hand, the drawings of pregnant animals magically dramatized the hunters' other preoccupation, increase of game. In this connection, the juxtaposition of male and female animals also suggests that the hunter desired by sympathetic magic to induce copulation and as a result fertility. In the Tuc d'Audoubert cave in France there is a clay relief of two bisons, the male about to mount the female; at the Roc-de-Sers, Charente, France, a mare is mounted by a stallion; in a wall engraving at Teyjat, Dordogne, France, a bull amorously follows a cow.

By 1952 seventy-one decorated caves had been discovered in France and thirty-four in northern Spain. In eastern Spain twenty-nine of the somewhat later rock shelters were found with painted rocks depicting, as well as animals, linear human figures engaged in hunting and other activities. Henri Breuil has stressed the fact that these decorated chambers were really chapels or sanctuaries. Situated in dark, mysterious recesses which could have only been dimly lit by flickering oil lamps or torches, they must have aroused a feeling of awe. He believes that the great felines at the entrance to Les Trois Frères cave constitute guardians, as do the strange monsters, half-ox, half-feline, at Tuc d'Audoubert. Lascaux seems to have been a summer sanctuary, since in it no reindeer or mammoths are depicted. Most of the caves seem to have been decorated in winter. As Breuil points out, "During the summer, life becomes secular as among the Eskimo. In contrast the coming of winter sees it lived, so to speak, in a continuing religious exaltation. This is the time to celebrate tribal rites, the initiation of adolescents into the tribe's traditions, its beliefs, into the rights and obligations of adults; the time, too, for magical ceremonies to multiply the useful animals, to destroy the great carnivores and to bewitch the game. It is the time to profit from the surplus accumulated during the good weather, to prepare the weapons and tools necessary for the summer expeditions, to prepare skins and furs, to sew clothes and manufacture receptacles of leather, bark and basketry indispensable for the gathering of additional nutriment. Would it not have been during this off season from the chase that the decoration of the sanctuaries was carried out? And in this skill which could only be acquired by great patience, at the price of moments snatched from an extremely arduous existence, for which the community must have seen to it that the artist was assured a life more or less free from economic cares, we may surely see a first attempt in the direction of the division of labor."

The artist consequently must have developed something of a priestly character. We have other evidence, however, that Upper Paleolithic man had developed the institution of the shaman or medicine man. The famous and often reproduced figure of the Great Sorcerer was found in the deepest part of Les Trois Frères cave drawn above a kind of rock pulpit about twelve feet above the cave floor. It is about thirty inches high and can only be reached by a narrow spiraling passage. The figure dominates the animals painted on the other walls. The costume includes a deer's horns and an owl-like mask with a sort of beard. It seems to be wearing skins with bear paws and sports a horse's tail. The legs are clearly human and the posture one of dancing. The picture may represent an idealized shaman under whose image the practicing magician would mount the pulpit to officiate before the tribe. Other representations of masked figures, always in the posture of dancing, include one with a mammoth mask from Les Combarelles, an engraving on a slate slab of a man with a horse's tail and deer's horns from the Pyrenees, a perforated bone slat with a figure wearing a chamois mask and skin from Teyjat, France, a naked ithyphallic figure engraved on bone from Mas d'Azil with an indistinguishable mask and, most suggestive of all, also from the Trois Frères cave, a figure wearing a horned mask and an animal pelt and holding either a bow or some sort of musical instrument, following two deerlike animals.

Mimetic dancing is common throughout contemporary hunting cultures. Nearly all the North American plains Indians danced buffalo dances. The Sioux regalia consisted of headdresses made from horned buffalo heads dried and used as masks. Little feathers or shells were added and a buffalo tail hung down behind. Forty dancers and singers took part. They hooked one another and imitated the buffalo's movements. The Ojibway said their buffalo dance was intended to heal the sick and increase the buffalo in time of scarcity. The Fox buffalo dance was described by one of the tribe as follows: "This is the reason a woman follows a man in the dance, it is because the old male buffaloes are the leaders. It seems as if the leader is in full control, verily he leads as he goes about. . . . The buffaloes are imitated in a way as they move along. This is why they dance in a circle when they imitate what they do, when they imitate their actions. It is as if the buffalo were doing it." A part of the accompanying song went:

> He feeds you,
> He feeds you,
> A buffalo.

The parallel is indisputable. Among the wealth of carved objects or "small art" that have been found in the caves are batons, with a hole through one end, which generally bear the image of some animal—deer, horse, bird and the like. Obermaier suggests that these objects, for which there seems to be no practical use, may have been wands used by shamans.

Another indication of ritual concerning animals appears in two engraved bone plates, one from Château des Eyzies and one from the Chancelade cave. In both cases formalized figures bearing what seem to be branches are paying homage to a buffalo head. The use of masks in the two engravings shows that Upper Paleolithic ritual involved social organization. Masks inspired respect and reverence in groups and the bison worshipers seem to be marching in a procession. The question arises: Are all of these objects evidences of totemism? This social form involves a relationship in which certain groups consider themselves to be descended from an animal or plant. Eating the totem is either taboo or only practiced on certain ritual occasions. Totemic peoples decorate their goods and utensils with pictures of their ancestral animals, and the large number of carved animals adorning the batons, spear-throwers, and various bone and ivory plaques of the "small art" could be interpreted as evidence of this phenomenon. Breuil discounted totemism on the basis that a limited number of animals is represented. This is, however, a weakly negative argument. There is no reason to suppose that a rudimentary totemism or pre-totemic mentality which might have sprung up thirty thousand years ago would be as fully developed as that which occurs among contemporary, or nearly contemporary, Australians or Iroquois. As Breuil says himself, "The relations established between man and animal are never simple but imply a mythicoreligious system well worked out from which the presence of superterrestrial entities cannot be excluded."

M. C. Burkitt describes the Tuc d'Audoubert cave with the two bisons as follows: "At the end of the gallery, probably not so very far from where the original entrance to the cave must have been, leaning against a natural block of rock, are two bisons modeled in clay. In front is the female, behind is the male. Both are about two feet long. Nearby on the right there is a semicircular depression, and on the clay surface of this depression can be seen marks as if somebody had been dancing on his heels round a tiny hillock that is to be seen in the center. Nearby on the floor is a very nice engraving of a harpoon. The whole gives one a strong impression that the site had been used for some cult or ritual purpose and further that the locality was not merely used once by chance but was a definite cave cult-shrine."

The indefatigable and dedicated Alfred Rust, who started life as an electrician and who rode from Hamburg to his diggings in Syria on a bicycle and eventually excavated the sites of Stellmoor and Meiendorf, has added to our knowledge of the reindeer hunters of the Mesolithic by investigating the summer camps from which they pursued their prey to the edge of the retreating ice cap. Both Stellmoor and Meiendorf lay on the shores of ancient lakes. In both areas, well out in the lake, skeletons of deer were found with a large stone of about twenty pounds weight wedged into the chest cavity.

In Meiendorf, the older site (15,000 B.C.), he found one; at Stellmoor (10,000 B.C.) thirty were recovered. One suggestion put forward was that, like certain Eskimo, the reindeer people stored their meat by sinking it in the cold waters of the lake. A second discovery at Stellmoor of a seven-foot pole, pointed at one end, with the skull of a reindeer buck with spreading antlers mounted on the other, shows that some ceremonial of the chase was probably practiced. It seems possible that the carcasses of does sunk in the lake were offerings. There is one difficulty, however. Hunters rarely have a surplus of meat and never among modern primitives toss away whole carcasses in this manner.

One other significant and fascinating series of finds poses a problem which has been only provisionally solved. One of the most familiar examples

of prehistoric art is the Venus of Willendorf unearthed while Hugo Obermaier was excavating a mammoth hunter site in Austria in 1908. A bril-
liantly stylized statue of a naked woman eleven centimeters high with
swelling pendent breasts, huge belly and exaggerated thighs and buttocks,
the sex clearly marked, the arms attenuated, and the extremities of the
legs almost pointed, it is remarkable for being almost faceless. The bent
head is without features and the plaited hair is wound around the head in
a sort of cap. As a work of art it expresses a massive femininity which reminds one of the work of the modern sculptor, Gaston Lachaise. The
Venus of Willendorf proved to be no isolated phenomenon. A whole series
of statues have been discovered in various French cave sites, in Italy and
Germany, and still more in eastern Europe and in Russia in the dwellings
of the tundra mammoth hunters. Significantly enough, very few sculptural
representations of the male figure have come to light. Although the female
type varies—in some cases the proportions being less massive, shading off
to rough cylindrical shapes with a knob for a head, bumps for breasts, and,
finally, in Russia becoming, according to Franz Hančar, a stylized object
topped with a thumb-shaped projection, keeping the bulging belly and
below it a roughly marked pubic triangle—the Willendorf type appears
fairly often. In the majority of cases the breasts, belly and buttocks continue to be exaggerated, the head is always featureless, though the hair
style is often carefully treated, and quite often the vulva is clearly indicated.

As sculpture the Venus figures are an expressive triumph, but what do
they mean? An often repeated interpretation is that they are generally
fertility symbols, related to a general desire for fruitfulness and plenty of
human offspring. Hančar points out that in a hunting culture a multitude of
children is no particular asset. Since food is dearly won, hunters are not
anxious for more mouths to feed. Then, too, it must be remembered that
hunting preliterates are not apt to generalize and certainly do not develop
abstract fertility symbols. The true mother goddess of increase is correlated
with vegetation cults. Hančar, working from the point of view that such art
must be an embodiment of the myths of its time and culture, exercised his
detective acumen upon the related objects and the setting in which the
sculptures were found. The most significant facts are available from the
eastern European and Russian sites, some of the latter having been excavated by Soviet scientists. In Kostjenki, Russia, for instance, a figure almost
as good as the Willendorf Venus was found in one of the oval dwelling
foundations (no doubt meant for a skin tent) buried in a squarish hole with
traces of fire, animal bones and red ochre. In the same site there was a niche
across from the hearth containing an ivory and a stone female figure. In
Gagarino, in the Ukraine, six figures of mammoth ivory were found near

the walls of the dwelling. Animal bones were also present. In Malta, in Siberia, in an aboveground dwelling site, figures were again found near walls associated with a hearth and burned animals' bones. Hančar feels that the association of the female figurines with the hearth and in the dwelling is significant. The mammoth hunters could not have pursued their game in the difficult winter weather of their period. Thus they were forced into a partially sedentary existence. During the hard winter months it is probable, as in many contemporary primitive homes, that it was the woman who did the serious work of curing hides and meat. It was she who developed the household industries which helped to make the family comfortable during the difficult season. With this type of domestication, Hančar argues that the woman became the symbol of the kinship group, the family clan mother. This would posit a matriarchal organization. The careful placing of the figures against the wall, the presence of red ochre (which we have seen is of ritual significance), the pointed feet of many statues which would allow them to be stuck in the ground and the holes found in others which would allow them to be hung, all suggest that the statues were cult idols important in the worship of the clan mother. The detailed treatment of the hair suggests that its style might be a clan identification, a device used by some modern primitives. Finally, if the huge bellies of the figurines are to be thought of as indicating pregnancy, Hančar points out that the pregnant woman is generally surrounded with magical significance.

In the Laussel cave in France three reliefs have been discovered, two of women, heavy-thighed and with pendent breasts, holding what seems to be a bison horn in their hands, and one of a male archer. Each of these figures appears on a separate broken stone slab. An ingenious reconstruction (by N. Zamjatnin) places all three together as part of one whole in which the women appear as symbols of beneficent hunting magic. Hančar cites the modern Siberian Tungus who celebrate a female hunting cult with small wooden female figurines which they call Dzuli. These represent both the human ancestors of the tribe and tutelary spirits. Protectors of the family and the clan, they are told to guard the home when the family goes hunting. The Tungus anoint them with grease and say, "Grant that we remain in good health. Grant that we kill many reindeer." There is a possibility, however, that such figures are a late borrowing from Chinese ancestor worship.

Since the Magdelanian hunters of western Europe were nomads who followed the reindeer herds, it is not surprising that scarcely any female figurines are found in their deposits. The hunters of eastern Europe and Siberia established their more permanent homes along watercourses, the migration routes of their prey, and thus were able to evolve a more settled way of life which may have resulted in the cult of the clan mother as sketched above.

Tantalizing and controversial as all these glimpses of man's spiritual activities in the Stone Age are, they are nevertheless vivid enough to convince us that human beings as emotionally, and nearly as intellectually, complicated as modern man already existed thirty or forty thousand years ago.

CHAPTER 4

Painted Pebbles

Western Mesolithic—developments in late Spanish Stone Age art—markings on pebbles suggest symbolism—similarity to Australian churingas—possible totemism and ancestor cult.

IT MIGHT SEEM farfetched to say that religion depends upon weather conditions, yet in a larger sense the statement is true. In the Mesolithic, or Middle Stone Age, which begins roughly about 10,000 B.C., important new climatic changes took place and these, in turn, were to drastically modify man's way of life. Whenever man's way of life is altered, his whole cultural pattern changes and with it his religious preoccupations. As the weather grew warmer and the ice cap retreated after the last glacial period, new vegetation appeared in Europe and the cold tundras began to be covered with the trees we now know: the birch and the willow, the pine and, finally, the elm, lime and beech. The reindeer retreated northward; the mammoth died out in Europe but lived on in Siberia. In more southerly areas, such as Palestine, rainfall grew less; because of increased difficulties in making a living, men learned to domesticate wild grain and thus agriculture was born. This marked a revolution in human culture and, as we shall see later, led to a period of migration.

The transition occurs with less of a break in such areas as that of Spain where the climatic change was gradual, and it is here that we can see most clearly an evolution from the Upper Paleolithic culture into the Mesolithic. While the reindeer hunters were moving northward and still pursuing their occupation (or also hunting the red deer), while colonists from the already agricultural peoples of Africa were moving north and building pile dwellings in the Swiss lakes, while northern pioneers (probably originally hunters) were settling on the shores of Denmark where they fished and left their bleached oyster shells and chipped flints in huge kitchen middens, in Spain the old hunting way of life was preserved for centuries, little influenced by changes elsewhere.

The Azilian culture, named from a cave in the Pyrenees, Mas d'Azil (which is related to a similar culture called Tardenoisian in France and central Europe), is the key to what was perhaps a new religious concept.

In the first place we must remember that in the eastern part of the Iberian Peninsula a late Paleolithic art developed which was remarkable for its treatment of the human figure. A similar style has also been found in North Africa. The bodies are of several types: some threadlike, some heavy-legged, some with attenuated torsos and short legs. They are drawn in silhouette, in black or red, nearly always in motion, often running frantically, taking part in group hunting activities, dancing, even collecting honey from a bees' nest. Animals, too, are generally drawn in silhouette. These people were cave dwellers but their pictures were always painted on protected but exterior rock surfaces. This suggests a new kind of outdoor ceremonial.

Hugo Obermaier has traced a metamorphosis in this art which gradually, as the centuries passed, changed from dynamic group scenes into a conventionalized expression in which the shapes of men and animals became schematized. The figures of men often lost their heads and were indicated by a straight line crossed by two opposed curves. Animals, too, were reduced to a few heavy strokes. Zigzag lines, circles with rays which may be sun disks or eyes, and rows of dots or lines also appear. A representative art has turned into emblematic signs; realism has given way to symbolism. It is not the first time that such sequences have been worked out archaeologically. In Mycenae a fairly naturalistic pottery decoration gave way to a formal abstract style. What happened in Spain should not be rashly interpreted to mean that the hunting culture had retrogressed. The appearance of a symbolic art may indeed indicate the development of a greater power of generalization, a modification in thinking.

At any rate, when we come to the Azilians a distinct note of condescension creeps into archaeological descriptions. Even V. Gordon Childe remarks, "The Azilians' equipment seems poor. . . . The only reminiscences of Magdelanian art are highly conventionalized figures painted on pebbles."

Many of these designs on the painted pebbles can be placed in a series, beginning with the realistic shapes that preceded them, to show an ultimate simplification, a symbolic shorthand. We should not suspect that they dealt with the human figure at all if we did not have the earlier data to go by. Working again from analogy, Obermaier suggested that the Azilian pebbles are very like certain ceremonial objects used by Australian tribes (also in a primitive hunting stage) called *churingas*.

What are churingas? They are ovoid stones or wooden slats which bear sacred symbolic markings. They were intimately associated with great totemic festivals involving elaborate decoration of the body, dancing and drama. The Arunta of central Australia believed that in the dim past, which they called the Alcheringa, their ancestors carried churingas about with them which were associated with specific totems. These totems were animal or plant ancestors of tribal groups and were connected with localized areas and landmarks, spots where ancestors had camped or died. It was thought that when a woman conceived a child near one of these totem spots the spirit of the ancestor entered into her and the child belonged to its totem.

If the Azilian pebbles were something like churingas, it suggests that these people were both totemistic and ancestor cultists. The Arunta of Australia have no specific gods other than the ancestral spirits, which are not exactly worshiped but rather invoked in ceremonies meant to increase the food supply. It was also maintained by various authorities that these Australian people did not recognize the function of sexual intercourse in producing children but ascribed conception entirely to the activities of the ancestral spirits. This belief, which has been often noted among contemporary primitives, should act as a caution when it comes to interpreting certain penis-shaped stone or clay objects as proof of phallic worship among Stone Age peoples.

The markings upon Australian churingas are certainly as enigmatic as those upon Azilian pebbles. The Arunta, for instance, said that repeated half circles could either mean a man sitting, squeezing dirt out of a grub, or the ribs of a lizard. Dots could mean tracks or eggs.

As has been said, the Australian ceremonials involved an elaborate decoration of the naked body. The art of the ancestors of the Azilians does show that the Stone Age people of this area wore fairly elaborate and varied headdresses, fringed belts, armlets, and leg ornaments. What the Azilian rituals may have been can only be conjectured. If they were indeed totemic, and if their emblematic art had some metaphysical significance, we can credit them with fairly complicated beliefs distinct from the sympathetic hunting magic which the Paleolithic hunters seem to have practiced.

The Near East

CHAPTER 5

Earth Mother and Bearded Bull

Sumer—clay female figures in the Near East—possible Neolithic fertility goddess—Sumerians develop irrigation and build temples—god as patron and owner of city—myths reflect growth of urban civilization—importance of fertility goddess—first myth of death and resurrection—bearded bull as pastoral god—Job theme and sadness of life—religion at the service of the state.

IN NORTHERN IRAQ certain headless, squatting statues of nude females were found which dated to some period in the fifth millennium B.C. In style they are somewhat reminiscent of the Venuses of Eurasia. They are, however, associated with sickle blades made of small flints inserted in bone or wooden handles which show that agriculture had begun.

In Jericho, in the Jordan Valley, grinding stones and sickles were found in a village site without pottery which may be as old as the sixth millennium. Here, too, was discovered a figure of a woman two inches high with a flowing gown gathered at the waist, the hands under the breasts, the head unfortunately missing. Shrines in the form of niches also occur in the ancient Jericho houses.

The Jericho figure is very similar to representations of a later Near East goddess who is associated with the earth, with sex, and with growing grain. E. O. James would see a line of development from the Paleolithic Venus to the Near East deity who is generally called a fertility goddess. If the clan mother, who may have been a female shaman, was a deity who brought increase in hunting, her relation to a female deity who symbolized the growth of vegetation (a fertility goddess) is tenuous. Quite possibly the latter had a separate history. Among preliterate tribes of the contemporary period, the earliest digging-stick agriculture is mainly carried on by women; in fact, O. T. Marsh credits them with inventing it. If agriculture in the Near East was first carried on by women, the attribution of a special vegetation magic to the female sex would be natural. From this to a vegetation goddess would be a matter of the gradual development of symbolic thinking. This explanation of the rise of the agricultural fertility goddess has, at least, the virtue of functional simplicity.

According to the present state of archaeological knowledge, the cultivation of crops began somewhere in the Near East and female figures turn up frequently in sites occupied by Neolithic farmers. At Hassuna for instance, in Assyria, west of the Tigris River, some of the steps from seminomadic cultivators, who planted until the soil was exhausted and then moved on, to truly sedentary village dwellers can be deduced from a series of stratified deposits. The earliest settlers left no traces of houses but sank large jars of pale pink pottery in the ground as storage receptacles. Rough querns or grinding stones prove that grain was ground into cereal. These people also left behind them what may be hoe blades, heavy flaked stone implements, and bones of cattle, sheep or goats which they may have domesticated. Six other superimposed villages of adobe houses testify to a settled existence. These houses consisted of three or four rooms grouped around a court. Their wooden doors were pivoted on socketed stones and in the courtyards stood round clay ovens in which they baked bread. Grain was reaped with sickles edged with flint flakes and stored in bins shaped like the earlier jars but now made of unbaked mud mixed with straw, coated on the outside with bitumen. The villagers also made pottery decorated with charming stylized animals. They, too, left behind them clay figures of nude women in sufficient numbers to suggest a cult. Although we have no way of knowing what rituals were practiced, it is reasonable to suppose that some concept connecting female fertility with fertility of the soil had begun to evolve. Subsequently a more highly developed fifth-millennium culture called the Halafian, first discovered east of the Tigris, produced a finer type of pottery. Wheat and barley were raised and two breeds of cattle as well as sheep, goats and pigs. The female figurines persisted, at first modeled in clay and later carved in soft stone. In addition, perforated obsidian amulets began to appear, some in the form of bulls' heads and double axes, two symbols which were to have a long history, often in association with the mother goddess. The Halafians also instituted the procedure of marking private property with clay seals upon which a magically protective design had been impressed.

Unfortunately for prehistorians, human culture seldom develops neatly in a straight line. Some areas progress with astonishing speed, others lag behind for thousands of years. There are gaps in the record; transitions are clear in some parts of the world and obscure in others. Often there is a complete break as a new people migrates from an undiscovered location, colonizes, and adds a completely new chapter to the story.

So it is with the first people to build cities in Mesopotamia. There seems to be no direct link between the various transitional Neolithic farmers and villagers such as the Halafians, in the Near East, and that energetic and inventive group which has come to be known as Sumerian. Apparently a non-Semitic, non-Indo-European ethnic group, they entered Mesopotamia probably from the Iranian mountains to the east prior to or during the fourth millennium B.C. There must have been Semitic settlers already in residence, probably with a culture similar to the Halafian, who were doubtless enslaved. Henceforth the history of the two ethnic groups is mingled but in the earlier period the Sumerians are dominant. In the valley of the Tigris River, at the head of the Persian Gulf, swampy lagoons and alluvial silt created enormously fertile areas, and it is here that the newcomers created the first known shrine, at Eridu, a square sanctuary built of long, prism-shaped bricks and dedicated to Enki, their water god. The temple was reconstructed seven times, each time on a grander scale, until it was practically a cathedral.

It appears that there were various groups of Sumerian colonists, each possessing a god or goddess, each maintaining its political independence. Since they shared a common culture, the gods were eventually assimilated into a pantheon. There is therefore no direct connection between their religion and the traces of a goddess cult among the Neolithic farmers (who continued their way of life in the north). When we come to consider the already sophisticated, written myths of the Sumerians, however, we shall find a full-fledged mother and vegetation goddess playing an important role in relation to lovers, relatives, friends and enemies.

Apparently the Sumerians soon learned to drain the marshes, control floods and irrigate desert areas by means of canals. Since they were able to construct monumental buildings, their agricultural economy evidently supported an urban population and their social structure was well enough organized to make cooperative enterprises possible. It appears that in the preliterate (or Ubaid) period most of the land of each community belonged to the temple of the deity and was tilled on behalf of the god. Probably the surplus of food was stored there, and it appears that temple construction, the cult ceremonies and the divine household were administered by professional priests. Nevertheless, alongside of, or, for all we know, connected with the official religion the old fertility ideas existed, for in this period clay figures of nude women with large hips, their hands holding their breasts, appear. They are sometimes adorned with necklaces and bracelets and decorated with black paint. Some of the figures are represented as nursing infants. Interestingly enough, the primitive Sumerian women were already wearing wigs similar to those considered fashionable by the predynastic Egyptians.

The Sumerians prospered, their colonies spreading across Mesopotamia to the Mediterranean coast, and, at the same time, their temples grew more imposing and their villages developed into cities. The temples were constructed in the form of a long rectangle with an altar at one end and an offering table at the other, with lateral chambers grouped symmetrically on each side of the nave. They were set upon a high mud platform faced with adobe bricks, their façades and sides broken by recessed buttresses between which ran horizontal bands of pottery mosaic sometimes painted in red, white or black patterns. Others had frescoes within depicting animals and human figures.

Meanwhile ideographic and pictographic signs had been developing from cylinder seals denoting ownership of property—the great step which divides history from prehistory—and when early in the fourth millennium the signs began to be used phonetically, written language was in the making. (As it happens, Egypt took this same step at about this time and indeed these two first urban cultures pursued a parallel course in the third millennium.)

By the fourth millennium the Sumerians had achieved city-states complete with royal governors who assumed the temporal powers which must have been originally assigned to the priests. These governors finally became local kings. The invention of the wheel made possible two-wheeled chariots and four-wheeled oxcarts used as engines of war. With the forging of bronze used for spears, daggers, harpoons, pickaxes and saws, Mesopotamia entered the Bronze Age. It is from the royal graves that we gain the most vivid impression of the luxury and multiplicity of expert craftsmanship achieved by this pioneer urban city civilization.

In the cemetery at Ur, Sir Leonard Woolley dates the earliest graves from about 3500 B.C. The area continued to be used up to about 3100, the beginning of the dynastic era. At first, commoners were buried in a square shaft, in a contracted position, wrapped in matting or in a wooden coffin, along with their personal possessions, holding a drinking bowl of pottery, copper or stone to their lips. Other offerings were placed outside the matting roll, the procedure indicating that the living-corpse idea probably persisted. As the culture grew richer and more highly developed, the grave goods of royal persons (who at first were called tenant farmers of the god and probably later identified with the god) became amazingly opulent. Gold and silver ornaments testified to Sumerian skill in metalworking; copper tools and weapons, alabaster vases, diorite and lapis-lazuli cups and bowls all accompanied these aristocrats in their houses of death. It was believed that if a man was not properly buried with appropriate gifts, his spirit would haunt the streets and attack travelers like a vampire. In later sophisticated times there was a concept of a shadowy world after death which was neither hell nor paradise, rather like the Greek Hades, in which the life of the dead was described as follows:

> Earth is their food, their nourishment clay;
> Ghostlike birds flutter their wings there,
> On the gates and the gateposts the dust lies
> undisturbed.

At any rate, grave goods would be thought of as a sustenance and a means of prolonging the life of the dead, as well as a protection for the living.

These royal graves were placed at the bottom of a shaft, walled with rough limestone and roofed with a corbel vault. Strangest of all was the discovery that not only inanimate things but servants as well were sent to share the living death of the master. In one grave the soldiers of the guard, wearing their copper helmets, lay in the passageway into the grave. Against one wall were found the skeletons of nine ladies of the court wearing elaborate golden headdresses, while in front of the entrance there were two four-wheeled carts accompanied by three bullocks which drew them, their drivers, and the grooms which led the animals. Queen Shub-ad was accompanied by her ladies in waiting, laid out in two parallel rows at the end of which lay the harper clutching his harp, decorated with lapis-lazuli and gold. Apparently these servants and slaves died willingly, perhaps by poison, as they were neatly and peacefully arranged. They cannot be regarded as sacrifices but rather as human grave goods. Woolley feels that the kings were probably deified but he also points out that there is no trace of such rites in the historical period and no real indication of human sacrifice. These attendants must have been resigned to self-immolation in order to achieve status in the otherworld.

Temple architecture continued to grow more elaborate. A shrine to the mother goddess Ninhursag, at Ubaid, had steps up to the entrance instead of a ramp, a porch flanked with wooden columns inlaid with copper, and a mosaic of mother-of-pearl, black shale and red limestone, a copper relief of an eagle god grasping two stags above the door, while along the outside walls marched a procession of copper statues of bulls and above them a frieze showing more bulls in relief.

By the third dynasty the temple, although its basic pattern remained the same, was elevated upon a tapering hill of baked bricks until the whole became a truncated stepped pyramid, a holy city and a fortress in itself, called a ziggurat.

But just what was the religion of these energetic city builders? Unfortunately we cannot trace the origins of their gods. The basis for official city-state religion seems to have been already well developed upon their arrival in Mesopotamia when each clan or tribe had its patron. This state religion is a good example of our initial definition of religion as a force that "expresses the unity of society and helps to create that unity." V. Gordon Childe has pointed out that historically there is a kind of natural selection of religions. Although the hunting magic of the Upper Paleolithic was undoubtedly consolatory and a force for binding the tribe together, it did not aid the Stone Age people to modify their environment. When their environment changed, they either changed with it, were absorbed by other peoples, or perished and their religion died out. The patron god of the Sumerians was capable of urban development, he embodied political authority, rewarded virtue, and punished social wrongdoing. Since his temple became a storage for surplus, specialization became possible and his guild of priests were able to become teachers and administrators. (All Sumerian schools were connected with the temples.) With the perfection of writing, legal codes were written down by the theocratic administrators, commercial pursuits regularized, and a mythology expressing national pride and self-justification was created.

The Sumerians were a practical rather than metaphysically minded people. It is interesting to see how the myths of their gods reflected the evolution of their new-found civilized arts and how clearly their gods were Sumerians writ large. Certain duplication and confusion of attributes among the gods seem to have arisen, since each patron deity tended to attract qualities and attributes of other gods as a matter of self-glorification.

The Sumerian cosmogony suggests that the primeval sea, Nammu, is eternal. It gives birth to a mountain, heaven and earth, which is separated into two parts by Enlil the god of wind and rain, in short, air. Life is conceived as a result of the union of earth, air and water. The myth is incomplete because the tablet is broken but it appears that at a drunken feast the gods discussed the fact that they had to work too hard and proposed to make man out of clay. An earth mother goddess created various human types including the barren woman and the eunuch, who was appointed to be the servant of the king—a curious rationalization of a practice which this first Oriental civilization may have invented.

The Sumerians possessed a host of gods, among them Ki who was possibly also Ninhursag, queen of the cosmic mountain, the queen who gives birth. She was a fertility, earth goddess. But Inanna, goddess of love, also shared fertility attributes; ritual prostitutes were attached to her temple. Nanna was the moon god, connected with astronomy and divination. Utu, the sun god child of Enlil, seemed to go to sleep at night and there was no mention of any boat or vehicle to carry him across the sky. Although he was connected with justice, he was less important (in early times) than Enlil, the weather god, or Enki, the water god, who was also god of wisdom.

When it comes to plants and animals, there is also duplication, since the fertility idea seems to take many forms. Enki is said to have begotten Uttu, goddess of plants. But Enki also sent Lahar, the cattle god, and Ashnan, the grain goddess, to earth.

> Lahar, standing his sheepfold,
> He is the shepherd increasing the bounty
>   of his sheepfold;
> Ashnan, standing among the crops,
> She is a kindly and bountiful maiden.

We also hear, however, of the shepherd god Dumuzi, and the farmer god Enkidu. A permanent villain was Kur, some sort of monster, given to throwing stones, who was identified with the underworld; he was the empty space between the earth's crust and the sea. He was also, however, thought of as a northern district, hence a hostile country, and destroyed in a certain myth by Inanna. This is therefore probably a symbolic echo of war with a neighboring state.

A myth in which the primeval waters misbehave, they do not water the fields and gardens but instead cause floods, evidently reflects the problems of irrigation which the Sumerians had to solve before they built their civilization. Ninurta, in his manifestation as an irrigation god, was finally obliged to build a stone wall to hold back the flood. Ninurta led the excess back to the Tigris, where it could be controlled.

It was also recorded that when Enki was asked for fresh water for Dilmun, a Paradisal land, which may have been an echo of the original home of the Sumerians, he provided it and:

> Her city drinks the water of abundance,
> Dilmun drinks the water of abundance.
> Her wells of bitter water, behold they
>   become wells of good water;
> Her fields and farms produce crops and grain.

Another proof of the close connection between Sumer's religion and its germinating civilization is the myth of the pickax which celebrates the invention of that useful instrument by Enlil.

> The pickax and the basket build cities;
> The pickax builds the steadfast house;
> The pickax establishes the steadfast house;
> It causes the steadfast house to prosper.

The house which rebels against the king,
The house which is not submissive to the king,
The pickax makes it submissive to the king.

It crushes the head of the evil plants,
It plucks at the roots and tears at the crown;
The pickax spares the good plants.
The fate of the pickax was decreed by father Enlil;
The pickax is exalted.

A myth which evidently mirrors cultural diffusion from one city to another deals with Inanna, queen of heaven and goddess of Erech, who paid a visit to Eridu, ruled over by Enki. She came to ask for certain "decrees of civilization." Enki was much taken with her and gave a banquet, serving barley cakes and butter together with plenty of date wine "with the face of a lion." Enki seems to have been overcome by the lion, for during the night of reveling he was persuaded to hand over a hundred decrees of civilization including such matters as: justice, shepherdship, kingship, music, carpentry, sexual intercourse, prostitution, masonry and metallurgy. Waking up, doubtless with a hangover, Enki became very angry when he saw that the decrees were gone from their usual place. He sent sea monsters after Inanna's boat. With the aid of her messenger, Nishubur, however, she defeated the monsters and bore off her bagful of civilization in triumph.

A number of concepts which first appeared in Sumerian mythology have been passed on by repeated borrowings until they entered the mainstream of European culture, thus bridging a gap of five millennia between these pioneer city folk and modern man. The hero Gilgamesh, who is listed as a Sumerian king, mythologically wears fifty-pound armor and carries a four-hundred-pound ax. He kills a snake which annoys Inanna by nesting at the base of a tree she had planted. As we shall see, in Babylonian literature his deeds are developed into an epic and in this epic the story of the flood is adapted from Sumerian sources. The Sumerian Noah is called Ziusudra and he is saved by the water god Enki.

Still more significant is Inanna's descent to the underworld. This is undoubtedly one of several fertility myths, a variation on the major theme in Sumerian religion. Inanna was determined to go down to the underworld to extend her power. She put on her queenly robes and her jewels and descended but she dreaded the enmity of her elder sister and bitter enemy Ereshkigal, goddess of darkness and death. Inanna herself was originally carried off to the underworld by Kur; Ereshkigal as an earth goddess is probably an alter ego of Inanna, for we shall see in versions of the cult elsewhere the fertility goddess is also equated with the death goddess. Inanna, the story goes on, told her messenger that if she did not return after three days he was to go to the other gods for help. She passed through the seven gates of the underworld, at each one of which some of her robes and jewels were taken from her. Naked, she stood before Ereshkigal and the seven judges of the underworld.

> Upon her entering the seventh gate
> All the garments of her ladyship's body were removed.
> "What, pray, is this?"
> Strangely, O Inanna, have the decrees of the
>   underworld been perfected.
> Then pure Ereshkigal seated herself upon her throne,
> The Anunnunaki, the seven judges, pronounced
>   judgment upon her;
> They fastened eyes upon her, the eyes of death.
> At their word which tortures the spirit,
> The sick woman turned into a corpse,
> The corpse was hung from a stake.

The messenger applied in vain to Enlil for help. Finally the water god created two beings who went down carrying food and the water of life, with which they sprinkled Inanna sixty times. When she revived she went up to earth guarded by:

> Small demons like reeds,
> Large demons like tablet styluses.

The demons would not release her until a substitute was found. Unlike the heroines of the Babylonian and Greek myths of resurrection, Inanna did not therefore rescue her lover-husband, Dumuzi, but instead, as a substitute for her, he entered the underworld and became an earth god.

Since, in this oldest known literature, the priesthood had not correlated the various stories, we find independent and parallel themes related to the same idea. The fertility goddess appears in various forms and in various episodes. As Inanna, her relation to natural increase is symbolized in her choice between the shepherd, Dumuzi, and a farmer god. Inanna inclines to the farmer.

> I, the maiden, shall marry the farmer,
> The farmer who makes plants grow abundantly.

The sun god favors Dumuzi who pushes his suit and overcomes his rival. Dumuzi becomes the Babylonian Tammuz, changing from a shepherd to a symbol of vegetation.

The Sumerian goddess Ninhursag, who parallels Inanna, stands for motherhood rather than erotic love. It is she who is associated with the bull symbol and whose temple possessed sacred herds. Even in the Halafian culture bulls' heads were found with the little clay female figures. Ninhursag's temple was surrounded with bull statues and a bull frieze. It appears therefore that the vegetation cycle centered about the mother goddess and the bull. The ancestry of the earth mother has been discussed; the derivation of the bull leads us into speculation.

Two statues dating from the third millennium, found in Umma, Sumeria, have been used to reconstruct the image of the bull-man. He stands erect, wears a beard and horns, probably had hoofs, and is ithyphallic (or at least the phallus is in a position reminiscent of that of the bull). Seals from Ur abound in bull images; one shows a bearded naked man embracing two upright bulls with human faces, horns and beards. There is also, from the same site, a golden amulet depicting a recumbent bull with a beard tied under its chin.

O. G. S. Crawford remarks that a bull cult would seem to have its home among pastoral communities, especially as there is no trace of it in the Paleolithic period. A virile bull deity is found in various parts of Mesopotamia, and he is generally related to the mother goddess as brother, son or consort. With pastoralism, which is believed to have emerged from hunting, there is bound to be an emphasis on the male sex. While the idea of increase of cattle may be tied to the fertility of the bull, he is also just as likely an expression of male potency and the male ego. It is noteworthy that among modern hunting and fishing primitives, religious activities and deity concepts are preponderantly male. The association of a procreant female figure with the fertility of the soil implies a fairly high level of generalized and symbolic thinking, as does the death and resurrection theme associated with the vegetation cycle. The Sumerians, however, were already sophisticated poets. It appears that there might be two impulses toward the formation of anthropomorphic gods: the female, agriculture cultist and the male hunter, pastoralist, and worshiper of male potency. In each case there may have been a connection with matriarchal or patriarchal social organization, depending on which impulse was dominant. If they both arose in the same culture or one was assimilated to the other, there would be a transition period, ritual marriages might be necessary to create a synthesis. There might also be a deep-seated sex antagonism, and indeed Geza Roheim sees it in the death and resurrection formula. He feels the sexual act, the loss of erection and semen, is identified by primitives with death. In other words, Inanna's male partner dies symbolically in coitus.

In general, the well-organized and highly practical Sumerian state religion implies a relationship of obligation in which man is the servant of his capricious gods. The beginning of a more philosophical questioning of the ethical scheme of the world is apparent in what is the first poem on the Job theme in world literature, a theme which was to be developed by the Babylonians in the lament, "I will praise the Lord of Wisdom," and made familiar to the modern world by the Old Testament.

The poem begins with an introduction in which it is stated that man should praise his god and keep him in a good temper. Then follows a catalogue of the misfortunes of a righteous man:

> I am a man, a discerning one, yet he who
>   respects me prospers not,
> My righteous word has been turned into a lie,
> The man of deceit has covered me with the South Wind,
>   I am forced to serve him,
> He who respects me not has shamed me before You. . . .
> I, the wise, why am I bound to the ignorant youths?
> I, the discerning, why am I counted among the
>   ignorant?
> Food is all about, yet my food is hunger,
> On the day shares were allotted to all, my
>   allotted share was suffering.

He goes on to complain that malignant sickness bathes his body and demands to know how long his god will leave him unguided. Like his Hebrew successor, the Sumerian poet finds no explanation for the contradictions of life, like him he contrives a pietistic happy ending in which the god relents.

> The evil fate which had been decreed for him
>   in accordance with his sentence, he turned aside,
> He turned the man's suffering into joy,
> Set by him the kindly genii as a watch and a
>   guardian,
> Gave him . . . angels with gracious mien.

In Sumer, by the historical period, a sophisticated religion had developed, mixed with a good deal of magic and divination. Although the gods were anthropomorphic, many seals showed animals in erect positions carrying out ritual activities. Although priests are often depicted as naked, it may be that the animal figures represent acolytes in masks and the skins of beasts. In Sumerian religion, therefore, there were probably survivals of what, for lack of a better word, we should call totemism or at least some cultic relation to animals. In general, however, the fertility principle is dominant, overlaid with the deity as patron of the city-state and organizer of specialized urban society. In this complex of religious practices the figures of the earth mother or fertility goddess and the bearded bull stand out. They were destined to have a long life in other cultures and in other areas.

CHAPTER 6

Divine Heroes of the Fertile Plain

Babylonia, Assyria and the Hittites—all three peoples borrow from Sumerian mythology and culture—development of the death and resurrection theme— Tammuz and Ishtar, fertility goddess bewails dying god—Enkidu in Gilgamesh epic as bearded bull—flood theme derived from Sumer—search for immortality and the coming of death—role of semidivine king in Babylonian New Year ceremony—fertility marriage—seasonal conflict—Hittite weather god as bull—first appearance of castration theme in Hurrian-Hittite myth— religion in support of master and servant ethos.

F OR more than three thousand years elements in the culture which we call Sumerian dominated the Near East, surviving conquest and political change. Along the river valleys green fringes of vegetation extended out into the desert where checkered fields were marked off by irrigation ditches. In their midst rose the cities with high walls, towers and battlements, pierced by gateways, behind which huddled a tangle of rather narrow and not too clean streets, lined with flat-roofed adobe houses. Another high wall enclosed the temple which, on its ziggurat, dominated the town. It has been suggested that the mountain origin of the Sumerians caused them, out of nostalgia, to build these man-made mountains of sun-baked brick.

A Semitic ruler united the Sumerian cities about 2350 B.C. to form an empire with Akkad as its center. His dynasty lasted a couple of hundred years, to be destroyed by invasions of barbarians whose inferior culture was lost in the greater one of the river valleys. The Sumerian kings of Ur again reunited and extended the empire, which once more collapsed under the impact of new barbarous Semites from the west. About 1800 B.C. a new Semitic dynasty ruling from Babylon put an end to the domination of the Sumerian aristocracy and carried the Mesopotamian civilization to its climax, modifying the basic culture with a new sophistication and perfecting the techniques of imperialism.

The new empire, enriched by pillage, developed a middle class of merchants and artisans, and spawned a bureaucracy to administer the complicated tax structure. In an effort to protect the small man from the extortion of officials, oppression by aristocrats, and robbery by soldiers, the Babylonians refined the Sumerian legal system. The great ziggurat of

Babylon rose in seven setbacks to a height of two hundred feet. Reliefs of bulls and dragons adorned the walls which flanked the Ishtar gate. On the roofs of palaces were gardens containing good-sized trees, the so-called "hanging gardens."

The Babylonians spelled out their own language in the Sumerian cuneiform and developed a money economy which stimulated the growth of trade. With the use of a medium of exchange, however, wealth began to be concentrated in the hands of great landlords who were also war captains. As a result, the price of barley rose steadily. It is clear that the small man's life was not greatly enriched by the increase of luxury enjoyed by the ruling class.

While the Babylonian empire was reaching its zenith, in the valley of the upper Tigris another Semitic people, the Assyrians, were also forging an empire and learning a great deal from the Babylonians. The Assyrians' chief interest was in war and conquest. In the second millennium they challenged the power of Babylonia. However, they succeeded only in the eighth century B.C. in becoming the supreme power in the Mesopotamian world. They built in stone, covering their palace walls with reliefs showing soldiers attacking walled cities, torturing captives, and carrying off women and children. Their culture they took over from Babylonia.

Many of their stone reliefs are in Western museums and from these their appearance is familiar to us. Tall hats and tightly curled beards and curiously modeled muscles distinguish them from their neighbors. The Babylonians wore long robes and square-cut beards while the Sumerians affected a flounced skirt which left the upper part of the body bare, a style worn by both men and women.

Still a third people, the Hittites, were also destined to build an empire in the Near East. Although earlier than the Assyrians, they did not reach the peak of their power until the period from about 1400 to 1200 B.C. Now for the first time we hear of the Indo-Europeans, nomadic hunters and warriors from the Asian steppes. The Hittites were a branch of this group which probably migrated into Anatolia (now Turkey) from somewhere near the Black Sea. They brought their own hieroglyphic writing which they reserved for such matters as the activities of gods and kings. They also used a cuneiform like that of the third dynasty of Ur for more mundane affairs. The Hittites, who called their country the land of Hatti, were eclectic. They borrowed much from Babylonia and also from the Hurrians, whom they eventually conquered.

The Hittites were remarkable for bringing the training of horses to a high level, using a light two-wheeled battle chariot which became a formidable weapon in their wars of conquest, and for developing the technique of working iron, a secret which became a monopoly. Their kings were less

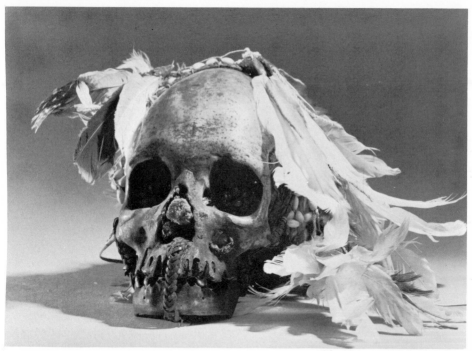

Asmat trophy skull from Papua, New Guinea, equipped with handle for carrying and decorated with feathers. Skulls found in the Paleolithic may have been preserved for similar reasons.

Gilyak bearbaiting ceremony, Island of Sakhalin. Bear skulls found in Paleolithic sites indicate ancient ritual connected with bear hunting.

Drawing of half-bison, half-man from the cave of Les Trois Frères.

Palimpsest of drawings from the cave of Les Trois Frères consisting of 25 bisons, 6 horses and 2 reindeer and the half-man, half-bison at the very bottom. From a stretch of wall below the Great Sorcerer, Upper Paleolithic.

The Great Sorcerer, cave of Les Trois Frères, Upper Paleolithic.

After Catlin, The Smithsonian Institution

The buffalo dance of the Mandan Indians of the North American plains, a magical ceremony to increase the game and ensure successful hunting.

The Willendorf Venus, Upper Paleolithic, Austria.

The American Museum of
Natural History

The American Museum of Natural History: photo S. Zamiatnin

Female figurines carved from mammoth tusk, from Gagarino, Russia, Upper Paleolithic.

After Breuil

Reindeer with web feet, half-stag, half-bison, followed by bison-man playing the musical bow, from the cave of Les Trois Frères.

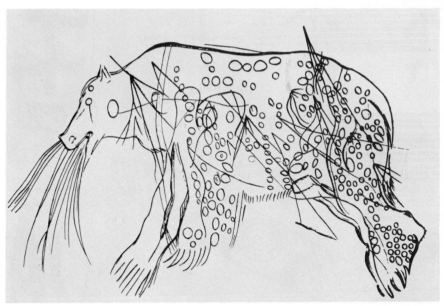

After Breuil

Bear, depicted as wounded, from the cave of Les Trois Frères. A form of hunting magic similar to that indicated by the clay bear, covered with the animal's hide and pierced with arrows, found in the Montespan cave.

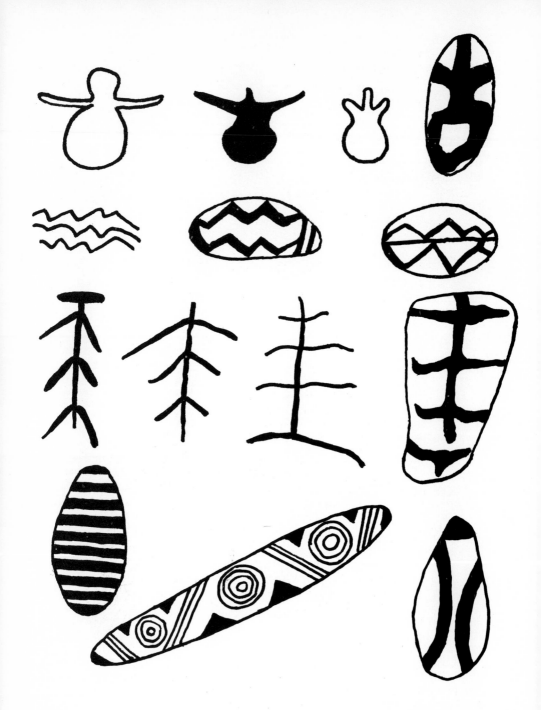

Top row: Three Spanish Mesolithic rock drawings and an Azilian pebble, all believed to be formalizations of the human figure. *Second row:* Spanish Mesolithic rock drawing and two Azilian pebbles. *Third row:* Three Spanish Mesolithic rock drawings and an Azilian pebble, also probably formalizations of the human figure. *Fourth row:* Arunta stone churinga, Arunta wooden churinga, Kaitish stone churinga, Central Australia.

Clay female figure from Tepe Gawra, Halafian period, about 3800 B.C. Probably a precursor of the fertility goddess.

The University Museum, Philadelphia

An offering to the fertility goddess Inanna, from a Sumerian vase about 3000 B.C.

Iraq Museum

The ziggurat at Ur, about 3000 B.C. The pyramid temple develops for the first time in Mesopotamia.

The University Museum, Philadelphia

Gilgamesh wrestles with lions, a double, bearded bull-man Enkidu between. Probably Late Dynastic Sumerian seal.

Museum of Fine Arts, Boston

Nude hero wrestles with bull, Gilgamesh wrestles with bearded bull-man, the bull-man Enkidu wrestles with human-headed bull. Late Early Dynastic Sumerian seal.

The sun god Shamash emerging from the gates of the East. Note third figure from the left is a bearded bull-man with horned headdress. Babylonian seal, about 2000 B.C.

The Metropolitan Museum of Art, Purchase, 1886

A bearded bull-man from Umma, Sumeria, restored, center, from statues right and left. Probably about 3000 B.C.

Left: The Hittite weather god, Teshub, from Zinjirli, second millennium B.C. (*After Gurney*) *Right:* Baal or El, chief Canaanite sky god, from Ras Shamra, second mellennium. Note bull's horns on helmet. (*C. F. A. Schaeffer and Mission Archéologique Française*)

Sumerian priest holding a libation cup, from Umma, 2600 B.C.

After Piggot

Top row: Two clay female figures, Kulli culture, south Baluchistan, second millennium B.C. *Middle row:* Bull from Kulli pottery. *Bottom row:* First two figures, female clay figurines from Rana Ghundai culture, northern Baluchistan, second millennium B.C. Third figurine from Harappa, Indus Valley culture, second millennium B.C. These may indicate the presence of a fertility deity.

Bearded priest or priest king from Mohenjo-Daro, Indus Valley culture, second millennium B.C.

*Archaeological Survey of India
and Art Reference Bureau*

Bull seal from Mohenjo-Daro, Indus Valley culture, second millennium B.C.

*Archaeological Survey of India
and Art Reference Bureau*

despotic than the priest-kings of Babylon, for like those of Sumer they were responsible to a council of nobles and in their feudal system all classes had privileges and obligations. Their art is clumsier and less distinctive than that of Sumer or Babylon. It depicts them wearing long robes or short tunics, conical or round hats, and peculiar shoes with turned-up toes. They had heavy curving noses and receding chins.

They infiltrated Anatolia at the beginning of the second millennium, building walled cities containing inner citadels with stone towers and battlements which were as important architecturally as their hollow-square temples. They dealt the power of Egypt a severe setback in the battle of Kadesh in 1296 B.C. By the end of the twelfth century B.C. their empire fell apart and by the eighth the Assyrians became the leading military state.

All of these ancient urban cultures were based on slavery; it was a result of such unpaid labor that they were able to accumulate reserves of wealth. The status of slaves varied. In Babylonia they were even allowed to go into business, owning property and trading with other slaves or free men. It must also be remembered that children born of slave mothers could attain their freedom and likewise slaves could buy their own freedom after undergoing certain rites of purification.

The ordinary citizen's home was very much like the sort of house which is still in use in primitive areas of the Near East. It consisted of a hollow square with a courtyard in the center into which the rooms opened. There was one doorway into the court and no windows in the external walls, merely channels for ventilation. This type of house was dictated by the hot climate. It had a flat roof which could be used for drying grain and other household activities. It was probably whitewashed on the outside. Often the door frame was outlined in red, the magical color we have met before, which was here supposed to keep out evil powers.

Indeed, even though these people had taken a great step forward in the direction of social and political organization and were rapidly improving their technology, magic was still woven into the texture of daily life. The primitive hunter repeats spells along with all his activities to ensure their success; these city dwellers were much concerned with divination, lucky and unlucky days for beginning their projects. Numbers, because of their strange mathematical properties, were regarded by the Babylonians with particular respect. The syllables of their language were given numbers, hence every proper name could be written in numbers. The perfect number 60 belonged to Anu, the father of the gods. The clay cylinder seals which have been recovered in such large numbers also mirror this belief in magic. Each individual had his seal with which he stamped upon his property some image or symbol of divine significance. Since the Babylonians had some five thousand gods, there were plenty to choose from. Many of these were duplications of the same basic divine entity; in fact sometimes one god was split up into as many as a hundred or so attributes which were all given names. At any rate, the protective value of the seal lay in the fact that the god whose image it carried would be angry if it were broken. Likewise there were a number of sacred symbols such as the sun disk, the crescent, maces, or arrowhead which were associated with specific gods and believed to be endowed with mana. In consequence, small replicas were used as charms, a practice which anticipates the symbolical significance of the cross, the six-pointed star, or the crescent. Babylonian magic and divination were carried over into other cultures influenced by the Near East and faint echoes of its methods still survive in the commercial astrological activities of modern times.

Two classes of priests were practitioners in these arts, the *ashipu* whose specialty was to protect individuals from the malice of evil spirits, witches, and sorcerers, and the *baru* whose task was to interpret omens and predict the future. Some of these doctors and dream analysts were poorly paid professionals who ministered to the daily anxieties of the average citizen. Those associated with the court and the temple could aspire to wealth and power.

The demons who caused human ills were sometimes the dead who had not been properly buried and sometimes offspring of Anu and Enlil or the gods of the underworld. Since the Babylonians believed in a science of magic by which the gods and the forces of the universe could be controlled, those who used such science for evil purposes were considered sorcerers. The penalty for this was death. The ashipu could perform rites to protect pregnant women, quiet a crying child, frustrate an enemy, or ensure favor with the king. Thus it will be seen that their activities were psychoanalytical as well as medical.

An interesting example of the connection between myth and practical treatment occurs in the following bit of dental magic:

> After Anu had created heaven,
> Heaven had created the earth,
> The earth had created the canals,
> The canals had created the marsh
> And the marsh had created the worm—
> The worm went weeping before Shamash,
> His tears flowed before Ea:
> "What wilt thou give me for my food?
> What wilt thou give me for my sucking?"
> "I shall give thee the ripe fig
> And the apricot."

"Of what use are they to me, the ripe fig
And the apricot?
Lift me up and among the teeth
And the gums cause me to dwell.
The blood of the tooth will I suck,
And of the gum I will gnaw
Its roots!"
Fix the pin and seize its foot.
[This was an instruction to the priestly dentist.]
"Because thou hast said this, O worm,
May Ea smite thee with the might
Of his hand!"

The text goes on to prescribe treatment, the incantation to be repeated three times.

Most treatment made use of the substitute, an animal, a clay image, or even an object such as a staff, a principle which has been handed down in magic to this day. When the treatment was said to take place in the "desert" the latter was meant as a symbol of the underworld from whose power the sick man must be freed.

Tying magic knots was another symbolical act; they could be used by a sorcerer to gain power over an enemy. The ashipu, in this case, untied them. He also undertook the task of protecting human activities from supernatural mischance. The most dangerous times in building a house were the laying of the foundation and its completion. The ashipu had to be present to recite the appropriate incantation and to bury amulets and figurines of gods or demons under the foundation. When the structure was completed he set out a clay figure of the brick god with provisions, in a little boat to carry him away, reciting an incantation which began "Brick-god, you are torn out, you are cut off, you are humbled ... " He and the builders were supposed to avert their faces and throw seven tablets to the right and seven tablets to the left into the river. Perhaps the ceremonies which occur when modern public buildings are completed are a dim reflection of these ancient practices!

The hard-working ashipu was in constant demand by the innkeeper whose business was bad, by the prostitute whose clientele was falling off, by the farmer who wanted more rain or was visited by a plague of locusts; for every human ill there was an appropriate spell.

Since there was supposed to be a magical order in the universe, the reading of omens was a highly developed science in which attempts were made to both control and predict the future. The Babylonian cosmos was animistic in the sense that all matter, every tree or stone, had a will and character of its own. The will of the gods worked through them and by prayers and incantation the divine will could be manipulated. Observable phenomena, on the other hand, indicated the direction in which events were moving. The baru priests collected such observations wholesale, as the vast accumulation of omen texts from many Babylonian sites proves. If a man intended to set off on a journey, build a house, or arrange for the marriage of his daughter, the baru was called in. Likewise, if the king contemplated war he would not be so rash as to provoke it until he had consulted the diviners.

One set of omens involved pure interpretation, the analysis of dreams and visions, unusual births, movements of animals and the course of the heavenly bodies. Sennacherib was told by the god Ashur (the head of the Assyrian pantheon) in a dream that he would conquer Egypt. Joseph's divination in Egypt is testimony to the diffusion of this concept through Palestine and the rest of the Fertile Crescent. The baru could also induce dreams by a process called incubation. A special chamber in the temple was set aside for this purpose. The client after dreaming successfully would then have his vision interpreted by the expert, who worked with an inherited body of tradition.

Multiple births or monstrosities were supposed to be highly significant, since birth in itself was a strange process. For instance: "When a woman gives birth to a child with the head of a lion, there will be a mighty king over the land. When a woman gives birth to a child with no right ear, the days of the prince will come to an end." Quaint indeed are the omens drawn from the behavior of dogs. "When a white dog pisses on anyone, poverty will overtake him; if a black dog does the same, sickness will seize the man; if a brown dog does the same, that man will be joyful."

A more active kind of divination consisted in mechanical procedures carried out by the baru. Oil or flour was dropped upon the surface of water in a bowl; from the shapes which it assumed omens could be read. "When the oil forms two circles, one large and one small, the man's wife will give birth to a boy." The connection with traditional Halloween folklore scarcely needs to be pointed out. Divination by consulting the internal organs of slain animals which began in the Near East spread all over the ancient world. In Babylonian psychosomatic theory, the heart was the seat of the intelligence, the bowels and liver of the emotions. Hepatoscopy or liver divination was highly developed. Clay models of the liver divided into more than fifty compartments were accompanied by detailed manuals explaining the significance of each area. "When the 'finger' is like the head of a lion, his servants will expel the prince, when the 'finger' is like a lion's ear, the prince will have no rivals." Another mechanical form of divination consisted in casting lots and studying the positions in which they fell, a system practiced by modern primitives in many parts of the world.

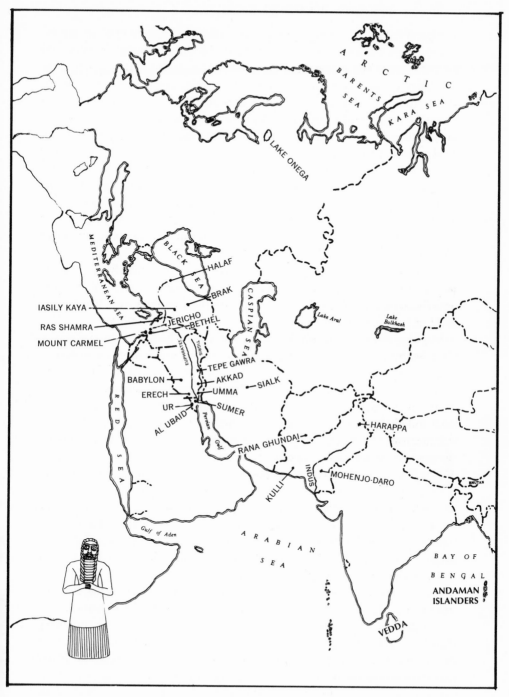

THE NEAR EAST AND ASIA

Divination by means of astrology was a science in itself and of course was based on observations which laid the basis for the subsequent development of astronomy. The planets and the stars were named for Babylonian gods; the body of traditional observation was written down in manuals which were probably compiled in the Sumerian era. The appearance and disappearance of the moon were considered to be portents, as was the conjunction of the sun and moon in the sky together. On the occasion of an eclipse of the moon, the Sumerian priests placed an altar at the gate of the house of their gods. "When the light fails they should cry aloud that catastrophe, murder, rebellion and eclipse come not near to Erech, the palace, the shrine of Eanna. . . . For a lamentation they should raise their cry. Until the eclipse is clear they should cry aloud." According to the month in which it took place, the eclipse was taken to portend social upheaval, floods, or agricultural prosperity.

Although it was not until the fifth century B.C. that the twelve signs of the zodiac, through each of which the sun passes during a month of the year, were established, already by 1300 B.C. the names of these signs had become emblems of certain gods who were, in turn, associated with stars and constellations. The casting of horoscopes therefore begins at Sumer, is developed by the Babylonians, and continues through European history to the present day.

While the Babylonian, Hittite and Assyrian peoples cultivated individual styles in art and in their way of life, they all made use of the Sumero-Babylonian cuneiform and, despite additions to and modifications of the pantheon, they shared basic mythological concepts which had been developed in the city-states of Sumer. In some cases missing portions of the myths have been restored by piecing together tablets from all three cultures. Consequently in various forms the ancient fertility ideas shine through the sophisticated elaboration of the priest-poets.

We have already seen Inanna as a goddess of love descending to the underworld and being allowed to return to earth when the shepherd god, Dumuzi, replaces her. Traditionally Inanna and deities like her may be either virgins, virgin mothers, or brides. The concept of her as a virgin seems to be an early one in which she is herself the fertile power of the earth, or the symbol may be split between Inanna and her alter ego Ereshkigal who is already dwelling below. The virgin-mother image is closer to Ninhursag. The lover, Dumuzi, as a shepherd is paired with Inanna, as a bull he is associated with Ninhursag. In the Babylonian myth of Tammuz and Ishtar, the lover has come to stand for the harvest, which the fertile powers of the earth produce, and also increase in general. The Babylonians created the image of the desolate mother, wandering in the barren fields or in the desolate sheepfolds or sitting in her temple wailing for her son and lover.

Tammuz, the dying god of increase, falls under a curse in midsummer, the season of drought when the rites were carried out.

> In Eanna, high and low, there
> They raise their voices in weeping, wailing for
>   the house of the dead.
> The wailing is for the plants, the first lament is
>   "they grow not."
> It is for the habitation and the floods;
>   they produce not.
> For the wedded ones, it is for the dying children;
> The dark-headed people do not create.
> The wailing is for the great river; it brings
>   the flood no more . . .

In this hymn the vitalizing power of irrigation is associated with Tammuz, who is involved with a water cult. A pantomime or possibly a rudimentary ritual drama took place. A wooden figure of the dying god was probably placed in a skiff and given over to the waters of the Euphrates or Tigris. Grain, sometimes spoken of as the body of Tammuz, was also thrown upon the waves. When the boat disappeared, a demon was supposed to have pulled the god under the waves. The earth mother's task was to arouse Tammuz from the sleep of death. This symbolization of the vegetation cycle was destined to be diffused over the world, appearing in Palestine, Egypt, and Greece and, indeed, the medieval myth of the Harrowing of Hell, in which Christ descends to liberate the virtuous prechristian worthies, echoes it. E. O. James sees it as the archetype of all deaths and resurrections.

By far the most important of the Mesopotamian legends is the great epic of Gilgamesh in which some unknown poet-priest about 2000 B.C. welded together a number of Sumerian episodes of independent origin into a culture-hero story which he endowed with a literary and philosophic significance.

As a historical king, Gilgamesh is listed as ruling during the first Sumerian dynasty of Uruk. As a mythological character, he is said to be the son of a goddess:

> Two thirds of his body is god and one third man;
> The shape of his body none can match . . .
> The force of his weapons has no equal . . .
> Gilgamesh is the shepherd of Uruk, the enclosures,
> He is our shepherd, strong, handsome and wise.

This hero is credited with building the city with its great walls. His energy and enthusiasm are so great, however, that he drives his people mercilessly until they cry out. His sexual appetite is also ravenous. The gods decide to create a counter-hero who shall divert some of his energies. Enkidu is described as a primitive being.

> The locks of his hair sprout like grain.
> He knows nothing of people or land;
> He is clad in a garb like that of Sumerquam
>   [a god of cattle and vegetation]
> With the gazelle he eats grass;
> With the wild game he presses on to the drinking place;
> With the animals his heart delights in water.

At the complaint of the hunter that he interferes with the capture of game and the shepherd that he leads away the flocks, a temple prostitute is sent to destroy his primitive power and to civilize him.

> When he waters the game at the drinking place,
> She shall take off her dress and lay bare her
>   attractions.
> When he sees her he will approach her.
>
> The prostitute saw the wild man.
> "This is he, prostitute, bare your breasts;
> Open your thighs that he may surrender.
> Do not prevent him from approaching;
> When he sees you, he will approach you.
> Open your dress so that without it, with
>   female wiles,
> You incite lust in him to lie upon you.
> Then the animals which he feeds in his fields
> Will change their habitation,
> When he bestows his love upon you."
> She did not prevent him from approaching her;
> She incited his lust with female wiles;
> He bestowed his love upon her.
> For six days and seven nights Enkidu coupled
>   with the prostitute.

The prostitute, impressed by his virility, urges him to visit the city. His erotic sophistication is thought of as endowing him with wisdom; in a sense it is the eating of the apple. Enkidu first fights with Gilgamesh, then becomes his dear friend. Ishtar makes advances to Gilgamesh, who rejects her. In revenge she sends the Great Bull of Heaven against the two heroes. This creature is so powerful that with a single snort he mows down a hundred men. When the heroes overcome him, Ishtar persuades the gods to kill Enkidu. As Enkidu is dying, he dreams of the journey to the underworld.

> On the road whose path does not lead back,
> Where dust is their food and clay their sustenance,
> Where they are clad like birds and dwell in darkness,
> In the house of dust which I entered.
> I looked at the kings and behold
> Their crowns had been put away.

Gilgamesh, inconsolable at the death of Enkidu, sets out in search of the secret of immortality. During his adventures he encounters the Babylonian Noah, Utanapishtim, the only man to become immortal. The latter launches into the story of the flood with all of the familiar details which were borrowed for the Hebrew version, including the specifications of the ark.

> I entered the ship and closed my door . . .
> For one day the tempest blew:
> Faster it blew and faster,
> As if in battle men were overcome;
> No man could see his fellow.
> Those in heaven could not distinguish men,
> Even the gods were terror-stricken at the flood;
> They fled and ascended to the heaven of Anu,
> The gods cowered like dogs and crouched in distress.

For six days and seven nights the storm went on, after which Utanapishtim sent out a dove, a swallow, and a raven. Enlil, the storm god, who had sent the flood, was angry that Utanapishtim had escaped but the other gods protested until the master of the air relented and made the Babylonian Noah immortal. (The flood was a very real thing in the history of the Sumerians, apparently an actual event, for they dated the reigns of some of their kings before and some after its occurrence.)

Gilgamesh is promised immortality if he can stay awake for six days and seven nights but, wearied by his travels, he immediately falls asleep for six days. He is about to leave in disappointment when Utanapishtim finally grants him a plant which he is to eat when he becomes old in order to renew his youth. Unfortunately on the trip back he comes upon a pool of cold water. He strips to bathe and while doing so a snake which lives in the pool smells the herb, eats it and gains the power to change his skin and thus rejuvenate himself, while to Gilgamesh immortality is lost forever.

The hero returns to his city and resigns himself to enjoy life while he can and to rejoice in the power and importance of the city he has built.

The poem is shot through with primitive themes. Enkidu with his hair like grain and his identification with animals reflects a mixture of fertility ideas. On a number of the cylinder seals of early dynastic times there appears an image of the bearded bull-man, upright and engaged in struggles with lions or ruminants or sometimes with a naked hero. It has been pointed out that Enkidu of this first part of the poem is a different sort of character from Enkidu the bosom friend of Gilgamesh in later episodes. It seems possible, as Henri Frankfort writes, "If at various times Bull-men appear in Mesopotamian art and fill a variety of functions (as attendants for instance of the sun god) they may well represent survivals or elaborations of a tradition which, though it was utilized by the authors of the epic, existed independently in Mesopotamia." Granting this, and in view of the lines in which Enkidu eats grass with the gazelles and drinks water along with the animals, there seems good reason to believe that the bull-man and the early Enkidu are one and the same. It is possible to go further: We remember that the prostitute with whom he performs such sexual feats is a representative of Ishtar. The coupling of these two ancient fertility spirits looks very much like a reflection of the association of what may be the two oldest gods of history, the earth mother and the primal deity of animal husbandry. The fact that Enkidu protects both the wild animals and releases the domesticated ones might be a reflection of the transition from the hunting of animals to their domestication. The Great Bull of Heaven is certainly our bearded bull once more (somewhere along the line he has become associated with the air god). When he is killed and Ishtar laments his bleeding thigh we are confronted with an echo of the dying god who is the illogical composite of vegetable and animal fertility. The flood myth is of course a separate story ingeniously worked into the texture of the epic. It probably germinated from an unusual season of storms which destroyed the irrigation system. The flood in the Mesopotamian myth does not come about as a punishment for sin but more as the result of the unpredictability of Enlil.

The loss of the gift of immortality through the misbehavior of an animal seems to be a widely diffused myth. Frazer elaborates upon it in *Folklore in the Old Testament*. An East African story recounted a visit to earth on which God addressed all living things and asked, "Who does not wish to die?" All unfortunately were asleep except the snake, the only one to reply to the divine question, and as a result the snake renews its youth by casting its skin. It is remarkable that the concept of renewal of youth by casting the skin is common to these myths of latter-day primitives and the Gilgamesh epic.

On the whole, we must admire the ingenuity by which the Babylonian poet has welded together this series of stories in order to sustain his main theme, the immanence of death. Already the sophisticated city dweller has

passed beyond the more primitive concept of the living corpse to the awful
sense of finality and a yearning for a renewal of life. Enkidu's vision of the
underworld is a bleak one; kings and commoners all are found in the same
dark and dusty place. The early episodes of the poem are skillfully organized
to display the superhuman vitality of the two heroes who nevertheless cannot vanquish the final enemy, while Gilgamesh's anguish and subsequent
journey achieve a great deal of dignity and power.

The Babylonian Genesis, called the *Enuma Elish* from its first line which
starts "When above," is particularly interesting as an example of the relation between Mesopotamian state religion and politics. Marduk, the patron
god of Babylon, as that city became dominant, had been advanced to the
role of king of heaven, replacing Enlil. In the *Enuma Elish* the glorification
of Marduk is the poet's chief aim and consequently a new version of creation results differing from that of the Sumerians. This fact also helps to date
the composition of the poem to about 1800 B.C. A primal male, Apsu,
standing for the sweet waters of the abyss, begot other hierarchies of gods
upon Tiamat, the salt water of the ocean. The primal sea therefore plays a
role similar to that in the Sumerian concept. The younger gods (before
heaven and earth had been named) became noisy and irritated their father.
He planned to destroy them, but was himself destroyed by his son, Enki,
the water god.

Ea and Damkina begot Marduk, the symbol of Babylonian supremacy.
He was extraordinarily beautiful, apparently on the theory that more of
everything was desirable since:

> Four were his eyes, four were his ears;
> When he moved his lips fire breathed forth.

Tiamat, however, determined to be revenged for the death of her husband.
She manufactured monsters.

> She set up the viper, the dragon, and the Lahamu,
> The great lion, the mad dog, and the scorpion man,
> Mighty storm demons, the dragonfly and the bison,
> Bearing relentless weapons, unafraid of battle.

The gods chose Marduk to be their champion, a role which he accepted
provided he be given the supremacy in heaven. At the banquet which followed, they were very merry,

> So that they sang for joy as they drank strong drink;
> Exceedingly carefree they were; their hearts were exalted.
> For Marduk their champion they decreed the destiny.

A long passage follows in which the power and pride of Babylon is symbolized in the epithets, dignities, and attributes which are heaped upon Marduk, the king of kings. When he went forth to battle,

> He held between his lips a talisman of red clay;
> An herb to destroy poison he held in his hand.

He destroyed the demons and finally killed Tiamat.

> The lord trod upon the legs of Tiamat
> And with his relentless club he split her skull.
> He cut open the arteries of her blood.
> Causing the north wind to carry it to far places,
> Like a mussel he split her into two parts;
> Half of her he set in place and formed the sky . . .
> Anu, Enlil, and Ea he caused to establish their
>   residence.

Later, after having created the sun, moon, and stars,

> Blood I will form and cause bone to be;
> Then I will set up lullu, "Man" shall be his name.
> Yes, I will create lullu: "Man."
> Service to the gods shall be imposed upon him
>   so that they may rest.

In short, as in the Sumerian version, man was created as a convenience to minister to the gods, a fairly clear rationalization of the citizen's duty to support the divine household of the god which included the priesthood and the king, a justification of the Mesopotamian social system.

The great Babylonian and Assyrian *Akitu* festival of the New Year (which had Sumerian roots) stressed the ceremonial significance of the king. For two thousand years this important *rite de passage* was enacted during the first eleven days of the month of Nisan in the spring of the year. Although the kings of Mesopotamia were never so completely identified with the god as we shall find them in Egypt, they were nevertheless sometimes thought of as divinely descended and in important religious functions they played a central role in cult activities. In the Akitu the king played such a role associated with basic fertility functions. The Babylonian Akitu can be taken as an archetype of the seasonal fertility drama which is repeated in other cultures.

Although the records of the ceremonies are fragmentary, and there is disagreement among scholars, some of whom are inclined to see more actual drama in the festival than others, the main outlines are clear. First a *Bit Akitu,* or festival house, was constructed on the outskirts of the city. The first four days were taken up with rites of preparation and purification. Prayers were said to Marduk; images were constructed; ablutions with water from the Tigris and Euphrates performed. The high priest recited the *Enuma Elish*. The fifth day was a day of atonement, for it was then that the king was ritually deposed. He entered the shrine of Marduk where the high priest removed his crown, ring, and scepter. He was struck in the face, forced to his knees before the statue, and obliged to make a negative confession announcing that he had not been negligent of his duties or failed in his service to the god. The priest absolved him, reinvested him with his royal regalia, and slapped his cheeks to make his tears flow. (As Theodor Gaster points out, among the Javanese natives as well as among the Khonds of Bengal and in Mexico tears are thought to reinvigorate the earth and even to serve as a homeopathic method of producing rain.)

Also on the fifth day the priests bound a bundle of forty reeds with a palm branch, laid them in a trench dug in the courtyard of the temple and led a white bull out beside it. The king set fire to the reeds with a torch, joining the priest in a prayer which began:

> Divine Bull, glorious light which lightens
> the darkness . . .

This is a reference to the constellation of the Bull, the reeds imitating the brightness of the stars. Since the king was a manifestation of Marduk it appears that the bull was here associated with a fertility aspect of the god.

While this ceremony went on, a kind of public drama was taking place in the city. Marduk in his Tammuz role was said to have disappeared, imprisoned in the "mountain" of the underworld, causing drought and desolation. The text, which is incomplete, mentions "fighting"; which probably means that some sort of dramatic spring and winter conflict went on. There was also lamentation and ritual searching for Marduk as the people ran about the streets in a frenzy. A "messenger" was sent to look for him and his empty chariot was sent careering down the road to the Bit Akitu. It is possible that a goddess also looked for him. There may have been a whole drama with a bloody puppet wept over by the goddess and the god magically restored to life by healing water. Marduk's son, Nabu, and the other gods of the pantheon arrived by barge on the following day. These were the images accompanied by their priests. The Babylonian images were of costly wood, plated with the divine metals, silver and gold, provided with large, staring, inset eyes. They were moved about in chariots or on barges and often their journeys from one city to another represented political dependency. The festival continued with the rescue of Marduk.

There is mention of a locked door: "They bored holes in the door and there they waged a battle." Nabu apparently played a leading role in the god's release on the eighth day of Nisan. It was then that all the gods (represented by their priests) assembled in the Chamber of Destinies in the temple to give Marduk his supreme power, his "destiny" by which he could renew the fruitfulness of the coming year. It is not clear whether there was an actual mimetic cult drama re-enacting the conflict with Tiamat or whether, as Frankfort suggests, some symbolic act such as the king smashing a pot with a weapon took place. But we do know that on this day the ritual concluded with a triumphal procession of the gods, no doubt driving chariots, bearing weapons, attended by their priests and acolytes with cult objects, the whole splendid parade bright with Oriental color, glittering with gold, silver, and jewels, and probably accompanied by barbaric martial music. On the tenth day the gods celebrated a victory banquet, the jubilation over the renewal of vitality, in the Bit Akitu. On their return the king and queen seem to have been joined in a ritual marriage in a chamber on one of the stages of the ziggurat, symbolical of the union of the earth mother with her consort. It seems probable that the king and queen spent the night in the temple and the marriage was sexually consummated. The Babylonian king and queen therefore became the representative symbols in this fertility magic. On the eleventh day the gods assembled again to determine the destinies of the year and on the twelfth returned to their own temples.

Frazer in his famous study *The Golden Bough* made much of the Babylonian symbolic yearly deposition of the king. He mentions another festival, called the Sacaea under Persian rule, in which a prisoner, condemned to death, was dressed in the king's robes, allowed to enjoy the king's prerogatives and his concubines, then was stripped of his robes, scourged and hanged or impaled. In this mimetic execution of the king he saw an example of the killing of the king as a fertility spirit when his vital powers showed signs of decline.

The body of myth and observance which has just been discussed was shared by the Sumerians, Babylonians and Assyrians. The Hittites, being eclectic, used three languages and the Mesopotamian cuneiform as well as their own hieroglyphic writing. In consequence, when they refer to a god by a Mesopotamian name, it is difficult to know whether he represents the same entity as that worshiped in Mesopotamia. Aside from borrowing from Babylonia, the Hittites seem to have absorbed something from the indigenous Hattic people and a great deal from their Hurrian neighbors. Their chief male divinity was the weather god who has many manifestations. It is possible that he was a combination of a number of local weather and fertility deities. His Hurrian name was Teshub and his wife was Hepat. A relief from the New Empire shows him in the form of a bull. Many images of bulls are found in small shrines. In other representations he stood upon a bull, or bulls pulled his chariot. This is the only case in the Hittite pantheon in which an animal stood for a god. Hans Güterbock wrote: "The weather god's sacred animal is the bull and, according to an older conception, he is the animal itself."

The Hittite sun goddess of Arinna was a true solar deity who sometimes outranked the weather god in importance. She was queen of heaven, protector of the king, and sometimes became an aspect of Ishtar. Actually the earth mother fertility figure is split up into various manifestations. Teshub's sister, Shoushka, is the Hurrian goddess of marriage and sexuality. Ishtar, too, was borrowed from Mesopotamia. Again, in the myth of Telipinu (the Hattic Tammuz), a son of Teshub, who disappeared and brought all life to a standstill, it is the goddess Kamrusepas who sends a bee to awaken him and remind him of his duty. Although Kamrusepas is a goddess of magic she plays a parallel role to that of the earth mother.

Hittite rituals were probably similar to those in Mesopotamia. There is a reference to a mighty festival at the beginning of the year at which the gods gathered to eat and drink and to "pronounce the life" of the king and queen. It has been suggested that this was a New Year's rite like the Akitu in which a sacred marriage of Teshub and Hepat took place.

Near the city of Boghazkeui, in Turkey, a deep cleft in the rocks called Iasily Kaya is one of the great shrines of the ancient city of Hatti. A strip of craggy wall about three feet high is hewn smooth and sculptured with two great processions which meet at the back of the cleft. The right-hand row of figures consists, with two exceptions, of robed women; the left is composed, with two exceptions, of male figures with the addition of a winged being; there are forty-five figures on the left and twenty-one on the right. The long procession of soldiers on the right, wearing conical hats and shoes with curled-up toes, appears to be running or dancing; the opposing women move at a more majestic pace. The male leaders of the dancing procession are images of Teshub, the weather god, in both general and local aspects. Among them is the priest-king. The leader of the procession of women is identified as a mother goddess, Ma or Ishtar, and her son, who stands for Tammuz. Both ride on lions. They are followed by local manifestations of the mother god and other local divinities. John Garstang is convinced that the whole great assemblage of Hittite divinities is a representation of a sacred marriage, the sky god united with the great mother. He suggests that it also may commemorate the marriage of Hattusil, a Hittite king, with Putu-Khipa, a daughter of the priest of Ishtar and herself a high priestess of the sun goddess of Arinna. The marriage was a political alliance, after a series of crises, which established the throne. If this interpretation is correct, the whole imposing sculptured procession is a proof of the state character of the Hittite fertility religion.

The Hurrian-Hittite myth of creation starts out with a mention of the familiar Anu, Enlil and Ea (Enki) and recounts a conflict between elder and younger gods somewhat parallel to that in the *Enuma Elish*. Written in prose, the early portion runs as follows:

> Then in the ninth year Anu fought against Kumarbi. Kumarbi, in the place of Alalu, fought against Anu. Anu could not endure Kumarbi's eyes any more; he escaped from Kumarbi's hand and fled. Anu, as a bird, flew toward heaven. After him Kumarbi rushed and he took Anu by the feet and pulled him down from heaven. He bit his testicles so that his manhood was absorbed into Kumarbi's entrails. When Kumarbi swallowed Anu's manhood, he rejoiced and laughed. Anu turned back to him and to Kumarbi he spoke. "Thou feelest joy within thine entrails because thou has swallowed my manhood. Do not feel joy within thine entrails. Into thine entrails I have laid a seed! First I have impregnated thee with Teshub, secondly I have impregnated thee with the heavy god, with Atanzah, thirdly I have impregnated thee with the heavy god, Tigris. Three fearful gods have I laid as seeds into thine entrails."

The rest of the narrative is fragmentary but it appears that Kumarbi was warned against Teshub and there is a possibility that Kumarbi eats one of his children. The castration theme appears here for the first time but it will be encountered later in other traditions.

The most important Hittite festival, analogous to the Akitu, was Purulliyas (of Hattic derivation) which also involved a ritual combat. It was so important that a king returned from a war to take part. Unlike the Akitu, it took place in autumn, which was the beginning of the Hittite year, a time when water was needed to relieve the drought. The myth indicates that the weather god has been deprived of his heart and eyes (hence has been symbolically castrated) by the water dragon. The weather god's son regains his father's organs and kills the dragon. At the end of the prose narrative there is a description of a procession of the gods and the enumeration of their seating at a banquet. A religious drama, similar to that of the Akitu, may have taken place.

Hittite religion, therefore, exhibits themes which run through all of Mesopotamian culture. A tablet, which makes the social aspects of the state fertility religion particularly clear, elaborates the metaphor of the master and the servant.

> "Is the mind of the people and the gods really different?"
> "No. The mind is the same. When the servant stands before his master he must wash and wear clean clothes and he gives him to eat or he gives him to drink. And then he [the master] eats and drinks some-

thing and he is refreshed in mind and is gracious toward him. If, however, the servant is neglectful and is not zealous, then his mind toward him is different. If the servant gives annoyance to his master then one kills him and mutilates his nose, his eyes, his ears. The master seizes him, his wife, his children, his brother, his sister, his relatives, his descendants, be they male or female slaves. Then one disgraces him in public and one takes no account of him and his descendants are placed with him."

In this formulation the god and the earthly master were the same. If the servant displeased the god, disasters and sickness followed; in the case of the master, cruel punishments were concretely dealt out. In the prayer of King Mursilis it is made clear that when a servant confesses his transgressions, if the master is in a good mood he will pardon him. Everything, however, depends upon the whim of the ruler. This, of course, is the germ of the inexplicability of a god's judgments which is developed philosophically in later sophisticated religious thinking.

The whole passage also reflects other aspects of the terrestro-divine master and servant relation. The command to wash and put on clean clothes of course symbolized ritual purification and ritual garments. The serving of food and drink is the core of religious observance. In the temple food and drink was offered to the god, a curtain was drawn while the deity ate, in order to lend the action mysterious significance, and later the food was discreetly consumed by the priests.

Since the relationship between the sacral king or priest, who owned the city-state, was a despotic one, the same relationship was reflected in the state religion. It is also notable that the concept of the sins of the fathers being visited upon their children is here carried to brutal extremes.

CHAPTER 7

The One God and the Many

Syria and Palestine—resurrection and conflict themes in Canaanite myth—Baal as bull-man, Asherah as fertility goddess—influence of Canaanite religion on that of the Hebrews—festivals related to local fertility cults—prophets as ecstatic shaman-diviners—unique intolerance of Hebrew monotheism.

AT TIMES we can clearly see how man's religion is shaped by his relation to the earth on which he lives, molded by the climate and the seasons. His desire and his imagination are given form and poetry by the forces of nature. This is especially true of the area comprising Syria and Palestine—the east coast of the Mediterranean, bordered by Anatolia on the north, Mesopotamia on the east, and Egypt to the south. It is a region particularly subject to drought and famine; in fact, no portion of the Near East has had such an uncertain water supply. The dry season lasts from May until late September and as a result the tension concerning the arrival of the rains has always been particularly great.

We do not know very much about the fertility practices of the earliest inhabitants. The Mesolithic culture in Palestine, known as the Natufian, which developed between 12,000 and 9000 B.C., yields very early agricultural implements such as sickles, with blades made of microliths, and stone hoes. The Natufians were already living in villages, in houses with stone substructures and dried brick walls. Burial practices included mass graves with nests of severed heads like that at Ofnet. In Jericho, around 6000 B.C., communities of probably the same stock practicing a more developed agriculture carried out a unique burial rite in which detached skulls were filled with clay, the eyes inlaid with shell and the faces carefully modeled with clay so as to suggest portraits, a forerunner of funerary masks which occur in more sophisticated form in Egypt.

In the centuries which followed, the Syrian-Palestinian area developed an urban civilization roughly parallel to the Halafian in Mesopotamia. During the end of the fourth millennium B.C. there began to be considerable cultural diffusion, influences from Mesopotamia spreading through Syria and Palestine down to Egypt. Since the Eastern Mediterranean coast was a connecting bridge between the Near East, Anatolia, Egypt and, eventually, the Aegean, it was destined to become a kind of crossroads at which conflicting political powers met and clashed while resulting cultural influences flowed back and forth.

It was during the middle and late Bronze ages (the second millennium B.C.) that a people of mixed ethnic stock, some of whom probably arrived as nomads from southern Mesopotamia, developed a common material and religious culture. They were called Canaanites, they spoke a Semitic dialect and, despite harassment and temporary conquests by the Egyptians, they possessed as distinct a way of life as the Hittites. Their identity was destroyed by conquering Hebrew nomads, who also probably moved upward from the southern Mesopotamian deserts, and the Philistines who may have been Greeks. After a period of eclipse, and an infusion of a new ethnic stock, they reappeared as the Phoenicians and played an important role in the Mediterranean. Phoenician religion, however, was basically that of the Canaanites with Egyptian and Greek borrowings.

The Canaanites lived in small city-states led by chieftains who were continually at war with one another. They built heavily fortified citadels of mud brick and stone which contained palaces and temples with stone towers and columns supporting two or more stories of mud brick. The ruling class lived in pretentious houses consisting of a single or double row of rooms built around a court, a style similar to that of Mesopotamia. The half-free serfs who made up the rest of the population lived in miserable hovels.

Burial was in family graves in subterranean caverns. Apparently these graves were not limited to one class, since a great variety of objects has been found with the skeletons, some far more costly than others. Occasionally individuals were buried singly in an underground chamber reached by a vertical shaft. Artistically the Canaanites were eclectic, the southern area heavily influenced by Egypt while some stelae are Mesopotamian in character. The pottery of Canaan ran to graceful jars coated with slip which was burnished to a metallic sheen.

A particular characteristic of the citadels was the massive gate with two or three gateways, each flanked by pairs of massive piers and towers. They were wide enough to admit one or two chariots. Despite these impressive fortifications, towns were destroyed again and again and sometimes abandoned for years before being rebuilt. Political unrest was constant and shifts of power took place continually. As early as the nineteenth century B.C. Egypt controlled the lower half of the area as far as central Syria. In the same century a migration of Aryan and Hurrian warriors with horse-drawn chariots swept into Palestine and even penetrated into Egypt. They were followed by the Hyksos princes (probably Semitic barbarians) who conquered Egypt and Palestine only to be driven out in the sixteenth century, at which time the Egyptians reconquered Palestine.

The Canaanites, therefore, never attained the political unity which was eventually achieved by the Babylonians and the Hittites, yet, strangely enough, although so much of their culture was eclectic, in the field of religion a remarkable literature attests the originality of their imagination.

It was not until 1929 that this wholly forgotten world of mythology was discovered at Ras Shamra, ancient Ugarit, in northern Syria. Here hundreds of clay tablets bearing a hitherto unknown cuneiform were unearthed by C. F. A. Schaefer. They appear to have been the archives of a temple and were stored in a building between the city's two great temples, one dedicated to Baal, the other to Dagon. When the script was deciphered, it was discovered that two languages were used, Canaanite and Hurrian. Parts of at least four epic cycles have been published and translated. Although the texts are in many cases fragmentary, it is clear that the fertility themes are similar to those already encountered in Mesopotamia, but they are developed in individual forms which had a considerable influence upon the Bible.

The Canaanite religion, like that of Mesopotamia, united church and state. The king apparently officiated in important festivals and there is some suggestion of a purification ceremony which he went through in the month of Teshrit before the fall harvest. Banquets for the gods were held in the temples as in Babylonia. The most important god in the pantheon was Baal, a weather god, a "rider on the clouds," associated with the sky and rain. As Gaster puts it, he is a being of energy and fertility who quickens a woman or the earth. There were many local Baals. El is the father god, equivalent to Enlil, who was represented as good-natured and benevolent. At times he and Baal were identified with each other. Above all, to quote Gaster, "Like El and his Near Eastern counterparts, Baal was popularly portrayed as a bull . . ." Thus once more we meet the bull-man as emblem of both animal and vegetable fertility. The mother goddess appeared in several metamorphoses; sometimes she was Asherah who was originally the wife of the supreme deity, El, but who could also become a rival to Anat for the position of Baal's wife. Further confirmation of the importance of the fertility earth mother is a number of oval pottery plaques impressed from a mold with the nude figure of Asherah holding lily stalks or serpents, the breasts and delta accentuated. The head is adorned with two long ringlets which are attributes of the Egyptian goddess Hathor. The style of the plaques themselves is borrowed from Mesopotamia. Nude figurines have also been found.

Mot was the god of aridity and death, and Yam, a water dragon, was lord of the sea and waters of the earth. Gods of the sun and moon were

Shemesh and Yareah, while a pair of twins, Shahar and Shalem, stood for dawn and sunset. Dagon was a god of crops.

The myths themselves give us a picture of a civilization, on the one hand barbaric and brutal, and on the other curiously sophisticated. The Baal cycle is particularly interesting in that it contains both death and resurrection and conflict themes. The poem begins with the quarrel between Baal and Yam, the water dragon. The latter demands of the gods that Baal be handed over with his gold. The gods are frightened but Baal says bravely:

> Oh gods on your princely thrones,
> Raise your heads from your knees,
> Truly I will cow those messengers of the sea,
> That delegation of the ruler of the streams.

Baal, using clubs symbolic of thunder and lightning, is about to finish off the monster when Asherah intervenes. Yam is forgotten for a while as Baal demands a palace worthy of his importance. When he obtains this palace he refuses to have windows installed for fear of Yam's return. He then gives a feast in which oxen, rams and sheep are slaughtered and wine is served to all the goddesses.

In other words, the passage describes the typical chieftain's feast which is also the basis of the ritual meal offered to the gods. Furthermore, the gods invited are those who preside over livestock, over civil authority, and the vintage, three aspects of community life to which attention is directed at the autumn festival when the god of rain resumes his power. This is also parallel to the divine victory banquet, after subduing the monster, in other parts of the Near East. After this Yam is knocked on the head and Baal consents to have windows installed, windows through which rain will fall upon the earth.

> Now, when the window is opened in the mansion,
> The casement within the palace
> Do thou, O Baal, open a rift in the clouds!

The second part of the myth cycle has to do with the summer season. Baal has boasted that he will also do away with Mot, the spirit of drought and sterility. The latter cunningly invites him to a banquet in the underworld (for which Mot's name is also a synonym). Baal shows fear and is taunted by Mot. When Baal finally cannot avoid the challenge he is advised to copulate with a heifer in the pasture to gain strength, an act that clearly dramatizes his bull origin and also identifies him with El.

> Mighty Baal obeys.
> He makes love to a heifer in the pasture,
> To a young cow in the field.

> He couples with it seven and seventy times,
> It is mounted eighty and eight times
> And it conceives and bears male offspring.

Baal disappears into the underworld, whereupon he is lamented by Anat who here plays the earth mother role. Dressed only in a loincloth, the Canaanite mourning dress, she wanders about in the fields and woods gashing her cheeks and wailing precisely as Ishtar did in Babylonia. She recovers Baal's body from the underworld and herself fights with Mot. Here Mot is identified with the spirit of grain.

> In a sieve she scatters him;
> In a fire she burns him;
> In a mill she grinds him;
> Over the fields she strews him . . .

Baal returns triumphantly and eventually destroys the older gods who were his enemies. Finally there is the usual feast of communion.

In symbolic ritual and myth the Near East peoples accepted sex and celebrated the beneficial mana associated with it. The Israelites reacted to the dangerous side of sexual mana and for the first time we encounter a puritanical religion and an attempt to create a far more abstract concept of divinity.

Efforts have been made to identify the Hebrews with the Habiru, a people who do not seem to have had a homogeneous quality, for no characteristic names predominate. From Semitic documents they appear to have been professional soldiers, at times laborers, even slaves. It is suggested that they were bands of mercenaries who raided defenseless towns, sometimes sold their services to warrior chieftains or, when the period was peaceful and the area well policed, worked at whatever jobs they could find. They were likely to have been a mixed group, some outlaws from their native cities, some refugees, some Bedouins in search of richer land. Since their wanderings were in Semitic countries, they acquired a predominantly Semitic culture. Kathleen Kenyon suggests that Abraham fits into this picture since he was a soldier of fortune and a wanderer.

It has been conjectured that the Israelite nomads entered Egypt during the reign of the Hyksos kings, who were probably ethnically kin to them. Although accurate dating is not possible, the Hebrews are assumed to have left Egypt about the time when the Hyksos rulers were expelled. In the thirteenth century B.C. the Israelites overran the Canaanite cities. Bethel probably fell in the first half of the thirteenth century; the actual destruction of Jericho has not yet been dated. By the end of the century, however, the Israelite tribes had destroyed the power of the Canaanites, had plundered and rebuilt many of their cities and had fused their own culture with that of the conquered people. W. O. E. Oesterley considers their own religion to have been originally connected with the moon, since desert nomads travel by night and orient themselves by the moon. The origin of their supreme god, Yahweh, is obscure. He does not seem to have been a vegetation deity but he does seem to have acquired some weather god aspects which link him with Baal, though priests of his monotheistic cult fought assimilation violently. Indeed, Yahweh appears uniquely intolerant of any sort of pantheon. The Israelites, in contrast to their Mesopotamian neighbors, retained an austere, spartan outlook which seems to hark back to the original desert pattern of life. Although the cults of Baal and the earth mother persisted among the Canaanites and at times found adherents among backsliding Hebrew tribes, the creators of the Biblical literature never ceased to attack the local fertility religion and were particularly hard on such institutions as temple courtesans and divine ritual marriage, which they regarded as mere prostitution, and the bull-man sexuality aspects of Baal, which they denounced as bestiality. The golden calf episode is an example of Hebrew worship of the bull. Indeed, within the Hebrew religion itself there was a dichotomy. On the one hand the cult of the prophets was antiritualistic and concerned with ethics and mysticism, and on the other a well-developed pattern of festivals was strongly influenced by both Babylonian and Canaanite antecedents.

Three important Hebrew festivals display elements which seem to be borrowed from Babylonian or Canaanite sources: Shabuoth (weeks), a midsummer rite at the beginning of the barley harvest; Sukkoth (or festival of the tabernacles); and Massoth, the festival of unleavened bread to which Passover was assimilated, a spring festival transferred to autumn. All these, despite historical rationalizations, contain familiar primitive elements. Passover, which was combined with Massoth, was celebrated at the full moon near the vernal equinox. Firstborn sheep were sacrificed, which suggests that worship of a lunar fertility deity must have originally taken place. Blood was also sprinkled on the tent posts, a magical usage to ward off evil night spirits. The persistence of this particular type of fertility festival was brought home sharply to the writer when he visited the highlands of Peru at the period of Carnival (fall, in the Sierra season). In a small Quechua village in the court of every household a ceremony was going on which certainly symbolized the sacrifice of a yearling sheep. While a mountain orchestra of flute, violin and harp played and the whole kinship group got ritually drunk on chicha, one of the men of the family clipped a piece of the ear from each of the year-old sheep. The severed bits of flesh were placed in a bowl containing coca leaves (coca is associated with the religious practices of the ancient Peruvians). When the celebrants were asked the meaning of the ritual, they told the writer it was to keep the sheep from straying. The real significance was plain to see in the person of the fertility deities themselves, a boy and a girl, around whose necks were hung gourds, fruit, biscuits and carnival streamers, clearly symbols of fruitfulness which transformed the little brown-skinned pair into incarnations of ancient deities, the equivalent of mother goddess and cattle god. When the operation was over, the sheep were driven out into the field while the man of the household flung a handful of rose petals over their backs. Here, indeed, was a practice (probably substituting sheep for the original llama) which had survived the state sun worship of the Incas and the imposition of Catholicism by the Conquistadores, a striking parallel with the kind of fertility worship which has just been discussed in the Near East.

The eating of the Paschal lamb at Pesach was of course a sacrificial meal, the aim of which was to achieve communion with the gods. The word Pesach itself means to dance with a limp (there was a Canaanite Baal of dancing), which shows that dancing must have been an important part of the ritual. Proof that Passover antedated the historical meaning ascribed to it appears in the fact that a date for the holiday was not fixed until the period of Deuteronomic writing; instead, in an earlier era it occurred at different dates according to the time at which the barley ripened in various parts of Palestine.

While Pesach was originally a pastoral festival, the feast of unleavened bread with which it was associated was agricultural, and probably contained in it a sense of New Year purification. Dough was commonly saved from an old batch of bread to start the new batch rising. By baking unleavened bread all the old impurities were eliminated and a fresh start was made. Also associated with this festival was the act of waving a sheaf before Yahweh, probably with an upward movement to make the grain grow high. Oesterley cites Jeremiah XLVII, 17-19, in reference to the baking of cakes. Here, in response to the denunciation of the prophet, the people reply that their fathers, their kings, and their princes burned incense to the queen of heaven, poured out drink offerings to her, and made *cakes* to worship her and since they left off they have "lacked all things," i.e., fertility has failed. Westerly sees this as proof the Israelites made cakes in the form of a woman to worship Ishtar (or Anat) and suggests that it may have been done at the festival of the unleavened bread.

The festival of weeks took place at the end of the barley harvest. In hymns, possibly connected with it, God is said to shine like light while Deber and Resheph go before him. Deber is the Babylonian pest god while Resheph is a Syrian storm deity called, in Babylonian, Ninib. In the Babylonian flood story there is a passage which runs as follows:

As soon as the first light of dawn appeared,
A black cloud arose from the horizon.
Romman thunders in the midst thereof,
Nebo and Marduk march before.
The throne bearers move over the mountains and plain,
Diban lets loose her mischievous forces,
Ninib goes pouring out rain.

The parallel suggests that sun and storm god concepts were borrowed from Babylonian sources.

Most important of all the agricultural festivals was Sukkoth or the feast of tabernacles, held in autumn in anticipation of the beginning of the next rainy season. It was thus also a New Year celebration. The tabernacles were arbors made of branches of palm trees, boughs of thick trees, and willows of the brook. According to E. O. James, behind this celebration lay the drama of the dying and reviving year god which also dominated the Babylonian Akitu. Those who would see a close connection feel that the Psalms, in which the enthronement of Yahweh was celebrated, must have been sung at this time. In xciii, "The Lord on high is mightier than the noise of many waters, yea, than the mighty waves of the sea." Again, in xcv, "For the Lord is a great God, and a great King above all gods. In his hand are the deep places of the earth; and the strength of the hills is his also. The sea is his and he made it; and his hands formed the dry land." The domination of the water suggests the conflict between Baal and Yam or Marduk and Tiamat. This is further strengthened by Psalm lxxiv, "Thou didst divide the sea by thy strength: thou brakest the heads of the dragons in the waters. Thou brakest the heads of Leviathan in pieces and gavest him to be meat to the people inhabiting the wilderness." If these passages are evidence of the familiar ritual combat, they may have had a relation to Sukkoth. The building of a green bower has been compared to the green bower constructed for the sacred marriage at the festival of Akitu. Added to this is the evidence in the Egyptian papyri from Elephantine that Yahweh was associated with Anat, probably as her consort, plus the references, earlier cited, which show that the worship of the queen of heaven was practiced in ancient times. This somewhat scandalous association for the monotheistic Yahweh has been suggested by Hooke as evidence that a sacred marriage took place at Sukkoth among the greenery. Waters were also offered to Yahweh at this time in a rainmaking ceremony.

Somewhat circumstantially, therefore, Sukkoth is seen as a modified Near East New Year festival possibly containing elements of ritual combat and sacred marriage, while numerous Psalms describing processions carrying the Ark and the enthronement of the Lord as sovereign of the universe reflect a borrowing of the sacral kingship concept and the enthronement and triumph of a young fertility god, as was the case of Marduk and Baal. Rabbinic literature records that on the second night of the festival a dance was held in the Court of Women in the Temple, together with a procession around the altar each day of the celebration in which branches of palm were carried and waved and a citrus fruit was held as a fertility charm. Of course the underlying concepts were overlaid with Yahwistic modification which tended to obscure their original meaning.

Alexander Heidel has compared the Babylonian creation with the version in the Old Testament. In both, divinities exist who are able to create matter. The earth is in darkness until the creators bring forth light. The land and waters must be separated. Finally man is created. When all is over, the Babylonian gods celebrate while Yahweh rests and sanctifies the day. The basic pattern is similar enough to indicate borrowing.

The Babylonian underworld and the Hebrew Sheol were also somewhat similar. The former was thought to be not far below the surface of the earth; Sheol was sometimes referred to as the grave and sometimes as a dwelling place of the dead. The Babylonians believed that all men without distinction went down to the underworld but the gods of the underworld parceled out better or worse dwellings depending on the status and earthly activities of the departed. In accordance with the monotheism of Yahweh, there was no underworld pantheon, although Sheol was also a place of darkness. There is a suggestion in later Biblical writing that the virtuous might look forward to a different fate, a hope interpreted from the phrase "gathered to his fathers."

Still another area of kinship between Sumero-Babylonian religious practice and that of the Hebrews has been recognized in the institution of the prophets, who were ironically enough the most violent antagonists of the fertility religion. Alfred Haldar traces a parallel between them and the divinatory priests of Babylonia, the barus, who were the mouthpieces of oracles and the divine word and who were accustomed to wield considerable power even in political matters. A Babylonian prophecy runs:

> If the king pays no heed to justice
> His people will fall into confusion,
> His country will be devastated.

The Babylonian priestly associations also included interpreters of dreams, as we have seen, and also a special group of ecstatics whose name, *mahhu,* means frenzy. The Babylonian diviners were well organized into guilds with sometimes the king as the head, sometimes a priest. They were accustomed to go forth in war, symbolically taking the god into battle, to prophesy the defeat of the enemy and to utter curses of a magic character. Haldar believes that the ecstatic character of Babylonian ritual has been underestimated. There was certainly dancing at the New Year festival; seal cylinders show dancing and also a metal relief depicts two nude dancing women, priests in animal disguise and musicians.

Numerous passages from the Old Testament show that the prophets were not isolated phenomena but members of guilds or brotherhoods, the Levites being a case in point. All the above activities were also performed by Hebrew prophets. Moses has many of the functions of a sacral king. Divination was practiced by watching signs, as in Isaiah XXI, 6.

> For thus hath the Lord said unto me, Go, set a watchman, let him declare what he seeth.
>
> And he saw a chariot with a couple of horsemen, a chariot of asses, and a chariot of camels; and he hearkened diligently with much heed:
>
> And he cried, A lion: My lord, I stand continually upon the watchtower in the daytime, and I am set in my ward whole nights:
>
> And, behold, here cometh a chariot of men with a couple of horsemen. And he answered and said, Babylon is fallen, is fallen; and all the graven images of her gods he hath broken into the ground.

Haldar would translate *watchman* as *seer,* and to him the episode shows the cultic leader "my lord" stationing a diviner to watch for omens. The movements of animals are a familiar form of divination. The seer reports what he sees and the head prophet then interprets it to portend the fall of Babylon. The prophetic guild is in an ecstatic state in I Kings XXII. Jehoshaphat gathers four hundred prophets.

> And the king of Israel and Jehoshaphat the king of Judah sat each on his throne, having put on their robes, in a void place in the entrance of the gate of Samaria; and all the prophets prophesied before them.
>
> And Zedekiah the son of Chenaanah made him horns of iron: and he said, Thus saith the Lord, With these shalt thou push the Syrians, until thou have consumed them.
>
> And all the prophets prophesied so, saying, Go up to Ramoth-gilead, and prosper: for the Lord shall deliver it into the king's hand.

This is interpreted to mean that the guild went into a collective ecstasy before the kings. The putting on of what must have been a bull mask suggests some sort of dramatic pantomime borne out by the expression "push the Syrians." There are very strong overtones of the bull-god, Baal, in this passage. The interpretation of dreams is, of course, a common form of divination in the Old Testament and there are episodes in which the prophetic guild influenced the succession to the throne as did their counter-parts in Babylonia. All of which is one more indication of how much the Hebrews borrowed from the general Semitic religious concepts of the Near East.

Despite conflicts with the indigenous religion, Yahwistic monotheism continued to develop ethically and philosophically until it led, in Western civilization, to more and more abstract concepts of deity. Efforts have been made to find ethical monotheism among contemporary primitive peoples but the evidence is not convincing. On the whole, the most ancient gods are unpredictable rather than ethical and pure monotheism simply does not exist. The concept of Yahweh seems to be the unique contribution of a nomadic desert people which was destined to play an extraordinary role in the history of Western civilization.

Meanwhile the basic fertility concepts of the Near East continued to be diffused and modified as new urban cultures arose on the lands and shores of the Mediterranean.

Europe — Neolithic to Iron Age

CHAPTER 8

Picture Book Without a Text

Crete and Mycenae—Mycenaean culture related to that of Crete with addition of Indo-European elements—female figures in Neolithic period—predominance of goddess or goddesses—mistress of wild animals and snake goddess—bird attributes, double ax and horns of consecration—possible bull cult—Hagia Triada sarcophagus and funeral cult—afterworld concept—Mycenaean burial rites.

WHO WERE the early inhabitants of Crete? There is something enigmatic about this people whose bright frescoes stare at us from the ruins of the great palace at Knossos. Builders of a luxurious civilization, curiously refined and, above all, peaceable, their art and their dress had a kind of elegance which is almost Parisian; indeed, Gordon Childe has called them the first real Europeans.

The green and fertile island of Crete is so located in the Mediterranean that it is easily accessible from Egypt, from Anatolia, and from Syria. Favorable winds and currents encouraged navigation; natural harbors invited trade and promoted a fishing industry. Blue sea, sheer mountains, green valleys between them, a strategic position on the trade routes—the island was a natural spot for colonization and the building of seaports. The earliest colonists that archaeologists have identified belonged to a late Neolithic phase of culture. As early as the third millennium they were importing obsidian from other Aegean islands which, in turn, were influenced by the Anatolian culture, best exemplified by Troy. The religion of these farmers and fishermen must have been similar to that of the Halafians in the Near East, for nude, soapstone and marble figurines of women, often with the hands on the breasts in the ancient earth mother posture, are found in Troy, the islands of the Cyclades, and in Crete. Often they are formalized, having a flat violin shape with a pointed projection instead of a head. Others are obese and remind us of the Old Stone Age.

When the Cretan culture entered the Bronze Age, aspects of both Sumerian and Egyptian culture seem to have penetrated the island. Whether these traits were the result of trading or whether there was an actual migration of proto-Egyptians who blended with other groups from Syria or Anatolia, we have no way of determining. It is clear, however, that commerce with the great centers on the Nile and the Euphrates had much to do with the development of the island cities.

The individual characteristics of the Minoan civilization appear by the second millennium, one of these being collective burial, a practice which did not occur in Mesopotamia, Egypt or Anatolia but which was common in the Mediterranean islands and among the Natufians of Palestine. At first the bodies were buried in caves, then in regular stone chambers, and finally in circular stone vaults entered through a low doorway with two large stone uprights. Eventually these tombs were roofed with corbel arches and became the great beehive tombs, or tholoi, which are so characteristic of the heroic age of Mycenae. It has been suggested that the shape of the tomb mirrors a type of round dwelling. Apparently when later burials took place little heed was paid to the earlier ones, which were simply pushed aside. Bodies were placed in the tomb in a flexed position and traces of fire are attributed to some purification ritual or sacrificial offering. At the same time individual burial in jars, or pithoi, grouped in cemeteries, also took place and became more general in later periods.

In the early Minoan period there was no great concentration of wealth, no fortification, a fact which testifies to the peaceable nature of these people; and religious rites were carried out in caves or at simple rustic shrines. There was no system of writing although seals were used to stamp export goods.

These seals, which served the same function as those of Babylon, were worn around the neck when cylinder-shaped, or were hung on the wrist or set in rings as beads. The hieroglyph or symbol on the seal, as elsewhere, became the germ of a script. The need for keeping records developed as Cretan society blossomed into a maritime trading nation. Sir Arthur Evans, who devoted his life to uncovering Minoan sites, distinguished what he called Linear A, an early system of writing, and Linear B, a true system of syllabic signs.

In the second millennium B.C. when Babylon and Egypt were already great powers, the island nation of Crete grew steadily from scattered villages to city-states and finally into an organized empire. Pottery reached a peak of craftsmanship in a flowing polychrome style which made use of plant motifs and sea creatures such as the squid and various species of fish. As Crete entered the Bronze Age, comfortable houses were erected and palaces arose in various cities, the greatest of all at Knossos whose king became the supreme ruler. Under his authority a dense population of towns and villages was united by a network of roads with guard stations. Meanwhile the widespread use of writing testifies to a well-organized governing and trading bureaucracy.

The Cretans grew olives, grapes and wheat, raised cattle, sheep and goats. They possessed the four-wheeled cart but did not develop the chariot, which would have been of little use in such a mountainous area. The wealthy individual, when he traveled, was carried about in a palanquin.

The typical Cretan house was similar to those in the Near East, rooms built around a central court with no outside windows. A well-organized drainage system and flush toilets strike a curiously modern note. The palace of Knossos developed into such a network of storerooms, living quarters, shrines, staircases and galleries, lined with the downward-tapering Minoan pillar, that it was almost a city in itself, a great religious, civil and commercial center. From Egypt in all probability came the art of fresco painting. Since the Cretan stone did not lend itself to graphic representation, the Minoan artists learned to paint on plaster smeared over the stone. At first they used a light-on-dark scheme which gave way to dark-on-light. The drawing is formalized, the figures in profile or semiprofile, but the whole effect is lighter and the subjects more lively than the rather solemn hieratic Eastern art. Processions of slim-waisted acolytes, party scenes, sports, and charming decorative panels of fish or flowers cover the palace walls. The Cretans excelled in delicate colorful detail but lacked a sense of balanced, planned composition. Their artists delighted in the human body; men are generally shown naked except for shorts or the codpiece, an article of dress which must have come from Libya, while the women are sometimes bare to the waist or wear a sort of jacket which bares the breast. Their elaborate flounced, full skirts are reminiscent of Sumeria.

Oddly enough, there are not many representations of boats. When shown, the prow was high and ended in a forked prong; sometimes there was a small cabin in the stern. They were propelled by both sails and oars and had a fixed rudder at the stern. Although the Cretans must have had to deal with pirates, there are no pictures of sea battles. Cretan weapons included a large figure-eight shield of hide and a broadsword. More typical were daggers and long rapiers which may have been used in formalized fencing.

The great palace at Knossos was destroyed in 1700 B.C., either by an earthquake or by invaders. It was then rebuilt. The civilization, at its height in the first half of the second millennium, finally fell in about 1400 B.C. The rise and fall of Cretan power, however, leads us to the development of the mainland and the complicated problem of its relation to the island.

In Greece itself in the Neolithic period, archaeological evidence shows influences from the Danubian area and also directly from the Near East, probably from Anatolia. The familiar female clay figures occur. A town culture with well-developed pottery and bronze tools, probably akin to that of early Crete and the Cycladic Islands, was flourishing on the peninsula at the beginning of the second millennium when new warlike people overran the mainland. They have been characterized archaeologically by their gray clay goblets and high-handled cups called Minyan ware. Various traits confuse the question of their origin. Their weapons were like those of northern Europe but their pottery suggests that of northern Iran. They seem to have brought the horse with them and their two-wheeled chariots resemble those of the Hittites. It is probable that they represented an early migration of the Indo-European people from Asia by way of Anatolia. All the evidence points to their being Homer's "fair-haired Achaeans."

The invaders destroyed some of the indigenous towns but soon blended with the native strains to build a fortified city civilization which has been called Mycenaean from the great city of that name first uncovered by Heinrich Schliemann. Within a few hundred years their culture took on most of the characteristics of that in Crete with certain local modifications. The invaders probably introduced the shaft grave, the great rectangular palace hall, and a primitive type of safety pin. Were these people the first Greeks and did the Minoan-Mycenaean civilization form the basis of the culture of the classical Greeks?

The answer leads back to the problem of Cretan writing. Although Arthur Evans collected a great store of seals and tablets, for decades he did not get around to publishing them and he was unable to decipher either Linear A or B himself. In recent years these seals have been made available to other scholars, with the result that in 1952 Michael Ventris broke Linear B and proved that it was an archaic form of Greek. Since many documents from Mycenaean cities and from Crete written in Linear B have now been translated, we know that the Mycenaeans were Greek-speaking and that they must have dominated Crete before the fall of Knossos since they had taken over Cretan writing and adapted it to their own language. This reverses Evans' view that the mainland culture had resulted from colonization by the Cretans. If Linear A, as Cyrus Gordon claims, is really a form of Canaanite, then many interpretations relating Cretan culture to the Near East are strengthened.

The Mycenaeans were active colonizers who established outposts even in Asia Minor at Ugarit and farther down the coast at Alakakh. There is now evidence both from artistic motifs borrowed from the Near East and from mythical elements handed down as far as the era of Homer that there was far more cultural interchange than used to be supposed between the great centers of civilization surrounding the eastern Aegean. Unfortunately the documents deciphered in Linear B have proved a disappointment in that they do not contain any literary or mythological material. They consist entirely of lists and inventories. They do give us more of a picture, however, of the feudal civilization of the Mycenaean city-states which, although they adopted much from Crete, must have retained characteristics which the Achaean invaders brought with them. The king, or *wanax,* was a priest or semidivine, as we should expect. He was surrounded by his counts, feudal nobility and military commanders. Below these were the mayors of various towns, charioteers in the army and able to rise to the nobility. They were responsible for the organization of the craftsmen and agricultural workers. There was an elaborate system of gift giving, both as rewards and on the occasion of promotions by the king; in return, the king received ritual gifts and taxes. Gifts were also given as a dowry and by suitors. This suggests the custom among primitive peoples in which the giving of presents has so much to do with status and kinship obligations.

The fact that craft guilds could hold land and that individuals could be promoted shows a certain social mobility which is nearer to the cultural forms of the Hittites than those of Babylonia.

While the Mycenaean Greeks were probably not literate until they came in contact with the Minoans, there is every possibility that they had a bardic court poetry. A figure of a singer with a lyre in a fresco is interpreted by T. B. L. Webster as the divine patron of such royal laureates who undoubtedly dealt with mythological and semihistorical material, shaped to glorify their masters.

What were the characteristics of the Minoan-Mycenaean religion which flourished in the Aegean and, as we shall see, sparked much of the intellectual achievement of the classical Greeks and the European culture which was heir to it?

Until the deciphering of Linear B, scholars were faced, in Martin Nilsson's phrase, with a picture book without a text. The material in the documents has only changed the situation slightly. Judging by the art of both the island and the mainland, both areas shared many basic ideas and we assume that there was a mingling of Cretan and Achaean concepts. From lists of offerings we now know that Zeus and Poseidon were worshiped in Knossos as early as 1500 B.C. and on the mainland, in Pylos, in 1300 B.C. At Knossos, Athena is mentioned once and Hera several times. This proves that several historic Greek gods were known to both cultures by the middle of the second millennium. Since the Linear A situation still remains unclear, we do not know with certainty what religious concepts were taken from Crete and given Greek names or, as Michael Ventris points out, how many Greek institutions developed with the trappings of Minoan art, ritual and social convention. Essentially, therefore, we still have a picture book without a text.

Once again archaeological detective talents come into play; but from seals, from frescoes, from cult objects, from the circumstantial evidence of

later Greek myth, we can only deduce the general outlines of Cretan attitudes. In consequence there are many unsolved problems and differences of
scholarly opinion.

One fact is indisputable: female figures are dominant in all cult representation. The Cretans never seem to have built actual temples. Many small
cult objects of bronze, stone and clay have been found in caves, among
them female figures, bulls, and other animals, the curious symbol known
as horns of consecration, and the double ax. Representations of shrines
delineate small three-chambered affairs which may have been placed on
rock terraces in the mountains. In palaces and houses, shrines are small
chambers containing the above-mentioned cult objects and, in addition,
libation vessels and altars. The indications are, therefore, that Minoan religion was chiefly an outdoor nature worship combined with domestic cults.

Since the Cretan goddess appears in more than one form and with various
attributes, the question arises whether she was a single supreme deity with
several manifestations or whether there was more than one distinct goddess.
Those who are impressed by the widespread distribution of the fertility
goddess in the Near East are inclined to feel that she represents the basic
female vegetation fertility principle. In the first place, the formalized nude
figures of the late Neolithic suggest an early diffusion of the ancient concept.
A second manifestation of the fertility goddess at Tel Brak in eastern Syria
has been found at what has been called the Eye Temple. This shrine, dated
at about 3000 B.C., was dedicated to the cult of Inanna or Ishtar and from
it have been recovered hundreds of clay figurines whose chief characteristic
is the eyes. They comprise the whole head and are underscored and over-
scored with lines which meet, suggesting eyelashes and eyebrows. It is believed that these figurines are votive offerings to the fertility goddess. Their
importance lies in the fact that the eye motif (sometimes combined with
breast protuberances and sometimes not) is found on pottery and in figurines,
and even engraved on rocks, all over the European area and that of the
Mediterranean islands. We shall meet this motif later but its importance for
Crete lies in the fact that a similar sort of eye treatment appears in some
so-called bell idols, female figures ending at the waist in a kind of cylindrical
pedestal, found in Cretan shrines. These figures are crude and archaic in
appearance, a style attributed to religious conservatism. Finally, the nature
goddess of Crete, who appears on seals and is depicted in more sophisticated figurines, wears a flounced skirt while her torso is bare. This flounced
skirt was worn by gods and goddesses in Mesopotamia in the third millennium, and a relief from Minet el Beida, in Syria, from the fourteenth century B.C., shows a goddess clothed in it, seated heraldically between two
goats who are nibbling at branches or ears of wheat which she holds in
each hand. The parallel with the Cretan goddess is striking, for the latter

is sometimes depicted between two animals, is often associated with a tree, and on one seal with something which resembles a wheat ear. Axel Persson, who inclined to the diffused great mother concept, also sees a connection with the great nature goddess of Asia Minor, Cybele Phrygia, who sometimes bears branches in her hands and who was associated with a sacred column or baetyl. Several seals with images of the Minoan goddess also show a baetyl which seems to be a part of the cult.

A burial urn appears a few times in connection with the goddess but the young male figure is very rare and there is no definite evidence that he is a Tammuz fertility spirit who dies and comes to life. It is clear, however, that there was a tree cult, probably of fertility, connected with shrines in a sacred grove and that priestesses danced ecstatically. Somehow the bare torso, the bell skirt and the arm postures suggest rotation of the hips and shoulders, perhaps a kind of hula.

Since Minoan-Mycenaean culture had a shorter development span than that of the Near East, it is unlikely that a unified mythology or theology existed. From the evidence of the seals which show a goddess accompanied by animals and a few which show a male figure, also heraldically placed, Martin Nilsson feels there was a Cretan mistress of wild animals and also a master of wild animals of lesser significance. Sometimes there are attendant demons who show signs of Babylonian origin. Since a goddess on Mycenaean seals sometimes carries a spear, Nilsson concludes that the mainland culture, which was warlike in contrast to the peaceful island trading civilization, transformed her into a war goddess.

For the snake goddess who was found in a shrine in Knossos, and elsewhere, Nilsson sees a different function. Tube-shaped vessels with snakes crawling along them as if drinking were associated with her. These were used to pour libations. Since no snake idols have been found in the open air, he concludes that hers was "a domestic cult, carried on in houses or in palaces." In peasant tradition in Albania and Serbia the snake is the protector of the house and sometimes fed milk. The same attitude is taken toward it by the peasants of Calabria and Lithuania. In Sweden snakes are allowed to live in cattle barns and are fed because they are supposed to bring good luck. The Roman house snake was also considered to be a kind of domestic tutelary spirit. In summary, Nilsson is convinced that the snake goddess was distinct from the tree goddess or mistress of wild animals and was specifically a guardian of the family and the house or palace.

In association with most of the Minoan-Mycenaean shrines are three other important symbols whose origin and significance are controversial. A bird is often shown perched on the bell idols or on domestic shrines and on double axes. Such birds are manifestations of the goddess. The double ax itself, which appears everywhere as a small cult object of bronze, lead or stone, and also painted on pottery and in friezes and within shrines, has been interpreted by some as the weapon of the weather god of the Near East. Teshub, however, carries a single, not a double, ax. There is no well-authenticated image from Crete of a male figure carrying it, and no real proof that the Cretans worshiped a weather god. On the other hand, it is associated with the nature goddess and female figures are shown holding it. It must also be remembered that we have seen it before in association with the bull's head as a possible votive object in the Halafian culture of the Near East. In Crete it is sometimes shown placed between the horns of a bull. It is also placed between the horns of consecration—the third controversial object—which adorn the tops of shrines, appear on pottery, appear within shrines depicted on seals, and have been found in shrines in the palace of Knossos and in those on the mainland. Sometimes these horns are alternated with bulls' heads in decorative friezes. Another interesting similarity is to the horned headdress of the Sumerian priests and the head of the Sumero-Babylonian bull-man.

The cultural complex, double ax, bull's head, horns of consecration which resemble bulls' horns, taken together with the bull-leaping game depicted so often in friezes, and strengthened by the Minotaur myth, do suggest that the bull had some special significance in Crete.

Ludolf Malten, in his study of the bull cult, traces its history in connection with sky and weather gods. In addition to the bull being a manifestation of Teshub among the Hittites and Baal among the Canaanites, it was spoken of as "the son of Shamash," the sun god of Babylonia. He points out that the Minotaur of Greek tradition was the result of the union of Pasiphaë with a bull. This also reminds us of the passage in the myth of Baal in which Anat bears a bull to Baal. Malten also considers the myth of Europa and the bull to be Cretan. Europa in Crete is connected with the earth goddess, while a second name for the Minotaur was Asterios, a name sometimes applied to Zeus, who was originally a sky god. Malten also discusses the story of Theseus and the Minotaur in the light of the bull-leaping game in which young male and female athletes, as shown in frescoes and on seals, seized a charging bull and performed a somersault over its back, a feat which no modern toreador would dare attempt. There is also some indication that the trick of bulldogging, bringing a bull to the ground by seizing its horns, exactly as performed by Western cowboys, was also popular in Crete. Malten suggests that the sacrifice might be modified into a gladiatorial game. In a sense it would be a battle between the god and the offering; if the leap over the horns failed, the toreador became the sacrificial victim. Since there were male as well as female bull jumpers, it is quite possible that the young athletes were originally war captives. Malten points out that in Babylonia the bull was *both* worshiped and sacrificed. The god himself was killed. The relation between the ritual death of a divine animal and sacrifice will be discussed later in the light of other cultures and in relation to the totemic heritage. It might be added here that bull sacrifice is recorded in Crete in the writing of a Christian author of the time of Constantine, Fermicus Maternus, who stated that in the worship of the Cretan Dionysus, a live bull (identified with the god) was torn to pieces and eaten by the worshipers, who then rushed through the woods in a wild noisy procession to the sound of flutes and cymbals, bearing sacred objects before them.

Malten finally connects the later Mithraic rites in which the initiate was bathed in the blood of a bull for fertility reasons with the historic fertility significance of the animal. "The bull and his sacrifice is deeply rooted in the agrarian thought complex, they belong to all the powers that are invoked in his area; hence their close connection with heaven, sun, rain, and especially in the Orient with the true bestower of all prosperity and fruitfulness."

When we come to a consideration of the Minoan burial rites and the cosmogony of this people, we face the fact that this was not a tomb-centered culture. The gaiety and luxury expressed by the frescoes, the attitudes of the people represented, the delight in flowers and jewels, the elegance of dress and coiffure, all suggest a cheerful people who succeeded in living for the day and dispensing with dark thoughts of death. Practically the only representation of funeral rites occurs on the famous sarcophagus from Hagia Triada, which has been the object of much contradictory interpretation. Nilsson suggests that it might be the tomb of a Mycenaean chieftain resident in Crete, because the mainland culture was far more concerned with funeral pomp than that of the island. It also appears to reflect some Egyptian influence. On one side, to the accompaniment of flute music, a bull is being sacrificed while a priestess dressed in a peculiar archaic hide dress of Egyptian style is offering libations before a double ax on which a bird is perched and near which arises a fertility tree. Two goats lie beneath the sacrificial table. On the other side three men march to the right bearing two bulls and a boat toward a stepped altar with horns of consecration and a tree behind it. A little apart from this shrine or tomb there is a rigid male figure which may or may not be an effigy of the dead man, again an Egyptian motif. Moving to the left is a lyre player and a woman with a basket, while beyond them a third woman pours liquid into a large bowl set between two columns surmounted by double axes and birds. On each end of the sarcophagus are chariots, both containing two persons, one drawn by horses, one by griffins. The griffin motif appears often in Mycenaean art and the chariot is not Cretan; hence it may show Mycenaean or Egyptian influence. E. O. James sees the scene as an indication that the fertility goddess was also a goddess of the dead or the underworld, as she is in some manifestations in the Near East. As a consequence, all her cult symbols appear while offerings are made to her in behalf of the dead. The dead man may also have been deified and the offerings could then be to *him,* while the chariots on the sides depict his journey to the celestial regions. The boat is a real problem. Since the funerary boat in which the soul journeyed is common in Egypt, one way out of the dilemma is to ascribe it to Egyptian influence. (An Egyptian statue of the twelfth dynasty, found at Knossos, indicates that there might have been a commercial representative stationed at the Cretan capital.) Once more the picture book is ambiguous and, lacking a text, we can only speculate concerning Minoan-Mycenaean concepts.

It may be, however, that the image of the Elysian Fields or Isles of the Blest was derived from Minoan sources, since Rhadamanthys (in Greek legend) who ruled there was said to be a brother of Minos and his name is definitely Cretan. The Isles of the Blest are agreeable and fruitful, in contrast to the probably Mycenaean concept of a shadowy underworld, and it would seem natural for a seafaring people who present as cheerful an appearance as do the Minoans to create such an image. The funeral boat on the sarcophagus would then be the vehicle for voyaging to the pleasant afterworld.

It is in keeping with the enigmatic character of the Cretans, who never took the trouble to record their mythology, that, although they were mariners and fishermen, the sea, except for marine decorative motifs, seems to have played so little part in their psychic life. We cannot assign any water divinities to them. Although Poseidon is mentioned in the records at Knossos and Pylos there are no images of him in Minoan art. It has been pointed out that the offering list to this god found at Pylos parallels to some extent the sequence on the Triada sarcophagus—one ox, two rams, wheat flour, wine, cheese, honey, unguent, two sheepskins. Ventris suggests that the sheepskins are to clothe the priestesses. Cups of gold are also listed like those carried by acolytes in the Knossos frescoes. On the whole, however, the evidence indicates that Poseidon was not originally Cretan.

The name of a goddess, Diwija, appears in connection with that of Zeus on records at Knossos; possibly she may be the original Cretan Mistress of Wild Things or the earth mother.

Both Minoans and Mycenaeans seemed to have lacked the historical sense of other barbaric cultures. Their graphic representations are not accompanied by any inscriptions; even their kings did not indulge in the permanent self-glorification of inscribed monuments. This fact makes it unlikely that undiscovered hoards of mythological literature remain to be unearthed like the tablets at Ugarit. The character of Linear B includes the possibility that it may have been written on linen or papyrus. If so, none of these documents have survived.

When the blended Minoan-Mycenaean culture became dominated by the mainland, as has been pointed out, burial rites became more important. The Minoan priest-kings were probably early capitalists; the kings on the mainland were heroes and warriors. Their great beehive tombs with corbeled chambers of carefully fitted stones were entered by a long passage called the dromos. Some were erected in an excavation in a hillside and many stood on a hilltop covered by an artificial mound. The most famous of these, the so-called Treasury of Atreus at Mycenae, was found by the enthusiastic classicist Schliemann. Tombs were used over several generations and filled with costly grave goods of Minoan style, some no doubt made by island craftsmen, others by mainlanders trained in the Cretan school. As would be expected, there is an abundance of weapons, spears, daggers, halberds, rapiers and helmets plated with boars' tusks, for battle scenes are common in Mycenaean art. Layers of ashes and charcoal suggest that there was a cult of the dead which consisted of repeated burning of sacrificial gifts. This may have been the germ of the hero cult which developed in the later history of Greece. Persson gives us a graphic reconstruction of the way in which these barbaric kings buried their dead:

> The king had had the tomb built during his lifetime for himself and his family. The chamber floor had been whitened with plaster—just as was done and is still done in houses of southern Europe. When the king died, his grave pit was hewn more than a metre and a half deep, out of the soft clay-slate forming the floor of the chamber. The bottom of the grave had been covered with a layer of plaster about five centimetres thick. Right in front of the door, about one metre from the entrance a rather deep square pit had been made over which great logs of wood were piled up to form a pyre.
>
> The funeral procession files through the long dromos into the chamber. The dead man is lowered into the grave and his indestructible treasure, cups of gold, silver and bronze, rings and engraved stones, weapons, etc., are laid on position. Those who follow him on his last journey throw other treasures at his feet as a last token of respect, swords, spears, knives, helmets, etc., exactly as in our own day flowers accompany the dead into the grave. I would again call attention to the confused heap of weapons found at the king's feet.
>
> But the dead man needed more perishable things with him in the next world, clothes and food, and so, in accordance with the Homeric expression "One heaped the pyre for him with goodly gifts." There

were finely wrought chests with mountings of gold and bronze and inlay or ivory and glass paste, fitted with costly gold-adorned materials, and there were pottery vessels and food and drink. One of the dead man's kinsmen takes a large vessel of wine, a stirrup vase, and shatters it against the logs of the pyre, so that the contents are poured out. The upper part of the shattered vessel falls into the fire; he stands there with the bottom in his hand, he throws it down to the dead man in the grave—so we found the fragments. Other vessels also have been shattered on the fire; the foot of a kylix has distinct traces of burning on the broken edges which appeared when it was broken in pieces.

The pyre gradually burns down—it is piled up just by the entrance and thanks to the pit under it there is a good draught—half-charred bits of wood, burnt gold and bronze mountings, burnt ivory, bits of glass and broken vessels filled the greater part of the pit.

Then the king's companions, his servants, his dog, and possibly his wife are laid in their places. [Persson found bones which seemed to indicate human grave goods.] The dead are covered with earth and before the covering slabs are put in place over the king's grave, a wooden stoup with rich bronze mounts is set down for him, the farewell drink. The large covering slabs are brought into position—to prevent the dead from walking—and more earth is thrown over the grave till it is filled to the level of the chamber floor. The other pits are filled in the same way and also the sacrificial pit over which the pyre had burnt. The chamber is cleaned and the sherds and such things which have not gone into any of the pits are swept out into the passage where we found them in the soil filling it.

The deep doorway is blocked with carefully piled stones, a last sacrifice, possibly some days later as in classical times, is burnt before the closed doorway—in many Mycenaean tombs a heap of charcoal and ashes has been found in just this fashion. The passage is filled in with soil to prevent the dead from coming out and injuring the living, and probably also to prevent the living from getting in and robbing the dead.

This is what the finds have to tell us of the funeral of the King of Midea.

All in all, though the archaeological picture of the Minoan-Mycenaean religion lacks details and in some areas tells us nothing at all, we have learned enough to see that this culture is a link between the great fertility religions of the Near East and the complex history of the gods of Olympus.

CHAPTER 9

Earth Mother
to Owl-faced Athena

*Greece—influence of Cretan goddess or goddesses upon the Greek pantheon
—earth worship archaic and orgiastic—Demeter, Persephone and death and
resurrection myth—Dionysus and Cretan Zeus as fertility figures—survival
of bull cult—hero cults and ancestor worship—Homer, magic and mana—
Indo-European sky and warrior gods—the horse and the animal-shaman—
Hesiod and archaic myth—castration theme—civil-war-in-heaven conflict
theme—Pandora and female magic.*

THE GREEK GODS, in most people's minds, are a combination of broad-browed marble statues and, when echoes of Homer still persist, rather naughty bedroom antics. These are the gods of hearty sophisticates whose religious practices were largely a kind of open-air picnic, prayers and pouring of libations being combined with the cooking of steaks over the sacrificial fire.

This is only one side of the many-sided Greeks. In their city-states there was popular and political worship, there were domestic and public gods and, along with the fleshly, athletic Olympians, darker and more primitive drives persisted which kept alive the mystically orgiastic element of the supernatural.

Archaeology has destroyed the old image of the virgin birth of Greek culture. We know now that the Hittites, the Canaanites, the Egyptians and the Greeks, bordering as they did on the Mediterranean, formed an international community, all aware of each other's cultures very much as France, England and America are today. In the past the mobility of ancient peoples has been underestimated. We must remember that they were as active in pursuit of pleasure and profit as we. Their business and sightseeing trips took them from one country to another; they hawked their gadgets and gaped at the sights and sometimes brought back strange customs, new ideas and foreign gods.

Behind the marble statues are the older ideas; it is these primitive origins with which we are here concerned. On the whole, the mysterious earth gods came from Crete or Asia Minor while the bellowing warriors are the contribution of the Indo-European horsemen.

After the fall of Knossos, perhaps brought about by the Mycenaeans, their heroic feudal chiefs ruled the Mediterranean, trading and colonizing at Tyrens, Syria, Sicily and Egypt. Then in about 1100 B.C. a new invasion of Indo-European horsemen overran the peninsula and destroyed the Greek cities. The result was a kind of dark age in which the old court life ceased and the artisans were dispersed. Gem cutting died out, writing almost disappeared, trade languished, the epics which Homer was to transform were only kept alive in such outposts as the colonies of Cyprus and Asia Minor. A new style of pottery called the geometric, which consisted of bands of decoration and few figures, provides a transition to the archaic Greek style which revived the human figure. The Minoan-Mycenaean religion was probably kept alive here and there, particularly at Tyrens, Athens and Eleusis where presently Greek temples were to arise on spots already hallowed by ritual. In this transition the old gods had either to vacate or to become absorbed into new deities who show their composite origin.

The old goddesses of Crete are linked to the new deities in various ways. Athena's owl relates her to the old fertility entity who had bird attributes. Athena's snake is reminiscent of those who attended the guardian goddess of the palace of Knossos. Artemis is clearly the ancient mistress of animals. She was a wild nature goddess who hunted and danced with her nymphs in groves and mountain meadows. She was also deeply imbedded in popular religion, generally a proof of antiquity. Dances in her honor were orgiastic, sometimes carried on by acolytes wearing masks. Animals were thrown into a fire alive, cymbals were clashed and, since both men and women took part in the rites, these were often erotic.

The oldest Greek goddess officially connected with the earth is Rhea but a large part of the female Greek pantheon shares or splits up earth and fertility attributes. In addition to Athena and Artemis, Aphrodite and especially Demeter are also the result of survivals, a blending and reshaping of Cretan worship with Near Eastern additions.

The familiar Demeter and Persephone myth stems from the Ashtar-Tammuz story. After her daughter was snatched underground by the lord of the underworld, Demeter wandered desolate over the sterile earth while mankind starved. Zeus finally interfered, ordering Kore-Persephone (she has both names) returned but, since she had eaten pomegranate seeds, she was compelled to dwell for one third of the year below ground, a month for each seed. The relation of this story to the death of Tammuz is clear; in this case the young god has disappeared, it is the earth mother herself who splits into two elements. Plouton, according to Homer and Hesiod, was the son of Demeter, which hardly accords with his role as god of the underworld in which he parallels the Sumerian goddess Ereshkigal. Nilsson, however, explains the myth in terms of the Greek harvest procedure. Corn (wheat) was stored in subterranean jars, or pithoi, during the barren season. Hence it was underground wealth and therefore the property of Plouton. Kore-Persephone's residence underground was symbolical of the same corn storage. When the jars were opened and the seed brought up, the corn maiden ascended to rejoin her mother, the old corn crop, and the Eleusinian mysteries took place. In the light of later creation of divinities from abstractions, and even animistically, and of the late elaboration of hero cults, this poeticizing of an ancient theme seems a plausible explanation. Persephone seems to have been a true underworld goddess, for she is sometimes thought of as Plouton's wife and perhaps is really related to Ereshkigal. Triptolemos is a still later addition. He was apparently an Eleusinian nobleman whose name, in folklore, was taken to mean "thrice plowing." Hence it is associated with the plowing of the field.

Little is known of what was actually done during the Eleusinian rites. The neophytes, after having undergone a course of secret instruction in what was to be revealed to them after being purified, were led in a procession to the sanctuary of Demeter. When they arrived they bathed in the sea and wandered up and down the shore with torches in their hands, dramatizing the desolate mother's search for her missing daughter. Then in darkness and in silence they sat on stools in the great hall, waiting for the sacred sights they must never reveal. The secret was well kept, for we really do not know what took place. James, quoting Hippolytus, who reports that an ear of wheat was reaped in a blaze of light and the birth of a divine child was announced, suggests that this is in keeping with the nature of the festival and also suggests that a divine marriage between Zeus and Demeter or Plouton and Persephone might have taken place. At any rate, the festival was grounded upon concepts similar to those of the Near East and assumed great emotional significance in the popular mind. At first a family cult, carried on by successors of the priest-king, it became democratized and transformed into a death and resurrection mystery with a suggestion of a blessed afterlife.

The cult of Dionysus which seems to have emanated from Thrace is also a blend of a very ancient ecstatic fertility concept and a late sophisticated yearning for immortality. The maenad followers of the god wandered in the forest, danced in the light of torches, saw milk and honey flowing out of the ground, and heard the bellowing of bulls. The god revealed himself in animal form. The maenads saw him in animals which they seized and tore to pieces, devouring the flesh raw. Phallic rites were also a part of this worship, the maenads carrying the phallus in processions. Much of this indicates that the god was a fertility bull, probably from Asia Minor, and the eating of his flesh is certainly a reflection of animal sacrifice.

Still more significant is the solemn marriage between the god and the wife of the King-Archon at Athens. According to Aristotle, this took place in a building which used to be the residence of the king and was called the Ox-stall. Evidently the fertility bull god of the East came into Greek religion by way of Dionysus and here we find a remnant of the sacred marriage between him and the earth mother still being celebrated.

Dionysus, however, is also represented as a divine child, a symbol of resurrection. Drawing upon this tradition, the culmination of mystical religion was Orphism, an eclectic and literate movement which rewrote mythology in the sixth century B.C. Orpheus, a mythical hero and poet who was said to have lived in Thrace, became a symbol of ethical and ascetic teachings. Hymns composed in his honor developed the concept of retribution and reward in another world, an ultimate synthesis of the mystical, ecstatic impulses which sought for an imaginative negation of the finality of death.

Much of the religious development which has been discussed is a modification in the archaic age of old beliefs, a modification which exhibits popular upsurges of religious feeling unknown to the rationalistic Homer. One of the most striking resurgences of ancient practice was the emergence of the hero cults. In essence this was a revival of the oldest religious practice, one which we shall see among modern primitives, the worship of the dead. In its earliest form it was a family affair. In the Neolithic it probably extended to whole tribes or clans, as evidenced in rites at megalithic graves. The Greeks of the archaic period were splitting up into small states often engaged in hostilities and ruled over by feudal barons who had replaced the more unified political system of Mycenae. Ancestors were now found for the whole community and the fictionalization of history gradually produced new cycles of myths about persons who became protectors of specific communities. They went forth to battle with their protégés and their myths were cited (and adapted) as evidence in legal quarrels between rival cities. Sometimes such heroes (Herakles for example) are clearly mythical creations, sometimes elaborate genealogies are developed (the family history of the Atreidae). Scholars have attempted to trace the historic elements in the heroic myths but the results are controversial. Actually the nostalgia for the Mycenaean heroic age gradually transformed the already fictional characters of the Homeric poems into saints very much like those of the Catholic Church. In fact, by the edict of Drakon in 620 B.C., they were officially ordained gods.

The cult of the heroes points up a more formal dichotomy in Greek religion, that between the Olympians and the earth deities. The Olympians are clearly enough a creation of a feudal aristocracy, reflecting its class distinctions. Their relation to men was personal and capricious as was that of the warrior baron to his retainers; they might help or hinder ordinary men. The Homeric conception of the underworld was a nonphysical place of darkness where all the sensual pleasures which made life worth living were denied the pale ghosts. In contrast the earth deities (some of whom might be earth manifestations of Olympians) belonged in an underworld which *was* the earth, where the hero pursued a diminished life in the tomb, the abode of fertility spirits. On the whole, the earth deities were more democratic and archaic, could be magically controlled and perhaps, as we have indicated, their qualities might be attributed to a different ethnic origin.

Their sacrifices differed from those offered to the Olympian gods, which were carried out in the daytime and in a classic temple generally on a height. The earth gods were worshiped at evening or at night on low, hollow, sacrificial hearths kept close to the earth. Sacrificial male animals, black in color, were held downward instead of upward, the blood being allowed to run into the altar so that the hero would have "appeasement of blood." The carcass was burned, for no living man was allowed to taste it. (The worshipers ate part of the Olympian sacrifice.) Since the hero was thought of as living underground, the worship often took place at the tomb or supposed tomb. Hesiod, who divided the course of history into five ages, describes the role of the dead as follows:

> Now that the earth has covered this generation,
> By decree of Zeus they become kind, earth-haunting spirits;
> Guardians of mortal men, they concern themselves with
> Justice and unfair dealings. Wrapped in dark mist,
> They roam the earth bestowing riches, for this kingly right
> Belongs to them.

The figure of Herakles is particularly interesting because it exemplifies a blend of the two cults. Herakles was supposedly the son of the mortal Alkmena and Zeus. He is mentioned in the *Iliad* and also in the *Odyssey*, in which his ghost is described as residing among the shadows in the underworld while he himself has been promoted to Olympus where he is married to Hebe and enjoys immortality. In this particular case the culture hero, who has made the transition to Olympic god, receives both Chthonian and Olympian worship. In addition to slaying symbolic monsters, his exploits include the civilizing achievements of draining swamps and road building. His boundless appetite, strength, and sexual prowess are characteristics parallel to those of folk heroes in other cultures. His good humor and earthiness endeared him to the common man, who worshiped him as a friend and protector-patron as the later Catholics did their saints. In Herakles, the Greek sense of democracy created the self-made god.

Another member of the earth group is Zeus whom we are here obliged to split into two parts. The warrior-horseman Zeus we shall come to later, but another character who acquired the same name was said to have been born in Crete in a cave from which a fire was seen to flash as blood from the birth streamed forth. A band of youths or hunter-warriors called Kouretes, said to have invented the armed dance, danced and clashed their shields as he was born. This Zeus is therefore thought of as leading a band of Kouretes in fertility rites. Nilsson believes that Zeus in Crete was reborn each year in accord with a fertility cycle in which the *death* of the god was forgotten. The divine fertility child in this, and in other legends of Asia Minor, is abandoned by his mother and reared by some animal; the Cretan Zeus was suckled by goats. There are parallel elements with the tradition of Dionysus which unite both gods to the child divinity theme.

When we search for archaic elements in Greek religion, the Homeric epics offer little evidence because they are not the product of priest-poets but of courtly minstrels. One belief, which does occur in the Homeric poems and is identified as ancient, is the concept of the *daimon*. The daimon, sometimes translated as "some god," is blamed for every sort of misfortune. Actually what is being expressed by this concept is a belief in mana, the intervention of a generalized supernatural power. It is the mana in the Greek world which also accounts for the creation of countless minor deities, often with no individuality, such as wood nymphs, water nymphs or sea nymphs. Another example is Hestia, the personified hearth fire. Mana, which may be helpful or hostile, accounts for the host of magical taboos which permeate even anthropomorphic cults. Impurity or disease could be wiped off or washed away. Women in childbed were impure and were excluded from the temple for forty days (an almost universal taboo among primitives); those who had had a death in the family were impure for twenty to forty days, even those who had looked at a corpse were temporarily excluded from the gods. Outside a house of mourning, a bowl of water was placed so that those who went out might purify themselves.

The drawing of a magic circle through which no evil may pass is exemplified by an agricultural rite. A virgin must walk around the farm with a cock in her hands to ward off weeds and injurious insects; these were even more effectively destroyed by a menstruating woman walking about in the garden. Curiously enough, exactly the same rite was noticed by Henry Schoolcraft among the Chippewa Indians in the early nineteenth century. A naked Indian woman ran around a newly planted cornfield at night to protect it from vermin or blight and to ensure a good crop. Since women have always been regarded by primitives as saturated with mana because of their sexual functions, it was this trait which was used to protect the harvest. Hesiod's poem, *Works and Days,* concludes with a later addition of a number of such taboos.

> Never stand erect and let water facing the sun . . .

> When at home do not approach the hearth fire
> With an unwashed body . . .

> When you return from an ill-omened burial,
> Do not beget children . . .

> Whoever crosses a river with unwashed hands
> And unrepentant, brings down the anger
> Of the gods who will soon punish him . . .

All of the above can be grouped together as states of impurity which offend the divine powers, the hearth fire, sun and river being thought of as gods. In addition

> If you are a man you must not wash in
> A woman's bath water; there is a heavy punishment . . .

and

> Never in the morning pour a libation of dark wine
> To Zeus or the other gods without first
> Washing your hands . . .

It is interesting to reflect that much of this purification magic was on the right track and has been substantiated by the germ theory of disease and the value of sterilization.

The Greeks did not lack sympathetic destructive magic. One of their favorite ways of harming an enemy was to inscribe a curse on a lead tablet. "May his tongue and his soul become lead that he may not be able to speak or act, and pierce his tongue and his soul," runs one example which was probably accompanied by jabbing some pointed instrument into the soft lead.

The group of deities and practices which has just been discussed belongs on the whole to the fertility area and, in all probability, entered the Greek cultural synthesis from the advanced agricultural and urban civilizations of Crete and Asia Minor. What elements can we ascribe to the Indo-Europeans?

In the first place, we shall find among the peoples of the steppe-warrior ethnic group gods reflecting those qualities prized by their worshipers; they are hunter-warrior, chieftain gods. Among the Greeks the most clearly Indo-European is Zeus. The Mycenaean bards made him a feudal overlord, quelling his turbulent vassals by personal strength. Just as the Hittites took the written names of Babylonian gods and either applied them to their own deities or absorbed the foreign concepts, so the name Zeus, used by the Greeks, covered a number of entities. As a weather god controlling the sudden and violent storms of Greece, hurling his weapon, the thunderbolt, he appears in a series of local manifestations—Zeus Lykaios, Zeus Laphistios, Zeus Akraios—exactly as does Teshub, the Hittite weather god. The weather aspect seems to be a basic Indo-European concept once the nomads settled down to agriculture, but behind this function are several others which are even older. Zeus Herkeios is a clan protector, a father-of-the-tribe figure, semantically related to the Aryan Dyaus-Pitar. He is also patron of the kingly office and the priest-king. In this aspect, Georges Dumézil, who has specialized in comparisons of Indo-European religions, sees him as magician and an upholder of law and order. Zeus demonstrates his clan-god side most clearly in that his altar, as Herkeios, stood in the courtyard, the area which could be defended. In Sophocles' *Antigone* he is also called the god of blood relationship, hence of the gens or clan. His magical aspect emerges most clearly in relation to his sacred oak at Dodona whose leaves revealed the future. In the *Iliad* he also sends divinatory birds and dreams in which the dead appear. Finally, in his role as judge, Dike, his daughter, who symbolized justice, sits at his side.

Eventually the Asian Apollo took over the divinatory side of Zeus and apparently also something of the legal and regulatory power. In this, Apollo perhaps reflects the ritualistic and divinatory priesthoods of the Near East. By joining with the cult of Dionysus he seems to have exercised a restraining influence over the wild and contagious emotionalism of the maenad train whose ecstatic excesses were so great that they have taken mythological form in stories such as that of the murder of King Pentheus. The divinatory aspect was of course exercised by Apollo through the Delphic oracle.

The second indubitably Indo-European god is Ares, who exhibits war-like courage—brute force carried to berserkir madness. Hesiod describes him in conflict with Herakles, "screaming aloud and flourishing his spear like a flame." Again:

> . . . and they met together with a loud yelling
> Like two lions who, over a slain buck rush at each other
> With a fearful roar and at the same time
> A noise of gnashing teeth . . .

We shall meet this brute frenzy among the other Indo-European peoples. It has also been suggested that the name Ares is Indo-European.

The third Indo-European-sounding divinity is Poseidon. Although he is generally known as a water god, first of streams and then of the sea, it appears that his more basic attribute is the horse. Ulrich von Wilamowitz-Moellendorf remarks that he remained a horse god even after his horse aspect was lost. In Arcadia it was said that Poseidon in the form of a horse coupled with Demeter as a mare. At Lycosura he was called Poseidon Hippios. He was also said to have created the horse by a blow of his trident on a rock. The horse symbol appeared upon the tomb of a hero. Not only was the horse introduced into Greece by the Achaean invaders, but through-out the steppe-warrior world the horse is important as a sacrificial animal and it is also associated with the leading warrior gods.

Still another area of Greek tradition which is linked with horse worship, and eventually totemism, is that of centaurs, satyrs and sileni. Dumézil has shown that *ghandarvas* of Aryan tradition, half-man half-horse demons, are active in spring festivals in India. The horse-tailed sileni are first en-countered in Asia. John Lawson, investigating Greek folk tradition, found that *callicantzari* are a kind of goblin descended from the centaurs, satyrs and sileni of classical times. Callicantzari are half-horse or half-goat, some as high as a house, some mere pygmies. They have huge heads and huge phalli, their leader generally being described as ithyphallic. They appear between Christmas and Epiphany but spend the rest of the time in the lower world. These creatures are both stupid and destructive. They break into houses, ruin furniture, urinate upon everything. Men whom they catch they beat or force to dance, while women captives are raped. They can be outwitted by setting them some absurd task such as carrying water in a sieve. The ghandarvas of India are also mischievous, somewhat stupid and outrageously phallic. The callicantzari are known to be shape changers. From this it is argued that they are probably a memory of sorcerers dressed in animal skins. The sileni and satyrs who caroused in the train of the god Dionysus were dramatized by initiates who wore the skins of animals. Orgiastic carousing in animal masks in winter festivals continued into the twelfth century until it was banned by the Church. Dumézil also comes to the conclusion that ghandarvas developed out of the memory of the ancient orgiastic sorcerer, or shaman. In north Siberian tradition there is much animal identification and supposed shape changing among shamans. Since the horse was introduced by the Indo-Europeans, it seems likely that the Greek centaurs, sileni and satyrs and the Aryan ghandarvas all have their roots in Indo-European religion in which the horse plays such an important role.

When we seek for archaic mythology, it is to the Boeotian poet Hesiod that we must turn. Although somewhat later than the Homeric writer, he reflects the conservatism of the rural mind. Hesiod deals with the same gods and heroes as Homer, but his poem, *Theogony,* has echoes of the priestly epic, particularly in its basic theme, the civil war in heaven, which we have already encountered in the *Enuma Elish* and the Canaanite poems. It, too, dramatizes a basic concept of the universe which is cruder than the sprightly fictions of Homer.

> In truth Chaos was born first
> And next came broad-bosomed Gaia . . .
> But Gaia's firstborn was one who equalled her,
> Ouranos, the starry sky . . .
> And after all of them clever Cronos came forth
> Most savage of all her children, who hated
> His potent father . . .
> Of all the sons the Titans were the most terrible,
> Hated by their father from the very beginning,
> As soon as they came forth he hid them
> From the light in the hollow womb of Gaia
> And Ouranos exulted over this evil deed . . .
> And Gaia, pressed from within,
> Groaned with pain and devised an evil plan.
> Quickly she made a sickle of grey flint . . .
> And in the hand of Cronos she placed
> The sickle with sawteeth . . .
> Then came great Ouranos bringing night with him
> And, eager for love, lay over Gaia
> And covered everything over
> And his son, from ambush reached
> With his left hand while he took in his right
> The long, sawtoothed sickle
> And quickly cut off the genitals
> Of his own father and let them
> Fall behind him but they were not lost.
> As many bloody drops as fell
> Were received by Gaia and, as the years passed,
> She gave birth to the pitiless furies
> And the huge giants . . .

The castration theme will be discussed with other Indo-European myths at a later point; here, however, it is interesting to note that the sickle is described as a gray flint and edged with teeth, which is of course the Neolithic tool and testifies to the age of the theme. The poem contains long passages of divine genealogy which remind us of the begat sections of the Old Testament. Since these catalogues include animistic spirits, major and minor gods, monsters, and personified abstractions, they reflect the heterogeneous nature of the material which is being welded into a synthesis by the sophisticated poet. The Cretan element which went into the composite figure of Zeus is fitted into the story as follows: Cronos takes Rhea to wife; she bears him various children whom he swallows. When it comes to the youngest, Zeus, Cronos is given a stone instead. Cronos was thus foiled in his attempt to prevent his son Zeus from replacing him as ruler. The actual civil war, however, then takes place between Zeus and the older generation of Titans. The latter are described as fifty-headed and a hundred-armed. They hurl powerful missiles, Zeus his thunderbolts.

> And the bolts of thunder and lightning
> Came close together, whirling one after another,
> From his mighty hand, while all about
> The crashing flames struck the fecund earth
> And great forests crackled, loud with flames
> And all the land boiled, both ocean currents and barren sea,
> As the hot steam enveloped the earth-born Titans
> And the blaze of the lightning and the thunderbolts
> Blinded the Titans' eyes, strong heroes
> Though they were . . .

The battle is described in great length, the archaic violence reminding us of Marduk's war with the older generation of Babylonian gods. Zeus, of course, is the victor, casting his opponents into Tartarus, beneath the earth.

A rather violent concept of the underworld is followed by a description of the realm of Hades and Persephone guarded by Cerebus and the River Styx. The general effect is of two traditions blended, the one a stormy cosmological concept and the other a more negative house of death derived from the ancestor cult and the vegetation myth. The civil-war-in-heaven theme appears to be fundamental in priestly myth making, for there are traces of it in Scandinavia, in Babylonia, in Canaan and, of course, in the revolt of Lucifer. Interestingly enough, Zeus is compelled to fight a second battle before the dominion of Olympus is established. This is with the monster Typhoeus, the offspring of Gaia and Tartarus (suddenly personified). The monster is described as having a hundred snake heads, fire glittering in their eyes. When the dragon is destroyed, wet winds flow from him. It is difficult not to see a parallel with Tiamat and Yam with Zeus as a rain provider since the wet winds emanating from Typhoeus would be storm winds.

Dumézil has analyzed the story of Pandora, which is included in both *Works and Days* and *Cosmogony,* as one of the fundamental themes in Indo-European mythology. He believes that the core of the story is not the theft of fire but rather the problem of immortality. In one of the Aryan Brahmanas a ghandarva (a half-horse demon) steals the sacred drink of the gods, soma, and hides it. This liquid is supposed to confer immortality. Since the ghandarvas were thought of as sexually voracious, a divine woman was created and sent to get it back. In another Indian legend yet another type of demon steals the food of the gods, amrita. While the demons are fighting over it, Vishnu, in the guise of a woman, appears, tricks them, and regains the divine food. Pandora is therefore the deceitful woman, parallel to the one in the Indian legends, who is sent to deprive men of the immortality-bestowing food.

> Now before this time the races of men
> Had lived on earth untroubled,
> Without labor and painful ills which bring death
> with them,
> (For wretchedness suddenly makes men grow old)
> But the woman removed the great lid with her hands
> And brought dire misfortune to mankind.

In Dumézil's view, sickness and age are equivalent to death and thus Pandora has deprived man of the gift of immortality. Ambrosia is transformed, by the poet, into abstract evils causing death.

Hesiod makes the legend a text upon which to preach a sermon against women. Although this is couched in terms of peasant misogyny, it is very likely a moralizing explanation of the very ancient taboos with which the female sex has always been laden. The irrationality with which one half of the human species has regarded the other as destructive and magically dangerous has already been illustrated earlier in this chapter and it is clear that the Semitic Eve fits into this tradition.

It was probably the particular history of the Greek states which hindered the development of a sophisticated monotheism. They were heir to the mythology of Homer and in the hands of this poet the gods had already become frivolously human. Moreover the city-states were never unified by an imperial power which could impose the all-powerful image of an emperor reflecting a single god as was the case in Persia. The Greek tendency toward rationalization was to lead to systems of philosophy. State hero cults satisfied the need for a local supernatural protector, in a sense an outgrowth of the clan god. The orgiastic and mystical tendency found a different outlet in the Eleusinian mysteries, the cult of Dionysus and finally the literary and ascetic creed of Orpheus, while the Greek peasant, as did most peasants in the ancient world, continued to cling to magic and archaic superstition.

Neolithic Island Cathedrals

Malta—unique megalithic temples—remains of stone statues point to fer-
tility goddess—oracular rooms—frieze of animals and remains of bones
proof of animal sacrifice—Hypogeum both necropolis and temple—incubation
chamber suggests divination by means of narcotics—possible ancestor cult.

WHILE the Fertile Crescent and Greece were developing so-phisticated religious systems, the devotional impulses of barbaric and still Neolithic Europe were concretized in a grave cult combining worship of a female goddess with the building of imposing stone structures which are the earliest architectural monuments of the area.

Before passing to northern Europe, however, an ancient civilization on another Mediterranean island demands some attention both for its intrinsic religious character and for the provocative combination of megaliths, or structures built of great stones, and the cult of a female goddess.

Malta and Gozo, rather barren limestone islands, are situated in the western Mediterranean not far from Sicily. Malta, the center of the culture, seems to have been colonized from Sicily where in the third millennium B.C. a village people bred goats, sheep and pigs, made competent pottery and buried their dead in caves or pit graves. At the middle of the third millennium B.C., the branch of this people which settled on Malta began to develop a way of life which lasted for over a thousand years. Judging from the artifacts discovered, during this period they suffered no invasions, lived in peace, and must have achieved a well-organized social system with a sufficient surplus to support a priestly class, a phenomenon unusual in human society before the introduction of metal industries. Remains of terraces indicate that they were ingenious in exploiting the limited agricultural resources of the terrain, and deep winding sledge or traves tracks still furrow the coraline limestone, revealing a transportation system. The ancient Maltans raised cattle and cultivated some sort of grain. Except for foundations, all trace of houses has disappeared. In all probability they were mere huts built of small stones or reeds.

For centuries all that remained of the Maltan civilization was a series of great stones jutting out of mounds of dirt around which the modern peasants worked the land. In the first decades of the twentieth century Sir Themistocles Zammit undertook extensive excavations and revealed the fantastic architectural monuments laboriously erected by the people of this simple peasant economy.

The temples of Hal Tarxien may be taken as typical. The ruins are situated on a cliff overlooking the harbor near Tarxien. (All these structures in fact were built on hilltops.) The basic ground plan was two ovoid bulges connected by a passageway, in outline not unlike the figure of the massive goddess associated with them. The floors were paved and the walls were built of large upright stone slabs, sometimes beautifully dressed in the later temples. The entrance and passageways were roofed with stone slabs, and capstones joined the sidewall blocks which were placed alternately broadside and edgewise. While the central court in each oval was unroofed, the side bulges or apses were covered with corbel roofs, as was the apsidial bulge in the center of the rear ovoid. The latest and largest temple in the series includes other rooms and divisions lacking the primitive clarity of design best exemplified in the middle structure. The whole complex was surrounded by a wall, and probably heaped over with a large earth mound or barrow. In front of Temple Three was a large semicircular paved court which afforded an area for ceremonial activities. On either side of the entrance a rectangular stone was recessed into a three-sided tray, the surface of which contained conical holes of different sizes. Since a heap of more than a hundred stone balls was found near them, Zammit conjectures that they might have been tossed into the holes in a sort of pinball divination game. Many other stone balls used as foundation for some of the stone uprights were no doubt also used as rollers.

Temple One, which is the oldest, contains no decoration; Three, which is the latest, exhibits a simple but effective decorative style featuring the running spiral or the branched spiral (also found in Mycenaean art), egg and dart and acanthus leaves. Temple Three evidently had an impressive façade of dressed stones which has not survived.

Within the main court of Temple Three, the base of a seven-foot stone female statue was found. Its general contours can be restored from a small stone image which was evidently a copy of it. The bulging figure consists of two ovoids, the headless top a unit of huge breasts and massive folded arms ending in tiny hands along massive thighs, and semi-squatting great pear-shaped legs ending in tiny feet. There was probably a hole between the shoulders for the insertion of a separate head. Such heads have been found, oval in shape, on which the eyes and mouth are incised as shallow lines, while the wavy hair may have been meant to represent a wig. The upper part of this figure was bare, the lower clothed in a pleated bell-shaped skirt ending in scallops. Some of the small images, however, are nude. At the left of the statue was a long stone settee with a back. In the apses there were various decorated blocks into which holes were bored and filled with stone plugs. A stone block in the court was also bored and when the plug was removed ox bones, marine shells, flint knives, broken pots, were found stowed inside the slab. Not far from the statue the pavement was deeply eroded by fire. A cylindrical vessel near it may have contained a libation or have been used to catch sacrificial blood.

In this temple a frieze on one stone altar depicted four goats (a type not now found in Malta), a pig, and a ram. Trilithon shrines, with flanking stone pillars on great decorated slab bases, were also found. Beyond the first court there was a niche filled with animal bones. In the second temple above a cache of animal bones, two facing bulls were carved in profile, below one of them a sow with thirteen sucklings. In the middle of the main court of the temple there was a large circular fireplace.

Temple One was distinguished by a hidden chamber with a wall containing a small window which could easily have been camouflaged, used, Zammit believed, to deliver oracles to worshipers. A small hole leading downward from the chamber through the wall to the outside room might have been used to produce an amulet or votive offering at the feet of the worshiper.

Subsequent excavations on the islands have shown that the earliest temples were simple structures which imitated the pattern of early kidney-shaped rock-cut tombs. Three phases have been identified: the earliest characterized by temples of simple form without decoration; a middle period during which architectural form and stone dressing reached their peak, probably enriched by Minoan influence, since baetyl altars and spiral decoration appear; and a final era of decline in which both planning and construction were inferior.

Three male clay figures in a fragmentary state show that priests wore a curled wig like that of a British barrister. The full face is rather Eastern-looking; the arms are folded over the bare chest and the lower part of the body is clothed in the same flounced skirt as the female idols (or priestesses), a style of dress reminiscent of both Crete and the Near East.

In a temple at Hagar Quim a room was found behind a conical pillar flanked by two slabs, in front of which a wedge-shaped block was set up. The wall of the room was pierced by a hole, indicating that in this shrine, too, priests gave oracular pronouncements. In one of the rooms at the same site the remains of the feet and legs of two more huge, corpulent statues in the same style as that at Hal Tarxien were found. Seven statuettes of female deities or priestesses were also recovered. Another temple, at

Mnaidra, is notable for a doorway, four feet by five, cut through a single great stone slab.

A structure near Hal Tarxien, the Hypogeum, was probably occupied from about the sixteenth century B.C. This temple (and tomb) was cut out of the underground rock and also made use of natural caves. It consisted of a large hall where worshipers could have assembled, an elaborate chapel, an oracular room and small cubicles. Evidence of the technique used in constructing this monument indicates that a hole was first drilled in the limestone with a flint tool fixed on a stick. The intervening rock was then knocked away with stone hammers and the surface smoothed by more pecking and finally dressed by rubbing with a hard stone. The stippled effect obtained in dressing the surface of slabs in some of the temples was achieved by boring shallow holes, probably with a bow drill.

In the Hypogeum, beside the oracular chamber, was a small oblong room pierced with a square hole. A deep low note uttered in this room resounded and vibrated in the large chamber. A red scroll and disk pattern on the ceiling of the latter proliferated into a network of branching curves. Zammit suggests that the small cubicles in this monument were incubation rooms used as in Babylonian divination. The devotees could lie on couches after having taken a narcotic and experience prophetic dreams. Evidence of this consists of clay figures of the familiar obese female lying in attitudes of sleep.

One of these figures, lying on its side, the head pillowed on the hand, is a particularly fine piece of modeling. Indeed, the graphic representations of the Maltan goddess, judging from the small examples, mark a high point in ancient art. The bodies of these ample women are treated with a magnificent simplicity; the balance of the monumental masses, the deliberate sophisticated distortion (worthy of Gaston Lachaise), create a style quite unlike that of Mesopotamia. It is a pity none of the great stone statues survives intact, for they must have been enormously impressive.

Although used as an underground temple, the Hypogeum contained many rock-cut tomb chambers. At its entrance there are traces of a megalithic structure. The Maltans sometimes buried their dead in rock-cut tombs but here the bones of more than 7,000 individuals have been recovered strewn about in the earth which filled the chambers when they were excavated. This has been taken to mean that the rites of the sanctuary had something to do with a cult of the dead, especially since bones have been found covered with red ochre.

Taking all of the evidence together, it looks very much as if the Maltan religion was a specialized branch of the earth mother fertility cult. Clearly cattle, sheep and goats were sacrificed. Friezes of animals probably represented sacrificial victims. The relief of the facing bulls and the suckling sow points to animal fertility and even hints at the familiar bull cult.

The connection between the mother goddess and the cult of the dead is strengthened by analogical relationships elsewhere. As Nilsson has pointed out in interpreting Demeter, in some Mediterranean areas the seed is buried for storage in underground jars or silos. This is the case in the Neolithic settlements of southern Italy. Since the dead were buried in artificially excavated pits, the resemblance may well have caused the connection between the goddess of vegetable fertility and a cult of the dead. However, it is well to remember that the dual personality of Inanna, the fertility goddess, and Ereshkigal, goddess of the underworld, goes back as far as Sumeria.

Up to about 1500 B.C. Malta, with its monumental goddess, was evidently a center of megalith religious worship and may well have been a link in its spread throughout Europe. After the middle of the second millennium B.C., the ceremonial centers were deserted and a meter of sterile silt shows a hiatus before the coming of another people of different ethnic stock possessing copper tools and burying the ashes of their dead in urns whose fragments are scattered above the relics of the Neolithic cathedrals.

CHAPTER II

Megalithic Missionaries

Neolithic Europe—distribution of stone grave and standing stones—possible Mediterranean origin of burial cult—missionary hypothesis—representations of earth-fertility goddess—meaning of menhirs—theory of substitute body— evolution of Stonehenge—earth cult and possible sun cult.

THE PLAINS of central, northern and western Europe are dotted with barrows, or heaps of earth, from which great stones project; sometimes the stone structures are free-standing, others have been fully excavated by archaeologists. In England they have been called giants' graves, in Holland *hunnebeds,* or beds of the Huns; folklore and early unscholarly speculation endowed them with an aura of magic and superstition. Likewise along the coast of Europe from Scandinavia to northern Germany and Holland and the Alps, on the Shetland Isles, through southern England and Ireland to Brittany and along the coast of Spain and Portugal there are countless monuments made up of single large, roughly dressed stones. Some stand singly and are called menhirs, some are arranged in groups and are fitted with capstones or they stand in large circles enclosed by a ditch or, as in Carnac, Brittany, hundreds of them line what appears to be an avenue. Very often the stones weigh tons and inspire wonder at the ingenuity of the primitive peoples who were able to move them. The relation between the stone chambers and the monolithic monuments is not yet entirely clear but similarities of archaeological material associated with them show that they are part of a complex of culture (related to that we have already encountered in Malta) which at one point was widely distributed throughout Europe.

Before the development of archaeology both menhirs and the stone structures were attributed to the Druids and fanciful accounts were given of their ceremonial activities. Folklore often identified them as the graves of legendary heroes. It was not until organized excavation of the stone chambers revealed datable artifacts that they were conclusively shown to be graves, Neolithic monuments, the last great achievement of the Stone Age.

But who were the builders of these mausoleums and where did they come from? The answer takes us into a complicated series of population movements which are not yet thoroughly clarified. The European Neolithic era produced many groupings which can be identified by complexes of artifacts but, lacking a written record, where the ethnic strains came from, how interchange took place, whether by conquest, trade or blending of different societies, is largely a controversial matter.

As we have seen, the first transition from Mesolithic hunting and gathering to the Neolithic probably took place in the Near East. Whether stock breeding or pastoralism stemmed directly from hunting, and cultivation of grain arose separately, resulting in an eventual mixture of the two economies, or whether both developed together, cannot be proved. The oldest Neolithic farmers practiced both in Jericho about 7000 B.C. It took several thousand years before stone axes began to be polished and the arts of pottery and weaving were added. The Sialk culture in Persia had achieved all these advances by about the fifth millennium B.C. Thereafter, as we have seen, urban cultures rose rapidly in the Near East, spread to Asia Minor and assumed new forms in the Mediterranean.

When we turn to northern and central Europe, civilization evolves at a much slower pace. Although the Mesolithic hunters no doubt did not die out or become absorbed all at once, the Neolithic settlements of what has been called the Danubian culture, which spread from Asia into the rich black loess lands from Hungary to Germany, Poland and Belgium, are of almost exclusively pastoral cultivators. A mixed group of native hunters and Danubian settlers probably pushed on northward into Denmark and Sweden where the Mesolithic fishermen had already ensconced themselves on the coast. No doubt here, too, a blending of societies took place.

Meanwhile other Neolithic farmers from the southwest, whose artifacts are sufficiently similar to those found in North Africa to suggest that this was their point of origin, pushed up into Switzerland, France, Belgium and Britain. On the Swiss lakes they built their wooden houses on piles. In Germany and southern England (Windmill Hill) they circled their encampments with ditches, quarried out of the chalk, and stockades. They, or the battle-ax people who amalgamated with them, also set up ritual circles of wooden posts, called henges, in England.

While the Neolithic peoples in the Near East built houses of sun-dried brick, the Danubians constructed wooden-gabled houses large enough to accommodate whole clans. (We are reminded of the longhouses of the American Iroquois.) After about ten years they moved on to allow the land to recover from cultivation and often returned later to build a new village on the old site, burning off the new scrub and repeating their cycle of living. Their pottery was decorated with spirals and meanders, their hoe blades, with which they broke ground for wheat and barley, and their querns, on which they ground the grain, were of polished stone. They used adzes for carpentry, while their neighbors and enemies of Switzerland employed axes. Against the inroads of the latter they dug ditches and built ramparts.

The Danubian pots seem to imitate gourds in shape, while the Swiss lake dwellers got their ceramic shapes from leather bags. Since both practiced agriculture without fertilizer, there was a constant search for virgin land and as a result a rather rapid spread of their societies. Although such groups were well enough organized to build defenses for their villages, there was not sufficient specialization to produce a surplus; households remained self-sufficient, trading, in some cases with the older hunting groups for antler axes, was no more than casual barter.

Among the Danubians, the dead were buried in a flexed position. Many clay figures of women suggest a fertility cult similar to that in the early Near East. Phalli of stone or clay are also found. Similar phalli also occur in Anatolia, the Balkans, in Malta and in England. It is customary to call them fertility symbols. Rather dubious artifacts of phallic shape, recovered from Paleolithic deposits, have been assigned a similar function. Somehow the explanation is not convincing. The female fertility figure has, after all, a long tradition in subsequent cult and literature. The isolated male organ has no similar history. In India, where sex organs are clearly worshiped, the vulva is also isolated. Once again caution must be used in assigning fertility ideas or a generalized desire for offspring to peoples who do not yet seem to have acquired great powers of abstraction. As will be shown later, it appears much more likely that the mechanism of potency, which is concretely allied to a pleasurable act, might well be considered magical. The phallic amulets, therefore, could be votive offerings in the hope of increased potency. In Malta, images of parts of the body have been found which may have been offered up in shrines in hopes of curing ailments. The Etruscans made similar objects.

Since the Danubians were organized on a clan basis, with only heads of households or elected chiefs as leaders, they preserved an archaic democracy. There is no trace of more pretentious establishments which could have been the residences of hereditary chiefs or kings. Judging from the practice of modern clan societies, the land would have been held in common. All in all, these first European peasants were a peaceful people; the only weapons they left behind were stone maces.

Did these peasant colonies of Europe build the megalithic monuments? They may have had some connection with them but there is a great gap between their simple inhumations and occasional cremations and the great stone cairns which apparently held whole families. These cairns have been typed and classified by various authorities who have disagreed as to the origins of the megalith burials. A study of artifacts has shown that there were two types of stone graves, the passage grave, a circular chamber with a corridor entrance, and the gallery grave, an oblong chamber often broken up into alcoves by partial partitions. The latter can be traced to the south and did not arrive in northern Europe until the middle of the second millennium B.C. Since the passage grave is highly developed in Spain, attempts have been made to derive it from that area. Glyn Daniel feels, however, that while there may have been single stone graves in early Spain, their subsequent development as collective tombs requires a foreign influence.

What could have been the reason for the spread of such stone mortuary architecture? W. J. Perry, who advocated the Egyptian origin of nearly everything in a book, *The Children of the Sun,* suggested that stone structures, which he located all over the world from India to the Pacific Islands to the Americas as well as through Europe, were the result of missionaries from the fifth dynasty of Egypt who had spread the sun cult while at the same time trading in metals. The Egyptian origin of the megaliths was not taken seriously, but the idea of missionaries, who were also prospectors for copper, did seem to fit because, although the tombs in various areas were similar in structure, the grave goods differed. No real movement of peoples seemed to be involved; all that was transmitted was a funerary cult. The similarity in style to the tholos tombs of the Mycenaeans (which were not, however, built of large stones), the occurrence of rock-cut tombs in the Mediterranean, and the similarities of construction to the temples on Malta were striking. Furthermore, in some chambers of the Malta temples there were porthole-like openings through which a man could just manage to creep. In the graves in Sweden, England, northeastern France, Belgium and northern Germany portholes were used as entrances, either bored through a single great slab or made by cutting semicircular holes in two stones. Decoration was also significant, for many of the tombs were richly carved. The running spiral and the repeated arc or circle, Mycenaean and Maltan motifs, turned up on the stones of tombs in Brittany and Ireland.

Finally, there were traces of a goddess cult everywhere. Daniel writes, "The great megalithic builders of western Europe were imbued by a religious faith, were devotees of a goddess whose face glares out from pot and phalange idol and the dark shadows of tomb walls, whose image is twisted into the geometry of Portuguese schist plaques and the rich carvings of Gavrinnis and New Grange. . . . I find it very difficult not to believe that our Spanish goddess and our oculi motifs do not come from the early goddess figures of Cyprus, Crete, the Cyclades, and western Anatolia."

Indeed, O. G. S. Crawford has traced the ramifications of this being whom he calls the "Eye Goddess" from Tel Brak, already mentioned in connection with Crete. In many areas her face appears on pots, sometimes with lines for hair or a necklace, sometimes with the double lines outlining the eye, sometimes with two nipple projections to indicate breasts. In Troy and also in neolithic Greece, Crawford finds traces of her on pots. In Spain and Portugal the eyes appear on stone plaques with chevroned or checked surfaces. In Spain there are also stone menhirs with the necklace symbol, repeated half circles, and tiny eyes or breasts. In Brittany there are other figures, which relate to the Spanish ones, either engraved on walls of tombs or on stelae. The eyes appear again in Irish passage graves. Finally, R. J. Atkinson has found a carving which he thinks suggests the same goddess on one of the monoliths of Stonehenge. While actual diffusion of a single deity cannot be proven, the distribution of the symbols is suggestive. The relation between the earth mother and the underworld has already been discussed in connection with Malta.

If the megalithic missionaries came from the Aegean they could have been sea rovers from about the middle Minoan period. The evidence indicates that they first invaded Spain, indoctrined the Neolithic peasants with their religion, and probably created a stratified society with themselves as overlords. If some were copper prospectors, many others were not, for tombs in Great Britain, Ireland, Scandinavia and northern France contain no metal objects. In southern France, Spain and North Africa bronze artifacts do occur. (Megalithic tombs are also found in Palestine, Tartary, Persia and India, and Crawford feels that symbols related to them occur in Africa, in Ethiopia and even on the Niger.) The Mycenaeans maintained some sort of trading contacts with Sicily, Capri, Spain, southern Britain and Ireland. Daniel writes, "Certainly religion played an important part in the life of the original megalith builders, even if I cannot see them as primarily missionaries. . . . They were surely looking for new places to live, new materials for life and perhaps also trade. . . . It is reasonable to suppose that the primary driving force of the megalith builders was a colonial and trading one and a prospecting one. . . ."

The achievements in Spain and Portugal are impressive. The circular burial chamber is sometimes over seven feet high, ending in a corbel arch. The passageway and the chamber were heaped over with a great barrow of earth. In front of the entrance was a circular forecourt with a slab wall, evidently used for ceremonial, just as in the case of the Maltan monuments. The great megalith of New Grange, Ireland, aside from the intricate carving on the stone slabs which includes representations of axes and ships as well as scrolls, circles and lozenges, is impressive for its huge mass. The barrow is two hundred and eighty feet in diameter. At some distance from it stood a ring of thirty-five monoliths, each five or six feet high. The corbeled burial chamber is twenty feet high and is ringed with three apses, each roofed with a huge stone slab. The passage entrance is sixty feet long and some of the stones of the great chamber are ten feet long.

The passage graves are generally in coastal areas. Their builders would have constituted a first migration from Spain along the coast of France to Ireland and England and eventually to Scandinavia. A second migration either from Spain or directly from the Mediterranean carried the gallery grave concept up through the middle of France to England and Scandinavia. Most of the gallery graves may have been built by the original Neolithic peasants after the absorption of the new stock. These colonizers, it has been suggested, were a separate sect of the megalithic religion. They penetrated as far as the Hebrides and the Orkneys and were the first agricultural settlers in these stormy and forbidding islands.

What was the megalithic religion? In all probability the great tombs were family or clan burial places; a family likeness has been discerned in some of the Spanish remains. The social structure was probably held together by kinship ties and a warlike chieftain. Daniel believes that G. E. Mylonas's reconstruction of Aegean funeral practice would apply:

> The dead, perhaps on a wooden bier, decked in his clothes and ornaments, surrounded by his belongings, and well provided with supplies to speed him on his way to the unknown, was left on the floor of the tomb. . . . Then the door was walled up, a libation or a toast offered by each participant in the burial, perhaps accompanied by the calling of his name, the dromos was filled in, a funeral feast was held, and a marker was placed to indicate the position of the grave. When a second death occurred in the family, the dromos was cleared, the packing of the doorway removed, the chamber was made ready and fumigated, and if the body of the first tenant had not entirely decayed, burnt offerings were made to propitiate its spirit and keep it in the grave. The second body was then laid in state on the floor. . . . Burial succeeded burial until the floor space was occupied and the bodies decomposed. Then room was made for the latest addition by packing the bones of ancestors in cysts, by sweeping them up against the sides of the grave, or by throwing them out into the dromos.
>
> The spirit of the dead was sentient and was around the grave as long as the flesh was in existence; the corpse was treated with respect; it had to be provided with supplies; it had to be given favorite objects that in life belonged to it; it had to be kept in the grave by walled doors. The moment the body was dissolved and was transformed into a pile of bones it no longer had need of anything; there was no danger that its spirit would reappear; the spirit had descended to its final abode never to return; the bones could be swept aside or even thrown out.

In Spain the objects found in the tombs which prove the trading activities of the megalith builders include dentalium shells from the Red Sea, ostrich eggshell beads, luxury and cult items in alabaster, ivory, and hippopotamus tusk from Egypt and Africa (which were probably exchanged for the gold, silver, and copper of Spain). Likewise early Minoan stone beads and a dagger from the second city of Troy have been recovered in Portugal.

While the megalith builders were penetrating Europe, other population movements were taking place. The discovery throughout Europe of a type of drinking vessel seven or eight inches in height with a curved bottom, ornamented in horizontal bands divided into checkers or zigzag meanders, made of thin, well-baked clay, is correlated with that of other artifacts. A polished stone wrist guard with gold-headed studs in the corners, and a bronze buckle showed that the beaker makers were also archers. They also were associated with a barbed and tanged arrowhead and a broad-bladed dagger.

The single, contracted burials of these people were found in small numbers all over the area colonized by the megalith builders. Their skulls showed them to be of a short, broad-headed stock unlike the natives or megalith builders, and indeed their graves were few in number and surrounded by graves of the indigenous people whose artifacts were sharply differentiated. The beaker folk were traced back to Spain and identified as bronzesmiths and bronze traders. They appear to have followed the megalith builders in the second millennium as small bands of peddlers. They were adaptable enough to have embraced the dominant religion, for they are sometimes found buried with their typical drinking vessels (which may have signified the invention of beer) in the megalithic tombs. In England they conquered the southern Neolithic peasants.

While the beaker folk spread through Europe from the east, another culture complex traveled westward. It is identified by beautifully polished stone tomahawks or boat-shaped stone axes of several types and a style of pottery of various shapes decorated with cord markings. The bodies associated with these artifacts were buried in a flexed position in a barrow, often one above another until the barrow became a high mound. The battle-ax culture is contemporary with that of the megalith builders and is spread from Scandinavia and England through northern Europe to Finland, central Russia and the Crimea. Since in the Kuban and northern Turkey richly appointed graves of warrior princes of this culture have been excavated containing gold drinking cups, sun disks indicating sun worship, and battle-axes of silver and copper dating from about 2500 B.C., it appears that a nomadic way of life, consisting of cattle and horse raising, developed on the steppes of the Ukraine. The typical ax, derived from the old antler ax of the forest hunters, was translated into copper and precious metals by

Eastern smiths for the southern outposts of the group. Those who migrated into northern Europe carried with them the typical ax imitated in stone with even the casting seams reproduced. They met and merged with the beaker people and megalithic and peasant cultures throughout northern and central Europe. A typical blended culture of this type flourished on the east coast of England in the second millennium B.C. The battle-ax people probably spoke an Indo-European language and those who see them as constituting an important population movement even suggest that they may have spread to Anatolia where they created the Hittite empire.

How did their culture originate? The explanation may be complex, as Gordon Childe suggests; descendants of Paleolithic hunters of the Russian plains could well have merged with a pastoral ruling class which developed out of the Danube settlements, to create the first Indo-Europeans.

It is clear that important cultural changes were taking place in Europe all during the end of the Neolithic period and the beginning of the Bronze Age. Collective burial in the megalithic tombs is, however, only one element of the religion expressed in stone monuments. In a study of the free-standing stone menhirs, Horst Kirshner first emphasizes that the megalith grave had cult significance. It was a "cultic spot at which the living generation could achieve a fruitful connection with the ancestors placed in it who were thought to be living beyond the grave." He cites the building of fires in graves (which was also common in the Aegean) as an example of the need for warming the dead body and keeping it comfortable because it was thought to maintain a kind of subdued vitality. The magical potency of the Greek hero lay in his bones and the place where they lay. Among the Teutons the idea prevailed that the soul dwelt in the grave and died as the body decayed. As we have seen, Mylonas attributed the same belief to the Aegeans. Contemporary Siberian primitives, such as the Samoyeds, also believe that the soul dissolves to nothingness when the bones molder away. It should be remembered that the Kanakas, cited in Chapter 1, believed that death was simply another kind of life and that the dead might return at any time. The idea of the dead disappearing with their material remains might represent one step beyond the metaphysics of the Kanakas.

Another aspect of the funerary cult, its fertility character, is attested by the symbols and images of the death-fertility goddess and also suggested by the forecourt which offered an amphitheater for dances and ritual activities. Kirshner also believes the dead themselves had a symbolic potency because uniting with them strengthened the traditional identity of the clan. This "double function of the graves as a strong house for the ancestors as well as a source of unconquerable strength from which the life of the clan in general is renewed as each of its members is strengthened" is echoed in many folkloric practices carried on by peasants of the regions where they are found. Both megalithic graves and the stone menhirs, which date from the same period, have been the center of such activities. Breton peasants, for instance, on Shrove Tuesday built straw fires at the menhirs around which the men danced with burlesque gestures, holding their penises in their hands. Barren women were in the habit of sliding down the stones of megalith graves or sitting under or rubbing themselves against menhirs in order to have children. Swords and knives were sometimes sharpened on menhirs to acquire magic potency; the sick were sometimes counseled to sleep under them (in the department of the Aisne) in the hope of waking up cured.

Assuming that both graves and menhirs had fertility significance, what was the specific meaning of the menhirs? They vary greatly in size, from a foot or two to fifteen or twenty feet, and they cannot have been gravestones since scarcely any burials have been found near them. On the other hand, some have been found with traces of offerings at their feet. Baetyls or small upright stones have already been mentioned in Cretan shrines and in the altars of the Maltan cathedrals. It has been said that such pillars represent the dwelling place of a divinity or spirit. Kirshner, however, believes he can trace a direct connection between the grave cult and the menhirs. He bases it largely on examples of small pillars found *within* megalithic graves in Carrowkeel, Ireland, and in Barclodiad y Gowres, North Wales. Also, at the foot of a menhir statue within a French megalithic grave, bones and potsherds suggested a funeral feast. There were rows of pillars within a grave at Morbihan, Brittany. In a later period, in the early Bronze Age, standing stones with flat stones near them, similar to altars, are found in grave mounds. Standing stones are also found in East German and Scandinavian cremation graves. Analogically, a Mycenaean grave at Nauplion about 1200 B.C. was found to be empty except for standing stones and a stone hearth with charcoal remains, animal bones and a sacrificial knife.

Kirshner feels that when the grave tenant's body was missing (sometimes because the individual was killed in battle) a substitute body had to be contrived in order to maintain the fruitful magic of the living corpse. The archaic Greek gold death mask, in his view, was a device to preserve the living corpse somewhat longer. The menhir, therefore, was originally a substitute *body* and not the residence of a divinity or soul—an enduring body symbolized by the strength and permanence of stone. The true gravestone embodies a different complex of ideas based on a later animistic concept of a disembodied soul which may take residence in it. The interior of the grave being a limited area, cult activity tended to draw the menhir outside where it might become the site of marriage and puberty ceremonies and where its size was no longer limited. The cup holes and grooves often found in menhirs might have had something to do with libations. The spread of free-standing menhirs apart from graves might indicate a development of fertility ideas in connection with the worship of ancestors. Small menhirlike statues of goddesses have been found in caves in France. Since the megalithic culture was more deeply rooted than the ensuing Celtic and Teutonic ones, it left a lasting impression transmitted in peasant superstition for centuries.

If the menhirs had fertility and funerary cult significance, the great number of standing stones in Brittany seems to indicate that the megalithic religion was of a complex nature. In the neighborhood of Carnac there are over three thousand such stones, the tallest of which once stood sixty-five feet and weighed at least three hundred and fifty tons. The most puzzling arrangements are the *alignments* which consist of multiple rows running in the direction of the midsummer sunrise. The alignment at Menac, which is the largest, contains 2,935 standing stones forming ten to thirteen parallel lines running for two and a half miles. The only parallel structure is the Ashdown site in Great Britain which contains about 800 megaliths spread over the irregular parallelogram the sides of which are 812 and 1,624 feet long. Excavation has not clarified the meaning of these outdoor temples. The orientation of the Menac alignment suggests sun worship. (Along the Peruvian coast near Ica there are arrangements of small stones in long lines which are said to have an astronomical orientation.) Certainly great crowds of worshipers could march between the stone pillars led by priests to carry out some as yet undefined ritual.

Greatest of all these monuments (and in a sense a summation of Neolithic practices as well as a transition to the Bronze Age) is Stonehenge on the Salisbury Plain of southern England, constructed in three phases, from 1900 B.C. to about 1400 B.C. The first phase of this edifice consisted of a ditch with a ring of holes inside, called Aubrey holes after their discoverer. Cremations were found in these holes, which also probably contained wooden posts. R. J. C. Atkinson conjectures that these cremation pits indicate that the earliest Stonehenge religion was a worship of the dead or underworld spirits and was practiced by the amalgamated people of the Windmill Hill culture. Other circles of this sort have been found elsewhere in Britain.

The second phase of Stonehenge consists of a double circle of bluestones set about five feet apart, eighty-two in all, which may have had capstones. This was demolished and a close-set circle of sixty bluestones arranged in its place. Strangely enough, these stones have been proved to have been quarried in Pembrokeshire, Wales, a hundred and thirty-five miles from Stonehenge. Using a concrete replica, archaeologists have demonstrated their probable transportation by a raft constructed on two dugout canoes, along the coast and up the Avon River, and finally by sledge to the site of the monument. To move the heaviest of the stones by sledge would have required one hundred and ten men.

Fragments of beakers around the stones indicate that this part of the monument was constructed by the beaker people. These people, as we have seen, were traders, and indeed one of their routes led from Ireland along the coast of Wales. Since they had already had some contact with the battle-ax nomads, who were sun worshipers, and they themselves sometimes buried gold disks with crosses on them in their graves, plus the fact that the bluestones definitely mark the line of the solstice, it seems that by this period Stonehenge was a solar monument. Buried surfaces in the center of the circle are compacted as if by dancing feet. Other circles, particularly the one at Avebury, follow the same pattern. The culture which the beaker people grafted upon the native one was seminomadic and pastoral with some sporadic cultivation. The appearance of warriors' panoply and battle-axes in their barrow graves indicates the emergence of a warrior aristocracy with some knowledge of metalworking. Their social organization must have been sufficiently centralized to permit the carefully planned and seemingly heroic undertaking of the transport of the bluestones. The work was done between 1700 and 1600 B.C.

Finally, the last great addition to Stonehenge was the arrangement of thirty bluestones in a circle with a horseshoe of fifteen inside it. Outside the whole structure a ring of great sarsen uprights was erected, each pair joined by a capstone, and an interior grouping of five still larger sarsen trilithons were set in a horseshoe, the uprights twenty to thirty feet high. These great boulders were carefully dressed with stone mauls. They were apparently set up by people of the Wessex culture of the early Bronze Age, in about 1500 B.C. These people buried their dead in a round barrow surrounded by a ditch and a bank. Their culture was a development of the combined beaker and local Neolithic societies, which had now entered the Bronze Age, for their richly equipped graves contained well-carved battle-axes, stone maceheads, and bronze daggers with gold ornamented hilts. They were both warriors and middlemen in the metal trade between Ireland and the continent. Their commercial connections are proved by the presence of amber beads obtained, not directly from Scandinavia, but from southern Europe on the long overland route from Jutland to the Mediterranean followed by the amber traders.

Not only were the trilithons a final triumph of engineering but the capstones were kept from slipping by mortise and tenon joints which suggest that the stonework imitated the framework of some earlier circular wooden building.

Most surprising of all was the discovery in the last few years of a number of significant carvings on the sarsen stones. A hilted dagger and a number of axheads were found on one. More axes were found on another. These are similar in type to the weapons carved in megalith graves in Ireland, Brittany, Norway and Sweden. The dagger, however, proved to be of particular interest, for it was of a tapering type with quillons at its base, a short hilt and a wide, flat-topped pommel. Daggers of this type were not indigenous to Britain but they were found in shaft graves in Mycenae up to 1500 B.C. This, and other objects in Wessex graves, prove contact with Mycenae. Atkinson points out that the great gate at Mycenae was not unlike the trilithons in construction, even to the use of mortise and tenon joints, and only the dressed stone architecture of the Mediterranean is comparable to the achievement of Stonehenge Three. Homer tells us that architects, like poets, were migrant workers, wandering from city to city. On the basis of the carving of the Mycenaean dagger and the evidence of trade between Britain and the Aegean, Atkinson hazards the suggestion that the Wessex chieftains might possibly have made use of a Mycenaean architect.

The final discovery was a weathered symbol on one of the fallen stones which resembles what Crawford calls the "box" symbol, a rectangle with a curved top and a projecting knob which may be the atrophied image of the great mother. Stonehenge also has certain features in common with the passage grave: for instance, the passage grave was sometimes surrounded by an outer circle of stones. The entrance to the grave was also essentially a series of trilithons. He writes: "If this theory has any foundation, Stonehenge would have been conceived as a sort of skeleton Passage Grave, or its sublimation. One could think of many reasons for building such a structure; if Passage Graves were the scene of rites and ceremonies it would be quite natural to wish to have a place for them that was not encumbered by a mound or cairn. Thus the temple might have developed out of the tomb, as in Malta."

What were the rites? Aside from burnt sacrifices, which seem to be generally associated with Neolithic religion, was there some pageantry connected with the fertility religion associated with the great mother? We have seen that in the Near East the earliest epics were probably based on dramatizations of fertility themes. We have, of course, no record of any oral literature current in Great Britain in this era. Some sort of drama, perhaps lit by torches and accompanied by music and dancing, may have been enacted in or around the great stone structure, celebrating the death and resurrection of the fertility goddess or her lover.

Sex, Stags, and Sun Ships

*European Neolithic to Bronze Age—carving in Camonica Valley as transi-
tion from Mesolithic—hunting cult—hints of pictographic language—from
stag to god—sun symbols—burial scenes—ithyphallic warriors—Scandinavian ships and sun symbols—weapons as magical phallic symbols—Russian
animal-headed figures—ceremonial significance of rock art.*

I T APPEARS THAT, given a clean, flat surface, human beings are
irresistibly impelled to draw or carve something on it. The
rocks of Europe, Africa and parts of Russia testify that this impulse was as
strong in men of barbaric ages as it is today when few lavatories, telephone
booths or even public monuments remain undecorated. Scholars generally
agree that the rock carvings of the Bronze Age bear messages of more
significance than those of the idle contemporary doodler, although occasionally a minority voice suggests that primitives might also have been
less than serious.

The continual repetition of certain symbols, however, the immense effort
involved in pecking out the countless figures large and small that have been
found in eastern Spain, in Scandinavia, in the Italian and French Alps, on
the shores of the White Sea, and even in Africa convince us that this art
holds the key to important elements in the material and psychic life of
groups which were just emerging from the Neolithic stage of culture and
were to finally develop ways of life about which we know something from
historic documents. Since the Bronze Age rock carvings are extremely
schematic, once more interpretation involves ingenuity and correlation with
artifacts and whatever analogical material anthropology and myth can
supply.

In Chapter 4 it was pointed out that the naturalistic style in cave painting
in Spain underwent a change during the Mesolithic; schematized figures of
men and animals appeared and finally turned into symbolic signs on the
painted pebbles of the Azilian culture. Paintings on sheltered rock walls,
however, continued into the Neolithic and Bronze Age; they preserve the

form of recognizable objects, exhibit relationships with Bronze Age art elsewhere and also (the Almería culture particularly) tie up with decoration in megalithic tombs of the second millennium B.C.

In the last decade an Israeli anthropologist, Emmanuel Anati, a pupil of Breuil, has undertaken the study of rock carvings in the secluded Camonica Valley in the Italian Alps. Here a people, strategically situated on the amber route which led from Denmark to the Mediterranean, lived undisturbed from the late Neolithic to the Age of Iron. Thus their art preserves a two-thousand-year record which links together the other transitional hunting and pastoral cultures of Eurasia. The one recorded in Russia, situated on the shores of the White Sea and Lake Onega, is contemporary with the Bronze Age in northern Europe but remains Neolithic in content. The Scandinavian area shows a transition from a late Neolithic hunting way of life to the Bronze Age in which datable weapons are depicted.

What are the characteristics which link together this northern and mid-European art which contrasts so strongly with the styles of the Near East and the Mediterranean? In the first place, from the compositional point of view it looks backward toward early cave art. The Paleolithic man painted collections of animals, sometimes in haphazard fashion, often superimposing one upon another. Occasionally he created groups for ritual or anecdotal purposes. Hunting or war scenes forced him to relate his figures. He was not particularly sensitive to the potentialities of the spaces which were his canvas. It was with the advent of representationally decorated pottery that the artist became aware of space limitations and was impelled to divide his canvas up consciously and to fit his shapes into a style appropriate to the area. Finally, with the growth of city architecture, space consciousness achieved new dimensions. The artist was forced to think still more in terms of related areas. If a wall was to be adorned, it must take its place as a part of the whole structure. Bands of relief automatically induced repetition and symmetry, as did gates or altars.

The carven rock art typically consists of myriads of figures and signs of various sizes crowded helter-skelter into an area (its confines dictated by the availability of the rock surface). There is in most cases no focus and no careful planning. Later artists superimposed their designs on older pictures. When certain areas are isolated one can see that there are anecdotal and ritual relationships, as in the Paleolithic period, and sometimes objects are repeated or arranged in patterns, but they are often drowned in a sea of other figures, objects, or enigmatic doodlings. Almost the only subordination is achieved by occasional very large figures which dominate an area. Whether this is conscious artistry, however, is debatable, for, in the case of the Scandinavian sites, the large figure is probably a god and hence magnified for emphasis.

Art and the stage of cultural development are closely correlated. All these barbaric peoples failed to build cities or decorate pottery with figures and therefore never developed the sense of organization and the ability to generalize in certain ways which arise with urban culture. This should be kept in mind in interpreting their psychology.

Another element noticeable in all the rock engravings is the schematization, a crude and childlike technique with the child's tendency to exaggerate whatever is of special significance to the artist. The contrast to the skillful naturalism of the Paleolithic is amazing and certainly indicates a major psychic revolution. Then, too, there is no real aesthetic evolution, as is particularly clear from Camonica. The same type of rugged sketching persists for centuries in all the carving; there is no progression in the direction of elegance or charm, proving conclusively that the major preoccupation of these artists was neither to achieve idealistic form nor to give decorative pleasure. Along with schematization goes a peculiar trend toward distortion. In late Spanish art Breuil has shown how a figure of a man turns into a pine tree. The branching antlers of a stag become towering fantasies or the stag atrophies into a comb-shaped emblem. In other cases the human figure is given a large dehumanized head, the head of an animal or a bizarre, outsized phallus. This is also true of the Russian rock pictures and to some extent of the northern European carvings.

Finally, there is in all cases a repetition of objects clearly to be identified as symbols. A few, such as weapons or representations of the sun, seem to be common to all rock engravers; special signs predominate in other areas. Anati points out that in Camonica art, symbolic signs, such as what is called (for lack of a specific interpretation) a paddle, the human figure cut off at the waist, and the stag with the branching antlers, are often gathered into groups of three or seven like words in a sentence. He identified fifteen signs which were often repeated. Images of animals which appeared with them might be considered substantives. There were also other groupings containing dots, bars, and curves which seemed to be numerals. (Mayan numerals consist of dots and bars.) Anati believes, and Herbert Kühn before him, that many of the rock symbols suggest early Minoan pictographs or the upper predynastic Egyptian signs from Merimde, the ancestors of hieroglyphic writing. Kühn speculates concerning the distorted Spanish figures. Oracle records from the Shang dynasty in China (the earliest Chinese writing) contain similar distorted figures which evolved into the character for ghost. The suggestion is made that the Spanish figures are symbols for supernatural beings.

In general, therefore, the character of the rock engravings indicates that all of this art is straining in the direction of written language, hence the disregard for aesthetic charm or idealized naturalism. A convenient analogy is the pictography of the American plains Indians. When Henry School-craft was traveling with General Lewis Cass in 1821, he described the creation of such a pictograph by his Ottawa guides. The Indians cut a sheet of birch bark, stretched it on the ground and drew with the point of a knife. Some of the crudely sketched figures had hats on. They stood for soldiers, while the Indian members of the party were drawn without hats. A man with a sword was General Cass. A man with a hammer was School-craft, who occupied himself with collecting geological specimens. Three columns of smoke meant they had built three campfires. A deer and a turtle showed what game they had killed. Eight guns showed what arms they carried. The bark picture was fastened to a pole with three hatchet cuts in it which meant they had been traveling for three days. The pole leaned northwest to show the direction in which they were going. The whole exemplifies a symbolic use of objects and detail to express thoroughly con-crete ideas.

European rock art, however, is extremely hard to decipher. The late Spanish drawings are the least identifiable. The Neolithic farmers of this area were perhaps a mixture of the old hunting stock plus some infusion of new blood from the Mediterranean, from which area a primitive pottery with incised line decoration was probably introduced. In the second millennium B.C., the people of Almería were working wood with polished stone axes and celts. They also made flat and round slate eye-idols which show that the fertility goddess had arrived. The culture was further complicated by the arrival of the megalith builders bringing with them their funeral prac-tices and copper tools.

The character of these rock paintings of the second millennium suggests that some religious practice was related to the old hunting culture. Out of masses of ladderlike images, dots, stripes, and vague emblematic signs, what emerges most clearly are a sun symbol which resembles a wheel, the stag with the branching antlers, numerous other unidentifiable animals, highly simplified human figures and others with huge hands upraised, possibly in a gesture of worship. These are sometimes associated with a group of animals. The stag is sometimes shown with a solid or rayed circle between its horns. A three-line schema of the human body, the two crosslines curved in opposite directions, is interesting because exactly the same shape ap-pears among the Camonica Valley carvings. Finally, a drawing from Los Letreros cave shows a man with horns, a strange excrescence on one of them, a pronounced phallus and what appear to be sickles in his hands.

The predominance of the stag and other animals in conjunction with the sun symbol suggests hunting magic combined with a new interest in the seasons. The demonic figure with the horns reminds us of the shaman from the cave of Les Trois Frères. The presence of the sickles suggests the emergence of agricultural magic. Above this figure's head are what may be symbols for the sun and the moon. Another half-human figure looks like the bust of a man raising large hands while a row of vertical lines point downward. It is possibly a rain symbol.

Breuil does, however, identify an elongated shape, with two extensions which might be arms and two dots which might be breasts, surrounded by oblong shapes pointing toward it, as a body laid upon the ground attended by mourners, in short a funerary scene. A parallel scene from Camonica, which shows the dead man with his weapons beside him in a similar relationship to mourners, lends strength to the interpretation.

We must turn to the Camunians, however, to get a clear picture of the general development of the European rock engravers. In the third millennium they are clearly an archaic hunting people with probably some admixture of Neolithic agricultural invaders. In Anati's words, "Old bands of semi-nomadic hunters who inhabited the fertile region of eastern Spain were thrust back towards the semi-desert zones of the Sierra Morena and the Guadiana basin. Other similar groups penetrated wooded regions like Galicia, the Fontainebleau forest, and today's Luxemburg; and they settled there where conditions were more favorable for hunting and the raising of livestock than for agriculture. In central Europe their counterparts filtered across the mountains to the depths of the Alpine valleys, where some of them maintained a cultural level of Mesolithic or archaic Neolithic character. It is to these groups that we should most often attribute the rock art of the Metal Ages and the Camunians probably counted among them." The Camunians, in other words, as hunters late in the third millennium, settled in an area which would never produce an agricultural surplus. They added some farming to their activities but with a stubborn conservatism clung to their old customs. They submitted to influences from Italian and Urnfield Bronze Age people (situated north of the Alps) and learned to make daggers, halberds and axes in about the sixteenth century B.C. From then on they developed a metal industry which resulted in trade with the adjacent peoples and the Mediterranean area. Daggers, spears, and a war chariot of Mycenaean type are depicted. They were thus possibly middlemen in the amber industry. At any rate they continued as hunters and miners. Around the sixth century, they absorbed ironworking from the Celts and by the La Tène period they became for all intents and purposes Celts. Through all these centuries, secure in their little valley which contained no wealth worth conquering, the Camunians built no cities, created no true writing system, maintained their conservative artistic tradition and stubbornly clung to the chase when logically the emphasis should have shifted to pastoralism and farming. They are thus a kind of slow-motion film reflecting events in north European culture.

One of the problems raised by engraved rock art is the extent of its religious significance. In Camonica Valley, division into periods and analysis of content show that there is a gradual process of secularization. The earliest phase consists of static arrangements of symbols or figures of men and animals. It is followed by larger groupings of a religious nature without real action, hunting scenes, and also maps and schematic representations of villages. In the third period action is recorded and, while religious ritual is important, the Camunian artist also set down genre scenes, herding cattle, plowing, weaving, building of houses, metalworking, war, erotic activity. On the whole, this secularization takes place in the Iron Age and dramatizes another psychic revolution.

Rock carvings in the Camonica Valley constitute a particularly rich record of religious activity. In the late Neolithic and Bronze period, the temple was probably a sacred grove, the carved rock itself might mark the spot and undoubtedly had magic significance. Priest and chief were probably the same in a society organized on clan basis. Dances and processions are the chief ritual acts portrayed. From the beginning, sun and stag worship predominate. The stag which appears continually in hunting scenes, instead of becoming subordinate to the bull in the later period when agriculture would have been more highly developed, supersedes it. The stag cult finally dominates even solar worship. Anati points out that hunting, although economically archaic, was a form of male expression. To this we will return later.

The sun cult begins with a simple representation of a praying figure and a sun symbol. At Mount Bego in the French Alps, the sun was associated with oxen. It is also so depicted in Camonica Valley. With far more regularity, however, the sun, which may be a wheel, a rayed disk, or a solid disk, is associated with the stag which may run toward it or even penetrate its circle. We have already seen the sun and stag in Spanish art. Strangely enough, the sun sometimes is attached to the phallus of a probably masked figure holding a spear. It also appears in ritual combats between two warriors and finally, in the last Camonica period, it adorns small temples and is held in the hand of a supernatural being. What, then, is its connection with the stag? Given its agricultural fertility significance in other cultures, when it is drawn with the stag it could mean that somehow the hunting magic and a new faith have merged. Rather than assume that some abstract fertility idea has joined the two cults, it would seem that rituals had simply merged, very much as the Christmas tree (vegetation fertility) has been merged with the celebration of the birthday of Christ. Another explanation will, however, be suggested later.

The stag cult provides a most important example of the development of an anthropomorphic deity. A scene shows a group of armed figures dancing around a large stag standing before a temple while a spirit in the sky kills the animal. Groups are also shown praying before a dog chasing a stag. Finally the stag god itself undergoes a transition from a clearly defined animal with branching antlers to a sort of centaur with the bust of a man arising from its back to, finally, a large figure human in form, crowned with antlers, wearing a sword, and adored by a smaller figure near which is a sun symbol. The anthropomorphic god, according to Anati, is festooned with a snake. Now the antlered stag of the Celts, Cernunnus, is sometimes represented with a serpent, and dances were performed around him near the small temples of this people. We have here, it seems, one complete case history in which an anthropomorphic god is assimilated to or develops from a totemistic relationship. The propitiatory behavior of the hunters takes us back to the bear cult, described in Chapter 1, and indeed countless examples of ritual eating of the totem, preceded by apologies and propitiation, can be listed from anthropological records. The gradual evolution through the centaur stage of course reminds us of Greece and of the animal demons of the Near East and Crete. Still more interesting is the fact that in the Iron Age of Camonica Valley, when human gods are fully born a group of demons appears, some half animal, one even with bull horns and a trident, seemingly much like the medieval devil.

Sacrifices are often represented in Camunian art, sometimes symbolically by the animal; sometimes other weapons are carved above the head of the officiating priest. The Romans accused the Celts of human sacrifice. One rock carving shows a figure apparently encased in a cloth or bag while an ithyphallic man is about to strike him with a sword. At the executioner's feet is an ax.

There are other symbols whose repetition shows their ritual significance. Birds appear to be guardians of the house or the individual. An oddly shaped implement, which has been labeled a paddle, appears everywhere. It seems to have been imbued with beneficent magic. The figure severed at the waist with hands upraised in prayer also appears as an emblematic sign, probably a favorably disposed spirit. Finally, the dagger symbol is carved so repeatedly that it evidently had cult significance. In the third period it is the attribute of the sun god. We know that the dagger cult was present in the Hittite area and in Syria and also had some relation to the megalithic religion. Sacred weapons will appear again in Scandinavian carving and in the Teutonic culture where they will be discussed further.

Toward the end of the Bronze Age, around 1000 B.C., the first battle scenes appear in Camunian art. Often they are combats between two warriors and their positions suggest the steps of a dance. They wear plumed decorations (priests in religious scenes also wear plumed headdresses).

Sometimes deities appear above them carrying the sun symbol. Since the Etruscans practiced gladiatorial combats at funerals and dead bodies appear beside the Camunian ritual combats, the inference is that the Camunians had absorbed a foreign rite. The warriors are often ithyphallic as is the heroic figure, sometimes on horseback, who now becomes common.

Throughout Camunian art a large proportion of male figures are frankly ithyphallic. In the majority of cases they appear in ritual scenes or scenes of some religious significance. We shall have more to say concerning this phenomenon when we come to the Scandinavian rock carvings.

Finally, the cult of the dead was evidently of importance among the Camunians. In the middle period, scenes show the corpse laid out on the ground, his weapons arranged around him, and prayers or dances performed by the mourners. Sometimes near an altar an animal is being sacrificed or the funeral scene may take place outside one of the small temples. In the last period the worshipers follow a four-wheeled wagon, bearing the urn which contains the ashes of the dead.

In summing up the evolution of Camunian religion, Anati makes the point that when anthropomorphic gods are fully formed, a fantastic supernatural also proliferates. Scenes of men attacked by demons become common; sometimes the hero defeats the monsters. He suggests that the Bronze Age peoples were often driven into the periphery of the more cultivated areas. It is possible that the Bronze Age demons might have been carried over into the folklore of spirits and fairies dwelling in secluded spots which continued into the Middle Ages and is still perpetuated in peasant tradition. Interestingly enough, E. B. Tylor cites the superstition that iron is a talisman against the machinations of elves and witches.

The rock engravings of Scandinavia were at first thought to have little connection with an earlier group of animal engravings which occur in the circumpolar region in northern Scandinavia and Russia from 8000–6000 B.C. up to the beginning of the Bronze Age, about 1600 B.C. These are in the Paleolithic tradition of hunting magic. Drawings occur with a kind of X-ray picture of the animal's heart, a line drawn to it from the mouth, a magical symbol exactly like that used by the Ojibway Indians in their hunting ritual and also parallel to the X-ray drawings made by Australian natives. It has now been shown that the distribution of these pictures overlaps that of the Bronze Age carvings to the south. It is even possible to trace a transition; the representation of motion dies out as the figures become more schematic. There is also a technical transition; the older pictures are more deeply incised, while the traces of color in the incisions show a connection with painted rock art. Later images are not so deeply incised and color disappears. The conclusion can be drawn that the Scandinavian

Bronze Age peoples, whose ethnic heritage probably included Danubian, beaker, and battle-ax strains, did inherit something from the culture of the old nomadic hunters.

The first period of northern cult carving proper parallels that of Camonica Valley in that the new expressive impulse begins with groups of symbols, the stag, the ax, the dagger, and above all, in this area, the ship. The second period exhibits crude human figures, sun symbols, and, as in Camonica Valley, bronze-hafted axes and daggers appear around 1600 B.C. Around 1200 B.C. datable swords can be identified. Unlike Camunian art, the northern cult carving does not seem to grow increasingly secular. There is, however, a progression from what seem to be ritual representations involving sacred symbols carried in processions to anecdotal scenes dominated by a huge figure, identified by Oscar Almgren as a god. The carvings cease roughly around 500 B.C., the beginning of the Iron Age.

Like their southern contemporaries, the northerners were pastoralists, probably seminomadic, practicing a limited amount of agriculture, and did not build cities or develop a pottery tradition with representational decoration. The tendency to stick fast in the pastoral stage of human development is explained by the less favorable climate of northern Eurasia which in this period was not suitable to advanced agricultural techniques. Hunting continued in these areas as an important part of economic activity, and also fishing, especially in Scandinavia where there was an expanse of coastlines and a relatively limited tillable flatland.

It is not surprising therefore that the boat is an ever-present object in northern rock carving. Indeed it appears thousands of times in southern and middle Norway, Sweden, and also in Denmark. The ship depicted is a long narrow craft, with high curving prow and sternposts, perhaps as long as seventy-five feet, probably without sails or a fixed rudder, the crew often shown as a series of mere stylized knobs. No sea fights appear; instead the ships are associated with the sun wheel symbol, often placed on the boat, with figures holding up their hands near them. Figures in the ships, more clearly cut, hold up axes; some appear to be dancing and playing the *lur,* an ancient Bronze Age curved trumpet, some even turn somersaults. Some figures are much larger than others. Occasionally there is a carving of a snake.

Almgren ingeniously connects these signs with latter-day folklore. In West Germany, Belgium and France, up until recent times, carnival ships were dragged about on wagons during the festival. With them were associated giants, dragons, and various grotesque figures. The carnival celebration is accepted as basically a fertility festival. The giant would be a reminiscence of the large figures in the rock carving, and the dragon of the snake. Also the wheel of fortune (so called in the Middle Ages) appears in the carnival and this, according to Almgren, would be a descendant of the sun wheel. Continuing the fertility theme, according to Tacitus the Teutons carried a goddess by the name of Nerthus about on a wagon. She was a deity of death and fertility. In Holland a Roman relief was discovered showing a Teutonic fertility goddess, Nehelennia, standing on a boat. The Greek god Dionysus was carried about on a ship-shaped wagon. The Egyptian sun boat which transported the sun god, Ra, over the heavens in cult activity, was carried about on land and symbolized fertility. Finally, in Trundholm, Denmark, a model of a gold-plated disk, ornamented with spirals, and an image of a horse were discovered, the two objects mounted on a six-wheeled vehicle, showing that their full-size originals were drawn in a procession. There were similar boat images among the rock carvings.

From this, and a great mass of additional analogical evidence, Almgren concludes that the cult boat bearing the sun symbol was drawn about on land or the symbol was transported in a wagon, in some sort of spring vegetation ceremony. In addition, a tree is sometimes seen in the ritual boat. This, too, is of course well established as a Near East and Mediterranean fertility symbol. The boat might be a sort of stage for a cult scene involving dancing and music.

Another element present in the Scandinavian rock carvings is the extraordinary ithyphallicism of a majority of the figures. This is even more strongly marked than in Camonica Valley. As in the Camonica area, ritual combats are shown with both warriors in a state of erection. Some scenes of copulation are also depicted and associated with them is a man with a bow and arrow. Almgren sees this as the ritual marriage of the Near East, with the archer representing the death and sterility deity. The presence of a figure with an upraised ax he connects with the Norse mythology in which an ax was placed in a bride's lap to consecrate a marriage. The whole complex of activity and symbol is considered to mean that the Near Eastern fertility cult was diffused in northern Europe, perhaps by Phoenician traders.

Nilsson has warned us of the danger of exaggerating the diffusion of religious concepts and also of imputing an organized mythology to a culture which has not had time to develop a long priestly tradition. It is true that the later Norse Baldur myth involving the death of a fertility god (but without his resurrection) reminds us vaguely of the Tammuz theme. We have no evidence, however, to prove that such mythology was already elaborated in the period of the rock carvings. The concept of fertility is often used too loosely and casually. There is no economic reason why a predominantly pastoral people should feel a pressing need to increase the number of human offspring. The association of male sexuality with the promotion of vegetation, we must repeat, requires a high level of abstraction.

That the vegetation goddess did reach northern Europe indirectly with the megalithic religion seems reasonably established by the appearance of her symbols in tombs. In all of the cultic rock carving, however, female figures are extremely rare. Since the people who made the carvings were probably of mixed ethnic stock, it is reasonable to suppose that their religion may have included more than one tradition. In the light of the Spanish paintings and the carvings of Camonica Valley, it seems that a cultural complex can be discerned which leads back to the old nomadic hunter, pastoral tradition. It is this which seems to predominate in the rock carvings.

The complex consists of the stag, the ax, the sun symbol, ritual combat, and persistent ithyphallicism; in other words, the religion of an exaggeratedly masculine hunting, pastoral, and warrior mentality. To apply the blanket word *fertility* to it is slipshod thinking. Scholars reared in a prudish Hebreo-Christian tradition tend to use the term fertility to render all sex expression respectable. They have been remarkably backward in absorbing depth psychology concepts which have long played a fruitful role in the sister science of anthropology.

A. E. Crawley pointed out decades ago that the functional biological crises were strange, dangerous, and hence magical. As has been mentioned in Chapter 1, the penis of a formidable enemy warrior was sometimes cut off and brought back as a trophy and worn to make the owner valiant. Far from being worried about fertility, hunters and warriors were concerned about preserving their masculine potency and courage. Hence they abstained from intercourse with women before hunting or fighting—coitus results in the loss of genital erection and hence a symbolic loss of masculinity. Eric Njoberg describes the making of stone phalli in northern Australia in connection with the subincision ceremony. While the specific purpose of subincision is not clear, it *is* clear that it has to do with the mysteries of male maturity and nothing to do with vegetation, since the Australian natives do not raise crops. Australian ritual, as Geza Roheim has pointed out, is shot through with phallic activity. Blood from the erect penis is used in every ceremony. Circumcision he considered to be a castration attack upon the pubertal youth by the old men of the tribe. The Maori of New Zealand, also hunters and above all warriors, equated genital strength with courage and both were supposed to be centered in the warrior's penis. Roheim goes so far as to attribute the male magician's sense of power to the tension of the penis in erection.

To return to the rock carvings themselves. From Camonica we have a clear picture of intercourse with a donkey, and on the rocks of Lake Onega in Russia there is a frank representation of pederasty. It would take considerable ingenuity to argue that these scenes have much to do with the spring festival.

Ithyphallicism is, of course, associated also with the Pans and satyrs shown dancing in Greek art. The half-animal Dionysian chorus seems an echo of the masked sorcerer of the Paleolithic; indeed, Hernández Pacheco explicitly connected them with certain orgiastic peasant dances in Spain. Several masked figures from the Upper Paleolithic, semi-animal in form, are depicted as ithyphallic. Thus it appears that male sexual tension was, in very early times, equated with magic and religion. Basedow testified that the Australian primitives in certain dances sometimes actually reached an orgasm.

The simplest explanation of the figures in the rock carvings, therefore, is that they are a reflection of the hunter-warrior-pastoralist tradition, portraying gods and/or worshipers with the same attributes. There is some evidence to connect this type of god with animal or half-animal shapes; he was possibly an early totemistic shaman who both killed and placated or represented the beast of prey. The purely hunting culture of northern Russia produced carved figures wearing animal masks or heads, holding spears or bows, and violently ithyphallic. Associated with them were sun symbols and images of elk or deer. In Camonica Valley, we have seen an animal develop into semi-anthropomorphic shape. In Spain a figure with huge hands upraised is seen surrounded by stags and hounds. Some of the Scandinavian figures either wear horns or a horned helmet.

A complicated and interesting scene from Sweden seems to unite two religious concepts. The stag is surrounded by hounds while the ithyphallic hunter contains a sun symbol in his body. The hounds are also shown aboard the sacred ship. (We are reminded that the Camunians were sometimes depicted in attitudes of prayer before their hounds in scenes of the chase.) Whatever the ship may have meant originally, here it seems to have become a generalized sacral sign like the Camunian paddle or the double ax of Crete. It has been combined with the hunting cult. Conversely, ships and axes sometimes appear in megalithic tombs.

As has been suggested before, the sun may have been merely assimilated to the pastoralist-warrior god. In Camonica Valley it is once seen appended to the phallus of one of the figures. Similarly the sun ship is shown attached to the erect penis of one of the Swedish figures. It is quite possible that it may have been a symbol of power. A widespread attribute of this deity concept, we find it in every area of rock art discussed.

The other constant attribute of the warrior-pastoralist is the sacred weapon, which may appear by itself or in his hands and is sometimes accompanied by an erection. Figures holding axes are found in Spain; the ax and the spear permeate Camonican art; they proliferate in Scandinavia; the spear and bow and arrow appear in northern Russia. The battle-ax was also the trademark of the battle-ax people who invaded central Europe. It is a fact that the pastoralists of the Eurasian steppes gave rise to the Indo-Europeans who contributed to the Hittite empire, the Mycenaean and Roman cultures, and to the barbaric Celtic and Teutonic cultures of middle and northern Europe. The concept of the warrior-pastoralist god just sketched fits perfectly with the omnipresent sky god of the Indo-Europeans. The sky god (also probably a protective clan god) would naturally wield some sort of a weapon, whether mace, ax, sword, spear, or club. It seems clear that the male ego aspects of this deity are more fundamental than his control of the weather. To take once more a psychoanalytic approach, weapons are classically equated with the penis. The Kiwai Papuan before going into battle chews a piece of ginger which has been kept for a while in his wife's sex organ. He then calls out, "My wife, all same lightning, straight where vulva I go." In other words, his weapons are to travel as directly as his erect penis into his wife. In Cape Bedford, New Guinea, the thunder spirit creates thunder by a rapid exposing of his sex. The expression for lightning is, "Thunder, his penis, ejects." Among the Central Australians, "In dream, or play, symbolism, ritual, and bad language, the spear is one of the most frequent penis symbols," Geza Roheim tells us. He further insists, "Thunder God Thor with his hammer Mjölnir hurls the ax with double aim. It is both an aggressive movement of the ego and a coition on the part of the libido."

From this it is not hard to understand the emphasis on phallicism. The state of erection was the supremely male condition—hunting, potency, and warfare are complementary forms of ego expression. In Bronze Age carving it would be descriptive of the god, the worshiper, or both. The nudity of the figures in the rock carving also has cultic significance. Sumerian and Babylonian priests in early periods carried out rituals naked. In European folklore tradition witches are often supposed to carry out their rites naked. The contradiction between ritual and reality is clearly shown in some Russian carvings of ithyphallic figures on skis.

Efforts to identify specific large figures carrying spears, axes, or hammers as Thor or Odin seem a rash undertaking. Scandinavian rock engravings are extremely schematic; certain emblems can be made out and certain activities discerned. Efforts to construct mythology, however, are purely subjective.

What was the precise purpose of this art? As we have seen among such peoples as the Cretans, the earliest place of worship was a cave or a wooded spot. The same seems to have been true of the Camonica Valley people in whose art we can trace a progression. For a people which worships out of doors the most permanent recording medium is the nearby rock. The pictures certainly record ceremonial acts. They would also perhaps come to stand for the actions they depict and therefore become an integral part of ritual. The Navaho Indians of the United States use magical pictures which they construct out of impermanent colored sand. The Australian natives likewise draw emblematic pictures which have ceremonial significance. Even the precursors of the Neolithic and Bronze Age peoples, the old hunters, as we have seen, drew magic pictures. As the worship grows more complex and the anthropomorphic gods become more specific, shrines come to be built which stand for the god's residence. We have a record of them in Crete and we see them on the Camonica Valley rocks. These shrines, however, tend to be small; they are not spacious enough to include worshipers, who continue to carry out their processions and dances in the sacred grove. And indeed the same situation continues for centuries among such nonurban barbarians as the Celts and the Teutons.

CHAPTER 13

The Magic of the Otherworld

Celts—warrior gods and clan providers—borrowed fertility goddesses—traces of horse sacrifice—shape changing—warrior's paroxysm—head taking—culture hero as magical protector—concept of the otherworld—magic used to coerce the supernatural.

THE WORD Celtic, from the time of Macpherson's inspired semi-forgeries of Ossianic poems to the period of the Irish revival and the lyricism of William Butler Yeats, has had connotations of misty romanticism. When we seek to penetrate the psychology of the actual historic Celts we are faced with all sorts of problems and perplexities. We know what their enemies, the Romans, said about them, but the Romans often depended upon hearsay and interpreted them in terms of their own cultural egocentricity. Since the Celtic peoples developed no writing of their own and transmitted their legends by word of mouth, the written versions we possess were recorded hundreds of years after their power had passed away.

The first question which arises is naturally: Who were they? The answer seems to be that they were the product of considerable ethnic mixture. As we have seen, there had been Danubian farmers in Europe by the third millennium B.C. In the early part of the second millennium what was called the culture of the beaker people (who were pastoralist and already working metal) met and blended with that of the battle-ax pastoralist peoples from the eastern Eurasian plains. The old nomadic hunters were certainly not extinct. We have seen from the Bronze Age rock carvings that an ancient hunter-pastoralist tradition spread through much of central and northern Europe. While, on the one hand, the agricultural way of life of the upper Danube also continued to spread in the Bronze Age and, with the development of cremation burial in urns, has been called the Urnfield culture, on the other hand there may have been a new influx of pastoralist warriors from the Pontic steppes about 800 B.C. There seems to be a new emphasis upon the use of horses, evidenced by bronze bits and bridle mounts in

Hungary and the northern Alps. We must remember too that at the end of the second millennium there were Indo-European incursions into Greece which broke up the Mycenaean empire and that in the same era the Hittite empire also fell, releasing the secret of ironworking which had been a closely guarded monopoly. The late Bronze and early Iron Age was a period, therefore, of population movement, especially of the Indo-European pastoralist-warrior.

The burials of the Urnfield people do not show any great stratification, but with the beginning of ironworking in middle Europe in the seventh century, graves of chieftains are found whose occupants are laid out in considerable state. The focus of this new Iron Age culture was in Bohemia, Upper Austria and Bavaria. It has been named Hallstatt from the first important site in Austria. These chieftains were buried with an iron sword and were laid out in a wagon or surrounded by the dismembered parts of a vehicle and plentifully provided with pottery and joints of beef or pork.

By the beginning of the fifth century B.C., the Hallstatt culture had spread over most of France and Switzerland, parts of Germany, the northern part of the Spanish peninsula, and the south coast of Britain. In T. G. E. Powell's view, the Celtic language accompanied it. The Hallstatt peoples were therefore Celts or proto-Celts. Henri Hubert is convinced that the continental Celts or Brythons split from the Goidels or Irish before the fifth century. The precise period of the invasions of Ireland, for there seem to have been several, remains controversial.

A second stage of Celtic culture called La Tène is named from a site on Lake Neuchâtel, Switzerland, which was probably a toll station and military post commanding the trade route from the Rhône to the Rhine. Here iron swords were found and many implements and objects ornamented in a baroque decorative style, involving a curving line, stylized animals and modified Greek motifs, all hallmarks of Celtic art from the fifth century to the end of Celtic power about 50 B.C. The La Tène style includes decorative goldwork and is marked by a fondness for coral and enamel insets.

The Celts at the height of their power dominated middle Europe, Great Britain and Ireland, penetrated Greece, took Rome in 390 B.C., and even invaded Anatolia to found a colony near Ankara. Archaeological, graphic, and historic evidence shows that they did not conform to any one physical type. Some were tall and round-headed, some tall and long-headed. The ideal of good looks, however, and the image preserved by the Romans, is of tall, blond, white-skinned warriors, clean-shaven except for long mustaches. Apparently they bleached their hair with lime and combed it back so that it stood up in a wild mane. They used at first round, then oval or oblong, wooden shields with a metal boss and wore either pointed or horned helmets. Some of the European Celts wore trousers which connected them with the equestrian warriors of the steppes; more general was a short, belted tunic and a cloak fastened with a decorated safety-pin type of brooch.

All classic authors agree that warfare was their prime interest and that they had strict codes of clan honor and social behavior. The Celts were organized on the patriarchal clan system, the tuath or tribe holding land, headed by a chieftain or king. Their farming villages look back to the Urnfield tradition, their cattle and horse raising testify to the continuance of pastoralism. In some areas they built timbered stockaded forts on hilltops. Their houses were round or rectangular with wooden or stone walls. Furniture was probably scanty; figures sculptured in a squatting position indicate that they habitually sat on the floor.

In war their chief mode of battle was hand-to-hand combat; in early periods the warriors fought ritually naked. In the fifth and fourth centuries they adopted the two-wheeled chariot from the Etruscans with whom they had trade relations. Chariots were the property of aristocratic chieftains who drove along the battlefront, flinging spears, shouting, and blowing horns. They then descended and went through the routine of boasting of exploits, lineage, singing war songs until they were worked up into a magical male frenzy, whereupon a general melee took place. This procedure is reminiscent of the scenes of challenge and personal encounter in the *Iliad*. The habit of fighting naked, which may have involved some notion of magical protection, is also characteristic of archaic Greece and the early Italian tribes. One of the Celts' less endearing habits was that of taking the heads of slain enemies and hanging them from their horses' bridles, or chariots. They were later hung in shrines or nailed to their house gables. This, as we have seen, is a very primitive custom which must originally have involved a magical accretion of strength and martial ardor from the vanquished antagonist.

The Celts were an eclectic people, judging from the characteristics of their art. Their early sculpture of anthropomorphic deities is crude and without style; later they adopted Graeco-Roman models. The metal decorative art with its prolixity of formalized and elaborate animal motifs is related to that of their Scythian neighbors of the steppes. In later periods traces of Etruscan influence appear.

As we would expect of a people made up of various ethnic elements and prone to accept local influences, their religion shows a diversity of characteristics and it is difficult to pin down the general outlines of Celtic worship. As Joseph Vendryes puts it, "The further you advance in the study of Celtic religion, the more you have the feeling that it continually recedes and rapidly evades you."

Perhaps a sketch of the Druid priesthood is the best introduction to the religious world of this people. The Druids, as a class, ranked next to the warriors. Theirs was not a hereditary organization but it seems to have been pan-Celtic, on the one hand suggesting men's clubs among contemporary primitive peoples and on the other priesthoods of other Indo-European groups such as the Magi of Iran, the Brahmins of India and the Flamines of Rome. The Druids married and participated in ordinary clan activities. In their priestly function they were teachers and judges as well as specialists in divination and ritual. There was probably a Grand Druid in Gaul and perhaps another in Ireland. The international character of their society was, next to a common language, the most unifying factor in Celtic civilization. Sensing this, the Romans stamped it out whenever they conquered the Gauls. The Druids practiced divination by listening to birds' cries, watching the direction of clouds, and consulting animal entrails. In Irish tradition they are magicians able to control winds and clouds and to cure the sick. The name Druid probably meant "Knower of the Oak," for their rituals were associated with oak groves in which, on the sixth day of the moon, they cut sprigs of mistletoe with a golden knife and sacrificed white bulls. We learn from Irish sources the choosing of a new king at Tara took place when a bull was killed and a Druid gorged on its flesh. He then fell into a trance while incantations were recited over him and on his reawakening he was able to decide on the rightful claimant to the throne. The rite was known as a "bull dream." Ecstatic frenzy is a shamanistic trait and once more suggests connections with the Eurasian steppes.

Magical frenzy is also a characteristic of the heroic court poet called in Ireland a *fili*. Poets, in Irish tradition, are capable of casting spells with their songs although as a class they were distinct from the Druids. Since there was no written language, the Druidic lore was handed down in rhythmical or alliterative literary forms, as were the heroic poems. Druid apprentices were trained for years to memorize this material, a practice analogical to that carried on by the Brahmins who transmitted the Vedic hymns in this fashion for millennia.

Celtic belief is shot through with the most archaic kind of magic. There is no evidence of ethical or philosophical development. From the myths and from glimpses of ritual practices, their magic assumed all sorts of fantastic forms, which, combined with shamanistic frenzy, create an image of a high-strung, aggressive, even sadistic people possessed of an almost demented imagination.

That the Celts practiced human as well as animal sacrifice is strongly attested by Roman reports. We are told by Lucan that to appease the god Teutates the victim was drowned in a cauldron of water, Esus required a victim hung from a tree, while in honor of Taranis a human being was burned inside a wickerwork idol.

When it comes to identifying gods and their functions, we are faced with considerable confusion. From dedicatory inscriptions on monuments in Latin, the names of four hundred gods are extant, one fifth of them female. Three hundred and five of these names are found only once! From this it is clear that many of the names represent local deities, perhaps manifestations of the same basic concepts. In some cases a Celtic name is coupled with that of a Roman deity, showing that some assimilation took place. The three gods mentioned above, which Lucan described as major deities, are very rarely mentioned. In fact the name Teutates is derived from Tuath, tribe, and merely means god of the clan.

In all probability there was no organized pantheon, just as there was no centralized Celtic political organization. Judging from Celtic ethnic history, there may well have been several elements predominant in their deities. Mythology shows that the male gods are largely warriors, magicians, colonizers, tribal protectors. The females are local earth mothers; some of them carry horns of plenty. We should expect that the Indo-European pastoral warriors would bring with them male clan gods, armed protectors of particular tribes. Such a god is Dagda of Irish tradition, whose name means the good god or protector. His attributes are what we should expect, a male power symbol, consisting of a huge club, and also a magic cauldron which is inexhaustible; in other words, a symbol of the never-failing prosperity which he maintains for his people. Another very ancient and probably Indo-European god is Belenus, the root of whose name means fire. The festival of Beltine was celebrated at the first of May when the cattle were put out to graze. The lighting of fire at this time has come down in European folklore as the rite of St. John's fire when cattle were driven between great fires to preserve them from disease. There is a god depicted on a cauldron from Gundestrop, Denmark, whose attribute is a wheel. Figures with wheels also occur on Hallstatt swords. These could well be symbols of the sun god, Belenus, an incarnation of male virility with the sun as a power symbol. Dagda, mentioned above, seems very close to Sucellos of Gaul whose attributes were a hammer and a cup (possibly inexhaustible like the cauldron). Dagda in Irish myth could kill nine men with one end of his club and restore them to life with the other end. He was a tremendous eater whose sexual prowess matched his appetite. Another semidivine hero in Irish myth was Fergus, who had the strength of seven hundred men, who used to consume seven hogs, seven vats of liquor, and seven cows, whose nose, mouth, and penis were seven fingers long, and whose scrotum was as big as a flour sack. Added to this phallic figure, we have mythological tradition which describes kings as proving their worth by means of orgies of food and sex. Still another male god was Lug, the long-armed, who carried a spear, and who was a skillful artisan.

To return to the female deities and their local fertility functions, we know that the earth mother predominated in the Near East and, by way of the Mediterranean and the megalithic missionaries, infiltrated into central Europe. There was also a female vegetation deity in the Danubian region. Celtic goddesses bearing the cornucopia of abundance are already Graeco-Roman. It would seem logical that the female vegetation goddesses reflect the agricultural elements with whom the pastoralist warriors amalgamated. The relation between the two is sometimes shown by paired names in which the male and female principles are mated.

Another element characteristic of Celtic mythology is the battle goddess who is also a magician and who either becomes amorous of the semi-divine hero or hostile to him, or both. In the myths the hero sometimes overcomes the battle goddess by his magic and sleeps with her; at other times he refuses her erotic advances and suffers from her hostility on the battlefield, or she sends champions against him. Here we are reminded of the episode between Gilgamesh and Ishtar.

A war goddess does not sound like a fundamental concept of an intensely masculine pastoral culture. Is it possible that mythical tradition mirrors two types of accommodation between matriarchal and patriarchal societies? One would be the peaceful marriage and the other an uneasy ambivalence, in which each distrusted the other's magic powers, symbolized by the struggle between the war goddess and the semidivine hero. The ambivalence and the sadism involved is significantly close to the classic Freudian view of the basic ambivalence in all sexual relations.

A third important element in Celtic religious imagery is the number of gods and goddesses with animal attributes or animal form. The god Cernunnus (whose name perhaps means horned) we have already seen merged with the stag god of Camonica Valley. Other gods have ram horns, the hero Ossian turns into a fawn. There is a horse god, Rudiobos. Cuchulainn himself, the semidivine hero of the Ulster epic cycle, derives his name from the word hound. Tarvod trigaranos was a three-horned bull. Perhaps there was a connection between him and the Brown Bull of the Cuchulainn cycle who is accompanied by fifty heifers with whom he coupled every day, with the result that each had a calf next morning. A hundred warriors are protected from the sun by his shadow and he possesses human understanding.

A mother goddess, Epona, is associated with mares and foals. In this connection, there is a significant Ulster coronation ceremony described by Geraldis Cambrensis. At a gathering of the whole people a white mare was led forth. The king then came before the people on all fours proclaiming himself a horse. The mare was killed, cut up and cooked, and a cauldron filled with the broth. The king bathed in this, and, while still sitting in the bath, ate some flesh of the mare and lapped the broth.

Roheim remarks that a man can attain union with his god both by coupling with it and eating it. In Aryan tradition the wife of a king, during the horse sacrifice, simulated union with the stallion; an act reinforced by a liturgy chanted by a priest which described the action. Here the sexual relation is reversed though the union with the animal still points to a totemistic concept. The horse symbolism belongs to the most ancient level of Indo-European religion. In this connection the incantation of a Yakut shaman is suggestive. The Yakut tribe, being a Siberian pastoralist group, is therefore a modern representative of the ancient Indo-European steppe culture.

The shaman's ceremony is carried out with the intention of curing a sick patient. He lies on a white mare's skin and shakes nervously. He then puts on his magician's coat which may be a female garment or be painted with symbolic breasts. He kneels on the mare's skin in the middle of the room and begins to beat the hand drum, at first softly, then violently until it sounds like a gathering storm. Then ventriloquistically the shaman sets up an increasing uproar of whistles, screams, shouts and bird calls to show he is possessed by spirits. Finally he chants:

> I, the mighty bull of the earth
> . . . horse of the steppes,
> I, the mighty bull . . . bellow.
> I, the horse of the steppes . . . neigh.
> I, the man set above all other beings,
> I, the man most gifted of all!
> I, the man created by the master all powerful,
> Horse of the steppes, appear! Teach me!
> Enchanted bull of the earth, appear! Speak to me!
> Powerful master, command me!

In the beginning, as Roheim points out, he is the bull and the horse himself. He identifies with the animal as his father in true totemic relationship. Finally the horse and bull become separate entities who completely subjugate the shaman.

In addition it must be mentioned that shape shifting occurs continually in the myths. Battle goddesses become ravens, eels, cows. An Irish poet-magician sings:

> I am the wind on the sea,
> I am the wave of the ocean,
> I am the powerful ox,
> I am a hawk on a cliff,
> I am a dewdrop in sunshine . . .

In the light of the Yakut incantation above, it certainly appears that shape shifting is distinctly related to a primal sense of the union between man and animal; in short, it is a mythic survival of a totemistic concept.

It is worthwhile examining the Cuchulainn epic cycle for its primitive religious characteristics. As has been said, the court bard passed on the lays or episodes by word of mouth for centuries until early Irish priests wrote them down, adding an occasional profession of Christianity to what is clearly archaic material. No written version is older than 800 A.D. Unfortunately the religious conservatism of the Celtic priests and bards, who did not accept writing, also stood in the way of an amalgamation of the episodes into an artistic and philosophical whole like that of Gilgamesh or the Greek epics. The repetition of heroic butchery often becomes tedious and epic dignity is frequently watered down to the level of fairy-tale fantasy.

As with most heroes, Cuchulainn's birth is unusual. In one version he is born three times. (Celtic gods were often shown with triple faces, a kind of triad of strength.) He is also considered the son of Lug. Dechtire, the sister of Conchobor, is his mother. While he is still a small boy he distinguishes himself by catching the fifty spears of his young companions on his shield without being hurt. His youthful feats win him an invitation to Conchobor's court but, since he arrives without warning, he is attacked by the watchdog, which he kills. When the king remonstrates, he agrees to take the animal's place, "guarding of thy cattle and substance and strong place." Hence he gets his name, which means Culainn's Hound.

The king offers him weapons but they all break when he bends them, and at last the king gives him his own. The boy sets out immediately and kills three champions. When he is challenged, "I will," says he, "take in my hand Conchobor's great spear, The Venomous, it shall pierce the shield over his heart and, after holing his heart within him, shall break three ribs in his side that is the farthest from me." This the boy also performed, and took the prince's head "or ever his body touches the ground." He thereupon hung the heads from his chariot wheels.

When Cuchulainn returns to court he is in such a battle frenzy that his uncle to calm him sends out twenty women of the court stark naked to meet him. (The priestly scribe has softened this episode to mean that his modesty is so great that he hangs his head and becomes calm. Obviously the primal meaning is that his sado-sexual excitement is so great that it takes twenty women to satisfy him.) After this he is plunged in three vats of cold water. The hoops and staves of the first burst asunder; the water in the second boils over; when he has finished bathing in the third, the water is left still too hot to touch.

The description of the young hero is slightly reminiscent of Marduk. "A beautiful boy indeed was that: seven toes to each foot he had and to either hand as many fingers; his eyes were bright with seven pupils apiece, each one of which glittered with gemlike sparkles. On either cheek he had four moles, a blue, a crimson, a green one and a yellow one. Between one ear and the other he had fifty clear-yellow long tresses that were as yellow as the wax of bees or like to a brooch of gold as it glints in the sun unobscured."

Cuchulainn is able to smooth a tree trunk into a chariot pole by drawing it between his toes and fingers until it is so clean a fly cannot perch on it. Episode after episode follows in which he kills champions. Then begins a confused struggle for the Brown Bull of Ulster which is supposedly carried off by Medv, the combined mother goddess and battle goddess. Her forces are the men of south and central Erin. Cuchulainn causes a hundred of her warriors to expire by merely shaking his weapons at them. Finally, after a parley, he is allowed to go on with his raid in her territory, with the proviso that he will only kill one warrior a day. In one of his subsequent struggles the hero's paroxysm is fantastically described.

All over him from his crown to the ground, his flesh and every limb and joint and point and articulation of him quivered as does a tree, yea, a bulrush in midcurrent. Within his skin he put forth an unnatural effort of his body: his feet, his shins and his knees shifted themselves and were behind him, his heels and calves and hams were displaced to the front of his leg bones, in condition such that the knotted muscles stood up in lumps as large as the clenched fist of a fighting man. The frontal sinews of his head were dragged to the back of his neck where they showed in lumps bigger than the head of a manchild aged one month. Then his face underwent an extraordinary change: one eye became engulfed in his cheek so far that it is a question whether a wild heron could have got at it, where it lay against his occiput, to drag it out upon the surface of his cheek; the other eye on the contrary protruded suddenly of itself so it rested upon the cheek. His mouth was twisted awry till it met his ears. His gnashings caused flakes of fire, each one larger than the fleece of a three-year-old wether, to stream from his throat into his mouth. The sounding blows of the heart that panted within him were as the howl of a watch dog doing his office, or of a lion in the act of charging bears. Among the aerial clouds over his head were visible the violent pouring of showers and sparks of ruddy fire which the seething of his savage wrath caused to mount up above him. His hair became tangled about his head as it had been branches of a red thorn bush, stuffed into a strongly fenced gap; over which, though a prime apple tree had been shaken, yet may we surmise that never an apple of it would have reached the ground but rather all of them would have been impaled each on an individual hair as it bristled on him for fury. His heroic paroxysm projected itself out of his forehead and showed longer than the whetstone of a first-rate man-at-arms. Taller and thicker than the mast of a great ship was the perpendicular jet of dusky blood which out of his scalp's very cranial point shot upwards and was scattered to the four cardinal points whereby was formed a magic mist of gloom resembling the smoky pall that drapes a royal dwelling what time a king at night draws near it.

When this has taken place, he leaps into his chariot and kills sixscore and ten kings. On his return he displays himself to wives, girls, poets and professors in all his beauty. Added to the earlier description is the detail that the hairs on his head were brown at the root, then red, and gold at the end. His seven fingers and toes had the grip of hawks' talons and hedgehogs' claws. He wore a gorgeous tunic and "in one hand he carried nine heads and also in the other which, in token of valor and skill in war, he held at arm's length and shook in full sight of the army."

In all of this sadistic carnage the most interesting element is the hero's paroxysm. It will be remembered that the Celtic warriors were in early periods accustomed to go into battle naked, boasting, hurling challenges and working themselves up into a frenzy. Apparently the passages in the epic are a magical exaggeration of this custom. Here is a description of a Maori war dance, before a battle, which has points of similarity: "The warriors are transformed for the time being into the most demoniac-looking beings it is possible to imagine. Every nerve and sinew is strained, the eyes roll wildly, or seem to stand forth from the head, tongues loll to an incredible extent. The warriors stamp with their feet until the earth trembles." Challengers then advance with jumping movements, distorted features and rolling eyes, every muscle straining. They shout defiance and throw their spears.

In these projections of the male ego there is the same shamanistic tension and trembling, the same distortion of the eyes and mouth. Also, according to the Polynesian epics, Maori warriors fought in a state of erection. The description of Cuchulainn's "swelling with great fullness like a breath in a bladder" seems to have a similar significance on the symbolic plane. The whole complex of sexual and warlike frenzy reminds us strongly of the ithyphallic contestants in the rock carvings. The Maori took trophy heads and were also cannibals. A passage from *The Death of Conchobor* runs as follows: "It was at that time the custom with Ulstonians to take out the brains from the head of every one that they killed in single combat and to mix them with lime water until they formed a hard ball." In boasting contests warriors brought them out and displayed them. The operation of removing the brains sounds very much as if at one time the Celts practiced brain cannibalism.

There are other Irish epic cycles and also considerable Welsh mythology and, while we do not know how much of this specific material was shared by the continental Celts, we can be sure that their myths were of the same tone and character. What emerges is a world of magic which always interpenetrates the real world. The attitude of the hero is one of constraint and manipulation of the gods. There is no placation or sense of ethical reward. The Celt got what he wanted by means of reckless violence, dominating the supernatural by supernatural means.

Anton van Hamel, interpreting Celtic folklore, feels that theism was weakly developed. The gods were apart and probably not personalized, while the culture hero or superman was the real protector of the clan and the land and dwelled in the real world. He points out that the hero was mortal, his *geis* or taboo was eventually doomed to be broken, causing his death. In this the hero fulfills Cazeneuve's definition of the magician whose own life is forfeit when he breaks the rules of order in availing himself of the power of the unusual. The myth, in van Hamel's view, operates through the magic of repetition. It becomes a power story to be used by the hero. Finn (the hero of a cycle parallel to that of Cuchulainn) is engaged with his warriors against three flocks of demon birds. A spell is finally used which forces them to kill each other with their beaks of bone and breaths of fire. It is revealed that the day on which this spell is used corresponds to another day when three mythical benefactors conquered demon foes. In other words, he who knows history can turn it to magical account. The Celtic hero is more or less equated with the ruler and, like the sacral king, protects the clan or the territory, heals the sick, and provides abundance, yet he requires no sacrifice or adoration. Curiously enough, the magic hound often is connected with abundance, giving forth any liquid required from its mouth. Perhaps the hound is an echo of a totem provider. Finn's animal is described as follows: "Its sides were white, its tail purple, its legs blue, its paws green, its nails red."

As we have observed in the case of the Greek Herakles, the hero is nearer to the people than a true god even though he may be semidivine. In the case of the early Chinese we also find that the gods are remote and little developed while the deified ancestor is the immediate protector of the clan. It is possible that the hero is a halfway stage between ancestor and god and in some cases he becomes arrested, the entity remaining magical and shamanistic instead of evolving into a true deity.

In Celtic mythology the concept of the otherworld was always present. Folklore records three invasions of Ireland, each succeeding group defeating those in possession by the usual combination of courage and magic. The

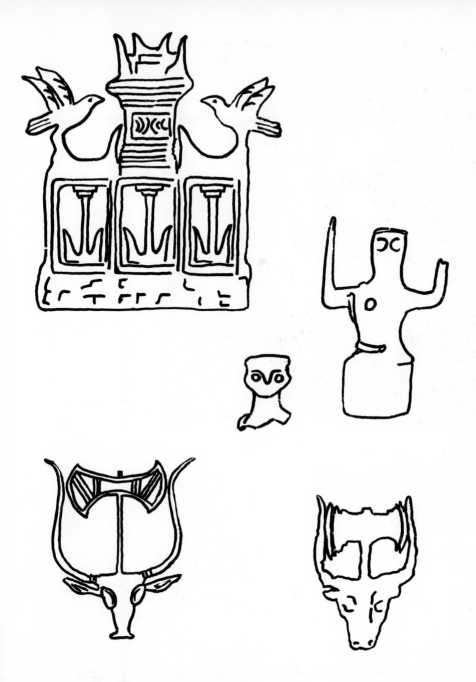

Cretan religious symbols. *Above:* A gold-leaf model of a shrine showing horns of consecration with small pillars (baetyls) and bird. *Center:* Two bell idols, clay images of a goddess of archaic type, second millennium B.C. (*After Nilsson*) *Below:* Intaglio bull's head with double ax, late Minoan; gold-leaf bull's head with double ax, Mycenae. (*After Cook*)

C. F. A. Schaeffer

Goddess of wild beasts, Minet el
Beida, Syria, 1400 B.C.

Eye idols from Brak, Mesopotamia,
about 3000 B.C. Probably symbols
of the fertility goddess.

*The Metropolitan Museum of Art,
Gift of the Institute of Archaeology,
University of London, 1951*

After Nilsson

Above: Impression of a clay sealing from Knossos showing Lady of Wild Beasts flanked by lions, shrine with horns and young male figure. Note similarity in theme to Minet el Beida goddess. *Below:* Gold ring seal from Candia indicating tree cult, a goddess flanked by two priestesses.

The Minoan snake goddess, ivory and gold, about 1600 B.C.

The sarcophagus from Hagia Triada, Crete, about 1400 B.C. Cult scene shows shrine with double axes and birds, votaries with offerings and the deceased next to his tomb.

Evidence of the fertility concept diffused among the Mediterranean islands. Marble Cycladic sculpture, third or second millennium B.C. Note in this and images which follow characteristic pose of hands at the breasts.

The Metropolitan Museum of Art, Rogers Fund, 1945

*Metropolitan Museum of Art, The Cesnola Collection;
purchased by subscription, 1874–76*

Terra-cotta female figures from Cyprus, second millennium B.C.

Marble Cycladic sculpture, third or second millennium B.C.

The Brooklyn Museum

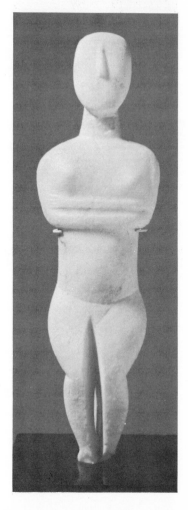

Sarcophagus from Cyprus, 600–550 B.C., showing Astarte, the Semitic fertility goddess, portrayed in a blend of Greek and Oriental styles.

The Metropolitan Museum of Art, The Cesnola Collection; purchased by subscription, 1874–76

The fertility concept culminates in Greek legend. Demeter, Triptolemos and Persephone, Roman copy of the Eleusinian Relief, a Greek work of about 450–440 B.C.

The Metropolitan Museum of Art, Rogers Fund, 1914

Greek centaur, probably a survival of totemism,
bronze, late sixth century B.C.

Herakles, a hero who achieved divinity. Archaic
treatment in limestone from Cyprus, about 600
B.C.

Exterior of an Etruscan tomb at Cerveteri, seventh to fifth century B.C.

Smiling at death, an Etruscan couple reclines on the lid of the sarcophagus from the Villa Giulia.

Air view of Hagar Quim temples, Malta, 2300 to 1450 B.C.

Figure, possibly a priest, reconstructed from clay fragment found in Tarxien temples, Malta, about 1450 B.C.

Valetta Museum

Sleeping woman, possibly a priestess incubating, found in Hypogeum, Malta, about 1450 B.C.

Valetta Museum

Air view of Stonehenge, Salisbury Plain, England. Second millennium B.C.

Passage grave, New Grange, Ireland, interior from center of burial chamber facing left wing. Note concentric rings carved on wall. Second millennium B.C.

Exterior view of New Grange showing barrow, entrance and circle of standing stones.

Stone at entrance of New Grange, Ireland.

Freestanding menhir from Bwlch, South Wales.

Model showing manufacture of "necklace idol" associated with Megalithic tombs. The circular necklace symbol may be related to designs on stones of New Grange.

After Anati, Camonica Valley, *Knopf*

The evolution of a stag god. *Above:* Centaurlike half-man, half-stag raises a sword. It is surrounded by four worshipers, 1000–800 B.C., Camonica Valley, Italy. *Below:* Fully evolved god with stag horns wreathed with snake accompanied by worshiper and possibly a sun symbol, 500–250 B.C., Camonica Valley.

Model of sun disk drawn by a horse from Trundholm, Denmark, probably second millennium B.C.

Carved stone from Engelstrup, north-western Zeeland, Denmark, second millennium B.C. Typical sun ship and several figures, between the two lower ones a sun symbol.

Panel of Gundestrup cauldron, Denmark, Bronze Age, showing Celtic stag god, Cernunnus, grasping a snake and surrounded by various animals including a stag.

Top row left: Ithyphallic warriors, Camonica Valley, Italy, 700–600 B.C. (*After Anati,* Camonica Valley, *Knopf*) *Top row right:* Ithyphallic warriors and sun boat from Sweden, second millennium B.C. (*After Almgren*) *Middle row left:* Figures on sun boat dancing and playing the lur from Tanum, Sweden, second millennium B.C. (*After Almgren*) *Middle row right:* Ithyphallic archer with animal head or mask from Karelia, Russia, second millennium B.C. or earlier. (*After Raudonikas*) *Bottom row left:* Stag, Tanum, Sweden, second millennium B.C. (*After Almgren*) *Bottom row right:* Stag, rock painting from Guadiana range, Spain, second millennium B.C. (*After Breuil*)

last group, the Tuatha de Danaan, defeated by the Son of Mil, took refuge in the hills, tumuli, and sometimes in megalithic tombs. They were considered to be the real gods. The otherworld was thus sometimes conceived as within the tumuli where the immortals feasted in their palaces. At other times it assumed the form of Isles of the Blest like those of Greek tradition. In *The Voyage of Bran* the hero is lured there by a goddess. The otherworld, however, has two aspects. When the hero is invited thither by a goddess who wants a favor from him, he is granted her love. He finds this world peopled by beautiful people, the *Side,* who do not age and can only be destroyed by violence, and are ruled over by Manannan and Tethra. The lands glisten with colored splendors; there is no sickness or sorrow; there is wine, laughter, and music. Its waters restore health; magic apples grow on the trees. If, however, the hero storms his way into the otherworld he finds castles to besiege, and monsters to overcome. There seems to be no contradiction between these two conceptions; they are both normal elements of the Celtic universe. Although, as has been said, the real world and the otherworld are in frequent contact, on the night of Samain, the 31st of October (the Celtic New Year and our Halloween), they were especially related, for there was an opening between the two which allowed reality and the supernatural to become one.

There are indications that the Celtic king had at least some semidivine attributes. Vendryes points out that a hero can give rise to a myth and probably the reverse process could take place. Llud Lavereint was for the British chronicler, Geoffrey of Monmouth, a king; in Ireland he was also a king but he has been traced to a divinity on a Gloucestershire monument. The Celtic king was disqualified for his office by any physical blemish. In early times he may have been killed by his successor. We may picture him sitting on hay or skins strewn on the ground, surrounded by his warriors, low tables before them laden with wine, beef and mutton, salted pork and baked fish. The court bard accompanies the meal with music and song. The reputation of a chieftain depends upon whether the bard praises or satirizes him. Despite the fantastic courage of these barbaric kings which enabled them to dominate Europe for centuries, in the end they were unable to unite into a nation. Their anarchic magic did not sustain them against the rising urban organization of Rome and the military genius of Julius Caesar. Ethnically and culturally, however, they contributed to the forging of Europe and Great Britain.

CHAPTER 14

The Magic of the Clan

Teutons—double religious tradition—dual pantheon—relation to rock art—
Indo-European warrior triad—Ziu as lawgiver—Othin as ecstatic shaman—
berserkir frenzy—Thor as culture hero—Loki as trickster—Baldur and death
of vegetation—ritual feasting and sacrifice—giants and menace of the under-
world—Götterdämmerung.

ODDLY ENOUGH, in the period which began about 1000 B.C. all
the Germanic peoples began to practice cremation. Apparently a major change in the attitude toward the dead had taken place. As
we have seen, the megalith builders and their contemporaries clung to the
pre-animist conception of the living corpse which had to be placated and
tended for at least a certain period. The cremation urns of the Europeans in
transition from the Bronze to the Iron Age were molded in the shape of
houses, consequently some part of the concept lingered, to the extent that the
dead were still provided with a symbolic home. The belief that the body
preserved a diminished life may, however, have given way to the idea
of an insubstantial spirit, detachable from the flesh but likely to linger
near its remains, which has been defined by Tylor as animism.

Ordinary burial was to return, but the introduction of cremation during
the early part of the first millennium B.C. deprives us of a good deal of
information concerning the development of that group of peoples which
it is convenient to call Teutonic.

Their specific culture was already in the process of formation during
the Bronze Age when the Swedish rock carvings we have already discussed
were made. Their subsequent history, in part, parallels that of the Celts
by whom they were held in check until about the second century B.C.
when the Celtic power was weakened by Rome. Then the northern tribes
began to expand until successive waves had rolled over all of Europe
to submerge the Roman Empire itself. These energetic barbarians expanded in two ways: small raiding parties of warriors made extended
marches, lived off the country, collected all the booty they could and re-

turned home; at other times whole tribes with their oxcarts, horses, families and goods moved wholesale into new territory. Disinclined to shut themselves up in fortifications, they placed their oxcarts in a circle around the camp at night, very much as the American pioneers did. In cultural level and even appearance they resembled the Celts. Like them, they attacked with a wild rush and much shouting. When they were defeated their women sometimes killed their children and committed suicide to avoid slavery.

Like the Celts, they practiced some village agriculture but were mainly a pastoral tribal people, the important chiefs being horsemen. The chiefs built large wooden halls in which they and their followers drank, feasted and slept. In the earliest period the Teutons were probably as disunited as the Celts, led by clan chieftains who, as their power began to grow, were called kings. A general assembly of free men, however, seems to have been a fairly old institution. It had the power to elect a war leader and later, particularly in Iceland, it became an early form of parliament.

The rapid rise of the Teutons is truly astonishing: at the beginning of the first millennium they occupied southern Scandinavia and a small portion of what is now northern Germany; between 200 and 800 A.D., all of Europe, part of Great Britain and some of the coast of North Africa were controlled by Teutonic bands, and eventually the Franks were to emerge as an amalgamated Teuto-Italic Holy Roman Empire. Their ethnic strain is still dominant in northern Europe today.

What accounts for their sudden eruption into history? In the first place, the rumor of sophisticated urban centers in the south full of booty certainly attracted these bandit-warriors. In the second place, improved standards of living resulted in early population explosions. Finally, the most pressing motivation of all was a great climatic change. The weather in the north was in the process of becoming colder and damper with severe winters unfavorable to cattle raising. Parts of the Baltic land areas, with the melting of the glaciers, were flooded. The coastal people were forced to move out. Indeed Roman tradition states that the Cimbri Teutons were forced to emigrate by a great flood.

In discussing the proto-Teutonic culture illustrated by rock carvings, it has already been indicated that the northern peoples were formed by an ethnic amalgamation of the megalith builders (carriers of the Mediterranean vegetation goddess tradition) with the pastoralist warriors of the steppes, the battle-ax people, plus an undefined infiltration of the ancient hunters.

A study of Teutonic mythology, as it has been handed down, supports this view of a mixed heritage. The masculine warrior aspects of the culture, however, are by far the strongest and it is these traits which characterize the magic of the clan and, according to Vilhelm Grönbech, are the key to Teutonic psychology. Though much of this interpretation depends upon Eddas and sagas composed by Norse and Icelandic bards and written down no earlier than 800 A.D., the material contained in these poems is much older and, by discarding what are judged to be later attitudes, a picture emerges of a somewhat gloomy, dramatic and bloodthirsty people who, despite their material civilization of the Bronze and Iron Age, were as psychologically archaic as the Celts.

In the first place, although politically the Teutons were independent and in their assemblies often disagreed with their king and sometimes set him aside, in social and religious behavior they were motivated by a profound feeling of unity. The luck or magic of the clan affected them all and the conduct of any individual could either maintain or impair it. This was reflected in the word *frith*—the loyalty between clan members, the unspoken bond which obliged them to support and defend each other and which forbade hostility between them. All relatives, in other words, were magically sacred; all outsiders were fair game. It is the opposition between the in-group and the out-group which still exists today on an international scale.

An exaggerated, almost hysterical conception of honor was tied in with this concept. Not to accept a challenge violated the honor of the individual and the clan. In this situation a verbal insult was equal to a blow. To help a kinsman avenge an insult was an unconditional obligation even though the kinsman had shown himself to be a worthless person. This, in turn, was connected with the sense of justice. All punishment was carried out by the clan. Characters in the sagas scheme and plot for years to avenge their honor. If they did not, they lost their status as clan members and to lose this was to become a social outlaw and practically nonhuman. Outlawry was worse than death. Still more important and more significant in the magico-religious sense was the fact that a stain on the honor could affect the health of the coming generation, kill the child in the womb, even render women barren.

The only way to avenge a slight to honor was to kill the offender or, if not the actual offender, someone of his clan with a wider reputation as a warrior. Women shared this magical clan psychology, fiercely reproaching their men if they were slow to take up a challenge. On the other hand, there were no sanctions against injuring a fellow clan member because such a situation was unthinkable. The greatest tragedy was a fight between siblings who were unaware of their relationship. In fact the very word *sib* also carried the meaning of peace.

Associated with the magic of the clan was the very ancient notion of name magic. The magic of the clan was handed down with its name; the giving of the name of an important warrior carried with it magic. To quote Grönbech, "Every kinsman felt himself as living all that one of his kin had once lived in the world, and he did not merely feel himself as possessing the deeds of old, he renewed them actually in his own doings."

Wealth was an affair of status; the treasure of a family or group was associated with its magic. If ravaged by an outsider it could cause disaster. The treasure of the Volsungs is a case in point, since it carried a curse with it. A parallel is the modern fable of the stolen Indian diamond which always brings bad luck.

The protocol of gift giving and receiving (which, as we have seen, probably also took place among the Mycenaeans) has interesting analogies among modern preliterates. The Teutons felt that failure to return a gift was no less than robbery. It put the receiver under profound obligation. Claude Levi-Strauss has pointed out that among very simple peoples in which food is a problem and famine often threatens, the sharing of goods is a moral duty. On a higher social level, as among the Trobrianders of the South Seas, there is elaborate ritual exchange of gifts on all sorts of occasions. This philosophy of exchange on a status level is no longer economic but total—even religious. It also serves the purpose of easing tension between aliens. As such it was also practiced by the Teutons. On the magical side some of A. E. Crawley's ideas might apply. He maintained that to the preliterate everything alien was dangerous. Contact with the alien had to be made magically safe. This was done by cross-inoculation. Each of two alien individuals took something from the other either actually or symbolically. The Teutons also made much of communal eating and drinking, both being an essential part of their religious rituals and, in the case of strangers, eating together cemented frith. To refuse such an offer was a deadly insult. Gift giving was also an important part of the marriage ceremony.

The concept of good luck or magic of the clan was also embodied in the leader, whose personal magic symbolized and affected the whole group. Since this was an essentially warlike people, success centered around sexual and physical vitality and victory in war. Thus disqualification of a king among either the Celts or Teutons because of some bodily defect was not a matter of failure to promote vegetation but of failure of male prowess, unfitness to lead and fight. There were cases in which a king was deposed because of defeats in battle and a child of his lineage put in his place.

Among the Teutons there was a fatalistic attitude toward personal and group magic. If it failed and sacrifices did not succeed in renewing it, this was an indication that the gods were unfavorably disposed. A person who lost his magic was *fey* (from Old English *faege*), a man who had lost his essential humanity and was touched with death. This idea of magic was not unlike that of an American Indian's *medicine* given him by his guardian spirit. The concept, however, only applied to the warrior class. Lowborn thralls were considered to possess no souls, no magic, no sense of frith, no privileges and obligations. Fortunately for the well-born, the spirits of ancestors could return in their descendants, carrying with them their special magic. For this reason it was customary to name children after relatives who were famous for their heroic deeds.

The principle of magic applied not only to goods in general but in a special way to weapons. The latter, as we have seen in several cases, had cult significance. A passage from an Irish saga, *The Battle of Mag Tured,* runs as follows: "Ogma unsheathed the sword and cleansed it. Then the sword related whatsoever had been done by it; for it was the custom of swords at that time, when unsheathed, to set forth the deeds that had been done by them. And therefore the swords are entitled to the tribute of cleansing them after they have been unsheathed. Hence also charms are preserved in swords thenceforward. Now the reason why demons used to speak from weapons at that time was that weapons were worshiped by human beings then; and the weapons were among the safeguards of that time." The word demons is of course the interpretation of the priestly scribe, while the word cleansing no doubt indicates some ritual of purification. The importance of Excalibur in the Arthurian cycle matches the supernatural effectiveness of Siegfried's sword in the *Nibelungenlied.* We have already pointed out the phallic significance of weapons as a form of male expression among warlike peoples. It is easy to see how the weapon becomes the sacred symbol par excellence of the luck of the hero and his siblings. It is testimony to the growth of the animistic idea that Norse mythology indicates the transfer of a weapon was fraught with problems. A man had to compel the soul of another's magic weapon with superior spells or else make friends with it before it would serve him. The Teutonic king had magic healing powers and, symbolically, his weapon possessed the same effectiveness. As we shall see from the *Poetic Edda,* a hammer laid in a woman's lap made her fruitful.

The cosmogony of the Teutons remains somewhat in doubt because of the late date of the literary documents. It has been argued that various elements are borrowings. The picture presented by the Eddic poems, however, has its own peculiar character and certainly reflects the religious imagination of the northern barbarian. The world appears to be tripartite. Midgarth, the residence of mankind, bends up in a rainbow bridge and leads to Asgarth, the home of the gods, where their mead hall, Valhalla, reflects the earthly life of a Teutonic chieftain. On the other side of Midgarth a pathway leads out from and in under the Outgarth. To reach it both the dead and the living must pass through deep valleys filled with the roar of icy, foaming torrents. The light grows dim, the road leads over damp, rimy hills where icy winds sweep down. Here monsters, neither man nor beast, may be encountered; flame darts from their eyes, their breath is acrid and destructive, their claws are fleshed in carrion. A giant eagle, Hraesvelgr, devours corpses. Here a house may turn out to be the legs of a giant; lank-haired sorceresses sit in caves. For a mortal to enter here and come out unscathed requires tremendous personal magic. The Scandinavian concept is modified somewhat to the south where the underworld is thought of as a region of darkness, an endless plain full of illusion. Blended with this image is that of the world ash, Yggdrasil. The roots of the tree run through Midgarth and penetrate Outgarth; between the two worlds the dragon, Nithogr, gnaws at its roots.

Concerning the origin of the world, according to the Teutons, we have only glimpses. Tacitus tells us that an earth-born god, Tuisto, had a son Mannus, whose descendants became the three primal Germanic tribes. The other hint comes from the *Poetic Edda,* "The Prophecy of the Seeress," which runs as follows:

> In earliest times did Ymir live,
> Was never sea nor land nor salty waves,
> Neither earth was there nor upper heaven
> But a gaping nothing and green things no-
>   where.

> The land was then lifted aloft by Bur's son
>   [Othin, Vili, Ve]
> Who made Midgarth and matchless earth;
> Shone from the south the sun on dry land,
> On the ground there grew the greensward
>   soft.

> From the south the sun by the side of the
>   moon
> Heaved his right hand over heaven's rim;
> The sun knew not what might be had,
> The stars knew not what stead they had.

> Then the gods gathered together for counsel,
> The holy hosts, and held converse;
> To night and moon names they gave,
> The morning named and midday also,
> Forenoon and evening to order the year.

Again we learn from the Grimnir episode,

> Of Ymir's flesh the earth was shaped,
> Of his blood the briny sea,
> Of his hair the trees, the hills of his bones,
> Out of his skull the sky.
>
> But of his lashes the loving gods made
> Midgarth for the sons of men;
> Shaped from his brain were the shifting clouds
> Which in the heavens hover.

The Eddic poems, although not welded together into a consistent whole like the *Enuma Elish,* nevertheless are echoes of very early religious literature. The Germans did not have an organized society of priests and hence the later shapings of the myths are literary rather than theological. From the above passages, however, it is clear that the creation of earth from the body of an elder god is strikingly parallel to the Babylonian story.

In Teutonic myth there is divine conflict but not in terms of generations; instead there was war between two hostile tribes, the Aesir and the Vanir. The Vanir group, after a first victory, then lost the war and peace was made involving the sending of hostages. Finally the two sets of gods were absorbed into the same pantheon. An analysis of this episode and the nature of the gods strongly supports the contention that there were two traditions in northern religion. The Aesir group of gods included Othin, Thor and Ziu (or Tyr), a triad of male warrior deities. The Vanir group included Njörth, Frey and Freya and Baldur, all of whom have fertility or sexual attributes. Njörth, a male god, is connected etymologically with Nerthus, the female deity whose image Tacitus described as being carried about through the fields in a cart to fructify the fields. The change of sex is a little puzzling and has not been satisfactorily explained, but at any rate Njörth is considered the father of Frey and Freya. Ithyphallic figures believed to be images of Frey have been found in Scandinavia and this of course reminds us of the ithyphallic warriors in the rock carvings.

The male sex of Njörth and Frey seems to mean that they, in part at least, were warrior gods. The ithyphallicism of Frey belongs to the warrior. An illogical fusion of two types of deity is perfectly possible. Except for Freya, the erotic counterpart of Frey, the goddesses are colorless and unimportant. It has also been pointed out that no goddesses at all appear in the oldest lays.

There is another possibility which might be considered in relation to the dual tradition and that is the amount of social stratification which existed among the Teutons. Thrall technically means slave but is extended to mean lowborn. In the episode of Rig, class distinctions are noted with full-fledged aristocratic bias. The peasant family is described as follows:

> In their hut happy, they had a brood:
> I ween they were hight, Hoggiver, Howler,
> Bastard, Sluggard, Bent-back and Paunch,
> Stumpy, Stinker, Stableman, Swarthy,
> Longshanks and Lout: they laid fences,
> Put dung on fields, fattened the swine,
> Herded the goats and grubbed up peat.

While this may be a later feudal image, interments among both Celts and Teutons attest that some individuals took greater riches into the burial mound than others. In the process of amalgamation it is possible that the local megalithic or Danubian population survived as a less privileged agricultural group. The Teutonic warrior is described as a lazy individual who gambled and drank when he was not fighting. If there was a peasant group, this, together with slaves, might well have been responsible for keeping alive some elements of the vegetation religion which were also partially borrowed by the overlords.

Georges Dumézil, who wrote extensively on Indo-European religion, sees a triad of ideas behind the gods of the steppe warriors. In his view, there is a father figure who is a magician, lawgiver, only secondarily a warrior, the supreme sovereign. The second element is embodied in the purely warrior type of deity. Finally there is fecundity. In his endeavors to find a coherent system of thought based on these principles he seems to impose a too rational scheme. Three male warriors, however, do appear frequently among the Indo-Europeans.

One of his triad is Ziu, whom the Romans identified as Mars and who is more ancient than Othin. He was probably the original father and sky god identified with the sun symbols, the circle, the wheel, the swastika, etc., which appear on so much of the metalwork of the Teutonic peoples. Ziu is considered to have been supplanted by Othin in the north while still maintaining his fundamental characteristics in the area of the lower Rhine where he determined the outcome of battle and administered justice. In the north, in the guise of Tyr, he is not a major god although he does retain some legal aspects.

Othin, who became the dominant god of the Teutons (German Wotan and Gauta of the Goths), the magical sovereign, is identified by his knowledge of the *runes,* magical signs later to be used in the formation of an alphabet. In the *Poetic Edda* we are told of Othin's ordeal as he hung on Yggdrasil to obtain this knowledge.

I ween I hung on the windy tree all of
    nights nine,
Wounded by spear, bespoken to Othin,
    bespoken myself to myself,

Upon that tree of which none telleth
From what roots it doth rise.

Neither horn they upheld, nor handed
    me bread;
I looked below me—aloud I cried—
Fetched up the runes and fell back then.

Thus Othin sacrificed himself to himself and underwent a symbolic death and resurrection, possibly equated with a shamanistic trance. The runes, which were dyed red, the ancient magical color, gave him the power to break fetters, stop spears, dull swords, kill foes, cure sickness and constrain women to sleep with him. Othin's weapon is the spear. We see here much of the shamanistic hero and little of the lawgiver. Othin is also characterized by the German word *wut,* frenzy, battle madness, which is extended with rather too much nationalist lyricism to poetic and creative madness.

A second aspect of Othin is the sexual one. Just as the Celtic warrior hero has a strong phallic character so do we find the Teutonic deity involved in a number of sexual exploits. He spends three nights with the giantess Gunnloth, coming to her significantly in the form of a snake. He also boasts that he slept with seven sisters.

With love spells mighty I lured witch women
And made them forsake their mates.

He also speaks of slaying "wanton wenches who warred in the mountains." The same complex of magic, hostility and sexual dominance is present as in the case of Cuchulainn.

There is also a connection between Othin and the *berserkir* phenomenon. This cult has a number of related elements which we have already encountered in Celtic religion: frenzy of the warrior, magic, and a relationship to animals. The berserkir were warriors dedicated to Othin who, as their name signifies, went into battle dressed in bearskins (nephednir were dressed in wolfskins) and fought with all the madness of wild animals. The *Yinglingsaga* tells us that "Othin saw to it that his men fought in battle without mail and in a frenzy; they were like dogs and wolves." The Othin warriors of the Chatti let their hair and beards grow until they were shaggy as animals. In the *Volsungasaga* Sigmund and Sinfjötli, who were Othin warriors, are characterized as werewolves. The berserkir madness has been compared to the Celtic hero's paroxysm. The werewolf legend, as has been pointed out before, is probably a totemistic survival.

Otto Höfler has traced a parallel to the berserkir theme in the folk material surrounding the legend of the Wild Hunt or the Wild Army. The first of these was a ghostly horde of frenzied warriors, often mounted, who swept by at night with frightful yells and shrieks. The Wild Army generally consisted of a mad hunter and his hounds, with or without followers. This apparition was associated with winter storms and was accompanied by the music of horns and bells. The leader of both these groups resembled Othin. Significantly these troops of demons were generally seen on Christmas Eve, Twelfth Night, Fastnacht. Höfler cites a number of details to show that the concept is a memory of cultic ritual. The music is especially significant since it might well accompany an actual ceremony (we are reminded of the lurs on the rock carvings). The association with specific festivals (Christmas being the Norse midwinter festival Yul) is another cultic clue and, finally, in some traditions the spirits demand bread or beer, clearly a religious offering. In both Teutonic and Russian areas, in folk tradition, bands of werewolves were said to roam on Twelfth Night, and in Sweden they could be distinguished from real animals by the fact that they sometimes broke into cellars and drank beer! The latter detail, of course, points once more to the idea of an offering and to humans in animal disguise.

There is a mass of European folklore tradition involving animal masks. Figures in skins and masks appear on the sixteenth-century carnival ship which is dragged about at Fastnacht. In Nürnberg in the Middle Ages the Schembartlaufers were wild figures in masks (often wolf masks) and skin costumes who indulged in orgiastic behavior. On a bronze plate from Sweden (circa 600 A.D.) two warriors are shown, one of whom wears a wolf mask, hide and tail, while he is armed with a spear and sword.

Othin himself is closely associated with the horse; horses were sacrificed to him; sometimes the leader of the Wild Army has a horse's tail. Othin is sometimes thought of as a horse himself. There was a further custom among the Teutons of setting stallions to fight each other after exciting them with a mare in heat. This was connected with pastoral fertility; if the horses bit well there would be plenty of offspring.

From all of this evidence Höfler concludes that both tradition and myth point to secret men's associations of a warlike character which carried on cultic activities in animal disguise. Parallel to them are the men's clubs among contemporary primitives. The germ of the warrior god such as Othin is therefore to be found in the totemic sorcerer, leader of a men's group in animal disguise; at first concerned with hunting magic, and later the chief of an ecstatic warrior fraternity. In addition, the Wild Horde in Teutonic folklore is thought of as composed of spirits of the dead, and Othin is often a death demon. This, too, fits since the men's club is often a center of ancestor worship, affirming the unity between the dead and living warriors of the clan.

The third figure in the Teutonic triad is Thor (German Donar). He embodies the warrior virtues, is a Herakles-like figure, and also can be compared to the Vedantic battle god Indra. He has aspects of the clan protector and fertility god in the sense of being a provider. Certain attributes remind us of the Celtic clan god. Like the clan god he carries a hammer, like Indra he is associated with a cauldron. In the "Lay of Thrym" in which the miraculous hammer must be regained from the giant Thrym, there occurs the famous passage which associates the weapon with fruitfulness. After Thor, masquerading as a bride to gain access to the giant's home, has eaten an ox and eight salmon (this lay contains some of the best low comedy in the Eddic poems) the giant speaks as follows:

> Said Thrym these words, the Thurses lord:
> "Bring the hammer the bride to bless;
> On the maiden's lap Mjölnir lay ye,
> In Vor's name then our wedlock hallow."

This, of course, indicates that the magic of the weapon was extended in symbolic fashion to the marriage rite. A cauldron appears in the "Lay of Hymir." In this poem Thor is sent to obtain the utensil from Hymir, who sets him various tasks. He succeeds in catching the world serpent with a bull's head for bait and kills it with his hammer. In the end he brings home the cauldron in triumph to be used for brewing beer in Asgarth. While it is not stated that the cauldron is inexhaustible, the utensil certainly suggests an aspect of Thor as a provider and clan protector.

Teutonic mythology is constantly concerned with conflict, the giants of the underworld being the antagonists. Who are these giants? Since they inhabit Midgarth, they appear to be parallel to the lords of the underworld in Near East mythology. They are not, however, exactly gods in the Eddic poems; they are more often misshapen demons, whereas the Asgarth pantheon consists of ideally perfect human beings. On the other hand, they are thought of as older than the gods; Ymir from whom the earth is made is a giant. This, of course, suggests a conflict with an older generation of deities as in Near East mythology. Eventually the giants perhaps become a dramatization of the northern fear of the lingering darkness and death with overtones of tribal warfare which was so much a part of Teutonic life.

The most enigmatic of all the figures in the Norse pantheon is Loki, with whom the myth of Baldur is connected. Loki is essentially a god without a cult. A great liar, small, quick, cowardly and clever, he is both hostile and useful to the gods of Asgarth. He does not seem to be one of them although he has sworn blood brotherhood to Othin. Loki often gets into trouble through his own curiosity; sometimes when he flies about in Freya's falcon feathers. He helps Thor get back his hammer (which Loki originally obtained from the dwarfs) and his most constructive act is the invention of the fishing net. Loki also entices away the horse of the giant who is building the walls of Asgarth, in order to make him break his contract. In this episode Loki assumes the form of a mare. As a result he gives birth to Othin's horse, the eight-legged Sleipnir. He is also accused of giving birth to other monsters, the wolf Fenris, the Nithhog serpent and Hel, the mistress of the underworld. In the Baldur story he plays a tragic role. Baldur, Othin's beautiful son, beloved by all, has dreams predicting his death. All living and inanimate things, except one, are sworn not to harm him. The one exception Loki discovers through a trick; it is the mistletoe. Loki prompts the blind Höth to take part in the games of the gods who are amusing themselves by throwing weapons at the invulnerable Baldur. Höth, given the mistletoe by Loki, throws it and causes Baldur's death. A messenger is sent to retrieve Baldur from Hel. He is told Baldur may return if every living thing weeps for him. Loki, in female shape once more, is the one exception. Loki is finally fettered by iron bonds to a rock while a serpent drips venom on his face. In the holocaust of the end of the world it is Loki who leads the forces of Midgarth.

Various theories have been put forward as to Loki's real origin. His basic character, that of the trickster and culture hero, finds its nearest parallel, strangely enough, in the mythology of the North American Indians. The American trickster is both an animal and a human being. He plays jokes on others but he himself is often outwitted. It may well be that the general concept of this god or demigod originates in a very ancient totemic situation. Loki's later role as the betrayer is undoubtedly a more sophisticated literary concept in which good and evil are more clearly defined. There are those who see in this a certain amount of Christian influence.

Our knowledge of the actual rituals of the Teutonic peoples is incomplete. Once more a picture must be put together from various sources. The Romans tell us of sacred groves in which sacrifices were carried out. The sagas suggest that small wooden temples were constructed near the feasting hall. The *horg,* or god's house, contained a stone block in the center for an altar. In some cases worship went on at the hearth in the homestead, where there may also have been an altar. The altar stone or *stallr* seems to have been connected with divination: in one case it is said to have revealed the future. Trees were important in the sacred grove, either as a symbol taken from the Mediterranean fertility cult or as a phallic emblem. We have seen that Othin sacrificed himself upon a tree. The Semnoni of the lower Rhine worshiped Ziu in the sacred grove, entering its precincts naked. The world tree, Yggdrasil, whose branches entered Asgarth and whose roots penetrated Outgarth, again may be of Mediterranean origin. We do know that prisoners of war were sometimes sacrificed by hanging them on trees in the sacred grove. We have already mentioned the tradition of the lowlands where the wooden image of Nerthus was carried about the fields in a fertility ceremony. Whether the ecstatic dance suggested by one or two of the rock carvings persisted in the Iron Age, we do not know.

The sacrifice of animals or men and the communal feast seem to be the core of the warrior religion. Many animals were killed and set to boil in huge cauldrons. Bowls or golden horns for drinking were passed slowly around from hand to hand. Mead and ale first appear in Europe among the Teutons, mead being perhaps the oldest alcoholic drink. It was brewed by mixing honey and water and allowing the mixture to ferment. As the assembled company drank to Othin or Thor there was a ritual order, the king receiving the horn first. The king may at one time have served as a priest as well. Divination was sometimes practiced at the *blot* or sacrifice by dropping twigs or chips and observing how they fell. The *Heimskringla* describes how all the blood from the beast of sacrifice was gathered in bowls and in these there stood twigs made like brooms with which both the stalls and the walls of the temple inside and out were to be reddened. The sacrifices to the gods were thought of as gifts and therefore put the gods under obligation. In addition, drinking to the memory of the dead, a unanimous act of their kinsmen, helped preserve the clan unity between the dead and the living.

The combat between Sigurd and Fafnir is an obvious parallel to the Baal-Yam conflict which Gaster believes was originally dramatic in form. Sculptured on the Gosforth Cross in England is a sacrificer with a drinking horn in his hand standing by the dead body of a demon. It suggests the ritual feast after the killing of the monster. So far, the evidence of cult drama is scanty.

A particular characteristic of Teutonic religion in its later phase is the fatalistic sense of doom. Although the cult of Othin created Valhalla, a haven for dead heroes in Asgarth, where they fought every day and returned to the mead hall in perfect condition to carouse all night, the sense of ever-present conflict leads to a conception of the outcome of the conflict. Probably the long, cold, dark season of the north inculcated the constant fear that the strength of the sun would not be renewed and eternal winter would prevail. This would be a parallel tension to that felt by the peoples whose great enemy was the dry season. Götterdämmerung, the twilight of the gods, is the poetic expression of this basic northern pessimism. After the final battle in which Thor is killed, the destruction of the world takes place.

> Neath sea the land sinketh; the sun dimmeth,
> From the heavens fall the fair bright stars;
> Gushes forth steam and gutting fire,
> To very heaven soar the hurtling flames.

The image is uncomfortably pertinent to our own times. Men cannot live without hope, however, and the gloom of the northern myth is softened by a final prophecy which announces that a new earth will rise; for the Aesir gods a new golden hall will be provided in which they shall "live forever in ease and bliss."

CHAPTER 15

Smiling at Death

Etruscans—relation of Etruscan deities to those of the Greeks—multiplicity of gods and lack of recorded myth—life in the tomb—journey to the underworld—dominance of divination—hepatoscopy related to that of the Near East—Etruscan determinism.

THE ETRUSCANS are another tantalizing people who have left us no decipherable written records. The rather short mortuary inscriptions can actually be read because the alphabet was largely borrowed from the Greeks, but scholars are only sure of the meaning of a few words. So far no relation to any other language has been established. Although proper names, some numbers and a few nouns and verbs have been puzzled out, the syntax of this strange and consonantal tongue is practically unknown.

The men and women represented in the art of this people preserve the remote archaic smile as if challenging us to penetrate their secrets, and indeed they seem to have exasperated outsiders from the time of the Romans, who slandered them, to our own time when the classicist, Moses Hadas, writes of the tomb painting: "The monsters, the gaiety, the unnatural colors all suggest a disregard of the limits of humanity. It is this disregard of ordinary limits, the conscious fashioning of a world unlike the familiar, which is characteristic of the Etruscan strain as a whole."

Although Dr. Hadas falls into the trap of Greek chauvinism, it is true that even the origins of the Etruscan people remain enigmatic. Sparked by Herodotus's statement that they came from Asia Minor, a whole school of experts has tried by linguistic arguments, evidence drawn from their customs, and by certain characteristics of their religion to prove that they represent an original invasion of Anatolian sea rovers. Other scholars see them as a gradual evolution of a primitive North Italian culture, stimulated by foreign influences.

About 1000 B.C., waves of Indo-European invaders poured into the Italian peninsula, bringing with them the technique of working iron, and

enslaved the local Bronze Age people. These so-called Villanovans occupied the area from north of the Apennines through the center of the boot
to below Rome. They cremated their dead and placed the ashes either in a
crude pot with a top like a helmet, surmounted by a bronze crest, or in a
circular ceramic urn shaped like a hut with a conical roof. Bronze and iron
daggers and swords were placed inside these urns in rock-cut pits; in the
case of women the grave goods consisted of jewels, combs, needles, and
other household objects.

Both the pot with the helmet and the conical hut relate to the Etruscans,
the first possibly leading to funeral portraiture, the latter suggesting the
shape of Etruscan tombs, themselves modeled on dwellings. By the eighth
century a new cultural impulse can be detected, probably set off by either
the above-suggested Anatolian invasion or peaceful diffusion. Cremation
and burial in pits gave way to luxurious burial in beehive-shaped tombs.
A simple geometric art began to be replaced by an elaborate representational one. At the same time that cities began to be built, Greek influences
and Greek imports appear, for the Greeks were already colonizing the west
coast at Cumae.

The new culture, which was now Etruscan, stands at the crossroads between the Greek and Roman civilizations. Despite Oriental and Greek borrowings it exhibits a curious individuality. At one time its art was brushed
aside as a mere offshoot of Greek tradition, but in recent decades the Etruscans have profited from an anticlassical interest in primitive art which has
elevated their productions in the critical scale. After a quaintly imaginative period of Etruscan study in the eighteenth and nineteenth century during which the culture became a literary hobby, modern archaeology has
finally begun to work on the unsolved problems in a systematic fashion.
Two contradictory literary appreciations of the Etruscans have helped to
publicize these ancestors of the Romans: a novel by Gabriele D'Annunzio
who, influenced by the demons and preoccupation with the underworld in
the later tombs, painted this people as melancholy, corroded by anxiety,
riding toward death, while D. H. Lawrence, impressed by phallic stones,
the gaiety of the banquet scenes and frank eroticism of some of the paintings, saw the Etruscans as carefree embodiments of the vital spirit, vibrant
with sensitivity and joy.

Since the Etruscans do not speak for themselves in writing, scholars are
obliged to make use of fragments of information set down by Greek and
Roman writers. Unfortunately, since they were writing about their enemies,
these writers are an uncertain source. They were prone to obviously propa-
gandistic statements such as that of the Greek historian Theopompus who
described both men and women as shameless erotomaniacs. Then, too, the
assimilation of Greek forms and mythological concepts means that a kind

of translation is necessary in order to distinguish what is basically Etruscan. The situation is somewhat similar to that of the Hittites and the Babylonians, for, as we have seen, the former attached Babylonian names to their own deities.

The Etruscans built city-states and a bronze and iron industry. As craftsmen and traders they developed an export trade which, in turn, led to the development of sea power. They traded with the Greeks on the west coast of Italy and with peoples in the western Mediterranean. At the peak of their power at the beginning of the sixth century B.C., they overran Rome and controlled the coast of the Italian peninsula as far as Naples. Expelled from Rome at the beginning of the fifth century, and then blocked in the south, they extended their power northward into Villanovan territory as far as Milan. Meanwhile, as a sea power Etruscans were disputing the control of the western Mediterranean with both the Phoenicians and the Greeks. Allying themselves with the Phoenicians, they at first defeated the Greeks and divided the western Mediterranean with their allies (who got the larger share). The Etruscans were able to dominate Elba and the coast of Sardinia. In the fifth century, however, Rome began to drive them steadily up the peninsula. By the end of the century, a defeat by Greek sea power destroyed their commercial sea routes and weakened them economically. While the Romans pushed on, inflicting a great defeat by taking the city of Veii in 396 B.C., the Celts, to the north, who had been customers of the Etruscans, trading tin for Greek bronze wine bowls and for Etruscan metalwork, developed an aggressive drive of their own. They swarmed into the valley of the Po and drove the Etruscans out of it by 350 B.C. The dying Etruscan power tried various local alliances with the Umbrians, the Celts, and even with the Greeks, but the Roman steam roller moved steadily on until by 265 B.C. the Etruscan nation no longer existed as an independent state.

The image of Etruscan life which we derive from their funeral art is largely a picture of the wealthy class which possessed a retinue of specialized domestic slaves. Prisoners of war and conquered peoples were both enslaved and there was a class of freemen, consisting of artisans and small merchants. Very probably the seamen and miners were slaves owned by wealthy nobles. Very little is known of Etruscan agriculture except for representations of tools and a few images of farm laborers and domestic animals. Large estates were no doubt extensively cultivated. The extent and importance of the mining industry is attested by great heaps of slag still to be seen in Tuscany today. Since ancient methods of smelting were not highly efficient, some of these slag heaps are being reprocessed by contemporary firms.

Cities generally consisted of a chessboard pattern of streets dominated by an acropolis and a temple. Houses began as a simple square or oval room with a gabled or pyramidal roof. They were next grouped in circles around a court. Finally in great houses a corridor gave entrance onto a court around which rooms were built. This became the atrium of the Roman house, in which the number of rooms increased. The furniture consisted of low beds covered with cushions, cushioned banquet couches, small tables, armchairs, benches and stools. The greatest luxury was expressed in decorative accessories: bronze tripods, candelabra, perfume heaters, statuettes, mirrors, silver goblets.

The Etruscans were a clothes-conscious people. The men sometimes wore only an embroidered kilt but their hair and beards were carefully dressed and probably scented. They also wore a hemmed mantle with embroidered or painted designs and, in winter, hung a heavy woolen cloak over their shoulders. Both sexes wore pointed shoes which remind us of those affected by the Hittites. The women were dressed in long tunics and heavy short mantles embroidered along their hems. Their hair style changed frequently. In one period they dyed it blond. There is something about the elegant sophisticated social life depicted in the banquet scenes which reminds us of the Cretans. Like them, the Etruscans were a nation with style.

Unlike the social relationships among the Greeks and Romans, in Etruria there appeared to be equality between husband and wife. The name of the wife sometimes figures in genealogies. The wedding ceremony was symbolized by placing a veil over the heads of the couple; the wife reclines beside her husband at banquets; the same mantle covers both diners, and even in the tomb the images of the married pair recline together on the sarcophagus, smiling at death.

The frescoes show that the Etruscan aristocrats enjoyed hunting, fishing and fowling and such spectator sports as wrestling. At their banquets they were entertained by ecstatic dancers of both sexes who performed to the music of the double flute, harp, and trumpet.

It is of course through their art that, like the Cretans, they speak to us across the centuries. Formalized heads on funerary jars from the sixth century B.C. already indicate an interest in the specific which was to lead to a school of portraiture. By trading and piracy, the Etruscans accumulated a wealth of luxurious foreign objects from Asia Minor and Greece. Early influences were Oriental but it was the Greek archaic treatment of the figure which left a most indelible mark on Etruscan style. The Etruscans were expressionists in the best sense. While the Greeks moved on to an idealized naturalism, the Etruscans kept the figure simple and in painting used flat areas of color. In sculpture we admire the slender attenuated shapes, the lengthened hands, the sense of tension which contrasts with the Hellenic spirit of monumental repose. Various cities developed special media: Chiusi created small bas-reliefs in which the movement of the dance is extraordinarily vivid; Veii produced terra-cotta figures with beautifully modeled archaic heads and sinuous treatment of drapery; Tarquinii was a center of tomb painting.

As the Etruscan civilization began to contract, its power weakened by military and political defeats, a kind of Götterdämmerung descended which is reflected in the art. Menacing demons appear in painting, eroticism increases, and the figures stretched out upon the sarcophagi become more naturalistic, in the end fat and debauched. Hellenistic influences finally creep in which dissipate the specific character of Etruscan inspiration.

Etruscan art, however, was not without influence in Europe. It served as a link between the sophisticated Aegean and the developing barbarism of the north; the sarcophagi with a figure outstretched upon them were precursors of those in the Middle Ages, influencing Romanesque art. The Etruscan portrait head is the precursor of Roman portraiture and critics have even discerned its influence in the Italian Renaissance.

Then, too, this people made no small contribution to architecture. The dome raised above the tomb is the precursor of the dome in Roman public buildings. The Etruscan temple was wider than long, of wood and brick, set upon a high platform of stone, reached by a stairway. It was divided into three chambers sheltering the major triad of gods, its entrance dignified by two rows of four columns under a projecting roof. Since there was no pediment, figures of gods were placed on the roof while friezes decorated the sides.

The attempt to reconstruct Etruscan religion strains the detective skills of both archaeology and literary scholarship. Throughout antiquity this people attained the reputation of being the most religious nation on record. This might be expanded to mean ritual-minded and supernaturally ridden. By the sixth century, however, most of the Greek pantheon had been absorbed and scenes from Greek mythology are depicted in Etruscan art. It is therefore very difficult to distinguish which were originally Etruscan gods. Since the testimony of Greek and Roman writers does not begin until very late, about the first century, it tells us little of the original character of beliefs which had been evolving for eight hundred years.

We do know that the Etruscans possessed sacred books which were revealed in a way that reminds us of the founding of Mormonism by Joseph Smith. The initial revelation took place when a farmer at Tarquinii plowed a deeper furrow than usual. From it a spirit emerged with the face of a child, but with also the gray hair and wisdom of an old man. This character, named Tages, was the grandson of Jupiter. The peasant uttered a loud cry, whereupon a great crowd assembled from all of Etruria, including the twelve kings of the city-states. To these kings Tages dictated the sacred books containing the secrets of divination and ritual. The revelation was completed by the nymph Begoë who taught more ritual laws and the technique of measuring. Her wisdom was deposited with the Sibylline Books in the temple of Jupiter. Although these sacred books must have accumulated orally and were probably written down at a later date, scholars consider that this material belonged to the oldest portion of Etruscan religion—it was called by the Romans the *disciplina*. Carl Clemen cites a Babylonian myth in which a half-animal, half-human being taught mankind the alphabet, measurement, how to build temples, and many other arts and skills. The analogy of course suggests Asian origins of the Etruscans.

Who, then, were the oldest gods? There are traces of an ancient mother goddess; very old funerary statues seem to show this divinity, protectress of the living and the dead. Pliny reported that the Etruscans worshiped an oak on the Vatican Hill of Rome, a fact which also points to the fertility religion as we have seen it represented in Asia and Crete. Still another bit of evidence which might relate to the same deity consists of pits found within Etruscan walls at Bolsena, near which were square masonry cists for votive objects. The pits consisted of a shaft about ten meters deep and one and a half meters wide, opening out in a globelike chamber with a diameter of four meters carved out of the tufa. Clemen mentions numerous offerings which indicated the *mundus* was a receptacle for the worship of an earth deity. Possibly this was the fertility-death goddess. The mundus concept was inherited by Rome in the form of a ditch surmounted by a vault which was supposed to be a channel of communication between the underworld and the world above. On certain days the mundus in Rome was opened and the spirits from below ascended to earth.

Another ancient rite which was inherited by the Romans is probably a modified form of human sacrifice. The Etruscans are accused of slaughtering prisoners of war as offerings. Also in the frescoes of a Tarquinian tomb there is a combat between a man armed with a club, his head enveloped in a bag, and a huge hound. Either one or the other is destined to be killed. This is thought to derive from gladiatorial games at funerals. When the Romans took over gladiatorial games they became secular and pointlessly cruel.

The first well-authenticated deities are the three known as Tinia, Uni, and Menrva, who became the Capitoline triad and who were imposed upon the Romans during the period of conquest to replace their Indo-European triad Jupiter, Mars, and Quirinus. The Etruscan gods became, in Latin terms, Jupiter, Juno and Minerva whose temple was erected on the Capitoline Hill supposedly by the Tarquin Etruscan dynasty. (Rome also owed its *cloaca maxima* to the excellent sanitation system introduced by the Etruscans and the organization of its army to the same people.) Since each Etruscan city had a triple temple, three gates, and three main streets, Roman authors maintain that there were three original tribes. In this case, each of the deities might have been a tribal god. After the triad came a sort of senate of high gods, then twelve gods who ruled the signs of the zodiac, and seven gods corresponding to the planets. Finally there were gods allotted to the sixteen regions of the sky, mapped on the bronze liver used for divination purposes, found at Piacenza. Some of these are equated with Greek deities, about others little is known. Tinia, Uni and Menrva of course appear and also Nethuns, the tridented sea god equated with Poseidon. Maris was Mars and the Etruscan Aphrodite-Venus was called Turan, a pre-Hellenic Greek name, meaning ruler. Fufluns was equated with Dionysus, Turms with Hermes-Mercury, Sethlans and Velchans, both gods of fire, shared the attributes of Hephaistos-Vulcan. Hercle was equivalent to the Greek Herakles, and Vertumnus was a purely Etruscan god at whose sanctuary in Volsini the great all-Etrurian religious and political meeting and festival took place once a year. Each of these gods was associated with a particular city. There are other gods, of which we have only the names, who were considered secret and mysterious and perhaps not individualized. Who were Pales, Favor, and Cilens? Turan is undoubtedly a manifestation of the old fertility god. Jupiter seems to be the familiar sky god, for he hurls thunderbolts, but we have no explanation for the phallus-shaped stones which are found at the entrance of many tombs.

The most puzzling problem concerns the mythology. How much of the Greek material, illustrated in painting and sculpture, was actually assimilated? What became of the native mythology of which we have no identifiable representations? We have no creation stories but we do have sufficient evidence to know that the concept of the underworld was extremely important. The idea of diminished life or the living corpse in the tomb is fully attested by the sumptuous mausoleums which imitated life and habitations aboveground. Graves were built to receive whole families, aboveground they were marked by stone cupolas, below the earth they branched and proliferated in veritable necropolises. Here the furniture, the jewelry, the weapons of the deceased, accompanied them in death. Upon the lids of their richly decorated sarcophagi their images reclined, surrounded by frescoes which depicted their favorite activities in life. The sumptuousness of the burials reveals a preoccupation with death and the fate of the body which rivals that of Egypt.

Along with residence in the tomb there existed the apparently contradictory concept of the journey toward the underworld. All the early representations show it as a pleasant journey, on foot, on horseback, in vehicles, or in boats, accompanied by winged spirits and armed acolytes, the dead person apparently tranquil and undismayed by the journey's destination. From the fourth century on, the concept becomes more complicated; foreign influences and the gathering pessimism of a dying culture shadow the picture with gloom. Eita and Persipnai (Hades and Persephone) rule over the scene, attended by such demons as Leinth, an androgyne without a face, or Tuculcha, a horse-eared vulture-nosed winged horror brandishing snakes. Charun, borrowed from the Greeks, with horse-ears and a hooked nose, his flesh blue as if decaying, carries a mallet to strike down his victims. He is believed to have influenced the medieval concept of Satan. At the same time scenes of massacre and torture appear. Along with the pessimistic idea of the underworld as a grim and gloomy place, there was possibly a late Orphic influence with some promise of resurrection. The Latin writer Arnobius quotes a passage from certain lost books which states that, "thanks to the blood of certain animals offered as sacrifice to specific divinities, the souls were deified and withdrawn from the laws of mortal condition." This concept does not seem to have been widespread. On the whole, Etruscan belief does not relate ethics to rewards and punishments in the afterworld.

This is all the more clear when the concept of the disciplina is examined. This was a fatalistic science of magic through which the Etruscans obtained glimpses of the foreordained course of events. The disciplina laid down in the sacred books, the *libri haruspici,* rules for divination by examining entrails, and in the *libri fulgurales,* the interpretation of thunder and lightning. The *haruspices* and *fulgurators,* priests trained in these schools of divination, were famous in the Latin world; they were even called in by the Romans when fearful of the outcome of their Carthaginian wars.

In the animal offered to the gods as a sacrifice, the liver, the seat of life, reflected the state of the world at the moment of sacrifice. As is demonstrated by the bronze liver of Piacenza, the sky was divided into sixteen parts, each with a ruling deity. The word *templum* was originally an Etruscan divination term for a particular part of the sky defined by the priest in which he collected and interpreted omens. During this process the priest looked toward the south. The templum also designated the place on earth devoted to the gods. The microcosm of the sheep's liver reflected the macrocosm. If a malformation of the liver was found in one of the "houses" of the gods, the haruspex could determine what deity had sent the omen, the meaning of the omen and what rituals would appease him if the presage was threatening. In the interpretation of thunder, the observer faced south; eastern areas were favorable, western unfavorable. Nine gods had the right to hurl thunderbolts but Tinia could throw three, the second only if approved by the celestial senate, the last and most dangerous only if so ordered by the highest gods. The point of departure of the lightning and its point of impact had to be studied, also the month, the day, the hour, and the object struck. The appropriate prayers and rites were then carried out to obtain the fulfillment of a good omen and to avert an evil one.

In addition to these sciences there were various other phenomena which were significant, such as a rain of blood, sweating statues, abnormal births among animals and human beings.

It will be seen from the above details that Etruscan divination is reminiscent of that practiced in Babylonia where hepatoscopy, interpretation of thunder, and the scrutiny of abnormal births all originated. This correspondence has been used as an argument for the Asian origin of the Etruscans. Clemen, however, feels that the two practices are not directly related but probably go back to the same source. Divination indeed even predates the Babylonian civilization, since Anu, Enlil and Ea were supposed to have taught divination by pouring oil on water.

The Etruscans also divided trees and animals into unlucky and lucky categories: anything unusual in the first meant misfortune; the second group, by the rhythm of its growth, regulated the development of human beings. In fact all of nature was thus connected by mysterious bonds. There was no ethical or philosophical aspect to this science of magic; it consisted entirely of arbitrary rules and rituals. The system was foreign to the Greeks, who sought to extend logic and human knowledge and laid the basis of true science. In contrast, the Etruscan world view led to an unreal formalism. A man was supposed to live for eighty-four years; up to seventy he might manipulate fate to some extent, but after that his destiny was fixed. For every activity there was an appropriate form, from building and consecrating temples to the organizing of armies, for every action in war and peace. Failure to consult the omens and to perform the prescribed rituals would result in failure of the undertaking and punishment by the gods. Furthermore, the Etruscans knew that their nation had a span of a thousand years, at the end of which it would decline and disappear, a prophecy which no doubt had much to do with the gathering gloom in the later centuries of the culture.

In short, this rather highly civilized people lived by a kind of academic tabulation of the most primitive world view, the view held by the simplest hunting and fishing preliterates of our own time, a projective interpretation of events based on no critical evaluation of repetition and stemming entirely from the imagination of a priesthood. It is no wonder that the Etruscans achieved a reputation for piety; their whole psychic life was bound up with a supernatural realm whose connection with the world in which they lived was entirely fortuitous. Obsessed by this system of superstition and otherworldly menace, it is surprising that they were able to maintain the joyous attitude in everyday affairs that much of their art reveals!

All of which goes to show that, for a time at least, almost any sort of religion is workable. In the long run, however, the charmingly anachronistic Etruscans were defeated in the power struggle because of this very failure to develop logical intellectual disciplines. Since they were never able to see their international position realistically, they did not feel compelled to unite their city-states. As a result they were no match for the vulgar, practical Romans with their cosmic power drive and their genius for organization. In the struggle for survival, in the Mediterranean world, irresponsible primitivism was already outmoded.

CHAPTER **16**

Binding on Both Parties

Romans—lack of true mythology—contractual religious mentality—gods and the calendar—numena and mana—animistic spirits—the Indo-European triad—Jupiter and weapon magic—high priest as sacral king—self-immolation—Mars and horse sacrifice—ancestor cult—funeral cult and public games.

AMONG THE ancient peoples of Europe the Romans possess the distinction of being the great borrowers. They borrowed the building arch, military organization, divination and the calendar from the Etruscans; art, mythology, the physical shapes of the gods, were derived from Graeco-Etruscan tradition; their money was modeled on that of the Greeks; their alphabet was derived from that of the Etruscans. Agricultural techniques were taught them by the Phoenicians. Under the empire they continued to borrow religious cults from Greece, Asia Minor, and Egypt. But all their teachers were conquered and became a part of their empire.

Their achievements in colonial and political organization, their efficient road building, their complex urban civilization, seem remarkably modern. Indeed, parallels have been drawn between the nature of their culture and that of the materialistic Western world of today. When we look more deeply into the religious side of their psychic life, however, we begin to see the archaic roots of the far-reaching commercial and administrative colossus.

The religion of the Romans presents two strongly contrasting characteristics: on the one hand, it is shot through with all sorts of primitive practices; on the other, the organizing and legalistic mentality of this people stamps it with a hardheaded contractual quality that is quite unique. In addition, far from remaining a fixed body of doctrine, it evolved in early historic times as a result of borrowings from both Etruscans and Greeks, to such an extent that it is not easy to distinguish what is distinctly Italic.

The ethnic strain which was to give the people of the Italian peninsula its character was compounded of several elements: early Neolithic, short, dark Mediterraneans, and probably more than one infusion of Indo-Europeans of the same stock as the Celts and the Teutons. The resulting mixtures, the Villanovan and Terramaran cultures among others, were overrun by the Etruscans in the beginning of the sixth century B.C. The early monarchic period is obscured by Roman rewriting of historical legend, but the expulsion of the Etruscan overlords seems to have come about a century later, along with a weakening of Etruscan power and a general movement among Italic peoples in which aristocratic families gained power and set up early republican types of government. Scholars also suggest that in this confused period of struggle the kings tended to make a kind of alliance with the plebeian warriors which eventually resulted in this group also becoming a political power.

With the consolidation and extension of the power of Rome and the domination of the whole peninsula (and eventually the European world) by its advanced urban civilization, religion became a part of the state but, judging by the testimony of Roman authors, it did not reflect social organization as coherently as did the city-state religions of the Near East.

Three warrior gods (the triad Jupiter, Mars, Quirinus) points clearly to the Indo-European heritage. Jupiter, like Zeus and Ziu, is related to Dyaus Pitar of the steppes. He has various manifestations: lightning, rain, thunder. Mars is essentially a warrior god, and Quirinus a war god of the Sabine tribe (which amalgamated with the Romans). Dumézil sees these three as embodying right (legality), force (war) and fecundity. He admits, however, that their myths and history have not been preserved. When the first two became identified with Zeus and Ares they acquired the Greek myths. The third was gradually assimilated to the founding hero, Romulus.

Dumézil maintains that Roman fictionized historical tales were a mythology reflecting some basic Indo-European themes. He attempts to interpret the combat of the Horatii and the Curatii as a variant of the combat of the hero against a triple-headed or threefold being such as Cuchulainn's fight with three champions, the Vedic god Indra's triumph over a three-headed monster, or Thor's defeat of the giant Hrungir with the three-horned heart. After the combat, the hero in unbridled martial fury kills a member of his own clan—in the case of Horatio, his sister who was engaged to one of the Curatii and wept for his death. This results in bloodguilt and the need for purification. Although at the service of the clan, the hero's frenzy leads him to break laws or taboos and he thus becomes a kind of scapegoat. Having carried out the warrior function, his victory contains a betrayal of the legal function. Finally, after a life of excess, including sexual excess, the hero dies voluntarily as a sort of self-sacrifice. To this theme of self-sacrifice we will return again.

Although some archaic survivals may be imbedded in it, Roman myth was chiefly concerned with glorifying and legitimatizing the state. Kings thus become culture heroes; their inevitable destinies were foretold by the various divinatory signs that were a part of the system of augury. The process is similar to the romanticizing of Lincoln or Washington, who are made the embodiment of all those virtues by means of which Americans consider themselves to have achieved greatness.

The absence of an identifiable ancient mythology makes for a certain lack of coherence in the Roman religious imagination. It is compensated for by the development of the calendar, first a lunar one of ten months with intercalated days and finally the twelve-month year still used by the Western world. The development of the calendar was motivated by a desire to regularize officially a tremendous number of festivals (even in early times some forty-five), many of them different manifestations of the same god, celebrations of very minor deities, and holidays of distinctly rural, vegetation character imported into Rome. In other words, the Romans made up for lack of creative imagination by organizing their gods into a bureaucratic system of carefully scheduled rites.

The multiplicity of gods resulted from a habit of mind which discovered *numen* in practically everything. The concept of *numina* approaches very closely to that of *mana,* the electrical god stuff that could be identified with a symbol, an instrument, an animal or a man.

For the Romans everything had a numen. It was not the spear that killed but the numen in it; it was the numen in the god that accounted for the deity's power. Numina had to be propitiated by offerings or constrained by magic ritual. The numen, it will be seen, is also related to the haminga, or magic, of the Teutons. The Roman concept, however, is developed into a curious structure of ordered primitivism. Not only anthropomorphic gods, but trees, plants, animals, men and women had numina and thus almost anything could develop into a deity with a name and, in turn, be given a festival date in the calendar.

The process is quite clear in the case of the god Terminus, to whom a sacrifice of a lamb or pig was made each year as neighbors came together and checked their boundaries. Anyone guilty of moving boundaries would be cursed by Terminus and, addressing the god, the invocation went, "whether thou art stone or stake planted in the field." Terminus was therefore nothing but a boundary marker. Now boundaries and private property are a late development of a well-regulated agricultural and legalistic urban culture, since clan territory is always held communally. This is substantiated by the fact that inscriptions to Terminus do not occur before imperial times. Thus it is that a legal concept is tied to an archaic magical idea and the whole given the name of a god. Another such god was Sterculius, whose name means dung and whose numen fertilized the fields. Silvani were projections of the groves; springs and streams also had their numina.

An interesting example of a merger of two kinds of religious thinking was the cult of Jupiter Lapis, or Jupiter the Stone. This manifestation of the god consisted of flint knives kept in a shrine. What was worshiped was the striking power (numen) of the stone weapon. An oath, sworn with the flint held in the hand, went as follows: "If I knowingly deceive, then may Jupiter without scathe to the city and the citadel cast me forth from my goods as I cast this stone." The speaker then threw away the stone. Another form of the same obligation consisted of killing a pig with the stone knife. Jupiter Lapis was then urged to strike the oath taker dead if he failed to keep his word even as the knife killed the pig. Here, of course, the magic of the weapon associated with the sky god (and a strangely primitive weapon for an Iron Age people) is made to serve the legalistic purpose of the Romans. Other weapon magic of the Indo-European sort is exemplified by the spears of Mars, kept in the Forum, and the armor of Quirinus which was ritually anointed by his priests.

A word analogous to numen and mana was *sarcer,* from which comes the modern term sacred. Anything sarcer belonged to the world of religion and the leap from it to the world of the *profanus* or secular had to be accomplished by means of definite rites. Sarcer was not identical with either good or bad. A thing which was sarcer could not be touched without being contaminated or contaminating. From this was derived the double meaning of sacred and cursed, to consecrate and to obsecrate. The oath taken with the sacred stone is an example. This duality shows that the concept is fundamentally the same as that of primitive taboo, the sanction surrounding anything containing mana. The most primitive prohibitions are thus religious but the Romans were in the process of making a transition from the religious to the legal. The codification of ancient superstition on their part has provided us with a heritage of law in which the practical has only gradually superseded the irrational.

The host of Roman gods created by these processes were distinctly lacking in human personality. Janus, for instance, who gave his name to January, looked both ways. He acquired an image with a face before and behind. He was both the spirit of doorways and the object of a domestic cult. In the city of Rome he had charge of gateways. He was probably linked up with rites de passage, a threshold, going from one state to another, a time of magical peril. The home, too, was protected from alien dangers by the doorway. City gates also had to be approached carefully; there was a right and a wrong way for an army to march through them. In this connection the legend of Horatius yields interesting information. After the crime of killing his sister, as we have said, expiation was necessary. His father placed a wooden beam across the road and made his son pass under this yokelike object with his head veiled. This rite can be traced back to the primitive idea that contamination could be removed by crawling through a hole in a stone (in the case of the Australians a lean-to of branches). It has been suggested that the arch of triumph was a development of the same theory; by marching under the arch, impurities which resulted from bloodguilt in warfare could be removed wholesale.

Vesta was the spirit of the hearth, a domestic cult perhaps originating merely from the fact that the hearth was used (as among the Teutons) as a general shrine. Vesta, in the form of an undying flame, was transferred to the Capitol, the hearth of the state, and tended by six Vestal Virgins. They were appointed to serve for thirty years, subject to various taboos, after which they could retire and marry. If they let the flame go out, they were beaten; if any one of them broke her vows of chastity, she was buried alive.

The practical aspect of the Mars cult is demonstrated by the fact that the god was not worshiped between October 19 and February 27, at which time the weather was too wet and cold for fighting. During March, the season for the beginning of campaigns, this god had a series of festivals. On the 23rd of this month a purification feast involved the playing of trumpets to drown out ill-omened sounds. Archaically interesting were the Salian priests (salii, leapers). They carried the ancilia, sacred shields, and lances, moved about the city led by a cantor, and stopped here and there to dance to a heavy triple rhythm, clashing the lances on the shields while at the same time singing the praises of the gods. They took part in horse races on March 14. It has been shown that the ancile or figure-eight shield was derived from the Mycenaean type; its form was exotic, which may have helped give it a sacred character. Although none of these objects have survived, gems and coins show them being carried to and from the sanctuary, hung on a pole. A still more interesting piece of archaeological evidence is a seventh century B.C. bronze urn found in a grave on the border between Latium and Etruria. On the shoulder and lid in two concentric circles are naked warriors wearing flat headdresses and performing a dance around what seems to be a chained bear. They are holding lances and small round shields. Especially significant is the ithyphallic condition of the warriors. We have here the whole complex of sexual excitement, martial mimicry and dance and hunting magic which has appeared among most of the European warrior cultures so far discussed. In October, to commemorate the end of the fighting season, a bloody rite was performed in which a horse was sacrificed to Mars. The head was cut off and the still-dripping tail was carried to the altar of Vesta. Horse sacrifice relates Mars to Othin, Celtic tradition, and the Vedic war god, Indra. When this ritual was completed the twelve ancilia were deposited in a sacred building on the Palatine.

In April there were festivals of Venus, who was originally a rural fertility spirit and was finally assimilated to Aphrodite; a peasant girl, in short, who became a queen of love. On May 7 to 14 the Vestal Virgins collected some sacred rye ears in which was the beginning of the harvest. Ceres, another grain goddess, also had her festival in May.

Quirinus, as a clan protector, was worshiped in June, as was Juno, goddess of birth and the family, who gave the month her name. Her festivals also carried over into July. In August Ops and Consus, also grain gods, had their festivals as did Neptunus, originally a fresh-water spirit who only took to the sea when he was identified with Poseidon. October was the month of Fons and Camena, spirits of springs and watercourses.

On February 15 a curious festival called the Lupercalia took place. Young men, priests of Faunus, the pastoral god, after sacrificing a goat, ran about the Palatine Hill naked except for a goatskin belt, striking women they happened to meet with bloody strips of the goat hide. This was popularly supposed to make the women fertile. The goat as well as the bull has a history as a male fertility symbol and thus what was evidently a rural pastoral rite was incongruously adapted to an urban setting.

The Romans also practiced the sympathetic magic so widespread among preliterates and still lingering in folk tradition today. Ovid describes the rites of the Feralia which were dedicated to the silent goddess, Tacita. The spell was woven by an old woman: "With three fingers she puts three lumps of incense beneath the threshold where the tiny mouse has made herself a secret path. Then she binds enchanted thread onto the dark magic wheel and twists and turns seven black beans in her mouth. Then she roasts in the fire the head of a sprat which she has plastered with pitch, pierced with a bronze needle and sewn up; she puts in also drops of wine, all the wine that is left she or her companions drink, she more than they; as she departs she says, 'We have bound the tongues of foes and the mouths of enemies,' and so she goes away tipsy."

A *tabella* was a tablet containing a spell and pierced with a nail in order to harm the person against whom the spell was uttered; it was of course similar to the Greek lead tablet. A gambler's petition went as follows: "I adjure thee, demon, whoever thou art, and require thee from this hour, and from this day, and from this moment, that you torture and kill the horses of the Greens and the Whites and that you stay and dash to pieces the drivers Clarus, Felix, and Romanus, and leave no breath in them." Having formulated this spell, the gambler peacefully bet on the red driver, sure that the rival chariots would be put out of commission. Actually the state religion frowned on such types of magic and made efforts to ban them.

The earliest places of Roman worship were sacred groves, caves or springs. Eventually small chapels or walls were built around the sacred spot. The first temple was traditionally built on the Capitoline Hill by the Etruscan kings. Later, large temples, borrowing from both Etruscan and Greek tradition, were constructed, and decorated with sculpture modeled on the art of the Greeks. The Romans created no images of their own gods; their human form was wholly Hellenic.

Actually the priest was ideally a magistrate, a war captain or the head of a household. Through all the official religion ran the contractual theme. Although sacrifices were offered to please the gods, the typical vow was an agreement; the worshiper bound himself to perform certain acts with the expectation that the legal conscience of the god would impel him to carry out his end of the bargain. *Pietas,* from which comes the adjective *pius,* which students of Latin will remember as coupled with the name Aeneas, meant not piety in the modern sense but duty. A person carried out a rite as if paying a debt. The gods were just and businesslike; in short, Romans. They were also sticklers for form. Here again legality and primitive magic united, for a slip in performing a rite invalidated it both as a legal document and a magic spell. In this, Roman tradition approached that of Indo-Europeans, the Vedantic in particular, with its letter-perfect oral transmission of religious literature over the centuries.

Another aspect of the magico-legal, contractual attitude of the Romans is seen in the attitude of this people toward foreign gods. Always hospitable to alien religions and thus differing from peoples of the Near East, whose gods went to war and conquered rival divinities, the Romans had a special ceremony for making a bargain with the deities of a besieged town. The commanding officer pronounced the *evocatio* in which he promised more worthy temples to the gods of the enemy if they would consent to change sides and take up residence in Rome.

The professional priests, the Flamines, associated with specific gods were, on the one hand, not a caste like the Vedantic Brahmins nor a highly organized society like the Druids. Although they were allowed to marry, they were extremely sacer and their lives were so dedicated to their offices that they had little time for secular activities. Even their wives. were subject to certain religious restrictions. The most important Flamines were those of Jupiter, Mars, and Quirinus, the head priest of Jupiter being hedged about with such a multitude of taboos that he seems a reflection of a sacral king. His nail parings and hair cuttings had to be buried under sacred trees; his head was always covered with a ritual bonnet made from the skin of a sacrificial victim, reminiscent of the Polynesian chief's head taboo. He could not mount or touch a horse; he could not eat leavened bread or drink fermented drink; at all times he had to be ritually pure and ready to sacrifice. He was not permitted to look at a weapon or a detachment of armed men. He could not wear knots or rings in his clothes and if he chanced to meet a criminal in chains he lost his position. If his wife died, he was also obliged to resign, for he was no longer the representative of a family.

One curious custom (which Dumézil identifies with the voluntary death of the hero) is also reminiscent of Othin's sacrifice of self to self and of the case of a Druid priest who turned himself into a cow and allowed himself to be slain by the enemy in order to gain a victory. This was the Roman *devotio* which was recorded on three historic occasions. According to Livy, the consul Decius, in 340 B.C. during an undecided battle between the Romans and the Latins, carried out the rite by veiling his head, reciting invocations and dedicating his life to the gods in return for a victory. He then leaped on horseback and plunged into the ranks of the opposing army. In this case they fled. The *devotus* could also be a rank-and-file soldier chosen by the general. In theory, if he did not die in battle after devoting himself, the rite was not properly carried out and substitute magic had to be used. If he was a soldier, a statue at least seven feet tall had to be buried and a sacrifice made. A curiously archaic statue of the sixth century B.C. from Capestrano may well be evidence of the rite. When the devotus was a general and survived he offered up all of his weapons to Vulcan. This type of immolation, especially in the light of the other Indo-European examples, is suggestive of the willing or enforced death of the king for the good of his people. We shall see later that the sacred hunt involves the killing of an animal by a royal huntsman and the animal is also totemically identified with its killer.

Of lesser importance than the priests were the diviners, or augurs, who consulted the flight of birds and the entrails of sacrificial victims. Since the custom was borrowed from the Etruscans, in times of great crisis, such as the Punic wars, Etruscan experts were called in to practice their pseudo-science. The Romans, however, were less interested in foretelling the future than in learning about the possibilities of enterprises already under way. Cicero, who was himself an augur, explains that since the dropping of excrement by a passing team of beasts of burden was unfavorable, the diviners ordered such animals to be unyoked while the ceremony was going on. Thus the practical Romans, unlike the anxiety-ridden Etruscans, made sure that prophecies would turn out favorably by a series of precautions and rationalizations.

The household cults, particularly ancestor worship, are considered to belong to the Indo-European heritage. Because there are no myths which give us a picture of the Roman underworld and there is no proof that ancestors became gods, some authorities refuse to see Roman practice as genuine ancestor worship. The rites, however, are similar to those of more primitive worshipers of the dead.

There was sufficient difference between the funerals of the rich and those of the plebeians to suggest that there might have been two traditions, one of the warrior aristocracy and the other of the indigenous inhabitants. No individual tombs are known until the time of Cicero. Earlier, the cremation urns were placed in niches in large cemeteries and also bodies were placed in niches in communal corridors. The Romans had the remains of a patriarchal clan system overlaid by social classes. There was a concept of the *genius* of the clan which, according to Herbert Rose, meant something like its accumulated tradition, perhaps nearly equivalent to the haminga or magic of the Teutonic clan. It was the duty of the son and successor to leadership of the gens, or clan, to breathe in the last breath of his dying father and thus to absorb the genius of the clan. A certain parallel can be seen in the beliefs of the matriarchal Ashanti of Africa who considered that the heredity of the clan passed on through the blood of the mother while the father contributed something more abstract, the *ntoro,* a word sometimes thought of as a spiritual quality and sometimes used to designate the semen.

After carrying the corpse from the house, rites of purification had to be performed to sweep out the pollution of death. When the body was borne to the tomb, pietas consisted of placing a sod upon it. The procession then returned home to observe a feast which was more in honor of the living than of the dead and consequently affirmed the unity of the clan. On the anniversary of the ancestor's death there was a renewal of offering of wine, water, milk, honey and oil on the grave, which was decked with flowers.

Inhumation graves have been excavated below the Forum, dating from the sixth century, a change in funerary custom which may indicate Etruscan influence. In early graves, traces of funeral feasts are found which lived on in the Parentalia. This was celebrated from February 13 to 21 and was followed by the Carestia. Both were family reunions with a communal feast in honor of the ancestors and an offering to the *lares*. There was originally a single *lar,* both an embodiment of the clan and a spirit associated with agriculture. On this occasion there is mention of the sacrifice of "black beasts" to the defunct parents.

That more than one tradition concerning the dead was a part of Roman belief is shown by the *lemuria* festival in May. The lemures were also ancestor spirits but thought of as merely tiresome entities who were anxious to return to earth and consequently needed to be exorcised by certain magical procedures. This attitude toward the dead is not unlike that of Bronislaw Malinowski's Trobriand Islanders of the South Seas. Finally, there was a third ancestor image, that of the *manes,* or good people, an undifferentiated designation for the hordes of the dead.

On the whole, the Romans do not seem to have been preoccupied with the afterworld. In the days of the republic there was a definite rejection of emotionalism in religion. The contract with the gods was faithfully carried out and the solid citizen went about his business. However, in the period of the decadence of the empire when Hellenism grew stronger, ecstatic emotional cults such as those of Dionysus or Orpheus infiltrated Roman culture.

Something should be said of the *ludi* or games which came to play an obsessive role in Roman urban society. Etruscan frescoes have been discovered showing funeral combat between warriors and, in Tarquinia, athletic scenes and chariot races as well as masked dancers. All these might have been the prototypes of the Roman gladiatorial games. Horse races in Rome, during the period of the Etruscan kings, led to the building of the Circus Maximus. In 264 B.C. a gladiatorial combat was staged at the funeral of Junius Brutus Pera in imitation of the Etruscan funeral custom. Several agricultural gods were honored at the Circus Maximus, suggesting some connection between the early games and vegetation ceremonies. By 216 B.C. the state had instituted the *ludi plebi* as a public spectacle. These festivals, celebrated in September and November, began with an offering to Jupiter and a solemn procession from the Capitol to the circus. This was led by a magistrate, dressed as Jupiter. Then followed competing athletes, Pyrrhic dancers, burlesque dancers, musicians, a grotesque troop of dancers gotten up as satyrs and sileni, naked except for goatskins, and a cortege of gods represented by their images. In the circus athletic competitions, chariot races and gladiatorial fights took place with interludes of dancing.

These games, which began as a religious festival, developed eventually into brutal and bloody combats between teams of warriors and prisoners, human beings and wild beasts, prisoners and Christians (wild beasts were even trained to rape women); the whole spectacle went on for days, cost immense sums and gratified the sadistic impulses of the Roman populace during the decay of Roman economy and the dissolution of the empire.

Asia

CHAPTER 17

Painted Pottery and Ritual Bath

India—Iran as transition from Near East to India—bulls and pottery tradition extending from Iran to western India—bull figure and clay female image in western India—connection with Indus Valley culture of central India—highly organized theocratic civilization—scarcity of human images—possible priest-king—clay females and animal seals—Shiva a deity of sex and lord of animals—ritual bathing in Indus Valley culture and modern India—connection with rivers and female deity—destruction of Indus Valley civilization by barbarians.

B EYOND the Mesopotamian plains, between the Caspian Sea and the Persian Gulf is a triangular area now known as Iran. It consists of mountain ranges sheltering narrow valleys and enclosing a central desert. To the north, a series of passes makes it accessible to the steppes; to the west, lowlands at the foot of the mountains connect with Mesopotamia; to the east, it joins Baluchistan and western India. Its geography has made it a crossroads through which cultural, commercial, and military contacts have taken place. It is the link between the Near East and East Asia.

Backtracking again in time, we find that in the fifth millennium B.C. when urban culture was barely taking shape in the Near East, on the edge of the Iranian desert, at Sialk, a remarkable pottery tradition arose. Bands of animals, birds, boars, and leaping ibex were executed in black paint on a dark red ground. They were drawn in a calligraphic style, full of action and admirably decorative. Almost immediately they were further stylized into abstract shapes. Indeed the sense of design is so sure that it makes the rock carvings of Europeans six thousand years later seem like the work of backward children.

The Iranian pottery tradition seems to have radiated eastward through Baluchistan and the Himalayas with local variations so that the late fourth-millennium Bronze Age cultures at Kulli, and Rana Ghundai, in northwestern India, appear to be connecting links between Iran and the great central Indian culture of the Indus Valley.

199

The Kulli culture which is found in tells, heaped-up village sites, displays a pottery in which stylized felines, cattle, ibexes and plants are drawn in black on buff. The dominant figures are elongated, the legs attenuated, and the eye consists of a large light ring with a dark center. In addition, clay figurines are found in the shape of humped cattle of the same type as depicted on the pots, birds, and also women with elaborate headdresses, necklaces and grotesque faces. These statues end in a flat pedestal at the waist. Similarly, at Rana Ghundai, cattle and black buck in black on buff or terra cotta are also stylized but in a different way, the legs and horns being elongated into calligraphic strokes to fill the band of decoration. Humped clay bulls also occur, and figures of women ending below the waist. The latter differ from the Kulli type, which often appear comic, in that the eyes are circular gouged-out holes and the mouth a grim slit producing a skull-like effect and in some cases the features are actually those of a skull.

In all the village civilizations mentioned above, some practiced cremation and some inhumation, and burials contain grave goods which prove that some form of cult of the dead was present. It is also logical to suspect from the interest in animal shapes that in the transition from hunting society to settled agriculture animal cults persisted. The humped cattle suggest that the bull was already a pastoral fertility symbol. It is also a link with the Indus civilization which will be presently discussed. Another link is the presence of the female figurines. The Kulli female figures do not have breasts; those from Ghundai do. Female figures and bull images, as we have already seen, are so widely dispersed through the Near East and the Mediterranean that it is extremely likely they would have cult significance here as well. A further interesting point, made by Stuart Piggott, is the fact that in contemporary popular Hinduism such small clay figures are to be met with as deities or votive offerings in rural shrines.

The peasant mountain communities of northwestern India more or less fill in the geographical gap between the great advances of civilization in the Near East and its parallel florescence on the plains of prehistoric India. In an area embracing a huge triangle eight hundred miles to a thousand on a side, twice the size of the kingdom of Egypt and four times that of Sumer, a great urban civilization attained maturity between 2500 and 1500 B.C. Because of the lack of trained archaeologists in India, and also of the difficulties of exploring and excavating in an area in which lush tropical vegetation completely covers ruins, little was known of this amazing culture until the 1920's when English and Indian scholars combined to begin excavations. In the forties the technique of excavation improved until we can now begin to form some picture of this ancient nation which, in spite of gaps in the record, is not altogether divorced from the India of today. Oddly enough there is no connected record which shows the gradual development of

Harappan urban civilization. A few sherds beneath the Citadel at Harappa suggest village settlement by people from Baluchistan, and Indus Valley pottery shows some affinities to Kulli ware. Sir Mortimer Wheeler suggests that small groups must have entered the plain from the mountains at various times but not until control of the flooding rivers was achieved by irrigation systems could extensive city building take place. Once this technique was developed, he believes, a sort of "explosive evolution" produced the remarkable achievements that characterize the precursors of modern India.

In the north this Harappan civilization included the Punjab, which is transversed by five rivers and is still a grain-growing area; in the south the land through which the Indus River runs is now desert requiring irrigation. The use of fired brick in the ancient cities proves that the timber resources were far greater in the past and consequently there was probably a greater rainfall. The Harappa community was evidently governed from two large capitals, Harappa in the north and Mohenjo-Daro in the south, which seem to have been parts of a united kingdom since they share a common ground plan. All through the area there are evidences of a centralized government, a planned economy, and no signs whatever of internal warfare. The careful preservation of street frontages implies hereditary land tenure; the standardized system of measurements indicates careful government control of building and commerce; and great municipal granaries show an economic foresight which reminds us strongly of the paternalistic state organization of the Incas. The Indus Valley culture seems to have lasted for a millennium virtually unchanged. Whether this was "isolation and stagnation," in Stuart Piggot's phrase, or a golden age, depends upon one's prejudices. Significantly, no shields, helmets, or any body armor have been recovered. A few rather fragile copper spears, dirks, stone maceheads and perhaps clay projectiles for slings constitute the only weapons discovered. The only defensive fortifications surround the citadels. There is no pictorial record of battles and not a single war memorial. Under the regimented Indus Valley organization a fairly high standard of living seems to have been maintained for a rather large middle class. So far, the inhumation graves which have been discovered reveal only pots and a few personal decorations and toilet objects; no aristocratic burials like those of Sumer with a wealth of lavish grave goods have been found. All in all, it seems to be a fact that the Indus Valley enjoyed a thousand years of peace before being disturbed by bloody and energetic barbarians. This tranquil conservatism, a legacy from the past, can still be discerned in the culture of modern India.

Like most ancient urban communities, it appears that the Indus Valley society was stratified. A slender, dark-haired, long-headed Mediterranean type (similar to that in most early agricultural settlements in the East and southern Europe) occurs alongside a short, dark, wavy-haired, thick-lipped type related to the inhabitants of Ceylon and Australia. These people still constitute the lower castes of India and may well have been the indigenous inhabitants who were conquered and dominated by the group mentioned above. Indeed a bronze statuette of a dancing girl, with Kulli hair style and jewelry, suggests that the people of Baluchistan were also Proto-Australoid.

Near the citadel of Harappa and also in Mohenjo-Daro, rows of standardized two-room cottages have been found paralleling narrow lanes. Since near them were brickworking floors with wooden mortars in the center for grinding grain and also metalworkers' furnaces, the chances are that these were the quarters of slave or coolie workmen. In all probability they were identical with the dark-skinned conquered natives.

The houses of the average city dweller presented blank walls on the outside; within the neat rectangles of the city blocks was an intricate network of two-story, patio-style establishments entered through narrow alleys. They were, however, nearly all furnished with baths which drained into street sewers. There were also rubbish chutes, indicating a municipal rubbish disposal.

Writing and art are generally closely related. The Harappans developed square seals with a perforated boss behind the seal face (unlike the cylinder seals of the Sumerians) carved out of steatite. These generally depict animals in profile; there are a few human figures. The animals are naturalistic and modeled with a sure touch and a stylistic elegance fully equal to the seal art of the Near East and differing from it, though the initial influence may have come from Mesopotamia. On the seals, on little copper tablets, on pots, a well-developed hieroglyphic script appears with about four hundred signs; but, since no inscriptions of more than twenty characters are known, it is probably another system of communication invented for commercial reasons. The language cannot be read and though the impetus may have come from Sumer, the characters are unlike any others which have been recorded. The shortness of these written documents makes it unlikely that mythological literature will be revealed when they are interpreted.

The Harappan culture reveals no civic art; no murals or reliefs decorate the unbroken expanse of brickwork. Yet, strangely enough, although only eleven stone figures have been recovered from Harappa and Mohenjo-Daro, those that have been found reveal the presence of a sophisticated tradition with no antecedents from which its development can be traced. Most of them were found either in the citadel or near a large building which it has been conjectured may have been a temple. Several badly weathered squatting figures suggest a stereotyped religious posture. The best example, from Mohenjo-Daro, is the torso of a man dressed in a robe decorated with trefoil inlays of red paste. The eyes were also originally inlaid. Since the trefoil motif has a religious significance in Mesopotamia, Crete, and Egypt, it seems likely that the figure represents a god or priest-king. The stylization of this head and of another, detached, but in a fair state of preservation, is distinctive. The modeling of the mouth is slightly reminiscent of the archaic Greek smile but the eyes are half closed and the hair and beard are given a straight-line treatment which contrasts strongly with the baroque curls of the Near East tradition. The effect is one of tranquil if somewhat superior assurance, which accords with what we know of the conservatism of the whole culture.

Two controversial four-inch male torsos from Harappa are entirely different; they are treated with a sensitive naturalism that is almost Greek. Because of lack of documentation their dating remains uncertain. There are also two bronze figures from Mohenjo-Daro, a dancing girl in particular, which represent another form of stylized naturalism.

Aside from these sculptural forms, a large number of small clay figurines have been found, mostly of animals and women, a few representing men. The pottery tradition is largely nonpictorial. A few birds and fish appear, one or two scenes with figures, while the recurring motif of the pipal tree may be of some cult significance.

What, then, can we deduce from the remains of the Indus Valley civilization concerning the religious practices of this remarkable people? In the first place, working with analogy once more, we can assume that secular life was a reflection of a theocratic organization in which the god or priest-king was the unifying force. In both city planning and craft industrial structure the Harappans seem to have been somewhat ahead of Sumer and Egypt. The temple of the moon god at Ur, for instance, controlled a clothing factory employing ninety-eight women and sixty-three children, but seventeen grain-pounding platforms have been found at Harappa and there were probably more. This, together with the workers' quarters, indicates a higher level of craft regimentation. The state granary, too, which in a moneyless civilization would be equivalent to the treasury, is a centralized affair at Harappa constructed of baked bricks (Sumer used the sun-dried variety) raised three feet from the ground on brick walls to allow for ventilation to prevent sweating and mildew. Ur gradually evolved planned streets from a wandering rural pattern just as New York combines a grid system with the diagonal course of Broadway. Harappa and Mohenjo-Daro, however, were built with a neat grid plan in mind from the first. The municipal sewage system and even the presence of bathrooms in some houses, a fixed latrine seat draining to a receptacle in the street, also testify to remarkable theocratic urban thinking.

In the Mohenjo-Daro citadel, a raised area with defensive brick walls and peripheral towers, there is a many-roomed building which may have been a priests' college, and a ninety-foot-square assembly hall. The most extraordinary monument is an enormous bath or tank thirty-nine by twenty-three by eight feet deep reached by stairs and surrounded by small cubicles and verandas. The bricks are made watertight with gypsum mortar and backed with bitumen. There was a drain for emptying it and a well from which it was filled. At one side are eight small bathrooms with individual tanks. It is conjectured that the large bath was for public cleansing while the eight small rooms might have been reserved for priests. This installation, together with bathrooms in private houses, points very clearly to a custom of ritual purification which must have been both part of a state cult as well as a private rite. Its significance is substantiated by the continuance of ritual bathing in Indian culture of today.

When we attempt to gain some sort of a picture of the deities worshiped by the Harappans, we must work from the stone sculpture, probably from sacrificial sites, and the small clay figures, which are widely dispersed, and, somewhere in between, the evidence of the seals. The terra-cotta female figures, though differing in detail, are clearly in the same tradition as those from the Kulli and Ghundai culture. The faces of the Harappan figures are sketchy and grotesque; many of the bodies, however, are nude with fairly prominent breasts. Others have elaborate headdresses, necklaces and some-times girdles. At times a child at the breast is suggested by a lump of clay and sometimes panniers are present on each side of the body in which traces of burnt oil or incense have been found. In all probability they are votive offerings of a domestic fertility cult. One seal also shows a plant issuing from a woman's womb and another depicts a river pouring from the same organ. If the goddess represents an ancient peasant household cult, the stone figures would probably represent the ruler of the official pantheon and the focus of the state religion. The seals present a variety of evidence. In the first place, they demonstrate clearly that animals still played an im-portant role in the Indus Valley religious imagination. Twelve hundred seals were found at Mohenjo-Daro alone. On these an oxlike beast with one horn (or with a second understood to be hidden behind) is very prominent. Short-horned bulls, humped bulls, the one-horned rhinoceros, the elephant and the tiger are also frequently represented. In front of all these a curious object often appears which looks like a bowl mounted on a pedestal. It has been variously interpreted as a manger holding fodder for the beast or an incense burner. Both interpretations suggest the animals were sacred. The importance of the bull is strengthened by the number of clay figures of bulls that have been found and the fact that no cows have been recovered. The emphasis on the bull both among the Harappans and on the pottery and in the form of figures in other Indian cultures earlier described certainly relates to the bull as a pastoral fertility symbol as we have found it throughout most of the Near East and parts of the Mediterranean. Occasionally a horned human-faced Enkidu-like figure appears on the seals.

Another human image found on three seals is a squatting male wearing a horned headdress, who in some cases has three faces. His arms are laden with bangles like those of the dancing girl. On one seal he is flanked by an elephant, a tiger, a rhinoceros, and a buffalo, while below the couch on which he is seated there are two goats. All of this connects this entity with the modern Indian god, Shiva, who in his Lord of Beasts manifestation also has three faces.

Horns certainly appear to have some ritual significance. Not only does the figure on the seals wear them but a squatting male clay figure with horns has also been found. On the seals a tiger is shown wearing horns and there is a curious composite animal which seems to be part elephant, part rhinoceros. We are reminded of the horned headdress of the Sumerian priests and the horns of consecration so prominent in Crete.

As from the Cretan seals, we get tantalizing glimpses of obscure mythology. However, there is no parallel tradition of later written myth from which it is possible to make informed guesses. Composite monsters are common, among them three-headed bulls and a triple-bodied tiger. Another recurrent creature has the face of a man, tusks of an elephant, the foreparts of a ram and the hindquarters of a tiger with erect tail. One scene defies interpretation—a deity of unclear sex with flowing hair and horns stands nude between the branches of a pipal tree before which a worshiper is kneeling. Behind the worshiper stands a goat with a human face, and below him seven clothed votaries with long pigtails and tall headdresses appear to be engaged in a ritual dance. This is repeated on another Mohenjo-Daro seal and on a seal from Harappa, while seven votaries appear alone on a third. The appearance of the pipal tree, which also has cult significance in modern India, probably meant that it was already worshiped in the Indus Valley. The discovery of cones and rings of stone may indicate lingam and yoni worship (the male and female sexual organs). This brings us back to the god Shiva whose significance it may be well to sketch.

In the first place, according to Alain Daniélou, this god's cult has always been the religion of the masses, in itself a proof of his non-Aryan origin. He represents creativity and eternal life and at the same time destruction and death. We do not know how much of the latter aspect he owes to the Aryan god Rudra, originally a storm god and a death demon, to whom he becomes assimilated. In his fertility aspect he gives birth to all forms of life when his seed is thrown to the winds. This aspect also tends to be hermaphroditic, a symbol of pure sexual desire concretized in the lingam and yoni. It is also said that he divides his body into two parts, male and female, which give birth to the universe. It appears from this that a female fertility god lurks somewhere in the background, perhaps the deity of the little clay figures. As Pashupati, Shiva is master of animals, and he sometimes has five faces. In this phase he may be encountered in the forest in the form of an animal or a hunter. He also steps on a lion to mount to the back of the bull, which is his symbolic animal. The bull is frankly an erotic image. Votaries touch the testicles of the bull image before entering Shiva's temple. The bull is also sometimes shown with a man's body. Finally, the ritual of this god is described in terms of the act of copulation, the orgasm being the moment of consecration, while sex pleasure is regarded as a divine experience. Taken together, the image of the seals and the presence of clay bulls and probably lingam and yoni create a strong supposition that Shiva is the ancient god of the Indus Valley. A final piece of evidence is the fact that the *Rigveda* once or twice refers to the aboriginal peoples as phallus worshipers and expresses Aryan disapproval.

In contemporary India the cattle cult is widespread. Cattle are not supposed to die an unnatural death; they are often fed long after they have ceased to be of any economic use. The beef eater is considered a barbarian. Cow manure and cow urine are believed to purify. Since in the *Vedas* beef eating is taken for granted, it appears that the special sanctity of cattle and the prohibition against killing them is more likely to derive from the Indus Valley culture. This taboo as well as the bull-man image of Shiva is suggestive of totemic ideas.

The other important link between the ancient past and India of the present is ritual bathing. The bathing establishments, public and private, in the Indus Valley culture prove that it was well established in pre-Aryan times. Stanley Rice writes: "There is nothing in nature perhaps more sacred in India than the rivers. It is not the Ganges alone which has this character; the Godavari, the Krishna, the Kaveri all share this attribute of divinity though the Ganges may be pre-eminent among them. And this deification of rivers is presumably testimony, if any were needed, to the value of water as personified in the rivers. In other words, the rivers embody the water spirit and to do reverence to them is to propitiate the spirit by which alone the fields can yield their produce." The Indus Valley culture was dependent upon irrigation and fertile fields; likewise we have the evidence of the seals on which a plant and water issue from a woman's womb. It does not seem improbable that ritual bathing originated in the worship of the river goddess, who may have been personified in the little clay figures. In India today the magic powers of water have received further elaboration. Bathing in the Ganges will purify to the extent of canceling sins committed in previous lives. Flowers are strewn on the stream as acts of worship; the water is carried to distant parts of the country and carefully preserved. To die in the water of the Ganges ensures immediate translation to heaven. For this reason dying persons are carried to the stream so that their feet may be placed in it or they may be immersed to the waist. When a man bathes in the stream it is impious for him to put his foot in it before he has taken up a little of the water, sprinkled it on his head and murmured, "Mother, forgive me." Bathing as a part of ceremonial purification is practiced in countless festivals.

From these similarities between the symbols of the past, as we glimpse them through archaeological discovery, and folk beliefs of the present, we can form some general notion of the religion of the Indus Valley. Sir Mortimer Wheeler writes that it was in all probability "a loosely knit complex of accumulated beliefs and observances, elaborately if implicitly graded, in which the lower grades may in fact have a greater hold upon the popular mentality than the higher. That is so in India today where the crudest animism and demonism still underlie the semi-philosophical and ethical concepts of the educated few; where the symbols of a higher thought are the awesome physical realities of the peasantry. Something of this duality or multiplicity would appear to have been present already to the Harappan society of the third millennium, as it is still present to the more evolved societies of the classical world."

The Harappan civilization fell with a rapidity which reminds us of the disappearance of the Cretan power. Toward the end there seems to have been a weakening civic energy; rebuilding of houses is shoddy in comparison with earlier periods. It is conjectured that the vigilance necessary to maintain the irrigation system declined. Finally barbarians from the northwest invaded Harappa. In the topmost layer of excavation, skeletons of men, women, and children have been found, lying where they were felled by axes or swords. The illiterate invaders became squatters, building a few houses with bricks robbed from the ancient town or putting up matting huts or tents. Probably among these people were the first Vedic Aryans, since the artifacts of these marauders are related to those found in northern Iran. The archaeological record, however, is not clear and literacy does not arise again for hundreds of years.

In order to understand later religious developments in India we must turn to the steppes and once more follow the activities of the ubiquitous Indo-Europeans.

CHAPTER 18

Despoilers of the Cities

Aryans—Indo-Europeans as conquerors of Iran and India—traces of common Indo-European mythology—triad of male deities—Indra and killing of the rain dragon—warrior frenzy and soma drinking—Varuna-Mitra as lawgiver—Asvin twins and Pushan as clan protectors—clan bonds strengthened at burial—horse sacrifice—sacrifice and sacred hunt—puberty ceremony as initiation into Brahmin priesthood.

SINCE nomads are cattle breeders and hunters, pasture land is the basis of their way of life. The boundaries of their territories are established by tradition and within these areas seasonal migration takes place. The immense plain which stretches from the western fringe of European Russia to the borders of China forms a single natural unit of grassland. A little before the historical period, parts of it were transformed into barren deserts unfit for habitation but open to travel and permitting tribal movements. In prehistoric and early historic times the entire region was rich in animal life. In Asia, elk, bears, wolves, leopards, bison and wild horses were abundant. In Europe there were wild boars, asses, goats, otters, beaver. Around the region of the central Dnieper, iron could be obtained and copper was mined in large amounts in Transcaucasia.

In Neolithic times when the Near East, Egypt, India and the Mediterranean were rapidly developing a complicated urban culture, the steppes were subject to intense cold during the winter months and torrid heat in summer, thus the area was less suited to advanced agricultural techniques. In consequence the people of the grasslands preserved a barbaric hunting and pastoral culture. In summer the parched vegetation of the plain in the Asiatic sector drove the tribes up into the lower mountain slopes, rendered fertile by heavier rainfall. In the autumn when the intense cold withered the mountain vegetation, the nomads returned to the plain. In time they developed a certain amount of agriculture. In southern Russia where the climate was less changeable, parts of the tribes may have remained more or less sedentary, allowing the rest of the group to migrate and return with the flocks and herds.

As a result of droughts and intertribal wars, the grassland peoples were often driven to undertake wholesale permanent migrations to other areas. Their way of life developed a turbulent, ecstatic, independent character. Knowledge of copper working and domestication of the horse made them into formidable warriors. Retaining a primitive energy and traditional mobility for thousands of years, they surged outward in waves, engulfing many of the more sophisticated urban peoples on the fringes of their home-lands and changing the course of history.

Oddly enough, the significance of this widespread cultural complex was first glimpsed in terms of philology. Nineteenth-century scholars, delving into the history of language, discovered remarkable resemblances between Latin, Greek, Persian, Sanskrit, Celtic and German. Many important words such as those for father and mother, horse and cattle were clearly related. Therefore philologists, sharing the nineteenth-century enthusiasm for large schematic interpretations of the world, posited a parent Indo-European language, an Indo-European race, perhaps even an Indo-European empire. Modern archaeology has shown that the story is complicated. The ethnic character of the steppe people is controversial and so is their point of origin. There never was any specific Indo-European nation although there may have been a loose confederation of tribes. The outlines of a parent lan-guage are, however, discernible though there is disagreement as to what prehistoric peoples first used it.

Interestingly enough, sometimes cultural traits, as they are diffused from a center, retain their primal character stubbornly at their farthest points of diffusion, while the parent area may undergo greater changes. Indo-European grammatical peculiarities have been identified in the Italo-Celtic languages, the Hittite, and the Old Irish. Similarly, traces of horse sacrifice practiced in ancient India have been discovered among the Celts, the Ger-mans, the Romans, the Scythians and even among the Altai Turks of mod-ern times. The primal warrior god of course occurs nearly everywhere the nomads are believed to have penetrated.

At any rate, it appears that during the second millennium B.C. the migrat-ing steppe tribes divided into two large groups. The Indo-Europeans proper penetrated into Thrace, rounding the Black Sea, and contributed, as we have seen, to the Mycenaean and Greek cultures. It is also possible that the battle-ax people, who moved into other parts of central Europe, were of this stock and, as has been suggested, conquered parts of Asia Minor to form the Hittite and Hurrian nations. Succeeding waves were to flow into Italy and central Europe, contributing to the formation of the Celtic and Italic peoples.

The Eastern branch, which has come to be called the Indo-Iranians, moved around the Caspian Sea to the bend of the Euphrates and established the kingdom of the Mitanni, which reached its peak around 1450 B.C. These nomads mixed with the Hurrians, who were already thoroughly Mesopotamianized, and blended their steppe culture with that of the local people. The importance of this group for Indo-Iranian religious history lies in a document, a treaty of 1380 B.C. between the Hittite emperor Suppiliumas with the Mitanni king Mattiuaza, in which the latter swears by Indra, Mithra, Varuna and the Asvins, the most important Indo-European gods, of whom we shall hear much more in India. In fact the branch of the nomadic peoples which moved into India in about the middle of the second millennium, and another group (of evidently the same ethnic and cultural stock) which was infiltrating Iran more gradually in the latter half of the second and first half of the first millennium, now come to be known by a new name, the Aryans.

The Aryans of Iran were eventually, after amalgamating with the local population, to contribute to the formation of the Persian empire, while the Aryans of India were to develop Hindu civilization. Indeed, in many cases the energy of the steppe peoples, when it came in contact with other elements of civilization, sparked new and vital achievements in human culture.

The invasions of Iran by the Aryans has been compared to Rome's struggles with the northern barbarians; border warfare, infiltration as mercenaries, weakening of the urban power, and finally domination by the invaders and an amalgamation of cultures. In India the Aryans themselves picture their conquests as violent and complete, followed by extermination of the inhabitants.

The Aryans are strongly reminiscent of the Achaean warrior princes in Greece with their love of horses and their chariot warfare, and in other respects they are perhaps similar to the more barbarous chieftains of the Beowulf epic. The society was stratified, with warriors and priests at the top, artisans and (in Iran) free men in the middle, and peasants and slaves at the bottom. Their literature describes chariots in such detail that a modern coachbuilder could turn out a replica. The Vedic Aryans drink and feast like Celtic heroes. They despise the dark-skinned aborigines, fighting them with bows and arrows. Hymns dealing with the war god Indra describe the destruction of cities.

> Armed with his bolt and trusting in his prowess
> He wandered, shattering the cities of the Dasas.

Again:

> Thou slewest with thy bolt the wealthy Dasyu, alone
> Yet going with helpers, Indra!
> Far from the floor of heaven, the ancient riteless ones
> Fled in all directions to destruction.

And in many similar passages:

> Indra smote down, Agni consumed, O Indra,
> The Dasyus ere noontide in the conflict.
> With his arrows he cast down many thousands
> Of those who gladly sought a hard won dwelling.
> Lower than any hast thou, O Indra, cast down
> The Dasyus, abject tribes of the Dasas.

The fact that forts and cities are mentioned, that the Dasyu are wealthy and called "riteless" (in other words having a different religion from their conquerors), all points to the destruction of the Indus Valley civilization. In the words of Stuart Piggott, "on circumstantial evidence India stands accused."

Vedic houses were of wood, rectangular in shape, with a thatched roof, divided into more than one room with possibly stall space for cattle and sheep as is still the case in some European peasant areas. The hearth in the center had ritual importance as the seat of domestic religious practices. While in Iran the Aryan princes built a palace and fortified the town with a wall and towers, in India the invaders seem for some time to have lived in villages. They did, however, construct meeting halls where men discussed the affairs of the community and sometimes gambled.

The grain grown by the Aryans was barley, sown in furrows plowed by attaching traces to the ox's horns. The main emphasis was, however, upon cattle. A war party (and we are reminded of Celtic mythology) was called "the horde seeking cows." "Slaying cows for guests" was hospitable behavior for an Aryan chief. In addition, mutton and goat flesh were eaten. Milk, curds, and butter were also important items of diet. Mead was drunk with enthusiasm and *soma* was made from an unknown plant by pressing it, filtering it through a felt cloth, and mixing it with milk. It was called *haoma* in Iran, was considered the intoxicating drink of the gods, became somewhat anthropomorphized and was the basis of an elaborate cult.

In spite of the emphasis on horses, riding was the exception; stirrups were not invented until late in the first millennium. In warfare the chariot was used much as in Homeric tradition; the charioteer drove while the chieftain used his bow. Chariot racing was also popular. The unfortunate team which drew the vehicle was, as elsewhere in the ancient East, harnessed to the central pole with an almost horizontal yoke, an inefficient device which half strangled the horses.

Our knowledge of this extinct barbaric people is derived generally from periods after they have settled down in conquered areas. In Persia one written document, the *Avesta,* retains a few archaic elements. This, however, apparently written down in the early medieval period, is already affected by the reforms of the prophet Zoroaster, and extols the great god Ahuramazda. It therefore reflects the superimposed political power of the Persian emperors and their effort to yoke together a diverse group of peoples and cultures under a state religion. Thus Ahuramazda is partly the religious embodiment of the Persian emperor, partly the sophisticated refinement of already philosophical religious thinking moving toward monotheism.

It is to the Indian documents that we must turn for a picture of early Aryan psychology and beliefs. Of the various early religious writings extant, the *Rigveda* is the oldest and most important. It consists of about a thousand hymns, spells and ritual texts—in English translation filling four volumes. Documents written on perishable materials have all disappeared but, thanks to the conservative Aryan tradition which opposed desecration of religious pronouncements by committing them to writing (as we have seen in the case of the Druids and Flamines), the material was committed to memory and for thousands of years transmitted through generations of Brahmin priests. The magical importance of retaining letter perfection has assured its authenticity. Actually the *Rigveda* and other later documents were not given written form until the late eighteenth and nineteenth century when such British scholars as Sir William Jones persuaded Brahmin priests to depart from the oral tradition.

Although there is no way of dating the composition of the *Rigveda* with certainty, there is a general agreement from internal evidence and the evidence of the Hittite-Mitanni treaty that the hymns were given literary form about 1500-1400 B.C.; in other words, at about the time of the Aryan invasion of India. Other documents such as the *Yajurveda,* the *Atharvaveda,* the *Brahmanas* and the *Upanishads* all relate to the *Rigveda* but are later in composition. Some of these add to our knowledge of cult practices; the *Rigveda* remains, however, the most archaic and primal source.

Descriptions of snow-capped mountains, great rivers and plentiful rainfall suggest that the landscape of the *Rigveda* is the northwest Punjab region. Since neither rice nor tropical animals are mentioned, this also supports the conjecture that the Aryans who composed the hymns had not penetrated any farther into India.

In form the *Rigveda* is quite unlike other early literatures. The hymns are short lyrical outbursts in praise of various gods. The narrative element is slight and consists mainly of references to warlike feats and supernatural exploits. Bits of concrete description flow into nature metaphors and enumeration of ritual practice. Conventional epithets and phrases applied to the various gods are repeated again and again somewhat in the manner of Anglo-Saxon kennings. The style, with floods of metaphor and symbolism, shows that the hymns were the work of fairly sophisticated literary (though illiterate) priests who developed their Sanskrit into a supple poetic vehicle and contrived advanced metrical schemes based on counting of syllables.

Was there an ancient Indo-European body of religious epic narrative and what became of it? As we have already seen, the material which has come down to us is contradictory and curious. Celtic material is late and folkloric. The Greeks developed two of the great epics of world literature. The Romans seem to have lacked the religious storytelling gift completely. The Teutons developed a late epic tradition which shows no episodic similarity to that of the Greeks. The *Rigveda* faintly echoes what might have been narrative, for some reason not fully recorded by the priests. A. B. Keith feels that the Aryans did not make idols or representations of their gods until they came in contact with urban peoples. The same is true of the Romans, and the Celts and Teutons also seem to have borrowed shapes for their gods from other peoples. This is rather to be expected of nomads who, since they do not build cities, do not develop sculpture or painting, their art consisting of decorative accessories. The habit of creating gods animistically is also Aryan, as we shall see from the *Rigveda*.

The most important element in the pantheon is the familiar Indo-European triad. The magical king and lawgiver is either Varuna or Mitra; the warrior-type, symbolizing force, includes Indra and Rudra; finally, the health- and abundance-giving clan-protector group is embodied in the Nasatya or Asvin twins and Pushan.

The Brahmin priesthood is a controlled ritualistic body which maintains the tradition of the Vedic hymns. Gandharvas are half-horse, half-human demons who are orgiastic, phallic and breakers of taboos. These demons are an ancient concept, probably allied to the trickster mentioned in connection with the Teutonic Loki who also can turn into a horse. Later we shall suggest a connection with the archaic tribal sorcerer.

In mythological tradition we may perhaps equate Varuna with the castrating parricides, the Greek Kronos and the Hurrian Kumarbi. The ancient Aryan father god, Dyaus, was killed by his son, Indra, to obtain soma. There are also traces of a ritual loss of virility in the consecration of a Vedic king. He pretends to kill the ravisher of his potency with arrows and cries, "Here I am, full of power and vigor." In one of the hymns of the *Atharaveda* there is reference to "thou, the herb, which the gandharva dug for Varuna when he has lost his virility, thou the herb which erects the rod, we dig thee!" Since the Indo-Europeans were exaggeratedly patriarchal, it is possible that oedipal conflicts were strong among this people, giving rise to a castration myth and reflecting political struggles between generations of a dynasty. The other possible primal myth is that of the maimed gods.

Dumézil points out that Othin was blind because he sacrificed an eye to obtain knowledge, while Tyr lost a hand in the mouth of the wolf, Fenris, because he placed it there as a gag when the gods were using legal trickery to subdue the monster. In Roman historical mythology there were two such heroes, Horatius Cocles (the cyclop) and Mucius Scaevola (left-handed or one-handed). The first paralyzed the enemy by his terrible glance and seemed immune to arrows. In this he recalls Othin's magical wisdom. Scaevola voluntarily burned his right hand in order to make the enemy Etruscans believe a legal lie. In a Vedic hymn the eyeless god, Ghaga, is mentioned and also Lavitar without hands; both of these were mutilated in order to save the other gods. These traces of a possible archaic common mythology uniting all Indo-European peoples are at best fragmentary and conjectural.

The chief deities of the Aryan despoilers of the cities, as we should expect, are male warriors and clan protectors; goddesses are unimportant and often merely a feminine form of the male god's name. The one exception, the goddess of dawn, is referred to as revealing creation with the sun's eye, as kindling fire, also dissolving into an abstract concept, bestower of "whatever wealth the dawns bring with them to bless the man who offers prayer and worship." She seems in every way a sophisticated poetic metaphor resulting from a late animistic tendency.

Of the male gods, Dyaus Pitar (Jupiter, Zeus), the primal sky god, is shadowy.

> Sing forth a strength bestowing song to lofty Dyaus,
> The bold, whose resolute mind hath independent sway.

Again:

> Dyaus is my father and my begetter.

He is then identified with a stallion whose seed is prolific. Dyaus is the father of Indra, who is sometimes called Dyaus-Indra, showing that the earlier sky god has been absorbed largely by his warrior son.

Indra is the most important and characteristic warrior god, in many ways equivalent to Mars, or Thor. He is a red-bearded "destroyer of castles" either wielding the bow from his chariot or in more mythological moments darting his thunderbolt. He is a great eater like the Celtic hero and a drinker of magical soma.

> Drinking deep draughts of soma, like an ocean his belly swells.
> Like wide streams from the summit of heaven,
> So also his excellence, great, many-hued and cattle-rich,
> Is like a ripe branch to the worshiper.

He is a clan protector and bestower of increase:

> Do thou, Indra, give us hope of beautiful horses and of cattle
> In thousands, O most wealthy one.

Called "master of bay horses," he is also a cattle raider. He is likewise identified with a horse or a bull, as is Rudra, a sort of alter ego, who as before noted later becomes assimilated to Shiva. Over all of his exploits a sky god image is superimposed. The breaking of the cattle pen in order to steal cows is equated with piercing the clouds to release rain. His most important and often mentioned exploit is the familiar killing of a water dragon, Vritra.

> Without feet or hands, still he challenged Indra
> Who smote him with a bolt between his shoulders.
> Castrated yet claiming manly vigor, thus Vritra
> Lay with scattered limbs dissevered.

Again:

> There as he lies, the water like a
> Bank-bursting river taking courage flows above him.
> The dragon lies beneath the feet of the torrent
> Which Vritra with his greatness had encompassed.

Since Vritra is also described as "stretched against the seven prone rivers" it appears that he both holds back the rain and the irrigation water while Indra in this manifestation becomes a rain god and a fertility god though there is no mention of reviving vegetation. It is quite possible that this fertility concept was borrowed from the aboriginal people.

Evidence of ecstatic, frenzied behavior of the warrior appears in the *Rigveda* in connection with soma, the divine intoxicant. Its effects upon Indra are described as follows:

> Like violent gusts of wind
> The draughts I drunk have lifted me.
> Have I not drunk of Soma juice?

> In one short moment will I smite
> The earth here and there in fury.
> Have I not drunk of Soma juice?

Elsewhere another hymn to Indra states:

> Strength much to be desired is in thee, Indra;
> The immortal dances forth his hero's exploits.

The inference is that some sort of war dance or ritual combat must have been part of festival practice, probably under the influence of soma.

Roughly a quarter of the hymns of the *Rigveda* are addressed to Indra, proving his dominance in the Aryan religious scheme, and indeed, surrounded by his seven followers, the Maruts, described as follows:

> Held in your manly arms are many goodly things,
> Gold chains are an your chests and glistening ornaments,
> Deerskins are on their shoulders, on the felloes of
> their wheels
> Knives; they spread out their glory as birds spread out
> their wings.

Indra is the image of the typical Aryan chieftain.

Mentioned less often, but interesting for his similarity to Thor or Dagda, is Pushan who drives a chariot drawn by goats, carries a spear, awl or goad, and eats mush because he has no teeth. He is described as a wonder-worker who feeds and invigorates, which makes him clearly a clan protector and provider of abundance.

Two gods, Varuna and Mitra, drive in the same chariot and seem to be almost interchangeable. Varuna exhibits the more kingly aspect while Mitra has more to do with legality. At times Varuna is identified with the moon and Mitra with the sun, yet both are associated with sanctions against breaking oaths like the Roman Jupiter.

> Whatever law of thine, O god, O Varuna, which we
> Because we are men, day after day violate,
> Give us not as a prey to death to be destroyed by thee
> In wrath. Because of thy fierce urges when displeased,
> Varuna, to gain thy mercy, with hymns we bind
> Thy heart as the charioteer his tethered horse.

It is this aspect of Varuna which the Persians developed into the authoritarian concept of Ahuramazda. Actually, even in the *Rigveda,* the gods are often assimilated to each other. For instance, Agni the fire spirit is invoked thus:

> Thou at thy birth art Varuna, O Agni,
> When thou art kindled thou becomest Mitra.

Agni is a good example of mana leading to animistic personification. Associated with the hearth, Agni as a fire spirit is also the fire of sacrifice. Agni is also apostrophized as "performer of the rite, invoker, administering priest," and "high priest of the gods." Agni has no personality yet he is invoked in floods of metaphor, given attributes of Indra, and is the subject of countless hymns. Clearly in deifying the fire of sacrifice and calling it a priest a kind of animism is involved. The magical ritual drink soma is similarly invoked. The Roman hearth spirit Vesta and the Vestal Virgins show that this is an old and continuing Indo-European trait which must hark back to the period before the Indo-Europeans and Indo-Iranians separated. We are reminded of the creation of the god Terminus in the following apostrophe to the sacrificial posts to which the victims were tied:

> Let those divine stakes which are standing here
> Kindly grant us wealth with many children.
> O men who lift the ladles up, hewed these and planted
>   them in the ground,
> Bring a blessing to the field, bear our precious gift
>   to the gods. . . .

In another place:

> Like swans in lengthened line, the pillars have come to
> Us arrayed in bright colors . . .
> Those stakes upon the earth with rings that deck them . . .

Stuart Piggott comments that the setting up of sacred posts in lines and circles took place during the Bronze Age in Europe (the English Wood-henge and the Armingall horseshoe are examples). The custom is associated with the battle-ax people who migrated into Europe from the steppes and whose culture may well have been a part of the Indo-European complex. Piggott says of Aryan burial that both cremation and inhumation are believed to have taken place. There is one hymn in the *Rigveda* which describes the burial of a warrior.

> Go hence, O Death, pursue thy special pathway
> Apart from that which the gods are wont to travel.
> To thee I say it who hast eyes and hearest;
> Touch not our offspring, injure not our heroes.
> As ye have come effacing Mrityas footstep,
> To later times prolonging your existence,
> May ye be rich in children and possessions,
> Cleansed, purified, and ready for sacrificing.
> Divided from the dead are these, the living:
> Now is our calling on the gods successful.
> We have come for dancing and for laughter,
> To later times prolonging our existence.
> Here I erect this rampart for the living;
> Let none of these, none other reach this boundary.

> May they survive a hundred lengthened autumns
> And may they bring Death beneath this mountain.
> As days follow days in close succession,
> As with the seasons duly come the seasons,
> Accordingly the heir fails not his forefathers,
> So from the lives of these, O Great Ordainer,
> Live your lives full and find old age delightful,
> All of you striving, one behind the other. . . .
> From his dead hand I take the bow he carried
> That it may be our power, might, and glory.
> There art thou, there; and here with noble heroes
> May we overcome all hosts that fight against us.
> Betake thee to the lap of earth, the mother,
> Of earth far-spreading, very kind and gracious,
> Young woman, wool-soft unto the gift-giver,
> May she preserve thee from Destruction's bosom.
> Heave thyself, Earth, nor press thee downward
> Heavily; afford him easy access, gently tending him.
> Earth—as a mother wraps her skirt about her child—
>   so cover him. . . .

Amid the often tedious repetition of bulls, rain clouds, soma drinking, and Vritra slaying, this hymn stands out in its classical dignity, a strong contrast to the usual profuse metaphoric style. In addition, a number of details reveal something of the Indo-European point of view toward death. In the first place, the reference to a boundary and to "death beneath this mountain" suggests a mound surrounded by a fence or array of posts, as Piggott has noted before. "Now is our calling on the gods successful./We have come for dancing and for laughter" suggests a festival which, if it does not involve games, is certainly a celebration for the good of the living. This is borne out by the invocation of riches and possessions together with the mention of the succeeding generations strengthening each other and carrying out their obligations to their ancestors. Here we see an affirmation of the unity of the clan spirit, as among the Teutons—the enriching magic of the dead. Finally, the taking of the bow from the dead hand to be "the power, might and glory" of the living suggests the magic of the weapon being passed on—evidently, as the hymn continues, to help the living heroes protect the clan against its enemies.

When we endeavor to discover where the dead were supposed to go, we have only fragmentary material. The Aryan conception of the world is not recorded in much detail. There are vague images of a dual divinity, sky and earth, at first united, then parted. There is also a triad idea, heaven, air, and earth. The *Rigveda* states that no bird can fly from heaven to earth. The *Atharaveda* maintains that the two wings of the sunbird flying to heaven are a thousand days' journey apart. A *Brahmana* hymn informs us that the distance can be measured by placing a thousand cows on top of each other. The sky is thought of as dark and watery, indeed often compared to an ocean, or the clouds are the cattle which Indra raids. Earth is a wheel (also the symbol for the sun), or heaven and earth are two bowls turned toward each other. One hymn, however, which has later philosophical trimmings, describes the world as having been made from a giant's body. The first human being was named Manu or Mannus, forefather of men and the first to sacrifice.

Rita was the physical order of the universe, the correct protocol of sacrifice, the moral law of the world. Sin, however, was thought of as a contamination, a magical mana concept rather than ethical. It could be removed by rubbing it off on a scapegoat or by water or fire purification. It was therefore close to the conception of disease which could be caused by rakshas (demons) and could be removed by the familiar method of passing through holes. In the *Rigveda,* Indra dragged Apala through the hole of the chariot, a cart and a yoke to cure her of a skin disease.

Great care had to be taken of the body at death, for it went into the next world. Since there was no discrimination between the virtuous and sinful, it was thought to go up to heaven in a cart or with wings. Another conception was of a path to the northeast guarded by four-eyed dogs (in the *Avesta*) who by barking kept dangerous demons away from the dead. Heaven was a place of light where there was much soma drinking and love-making. Presided over by Yama and Varuna, miraculous cows provided everything needful: milk, honey, and soma.

On the whole, the official attitude of the Aryan toward his gods was that of bargaining, familiar to us from the Roman tradition. Sacrifice was offered to attract the god's attention and to promote good will so that he might reward his worshiper. Evidently the independent character of the individual in Indo-European society is here reflected in contrast to the servant-master relationship which we have seen in the Near East.

There were countless festivals at various times of the year, some domestic ones presided over by the householder, others regulated by the priests. Milk, grain and cakes were offered to Agni and Soma at the domestic hearth, at the new and full moon and various seasonal dates. Animal sacrifice occurred in connection with other rites or separately. Considerable protocol surrounded the post to which the victim was tied. The sacrifice, a goat, cow, or sheep, was bathed and tied by a string fastened to the left forefoot, passed over the back, and again fastened to the left horn. Hymns were repeated, the victim was anointed with butter, a fire was lit. Then the animal, facing west, its feet to the north, was strangled or pierced without a sound. After more ceremonies it was cut up. The priests and sacrificers ate parts of it, partaking of its divine essence. The latter conception, of course, has overtones of totemism.

The most important and apparently universal Indo-European sacrifice, only performed by the king, was the horse offering. In Vedic literature there are elaborate descriptions of this event which was supposed to provide abundance for the whole nation. There was a prelude in which the horse was led into standing water. A man of low class killed a four-eyed dog and let it float on a mat under the horse. The sacrificer said, "He who will kill the horse attacks Varuna: away with the man, away with the horse." The next step, which also seems mythical, was to release the horse to wander for a six-month or year period, guarded by four hundred warriors who kept it from bathing and having intercourse with mares. Meanwhile the priests and sacrificers sang hymns and told tales of ancient kings. When the horse returned, the king was hailed as one of the gods. Then supposedly a great number of sacrificial animals were symbolically tied to posts to be later released. The queen anointed the stallion and placed gold pieces in its mane. The horse was then covered with a garment and killed. All the queens present went around it from left to right and in the opposite direction three times. When the chief queen and horse were covered with a garment, symbolic sexual intercourse took place while the priest and the other women present carried on a ribald dialogue. The latter part of the rite is not mentioned in the *Rigveda* where the ceremony is described in the following hymn:

> Slight not Varuna, Aryaman, or Mitra,
> Ribhukshan, Indra, Agni, or the Maruts,
> When we declare amid the congregation
> The virtues of the strong steed, god-descended. . . .
> Invoker, ministering priest, atoner, fire-kindler, Soma-
>   presser, sage, reciter,
> With this well-ordered sacrifice, well furnished,
> Do ye fill full the channels of the rivers.
> The hewers of the post, those who carry it, and
> Those who carve the knob to deck the horse's stake;
> Those who prepare the cooking vessels for the steed—
> May the approving help of these promote our work.
> For the region of the gods the charger
> With his smooth back comes forth; my prayer attends him.
> The singers and the sages rejoice in him.
> A good friend have we won for the god's banquet.

May the fleet courser's halter and his heel-rope,
The headstall and the girth and the cords about him,
And the grass put within his mouth to feed him—
Among the gods, let all these, too, be with thee.
That part of the steed's flesh the fly hath eaten,
Or is left sticking to the post or hatchet,
Or to the slayer's hands or nails adhereth,
Among the gods, too, may all this be with thee.
Food undigested steaming from his belly
And any odor of raw flesh remaining,
Let the sacrificers set this in order
And dress the sacrifice with perfect cooking. . . .
The starting place, his place of rest and rolling,
The rope with which the charger's feet were fastened,
The water that he drank, the food he tasted,
Among the gods, too, may all these attend thee.
Let not the fire, smoke-scented, make thee crackle,
Nor glowing cauldron swell and break to pieces—
Offered, beloved, approved and consecrated—
Such a horse do the gods accept with favor. . . .
If one, when mounted, with excessive urging
Hath with his heel or with his whip distressed thee,
All thy woes, as with the offering ladle
At the sacrifice, I banish with my prayer. . . .
Let not thy dear soul burn thee as thou comest;
Let not the hatchet linger in thy body.
Let not a greedy, clumsy sacrificer,
Missing the joints, mangle thy limbs unduly.
No, here thou diest not, thou art not injured;
By easy paths unto the gods thou goest.
The bays, the spotted deer are now thy fellows
And to the ass's pole is yoked the charger.
May this steed bring us all sustaining riches,
Wealth in good cattle, good horses, manly offspring,
Freedom from sin may Aditi vouchsafe us,
The steed with our offering gain us lordship.

The whole hymn is interesting in that the symbolic and metaphoric Vedic style is here discarded in favor of a thoroughly realistic description of the barbaric and primitive process of sacrifice. The rude and bloody scene of Aryan feasting is vividly set before us. In addition the rite is shot through with archaic elements. The totemic basis of the festival could not be more clearly indicated. In the first place, the expressions of affection toward the animal and the assurances that it is not being hurt, that all its past sufferings are being wiped out, remind us strongly of the Ainu ceremonies cited in connection with the Paleolithic bear cult. In the second place, the horse is called god-descended. Since we know that it was associated with Dyaus and Indra and, from other sources, that the queen had ritual intercourse with it, we have here what appears to be an equating of king, god, and animal. In the hymn we are told that the killing of the divine animal will produce more water, cattle, horses, human offspring, national wealth and freedom from sin. Hubert and Mauss's views on sacrifice are particularly interesting in this connection. They stress the rite as a ceremony of transition from the profane to the divine in which various forms of purification must lead in and lead out. They also point out that the sacrifice is confounded with the sacrificer. (We have already met the idea of self-sacrifice to oneself among the Indo-Europeans.) They write: "The identification becomes such in Hindu sacrifice that from now on the future destiny of the victim has a sort of reciprocal effect on the sacrificer." The act becomes a divine crime or beneficent sacrilege and for this reason the animal must be placated or mourned as a relative. Also, in Cazeneuve's view of magic, the magician braves the destructive effect of mana and offers himself as a victim in order to control the abnormal, the forces beyond the human. The dangerous part of the divine aspect, the spirit of the animal, if all goes well, and the rite is letter perfect, goes peacefully to the gods and the subsequent purification provides a safe exit from the ambivalent sacred condition for the priest. Why is death thought to ensure fertility or abundance? Cazeneuve would see death as the height of the abnormal, hence especially charged with mana. From the psychoanalytic point of view, a ritual killing may well satisfy group hostilities, leaving a sense of well-being. This, of course, leads to the death of the hero and the purgation of tragedy. Cazeneuve sees the magician as pursuing an individual suicidal adventure. In a later form of society in which kingship or chieftainship has developed as a symbol of the group, the sacral king emerges. The sacral king is, of course, identified with a god. Out of this whole complex comes the killing of the god or rather the self-suicide of the god. "Priest or victim, priest and victim, it is a god already formed who acts and suffers at the same time in the sacrifice."

In this connection, Helmut Straube's studies of animal dress in Africa throw interesting light on the warrior-hunting psychology. In the first place he finds that in puberty ceremonies both the leader and the neophytes assume animal dress. A mythological murder and rebirth takes place. At circumcision ceremonies among the Sahel of west and central Sudan, a mythical leopard attacks the sexual parts of the boys. Among the Luba, the leaders of the ceremony roar like lions as they operate upon the boys. The drum or bullroarer is often the voice of the animal. This Straube finds strongly totemistic, especially since secret societies among the Luba have a lion totem. He feels that these rites stem from an ancient god-killing ceremony re-enacted in initiation in which initiating animal, initiate, sacrificer and victim are all equated. The leaders of men's clubs in such rites even wear cats' claws on their hands. Parallel to these activities, Straube finds that all over Africa the sacred hunt is related to sacral kingship. The regal animal is killed by a chief or king in animal clothing; again sacrifice and sacrificer are one. Between the ritual hunt and sacrifice "stands the mythological ancient being which has taken shape in the king and in his totem animal which must suffer the mythical death which alone guarantees rebirth and new life." These conclusions certainly apply by analogy to the Aryan horse sacrifice.

One other element of the poem characteristic of the religious outlook of the Aryan people is the attention paid to ritual detail and the magical importance attached to the post, the heel ropes, the pots and cooking utensils. Throughout the rite there is an attribution of mana to these objects which leads to the creation of animistic deities.

Magical practices played an important role in Aryan life and still continue to do so in India today. When a child is about to be born all knots are loosened and all doors opened. The father breathes three times upon the baby, probably to transmit his spirit. After the first pregnancy there is a ceremonial parting of the wife's hair, at which time the husband hangs fruit around his wife's neck. It has been suggested that this is an agricultural allegory.

Particularly interesting is the transferral of archaic puberty ceremony taboos to the relationship of Brahmin priest and pupil. The pupil is accepted in his eighth year after purification by bathing, putting on clean garments, and lighting the ritual fire. The period of learning is not fixed but might last as long as forty-eight years, twelve for each *Veda*. During this period asceticism is practiced; the scholar sleeps on the ground and has no intercourse with women. For the first few days after ending the discipleship, the student eats no flesh, does not drink from clay vessels and is not allowed to speak to or even look at a woman. Mention of certain names and the sight of dogs or corpses are also taboo.

Much of the popular belief reflected in later Vedic documents may well represent assimilation of magical practices from the Indus Valley inhabitants. In the light of recent discoveries it becomes clear that ancient India was an amalgamation of Aryan and Harappan tradition. About 300 B.C., Megasthenes, a Greek traveler, described the civilization of northern India as a bureaucratic state with a civil service and an elaborately departmentalized army, ruled from walled towns. The society was literate and highly organized. The city council carried on public works such as road building and irrigation and even collected a sales tax! The despoilers of the cities after plundering the peaceful dwellers of the towns had settled down to absorb the more advanced civilization of their victims.

CHAPTER 19

A World of Animal Shapes

Scythians—possible relation of animal style to Paleolithic art and totemism—Scythian pantheon with deities similar to Indra and Mitra—weapon worship in Indra cult—human sacrifice—strangling of sacrificial animals—possible reindeer cult from horse headdress and antler evidence—sati burial at funeral of chief—shaman diviners.

FROM BURIALS in southern Russia, Siberia and Mongolia, figures of deer and hordes of eagles and felines imbued with a curious vigor have been recovered. They are the work of those steppe tribes which retained their archaic nomadic society and developed this way of life until they reached a relatively high barbaric level. These formalized yet vital images of animals in wood, metal, and in textiles are found on dagger sheaths, bow cases, quivers, shields, on cheekpieces of bridles and frontlets, on saddles, on the ends of wagon poles, on standards, on metal plates sewn to clothes, on belts and buckles, on cups, bowls and mirrors; on all of the material objects, in short, that a wandering people carried about with them. This remarkable decorative art has been called "the animal style."

While this minor art is beautifully adapted to its ornamental purposes, it clearly reflects the psychic world of its creators. It is quite distinct from animal art developed in Mesopotamia; in the west it clearly influenced the Celts and the Scandinavians and to the east it penetrated to the Mongolian area, influencing the art of the Chou dynasty (1100–250 B.C.) and, later, that of the Han dynasty (202 B.C.–220 A.D.). Since these nomads had no written language, the meaning of the Scythian animal style must as usual be interpreted from classical documents, from archaeology and by comparison with anthropological material.

In the first place, the designation Scythian is a convenient blanket term for the nomads who dominated the vast area of grasslands which constitutes central Russia today. Russian archaeologists apply the term to the tribes which inhabited the area of the Dnieper Valley and the north shore of the Black Sea, but the discovery of frozen burials full of well-preserved artifacts, even including embalmed human bodies, in Pazyryk in the Yenisei Valley of Siberia has shown that the peoples there also possessed the animal style; indeed in one case the distinctive shapes were tattooed on the body of a buried chief. The people of Pazyryk also buried horses in their graves, as did the western nomads, and possessed a culture in every way similar to them. In addition, the tribesmen who harassed the Chou dynasty of China were probably the ancestors of the Huns and they too were bearers of the style. Since it is known that all of these steppe warriors spoke a basically Iranian language, and it is generally agreed that ethnically the majority were Indo-European, we are here dealing with a fairly unified cultural complex which persisted for roughly two thousand years (1700 B.C.-200 A.D.).

What sort of people were the Scythians? A vase of Greek workmanship which tallies with the finds at Pazyryk shows us long-haired, bearded, Aryan-looking men wearing close-fitting trousers tucked into soft high boots. The upper garment is a belted tunic. In some cases peaked hoods were worn which were tied under the chin. These garments were decorated with appliqué work and embroidery. Patriarchal and polygamist, the Scythian men were intrepid horsemen. While they galloped onward their women and children were transported in four- to six-wheeled wagons, drawn by oxen in south Russia, by horses in Siberia. Apparently they lived in tents or, when on the move, in their covered wagons. The tents were made comfortable with felt hangings and the ground under them was covered with rugs upon which the tribesmen sat cross-legged.

The Scythians were inveterate warriors who took scalps and heads (an old Indo-European custom, as we have seen). They harassed the Persians, the Medes, the Kingdom of Urartu, and the Greek settlements in Asia Minor, and sometimes mixed with local peoples in the South Russian area, took to sedentary life, and picked up some Greek culture. Likewise there was some give and take between them and the Mongolians to the east, for Mongolian ethnic types in the Pazyryk graves indicate intermarriage, and artifacts of Chinese style have been recovered in the same burials.

Although the Scythians were pastoralists and practiced some spasmodic agriculture, the animal style shows how firmly they were attached to ancient hunting traditions. Some efforts have been made to see the origin of the style in the Near East; more convincing suggestions by Russian scholars relate it to northern Siberia on the basis of similarities to Eskimo carving in wood or bone. Indeed, a number of carvings in wood have been recovered from Pazyryk and Sir Ellis Minns described the process of goldworking in the Black Sea area as follows: "I believe that the pattern was cut in wood, from it a negative mould was made in clayey sand and from this was taken a positive bronze casting to serve as a die. Upon this the gold plate was hammered." If we assume that the Indo-

European steppe people were descendants of late Paleolithic hunters, the Scythian group may well have preserved some very archaic elements of the Paleolithic psychic heritage along with later anthropomorphic conceptions. Keeping this in mind, let us consider some of the conjectural interpretations of the animal style which would see in it survivals of very ancient religious attitudes.

An emblematic animal on a stave is found in shamans' graves in Siberia and on their magical wands. The same use of an animal shape on top of a standard or pole occurs in Scythian graves. The Hungarians (who were related to the Scythians) placed the figure of a wolf on the top of a banner pole to signify they belonged to the wolf totem. The Huns made use of a wolf, and also the wolverine appears to have been a totem animal among them; the Chinese designated them by its name. There was a myth among the Huns of a winged wolverine which sought out and killed the elk and then led the ordinary wolverine to the game. A. Alföldi sees the winged wolverine as a sort of super totem who finds game for the rank-and-file warriors of the tribe. At any rate, the omnipresence of animal shapes does suggest the totemic badge and the continual recurrence of certain themes is certainly not accidental.

Another interpretation of the animal conflict theme, suggested by J. G. Andersson, is that the Scythians trained eagles and leopards to hunt. His only supporting evidence is the fact that falconry was known in China about the seventh century B.C. and in Greece in 440 B.C., and Marco Polo reported that Kublai Khan had hunting leopards which caught asses, stags, bears and boars. He also feels that the wolflike animals attacking their prey represent large hunting dogs. It is true that horses are often shown attacked by a wolf dog or a feline, that the deer is often struck down by an eagle or a wolf dog, and the eagle also attacks a yak. The reason for such representations would be, according to Andersson, mimetic hunting magic analogous to that of the late Paleolithic. He cites, as further evidence, the multiplied image of one animal in many Scythian designs which he regards as charms to increase fertility. In addition he finds a few examples of copulating animals in Scythian art which he compares to the famous engraving from Dordogne of the bull following the cow. Finally he mentions the Paleolithic batons tipped with animal figures which were probably charms for success in hunting and compares them with the Scythian utensils also tipped with animal shapes. It might be pointed out here that the animal tattooing on the body of the Pazyryk chieftain could not have been done for aesthetic or status reasons, since these nomads lived in a relatively cold climate which would compel them to go about fully dressed. It would seem likely, therefore, that the designs had a magical significance. Indeed they recall the tattooing practiced by the Indians of the northwest coast of America. Here, too, a formalized animal style is stamped upon every phase of the culture and in this case we know that it stemmed from the totemic and mythological concepts of its creators. On the whole, it seems very probable that totemism and magico-religious belief must have lent energy and distinction to this remarkable art form reflecting a world of animal shapes.

As we should expect from Indo-European tradition, Scythian art rarely deals with human beings. The exception is what has been called the "great goddess." This deity, however, was worshiped in the Black Sea area before the arrival of the Scythians. In some representations she is distinctly Mesopotamian-looking while in others she appears more or less Greek. The only Siberian evidence for her cult is a hanging from Pazyryk which shows a seated figure (which may or may not be a woman) with a mounted warrior in front of it. The seated figure is beardless and wears a long robe but there are other representations of Scythian *men* in long robes and some bodies found in the tombs were beardless. The warrior, moreover, is not a Scythian type and nothing in his posture suggests adoration, so this could be a secular scene. Judging from the Indo-European tradition of male deities, the great goddess is very likely a borrowing from the Near East and the fact that she is the only consistently represented human being also suggests that she is a foreign intrusion in a culture which did not make images of its anthropomorphic gods.

For evidence of other Scythian deities the Greek historian Herodotus is the only source and since much of his testimony concerning the Scythians has been corroborated by archaeology, he is probably reliable. The chief war god and the leading figure of the pantheon, whom Herodotus calls Ares, is probably Indra. Apollo or Oitosuros, in a Greek inscription, has been identified with Mitra. Zeus-Papeus would be equivalent to Varuna, while Tabiti, regarded as female, was the goddess of fire, similar to the Roman Vesta and the Aryan Igni. The deity called by Herodotus Poseidon would doubtless be a horse god.

According to Herodotus, Ares-Indra, to whom most sacrifices were offered, was worshiped in the form of an old iron blade. Since the Scythians had no temples, they built a square platform of faggots to which they added fifty more cartloads each year. On the top of this they stuck the iron blade to which they offered horses and other animals. The use of a blade as a symbol for the god is interesting, particularly as we have encountered so much weapon magic in other areas of Indo-European infiltration, notably in Italy where Jupiter was equated with a stone knife. The Greek historian goes on to say that one in a hundred prisoners of war were also sacrificed to this god. First they poured wine on the heads of the prisoners, then cut their throats and let the blood drip into a vase.

They carried the vase to the top of the platform and moistened the blade with the blood. While this rite was being carried out, the sacrificers below cut a shoulder and arm from each victim and flung it in the air. The bodies and arms were left where they fell. Herodotus stresses the fact that this practice was unusual, sacrificial animals were killed in a different way. Their front feet were tied together; then the sacrificer stood behind the victim, pulled the cord and threw the beast, at the same time invoking the god to which it was to be offered. A cord was then looped about the animal's neck and it was strangled by twisting the cord with a stick. This was done without lighting a fire or any preliminary libations. The procedure resembles that of the Aryans who also strangled their sacrificial animals. The Scythians cooked the flesh of the sacrificial beast in a large cauldron, first having removed the flesh from the bones which they burned under the cauldron because of the scarcity of wood.

Probably one of the most recurrent images in the animal style is that of the reindeer. It appears very often in a crouching position, the legs folded under the body. It has been suggested that this is a ritual attitude, either of the animal wounded in the sacred hunt or of the sacrificial victim. An interesting find in the burials at Pazyryk consisted of headdresses for horses surmounted by mythological elements, two of which clearly transformed the horse's head into that of a stag, for they were surmounted by antlers. It has been suggested that this represents a survival of an elk or reindeer cult and a transition to the horse cult. A fourth century B.C. vase from Chertomlyk, of Greek workmanship, shows scenes of breaking wild Mongolian ponies. This indicates that as well as breeding horses the Scythians captured wild ones until fairly late in their history. If the Scythians sacrificed both reindeer and horses, it appears that the evolution of their religion may well illustrate Helmut Straube's suggestion that the ritual hunt and death of a totem beast was gradually transformed into the sacrifice of a domestic animal, since the horse, whose flesh was sometimes eaten by the nomads, was at some stage in their history a wild animal and later a domestic one.

The reindeer cult must be the basis for the importance of antlers in ritual practice. A. Salmony points out that a hanging found in the Pazyryk burials shows a horned man, the horns fancifully developed in the same style as some reindeer-headed finials. The Indians of the upper Punjab are said to have borrowed a myth from the Scythians involving worship of deer to which they were bound by "religious parentage." In China, in late Chou culture, wooden animal and human heads surmounted by deer antlers also testify to a deer cult which may or may not have been borrowed from the Scythians. A fourth century B.C. Chou bronze also depicts antlered figures dancing toward each other. Salmony also alludes to the famous horned sorcerer of the Trois Frères cave as indicating that the dancing shaman wearing horns is a link with very early hunting practices. On the whole, the evidences of a reindeer cult add to the presumption that the animal style has its roots in ancient totemic attitudes.

Herodotus describes the Scythian funeral procedures in considerable detail and this detail has been corroborated by the finds at Pazyryk. The body of a chief was emptied, cleaned and stuffed with embalming herbs and borne to the burial chamber on a cart surrounded by the whole tribe wailing and slashing their flesh. The journey was supposed to circumscribe his dominions and lasted forty days. The body was lowered to a bier which often had standards surmounted by animal figures at its corners. In the ditch around the burial were placed the strangled bodies of the royal concubines, the cupbearer, the cook, the groom, the secretary, the herald, the chief's finest horses and the best of his goods such as his golden cups, jars filled with wine and oil, and his great cauldron filled with meat. This burial of human grave goods is of course exactly similar to the famous finds at Ur. Herodotus goes on to report that a year later fifty men and fifty horses from the chief's bodyguard were strangled, embalmed and stuffed, and the riders, mounted on their horses, impaled on posts in a circle around the barrow and left to disintegrate. No trace of such bodies has ever been found but the circles of posts which are associated with the burials of the battle-ax people and the Aryan references to circles of posts do suggest that the placing of some sort of offerings on posts around a grave might be an ancient Indo-European custom.

The Pazyryk burials, because the ground below the barrow froze permanently, have preserved the rich grave goods interred with a nomad chieftain. From seven to sixteen horses accompanied these equestrian aristocrats. Some of the offerings were wild Mongolian ponies but, in each case, one elegant thoroughbred was also interred. One chief was placed in a coffin hollowed out from a tree trunk on which were incised figures of tigers. Sheepskins, vessels of wood, clay, and skin, small tables, and even rich felt wall hangings were included in the furnishings of the burial chamber.

If the animal art points to Siberia, the Scythian shamans with their pointed hoods and feminine (or invert) behavior also seem very North Asiatic. They were said to practice divination by untying a bundle of twigs and placing them in groups. If a king or chief fell ill it was believed that some shaman must have bewitched him. Whoever was accused by the other wizards consulted was placed on a cart piled with brushwood and burned to death. The method of taking oath is strongly reminiscent of weapon magic. Wine was poured into earthenware cups and mixed with blood drawn from both parties. Into this mixture were dipped a sword, arrows, an ax and a dart. It was then prayed over and drunk by both parties and the chief of the tribe.

The Scythians, after dominating the steppe area for so long, inexplicably disappeared from history in about the third century A.D. Their place was taken by the Slavs whose ethnic origin is controversial but who seem to have inherited a good deal of Scythian tradition. The animal style, however, like the echo of a bell note, continued to resound in other areas for hundreds of years. The Celts carried traces of it to the British Isles. In central Europe, the Germanic peoples brought certain traits, specifically the large-beaked, round-eyed Scythian bird, into the decorative art of the Middle Ages.

CHAPTER 20

Oracle Bones and
Grandfather Tuesday

China—Bronze Age Shang empire discovered through oracle bones—divination techniques—dominance of ancestor worship in terms of clan—funeral goods—head taking and human sacrifice—Chou period records on bronze pots—poetic record of ritual meal in ancestor worship—rain deities and dragons—diffusion of rain cult to Pacific and possibly Middle and South America—traces of male sky warrior god—culture hero myth—shamanistic ritual.

CHINESE MEDICINE has played a strategic role in the archaeology of the Far East. A highly primitive theory of disease which involved prescribing ground dragons' bones resulted in the destruction of many prehistoric relics but, on the other hand, also brought such objects to the notice of specialists who were thereby led to important sites. The teeth of the Chou-k'ou-tien man were first sold to G. H. von Königswald by a Chinese druggist. This led to the uncovering of valuable data concerning Paleolithic man in Asia. The most spectacular discovery, however, emanating from the pharmacopoeia was that of the "oracle bones." These were strips of bone with characters scratched upon them which finally came into the hands of antiquaries who recognized the writing as an early form of Chinese. Eventually, at the turn of the century, they were identified as records of the royal archives of an ancient and highly literate civilization which extended over the entire central plain of China to parts of the Huan and Yangtze river basins.

Excavation did not begin until thirty years later because of the unsettled state of China and because of strong religious sanctions against the excavation of graves. Despite interruptions during the war with Japan, the fall of Chiang Kai-shek and the formation of the People's Republic, excavation of sites in North China has gone on since 1928 until we now can form a picture of a great culture as significant and sophisticated as that of Mesopotamia or Egypt.

232

What were the oracle bones? Actually they were an important element in religious divination. A scapula or flat portion split from the leg bone of an ox (later a tortoise shell was used) was scraped thin and heat was applied to the back until a T-shaped crack formed. Meanwhile a question was asked. From the crack a yes or no answer was derived, how we do not exactly know. Fortunately for archaeology, however, the question was then written down on the bone, which was preserved in the archives. The earliest Chinese written records therefore are of a religious nature and tell us much more about the psychic development of the people than, for instance, the administrative details which have been obtained from Cretan Linear B.

Excavations of the ancient capital at An-yang and some of the outposts of this empire, together with investigation of the Neolithic background, have proved a continuity of development unique in world history. Despite earlier attempts of diffusionists with a Western bias to attribute cultural advances to invasions or Western influence, archaeology has now shown that Far Eastern civilization is an individual creation of the Mongolian people. Despite gaps in the record and a temporary appearance of a painted pottery, which seems a Western intrusion, certain traits such as bone divination, the domestication of horses and cattle, pounded earth walls, black pottery and white porcelain ware are peculiarly local. In particular a tripod pot, called the *li,* was made of pottery in the Neolithic and persisted into the historical period where it was cast in bronze. Even bronze casting, which was thought to be a Western borrowing, has now been shown to have evolved gradually and independently in the Far East.

We shall consider here only the religious developments of the two earliest periods of the Bronze Age known as the Shang and Chou empires. The first, the culture of the oracle bones, is now dated from about 2500 B.C. to 1100 B.C. The second, resulting from conquest by and amalgamation with a more barbaric people, runs from about 1100 B.C. to 250 B.C. In these two millennia the basic character of Chinese civilization, its typical social structure, art, religion and philosophy, was created and has persisted through the centuries without major changes until the advent of the Communist regime.

The Shang capital was created in a bend of the Huan River which protected it on two sides. On the other sides there was a defensive wall. Neolithic houses were crude beehive-shaped affairs, dug into the ground, roofed with lumber and sodded. The Shang period saw the development of an architecture which has continued to be used in later centuries. The soil of the area, a fertile loess, when pounded becomes as hard or harder than the sun-dried brick of Mesopotamia. The Neolithic people sometimes made walls of it. The Shangs created a raised terrace upon which they set three rows of wooden pillars, and stones under each for a base. The pillars supported a gable roof which was covered with matting and plastered with mud. The walls, either of pounded earth or more perishable materials, were sometimes decorated with polychrome. A poem from the Chou period describes the building process.

> They bound frames for the earth
>   exactly over one another;
> T'o, t'o went the pounding—
> Impervious to wind or rain,
> Offering no cranny to bird or rat,
> A fine dwelling is laid for our noble
>   lord . . .
> Level and smooth is the courtyard
> And lofty are the pillars around it.

The largest building unearthed in the capital was ninety-six by twenty-six feet. Near the larger buildings, which probably constituted the palace area, the remains of what seems to have been a district of artisans were found, perhaps controlled as a royal monopoly. Slag, ash, broken molds, all the by-products of bronze casting, were grouped in one spot; in another, knives, jewelry, stones such as jade; in still another arrowheads, ladles, hairpins and carved bone.

Treasure pits containing pottery, bone and mother-of-pearl carvings, gold, jade, and strings of cowrie shells were also excavated. These little shells (which have turned up in burials all over the world from the time of the Paleolithic and are considered by some writers to have fertility significance because the opening of the shell looks something like the vulva—a dubiously abstract idea) were used by the Shangs for money. Since they were imported from the coast, they were relatively scarce and hence valuable. Likewise they were small and portable. In the Chou period strings of ten were presented as rewards to the king's deserving vassals. A gift of ten strings warranted presentation in the temple.

All of our knowledge of Shang civilization comes from the remains and records of an aristocratic feudal class which must have formed early in the history of the culture. As in other Bronze civilizations, chariots were used by the king and his nobles with the difference that, in addition to a team yoked to the pole, two outside horses attached by traces were added to the vehicle. In warfare it contained a driver, bowman and spearman. The king himself rode in a sort of flagship with a standard-bearer and a drummer.

Judging from the rare representations of the human figure in marble and jade, the Shang people wore fitted clothes with sleeves (and perhaps even trousers) made of fur, silk, and other fabrics, decorated with embroidery in characteristic Shang motifs. One jade statue shows a man wearing a tall, crownlike headdress and a robe reaching to the feet.

Shang art ranged from wood carving, bronze casting, small carvings in bone, ivory, mother-of-pearl or jade to larger carvings of animals and men in marble. The motifs consisted mainly of stylized animals and the running spiral or running blunt-edged square. Among figures of single animals the antlered deer is most common. The Shang animal style includes oxen, tigers, birds, cicadas, dragons and, particularly in the later period, composites. Among these is the double mask with raised eyes, a generalized creature which, when viewed from the side, becomes an animal's body in profile, the ear, horn, and half the crest stylized in spirals and rounded angles. This particular and unmistakable style radiates into the Pacific and perhaps into the Americas.

The clan system evidently prevailed in the Shang period and on into the ensuing Chou empire. Some two hundred Shang aristocratic clans have been identified. The Shang rulers were all of one family but, strangely enough, the throne went from older to younger brother and only to a son when the older generation had been exhausted. As offerings were made to several "fathers," it has been conjectured paternal uncles were so designated. In a sense China has ever since been dominated by an archaic social form, for the cohesiveness of the clan has persisted in the family group and the unifying force has been that most primitive of religions, ancestor worship.

The importance attached to burial testifies to the emergence of the familiar type of living-corpse ancestor cult which we have encountered in so many other areas. The royal tomb was a pit; the largest found was forty-three feet deep and sixty-five feet square. In the center of the pit a wooden burial chamber about ten feet square was erected, the sides of which were often finely carved or decorated with polychrome elements of the characteristic style. Four stairways led down into the pit. Rich grave goods accompanied the ruler to the other world, bronze dagger-axes, round shields, leather armor reinforced with wooden slats, and bronze helmets. Particularly interesting was the discovery of thirty-eight horse skeletons with bronze-ornamented harness in a single pit. Remains of chariots have also been recovered from graves. The whole area outside the wooden burial chamber was filled in with layers of pounded earth until the surface was reached. The Shangs were content with a level surface above the burial pit but in a number of Chou tombs a pounded-earth pyramid was erected, sometimes twenty-five to forty feet high and fifty to eighty feet square, forming an impressive series of monuments on the treeless plain of north China.

Throughout the period of the Shang empire a series of wars was carried on with barbarians to the north and west. The captives taken in these wars were often referred to as Ch'iangs or sheepherders. A pictograph shows a symbol for a man with a knife severing his neck. Together with this evidence, special pits have been found containing thousands of headless skeletons, sometimes with the wrists crossed behind the back as if tied. The skulls were buried in separate pits. Small bronze knives and axes accompanied these skeletons. The probability is, therefore, that war captives were sacrificed in great numbers, the technique of beheading reminding us strongly of the customs of the Indo-Europeans. The presence of a number of victims near a royal tomb indicates that they were offered up at the death of the king.

The Shang civilization was maintained on a high level of literacy; identification of the symbols for book and writing brush shows that, in addition to the records on the oracle bones, books existed, probably written on slips of bamboo, a perishable material which has not survived.

In the end, as so often happens, the urban culture was overrun by the same barbarians it had so often repelled. The Chous who captured Anyang were of the same Mongolian stock as the Shangs, their language was so similar that they were able to appropriate the writing of the conquered, and indeed they adopted practically all of their civilization. The Chous did not refer to their own ancestry beyond the great-grandfather of the conquering leader, Wu. They reinforced the feudal system, parceling out the various areas of the empire to friends and relatives of the ruling house, even leaving a descendant of the Shang royal house to govern part of it.

The Chous took to literacy with enthusiasm. They were great letter writers, record keepers, and also accomplished poets. The art of bronze casting, perfected by the Shangs, under Chou rule took on a special function. Bronze pots and bells became commemorative objects and lengthy inscriptions were engraved upon them, telling us a great deal about the emerging Chinese culture. Such bronzes were given as wedding presents or by the king to his vassals; they were used for sacrificial purposes and they recorded military actions. Treaties, genealogies, history, deeds, dedications to ancestors, and whole books on such subjects as music, archery, divination and, above all, poetry were engraved on the enduring bronze, "for ten thousand years, forever."

A picture of early first millennium B.C. sophistication emerges which, despite traits here and there reminding us of heroic ages elsewhere, is curiously modern in the sense that it reflects a serenely personal and secular world outlook.

As Te K'un Chang points out, man was the center of the universe. The world of the heavenly gods was above, that of the earth spirits below. By means of offering and sacrifice man could associate himself with the other two. In death he could enter all three. Supernatural powers took care of man and could, with proper ritual precautions, be made to do what he wanted as long as his powerful ancestors were on his side.

> They confer upon you abundant blessings;
> Each as it is desired, each as sure as law.

Reliance upon ancestors and the maintenance of the clan unity was the basis of all security and the guarantee of all abundance.

The examples of poetry here used to illustrate the early Chinese world view are taken from *The Book of Poetry,* an anthology which mainly dates from the early Chou period. Some of the material undoubtedly stems from the Shang era and indeed the form and technique of verse is so highly developed that it must have had a long tradition behind it. There is scarcely any trace of the heroic oral style with its standardized kennings or epithets which made composition easy for the bard in Bronze Ages elsewhere. If there ever was a heroic oral literature, even in the Shang period, it appears to have been replaced by composition in writing, for *The Book of Poetry* abounds in specific imagery, vivid observation, acute expression of subtle shades of emotion and mood, delicate symbolisms found nowhere else in the world in such an early period of civilization. They seem contemporary, and indeed they are, for Ezra Pound and the American imagists were deeply indebted to the Chinese classics.

Ancestral spirits were sometimes thought of as roaming about the earth and, if not satisfied, dangerous. Their names were taboo. In sacrificing to them the name of a day of the week was used, in the case of the oracle bones, and thus prayers might be offered up to or questions asked of "Grandfather Tuesday." The Shangs offered only animals: ox, pig, sheep or dog; there is no reference to horse sacrifice although the burials are suggestive. Liquor was used in Shang ritual, probably a sort of beer made from millet. Under the Chous various vegetable offerings were added. In Shang practice the spirits were thought to drink the blood of the victim precisely as did the Greek ancestral spirits. The temple was called the House of Blood. The Chous also used to designate a member of the family to represent the spirit of the forefather and to play a special role in the ceremony.

The questions asked of ancestors on the oracle bones concerned such matters as favorable days for journeys, hunting, carrying on war, success in war or hunting, good or bad harvest, the outcome of illness and even such simple queries as "Will it rain tonight?" very much as the modern New Yorker dials WE 6-1212. There may have been some sort of tally kept because, in the case cited, the bone also recorded the statement "It did rain." The Chous abandoned bone for the tortoise shell. They often carried one about with them on journeys, using it more than once.

A complete account of the ancestral services in the family temple is recorded in a poem which is worth quoting extensively.

> Thick grew the tribulus
> But they cleared away its thorn bushes.
> Why did they do this of old?
> That we might plant our food and sacrificial
>   millet,
> That our food millet might be abundant,
> And our sacrificial millet luxuriant.
> When our barns are full
> And our stacks can be counted by tens of
>   myriads
> We proceed to make liquor and prepare food
> For offering and sacrifice;
> We seat the representatives of the dead and
>   urge them to eat—
> Thus seeking to increase our bright happiness.
>
> With correct and reverent deportment,
> The oxen and sheep all purified,
> We proceed to the winter and autumn
>   sacrifices.
> Some flay, some boil, some arrange
> The meat, some adjust the pieces.
> The priest sacrifices inside the temple gate
> And all the service is complete and brilliant.
> Grandly come our progenitors;
> The spirits happily enjoy the offerings;
> Their filial descendant receives a blessing—
> They will reward him with great happiness,
> With myriads of years, life without end. . . .
>
> We are very much exhausted
> And have performed every ceremony without
>   error.
> The able priest announces the will of the
>   spirits
> And goes to the filial descendant to convey
>   it.

"Fragrant has been the sacrifice
And the spirits have enjoyed your liquor and
  food.
They confer abundant blessings upon you,
Each as it is desired, each as sure as law.
You have been exact and expeditious;
You have been correct and careful;
They will ever confer upon you the choicest
  favors,
In myriads and tens of myriads."

By the time the Shang civilization had developed from its Neolithic roots, it appears that various cultural streams had already been synthesized. Ling Shun-Sheng feels that two complexes can be distinguished. One is a maritime type which is diffused from the south and ties up with the Oceanic peoples. It is distinguished by beads, use of shell, the boat, and domestication of the dog. The other animals associated with it are the fowl and the pig. The second element, which entered from the northwest, brought with it jade and bronze working, horse and vehicle, elaborate garments. The animals which were a part of this way of life were the horse, ox, and sheep. Shun-Sheng traces the eating and sacrificing of dogs throughout the Pacific area to Middle America and North America.

Arguing from the three or four carvings of human figures from Shang sites and from tradition, Li Chi adds further details. He connects a squatting figure with the black pottery makers of the east coast, and also a second figure, nude except for an apron but with tattooing depicted on the body. A third piece of sculpture shows the pose of sitting on the heels, developed from kneeling (kept alive in Japanese tradition), which he feels was characteristic of the Shangs. This custom would also be typical of the Western cultural component which he ties up with the painted pottery and possibly the legendary Hsia dynasty traditionally supposed to antedate the Shangs. The latter, in his view, were originally a hunting people who developed the pastoral stage and, having conquered and absorbed the contributions of the other group, retained their old hunting habits as an aristocratic pastime. The animal style which began, like that of the Scythians, as wood carving, would be their contribution; the spiral and blunt square or meander patterns would be Eastern.

Another diffusionist study (by Lou Wing-Sou) draws parallels between the ancient Chinese rain cult and similar practices and beliefs in Middle America among the Nahua peoples of Mexico and the Southwest Indians of the United States. The Shangs worshiped two major rain deities: the dragon whose symbol is interchangeable with that of the snake, and Leikung, Lord of Thunder. The snake is sometimes regarded as an ancestor; in one legend man is born of twin snake deities. In some areas of China the creation legend describes man as born of a snake egg. The image of the dragon becomes elaborated in Chinese art until it is often a composite with a frog, horse, or even an elephant head. The dragon rain god is thought of as divided up into four elements for the points of the compass, with a fifth central unifying element. The four rain dragons are associated with four colors: N—black, E—green, S—red, W—yellow or white.

To return to the problem of the origins of Shang religion, the fact that rainmaking is shared by the dragon and an anthropomorphic god of thunder, Leikung, is also significant. Leikung sometimes carries an ax or thunderbolt (as do the Mayan Chacs). He may also ride upon the dragon or even appear himself with a dragon's body. It seems as if two concepts were involved. To trace them further involves a glance at the Shang pantheon.

In a feudal position as ruler of the heavens was Ti, the symbol for whose name is also the symbol for king. The wind god was called the Envoy of Ti and Ti himself was sometimes called Shang Ti or great Ti. Ti was concerned with war, rain, and abundance in general. He was the central element in the four-element-with-a-central-ruling-power scheme which was paralleled by the earthly ruler, whose people were also divided into four groups. It therefore appears that Ti is very much like Leikung the thunder god. His other attributes also link him with the male clan-god-warrior concept whose image we have encountered among the steppe dwellers. It would seem therefore that the anthropomorphic sky god was assimilated to a dragon rain god and the whole synthesized in the rain cult.

Wing-Sou suggests a nomadic infiltration from the northwest into the Shang area about the end of the third millennium B.C. Although it is argued that there are almost no pastoral images in *The Book of Poetry,* we have seen that this is a late, sophisticated literature. Other traits in Shang culture do suggest nomadic psychology; the emphasis on animal sacrifice (vegetable offering only comes in later Chou times), development of the chariot and use of the horse, horse burial, an animal style in art, human sacrifice by beheading, as well as Ti, a warrior-sky god. Then, too, the emphasis on hunting as an aristocratic pastime is connected with the one significant bit of evidence, a sentence from one of the oracle bones: "The king must shoot an arrow into the bull for sacrifice," certainly hinting at the sacral hunt which, as we have seen, may be the origin of the sacrifice of domestic animals.

The earth deities, whom we would expect to be a separate cultural component, are not personified except when they blend into ancestor images. She or Tu was an earth god whose sex is not clear. The Chous heaped up a mound to symbolize this deity. Aside from these abstractions, sacrifices were made to the Huan River and the Yellow River. The sky gods were not clearly personified either, nor were they sacrificed to directly; they had to be reached through the ancestors as intermediaries.

Myth making as exemplified by the Chou records seems to take a historical direction; the deeds of early kings are treated in legendary fashion.

> Great is Ti,
> Beholding the lower world in majesty
> He surveyed the four quarters,
> Seeking for someone to give stability to the people.

Needless to say his choice was the Chou dynasty.

One ode, however, is a good example of late animistic myth making. It records the birth of the millet.

> The first birth of our people
> Was from Kéang Yuen.
> How did she give birth to our people?
> She presented a pure offering and sacrificed
> That she might no longer be barren.
> She trod on the print of Ti's big toe.
> In the great place where she rested
> She became pregnant; she lived in retirement;
> She gave birth to and nourished
> And this was Lord Millet.

The millet plant seems to have been identified with a Chou ancestor. The ode continues with a curious combination of personification and metaphor.

> When she had fulfilled her months
> Her first born came like a lamb
> With no bursting or rending
> With no hurt or harm—
> Showing how magical he would be.
> Did not Ti give her comfort?
> Did he not accept her pure offering and sacrifice
> So that early she brought forth her son?
> He was placed in a narrow lane
> But the sheep and oxen tenderly protected him.
> He was left in a wide forest
> Where he was met by the wood cutters.
> He was placed on cold ice
> But a bird screened and raised him on its wings.

When the bird flew away
Hou Tseih began to wail,
His cry was long and loud
So that his voice filled the whole countryside.

When he was able to crawl
He looked majestic and intelligent.
When he was able to feed himself
He took to planting large beans.
The beans grew fat and tall;
His paddy-lines were close-set;
His hemp and wheat grew strong;
His gourds yielded abundantly.

The poem ends with the statement that the child gave his people millet which was carried home for sacrifice and explains how it should be offered to him with the fat of a ram.

Interesting elements in the poem are the miraculous birth and the abandonment of the baby which is subsequently protected, also magically—details which occur in the biographies of heroes among so many peoples in other parts of the world, for instance in the tradition connected with Zeus and Herakles.

If ancestor worship became the synthesizing element in Chinese religion and was practiced, as we have seen, with a kind of Apollonian tranquillity and with magical insistence upon perfection of detail which would be automatically rewarded, there are nevertheless traces of more orgiastic practices. Dancing is often referred to as a part of ritual.

We sacrifice to the land and the four quarters.
That my fields are in such good condition
Is a matter of joy to my laborers.
With lutes and drums beating
We will invoke the sovereign earth
And pray for sweet rain . . .

Wing-Sou points out that fires were kindled in the rain ceremony to the accompaniment of the beating of drums and dancing. We know something of the musical instruments thanks to the excavation of the Shang tombs. The ocarina of bone or pottery encompassed the first five notes of the major scale; drums were made of hide and wood or bronze decorated with characteristic Shang motifs. Chiming stones which were struck together came in threes and were often made of jade. Bronze or pottery bells were tub-shaped with handles; these, too, often came in sets of three, decorated with the mythical animal mask. Apparently both pentatonic and tritonic scales were used together. One ode suggests that even the sacrificial knife was ornamented with bells.

The shamanistic character of the dancing is best exemplified by a song which describes what has been suggested is an exorcist in the process of driving out disease.

> Easy and indifferent! Easy and indifferent!
> I am ready to perform all the dances
> Yonder, when the sun is in the median,
> Yonder in that public place.
>
> I, large as a giant,
> I dance in the ducal courtyard;
> I am strong as a tiger;
> I hold the chariot reins in my grasp like
>   ribbons.
> In my left hand I hold a flute;
> In my right a pheasant's feather.
> I am red as if I were painted:
> The duke gives me a cup . . .

The phrase "strong as a tiger" even suggests that the dancer might be wearing a tiger mask. The reference to the midday sun must have ritual significance and the cup is, of course, both for ritual drinking and pouring a libation.

Like that of so many of the early civilizations we have been discussing, the Shang culture is a strange mixture—on the one hand human sacrifice, and on the other delicate love poems and a keen appreciation of the beauty of flowers. The court life of these ancient Chinese was certainly brilliant and dynamic, and its sights and sounds are preserved for us by the enduring magic of their verses.

> The princes are coming to court;
> I see their dragon flags—
> Their dragon flags are moving in the wind
> While the sound of their bells comes, hwuy-hwuy.
> There are the two outside horses; there are the
>   chariot teams—
> Proof that the princes are coming to court!

Africa

The Eye of the Falcon

Egypt—traces of early totemism—possible invasion and "dynastic race"—early cow sky goddess—animal gods from totemism—development and function of the sacral king—multiple animal symbolism—varied mythological tradition—unifying role and power of sacral king—castration theme in mythology—mana unites pantheon—development of grave cult—priesthood and ritual—divination and magic—sadness of life theme.

PYRAMIDS AND MUMMIES have long been synonyms for the most ancient form of civilization. In recent decades, however, since the investigation of Sumer, we begin to realize that the great culture of the Nile must have owed a good deal to the Tigris-Euphrates Valley. Yet, as the earlier layers of occupation have been unearthed, the puzzle of Egypt is far from being solved. How did a great theocratic empire arise in a span of time which, in comparison with events elsewhere, seems much too short?

As it has been worked out so far, there are several episodes in the story which are clear enough. The earliest traces of agriculture are found on the shores of an ancient lake just south of the Nile delta. Here in the fourth millennium B.C. there were hunters who did a little farming with the familiar flint-edged sickles. They also kept cattle, sheep and pigs, and stored their grain in coiled baskets buried in the ground. We know that they lived in villages since their flimsy huts were arranged in streets. They buried their dead in simple pits with few grave goods. Somewhat farther up the Nile at Badari, other hunter-farmers, a little later in the fourth millennium, buried their dead in oval trenches and wrapped the corpses in linen. Badarian women were sophisticated enough to plait their hair and put combs decorated with animal figures in it. Palettes containing red pigment suggest the use of cosmetics. From now on, palettes of stone will play an important role in the archaeological story. One curious habit of the Badarians which suggests a connection with later Egyptian customs is that of burying domestic animals, especially cattle, wrapped in textiles.

On top of the Badarian strata came the Naqada culture—by now small towns were in existence. Crude figures of animals were painted or scratched on pottery so frequently that they look like totem symbols. It seems then that each of the towns developing along the Nile valley was perhaps inhabited by a single clan.

After this we move to the mid-Nile region where irrigation for agricultural purposes began. In this period, the Gerzean, boats made of bundles of papyrus were plying the river, cast copper was used to make weapons and, for the first time, there is proof of a connection with the Near East. A copy of a Sumerian cylinder seal, stone axheads and knives technically similar to those made much earlier at Jericho, show that trading must have been going on. A knife handle found at the end of a desert route to the Red Sea shows a naval battle on one side and on the other a figure grasping two lions exactly like that on a basalt stele from Erech, in Sumer. All this takes us to the end of the fourth millennium, at which time urban civilization was already flourishing in Mesopotamia.

Now comes the big jump and what seems like an acceleration of history. Around 3200 B.C. we have evidence of an Egypt united under one king; cities have been founded, writing has been invented, imposing brick tombs have been constructed for kings and aristocrats, sculpture in the round has been achieved, and the main outlines of Egypt's complex religious institutions can already be discerned.

How did it all come about in the space of less than a millennium? No architectural sequence has been found, leading from the villages to cities with great tombs, like that worked out in the development of the Sumerian temple.

One solution is the theory of an invasion by a "dynastic race." The testimony of the knife handle has been adduced; in the sea battle depicted, Egyptian ships sail on one side, on the other those with high prows and sterns of Mesopotamian design. Graves also show that burials in northern Egypt contained skeletons with larger skulls and larger over-all dimensions than those of the early hunter-farmers. The difference in burial customs between the new rulers and the commoners is also striking. Mesopotamian invaders might have entered Egypt in a series of waves either from the delta in the north or at mid-Egypt near Coptos. Various states would have resulted, with struggles for leadership, and this is borne out by tradition which tells us that there were two kingdoms, one in the south and one in the north, with the latter at first dominant. Carved stone maceheads preserve records of these wars which ended with the south triumphant. The ruling group which unified the country was traditionally known as "the followers of Horus" (the falcon god). If the invasion theory is correct, these would have been of Mesopotamian stock. At any rate, a stone palette shows a certain Narmer, already in the traditional stance of a triumphal Egyptian monarch, wearing the crowns of both north and south, about to beat a prostrate enemy over the head with a stone mace. Narmer apparently married a northern princess to consolidate his position and either he or his son Hor-aha was the founder of the first dynasty and given the ceremonial name of Menes. Menes established a new capital for the united country at Memphis.

Eventually it was the institution of the sacral king which created a coherent nation. We have seen the ceremonial identification of king and state in Sumer and Babylonia; in Egypt kingship was total. Not only was political power identified with sacral authority but economic life as well. Private ownership was only a temporary grant from the monarch who could revoke the holdings of his vassals at will. Hence all trade was a royal monopoly controlled by the state. Likewise every official was subservient to the sacral state and obliged to carry out whatever function was assigned to him.

A literate priesthood shaped official mythology to strengthen the royal office. The king was identified with the gods of creation. He was the impersonation of *maat* (order, justice, truth) and the enemies over whom he always triumphed represented chaos and evil. Thus in mythology Set, who had once been the beneficent god of a large group of the population, was turned into a symptom of evil disorder. In the static Egyptian world the only dynamic was the cycle of the seasons. The king was not thought of as a personal despot but as an unchanging symbol. An instance of this is a stele depicting the triumph of the king over Libyan chiefs whose names are enumerated. Two hundred years later another king is shown defeating the same list of chiefs! The king was supposed to possess magic powers of divination; myths recounted miraculous omens before a successful battle. The world in this framework was totally Egyptian-centered; Egyptians, symbolized by the divine majesty, were always right; aliens, symbols of disorder, were always defeated in war. By this time it will be seen what a curiously close parallel prevails between the ancient Egyptian and the modern Marxist state. The self-centered assumption of perfection is familiar and the complete dedication to the state only differs in that the Egyptians justified it by supernatural explanations. Ancient man was able to muster his loyalties to what he believed was the highest good of the community in terms of poetic metaphor and visual symbols, while the modern citizen is motivated by abstract political theory. It is significant that there are no indications of popular uprising in Egypt even though the army and the labor force were also the personal property of the king and the building of massive tombs and continual wars of conquest must have constituted an onerous burden. The fact remains that the institution of the sacral kingship held the country together for three millennia, far longer than any other barbaric state on record.

As the problem of animal gods in Egypt involves totemism, the character of both religion and the state can only be understood in terms of primitive origins. V. Gordon Childe, in writing of the predynastic villages of the Badarian-Naqada period, remarked, "They appear grouped in apparently autonomous villages each perhaps occupied by a totemic clan. Later the totems, the animals, plants or natural objects from which the villagers may have believed themselves descended, became the emblems and standards of the counties or *nomes* into which Egypt was divided in historical times." Finally, to the late Gerzean phase "belong a series of ivories and slate palettes carved with pictures of animals in combat, mythological versions of struggles between totemic clans and in particular the victories of the Falcon clan."

The nome symbols in the prehistoric epoch decorated vases, ships and primitive constructions and persisted in historic times. On the Hunters' Palette the falcon standard is carried at the head of a procession. The standards even reach out hands to grasp prisoners. The nome symbols have been identified with local animal gods; for instance, that of Assiut was the wolf, while Bast, the cat or lioness, was none number ten of the north. According to Jacques Vandier, "This ensemble of circumstances can only be explained if the ensigns discussed represent the oldest gods of Egypt and it is logical to consider that the nomes originally constituted not just administrative divisions but zones of religious influence." Later came a growing anthropomorphism, animal-headed gods appeared, and finally the animal attribute was reduced to a symbolic headdress such as horns.

The oldest god represented in sculptural form, that of the ithyphallic Min, is human. Now stone statues of Min were found at Coptos and date from the Gerzean phase. Coptos, it should be remembered, is at the termination of a trade route across the Red Sea which may possibly have been a point of Mesopotamian invasion. Henri Gauthier, in his study of the cult of Min, describes the god's festival in which a white bull was sacrificed with special dances and hymns at harvest time. It is clear from the texts that Min was identified with a bull. It will be remembered that the bull-god image from Umma, Sumeria, was also ithyphallic.

The falcon was already the god and nome symbol of Hierakonpolis before the unification. The conquering kings assumed the symbol as an emblem of royalty. The falcon was not the only animal symbol identified with the conquering kings. On Narmer's palette we see a bull personifying the king trampling on a defeated enemy and destroying a fortified enclosure. Likewise on both sides of the top of the palette are cows' heads with human faces. Another ceremonial palette, in fragmentary form, shows the divine bull in the same attitude of conquest. In addition, during the first dynasty the bull god Apis, associated with Memphis, appears in a fertility ceremony. Judging from the double bull depicted on the Hunters' Palette and the fact that the bull was the insignia for the tenth nome of the south, bull worship existed before the unification. The association of the divine king with the bull god, however, is remarkably similar to the state of affairs in both Mesopotamia and Syria. It might well be that the concept was a pre-unification importation (like the cult of Min), or, if the dynastic race theory is accepted, that the invading chiefs were divine bulls and the cult was assimilated to a less developed indigenous use.

If Min be ruled out as a foreigner, there is, however, evidence for an early goddess. Three nude female figures, with the delta outlined, have been recovered from the Badarian site which remind us of the figures found in Neolithic areas elsewhere. From the Naqada level large-hipped female figures in limestone occur. The Gerzean culture indicated more of a break in tradition and seems to have been spread by conquest. From this level, figures of a goddess with upraised arms, sometimes tattooed with animal and chevron designs, have been recovered. A stylized female figure in the same posture appears on pottery. Moreover, the ceremonial slate palettes began to show both the head of a cow, horns, ears, and the tuft of hair between the horns marked by stars, and also a female figure with upraised arms, stars marking the hands, head, and breasts. Thus both cow and female image appear to be equated with a constellation. A connection between this and the Nut-Hather concept of the mother goddess in later Egypt (Nut is depicted as the sky bending over the earth, her body spangled with stars, and also as a cow with the sun boat sailing below) suggests a continuous development from very early times. A Naqada standard, depicted in a rock drawing as a pole with a cow's head on top, also may be evidence of the early cow-mother cult. There is again a possibility of influence from Mesopotamia. At Al 'Ubaid a mother goddess who became Ninhursag was the guardian of the fecundity of the fields and from her was drawn holy milk which nourished the sacred dairy herd at the Lagash temple. The temple of Ninhursag at Ur dates from the first dynasty of the late fourth millennium but her worship is so elaborately established that it is evident the cult must have existed for a considerable time. It could therefore have predated the cow-mother cult in Egypt.

Cattle have played and still play an extraordinary role in religious life among the Nilotic and Bantu tribes of East Africa. It seems that they did so in ancient Egypt. If in Mesopotamia the heritage from the pastoral age was an emphasis on the bull, in Egyptian civilization both cow and bull continued as important symbolic elements in psychic life. Undoubtedly environment had something to do with creating different lines of development. The Mesopotamian rivers were prone to unexpected flood, rain was often unpredictable and sometimes torrential. The Mesopotamian outlook was in consequence dramatic, shot through with doubt and fear, and pessimistic. The sky god was a thunderer, a bellowing bull. In contrast, the Egyptians were used to clear, cloudless skies in which the stars were prominent. The Nile flood came predictably every year bringing fertility with it. The Egyptians' static view of life was conditioned by this dependable rhythm. They had no need of a rain god or a thunderer. In fact their notion of rain was "the Nile in the sky." Their chief sky god was the star-tattooed, life-giving body of a woman or a cow.

The fact that the Egyptian harvest festival was connected with Min, the ithyphallic bull, suggests foreign influence. The equating of Osiris who is killed and resurrected with the sprouting grain and Isis's role in resurrecting him, although it takes a special Egyptian form (conditioned by the Nile flood and the role of the sun), parallels the Mesopotamian death of the god although Osiris was not originally a grain spirit.

Even though both Min and the cow-mother seem to have achieved human form in predynastic times, this in no way precludes the parallel development of animal gods from the totemic nome symbols. The evolution of culture is never particularly consistent and, in the religious sphere especially, the concrete and the abstract, the archaic and the sophisticated, can and do exist side by side; indeed the religion of Egypt is a notable example.

In this connection something should be said concerning Egyptian inconsistency and the mythopoeic imagination. It is clear that Egyptian religion grew out of many cults and diverse elements. Conflicting myths and images appear in the same ritual documents. Henri Frankfort points out that the myth-making imagination is emotional thinking, a process in which logic plays a minor role and consequently conflicting ideas and images do not disturb the primitive or barbaric worshiper. Actually this is a point which has been stressed by literary critics for the last forty years. Modern poets have consciously made use of multiple and even apparently conflicting imagery. What the poet is doing is using qualities in the images which emotionally relate to the concept he is creating. Similarly, for the Egyptians, the sky could be a goddess with hands and feet touching the earth, or a cow, or an object supported on four posts, or a marsh of rushes. All of these images represented some part of their feeling about the sky. In the same way the king, in the Pyramid Texts, goes up to heaven in various forms.

> Upon the empty throne which is thy boat, O Re,
> The king has flown as a cloud to heaven;
> The king has kissed the sky as a falcon;
> The king has reached the sky as a grasshopper which the
>   sun makes invisible.

These images contain emotional value as symbols; the falcon, for instance, standing for the sun, royal triumph, and absolute power, while the bird form was associated with the Ba, the immaterial spirit which survived death.

To return to the divine king, the central focus of Egyptian religion, there is a reasonable amount of evidence for a totemic origin of his power. Alexandre Moret argues that the development of central authority is gradual. Among the totemic clans of Australia the old men wield a generalized authority in ceremonial matters. In the Iroquois clan system, personal prestige resulted in elective war chiefs and sachems. Among the Northwest Indians of America, as the tribal chief accumulated wealth through inheritance and potlatch ceremonies and the totem became a family crest, his prestige was dependent upon his magico-religious experience. His position was also hereditary. Moret believed that in Egypt "the chief sorcerer of former days, becoming step by step the priest king, now rises to the rank of god king."

That the divine king's office derived much of its force from a long tradition of magic is made clear by the Sed ceremony. This sometimes took place thirty years after the king came to power or, in earlier times, at shorter intervals. It appears to have been a symbolic development of the rite of killing the ruler when his vital powers declined.

It was Frazer who first suggested that the Egyptian king was ritually killed. C. G. Seligman, investigating the Nilotic tribes among whom sacral kingship seemed to be either related to Egyptian culture or derived from it, cited actual cases of such ritual murders. Apparently among the Shilluk the king was strangled when his sexual potency failed. Among the Dinka, the aged rainmaker chief was laid in a cell built in a grave. He ate millet and drank milk, then threw the remainder to the east, and announced that he was going to his fathers but he left food for his children. A cow rope was placed around his neck. He held a spear in his hand. This was taken by his son, whose task it was to strangle him.

In the Sed festival special buildings were erected in which the king changed his dress and insignia and in which purification rites took place. Various civil and religious dignitaries were gathered together. The statues of the gods arrived from all over the country on barges. (We are reminded in some respects of the Babylonian Akitu.) The king visited a number of shrines and paid homage to the gods. Among the priests who officiated in the ceremonies were the wolf nome followers of Upwauet who wore caps adorned with the head and tail of a wolf (another reminiscence of totemic-sorcerer dress), and the worshipers of the crocodile, Sobek, also a nome god. The king eventually paid a visit to the shrine of the bull, Apis, and then anointed the wolf standard. He then changed into the archaic kilt with the bull's tail. The central episode was a ritual race or dance four times around the boundaries of a "field" which symbolized Egypt. A goddess clapped her hands in time to his steps, while the wolf standard was carried behind him. The four circuits had to be completed once for the north and once for the south. This constituted a reassertion of his authority and a magical rejuvenation of his fertility-giving power. In the final act of the ceremony the king shot four arrows, one to each point of the compass. The god Set is shown guiding his bow. Since there is no mention of Osiris in this ceremony, it probably dates back to the early years of the unification.

The unquestioned acceptance of the authority of the sacral king can therefore be best explained as the result of clan and tribal unity, always authenticated by magical tradition, in terms of a single symbolic figure. In time this figure came to be strengthened by the association of several theological systems. Emblems which were originally derived from psychological identification with animals came to assume a more abstract significance just as the cross, the star, or the crescent became a psychic focus in existing religions.

Before discussing the hieratical meanings of the animal symbols it is necessary to examine the general theological systems which were developed by the priesthoods. As the nomes were grouped together, pantheons tended to form, and as priesthood and royal power grew, various local gods were elevated to cosmic status. Some cosmic ideas, however, may have already existed, as in the case of the sky goddess or cow-mother. Central to all organized thinking was the falcon, Horus, the emblem of royal authority. He was identified with the sun, Re, and in turn associated with the worship of the sun disk which was maintained by the priesthood of Heliopolis. The final result was the disk with wings. In the earliest cosmology Nut, the sky goddess, and Geb, the earth, formed a couple who gave birth to Re. Each day Nut received Re, hid him during the night and gave him forth at dawn. The priesthood elaborated this still further. According to their system the sun, self-created, came out of liquid chaos, Nun. He was called both Atum and Re. By masturbating he created the first couple, Shu and Tefnut, air and moisture. These two gave birth to Geb and Nut and they, in turn, to Osiris, Isis, Set and Nephthys. Significantly, when the sun emerged it rested upon a mountain near Heliopolis, which gave this area the right to govern the world. (The mountain is also equated with emerging mounds of Nile mud which appear after the fertilizing flood begins to subside.)

Sometime during the second dynasty a significant rebellion took place, led by a chieftain of the god Set, a nome god from the south. It has been suggested that Set was a symbol of the indigenous people rebelling against the dynastic race. Actually the Set animal is a puzzle. Its body when seated is distinctly doglike, but its tail always stands up straight and is either forked at the tip or tripartite. Its head terminates in a curved drooping snout while its ears are erect and square at the top. Various unconvincing attempts have been made to identify it as a mouse, jackal, anteater, greyhound, okapi, or giraffe.

The Set rebellion is significant for cosmogony because a rival theology in connection with it emanated from Hermopolis. In this system four couples, four frogs and four snakes, created an egg. The egg was placed on a mountain near Hermopolis and from it the sun emerged. The latter detail, of course, was to prove that the center of world power belonged in the south instead of at Heliopolis.

When, during the unification, Memphis was established as the capital of the whole kingdom, it became necessary to make the local god, Ptah, a part of the system. This god, who was always anthropomorphic, seems to be a late creation. He produced Atum-Re from his tongue, teeth and lips. It is stressed that this creation by the word is a more abstract and intellectual concept than the earlier onanistic one.

The Egyptians often assumed a coercive attitude toward their deities, even threatening them. In a so-called "cannibal hymn" the deceased is depicted as a magician who "eats the magic and devours the glory" of any gods who may oppose his entry into the other world. The average Egyptian felt himself surrounded by many forces, some friendly, some unfriendly. He was obliged to be careful not to arouse the latter and when he did he had recourse to magic to control them.

The Egyptians, being inherently symbolic thinkers yet with a penchant for the concrete and specific, created a kind of animal rhetoric. Strangely enough, the lioness goddesses seem to assimilate easily to the peaceful mother concept, even to Hathor. Both the hippopotamus and the crocodile had a dual nature. In their harmful manifestation they were associated with the hostile element in Set. The crocodile was particularly shameless, aggressive and greedy. The jackal, Anubis, became the god of the cemetery, perhaps because it devoured corpses. The ibis, the heron and the Nile goose, being winged, tended to be symbols for the spirit or soul. The ibis eventually developed into Thot, the scribe and moon god. The snake goddess, Wadjet, was a protector and fertility symbol which became the Uraeus on the red crown of northern Egypt, and Nekhbet, the vulture goddess of southern Egypt, was the tutelary goddess of the white crown. Animals thought of as generated from the earth were used as symbols of Atum-Re, among them the frog which emerged from the Nile mud and the scarab beetle which rolled a ball of dung containing its eggs and thus provided a ready-made image of the sun. The tendency toward monotheism which developed as Egyptian civilization grew older was achieved not by simplification (Ikhnaton's bold attempt to introduce the sun disk was rejected) but by making all minor symbols equivalent to a few major ones; in other words, everything stood for everything else, and the whole complex structure became a kind of pantheism through polytheism.

This gradual interweaving of themes comes about with the development of two chief mythological cycles. The first, dealing with Re, is largely the creation of the Heliopolis priesthood. Re is repeatedly menaced by rebels both human and divine. Vandier suggests that this is a reflection of both political tensions and the periodical disappearance of the sun. A council of the gods including Shu, Tefnut, Geb, Nut and Nun urges him to direct his eye toward the rebels. He does so and makes them flee to the desert. Hathor is sent down to continue the fight. She proceeds to massacre mankind. Re, deciding that some should be saved, is obliged to find some way of diverting Hathor. He spreads a red beer over the fields. Hathor, returning the next day to continue the destruction, tries the beer, acquires a taste for it and drinks so much that she is no longer able to recognize the men whom she wishes to destroy. Re's troubles continue, however, until he decides to retire from the government of the world. His daughter, Nut, the heavenly cow, carries him up to heaven on her back but gets dizzy in the process so that her stomach has to be held up by Shu. This explains the arrangement of earth, air, sky, and sun. Re is succeeded by Shu who, in spite of a beneficent rule, has to fight with the sons of Apophis (these symbolized enemies on the eastern frontier). After a brilliant victory he falls ill and a palace revolution causes him to turn over the throne to Geb and to join Re in the sky. Geb also becomes involved in warfare and tries to use the Uraeus serpent against his enemies but the serpent turns against him, kills some of his courtiers and bites Geb. The latter is miraculously cured, re-established on the throne, and pacifies the country.

Other tales are concerned with the eye of Horus. Horus as the defender of Re in one version campaigns against the hippopotamuses and crocodiles of Set. In another version he is involved in personal combat with Set, who tears out his eye. Horus, in turn, tears off Set's testicles. Set is finally vanquished and forced to return the eye of Horus. One of Horus's eyes is the sun, the other the moon. It is interesting that the conflict-in-heaven theme here appears with a kind of double castration elaboration, once more proving that profound sexual rivalry shapes a good deal of primitive mythology. We shall see another example of this presently.

Another myth cycle, which probably arose later, is believed to have a historical germ. Basically the Osiris legend deals with a king whose brother Set kills him out of jealousy. His wife, Isis, has a posthumous child, Horus, who, when he grows up, avenges his father. To this factual base was added the dying-god-who-is-resurrected theme but symbolizing both the birth of the grain after the Nile flood and the entry of the king (and, later, all Egyptians) into eternal life. According to the elaborated myth, Set aided by Thot traps Osiris and kills him, sometimes throwing him into the water, sometimes tearing his body to pieces. The gods are saddened by his death, Isis his wife being inconsolable. She and Nephthys wander through the entire country seeking the body of the dead king. It is finally found, Nut puts it together, and the gods give it life. Isis, in the form of a vulture, settles on the dead body of her husband and becomes miraculously pregnant, giving birth to Horus. When he grows up, his struggles with Set take place. Although the outline of Isis's search for the dead king is vaguely reminiscent of Mesopotamia, she, too, was not originally a creation of the vegetation cycle. She is believed to have originated as a personification of the royal throne and also as a goddess of a local town close to the home of the Osiris cult. She also assimilated the maternal qualities of the Hathor-Nut entity. Actually the assimilation of god to god is best understood in terms of the Ka which was a general power, spirit or supernatural force which inhabited both gods and men. If this be defined in terms of mana, then, since the gods shared the same supernatural force, it was easy to think of one in terms of the other.

Egyptian mythology, however, did not lead to a religious epic literature. Apparently the epics remained an oral folk creation, a body of legend which was drawn on by the priests as they spun their complicated theology. There is a certain parallel to the *Rigveda,* in that myths can be pieced together from the funeral hymns of the Pyramid Texts. A New Kingdom story of the struggle between Horus and Set is interesting for the archaic elements which still persist. In the *Contending of Horus and Set,* the Ennead is the council of nine gods consisting of Atum, Shu, Tefnut, Geb, Nut, Osiris, Isis, Set and Nephthys. The last four are the offspring of Geb and Nut but during the tale Set is sometimes regarded as the older brother of Horus, and at times as his uncle. It is as an older brother that he first comes before the Master of the Universe (Atum-Re) and claims the throne since Osiris now dwells in the other world. Horus is disqualified because he is a little child with weak legs, but he loudly claims the throne. Thot, who is acting as court clerk, agrees that Horus is in the right. Atum-Re angrily favors Set but Isis is delighted. Set, who is characterized as a stupid lout, wants to fight it out as the council vacillates. The goat god, when consulted, suggests writing a letter to Neith (another manifestation of the sky goddess and here described as Re's mother). Neith writes back that Horus should have the throne but Set's possessions should be doubled and he should also receive Anat and Astarte (borrowed from Canaan) as a part of his consolation prize. The sun god is still angry, at which point an obscure god, Babai, rises and insults him, saying his shrine is empty. The sun god leaves the council to sulk; the latter expels Babai and goes to its tents.

> And the great god passed a day lying upon his back in his arbor, and his heart was very sore and he was alone.
>
> And after a long space, Hathor, the lady of the southern sycamore, came and stood before her father, the Master of the Universe, and she uncovered her sex before his face.
>
> And the great god laughed at her.

Her gesture, which reminds us of a burlesque show, is so hilarious that the sun god's good humor is restored and he goes back to work. Horus now uses the argument that Set is his uncle and not the direct heir to the throne; the Ennead is split and Isis curses the council. Set, in a very Ares-like mood, announces that he will take his 4,500-pound scepter and kill one of the gods a day, and besides he will not contend in the tribunal as long as Isis is present. They accordingly move the court to Island-in-the-Midst, giving strict orders that no woman is to be allowed to land.

> And the Ennead crossed over to Island-in-the-Midst and they sat down and ate bread.
>
> Thereupon Isis came and she drew nigh unto the ferryman as he sat nearby in his boat and she had changed herself into an aged woman and she went along bowed down. And a little ring of gold was on her finger. And she spoke to him: I have come unto thee that thou mayest ferry me across to Island-in-the-Midst, for I have come with this jar of flour for the little lad. He has been looking after some cattle in the Island-in-the-Midst for five days until today and he is hungry.
>
> And he spoke to her: It was said unto me, do not ferry any woman across. And she spoke to him: Was it said to thee on account of Isis, this that thou hast told me? And he spoke to her: What wilt thou give me that I may ferry thee across to Island-in-the-Midst?

First she offered him a loaf which he refused but finally succeeded in buying him with the gold ring.

> And while she was going beneath the trees, she looked and saw the Ennead as they sat and ate bread in the presence of the Master of the Universe in his arbor.
>
> And Set looked and he saw her as she was coming from afar off.
>
> Thereupon she uttered an incantation with her magic and she changed herself into a maiden with fair limbs and there was not the like of her in the entire land.

And he loved her sorely.

Thereupon Set rose up, and he sat down and ate bread with the great Ennead and he went to overtake her and no one had seen her except him.

Thereupon he stood behind a tree and he cried to her: I am here with thee, fair maiden. And she spoke to him: Nay, my great lord! As for me I was the wife of a herdsman of cattle and I bore unto him a male child. And my husband died and the stripling came to be after the cattle of his father. [Throughout the story there is a pun on the word cattle which is the same as the word for kingship.] Then a foreigner came and he sat down by my byre and thus he spoke to my son: I will beat thee and I will take away the cattle of thy father and I will cast thee forth. Thus he spoke to him. But my wish is to make thee act for him [my son] as a champion.

And Set spoke to her: Shall the cattle be given to a foreigner while the son of the good man is yet alive?

And Isis changed herself into a vulture and she flew up and perched on top of an acacia. And she called to Set and she said unto him: Weep for thyself; it is thine own mouth that hath said, it is thine own cleverness which hath judged thee. What aileth thee now?

And he stood aweeping . . .

Set went blubbering to the council, repeated the story, and was told it was his own fault. He still complained, however, and got the ferryman beaten. The wandering tribunal then met in the mountains. At this point the sun god changed sides and gave Horus the crown. Set screamed that the crown should be taken off, and Horus should be thrown into the water so that they could fight. The sun god obligingly agreed. In the form of hippopotamuses they had a contest to determine who should stay under water the longest. Isis became worried and tried to harpoon Set but hit Horus. She freed him and harpooned Set. The latter now appealed for mercy as her brother. She released him.

Thereupon Horus, the son of Isis, was angry with his mother, Isis, and he went forth and his face was savage like a panther of Upper Egypt and his chopper of 16 pounds was in his hand. And he removed the head of his mother, Isis, and he put it in his bosom and he ascended into the mountains.

Thereupon Isis changed herself into a statue of flint with no head.

The sun god demanded that Horus be punished. Set pursued him and found him under a tree and wrenched out his eyes, which became lotus bulbs. Hathor cured his eyes with gazelle's milk. The sun god then told

Set and Horus to be quiet for a while. Surprisingly they went to bed together.

And in the night Set caused his member to become stiff and he made it go between the buttocks of Horus.

Thereupon Horus put his two hands between his thighs and he caught the seed of Set.

Thereupon Horus went to speak to his mother, Isis: Come unto me, O Isis, my mother and see this which Set has done to me! And he opened his hand and he caused her to see the seed of Set. And she cried out aloud, and she seized her knife and she cut off his hand and she cast it into the water. And she drew out for him a hand of like worth.

Thereupon she took a dab of sweet ointment and put it upon the member of Horus.

Thereupon she caused it to become stiff; it was put into a pot and he made his seed to run down into it.

Thereupon Isis went with the seed of Horus in the morning to the garden of Set and she spoke to the gardener of Set: What herb is it that Set doth eat here with thee? And the gardener spoke to her: He doth not eat any herb here with me except lettuce. And Isis put the seed of Horus upon them.

And Set came after his fashion of every day and he ate the lettuce which he regularly used to eat.

And he arose pregnant with the seed of Horus.

And Set went to speak to Horus: Come, let us go in order that I may contend with thee in the tribunal.

Thereupon the two went to the tribunal and they stood before the great Ennead and they were told: Speak concerning yourselves.

Thereupon Set said: Let there be given unto me the office of ruler, for to Horus, the same that standeth here, have I performed mighty deeds of war against him.

Thereupon the Ennead cried out aloud and they belched and spat before the face of Horus.

Thereupon Horus laughed at them.

Thereupon Horus made an oath to god, saying: False is all that Set hath said. Let the seed of Set be summoned that we may see whence it will answer. And let mine own be summoned that we may see whence it will answer.

Thereupon Thot, the lord of divine words, the scribe of truth, of the Ennead placed his hand on the arm of Horus and he said: Come forth, thou seed of Set! And it answered him from the water in the fen.

Thereupon Thot placed his hand upon the arm of Set and he said: Come forth, thou seed of Horus!

Thereupon it spoke to him: Where shall I come forth?

Thereupon Thot said to it: Come forth from his ear.

And it spoke to him: Shall I come forth from his ear, I who am a divine effluence?

Thereupon Thot said to it: Come forth from his forehead.

Thereupon it came forth as a sun of gold upon the head of Set.

The story continues with more conflicts between the two contestants.

Aside from the sophisticated relish in a bawdy tale, the tale combines the incongruous magic of the folk legend with truly archaic violence. The cutting off of Horus's hand and his mother's head is as brutal as the cosmic creation myths and apparently no contradiction was felt between it and the protective mother-and-son relationship which is the substance of the narrative. The symbolic castration of Horus appears again with the elaboration that his eyes become lotus bulbs. More curious is the sodomical episode with the subsequent pregnancy of Set after swallowing the seed of Horus. The parallel with the Hurrian Kumarbi myth is striking. Efforts have been made to find a record of actual abuse of war captives but Set's boast may be merely a metaphor.

The castrating by swallowing of testicles causing pregnancy which is related to the swallowing of semen could well carry us back to ritual cannibalism. We have already seen that the penis of a vanquished warrior is sometimes removed to be used as a charm to promote virility and courage. In one of the episodes of the Egyptian coronation drama, Horus is handed two maces which symbolize Set's testicles torn off by him in their conflict. Horus is told, "Engraft these testicles upon thyself! Thereby increase still more thy potency!" When Kumarbi swallows his father's testicles the same magically cannibal idea may be behind it. In the case of *The Contending of Horus and Set* the added elaboration of sodomy seems to show that in ancient mythology there was a deep-rooted drive to reduce competing males to female status which could be dramatized either by castration or sodomy. It has been mentioned before that Geza Roheim considered circumcision to be a symbolic castration attack upon the young men of the tribe by their elders. There is a moderately well authenticated report that in ancient times the Hottentots of South Africa removed one testicle from their youths in the puberty ceremony. The Wahehe (northeast coastal Bantu) after a battle place the testicles of the men they have killed on their spearpoints and display them to their chief, while the Bantu of Rhodesia cut the testicles from slain enemies and eat them. It is said a coward would then be forced to vomit but the heart of a brave man would be strengthened. Apparently hostility and sexual assault are fundamentally associated.

The myth just cited combines the Horus-Set dualism with the Osiris story and the ever-present theme of royal authority. In the eclectic Egyptian religion, ancestor worship and the cult of the dead both centered about the divine king. As we should expect, funeral cults are present in predynastic times. In the Naqada burials five skulls were found set up on a pile of stones like those of Monte Circeo, and headless skeletons were also recovered. The Osiris myth mentions that when the god's body was dismembered by Set the head was said to have been preserved and buried at Abydos, placed in a coffer surmounted by two plumes and mounted on a staff. This may be a memory of ancient head veneration. Although the head was not removed after mummification was adopted, in the fourth dynasty a substitute head sculptured in limestone or mud was placed in the burial chamber to secure continuance of this most important part of the body when the actual corpse decayed. This is probably the origin of the portrait statues which appear in so many tombs.

Mummification began in primitive form by wrapping the body in linen. The Badarians did this to cattle; later, the kings of the first dynasty were also carefully wrapped. In the second dynasty the bandages were molded to the face, torso and limbs in such a way as to preserve the shape of the flesh after the body had decayed. This was done by soaking the linen in gummy material. The features of the dead were thus modeled in detail as were all of the limbs, even the fingers and sexual parts.

The *mastaba,* or sun-dried brick tomb, which was used through the archaic period and preceded the pyramid, began as a shallow pit in which a series of brick-walled rooms were erected; the central one was for burial, the others held grave goods. This was roofed with timber beams and the mouth of the pit filled with rubble. Above this, on the leveled ground, the mastaba was a rectangular mass of brickwork containing rooms for the deposit of less valuable grave goods. The exterior was recessed in elaborate panels which foreshadowed the pylons of the later stone temples. It was also gaily painted in patterns derived from the woven matting which was used on the external walls of dwellings. On the north side of the building there was a long oval brick structure which contained the wooden funeral boat provided to take the spirit of the owner on his voyage with the sun god. The graves of commoners were simply oval pits with rounded corners surmounted by a low mound, containing a few simple grave goods.

Just as in the early barbaric stage of Sumer and of the Shang culture, human grave goods accompanied the dead king. These were the king's retainers, officials, and women of the harem, placed in subsidiary graves around the royal tomb. In the burial of Zer, the second or third king of the first dynasty, there were 338 of these. G. A. Reisner wrote:

> In the case of ordinary subsidiary burial the person dies an ordinary death and is buried in a grave prepared by the king or master in anticipation of his death. In the case of sati-burial the person is buried alive or put to death at the funeral of his master. The only difference is that the sati-burial permits the person concerned to pass at once with the master into the world of spirits and to continue without interruption his service to his master.

Sati burial ceased in the pyramid age but a symbolical remnant lingered; the images of servants occupied with their tasks have been recovered from later tombs. In 1923, however, Reisner excavated the tomb of an Egyptian governor of a border station at Kerma, in Nubia. Here in the provinces the custom had lingered in Middle Kingdom times in its cruelest form. There was no mummification, but the body of the aristocrat reclined on a bed and around it lay the skeletons of harem women, nobles and attendants and also a certain number of skeletons of rams. Altogether, Prince Hetzefa took nearly five hundred people with him into the spirit world. The bodies lay in convulsive positions produced by fear and the agony of suffocation. One young woman had crept under the bed. Yet such was the strength of their religious belief that they had immolated themselves willingly. Reisner envisaged a great crowd at the funeral rites who, at the end, rushed in with baskets of earth and accomplished the ritual murder in a few minutes. After this they all took part in a funeral banquet at which many oxen were slaughtered.

Thus the old diminished-life concept lived on and proliferated with the multiplication of grave goods and the elaboration of ponderous tombs for royalty and aristocrats while, at the same time, theology and myth elaborated a nonmaterial resurrection in the sky. Added to this and growing more important in later times was the Osiris theme.

The Pyramid Texts, however, indicate that the king's journey to heaven was fraught with certain dangers. The otherworld is faintly indicated as subterranean in some early inscriptions but later the stellar concept becomes dominant. Although the king was already a god, some purification was necessary. The king ascended, generally as a bird, to the eastern sky on the way to the marsh of rushes. There was a lake in the way. He was interrogated by the helmsman of the sun boat as to his credentials. Here he was able to use magic. He passed on in the boat to become the equal of his divine father the sun god who traveled in the boat over the sky.

The king is purified in the Marsh of Rushes.
The hand of the king is the hand of Re, Nut takes his arm;
Shu lifts him up, Shu lifts him up.

O Geb, bull of Nut, the king is a Horus, heir of his father . . .

Having been assimilated to the god, the king sat on his throne and exercised his old privileges. His subjects were probably the privileged aristocrats who were thought of as becoming the stars surrounding the North
Star, a symbol of permanence because they never set. The king's ancestors
played a role in helping him to ascend to heaven and, since they were
also divine, he merged with them at death. When he became identified with
the sun he avoided extinction by becoming a part of the sun's rhythm; as
Osiris he also avoided the finality of death by becoming a part of the
vegetation cycle. Osiris likewise stood for every dead king.

The divine king was thought of in highly concrete terms as the son of
the sun god. At the time of his conception, the god actually entered his
father and physically impregnated his mother. At the same time he was
also thought of as self-created in terms of being the bull of his mother.
In other words, the sun god enters his mother, impregnates her, re-creates
himself and is suckled by her in terms of the cow-mother. Thus the resurrection of the king and the funeral cult combined the solar theme, the
Osiris theme and the cow-mother theme which was probably the oldest.

The intertwining of the various symbolic themes in their most baroque
form is also exemplified in the coronation play which was written down
in 1970 B.C. but which is considered to date to the beginning of the first
dynasty. It is therefore the earliest drama known. Two other plays of the
same ritual nature are extant and all show that Egyptian dramaturgy, perhaps because of its static view of life, never got beyond the germinal
quem quaeritis type of action which is familiar to us from the Middle Ages.
In other words, it is a scenario for a series of ritual episodes but there are
no real characters, story, or development. The coronation play was celebrated in conjunction with New Year ceremonies during a royal cruise by
barge down the Nile. It was enacted at several cities; indeed some of the
episodes are designed for particular cities, the king at each site paying
homage to the god of the town. Both the Horus and Set conflict and the
Horus succeeding Osiris themes are merged with the real king's succession.
Actually all scenes are equivalent although the symbols and properties
change. The forty-six which are extant consist of a description of the
episode, a mythological explanation, a sacred conversation and stage directions. Horus's eye or eyes are returned to him fourteen times in various
forms. As grain and as loaves of bread, their fertility significance points

up the fact that the original loss of the eye was symbolic castration. The play is full of mana; like the Sed festival, its rituals have magic efficacy; fertility is reasserted, and the new king integrated once more into myth and administration as the sacral unifying force which dominated all of Egyptian life.

The priesthood which played such an important role in the development of the complex Egyptian religious observance was divided into hierarchies. At Memphis and Hermopolis the high priests had many honorific titles. They represented the king in carrying out cult activities. They were actually chosen by the king, but a complicated performance was publicly staged in which they were oracularly chosen by the god. Their assistants constituted the highest rank; below these were less important functionaries who tended the statues, and lectors who read the liturgies. Pious laymen contributed part-time service and also material goods to satisfy the needs of the priesthood. Among the women attached to the temples were concubines of the gods (probably sacred courtesans), singers, musicians, and dancers.

The earliest temples were not different from the private dwelling house, huts surrounded by a fence before which were planted tall standards with banners. The sun worship at Heliopolis took place in an open court containing an obelisk with an offering table at its base. Outside was a great solar ship of dried brick. There is little record of the baked-brick temples equivalent to the mastaba tombs but they must have been built with recessed façades like the palaces. Finally the great stone structures, with gates flanked by recessed stone pylons, on whose tops staffs and banners were placed, were developed in the shape of a closed court with pillared colonnades; inside them were rooms for the altars and statues of the gods.

Although the enumeration of the many observances which took place at the innumerable festivals such as the Sed, the harvest festival of Min, the returning of Horus's eye, etc., creates a picture of interminable repetition and piling up of detail, it must be remembered that the need for entertainment, group participation, and release from deepest tensions was all satisfied together. And indeed such a celebration as the Feast of Ofet, in which a great procession of decorated barges was propelled up the Nile to the temple of Luxor, bearing whole series of dancing troupes, foreign folk groups such as Libyans in leopard skins, as well as sophisticated Egyptian ballerinas, must have been a satisfying national holiday.

The religious observance which we have been discussing nearly all stems from the early dynastic period, centers about the divine king, and was largely carried on by the privileged groups. After the invasion of the Semitic Hyksos, faith in the monolithic regal organization was deeply shaken. A certain amount of democratization took place. The popularization of the Osiris cult resulted in a more general belief in the continued existence of the average man after death. *The Book of the Dead* elaborated the problems of the soul facing the judges in the other world, and the magical recipes by which it proved its worthiness for afterlife increased. Although some ethical concepts were in evidence, the emphasis tended to be upon the spell which would neutralize the judges and not upon penitence. Similarly, the daily ethic as taught in various didactic essays was a kind of enlightened self-interest plus the idea that antisocial behavior disturbed the cosmic maat or divine order.

Magic, as in other early civilizations, remained the solace of the populace. Amulets were carried to promote health, prosperity and physical charm. There were treatises on lucky and unlucky days. For instance: "First month of inundation, day 26. Bad, bad, bad. Do not do anything on this day. It is the day when Horus fought Set...." The blood of a tick taken from a black dog was considered very effective in gaining a woman's love. Since medicine was mostly magical, there were charms against crocodile, serpent and scorpion bites. One of the latter runs as follows: "Come, O my mother, Isis and my sister, Nephthys.... Speak against the bite of the orphan girl. Whether the bitten die or the bitten live, it is Thot who replies. *To be recited over a pellet of barley bread, onions and ochre, heated and put on the place of the bite*. It will not spread. End."

Magicians were mostly the lower order of priests, especially the lectors. It was probably one of these who compiled the dream book. There were two kinds of dreams, Horus dreams and Set dreams, and both types were divided into good and bad omens. When a man awoke after a bad Set dream he recited an invocation to Isis which ran in part: "Come to me, come to me, my mother, Isis.... 'Here I am, my son, come out with what thou hast seen in order that thy afflictions throughout thy dreams may vanish and fire go forth against him that frighteneth thee....'"

The symbolism of the dreams is particularly interesting as representing the anxieties and values of the average Egyptian. Since there were few repressions in the area of sex, the images differ considerably from those listed by modern psychoanalysts. They center largely around eating, drinking and copulation. The formula went: If a man see himself in a dream

Copulating with a cow:	Good; passing a happy day in house.

Obviously the cow meant Hathor, a beneficent deity.

Eating dung:	Good; eating his possessions in his house.

This perhaps suggests the dung beetle which was a sun symbol.
Two items are, from the modern point of view, very funny.

Uncovering his own arse:	Bad; he will be an orphan later.
Seeing a woman's sex:	Bad; the last extremity of misery is upon him.

Frankfort stresses the gap between the popular reliance upon magic (which grew as official theology became more abstruse) together with the unimaginative survival of the concept that life after death was a mirror of material existence, and the more abstract idea of the hereafter in the Pyramid Texts. The same contrast can be pointed out between the dream book and a prose and verse lyric entitled *The Man Who Was Tired of Life.* This work is late in composition, an example of New Kingdom pessimism, and a parallel to the Job theme in the Near East. It is one of the finest examples of Egyptian lyricism. In the beginning the gods are invoked in prose: ". . . May Thot who pacifies the gods judge me, may Knons defend me even he who writes truly; may Re hear my plaint . . ."

Some of the best stanzas of the poem run as follows:

> Behold my name is detested,
> Behold more than the smell of vultures
> On a summer day when the sky is hot.

> Behold my name is detested,
> Behold more than a woman
> About whom lies are told to a man.
>
>   · · ·

> To whom can I speak today?
> Hearts are rapacious
> And everyone takes his neighbors' goods.

> To whom can I speak today?
> Gentleness has perished
> And the violent man has come down on everyone.
>
>   · · ·

> Death is in my sight today
> As when a sick man becomes well,
> Like going out of doors after being shut in.

> Death is in my sight today
> Like the smell of myrrh,
> Like sitting under an awning on a windy day.

Death is in my sight today
Like the perfume of lotuses,
Like sitting on the shore of the Land of
Drunkenness.

The final resolution of the suicidal mood is in prose:

What my soul said to me: Hang complaining upon a peg, my comrade and my brother; make offering upon the brazier and cleave to life according as I have said . . .

Thus, despite the vast and complicated ideology by which the Egyptians endeavored to persuade themselves that man was integrated with the cosmos and that human existence was eternal, despite the magic, the anxious mummification, the piling up of grave goods and the heaping up of great stone tombs, for the actual evils of life stoicism was the dusty answer.

CHAPTER 2 2

The Mantis and His Friends

Bushmen—ancient hunting culture and Bushman art—lack of clearly defined deity—archetype of the trickster-shaman, the Mantis—animal mythology and animal identification—mimetic dances and increase of game—fear of the dead and avoidance of burials.

AFRICA, vast continent that it is, on the one hand contains the ruins of one of the great barbaric urban civilizations and on the other the living remnants of the Middle Stone Age. In the deserts of the southwest a handful of people whose ancestors once populated all of South Africa still pursue the hunter-gatherer way of life although the game is fast vanishing and persecution by more powerful tribes and the Boer farmers has thinned their ranks to a shadow of their former distribution.

The history of the Bushmen, one of the oldest peoples still living in the world, takes us into the Paleolithic of Africa. South Africa has the distinction of having been the home of the earliest transitional manlike life form, the man-ape or Australopithecus. This shaggy but upright tool user is not considered to be in the direct line of modern man's ancestry. Early Stone Age types of man equivalent to those in Europe appeared, however; indeed Grahame Clark believes that the first true men, who developed the hand-ax culture, evolved in east-central Africa. Pre-Neanderthal and Neanderthal types pursued and ate giant baboons, giant pigs, a large kind of horse, hippopotamuses, and left their flaked tools behind them. Some of these early strains died out until, by the Middle Stone Age of Africa (equivalent to the Upper Paleolithic of Europe), the fossil human types are divided into Australoid (having features in common with the aborigines of Australia) and Bushmanoid, the remote ancestors of the present-day Bushmen. Closely resembling the Bushmen in physical type (except for larger stature) and some cultural characteristics are the Hottentot, who were probably originally of the same stock but interbred with the Bantu from whom they obtained cattle and fat-tailed sheep.

Judging from prehistoric remains, people of Bushman stock inhabited

269

all of South Africa and up into the eastern area. Their digging-stick weights have been found in Uganda and the southern Sudan. Their distribution can also be traced from paintings which adorn flat stone surfaces and caves, paintings of animals and men in red, yellow ochre, claret, purple and white.

The discovery of this widespread and remarkably rich legacy of primitive art aroused much scientific discussion and disagreement. It was studied by such experts as Hugo Obermaier and the Abbé Breuil. Bushmen have been able to interpret some details of the pictures and, according to G. W. Stow, the last Bushman painter was killed by the Dutch for horse stealing in the eighteen-sixties. He had ten small horn pots hanging from a belt, each containing a different color. This establishes a link with the surviving Bushmen. Analysis of hundreds of sites has shown that there are many styles and distinct traditions. Some authorities have insisted that the paintings are all recent, others such as Henri Breuil feel that the tradition at least goes back to the African Middle Stone Age (10,000–8,000 B.C.). Some of the painting show a marked similarity to the Paleolithic art of eastern Spain. It is probable that some line engravings are all that have survived from the very early period.

The existing Bushmen are particularly interesting, however, in that they are actual representatives of the mentality of the Paleolithic era. Unfortunately anthropological descriptions are often vague and contradictory. When the Bushmen were first encountered by the Dutch, the latter took no interest in them as human beings. In fact the notorious apartheid program was promulgated from the earliest colonial days. The Bushmen, although nomads, were accustomed to hunt in certain areas, each band controlling a specific amount of territory. When the settlers took over the land, they drove off or killed the game, and the Bushmen, who had already been pushed south by the Bantu tribes, found themselves facing starvation. In revenge they attacked and killed the white men's cattle and tortured their Hottentot servants when they caught them. The result was a war of extermination. The Bushmen bands were so reduced in numbers that according to Victor Ellenberger's estimate there are no more than 50,000 left today. The fact that Boer farmers were also accustomed to capture them and subject them to forced labor has made them all the more shy of the whites.

By the time George W. Stow and the Bleek family began to record Bushman folklore in the late nineteenth century, traditions were already fragmented, and none of these admirable pioneers undertook systematic studies. The chief difficulty in obtaining an accurate picture of the cultures of modern preliterates arises from the fact that the earliest studies (before their traditions are distorted or destroyed by contact with technological civilization) were carried out by untrained observers with a strong cultural bias.

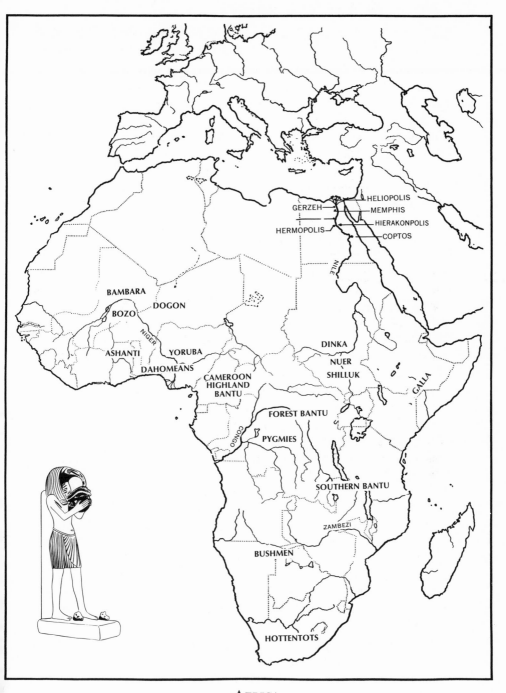

AFRICA

In the area of religion particularly, the subjectivity of the observer is a great handicap. The word *god* is used indiscriminately with Christian or classical associations, with the result that no accurate idea may be formed of the precise psychology of the people described. In the case of the Bushmen, all that can be done is to compare various reports and search for areas of agreement.

Bushmen are small people, the men seldom more than five feet tall, the women shorter. They are slenderly built, swaybacked, often with distended bellies resulting from an uncertain diet and periods of gorging when food is plentiful. The buttocks generally protrude, the women, particularly, often being steatopygous, a characteristic which is clearly depicted in the rock art. Their skins are yellowish brown and their hair tends to form little tangles known as "peppercorns." In profile the Bushman face is extremely flat, the nose having little bridge and the jaw being slightly prognathous. The men traditionally wear a small penis covering drawn tightly between the legs and tied to the waist string at the back, the women a small apron in front and a large one in the rear. They rove about in search of game during the day, returning to the water holes at night. Often for shelter they do no more than weave tall grass together to keep off the wind. Sometimes they construct a simple dome-shaped hut of twigs and grass. Building the hut and gathering food is women's work; the men are concerned with hunting.

The modern Bushman's tensions arise from scarcity of food and water. The Kalahari desert area of central South-West Africa is described by Elizabeth Thomas as follows: "From March to December in the long drought of the year, the sun bakes the desert to powdery dry leaves and dust. There are no surface waters at all, no clouds for coolness, no tall trees for shade, but only low bushes and grass tufts and among the grass tufts grow brown thistles, briar, the dry stalks of spiny weeds, all tangled into knots during the rains, now dry, tumbled and dead." June and July is winter, eighty degrees during the day and freezing at night. In this season the Bushmen wear a kaross or skin cloak. The rainy season begins in December and everything flowers lushly. By August even the water holes which have lingered, hidden in the long grass, dry up.

Like their Paleolithic forebears, the Bushmen are gatherers and hunters. They eat every sort of live thing: eland, antelope, quaggas or hartebeest when they can get them, but Elizabeth Thomas describes the cooking of a turtle, a lizard, and a rabbit, while ants' eggs (actually larvae) are known as "Bushman rice." Small wild melons and a kind of cucumber help provide liquid and in very dry seasons certain roots are dug from which moisture can be extracted. Water is so scarce during the dry season that they save their own urine to dress skins.

Reports of actual religious observance are somewhat contradictory. Kaggen, the Mantis, is a trickster but also something of a culture hero. Various deities called Xamab, Heiseb and Huwe all tend to be equated with him. Under these names he is spoken of as a rainbringer, the first man on earth or a forest spirit bringing good luck in hunting.

Since no details of ritual, cult or worship are reported in connection with any of these beings, it would seem that the epithets sky god, creator god or high god are out of place and should not be used. A creation story which is reported in two versions makes mention of no divine agency. The animals and men lived in a hole in the ground. In one version the men quarreled so that the animals were driven out. Then the men quarreled among themselves and drove each other out. The men are told they must not make a fire or they will frighten the animals. It gets very cold during the night, however, so that they are obliged to make one. The animals, who had formerly been able to talk, are frightened away and lose the power of speech. Only the domestic animals remain with the men at the fire. The addition of the domestic animals is of course late but the concept of emerging from a hole in the ground is held by many preliterates.

The only authenticated accounts of worship are in relation to the moon and the stars. Although Samuel Dornan says he found no sky worship, Dorothy Bleek records a prayer to the moon which runs as follows. The right hand is raised:

> Ho, my hand is this,
> I shoot a springbok with my hand
> By an arrow.

> I will lie down,
> I will kill an early springbok
> Tomorrow.

> Ho, moon lying there
> Let me kill a springbok,
> Tomorrow.

> Let me eat a springbok;
> With this arrow
> Let me shoot a springbok;
> With this arrow
> Let me eat a springbok;
> Let me eat, filling my body
> In the night which is here;
> Let me fill my body.

> Ho, moon lying there,
> I dig out ants food
> Tomorrow
> Let me eat it.
> Ho, moon lying there,
> You must look at this arrow
> That I may shoot a springbok with it tomorrow.

The star Canopus is known as Bushman's Rice and is prayed to for this food. Bushmen are also said to point a burning stick at it and to ask for warmth in winter. The fact that the moon is created, in another myth, by the Mantis throwing his shoe into the sky indicates that the heavenly bodies were not anthropomorphized and that no real hierarchy of deities is present. The creation of the stars is also explained by a just-so story. A girl who was undergoing her puberty rites (a time when a woman is especially imbued with mana) became angry with her mother because her mother would not allow her to eat a root which was taboo at this particular time. The girl picked up the food and threw it into the sky. Some ashes were adhering to it and these became the Milky Way. The rain bull is thought of sometimes as an actual bull which lives in the water. According to one myth he courted a young woman of the Early Race. (The Cape Bushmen say they were preceded by this people.) The young woman said, "Who can this man be who comes to me?" She put buchu (a powdered aromatic plant used as a drug) on his forehead while he held her child. She mounted on his back and he took her away. The buchu scent put the rain to sleep. Meanwhile the girl escaped. It was also said that a girl killed the water bull's children, whereupon a whirlwind sprang up and carried her whole family to a spring where they were turned into frogs. Powerful sorcerers were supposed to be able to capture the rain bull and lead it about the land in order to make rain fall in the area it had traversed. When shown certain rock pictures which portray fabulous animals, the Bushmen also identified them as rain bulls. Here again, however, the supernatural being is not worshiped and is certainly not a deity.

The one well-characterized supernatural individual is Kaggen, the Mantis. He is the special protector of the bovids. The Bushmen say his head resembles the head of a hartebeest, which perhaps explains the association. They also say he sits between the eland's horns and torments men who shoot at it. Kaggen has a wife, Dasse, the rock rabbit, three children and an adopted daughter, Porcupine. Porcupine has two children, Kwammanga, who does not seem to be an animal and who is brave and self-contained, and the Ichneumon (mongoose), who is clever and a know-it-all. All these characters were once people of the Early Race who became animals.

A sketch of some of the myths will indicate the nature of the Bushman supernatural world. The myths were taken down by Heinrich Bleek in the Bushman language. It was he who worked out the grammar and devised symbols for the peculiar clicks made by sucking with the tongue which are a characteristic of Bushman speech. The repetitions which he recorded carefully are typical of preliterate oral composition.

In one tale Kaggen assumes the form of a hartebeest. Some Bushman children kill him and cut him up with stone knives. As they are carrying the game home the pieces magically assemble, actually running together. "His body was red, when he had no hair, as he ran swinging his arms like a man." The mention of stone knives testifies to the antiquity of the story, for the Bushmen have now lost the technique of chipping although one or two encountered by Europeans in the past were still able to demonstrate it. Likewise they no longer tip their arrows with stone but make fragile bone-tipped projectiles which they poison with plant sap or the larvae of a particular beetle.

The baboons steal the Mantis's grandchild, remove its eye and play ball with it. Mantis seeks his grandchild, finds the body and anoints it with the sweat of his armpits. (This is a practice which is used to cement brotherhood and certainly bears out Crawley's theory of cross-inoculation to avoid the danger of the alien.) Kaggen is beaten by the baboons but he flies off with the eye and puts it in water. He comes home covered with wounds, only to be lectured by the Ichneumon. The child, however, regenerates from the eye which was placed in the water (again a castration theme).

A second baboon myth, cited by Victor Ellenberger, has it that Kaggen's son is killed when he comes to cut bows which the baboons shrewdly suspect are to be used against them. After the murder the baboons dance and sing. When Kaggen comes to investigate he makes them dance and sing the song which goes, "Kaggen thinks he is very clever." While they are dancing, the Mantis sticks wands in their rear ends. They had formerly been men but now, being provided with tails, they become baboons. Ellenberger suggests that a baboon dance may derive from this myth.

Kaggen has created the eland and feeds it honey. Ichneumon spies on him and discovers that the eland is eating all the honey. He reports, "O Kwammanga, a strong thing it is that keeps eating the honey; it is not small, it is big, it is dark, it has gone into the reeds." The family plots against Kaggen and shoots the eland. They cut up the meat. Kaggen tries to interfere but his arrows return to him and the others finally beat him with a club. He pricks the eland's gall which they have hung on a bush, letting out darkness which covers him. In order to create light he throws his shoe into the sky. "That is why the moon shines out at night. That is why the moon is cold, because it is a shoe, it is leather. It is red because it has earth on it, the dust which the Mantis walked on."

Kaggen, who continually gets into trouble through heedlessness, nevertheless has magical powers. Once when he was feeding a little springbok honey, the elephant mother stole the child and swallowed it. Kaggen went boldly into the elephant camp and demanded it back. "The Elephant said he should not carry the child off, but the Mantis answered that he meant to get the child out. She replied, 'How will you manage to take the child out?' The Mantis said, 'I will get into your mouth.' And the Elephant replied that she would spit him out. Then the Mantis said he would get under her fingernail and the Elephant replied that she would pick him out. Then the other elephants closed in on the Mantis as he sat there talking but he got into her navel and the other elephants who were standing around stabbed at him with their spears as he went in at the navel. Then the Mantis reached the little springbok in the Elephant's inside and with a skin he slung it on his back. The other elephants stood around ready to stab him when he should bring the little springbok out. The Mantis cut the Elephant's inside to pieces and while the other elephants were waiting for him at the Elephant's navel, where he had gone in, he came out at the Elephant's trunk, came out above her head carrying the little springbok on his back while the Elephant fell down dead. Then an elephant said, 'The Mantis has really come out there, on our mate's head.' And they ran together closing in on the Mantis, for they meant to stab him to death. And then the Mantis spoke as he flew away with the little springbok; he said, 'Can you equal me? I am the Mantis from whom you tried to steal his child, whom you cannot rival, for he is an enchanter from whom you tried to steal his child.' And when he had thus spoken to the elephants he returned home."

Kaggen learns from a bird, the Korotwiten, how to dive into ants' holes and to bring up a whole karossful of ants' eggs. Having learned this, "Then the Mantis broke the bow across his foot, he snapped an arrow in two, he tore up the quiver and broke the digging stick, he also struck and split the digging stone [a doughnut-shaped stone used to weight the stick], he struck and broke the digging stick around which he had placed the digging stone in order to dig Bushman rice." Delighted with his emancipation from hard work he says, " 'Tell me, why is it we always seem to have been digging? Our hands were sore because we dug, while we might have done like this.' " The Korotwiten tells him he must be given a share. Kaggen ignores this demand. Kwammanga also tells Mantis, through Ichneumon, to give a share to the bird or the ground will become hard for him. Kaggen refuses because he says the bird has plenty of rice. "And the Mantis woke up early, he went out early to seek an ant-heap which he had found. And he went along, he reached the ant-heap, he went to hover over it. And he kept hovering there, he dropped down, he tried to dive in, he plunged onto his forehead. He got up again for he thought he did not seem to have entered the hole properly. He got up again, he again hovered, he dropped down, he again crashed to the front of his head while the blood flowed. And he got up, he crept home." After this he is once more condemned to hard work. The Ichneumon, who had relayed Kwammanga's advice, says I told you so. But as for Kwammanga, "Because he would not speak in haste, he had spoken to the young Ichneumon. He was silent, quite silent."

The sun is described as the All-Devourer. Kaggen makes the mistake of inviting him to eat some sheep, whereupon he eats up the bushes, the water and all available meat, burning them with his tongue. He even eats Kwammanga and the Mantis. Finally the children cut his stomach open releasing bushes, sheep, Kwammanga and Kaggen.

The character of Kaggen that emerges is part trickster, part culture hero and part sorcerer. His misadventures remind us very strongly of those of the North American counterpart who, as was pointed out in connection with Loki, presents very archaic characteristics. Kaggen is also suggestive in that he reflects the magician with supernatural attributes who perhaps leads eventually to the shamanistic god.

The Bushman doctor-magician is considered to be a shape changer. Those who become antisocial and practice harmful sorcery often take the form of lions. Some have certain powers over game just as Kaggen is a protector of the bovids. They do not wield political authority and while it is possible to learn the trade through apprenticeship, in many it is considered to be an inborn talent. In some cases they suck disease from the patient in terms of a splinter of bone or wood. Elizabeth Thomas explains that medicine dances warm the shamans so that they can purge evil and cure a mysterious "star sickness." The magicians are possessed. They "fall into a trance, shudder and shriek and roll up their eyes into their heads, fall into the fire and are not burned, and when they rub their fire-warmed hands on you to cure you, their hands are hot and dry and flutter like moths, and presently the star sickness leaves you, and enters the bodies of the medicine men, and is shrieked into the air, hurled back to the spirits of the dead who brought it."

The dances are a major part of Bushman life. On evenings on which they are feeling happy they dance far into the night, every boy old enough to walk taking part. The women sit in a circle and sing as well as clap. On their legs the men wear as many as sixty dry beetle cocoons, each containing twenty ostrich eggshell fragments and serving as rattles. Countless representations of figures wearing animal headdresses and tails in rock paintings indicate that formerly the regalia of shamans was more elaborate. (We are reminded of the figures with animal heads and tails in the European rock carvings.)

Dances can be purely social or magical or both. Gai, one of Thomas's informants, in the midst of a dance suddenly began to move faster and faster, flung his arms into the air and with a piercing shriek crashed to the ground. When he came to, he ran about, shrieked, and rushed through the fire, washed his hands in the flames and went about sucking evil from the group. He finally fell exhausted and was dragged into the shade.

A number of dances are concerned with animal mimicry. An ostrich dance is reported in which the Bushmen imitate the animal fighting or mating. In connection with this it is interesting to note that the Cape Bushmen wore feathers and carried a long curved stick to represent the animal's head when they stalked it as game. A cave painting also shows a Bushman thus disguised among a flock of ostriches. It seems very likely that this type of hunting disguise leads directly to animal disguise in the dance.

Although there is no specific ceremony described in connection with the initiation of boys, the Naron Bushmen take them into the bush after they have killed two or three head of big game. The boys are generally between the ages of eight to twelve. Under the tutelage of medicine men they spend a month undergoing hardships. They are allowed to eat only roots and berries, are taboo to all women and spend every night singing solemn songs and dancing. A spirit who is sometimes called Huwe often appears.

Courting dances or dances connected with the girls' puberty ceremony also involve animal mimicry. In one a chief moves about to represent a buck while the women offer themselves sexually, dancing in a circle around him. He would now and then take one of them apart from the circle and mimic animal intercourse. One report connects it with the girl's puberty ceremony in which the girl herself lies on the ground in the center of the circle while the other women dance in a line about her and a man wearing short black wooden eland horns behaves like a bull, every now and then taking one of the women aside and pantomiming intercourse. Bleek describes the same dance among the Naron in similar terms. It would appear that female fertility is thus equated with increase among the game animals. Since the Bushmen can in some degree be compared to the Upper Paleolithic artists, this type of ceremony might by analogy throw some light on the pairs of mating animals sometimes depicted in the European caves.

These mating dances, together with Thomas's testimony that the Bushmen know the function of male semen, would indicate that these people differ from those Australians who deny or minimize the male role in procreation. One recorded myth does seem to point to a period when the process of reproduction was either not understood or not acknowledged.

It tells of an age of innocence when there was no war, no eating, no bearing of children, no dying. Then one day a woman complained of a bad pain in her stomach, so bad that she had to lie down. The other women were kind to her and did what they could but the pain got worse. After a while a little man came out of her just like herself. The other women were very frightened. Thinking her a witch, they ran away. What she had done was something new and they did not like it. They evolved a clever plan to kill her which consisted of feeding her corn and pumpkins, which, since no one had eaten them before, they hoped would kill her. Instead of dying she ate and got fat and so did the little man. The women finally returned, got to like the little man and soon learned that food was good to eat. This same story is recorded as told by the Amazulu who may possibly have borrowed it from the Bushmen.

Divining bones used by the Bushmen to learn whether enterprises will succeed or fail, are either four pieces of wood or bone, or fruit stones, two male, and two female, often with dots or lines painted on both sides. They are carried in a skin bag and when they are used they are anointed on both sides with medicine carried in a horn around the neck. They are blown on, turned in the hand like dice and thrown on a flat spot. By their positions on the ground the owner knows whether his luck will be bad or good and whether to persist in an enterprise. There is some doubt as to whether the Bantu or the Bushmen were the first to use them.

In the Bushman's attitude toward the dead we again discern certain parallels with the evidence from the Upper Paleolithic. In some cases the deceased is buried in a sitting position with his hands between his knees. Thomas says the body is bound with arms crossed over the chest, knees raised and bound and ankles bound. In excavated Hottentot graves in the Cape, the corpse is sometimes found lying on the left side with two large flat stones placed directly upon it, sometimes with human figures painted upon them. These details observed in Paleolithic burials, contracted position and stones upon the corpse, have been interpreted as fear of the spirits of the dead. This is corroborated by what is known of Bushman attitudes. In the first place, like many preliterates they do not feel that death is normal and, if it does not occur by violence, ascribe it to harmful magic. In some cases those who have not died a good death, without pain, are considered to have been bewitched and are not even buried, but simply abandoned. Normally the deceased is buried with some personal possession. Sometimes there is a funeral feast and funeral singing. The mourners are careful to stay upwind of the grave because the spirit blows downwind after death and is harmful to the living. Whirlwinds are thought to contain the spirits of the dead. Some Bushman groups then abandon the neighborhood and never mention the name of the deceased again. Apparently Bushman fear of the dead may lead to rather hasty burial because there are stories of those who have emerged from the grave. One of these tells of a man who arose from the grave and was seen by his mother. He, however, ran back to his habitation in the earth and magic had to be used to make it possible for him to rejoin the living and to become normal again.

The same theme is treated mythologically. Heiseb, the trickster of the Heikum Bushmen, had a son who pretended to be dead because his father would not let him eat certain berries. Heiseb decreed that for the dead there was only burial and consequently buried his son. The son arose from the grave during the day but returned by night. He was found by his mother, who brought him home. Heiseb remarked, "Nevertheless the dead shall remain dead." He killed his son and from then on in the grave there was only death. Another myth concerning the origin of death involves the moon and the hare. It is an example of the perverted message which we have encountered before. The moon, it seems, once appeared to a young hare, telling him not to cry for the death of his mother, for she would return again just as the moon dies and is re-created. The hare was instructed to deliver this message to mankind but he distorted it and told men that they would die and never return again. In one version the moon, in another the men, were so angry with the hare that he was struck and his lip split. Since then death has existed on earth.

Various authorities speak of the adornment of the corpse's head with buchu and red ochre, which also reminds us of the use of red coloring matter in Stone Age burials. On the whole, all testimony agrees that the Bushmen do not worship the dead, although awareness of them and fear of their influence play an important part in their psychic life.

Allowing for the fact that Bushman culture has undoubtedly been weakened since the period of contact with the Bantu and the Europeans, it does appear that on the whole their institutions represent archaic and rudimentary social forms. Since their typical supernatural is the Mantis, who is not worshiped, it is clear that their psychic life is mainly concerned with animal magic and the image of the shaman writ large who, in turn, is vitally connected with animals. It seems unlikely that they ever possessed a well-developed totemic system. It does appear that theirs is a kind of pre-totemic mentality in which the distinction between the animal and the human is never very sharply drawn. Kaggen, as we have seen, changes from animal to human form just as the sorcerer is said to do. In addition, throughout the myths animal and human attributes are constantly mixed. Although Kaggen crawls out through the elephant's trunk, the other elephants menace him with spears. When the Mantis tries to steal the hyena child in order to eat it, he is thrown into a fire, which shows that the hyena family employs the fire for cooking. Examples of this sort of mixture abound. Then, too, the belief that animals were once human beings who have lost the power of speech adds to this double image. Thomas also reports that the Gikwe believe the gemsbok people live in the south. If a Bushman draws his bow at them, they say, "Do not shoot at us, we are not gemsbok." Wilhelm Bleek also records a belief concerning the antelope seen near the place where a person has died. "We respect the antelope, for the antelope is not a mere antelope. Its legs seem small, it is the person who has died, and it is a spirit antelope." This belief also occurs very often among tribes which are definitely totemic.

A series of paintings on the rocks of Nyasaland reproduced by Roger Summers shows distinctly groups of entities which combine the attributes of bat and human being and crocodile and human being. Dances in which the sexual activity of eland and human is blended also blur the lines between the animal and anthropomorphic form. We are dealing, it seems, with a world in which the primitive respected the animals which provided him with food and recognized their kinship with himself. He emphasized this kinship in his magical rituals, and when he made up stories about natural phenomena, the entities which peopled them were somewhere between the animal and the human. In the rock painting the recurrence of a large animal of one species or another surrounded by dancing figures or figures possibly engaged in ritual activities indicates that specific groups took part in ceremonials connected with a particular creature, probably more elaborate ceremonials than the contemporary Bushmen have preserved. It is also possible that the shape-changing or animal-human double image may well be an older idea than the more highly organized totemic notion of descent from a particular beast ancestor which eventually leads in many cases to clan structure and elaborate marriage prohibitions. It is easy to see, however, that the need to study animals carefully in order to kill them for food leads to empathy and a deep understanding of their behavior and when the chase is carried out in skin or feather disguise, in bird mask or horned headdress, identification easily follows. That the sensitivity of the primitives like the Bushmen toward animals differs greatly from modern humanitarianism is attested by Elizabeth Thomas, who was made uncomfortable when her primitive friends began to cook a turtle in its shell before it was dead. Although the inhabitants of the beast world must be reckoned with as spirits and as realities, although they have often to be treated with magical precautions, there is no sentimentality toward them as nutriment in the bitter struggle for existence which the hunter faces every day of his life.

The Bushmen share a number of fundamental taboos with many other primitive peoples. Women and men sit on different sides of the hut or shelter. If a woman sits where a man has been she will run the risk of a diseased vagina; conversely, if a man occupies a woman's place he will become impotent. Intercourse must be avoided when a man sets out to shoot an eland or a giraffe or the poison on the arrows will not work. A Bushman woman gives birth secretly in the bush and if a man inadvertently steps over the spot he will lose his power to hunt. Schapera cites an interesting and unique custom in regard to chiefs which suggests that they, too, have certain magical powers. The chief is supposed to make the fire, using the fire drill, because only he can make sure it will bring health and happiness. Persistent ill health means that the chief must make a new fire. Meat killed by the bow and arrow must be ritually tasted by the chief. It is then shared by the whole band, ritually divided according to tradition, only certain parts being eaten by women.

The amputation of the little finger of the boy's right hand is explained as follows: "The little boy feels that he is a little boy, he has this hand cut, his male arm, for they shoot with this hand." The girl was sometimes deprived of the joint of the left hand. Taken together with the custom of excising one testicle, recorded by one of the older writers, the finger operation seems to be a kind of symbolic castration.

Today the majority of the Bushmen, inhabiting the inhospitable desert land, suffer continually from lack of water. At times during the worst of the heat and the drought, when there are only traces of brackish water left in the salt pans, they dig shallow pits which they line with melon pulp moistened with urine. They lie in these during the day to conserve their forces and only gather food by night. From this it is easy to see why water becomes magically important. Kaggen regenerates his sister the Blue Crane by placing one of her feathers in the water and also his grandchild by placing the child's eye in the water. C. G. Seligman cites a report that the sorcerer's strength resides in the dirt and grease of his body and that if he touches water he will lose his power; thus the water is clearly felt to be full of the ambivalence of mana. Since the Bushman formerly inhabited less desiccated areas, it may well be that much of their rain magic and rain prayers are a late development of their culture, while the hunting rituals would constitute their oldest religion.

Although the ancient population of the Bushmen has been decimated, there is some indication that their numbers have begun to increase slightly in recent years. If so, perhaps the sad prophecy of an anonymous tribal poet is not destined to come true. "The wind does thus when we die, our own wind blows; for we who are human beings possess wind; we make clouds when we die. Therefore the wind does thus when we die, the wind makes dust because it intends to blow, taking away our footprints, with which we had walked about while we still had nothing the matter with us and our footprints which the wind intends to blow away would still be plainly visible. For the thing would seem as if we still lived. Therefore the wind intends to blow, taking away our footprints."

CHAPTER 23

Spirits of the Rain Forest

Pygmies—ancient hunting culture—dependence on and influence by the Bantu—early form of totemism—creator and culture hero—megbe as mana —shamans—elephant dance—ritual of the horn—initiation rituals.

TALES of "little people" abound in mythology and folklore. In many areas they are no more than a fantasy memory in popular tradition. In other parts of the world they actually exist. The Pygmies of Africa, when they were first discovered by Europeans in the mid-nineteenth century, were thought to be a degeneration from average-size Negroes. Physical anthropology and archaeology have shown that they represent a separate ethnic strain with a long history; indeed, like the Bushmen, they are one of the oldest living peoples of the world. The Sangoan culture of Upper Paleolithic times has been identified with their ancestors; their artifacts are found through central Africa west of the great lakes as far south as the edge of the ancient Bushman distribution. The focus of this culture has always been the great rain forests of the Congo. After the hunting-gathering way of life was adapted to the woodlands, the Stone Age tools of the Pygmy ancestors tended to become instruments for working wood. Until about 2,000 years ago, this people roamed the forest undisturbed; after that, agricultural Negroes penetrated their territory from the north, the northeast and the northwest. Since the invaders had a more advanced economy the forest dwellers quickly began to exchange game, forest products, and ivory for bananas, more efficient tools, and especially iron. As a result a strange symbiotic relationship occurred, which has continued and intensified up to the present.

Instead of being absorbed, as generally happens, the Pygmies retained their nomadic way of life, modified by the products they obtained from the Negroes. They have made no effort to learn the techniques of ironworking or agriculture, have continued the barter system, and have attached themselves to particular Negro chiefs or headmen upon whom they are semi-dependent and, although they roam the forest in search of game, they remain in the particular area controlled by their "patron." The relationship is reciprocal, with the Negroes politically dominant; some of their psychic and ceremonial culture has been absorbed by the Pygmies who are distinctly treated as second-class citizens.

Some absorption, it is true, has taken place. The Batwa of Ruanda are already Pygmoid rather than truly Pygmy. The Bambuti of the French Congo and the Babinga, formerly under Belgian control, however, are pure in physique and culture. Intermarriage takes place, but while Pygmy women are willing to become secondary Negro wives in order to enjoy the relative comforts of village life, Negro women are not anxious to undertake the hardships of the forest. Since children remain with the paternal clan, this state of affairs means that the roving Pygmy groups remain relatively unmixed.

The average Pygmy male is about four feet four inches tall, the women being somewhat shorter. The legs are short while the torso and arms are very long. Hair is of the "peppercorn" type like the Bushmen's, skin earth brown, while the characteristic nose, very large, fleshy and triangular in shape, is deeply indented above the bridge.

The rain forests in which they live are wooded with giant trees which keep out the sun. Below them there is thick underbrush, intertwined with lianas, and sometimes swamp. In the drier season it rains for an hour or two every other day; in the rainy season, from April to November, the rainfall is greater. Although the forest is steamy and moist, with temperatures from 80 to 90 Fahrenheit, at night it grows cool, making it necessary to build fires around which the Pygmies sit for warmth.

The rainstorms often take the form of crashing thunder showers with hurricanes following in their wake. The noise of rain and thunder is deafening; the great trees creak and groan and sometimes fall as leaves and branches whirl through the camp of the tiny hunters. It is not surprising, therefore, that the Pygmies, in contrast to most people we have been discussing, are concerned with averting rain rather than praying for it. They blow a magic *segbe* whistle, made from the wood of a tree which has been struck by lightning, which they are convinced diverts the strength of the storm.

The characteristic sound heard on approaching a Pygmy encampment is the tapping of the ribbed handleless mallet used to make bark cloth, their only textile. The bark is laid on a log and pounded to make the penis sheath worn by the men and the aprons hung at the women's waists. When the men wish to adorn themselves for the dance they stick leaves in the rear of their G-strings which stand up and make them resemble little roosters.

Pygmy camps are set up in a circle in a clear space under the trees. The house, constructed by the women, consists of saplings stuck into the ground, bent over and interwoven with withes to form a little dome. Upon this the large leaves of the phrynium bush are laid like tiles, the stems being pierced and tied to the skeleton. Generally one side is left open; in some groups a tunnel-like entrance is added. One of the real menaces of forest life are the voracious army ants which pour through the camp in a horde like a river devouring every living thing in its path. These creatures can only be turned aside by fire. If their columns move through the huts, the inhabitants are forced to abandon them until the scourge has passed.

In the center of the encampment the fire is made and the area about it is reserved for dancing. Although all life revolves around food getting, there is sufficient nourishment so that Pygmies seldom go hungry. The women's task is gathering fruits, nuts, a tuber something like a wild potato, and particularly such delicacies as giant snails, and caterpillars, which they skin and sauté over hot coals, and termites. The men set forth in the morning to hunt whenever the weather permits. Sometimes the women join them in the net hunt. In this case nets of lianas are set up and the women act as beaters, striking the ground with bundles of saplings and emitting shrill yodelings which signal the type of game spotted; the men shoot the game, when it rushes into the nets, with either wooden arrows or arrows tipped with iron heads obtained from Negro smiths. Game animals include dwarf antelope, okapi, hippopotamuses and even elephants. Through association with the Negroes, Pygmies obtain bananas and yams as well as occasionally clay pots.

To obtain such benefits Pygmy women sometimes work for the Negroes. The men are occasionally forced to hunt by their patrons when they are not anxious to, and the Negro greed for ivory results in the death of many small elephant hunters. In such cases, Schebesta reports, a certain compensation is paid to the family. Although much of the symbiosis smacks of exploitation, there are also psychic ties between the nomads and their patrons. The Bambuti have taken over circumcision from their Bantu neighbors. When the ceremony is performed on pairs of Negro and Pygmy boys, their blood drips together on the ground and this creates a blood brotherhood which lasts for life. Each bewails the other's death and the Negro often buries his small companion. On the other hand, Noël Ballif reports that when he engaged a guide to take him to a Babinga encampment the man said, "Why the Babinga? They are dirty, they are ugly, and they stink." Apparently the odd relationship varies greatly from that of Ruanda, where the Batwa are a sort of integrated lower level in a stratified kingdom of three different ethnic strains, to the looser connection of the Babinga and Bambuti in which the forest hunters are tied to their patrons by some ritual unity and the desire for salt, tobacco, yams, bananas, sugarcane, tools, iron, drums (which they borrow), and perhaps also by an unconscious desire to submit to father domination since they have no chiefs who wield political authority, while the Negroes do. Another aspect of this almost feudal relationship is the fact that the Pygmies fight on the side of their patrons when the latter go to war. Efforts have been made to find grammatical traces of a specifically Pygmy language, which they must have once had, but today they speak the language of their Negro neighbors.

Pygmy religion is unquestionably an area of confusion and controversy. Two factors have caused this situation. In the first place, it is not easy to separate indigenous custom from what has been absorbed from the Negro patron, and in the second place the theories of the Vienna School of anthropology founded by Father Wilhelm Schmidt have strongly affected the reports on Pygmy culture.

Schmidt, in 1912, embarked on a many-volume work based on the premise that the Pygmies were the oldest of peoples and therefore their religious belief would shed light on the very basis and origin of the idea of God. Schmidt stimulated research among the Pygmies by Catholic missionaries and he based his theories on their findings. In brief, he posited a kind of contrary evolution. The Pygmies, possessed of the least material culture possible, were supposed to show the primal type of spiritual development, worship of a supreme being. This was Ur-monotheism. With more elaboration of material culture, as among the Negroes, the purity of this monotheism became corrupt and degenerated into animism, ancestor worship and magic. As it happens, up to the present, there have been few studies made of Pygmy religion by secular fieldworkers. As Schmidt's most astringent critic, J. J. Fahrenfort, warns us, "Precisely in the religious area is there a great danger that primitives, who so easily lie, by succumbing to leading questions give the sort of answers which they feel will please the questioner."

Among the Pygmies a creator god is reported, called Mungu, who sometimes seems to be a first ancestor and sometimes a culture hero. He may have five or six other names. A similar or equivalent supernatural who also has alternate names is Tore, a spirit of the woods, lord of animals, master of everything and bringer of death. His name is also sometimes given to the dead.

Mungu is the possessor of the totality of *megbe,* or mana. But the totem is also the possessor of the primal megbe and the clan members derive megbe or mana from it.

The variety of names and variety of descriptions of these supernaturals negates any fundamental monotheism. Tore, for instance, in the northeast is a small creature who lives in the liana or a tree in the forest and goes *é é é* at night. To meet him is to die. Other Pygmies say he is a short anthropomorphic figure whose head ends in a spine or, again, he is large, hairy and bright.

None of these creatures is actually worshiped, which also negates any formalized theological concept. It must be remembered that individuals create mythology and these individuals may be, in the first place, merely good storytellers. Afterward the theologically minded intellectual, the shaman, tends to standardize certain religious concepts which are handed down from generation to generation if there is a well-knit tribal organization. The fact that Pygmies, like the Bushmen, roam about in isolated hunting bands would militate against a unified theology.

Though the moon is sometimes associated with Mungu, the Babinga Pygmies associate their chief supernatural with lightning and the rainbow. The same group speaks of a great elephant, Gôr, higher than the forest trees, father of all the elephants who, when he drinks, empties a river at a draught. He is all white, upholds the sky on his shoulders, and his voice is heard in the thunder. The Babinga refrain from sexual intercourse during a thunderstorm for fear of irritating Gôr. Since Gôr sends the elephants to the elephant hunters, they offer him the fat of a newly killed elephant or put some of the meat on a leaf. The same thing is sometimes done for Mungu and sometimes for Tore. The totem may be invoked before hunting. Otherwise there is no specific cult for any of the spirits.

There is another aspect of Tore, described in connection with a leopard society, a secret society composed of men who possess a long wooden trumpet, which they blow into a pot with water in the bottom to represent the leopard's voice. The uninitiated and especially women and children run away and cover their eyes so as not to see Tore, for fear of dying. The Bambuti rationalize the society as a punishment for shrewish wives but it may be influenced by Anyoto leopard men of the Babali Bantu whose rites include murder and cannibalism. Schebesta feels that the Negroes took over the society from the Pygmies.

On the whole, therefore, the Pygmies believe in a number of supernatural beings whose attributes vary from group to group. These supernatural beings have the attributes of culture heroes, are sometimes primal ancestors, sometimes have creative powers and are sometimes associated with the spirits of the dead. It also appears that they can take the form, or have the form, of certain animals, and exercise control over rain or hunting. All these elements parallel to some extent what has been noted among the Bushmen. Perhaps the character of these spirits can be made out more plainly from folklore. To begin with, there is the myth of obtaining fire. In one version the chimpanzees are the original proprietors of this commodity. A Bambuti Pygmy was once well received by them and, enjoying the warmth, decided he would steal a firebrand. The following day he arrived with a long bark train hanging from the rear end of his G-string. Only chimpanzee children were at home but they received him and served him bananas. As he moved about the blaze his train was in continual danger of catching fire. The chimpanzee children said, "Look out, it will take fire." He replied, "It doesn't matter, it is long enough." Eventually it did catch fire, whereupon he ran off. The children set up an outcry, alerting the elder chimpanzees who chased the thief. When they arrived at the Pygmy camp the fire was burning brightly. "Why did you steal it instead of buying it honestly?" they cried. They were so angry because the Pygmies had stolen fire (and bananas) that they retired to the woods, did without both, and ate wild fruit.

A second version of the theft of fire attributes the ownership to Tore, who has a mother and who is accustomed to take his ease in a magic swing. Some Pygmies seized fire and ran off with it while Tore pursued them on his swing. He swung up to the sky and down to the valley, he swung from mountain to mountain, but in vain. When he returned home he found his mother lying dead. As a punishment he decreed that men should also die.

Since many of the Pygmies do not make fire themselves but get it from their patrons, these myths reflect cultural borrowing. The fact that the fire is in one case in the possession of the chimpanzees and in the other belongs to Tore certainly shows that the personages in Pygmy myth have no fixed characteristics and also that Tore is on a level with, or interchangeable with, mythical animals. Likewise the just-so story element is mingled with magic.

Apropos of the importance of the leopard, Schebesta reports that a member of the leopard clan said that their ancestral leopard had a very large family. One day he said to them, "My children, you are to go into the village and settle down while I stay in the forest and hunt for food." Before they departed, he gave them the Tore trumpet so they might be able to imitate his growl. When the body of a member of this clan was lowered into the grave, an elder cupped his hand over his mouth and imitated the growl of a leopard. A part at least of the dead man's spirit was supposed to be reincarnated in a leopard. The same informant said he had seen a leopard cub sitting on a new-made grave. This, of course, is parallel to the Bushman belief that the dead may appear in the form of an antelope.

Finally, Schebesta records several episodes of the Arebati cycle in which Arumei, the chameleon, seems to be interchangeable with the creator god. Originally the earth was above Arebati who lived with the moon and the lightning. Dust and dirt from the earth above fell down and contaminated his food. Arebati commanded the lightning to find a habitation above the earth. With a great crash the lightning divided the earth and traveled upward into the sky followed by the moon. Arumei, the chameleon, climbed up to the tops of the highest trees and is therefore near Arebati. One day Arumei heard a murmuring and twittering in the branches of a *tii* tree. When he dug around the roots, a wide stream flowed from it which distributed itself through the earth. At the same time the first two human beings appeared, Uti and Mupe. But Arebati is also said to have created everything and, a further contradiction, the first human, who may have been the chameleon, is said to have named the trees which were engendered from the primal tii tree which he himself planted. Unfortunately there is no way of knowing if Schebesta has failed to record the details of Pygmy mythology through lack of literary sensitivity, or if the Pygmies simply lack the coherent storytelling talent of the Bushmen. From the Babinga come fairly elaborate stories told by traveling raconteurs. The following is more secular than religious: Kmvum was asked for wives by the Pygmy men because they were tired of their own cooking. Kmvum sent them all off to hunt. They came back with a variety of animals. The creator god said "Arise," whereupon each animal came to life as a woman, each with the character of the animal from which she had been made. The men had caught many monkeys and porcupines but no elephants and consequently there were no intelligent women. When the storyteller finished this tale the female members of his audience were all in favor of beating him. There are also animal fables in which the small animal outwits the large; the tortoise or chameleon, for instance, triumphs over the elephant. In style these are very reminiscent of the Br'er Rabbit stories of American Negro tradition.

On the whole, it appears that there are rudimentary stories about semi-animal culture heroes but the shamanistic and trickster character is not so developed as among the Bushmen. This does not mean, however, that ecstatic magical practice is lacking. Schebesta describes in detail magical divination which took place when some goods had been stolen from the camp. The magician held in his outstretched hand an antelope horn smeared with beeswax containing a magic draught. After a while his arm began to tremble more and more violently. He then lost consciousness and went into a trance, "in the throes of which he flung his arms about, howled, whined, and behaved like one possessed by an evil spirit. . . . Then he suddenly got very violent and it looked as if he were about to smash up the whole camp. Those nearest to him thrust him forcibly out of the hut. Once outside, he hurled himself on the ground where he writhed convulsively, flinging his arms about but without relinquishing his hold on the antelope's horn which he held tight in his viselike grip." The magician pointed and muttered but did not speak the name of the thief. A second man seized the horn as the drums began to throb again. This magician went through the same procedure but finally ran for half a mile to the Negro village, ran into a hut, and denounced its inhabitants. The horn had to be snatched from his hand before he became normal. This *dibo* ceremony was practiced by both Negroes and Pygmies but, since it seems archaic, may well be authentically a part of Pygmy culture. It is used to catch thieves, murderers, and witches. Anne Putnam describes an episode in which a similar diviner had accused an old woman of having caused the death of one of the band through witchcraft. The old woman was being beaten so severely that the white woman had to intervene to save her life.

The concept of an entity of the woods who is also a bringer of death and even a spirit of the dead seems to be rather mixed, as if several elements were combined in various complexes. It is possible that there is an underlying spirit of the forest who has to be propitiated in order for hunting to be successful. Schebesta describes the placing of leaves on a fire to cause smoke, thereby preventing rain which spoils the possibilities of the chase—simply a magical rite like the blowing of the segbe whistle. Pygmy hunters also carry amulets; an antelope horn or a shell holds a bit of the totemic animal: horn, bone or hair. These containers are hung at the neck or belt. Ballif describes a rite in which the hunters tie a liana around a tree trunk and stick leaves in it, naming each for an animal. They then cut the liana and cry out, "We are pleased!" This is to multiply game in the nets. Babinga hunters also invite the Edzengi to see them dance after they have killed an elephant. The actual ceremony is derived from their Bantu patrons, the Banzombe. Edzengi is a dancer completely enveloped in a cloak of raffia hung from a pole from which are hung the amulets ordinarily worn about the neck and right wrist of the hunter—antelope horns and two little iron bells. The other hunters dance around this apparition and sing. Some of them carry branches with ribbons of raffia with which they stroke the Edzengi. The latter, gyrating continually, rises higher and higher above the other dancers. Several times it drops flat, seems to recuperate again, whirls once more and finally bounds into the forest. Ballif writes that the Edzengi is not the elephant "but the collective symbol of animal life which alone allows the Babinga to survive in the forest." This is a shrewd observation which suggests that an archaic hunting magic (the amulets hung from the pole) was eventually given a name and treated as an entity which could be dramatized. The various names given to the hunting spirit could well include some borrowed from the Negro peoples. On the whole, this entity seems similar to Huwe of the Bushmen. The concept of the Tore upon which it is death to look seems to stem from the secret-society development, in view of the trumpet and leopard myth. Since Tore is also lord of the dead and the dead are said to become Tores, it appears that still a third element has here joined the complex.

All writers agree that all Pygmies are totemistic. Schebesta feels that totemism is indigenous because of the dominance of the animal and some differences between the Pygmy attitudes and those of the Negroes. Pygmy clans are not localized, clan groups being split up among different bands. Among separate bands there is rivalry and antagonism; indeed, Schebesta found that two groups with different patrons quarreled continually when they camped near him. As a result there is local patriarchal exogamy between family groups but not between clans. Also the unity of the clan is only affirmed in totemistic ceremony. We have here, therefore, an example of totemism divorced from marriage classification which may well be an early stage of the institution. Several family groups may have the same totem but the totem has no fixed locality and no clan chief. Strict taboos are observed against killing or eating the totem and also even touching it; all members of the clan will suffer if infractions take place. The totem is thought of as an ancestor, a protector, an aid in hunting, and as full of the vital mana which infuses all of the members of the clan. Likewise, as already noted, the clan members are thought to fuse with the ancestral totem in a sort of incarnation after death. Since the totem is invoked and offerings given to it before a hunting expedition to ensure success, and bits of the totem are used in amulets, this layer of Pygmy religion may well be the oldest, leading to or associated with the spirit of the forest. The Pygmies therefore differ from the Bushmen, among whom no offerings are recorded. The basic idea, however, does appear in the story of Kaggen and the Korotwiten, for here Kaggen comes to grief for not giving the helpful animal its share of the food obtained.

The bond between the animal and the clansman is also illustrated by what is supposed to happen when a leopard Pygmy meets his totem. He says, "Father, let me pass." The leopard switches its tail and refrains from attacking him. Chimpanzee, crocodile, hippopotamus, iguana, and pangolin are listed as Babinga totems but, strangely enough, the most usual food animals, deer, antelope or elephant, do not assume this function.

Aside from the ecstatic divination and hunting magic, the Pygmies also cast the bones, in this case pieces of tortoise shell. The female ones, the wife and the young woman, are notched at the end; the males, the headman and the boy, are pointed. If they fall close together, circumstances are favorable to an undertaking; the direction in which they point is also significant. Different configurations of the bones have archaic names whose significance is already forgotten. Such divination is extremely archaic, artifacts of this sort having been found in Auvergne in Neolithic levels. Other forms of magic are ointment rubbed on the eyes of hunters to make them see better, the juice of certain leaves, chewed and squirted on the body of the beloved to act as a love charm.

If we compare the Pygmies, as an archaic people, to the Bushmen, they seem to have advanced further on the path of organized totemism. Their graphic and narrative imagination, however, appears to be inferior. Although wood is plentiful in their environment, no indigenous style of carving is mentioned and painting is limited to body adornment.

Colin Turnbull, in a study of initiation among the Bambuti, clarifies the distinctions between Bambuti customs and those of their Negro patrons. The group which he studied were far less dependent upon the Negroes than those described by Schebesta. Although the Negroes carried out the circumcision ritual for both groups, there was no pairing and blood brotherhood. The Pygmies continually criticized the Negroes for being too harsh with the boys, slighted the food taboos, burlesqued some of the dances and even broke up the ceremony to take their sons hunting. It was Turnbull's impression that the Pygmies tolerated the ceremony for its status value among the Negroes. While the latter were convinced that bird spirits and ancestors appeared during the dances, the Pygmies exhibited no emotional involvement. Although the Negroes were using the ceremony to assert their superiority, they were unable to control their Pygmy neighbors, who stubbornly adhered to their own values.

The Pygmies, much like the Bushmen, have their own initiation for adolescent boys which takes place when the boys have killed an animal large enough to be ceremonially divided. The initiation society is called the Lusumba and possesses a Lusumba horn. Circumcision does not admit boys to this organization; initiation involves undergoing hardships in the forest at about the age of fourteen. A part of the ceremony consists of sacrification above each eye. When hunting has been bad the Lusumba society is called out and sings songs through the horn to the spirit of the forest. All this sounds very much like the Tore leopard society Schebesta describes.

Another name for the horn appears to be the *molimo*. Sometimes it is a length of bamboo but in more important ceremonies it used to be a fifteen-foot hollow tree trunk or bamboo. Contemporary Pygmies substituted an iron drainpipe which was hidden in the forest and brought out with a certain secrecy and given a drink by placing it in a stream. (In the past this was done to tighten up any cracks in the wood, but tradition prevailed with the iron pipe.) The whole village collected food for feasts on evenings when the molimo was played and the women and children shut themselves up. The instrument was blown from far off, sometimes imitating a leopard's voice or other animal's; sometimes it was actually sung through, while the group at the fire answered in chorus. It was then brought into camp, passed through the fire, ashes were rubbed on it, and then it was borne into the forest by two dancing men. A feast followed. At times during the day bearers of the molimo attacked and destroyed the hut of someone who had committed some transgression against the group.

The ritual seemed to consist entirely of simple songs requesting the good offices of the spirit or animal of the forest, who was supposed to be asleep and in need of awakening. The molimo ceremonies went on every night for two months. The attitude toward them, as described by Turnbull, was relaxed, mildly religious but also partly social and recreational, expressing a happy belief in the unity between the little people and their natural environment.

The girls' initiation society is called the Alima and also has special songs sung to the spirit of the forest. The girls are sequestered in a special hut and painted with white designs. This takes place after their first period. The girls remain in the hut for some days while the whole village seethes with excitement. As the erotic singing goes on, the girls' lovers try to enter the hut. A battle ensues, the old women armed with whips and lianas and shielding themselves with baskets. The men wield sticks and stones. In the old days bows and blunt arrows were used and some injuries occurred. The aspiring lover is urged on by the men who support him. It is considered a proof of virility if he succeeds in fighting his way into the hut. When he enters he either sleeps with the girl or goes out again through the back entrance, depending on whether the girl is willing or not. Turnbull corroborates this description.

The similarities between the Bushmen and Pygmy initiation ceremonies and their general religious practices set them apart from the Negro peoples whose psychic world is pervaded with ancestor worship. Since these small hunting peoples are indeed a survival from the dawn of prehistory, their relatively simple ceremonies express an involvement with nature and a magical adaptation to the hunting way of life, which precedes the more complicated theologies of an agricultural village and fully evolved clan society.

CHAPTER 24

The Tyranny of the Tree

*Bambara—origin and development of true Negro culture in West Africa—
ancient kingdoms and unusual development of mythology among the Sudanic
tribes—Bambara dualism and sexual myth—symbolism pervading whole culture—initiation and circumcision—men's societies as ancestor cult—role in
punishing witchcraft—dramatic element in ceremonies—survivals of totemism—ancestor cult and funeral rites.*

I<small>T IS</small> only recently that botanical studies have revealed a new
ancient agricultural complex, an unsuspected center in which
early man made the breakthrough from hunting and gathering to settled
cultivation of the soil. Careful investigation of the distribution of domestic
plants and the dates of their appearance in various cultures indicates that
fonio (a wild rice), pearl millet, sorghum, the cow pea, a type of peanut,
the Guinea yam, okra, the fluted pumpkin, the watermelon, cotton, the oil
palm, and sesame were all developed in the Sudanic region of West Africa.
In this territory along the upper Niger, which is considered the center and
point of origin of Negro civilization, recent investigation has also revealed
an unsuspectedly sophisticated and elaborate metaphysical religion and the
rudiments of an indigenous written language. As George Murdoch points
out, prejudice has been one of the obstacles in recognizing the significant
contributions of the Negro ethnic strain to man's cultural history.

The true Negro is thought to have evolved from a Paleolithic form of
man who also gave rise to the Bushmen, each group following a different
evolutionary path because of different environment. Since there is a lack
of archaeological studies in West Africa, there is no detailed picture of the
course of the Neolithic in this area, nor can the Negro agricultural revolution be accurately dated. Because the Sudanic domesticated plants had
spread to the Nubian border by the end of the fourth millennium B.C. (a
time-consuming diffusion from tribe to tribe for 3,000 miles) and also because it takes at least a thousand years for agricultural techniques to develop from their first tentative beginnings, George Murdoch concludes that
the Negro agricultural revolution must have taken place before the fifth
millennium. Eventually the Negro stock was to spread over more than a

third of Africa, diffusing its culture and interbreeding with both Bushman and Caucasoid peoples. The Pygmy group also reached south Asia and Oceania.

The Negro human type averages fairly tall, about five feet eight, the skin is dark brown, the hair woolly, the nose broad and the jaw somewhat prognathous. The skull is generally long and ovoid. The lips tend to be very full and somewhat everted. The Mande group on the Niger number about two million, and closely related in economy are the six million Voltaic peoples to the south on the River Volta. Of these groups, the Bozo, the Dogon and the Bambara all share a similar basic world view. We shall discuss the Bambara in detail because their religion has been most carefully studied.

In the first place, it must be remembered that, although the Sudanic Negroes originated their own civilization, in the past couple of thousand years cultural contacts both hostile and mercantile have taken place which have modified the local customs and stimulated social development. Contact with the Neolithic peoples, the Caucasoid Berbers of North Africa, gave them fowls, donkeys, goats, sheep and cattle, although the Mande did not adopt the practice of milking and rejected most of the northern food plants. Early in their history they achieved centralized political forms; Ghana was a kingdom which had existed from about the fourth century. In 1067 A.D. it had a king at whose funeral there were human sacrifices and who was succeeded by his sister's son, which suggests a primal matrilineal system. Not only did the Sudanic peoples arrive at political unity but they also set up fluctuating empires. Ghana was destroyed by a Berber invasion but followed by another Sudanic state, that of Mali, which conquered Timbuktu and dominated all of West Africa from the rain forest to Senegal and maintained diplomatic relations with the Sultan of Morocco and the King of Portugal. This empire began to break up in the late fifteenth century. The Bambara had become independent of Mali in 1670 and set up their own states of Segou and Kaarta, finally occupying Timbuktu. They were conquered by the Fulani of Masina. The Arab leader Hadj Omar introduced the Moslem religion but the Bambara were finally "liberated" by the French from "the cruel Muslim occupation," as a French author puts it. Ironically enough, the French promptly executed the Bambara king who revolted against them in 1893 when the country became a French colony.

The Bambara live in compact villages or towns of circular houses of mud or sun-dried brick with conical thatches. These are grouped in courtyards surrounded by a hedge or wall. The towns themselves in the warlike period typically had three walls, one surrounding the gardens on the outskirts, one circling the town proper and one around the chief's houses. Among the chief's houses there was an arsenal containing arms and ammunition.

Bambara settlements are situated near the Niger on the riverine plains fringed by small forest growth. There is rain from April until June, the annual Niger flood depending on the amount of the downfall. The Bambara subsist mainly by agriculture with subsidiary hunting and gathering. Their technique is chiefly shifting hoe cultivation. Although some irrigation takes place, Bambara economic development has never reached the point of surplus which results in a high degree of specialization and advanced urban development. Their stage of culture can be thought of as parallel to that of the Celts or Teutons since they forge iron tools but, in contrast to the ancient European barbarians, they have taken a step forward into settled cultivation, having never possessed the mobility bestowed by the horse and vehicle. Their clan structure is now patrilineal, kingship being based on a dominant clan.

Practically nothing was known of the intricacy of this people's spiritual development until recent decades because, in the first place, their mythology was secret and esoteric, possessed only by old men and certain initiates, and in the second place the attitude of early investigators was affected by European cultural bias.

The Abbé Joseph Henry, who first described their religion in 1910, wrote of the typical Bambara as obstinate and incurious. "To squat under a leafy tree and pass the whole day chatting or in a half stupor is his dream and constitutes his happiness. Lazy, do-nothing, when he has enough in his storehouse to feed his family, he believes he has accomplished everything. The head tax, the fetish cult above all, force him to shake himself out of his lethargy; but he has figured it all out, he works to get what he needs and then stops." Henry was influenced by Schmidt's theories but his obvious bias prevented him from making any attempt to penetrate the meaning of Bambara religion. His descriptions of ritual are colorful and full of clerical disapproval. One or two other descriptive accounts were published but it was not until the 1930's and 1940's that a new group of trained French anthropologists, under the direction of Marcel Griaule, succeeded in gaining the confidence of the initiates and penetrated an extraordinary world of symbolism which unified all categories of social behavior. Studies among the Bozo and Dogon revealed that related tribes shared this amazing psychic development.

In the first place, it is necessary to keep the outlines of the intricate Bambara creation myth in mind, since it is the basis upon which the rest of the religious practice is built. Step one is the conception of a universal void containing motion. This motion became double (twinship pervades the whole story) and emitted a cold rust which formed hard, brilliant bodies. The twin motion determined the points of the compass and emitted vibrations. These vibrations were signs for everything; the symbol was created before the thing. From the primal motion consciousness detached itself.

In step two the *yo,* described as an interior voice, began to work through numbers. Altogether the world had twenty-two terms. There were seven for man: three male which symbolized the penis and testicles, and four female, the four lips of the vagina. Yo thought of the present world and also a world to come. "In the world to be all the words will be changed. Solidity has not been realized in this first creation but the universe will be made in the solidity of the word. The course of Yo, the work of Yo, the sleep of Yo will penetrate all beings. The second world is a new world, the new world is the world of a word." This curious text is repeated in discussions after religious ceremonies.

The creation of abstract ideas and emotions followed and after this the first concrete being. This was Pemba who existed for seven years in a whirl-wind, dropped to earth as an acacia seed, and grew into a tree. The opposing twin entity, Faro, was created at the same time as vibration. This turned into water dripping to earth, leaving behind a space which became the spirit of the air, Teliko.

Faro, who often appears as an androgyne, gave birth to twins on a bare hill. Grass began to grow and dew formed a spring. Faro created fish and other water animals. The twins were the Bozo, a fishing people who could live in water.

Pemba, meanwhile, was also creating. He spat in the dust, lay upon it, and created a grotesque female, Mousso Koroni, animal-headed, with long ears, a human body and a tail. Then a curious reverse process took place. Mousso Koroni lay upon Pemba and without being penetrated by him impregnated him with female sexual fluid and was herself fertilized, giving birth to animals and plants. All these creatures, as well as the offspring of Faro, at this point revered Pemba, the male tree.

Faro's human beings were immortal. They grew pubic hair at the age of twelve, hair in the armpits at twenty-two, beards at thirty-six, and at fifty-two their hair became white, signifying they were adult. Seven years later they became thin and old. They spoke no language, went naked, but scar-ified their faces with signs for the penis and testicles and the four lips of the vagina.

The next step was the coming of hostility and evil in this mythological era. Pemba, the tree, demanded the love of all women so far created. Mousso Koroni became jealous, ceased to cooperate with Pemba and raged madly through the universe. She had been mutilated by Pemba in a way equivalent to excision of the clitoris. Now in her madness she circumcised and excised men and women with her teeth and nails. She betrayed Pemba's secret wis-dom and made all she touched, including the earth, impure. Pemba, in a police action, pursued her in vain. Faro, being appealed to, caught her, but she refused to submit, introducing misfortune, sickness and death into the world. Although she died in misery, in her efforts to survive she invented agriculture and gave it to mankind.

There followed a new era in which Pemba's tyranny became excessive. To renew his strength, the tree needed the female liquid from all women. In the course of this coupling, a woman was deflowered with loss of blood. This created an abnormal bloodthirstiness in the tree but in return for this exaction it offered rejuvenation to men at the age of fifty-nine. Men gave Pemba blood from their right wrists. After they had endured having their pubic hair plucked out without murmuring, they became young again. For women a different process was used. All virgins were deflowered by a priestess of the tree who allowed their blood to run down the trunk. Then at fifty-nine they automatically became young again. They were once more deflowered and thereupon able to give birth to animals and vegetables. The tree also received offerings of menstrual blood.

As its appetite for blood increased, it devised a new system. It ordered wooden penises of various sizes made and inserted into its trunk. From these women experienced great pain but also extraordinary pleasure. The tree now taught mankind the secret of fire but it continually demanded more blood both of men and animals. Human beings were seriously weakened by loss of blood and lack of food.

Faro, at this point, took a hand. He taught a woman to eat a tomato and thus regain her strength. (This element in Bambara theology must have been introduced no earlier than the fifteenth century when the tomato was imported by the Portuguese from South America.) The tomato fortunately contained seven seeds, three for the male and four for the female principle. Faro decreed that the tomato should cause conception and Pemba should create no more.

This precipitated war in heaven. The tree uprooted itself, and went forth to battle. It was defeated by Faro but in defeat cursed mankind with hate and sickness. At this point, however, Teliko, the spirit of the air, also made a bid for power. Faro took him on, destroyed his testicles and broke his right arm. Up to this point all creatures had supple limbs but after the mutilation of Teliko they had jointed limbs and fewer twins were born.

From now on Faro assumed command of the universe and created order. He ordained the seasons and, through vibrations, created seven heavens, in the seventh of which he resides.

The tree, however, was not entirely without power. Some old men continued to worship, gave him all their blood, and were turned into birds. These were the first ancestor spirits; they concerned themselves with fire and were particularly worshiped by blacksmiths and magicians. In scorn of

Pemba a man lopped off one of his branches. He was pursued by a vengeful force, *ayama,* which killed him. The tree told men that henceforth they would all die.

Faro then took men under his protection, gave them rain and the Niger River and instructed them that water was sacred. He also established the different classes of animals and ranks of men, including slaves.

The symbols of this frenzied and violently sexual creation story with its mixture of abstract and concrete, subtlety and barbarism, run through all of Bambara life, operating on various planes. Although Pemba is not worshiped, a piece of wood with a groove in it is his chief symbol, the *pembele.* This is the universe, one side heaven, the other earth. The groove symbolizes the grave. Three groups of twenty-two engraved lines stand for the twenty-two terms of Yo. Two groups of seven lines are the paired male and female numbers, Pemba and Mousso. The pembele is used in domestic worship as an altar, and the circumcision board is also called a pembele.

Mousso Koroni symbolizes the impure earth and night sorcery. In memory of her bestowal of agriculture, when the grain is brought in, an old woman in rags rushes about from west to south and from east to north, simulating her madness, and then goes to sit with the threshers. The sun is Pemba, red from pursuing Mousso Koroni, and the stars are his dilated pores. When clouds gather for rain they also stand for Mousso's mad course through the sky. The impurities of the earth are removed by cultivation.

Faro, who stands for law and order, is the major supernatural entity, symbolized in basket weaving by seven spiraling tiers of strips. The spiral is order and also the vibrating principle. Hats and masks are constructed on the same design. Tomatoes and cooked cereals are Faro's offerings. He is manifested in the rain and the thunder, the latter being thought of as an ax thrown from the sky. Neolithic axes are buried under altars. One of Faro's helpers, a primal blacksmith, lived when artisans did not know the use of tongs and held the red-hot iron in their hands. This blacksmith's wrists were broken by the hammer of a clumsy apprentice. Faro took him up to the seventh heaven. The kokoni fish and the tomato remain Faro's attributes. Since water is sacred to him it is taboo to carry gold or copper across a river. Food or gold must be offered to him; he is master of riches. According to Germaine Dieterlen a menstruating woman is taboo to anything or anyone connected with Faro. "He represents in the human microcosm human will and intelligence coming to control the drives of sexual instinct symbolized by the virility of the tree, the violence and disorders of emotionalism expressed by the vertiginous chthonian voyage of Mousso Koroni. . . ."

In the human being these three beings are represented as vital principles.

Faro is the *dya,* Pemba is the *nyama,* Mousso Koroni is the *wanzo.* Different balances between them create different psychic states.

Conception is thought of as taking place after a woman eats a tomato. An embryo begins to form in her body. She then has intercourse with her husband to shape the embryo into human form. She takes in the upper part of her husband through her eyes, the lower part through her sex. The semen is thought to grow in the man's joints. It is pointed out that after intercourse his joints feel weary.

The *dya* is the double, the twin of opposite sex, seen as reflection in water or in a mirror, or the shadow. A crocodile can harm a man if he seizes his dya in the water. The *ni* is a second spirit principle which can be seen beating in the fontanelle of a baby or in the pulse. It leaves the body during sleep and enters the sixth heaven from which it returns bearing dreams. Animals have both dya and ni, vegetables only a ni, except for the sacred tomato.

Tere is the personality, a kind of gestalt which can be read in the form of the body. It reflects Mousso Koroni's condition when pursued by Pemba. Only domestic animals have tere. At death it leaves the body, becomes nyama, and can attack anyone who was responsible for the death of its owner. *Wanzo,* which comes from Mousso Koroni, is a bad vital principle, situated in the prepuce and clitoris, which is why they must be removed. At this time it drips out with the blood lost and is captured in the masks of the Ntomo (the society of the uncircumcised).

At death the ni is captured by the head of the family and transported to the domestic altar. It will then animate the dya of the dead man's heir. Ceremonies cause the nyama of the dead to join the benevolent forces of the ancestors.

With the family name given to a child, comes the animal or vegetable taboo. This taboo is rationalized by stories in which animals have been helpful. For instance, a man was once captured by a crocodile, dragged underwater, and left in its lair. Some sand began to fall on his face. He saw a beam of light. It turned out that an ant lion was dropping sand to show him the way to freedom. He succeeded in enlarging the crack so that he was able to escape. Henceforth the ant lion was taboo to his lineage. Again another fable tells of a crocodile who came up on the bank of the river and left food for a certain family. Eventually it turned out that it was a reincarnated ancestor. It, too, became taboo to the grateful family. A third story tells of the early history of the Diara men. During a period of famine two of these men grew claws and became semibeasts. Once when they were sleeping together one raped the other. The victim of this attack gave birth to lion cubs. Lions are therefore taboo to this lineage.

The basic mythological symbolism is very clearly exemplified in the techniques of daily living. Woven cotton cloth is made in various striped and checked patterns. White stands for Faro. Those who dress in it are following religious rules, the word of Faro. Indigo, embodying Mousso Koroni, is obscurity and impurity. Women wear it when their menstruation is over and they are resuming sexual intercourse with their husbands. Those who die under a taboo are buried in this color. It is taboo to anything connected with Faro. Red signifies blood and is worn by hunters. Little boys wear shorts woven of three bands of color, the male number.

Circumcision preparation takes place in the Ntomo society which is something like the circumcision "schools" we shall meet among the Bantu. This group meets outdoors at the foot of the tree which contains their patron spirit. The boys, from seven to fourteen, are sometimes beaten, perform masked dances and sometimes represent men and women, mimicking sexual intercourse. They are prepared to undergo the operation of circumcision without showing pain. At the beginning of the rite, called the *soli,* the whole village drums and dances. The actual cutting is done at dawn. The prepuce is tied with a fiber, laid on the pembele, and the knife struck with an iron weight. The penis is also scarred twice, which is supposed to give the organ strength. The boys all then bleed together in a hole to get rid of their wanzo. A circumcision bonnet with ritual marks is put on their heads. The loss of prepuce symbolizes the removal of the female principle; the loss of clitoris stands for the removal of the male principle. The clitoridectomy operation is done in daylight; while it is taking place the victim is supposed to sing and show no pain. The seclusion of the boys after the rite is ended on the sixth day with another fiesta, including much feasting and drinking. On the seventh day the boys are given men's costumes. Brandishing lances, they simulate warlike acts. The group which goes through the soli together is separated into pairs, each pair being blood brothers for life. At the very end of the ceremony they jump three times over the fire, which means that the wanzo has joined that of the boys of last year and also indicates that masculinity has been achieved. During the final fiesta the girls lie on a piece of striped cloth between the legs of their mothers, a sign of their birth as women.

Blacksmiths play a curious and important role in Bambara culture. They are a sort of endogamous caste with special ancestor cults. They are supposed to have received certain secrets from the eight bird ancestors, such as the proper way to build altars, techniques of protecting their hands from fire, and forging and consecrating the circumcision knife. It is they who perform the operation of circumcision. They possess magical powers, and are able to turn into animals or plants. Hyenas are sometimes thought to be their ancestors. The forges symbolize the blacksmith, the furnace is his body, the fire his head, the bellows his testicles, the blowpipe his penis.

Any failure to follow the taboos connected with ironworking would cause the blacksmith to become impotent because the bellows are his testicles. What is said to be the first forged iron ax is used on the altar at which ancestral sacrifice takes place. The anvil is placed in a public spot since before it such judicial matters as solemn oaths and marriage arrangements take place. Sexual activity near it is taboo but the spirits of the forge are sometimes evoked by sterile women to remedy their condition. The blacksmith also has a role in agricultural ceremonies and is generally the head of the Komo society, the most important men's organization.

The wives of the blacksmiths are the potters of the community. They have an organization of their own and a special altar. They can only become members of this society after excision and while still virgins, and are publicly examined to make sure of the latter fact. Sexual intercourse is taboo just before going to work. On the same day that the blacksmith is making an offering to his altar they also carry out ceremonies before their own which contains the same spirits. They strip and "present their sex before and behind" to the altar, this gesture symbolizing their submission to the spirits subordinate to Faro. Still naked, they circle a heap of cinders left over from the previous firing. They then build a large fire which attracts bee-eater birds. These they shoot down with slings, burn to ashes, and mix the ashes with oil with which to anoint their bodies before purifying themselves by going through the flames. The potters also perform the operation of clitoridectomy upon the girls of the tribe at puberty.

There are various types of altars at which sacrifice takes place. Family altars generally are placed in the storehouse of tools and weapons. Designs symbolic of the universe from the Faro myth are done in ochre on the walls. There are altars for the head of the house, for his son, and for war. In the court of the chief's residence, where his throne is set, various wooden objects are planted in the soil above the body of an albino. Apparently in the past, human sacrifice was carried out in times of national crisis. An albino was generally chosen; being unusual, and conceived during sexual intercourse at midday, which was taboo, he was therefore especially full of mana.

Outside the village are sacred trees or rocks containing spirits. Often an animal such as a crocodile, female donkey, or monkey is associated with such shrines. The offerings include cotton cloth, kola nuts, chicken or sheep. The animal associated with the shrine must be fed and protected.

Charles Monteil describes ancestor sacrifice as follows: The head of the household squats in front of the door of the room containing the altar, "his head covered, holding a chicken in his hand." He speaks to the last deceased: " 'I offer you this chicken in my name and in the name of my children. In agreement with our dead fathers and mothers preserve us from dya-eating sorcerers and the evil deeds of the wicked; protect us against sickness and calamity, keep us in health, give us faithful wives, healthy children, make our farming successful, give us rain. . . .' "

Sometimes a specific request is made and in this case the behavior of the sacrifice is used in divination. The officiant cuts its neck and lets the blood run on the wall of each side of the window of the room containing the altar. He throws the chicken a little way and watches the position in which it dies. If its feet are toward the sacrificer, this is a good sign. Divination includes examining animal viscera. When a man has been on a journey he examines a sacrificed cock; if the testicles are normal his wife has been faithful to him. Twenty-two bones are cast which are in part bones but also include other objects such as shells. A very complicated system of interpretation is used which is intricately based on the creation myth.

An important part of Bambara psychic life (and of most African tribes of Negro or even partially Negro stock) is the ritual of the various secret societies. In these Faro is worshiped through the intermediation of the patron spirit. The most important of these groups is the Komo organization. It is headed, as has been mentioned, by the blacksmith, who must be a man of honesty and integrity. The altar is a hut outside of the town containing shelves on which are *boli*. These objects are more or less altars, symbolic of the universe and a résumé of the psychic force of the society. The hut is very taboo to all except adept initiates, and particularly to women. Boli number one is a sack containing grain always kept wet with sacrificial blood. The second boli has grain and gold in it, the third an engraved stone used for war magic. Monteil describes them as covered with fetid blood, feathers and viscera, on the whole nauseating objects to the European who is not affected by their symbolism. On the floor are small altars into which are stuck animal horns containing ritual powders. On the walls of the sanctuary are designs symbolizing the creation myth. The mask incarnates Komo, the spirit of the organization. Its wearer is appointed for each ceremony by the head of the society. By use of the mask and by dancing, the Bambara leave the ordinary world and enter the supernatural one. The mask itself may be human or animal; among the latter shapes, panther, stork, eagle, elephant and vulture appear. It is made of wood or skull bone (human or hyena) and painted white, black and red. Sometimes it is ornamented with wild duck feathers or a beard. It is said to be the face of the ancestor which is supposed to frighten uninitiates. "The eyes of the mask are big so that Komo may see and unveil all; the nostrils are wide for he must smell and sense good and evil things. The mouth is twisted for Komo does not speak, he only whistles and sings. The ears are huge so that he may hear everything, even what everyone secretly says in his heart. The chin of the mask is square, is a sign of purity, decision and clairvoyance." A costume of strips of wood with sleeves ending in copper hooks impregnated with viper poison is also worn. It is taboo to women or uninitiates. The mask wearer is made drunk on beer, carries the boli in a bag and a whistle between his teeth. An officiant goes before with a special iron bell to warn noninitiates to run away. Monteil speaks of the voice of the Komo being the sound of a metal trumpet. In his description the mask is carried on a stick while the bearer is hidden under a mantle covered with guinea hen and chicken feathers. "He creates, in the firelight, the illusion of a fantastic being whose cries, transmitted by the horn, freeze even the faithful initiates with fear." Monteil describes two annual ceremonies in which the procession circles the village with an orchestra of drums, flutes and metal striking bars. The other officiants wear costumes of palm leaves and hemp fibers surmounted by a hood with eyeholes which has a red ochre wooden crest and sometimes a bird's beak. The torchbearers wave their flares and shriek like madmen; the orchestra plays and echoes Komo's wild hoots. According to Germaine Dieterlen, the real adepts are taught secrets of the cult and the boli on penalty of death if they reveal them. The secret lore is taught through the medium of symbolic designs traced on the floor of the Komo hut. Komo's poisoned hook is used upon maleficent sorcerers who are sometimes revealed by the mask. Komo wounds the victim, who subsequently dies and is thrown to the hyenas, denied burial. If a virgin inadvertently approaches the night ceremony (which is taboo to women) she may be killed by Komo in memory of a former annual sacrifice of virgins to Faro. The mask only appears in night ceremonies. The Komo society has power over all village matters and has influence in all social ceremonies, since its chief is generally a diviner. Initiates of other villages attend appearances of the mask. Its festivals become social affairs at which myths are told and marriages arranged. The society also plays a role enforcing social privileges and obligations and takes part in administering justice.

The Kore or Kwore society is perhaps next in importance, for it is concerned with rainmaking. The society is proprietor of the communal millet fields. It is taboo to all women. The members possess a sacred tree near the village at which they sacrifice in May on first hearing thunder. They decorate the tree with creation designs. This is to purify the sky where the clouds stand for Mousso Koroni's mad progress. New members are initiated with considerable flagellation and the pembele is told the story of Mousso Koroni. At the end of winter the anniversary ceremony takes place. Dressed only in penis sheaths, the members dance around the sacred tree and burn each other with torches. Bruises and burns commemorate certain combats of the spirits in the sky to obtain rain. In the center of the town these costumed spirits appear on wooden horses. They dance and sing while they continue to whip and burn each other and throw pepper powder in the faces of the other dancers to recall the burning skies and the storm winds. These

Kworedugas or clowns speak a comic language and make up witty strophes of a satirical nature. The disapproving Abbé Henry describes the ritual: "Two or three tatougoula start the dance with a torch in each hand. They singe their backs, breasts and armpits and make a thousand sparks rain on their heads and hail on their skins before they go out. They devote themselves above all to their dirty songs; they become aware of their gourds with holes in them which they shake with rage and more than one dancer gets scorched. . . . And when the torches are burned down, they squat before the great drum, shake their burnt handful of straw and it is now an obscene gesture that provokes choking laughter, a hou! hou! from the *souroukou,* a roar from the *ajara,* a snigger from the *soula* and around the gourds cries of encouragement, '*O do,* that's it!' "

The Kworedugas also amuse the public with a kind of theater; they mimic sexual intercourse between men and women or carry dolls with exaggerated sexual parts with which they mimic the same act. Similar puppets are made by agricultural workers and used in skits. In fact these clowns seem to suggest that among the Bambara a sort of germinal Aristophanic drama exists.

There are numerous other societies, among them that of the Nama, which is the hyena. The officiants wear headdresses of wood in the form of fantastic birds. Monteil speaks of a possible sacred marriage rite but gives no details. The Nama procession traverses the village in order to drive out sorcerers. The procession preceded by the warning bell discovers in some of the huts objects made by the shadow-eating sorcerers. If these are identified, they are chased and said to expire near the Nama hut.

Burial ceremonies involve ancestor worship and references to the basic mythology. The dead man is washed and wrapped in a supple piece of matting. The women wail loudly accompanied by singing and handclapping. Care is taken not to touch the dead because of the impurity of the corpse. According to Monteil, the body is laid out under a shelter in the courtyard where members of the family come to pay their respects, ask pardon, and confess their faults. The individual mourner says, "Pardon us, don't be angry, we love you, we respect you, be happy and protect us." The wailing chorus adds, "Give us rain in the winter season, render our harvest abundant, make our house prosperous, give us many children, women, and riches." The head of the family passes his hand over the face of the dead to receive his nyama which he gives to the pembele by rubbing the groove in it, whereupon it joins the benevolent ancestral forces. His name, ni, and double will be given to a child born to the family. A sacrifice is made so that the dead man will leave his family in peace and be good to them. If the departed is a chief or an important person, the Komo head speaks to him by whistling in his ears. At the grave, water (sacred to Faro) is poured on the head of the dead man with an invocation as the matting is removed.

As the grave is filled up the chorus of women claps and sings, "Our *Fa* [head of family] is dead. Young men fill the grave so that no sorcerer, hyena, or wild beast may remove it." Sometimes a chicken is put into the grave to keep off misfortune. The matting is burned. A piece of the shroud may be kept for its magic properties.

When the family returns home the dead man's dog is killed. Monteil writes that sometimes a dog is bought for this purpose, which suggests that this is really a dog sacrifice. The mourners eat a communal meal and food is given to the poor. For eight days the family stays at home, then the house is purified. The wife of the dead man cannot be purified until the end of the moon. At the fortieth day the flesh and bone of the corpse are believed to separate. This is the real end of the mourning period and the date at which a new Fa or chief is chosen. (Such a belief concerning the state of the body suggests a survival of the diminished-life concept and perhaps throws light on the attitude of the megalith builders toward the body.) If all burial rites are not strictly observed, the nyama of the dead may injure the members of the family.

Interestingly enough, the Bambara, Dogon and Bozo tribes all employ symbols connected with the mythology, which are often painted on the sanctuaries. Symbols have also been found painted on rocks. There are two systems, one representing vulgar or common knowledge, and the other the more secret esoteric lore. There are 266 such ideograms which represent the names of things and abstractions. Sometimes they are engraved on gourds burned in the fields during agricultural ceremonies; some are engraved on the front of the Komo masks. Others are used in the circumcision ceremony. The 266 signs were those which were created in the beginning before the things themselves were created.

Some of these signs were said to have been used formerly for royal messages, engraved on gourds or pieces of wood serving as safe conducts or administrative reports. Some are supposed to be still so used by certain chiefs. If this is the case, the Sudanese seem to have hovered on the verge of a true written language; but the religious aspects overshadowed the practical uses and prevented further development. In this respect the symbols parallel the Teutonic runes.

In general it appears that the metaphysical unity which pervades Sudanese life was a gradual and conscious blending of various elements. An early layer of animal magic and probably totemic concepts survives from an archaic hunting phase. We have seen that certain animals are associated with sacred trees and are taboo. The animal masks used by the secret societies are significant, the Nama organization even being named for the hyena. Although hunting is not an important activity today, Monteil states that hunting magic is still used, and sympathetic materials such as horns, hair, tails and excrement are employed in amulets. L. Tauxier also stresses the belief in shape-changing sorcerers. Some are credited with being able to turn into leopards. They then go forth at night to catch and eat human victims. Finally, the mythological stories which rationalize lineage taboos generally involve the prohibited animal with an ancestor. Concerning this, Tauxier writes: "I believe that this conception is a current and recent one which only masks a more ancient concept which we find among races of Africa more primitive than the Bambara, that of an ancestral relationship between the sacred animal and the clan."

Judging from the lack of an ancestor cult among the Bushmen and Pygmies, and the widespread relationship of this cult to organized clan structure all over Africa and elsewhere, it is a later development which parallels increasingly complex social organization.

The third element is the secret society which exhibits shamanistic traits on the one hand and on the other is related to the animal symbol and is a form which begins to suggest the worship of an individualized nature spirit. Although the Bambara creation mythology and symbolism, which weaves all this together, does not appear to contain Islamic borrowings, contact with the Arabs may have been a stimulus to abstract thinking. It is all the more surprising to find such a structure in a group without an advanced urban economy or a unified priesthood. Possibly the priesthood in the time of the empire was more organized than it is now.

In any case, the discovery of such an elaborately organized psychic life in the Sudan area suggests that in other preliterate cultures there may have been or still are unifying concepts which investigators have so far overlooked.

CHAPTER 25

"You Will Eat Grasshoppers..."

Bantu—largest group in Africa—cattle and male expression—slash-and-burn agriculture—abstract creator concept—secular character of ancestor worship —importance of shaman—his role as rainmaker and diviner—circumcision as assault—survivals of totemism.

S HAKA, paramount chief of the Zulus and empire builder, instituted the custom of taking his morning bath publicly while holding court. First he was soaped with a millet paste, then washed, all the while chatting with his councilors. Cosmetics were then brought, red ochre paste which was rubbed into the skin, followed by anointing with native butter until his beautifully built six-foot body shone with a ruddy silky gloss. He was then dressed in a kilt of furry tails, armlets and leg ornaments of white cows' tails, and a tall headdress of red plumes was placed on his head. His chair of state consisted of a huge roll of matting while beside him stood a page boy bearing the regal umbrella which consisted of the great oval white oxhide shield. Shaka in the first half of the nineteenth century, by dint of administrative ability, clearheaded rationality and personal honesty and courage, elevated himself to a paramount chieftaincy which controlled 200,000 square miles of Southeast Africa mostly in what is now Natal. He created an army of 50,000 men as well disciplined as the Roman legions. Shaka is an outstanding example of the warlike Bantu leaders who made this people the dominant group in Africa.

The Bantu-speaking tribes occupy roughly a third of the continent. From the Congo rain forests through the great lakes to the upper reaches of the Nile, along the east coast through South Africa to the Cape, this great aggregation of peoples represents waves of migrations of Negro stock carrying with them a basically unified culture. From the Nigerian plateau the Negroes spread northward and eastward, mixing with Caucasoid and Bushman stock. By about the sixth century A.D. they had reached the great lakes and upper Nile from whence they began to flood down the eastern side of the continent, rather as the Celts and Teutons overran Europe, driving the Bushman aborigines southward and engulfing the Pygmies. That the Bantu of South Africa were for a long time exposed to Bushman contacts is proved by the existence of clicks in Xhosa, Zulu and Swahili dialects.

The Bantu are tall, strongly built, lighter in color than true Negroes, the lips being thinner, the nose less broad, sometimes even aquiline. They all practice agriculture and use iron, their way of life varying with their physical environment.

The Cameroon Highlanders of the West Coast occupy swampy valleys with rivers running through them. The men are concerned with hunting and fishing and raise some cattle and pigs, leaving most of the agricultural labor to the women. In the rain forests of the Congo, where during windstorms roofs are carried to unbelievable distances and trees are snapped like matches, in the rainy season the rivers flood, pouring into lakes and over the plains. When the rains are over, the water drains back into the rivers, keeping them more or less navigable. In consequence, the rather small villages of the forest Bantu, consisting of thatched huts either conical or rectangular in shape, are situated on rises near the riverbanks, the streams serving as highways for dugout canoes. Hunting and netting fish are important activities, and, as we have seen, these forest groups sometimes also employ the Pygmies to hunt for them. Slash-and-burn agriculture is carried on where the riverbanks are fertile, the men doing the clearing and helping to weed while the rest of the work is assigned to the women. The Lele of the Congo, who live in the grasslands on the edge of the forest, still cling to a woodland psychology. Men's societies and most of the magical practices are concerned with hunting and rituals of dividing up game, yet the men also engage in weaving and sewing raffia squares which are used as currency.

In West Africa the Bantu absorbed the cattle complex from the north and carried it southward. Among these groups hunting ceases to be an important form of male expression and pastoralism takes its place. The cattle kraal is generally taboo to women. Boys are the cattle herders and cattle are status symbols. A ceremonial gift of livestock called the *lobola* takes place before a man obtains a bride. Although beef is eaten, animals are nearly always slaughtered solely on ceremonial occasions. Here, too, the major part of the agricultural labor is carried out by the women.

In the Transvaal, in July, the heat abates although the rain is not yet due. The mahogany and sala trees turn a delicate green, the sandy dunes are covered with blossoms and the marshes with pink and white lilies. The women set out for the hills and marshes carrying hoes with handles two or three feet long. They cut down the small trees with axes and burn the bases of large ones. Breaking the soil and burning the weeds goes on through August, September and October. In the wet hollows of the marshes, roots and stems are cleared away, small canals dug and sowed with rice, and pumpkins are planted in the weed heaps. Stems of sweet potatoes are set in the borders of the canals. When the rain comes in September, maize, mealie seeds, peanuts and beans are sown. Junod describes the women at work in communal groups: "Some fifty black bodies toiling vigorously, making the sand fly, their hoes working with marvelous rapidity, each one urging the other to greater exertion and all hurrying to finish the job! They know there in the hut ten big jars of beer brewed to a nicety await them, and that they will have a good time at midday, when the heat will be unbearable and the work done."

In November, December and January the whole village turns out to scare away the birds which descend on the crops in swarms. During this period weeding also takes place. At harvest time the maize is threshed by beating it with sticks on stone and clay threshing floors in the middle of the field.

In the area between the Drakensberg and the sea and down to the Cape, the Bantu peoples live in kraals or family groups with separate huts for the wives of the head of the family and their children. Although the Bantu clans which ramify through villages and towns are now patriarchal, Murdoch in many cases finds elements of structure which show that descent was orig-inally traced through the female line. The Bantu owe their unity to their loyalty to the office of chief. Kraals are grouped in subunits with subchiefs all owing allegiance to a central authority. There are now towns, in some cases with a population of several thousands. When such large groupings take place, the cultivated land and the grazing areas may be as much as a day's travel from the town.

In the region of Lake Victoria, a terrain of river valleys and hillsides dotted with umbrella-shaped acacias, aloes, wild figs and grotesque-looking sausage trees, individual kraals, high on the sides of valleys, consist of the familiar circular mud huts with conical straw roofs surrounded by fences of thornbushes. Near them are banana groves, maize and sorghum fields. Along the winding roads which crisscross the sides of the mountains, the women trudge bearing boxes and baskets filled with fruit or pottery.

The Bantu ability to dominate other peoples and to occupy such large areas of Africa is no doubt due to the institution of unified authority. Al-though Shaka and other war chiefs rose to their positions of importance through personal qualities, in the Congo area we also find the institution of divine king. The ruler of the Kongo tribe maintained a capital at San Sal-vador, so named by the Portuguese, who created a colonial domain in the forest in the fifteenth century and profited from the fairly widespread Bantu institution of slavery. This monarch was an absolute despot with a ritual relation to the land. He was also highly taboo; no one might look upon him eating or drinking on pain of death. The symbols of his office included an ivory throne, a white cap and a zebra's tail. Surrounded by a court consisting of slaves, pages, a large harem, a chief priest and a royal executioner, he exercised the supreme judicial power and possessed the exclusive right to inflict the death penalty. The king appointed provincial governors and district chiefs, mostly his own relatives. When he died, a sacred fire which had been kept burning throughout his reign was extinguished, his corpse was mummified by smoking and wrapping in cloth, and interred with human grave goods.

The Lovedu of Basutoland in South Africa have actually a divine female "king," the male ruler having been replaced some generations back by a woman. As is often the case elsewhere, the ruler must be physically perfect and controls the rain through special medicines and charms. She cannot die a natural death, for her vital forces must not be allowed to fail; she therefore commits suicide. Since she is a king she takes no husband but marries a number of wives. Her heir is chosen from among the children of the wives while her own sex life is secret and promiscuous. Despite this curious and exceptional substitution, Bantu psychology is strongly male-dominated; the warrior ideal is necessarily strong in a people oriented toward conquest.

Although all of the Bantu practice agriculture and this social activity is carried on chiefly by women, the Africans do not seem to have developed the idea of a female spirit of fertility, nor has their possibly archaic matrilineal society had any effect on their religion. The main features are a vaguely defined creator entity, minor spirits often associated with men's societies, magicians (divided into beneficent diviners and healers and maleficent sorcerers), hunting magic and totemism.

The Bantu concept of a creator god who is also an ancestor or first man has caused considerable discussion and controversy. The cultural bias of European fieldworkers, many of whom have been missionaries, has tended to elevate this entity to Supreme Being. Unfortunately the creator spirit of Africa does not behave like a respectable Western patriarchal divinity. Although he is often said to have created all things, he has done nothing since. He has no moral attributes and he is not worshiped by the majority of tribes. In most cases there is no detailed mythology connected with the creator god; he is anthropomorphized only in name and plays no role in the daily life of the people. Indeed, the concept of divinity among the Africans should be approached without preconceptions and prejudiced terminology. An analysis of actual statements by Zulu informants, which Canon Henry Callaway recorded with remarkable objectivity in the last century, helps to define Bantu psychological attitudes. Unkulunkulu is the old, old one. "The old men say Unkulunkulu is the first outcomer, for they say he came out first, they say he is the source of being from which all men broke off. Unkulunkulu is; he made the first men, the ancients of long ago. . . ." Further efforts to clarify the nature of the entity produced the following: "To us black men Unkulunkulu is a stalk of maize. It may produce the ear, it can be plucked, and the stalk be left, and decay in the place where it grew; the grains of the cob are Unkulunkulu. . . . And we black men did not say that Unkulunkulu was in heaven; we said he came to be and died; that is all we said." From this it seems that Unkulunkulu was the primal creator and the created, which is capable of reproduction but itself dies. In other words, Unkulunkulu is a name for a process. Another concept expressed by a Zulu informant is that "All things, as well as Unkulunkulu, sprang from a bed of reeds—everything, both animals and corn, everything coming into being with Unkulunkulu." The only specific action attributed to Unkulunkulu is the sending of the perverted message. He told the chameleon to go to men and say, "Let men not die." The chameleon set out but loitered on the way. As it went, it ate the fruit of a bush called Ubukwebezane. After a while Unkulunkulu sent a lizard after the chameleon. The lizard ran quickly, for Unkulunkulu had reversed himself and told it to say, "Let men die." The lizard returned before the chameleon had reached its destination. The latter finally arrived and shouted, "It is said, let men not die." Men, however, answered, "Oh, we have accepted the word of the lizard. We cannot hear your word. Through the word of the lizard we will die."

Other informants gave Unkulunkulu a wife who also came from the reeds, but there were no details concerning her. It seems probable the word Unkulunkulu is simply a concrete way of thinking about the process of creation. The Zulus also speak of male and female sky or heaven depending on its helpful or harmful qualities. Here there is no question of a sky god, it is simply the preliterate's tendency to use concrete expressions to designate abstractions for which he has not developed a specific vocabulary. In this connection J. H. Driberg writes of the creator god idea: "The universal power to which I refer is a concept world-wide in occurrence, and appears under a number of names both in Africa and elsewhere, the best known of which (as it has received most literary expression) is mana. This spiritual force consists of an abstract power or natural potency, formless as the ether, all pervasive and definitely never regarded anthropomorphically . . ." He finally concludes: "In point of fact the 'High God' idea does not exist in Africa . . . the African has his power concept. . . ." We have met the mana concept many times before and recognize it as the ambivalent power felt to reside in the unusual, a supernatural order of force which can be either helpful or harmful and which can be channeled by the magician for weal or woe.

The mana concept best describes African psychology, as can be seen from further exploration of the Zulu supernatural world. Since Unkulunkulu created man he is also responsible for the Amatonga, all men who have died, to whom the Zulus pray. After death a man is summoned by the Amatonga. "When anyone dies among black men, they lament very much and make a great noise and when he is buried, all his things are taken and a large fire kindled to burn them; not a single thing he wore on his body is left, all is burned, for they are afraid to wear the property of a dead man. . . . When a man dies among the black men the grave is covered over with branches. The person to whom the dead man belongs watches over the grave continually. If a son has died, his father watches the branches constantly that when they see the branches are rotten they may be satisfied knowing that nothing can now disturb the remains for they are rotten. And if he observes a snake on the grave, the man who went to look at the grave says on his return, 'Oh I have seen him today basking in the sun on top of the grave.' " This, of course, indicates both fear of contamination by a dead man's possessions, the belief that something living lingers in the body until it decays, and also the belief in reincarnation in animal form which we have already indicated as a characteristic of totemism. If no snake comes out, cattle are sacrificed so that the spirit will come back and prove it is not angry. The Zulus worship the dead (a man's father especially, "for they know him best") because the spirit of the dead can cause misfortune, disease and death, if he is angry; prosperity, fertility and success in war if he is kindly disposed. "And if there is illness in the village, the eldest son praises him with praise-giving names which he gained when fighting with the enemy, and at the same time praises all the other Amatonga; the son reproves the father, saying, 'We for our parts may just die. Whom are you looking after? Let us die, all of us, and you will see whose house you may enter. You will eat grasshoppers; you will no longer be invited to go anywhere, if you destroy your own village.' "

This passage illustrates another point made by most observers concerning ancestor worship. It is not carried out in any mood of awe or reverence. There is no great separation between the real world and the world of the ancestors and there is no sharp dividing line between the dead and the living. The clan, as we have seen in other cultures, consists of both living and dead, the reservoir of supernatural power or mana pervades both branches. The African asks, beseeches, and expostulates with his dead ancestors as he would with his live kin. Among the Kavirondo the dead are talked to as in life, a wife sometimes even stops wailing to scold the dead, and no religious awe is shown. Junod writes, "If the gods were actually old people still living, they could not be addressed with more familiarity." Just as a Bantu youth moves from one age set to another, so the adult in a rite de passage at death moves on to another kind of status, frightening and different, it is true, but nevertheless leaving the dead still present in the world, affecting and a part of his kinship group. The ancestor still subscribes to the network of privilege and obligation of kinship and gets a special portion of good just as the living elder does. In some cases, in which the soul of an ancestor is supposed to be reborn when the name is given to a child, the living force of the clan is here clearly put in circulation again. The concept of mana, although not concretized by most of the Bantu, is nevertheless sociologically a useful way of understanding the African point of view. The omnipresent mana can operate as follows: (1) A man living or deceased can reinforce or diminish the being of another man; (2) the vital human force can directly influence the inferior force which resides in animal, vegetable or mineral beings; (3) a rational being (spirit, ancestor, or living man) can act directly upon another rational being by communicating this vital influence to an inferior force in an animal, vegetable or mineral.

The confusion in the minds of Western observers arises from the fact that the preliterates who arrive at a fairly complicated transitional or agricultural way of life begin to deal to some extent with abstractions but possess a concrete vocabulary. Hence the ambiguity concerning "spirits" which seem to be neither gods nor material things. The African denies that he is worshiping a tree or an animal; it is an indwelling spirit with which he is concerned. In most cases the spirit has no anthropomorphic form, its worshiper is grasping at an abstraction but his habit of mind and life demand something concrete to symbolize his feelings, hence the offering placed at the foot of the tree. This process is not a simple one, however, since this fluid state of intellectual development leads in various directions. The human mind, even in areas which are the province of emotion rather than logic, still yearns for order and system, hence even the supernatural processes become classified; the psychic activities of man are divided up into several souls (dream soul is fairly close to the unconscious), magic is elevated to a pseudo science. As has been said before, the abstraction, in order for the preliterate to handle it, must be given "a local habitation and a name," very often a human name. Various degrees of anthropomorphism result. In Africa this can be seen in connection with elements in nature. Rain, a river, iron, even a pestilence, are significant in the lives of the worshiper and hence fraught with mana. Once given a name, the human tendency to create fiction can lead to concrete personality. Likewise certain ancestors, war leaders, rainmakers, shamans, inventors or culture heroes become set apart from the kinship network and hence are on the way to divinity. Sometimes there is crossing between the ancestor deity and the incipient nature deity. Junod cites an ancestor of the Thonga, Makanetu, who is also the sea. In summation, the chief problem which has stood in the way of understanding early religions has been a lack of semantic sophistication. The local and specific forms which belief and ritual take, however, are based on temperamental, environmental and historical factors which can only at times be made out.

If the ancestor cult is the chief form of worship among the Bantu, it is, as has been pointed out, relaxed and secular. Shrines are relatively simple altars set up in huts, a group of stones in the court of a compound, sometimes an altar in the center of the village. In most cases no temples are built. Among the Lunda of the Congo where hunting magic seems to have been crossed with the ancestor cult, a small pathway leads to an anthill terminating in a forked stick on which are hung shreds of cloth or bits of animal entrails. The Thonga make their offering to a tree or a branch stuck in the ground. They place before it beer and woven cloth while the eldest male utters the invocation and uterine nephews kill the sacrificial fowl. Some of the forest Bantu carve crude wooden images which are placed in huts.

The Bantu ideas concerning another world are not universally concretized. The Thonga believe that their forebears reside either under the earth carrying on their activities as in life, or in a sacred wood. Ofter there is an idea of a gradually changing status. The Kavirondo Bantu, who believe the heart is consciousness and vitality and the shadow more or less the soul, conceive of the soul as looking like smoke, and for many years sensitive to any harm the body may suffer. For the first few days after death the shadow sits on the roof of the granary or in a tree. Later it goes beneath the earth or to the west, where it maintains the same status as in life. In the past, human grave goods sometimes accompanied a chief. Among the Zulus, "They cut much firewood and as there were oxen, too, the chief's ox with which he made royal festivals was killed and with him . . . when the fire was kindled the chief was put in; and then his servants were chosen and put into the fire after the chief; the great men followed, they were taken one by one. They said so-and-so is fit to go with the chief." Ten young girls were obliged to undergo sati burial in 1857 with the corpse of Shaka's mother. Countless warriors were also killed, and indeed so disturbed was this chief by the death of his mother that he became partially unbalanced and undertook an orgy of killing.

In some cases it is felt that the ancestors are inimical for about a year and then they become reconciled to their status and join the helpful kinship group. The Kavirondo burial rites include dramatizing of incidents in the dead man's life with expressions of honor and respect, and a great dance takes place at which he looks on. The cooling-off period in which he is dangerous lasts several months during which daily food offerings are made. They are at length given up as he passes to the other world. His hut may be torn down or a rafter from it buried in a swamp to keep him from returning. Indeed the constant ambivalence toward the ancestor reflects the classic and basic ambivalence which the psychoanalyst sees in the parent-and-child situation.

The communications of the ancestors often take place in dreams, and through various forms of divination. At times the dreams are explicit, at times they must be clarified by a professional who uses divination. The professional may also receive direct communication through the voices of familiar spirits. The professional magician or diviner, whose trance performance has already been described among the Bushmen and Pygmies, is a continent-wide phenomenon in Africa. His status varies in different Bantu tribes. Sometimes he is an ecstatic shaman, sometimes he merely casts the bones; among the Tembu the profession is divided into herbalists and healers and diviners. Among the Zulus the shaman is concerned with rainmaking and averting the damage caused by severe storms and hail. Although he may undergo training, he generally has a psychic predisposition toward disassociation and hysteria. He generally feels the call in the form of psychic disturbance which leads to apprenticeship. The Zulu description of this process is remarkably dramatic. He begins by dreaming. He "dreams continually of many snakes encircling his whole body while he is in a pool of water. He quits the water heavy with snakes. . . ." Other symptoms follow. "He begins to be delicate, not having any real disease but being very delicate . . . he dreams of many things and his body is muddied and he becomes a house of dreams. And on awakening he says to his friends, 'My body is muddied today; I dreamed many men were killing me; I do not know how I escaped and on awaking one part of my body felt different from other parts; it was no longer alike all over.' At last the man is very ill and they go to the diviners to inquire. The diviners do not at once see that he is about to have a soft head." However, when he remains ill for as long as two years, when his hair falls off his body and becomes scurfy, and he yawns continually, they recognize the signs which gradually become more acute. "He habitually sheds tears, at first slight, and at last he weeps aloud and in the middle of the night, when people are asleep he is heard making a noise and wakes the people by singing; he has composed a song and men and women awake and go out to sing in concert with him. They are afraid he will die but he goes on singing. . . . Perhaps he sings till morning, no one having slept. The people of the village clap their hands in concert till they are sore. And then he leaps about the house like a frog and the house becomes too small for him and he goes leaping and singing and shaking like a reed in the water and dripping perspiration." He finally goes to a diviner who purifies him with emetics. Ancestor spirits speak to him by whistling, telling him what to do. His divination ability is then tested by the tribe.

Among the Bantu tribes where there is tension over rain, the magician plays an important role as a rainmaker, and even in the Kavirondo area where rain is plentiful his office is also important, indicating perhaps that local tradition stems from a different region. Not only do such magicians bring rain but they also control the bad effects of storms. Actually lightning and thunder are considered to be a bird which deposits its urine in the ground. Magicians use portions of this bird after killing it to help in their magic. It is variously described, sometimes with wings so large that one could cover two men. The concept is interesting because of similar lightning or thunderbirds in other parts of the world. A Zulu informant discussed it as follows: "A man may think it is red; again he sees it is not so, it is green. But if he looks earnestly he may say 'No, it is something between the two colors as I am looking at it.' While I was living in Umsunduzi I myself saw a feather of this bird; and at length I saw one of its feathers. The man to whom it belonged took it out of his bag; and truly I saw it and said 'Indeed it is the feather of this dreadful bird.' He also showed me one of its bones; it was like a bone in which are many little blood vessels and many little gray lines." The emotional attitude surrounding the process of controlling the sky is dramatized by the same informant. "I was sitting in the doorway while it was thundering very much, and my brother who is a doctor entered the house running and took down his shield and his string of medicines and went out. When it thundered aloud he, too, shouted aloud and whistled. I asked my mother what the man was doing. She replied 'Do not speak for when it is like this, no one any longer speaks. He is a heaven-herd.' So I was silent and I thought he would die for the sky cast down many hailstones and I heard them striking on his shield; it was as though maize had been thrown on him. But although he resisted very much he did not enter the house. And as regards the lightning in a like manner the sky resisted him; but he did not enter the house until it was bright again." Other practitioners blew a special whistle or flute, covered with lizard skin with coral beads imbedded in the end, and told the sky to go away. The Kavirondo sky control involves a magic stick.

The life of a rainmaker is not always one of riches and honor (consisting of presents of goats and cows), for if he fails in his duty he is charged with intentional malpractice. The Kavirondo rainmaker fills pots with water in a secret place. In 1933, in North Kutosh, this was done but the sky cleared before rain fell. The rainmaker left town but his two sons were caught and beaten. When asked why they had not simply denied their power, they replied they would rather be beaten occasionally than give up a profitable profession.

Although the professionals just described engage in socially approved activities, the concept of harmful magic, or the bad side of mana, is also universal. Africans share the usual disturbed attitude toward death found among most primitives. It is understood that death may result from natural causes, but the unconscious refuses to admit it, any more than disease can be accepted as a normal hazard. Even granting that old people do die from general decay, the precise moment and particular circumstances under which death takes place are attributed to witchcraft. Thus the Western idea of *chance* is not accepted by the African; the supernatural power governs every event specifically. As a result, the drama of the unconscious is expressed in the fear of harmful magicians. Among the Kavirondo, who are particularly apprehensive concerning black magic, the evil tendency is passed down matrilineally and some clans are accused of having particular aptitudes. A man may be a black magician in spite of himself, his shadow going forth to create trouble without his knowing it.

The Thonga, however, believe that there are secret societies of such persons, dedicated to eating human flesh. (All over the world dangerous spirits are associated with cannibalism.) The Thonga also believe, as do the Bambara, that a wild beast remains while the sorcerer withdraws from his or her body and flies at night. They tell a story of a man whose father told him to beware of his wife, that he must stab her while she slept, for what lay beside him at night was not real. The man stabbed the simulacrum, and it immediately turned into a hyena which ran off defecating and howling. In the morning something fell from the roof of the man's hut— it was his wife, wounded in the leg and still sleeping. This belief seems allied to the belief that human beings are reincarnated as animals and is strengthened by the actual behavior of such secret societies as those existing among the Baluba of the Katanga area. The Batambo society's only purpose was torture and revenge. W. F. Burton says, "They pretend to be lions and tear their victims at night with an iron instrument. It is said they put wooden imitations of lions' pads on their feet."

The Kavirondo, being experts in these matters, are sure that evil sorcerers dance naked at night around the house of their victims. Any such caught by the villagers are put to death by running a sharpened stake up the anus. Other groups call upon beneficent magicians who are specialists in witch finding. Junod noted that the typical witch finder of the Thonga or Zulu groups carries shields and arrows and a gnu's tail containing special drugs and decorated with copper wire and beads. Cow horns full of medicine hang at his waist over his bead girdle and panther-skin kilt, and on his head is a great feather headdress. "He falls into a condition of extreme nervous excitement and ecstasy, and inspiration. He brandishes his tail, dilates his nostrils, inhales the air on all sides as if to smell the spot from whence the evil influence has emanated, then takes to his heels in a certain direction, the assembly still clapping their hands and singing." He finally enters the hut of the accused and plants his *assegai* where the incriminating magical equipment is to be found. Questioning and ordeals of poisoning or intoxicating drinks are also used.

Still another function of the magician, that of divining, to unmask witches, is also carried out by specialists. There is an uninspired type of divining in which the seer asks questions (much as the modern crystal reader or palmist) while the client beats the ground when the guess is near the mark. This type of clairvoyance is not much respected. Casting of bones is of course widespread. A variant used by the Kavirondo is pebble divining. A flat oval tray contains four to six pebbles, bits of charcoal, the horntip of an antelope. At first bad influences are driven out of the hut by the use of gourd rattles. Then the diviner, while mumbling the names of the client's ancestors, swings the tray in his right hand with a rotary motion. If the pebbles all drop off, the ancestors are not responsible, but if some stick (as they can be made to do by centrifugal force) the ancestor named when this happens is causing the trouble. Günter Wagner felt that the diviner showed quick perceptions and, by certain leading questions, was able to discover what the client suspected. He then proceeded to confirm his customer's suspicions, thereby reducing his anxieties. The typical African consults his diviner before any undertaking rather as a Western sophisticate might ask the opinion of his therapist.

Most of the Bantu practice circumcision, surrounding it with so much ritual and taboo that the ceremonial becomes a matter of great social importance. It is probable that several ideas and drives enter into the complex. In the first place, it is clearly a rite de passage (or ceremony of transition) into adult responsibility in the community. Even though it may take place late in life (among the Kavirondo from twelve to thirty) responsibilities and privileges are withheld until it has been experienced. Men who for some reason avoid it have no status. In some cases there is a "circumcision school" in which the boys are taught practical arts such as hunting and are initiated into sexual matters, very often in terms of bawdy songs. In other tribes there is a dramatization of death and resurrection, indeed in most cases when the boys appear after the operation or during their dances in the ceremonial period they are decorated or daubed with white clay and supposed to be unrecognizable. The presence of an animal spirit or the pretense that the officiants are animals who do the actual circumcising, which occurs among the Baluba and even among Junod's plains Sotho, carries us back to an earlier hunting phase in which an animal (and human) totemic victim was probably ritually killed. Junod describes eight "lion men" heads covered with lion manes, sitting in front of eight boys. The boys are hit on the head from behind; when they turn their heads the lion men rapidly cut off the prepuce. The period of seclusion and ordeal

Predynastic Egyptian pot, Gerzean period, fourth millennium B.C., depicts what may be an early goddess accompanied by two males.

Predynastic clay female figurine in a dancing pose similar to the preceding, same period. Possibly another image of an early goddess.

Palette of King Narmer, probably first dynasty, third millennium B.C. First sacral king to unify Egypt, he wears crowns of North and South, totemic nome standards are carried ahead of him. At top human-faced cows may indicate coalescence of early goddess with cow. At bottom the king as a bull destroys a city and tramples upon his enemies.

The Metropolitan Museum of Art, Dodge Fund, 1931

In Egypt the pyramid becomes a tomb. First Egyptian pyramid, tomb of Zozer, third dynasty, third millennium B.C.

Ewing Galloway

Animal-headed gods of Egypt, probably of totemic origin. *Upper left:* Horus, the royal falcon, wearing the crowns of Upper and Lower Egypt. *Upper right:* Wolf god, probably nome from Upwaut. *Lower right:* Sakhmet, the lion goddess. *Lower left:* Thoth, the ibis god, the scribe.

After Summers

Rock drawings attributed to Bushmen from Mashonaland, Africa. Animal identification suggests early ritual. *Top left:* "Bat" man. *Top right:* Animal-headed entity with tail. *Below:* Four "crocodile" men greeted by bowing worshipers.

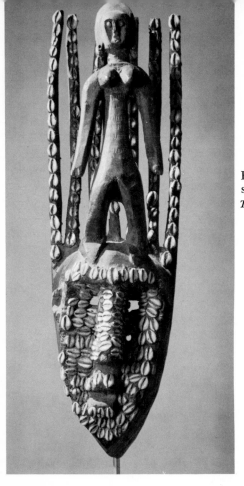

Bambara initiation mask used by boys' N'toro society, West Africa.
The Museum of Primitive Art

Bambara Komo society mask in the form of a bird's head, West Africa.
The Museum of Primitive Art

Zulu shaman fighting an oncoming hailstorm, South Africa.
The American Museum of Natural History

Image of Egungun headdress representing the trickster, Legba, Dahomey, West Africa.
The Museum of Primitive Art: Photo by Charles Uht

Fertility doll, Ashanti, West Africa.
The Museum of Primitive Art:
Photo by Charles Uht

Carved wooden stool in the form of a leopard believed to contain an ancestor's soul, Ashanti, West Africa.

The Museum of Primitive Art:
Photo by Charles Uht

Photo Spencer, National Museum of Victoria

Medicine men at work. Shaman at left conducts the examination; oldest medicine man of group sits on right. Diagnosis, a dead man's bone had gotten into the patient's body. Treatment, blowing in sick man's ear, singing over him and sucking to remove foreign matter from body. The patient died. Warramunga tribe, north-central Australia.

Man runs from hiding place in the scrub carrying a bundle of decorated grass which represents the Wollunqua snake, a totemic ancestor similar to the python of Arnhem Land. Warramunga tribe, north-central Australia.

Photo Spencer, National Museum of Victoria

Photo Spencer, National Museum of Victoria

Laying the Wollunqua snake to rest. The Warramunga believe thunder is his voice and it is hoped he will bring rain. White areas are made with grass-seed down instead of eagle down. The snake, in the dream time, stretched out 150 miles from his water hole, performed various ceremonies with his head, and left spirit individuals behind.

Ceremony connected with secondary burial. Body first placed in a tree, a year later some of the bones are buried in an anthill. One armbone is wrapped in bark cloth and decorated. The women of the tribe crawl through trench between men's legs, last one bearing the armbone. It is afterward buried with an emblem of the totem, the Wollunqua snake. Warramunga tribe, north-central Australia.

Photo Spencer, National Museum of Victoria

Men's house showing a shrine with trophy skulls and shields representing ancestors, Urama tribe, Papua, New Guinea.
The American Museum of Natural History

Urama taboo goblins who perform a dance around trees or gardens making them taboo and conserving the food for ceremonial feasts. Tall men's house in background.
The American Museum of Natural History

Masked dance (taboo to women) performed at boys' initiation ceremony by Fly River tribes of Papua, New Guinea. Masks are of bark cloth, dancers assume role of oracles and answer questions.

Boys wearing raffia costume used in initiation ceremony, Asmat tribe, Papua, New Guinea.

Marine spirit, Solomon Islands, Melanesia.

Malanggan, carving used in initiation and burial ceremonies, New Ireland, Melanesia.

Maori war dance showing grotesque faces made by participants which are intended to frighten the enemy, related to "warrior's paroxysm," New Zealand.

Easter Island stone heads connected with ancestor w

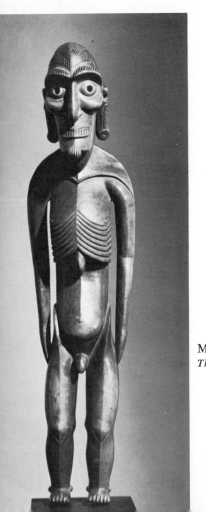

Male ancestor figure from Easter Island, Polynesia.

may take several months and involve considerable expense (hence it is often postponed for years until enough candidates are ready). It is marked by sadistic features in nearly every case. Among the Sotho, the boys are beaten daily, kept naked, given repulsive food, and made to suffer from the cold. Schebesta describes the actual operation among the forest Bantu as a violent assault in which a crowd of masked figures snatched the frightened boy from the protection of his mother. Among the Kavirondo the operator is painted red, black and white, wears a leopard skin and iron rattles on his legs. He is extremely fierce-looking and dances threateningly, waving the knife to frighten the boys, who are not supposed to show fear and even try to beat the operator. If a victim does show pain, his father is so humiliated that he runs away and hides in the bush. The brutal treatment of the boys, taken together with the operation itself (and the knocking out of two front incisors which often occurs about the same time), is probably once again a dramatization of unconscious drives, in this case the sexual rivalry between the adult males and the youths just entering manhood. As Laubscher writes: "The amount of sadistic pleasure exercised in beating the boys with the consent of the elders seems to gratify some unconscious hostility which their elders have against them. . . . It is not unlikely that at one time circumcision and castration had a similar connotation. . . ." C. G. Seligman, who points out that the psychoanalyst considers dreams concerning loss of teeth to show castration fear, has studied the distribution of the excision of teeth and circumcision. On the whole, except where there is a crossing of cultures, they tend to be mutually exclusive, which indicates that one is equivalent to the other.

Another element in the ceremony is the fact that it is so rigidly taboo to women that the boy is supposed to reject his mother and undergo a toughening (originally no doubt in preparation for war) during the ordeal, and the general stress upon male sexuality throughout. It is clear that the ceremony expresses an ambivalence, on the one hand a hostility toward and a symbolic castration action against the young male sexual rivals, and at the same time an acceptance of them into the male semihomosexual world with its fear of contamination by the female.

Although animal themes have recurred constantly in Bantu culture, clearly defined totemic clan structure is not as apparent as in other parts of the world. Probably all the southern Bantu were originally totemic. Numerous taboos concerning eating specific animals and the widespread belief that ancestors return in animal shape, which we have already seen in the case of the Zulu ancestor snake, are found among them. The forest Bantu, including the Baluba, Basonga and Bakongo, are also totemic and the Kpe of the Cameroons who are geographically near the origin of the Bantu peoples, possess a *Male* elephant society which is extremely significant. Members of this organization, which is exclusively male, possess elephant doubles. The aims of the group seem to be merely to revenge themselves upon enemies and to practice magic. In the form of their doubles they are supposed to travel great distances with miraculous speed. Before their dances they enter their animal bodies and damage planted fields to show their power. The dance itself depicts a group of hunters seeking elephants. After the hunters have danced a preliminary passage, the animals appear. Edwin Ardener describes them: "They are dressed from the waist down in large spreading skirts of palm fronds. The rest of the body and head and arms are completely enclosed in a loose headdress of sacking with a shaggy covering of palm fiber dyed red. From the upper part of this extend two long 'tusks' made of ironwood apparently held from inside by the dancer. The whole headdress is extensible to twice its length by holding the tusks at arms' length above the head. In addition each dancer wears strings of shells of a certain seed round his ankles with which he makes rhythmic rattling sounds as he stamps his feet." The mimic elephants rush about and make aggressive movements with the tusks at the hunters.

The Male institution seems to combine both extremely primitive and more recent elements. The mimetic hunting dance and the identification with the elephant take us back to the archaic practices of the Bushmen while the magical and hostile activities of the society remind us of the more complex organization of the Bambara.

On the whole, the Bantu tribes display survivals of the earliest forms of hunting magic, together with ancestor worship and the shaman magician, which are nearly universal in Africa, and are perhaps almost as old, and also the phenomenon of men's societies which are important in all true Negro cultures. Bantu religious activities are less complex than those of the true Negro groups of West Africa or the Nilotes of the upper Nile tributaries. They therefore remained in a more or less transitional phase, perhaps because of the mobility of these groups during their period of expansion.

In order to study the most elaborate structures of ritual and ceremonial which the African peoples have erected upon the simple slash-and-burn agricultural economy, we must turn to the West African area of the Dahomeans and the Yorubas and to the Blue and the White Nile, the abode of the Shilluk, Dinka and related pastoral peoples.

CHAPTER 26

The Divine Rain King

Shilluk—Egyptian influence on sacral king—death when physical vigor fails —Nuba shaman as step in development of divine king—totemic relationship to cattle among Shilluk and Nuer—Shilluk mythology in support of regal authority—installation of king as rite de passage for nation.

THE SHILLUK of the Upper Nile deform the horns of their cattle by training one of them to grow forward over the animal's forehead in exactly the same way as did the Egyptians, who depicted them thus in tombs dating from 2700 B.C. The Shilluk also have developed the institution of the sacred king to a point where it dominates their religious and political life. Just as in Egypt, the prosperity and fertility of the country depends upon the magical powers of the divine monarch.

This people together with the other pastoral groups of the White and Blue Niles represent an influx of Negro stock combined with Caucasoid elements. The original invasions from the west probably took place during the fourth millennium B.C., bringing with them elements of Sudanic agriculture. These Nilotic peoples evidently derived the cattle complex from the north by way of the Nubians and probably also acquired other elements of Egyptian civilization, including the sacral kingship. According to Seligman, the Egyptian influence is strongest among the Shilluk, weaker among the other Nilotic peoples, and probably was transmitted through the great lakes in the direction of the Congo where, as will be remembered, there are Bantu sacred kings.

The Nilotes are tall, slender, long-legged, Negroid, but often have aquiline noses, indicating a large mixture of Caucasoid blood. The men go naked, wearing no genital covering, and among them circumcision is regarded as a disgusting foreign custom. They are generally considered to be a proud, self-respecting group of peoples which clings determinedly to its ancient customs. Indeed the complicated ceremonial surrounding the Shilluk *reth,* or king, has survived Arab and Turkish conquest and persecution.

The country inhabited by these peoples consists of swampy savannas bordering the rivers. The tribes are all basically pastoral, the Shilluk less so since depredations of the Egyptians cut down their herds and forced a greater dependence upon slash-and-burn agriculture. The Dinka and the Nuer, with whom the Shilluk used to carry on intertribal war, drink the blood of their cattle ceremonially; the Nuer in particular raise the cattle cult to a complicated social institution. South and west of the White Nile the Nuba, who inhabit a hilly country, retain Negro features and more Negro traits, probably predating the Egyptian influence which modified the culture of the invaders elsewhere.

Shilluk houses are conical, thatched with grass. They are grouped in hamlets of a single clan, presided over by a chief. The village is horseshoe-shaped, the central space being used to tether sheep and cattle. There is only an occasional shade tree. The village population begins to stir before dawn. Some fires are made; any leftover food is eaten. According to the season the inhabitants then go to the fields to plant or cultivate. Various crops of millet are sown, one in April at the beginning of the rainy season. When the crops are nearly mature the children are left in the fields all day to stone the birds. In the dry season, an hour after sunrise, cattle and goats are tied up and milked. A few hours later they are driven off to pasture. Before this, some of the women have arrived from the water hole with pots of water on their heads. If there is a shady tree the old men gather and gossip and doze under it. The cattle are driven back to the village for a mid-day milking and shortly after this a light meal is eaten. The cattle are brought back again an hour before sunset; all of the herding and milking being done by the men who, however, share the field labor with the women. At sunset the main meal is eaten, after which dancing may take place or else groups sit quietly and talk.

Although the Shilluk conceive of various nature spirits and a remote creator god, Juok, ancestor worship is dominant and specifically the ancestor cult of the divine king. The mythology which rationalizes this belief is partly historical. Nyikang is supposedly the first Shilluk king (in 1932, thirteen generations removed from the reigning monarch). He is sometimes said to be descended from a great white cow or a crocodile, and has magical characteristics; he was supposedly able to blind his enemies. Nyikang is said to have led his people to their present territory from the southwest after a quarrel with his brother about the succession. He entered the domain of another tribe and married the daughter of the ruler, by whom he had a son, Dak, who was quarrelsome and something of a trickster. Nyikang was defeated in battle and disappeared in a whirlwind. He was succeeded by Dak. Another son, Cal, was a coward. Images of all three appear at the installation of the reth. In the past, Shilluk kings were said to marry their sisters.

This custom and the notion of descent from a cow both suggest the Egyptian heritage. Nyikang is manifest in every succeeding king and also in certain animals and in a wooden image in a shrine at Akura. Epileptics are possessed by him. He made people for his kingdom out of insects, fish, and animals. In another version of this tradition he saw that men were masquerading as animals and turned them into the men they really were. He also established totemism. On the rare occasions in which Juok is worshiped, he is approached through Nyikang. Juok in fact clearly represents the mana principle, for "anything the Shilluk cannot understand is Juok."

The king, as a manifestation of Nyikang, is treated with ambivalence. On the one hand, he is supposed to be omnipotent (although reduction of herds has reduced his cattle prestige) and even his sons should address him with their faces averted, the hand hiding the mouth and lower part of the face. He is also magically responsible for rain, fertility of crops, and prosperity. On the other hand, as has been mentioned before in connection with the Egyptian Sed ceremony, he was probably killed if he failed to satisfy his wives sexually or allowed the state to undergo some major misfortune such as famine, an epidemic, or a defeat in war. There are two versions of his death: one, already cited, in which he is walled up in a hut with a young virgin and left to starve and suffocate, while the other tradition states that any regal son had the right to kill his father at night and ascend the throne. In the past the reth is described as left alone at night with his wives and no guards. He was supposed to have spent his time in sleepless watchfulness, prowling fully armed, peering into the shadows or standing silent and tense in some dark corner. Although some authorities have questioned the violent ritual death of the king, evidence from the period of interregnum, before a new reth is installed, indicates that it was a period of special danger for the new monarch and that he continually feared attack by rivals. Also in neighboring tribes the same tradition of ritual killing by a relative exists.

The worship of Nyikang, the reth's ancestor, takes place in sacred huts or tombs scattered throughout the country. Drums are placed in the center of the village around which as many as a hundred men and women dance, the men with spears, the women with hippopotamus-hide whips, moving in surging spirals around the drums. The priesthood consists mainly of old men with epileptic tendencies and wives of the king who have passed the menopause. At various times during the ceremony a speech is made to Nyikang begging him not to let the birds eat the millet. The culmination of the rite is the spearing of a bull by the king. If it goes toward the river in its death agony, falls on the left side or near the shrine, it is a good omen. Since the Shilluk do not practice circumcision, initiation merely consists of a great ceremonial dance at which the young men display their virtuosity, dramatizing situations from everyday life and indulging in humorous mimicry.

Although the Shilluk are less cattle-conscious than their neighbors, they do share to some extent the peculiar psychic relationship which seems to be connected to Egyptian attitudes. Bullocks are sacrificed in all important rituals and horns are set upright on burials. A curious parallel to this is seen at Sakkara in the tomb of Uadji, the third or fourth king of the first Egyptian dynasty. Here a low bench ran along the east façade upon which was arranged a series of approximately 300 bulls' heads modeled in clay surmounted with real horns.

The Shilluk also make a practice of assigning a special bullock to each boy as a favorite and pet. The ultimate development of this custom takes place among the Nuer. Like the Shilluk, they make marriage payments in cattle, use milk and beef (the beef cattle are only killed on ceremonial occasions), sleep on cowskins, burn dung to keep the flies away, and in general are dependent upon their herds. Unlike Bantu cattle, Nuer herds are not taboo to women, who do the milking. The special male relationship, however, is formalized in the presentation of a bullock to each boy on initiation. From this animal he gets an ox name. The creature is his friend and companion. In the words of Evans-Pritchard, "He plays with it and fondles it. He composes poems about it and sings them to it, and he gets a small boy to lead it around the camp in the morning or evening as he leaps behind it chanting poems. He walks among the cattle at night, ringing a cattle bell and singing of his kin, his loves, and his cattle, and he praises this ox among all other oxen. He makes tassels to hang from one of its horns, and he loves to see it toss the tassel in the air with a sweep of the neck. He acquires an iron bell to hang around its neck, and no music, unless it be the ox's lowing, is sweeter to his ears than its tinkling in the pastures. He goes to the edge of the camp to meet it when it returns from grazing in the evening. He is never tired of describing its points, and as he does so, and also in dancing, he may hold up his arms in imitation of its horns. Should the ox die he is downcast, and should he die it must be sacrificed at his mortuary ceremony."

A part of this relationship is clearly that of a male power symbol (when the beast is given to the boy it is not yet castrated) roughly equivalent to a Western boy's first car. Acccording to Evans-Pritchard, it also has a deeper significance. A kind of identification takes place through the ox name; in Nuer poems it is sometimes not clear whether it is the man or the ox which is being discussed. The ox is also thought of as having a sacral connection with the ancestor spirits and the supernatural world in general. The Nuer word for Juok is Kwoth which can be singular or plural, localized in ancestors, totems or cattle, and also generalized as an omnipresent creative spirit; in short, the concept which we have repeatedly characterized as mana. The sense of mystical identification and the male relationship certainly appears to be a pastoral elaboration of the ancient totemic connection between man and beast.

To return to the Shilluk institution of the divine king, the neighboring tribe of the Nuba may perhaps throw some light on the magical origin of this ruler and upon one line of deity development. Among this people shamanism is dominant. The Nuba magicians do not rely on music and dance but go into trance through self-hypnosis. They are not possessed by ancestor or nature spirits but by certain inherited entities who are given names and offered beer. As we have seen among the Zulus, the magician feels his call through a violent fit in which he yells and trembles. He finally runs off, wanders in the bush for some time, then comes home and digs a hole with his hands like a dog near his house. He remains in his hole without food for three or four days. On the fifth there is a ceremony of consecration by an already initiated shaman in which the neophyte steps over a goat which is afterward sacrificed. He must abstain from sex for a month, not because sexual activity is impure, but because in the Nuba view it would cause his possession to become unbearably severe. The shaman when consulted professionally induces automatic activities, retching, groaning and finally going into a trance in which he speaks with a different voice and makes enigmatic pronouncements that must be interpreted. S. F. Nadel, who observed seven of these séances, maintains that two were simulated, two started so and became genuine while three were genuine dissociation from start to finish. The general effect of the shamanistic séance was that of a psychoanalytical session; guilts were brought out into the open and catharsis achieved by pointing out ways of atonement (by proper sacrifices). From the social point of view the shaman played an important role in upholding the authority of the chief. According to Nadel, some generations back the *chief and shaman were one.* Later they tended to be two brothers. It appears, therefore, that the earliest priest-shaman may well have been a phase in the development of the divine king. It is easy to see that if the secular and magical offices were not split up and he retained both, and strengthened and deepened their significance by assimilating the ancestor cult to them, a sacral monarch would result.

The integrating power of the Shilluk reth and his significance for the nation is best exemplified in the installation ceremony, which merits a detailed description.

In the first place, the whole affair is a true rite de passage both for the reth and the nation. As in Van Gennep's classical description, the transition of Nyikang from one ruler to another is a threshold which must be safely passed, a period in which both new ruler and nation are particularly vulnerable. The death of the old reth leaves an interregnum of a year during which Nyikang has no home. There is danger of civil war, a general feeling that the fertility of the land is imperiled, that rain may not fall, and that the reth-to-be may be killed by a rival. In modern times, in which the king is no longer killed by his successor, a sort of electoral college made up of influential chiefs from the most important provinces meets to choose the new reth. Actually a horse-trading compromise results and office often passes from one lineage to another. In theory, however, Nyikang makes his will known in a divination ceremony in which stones are cast into a fire. This exactly parallels the appointment of the Egyptian high priest and the Catholic Pope. The reth then raises an army in the southern province while the priests of Nyikang remove his effigy and those of Dak and Cal from their shrine in the north and also collect an army. The image of Nyikang is a conelike body of bamboo surmounted by a tuft of ostrich feathers; it only leaves the shrine at the installation of a reth. A new image is constructed for each new ruler. The Dak image, which is of black ostrich feathers with a shorter body mounted on a long pole, often travels about the country.

Nyikang sleeps at night in a forked stick which is carried behind him. Both images pause in the villages they pass through while dancing and singing take place. Meanwhile the reth feels in great danger both because of possible rivals and because Nyikang is resentful of the approaching seizure of his powers by a man who may be unworthy. The reth flies from his capital of Fashoda to a neighboring village which ceremonially resists his entrance. He conceals his identity by hiding in a ramshackle hut. At the same time Nyikang's spear and ceremonial beads are brought to Fashoda. A period of amnesty for adulterers and seducers follows in which they atone for their faults by offering sheep. When the reth comes to the capital with his army he first steps over a white sheep; beside him, on the march, the spear of Nyikang is carried wrapped in a white cloth. On the way to the battleground there is a watercourse. If there has been much rain he is obliged to enter a canoe after stepping over a black bull. The armies advance toward each other, Nyikang continually turning back and then advancing, to symbolize his doubt as to whether the new reth is worthy. The reth is joined by Nyakwer, a little girl who is his symbolic bride. A danced conflict then ensues in which whips and millet stalks are brandished. When the dust dies down, the reth is clasping the body of Nyikang but his army has been put to flight and he is accompanied only by the Nyakwer. The reth and the image are then lifted and carried to the shrine of Nyikang near which the sacred stool has been set covered with a leopard skin and a white cloth. The image is first placed on the stool and then the reth, an action which symbolizes the passing of power. A white cloth is held up in front of the reth who meditates for twenty minutes. During this period he is seized with a fit of trembling and goes into a trance, a token shamanistic performance which indicates that he has been possessed by Nyikang. He then retires followed by his child bride, undergoes purification, and a ritual fire is kindled. For two days nothing further occurs, then on the fourth day the Nyakwer is stolen by Nyikang. The reth marshals his forces and goes to the shrine where he demands her back, saying, "Have I not married her with cattle?" He has a second battle with the retainers of Nyikang during which Cal (a rope body with gray female ostrich feathers) appears. Stalks of millet are thrown like spears. The girl is recaptured, hostilities cease, and now Nyikang accepts the reth. The three effigies return to the shrine, are not seen again, and later travel home.

On the final day occurs the planting of the spear. The Nyikang's silver shield adorned with bells, his long spear and the sacred stool, all wrapped in white cloth to conceal them from the gaze of ordinary men, are brought out of the shrine and taken to the bottom of the hill where the chiefs of the kingdom are waiting. The stool is set upon a giraffe skin. Shortly afterward the reth appears dressed in white and wearing the skin of the female Mrs. Gray antelope and a new ivory armlet especially made for the occasion. After stepping over a sheep, he walks down the hill accompanied by Nyakwer and a small party of attendants. He is protected by the royal fan, made from the wings of a saddle-billed stork in the form of a shield. When he reaches the stool he is lifted onto it by two members of the Ororo (a lineage which has been degraded from royal rank to cut down the number of pretenders to the throne). The bearers of the fan hold it over the reth's head to protect him from the sun while the bearers of the shield, spear, and drum stand in front. When all is ready, the shield bearers advance toward the rows of chiefs, shaking the shield so that the bells jingle, and mark out the first speaker.

The chiefs speak in turn, each one leaving his spear planted in the ground when he is finished. They urge the new ruler to rule well, provide good crops and good fortune. When they finish, the reth arises, answers them, stabs a sacrificial bull with his spear, and departs. He is now secure in the occupation of his throne, the spirit of Nyikang has entered into him and will henceforth rule through him ensuring the prosperity of the Shilluk nation.

CHAPTER *27*

The Sacred Dung Heap

Galla—Caucasoid people showing Near East and Egyptian influence—castra-
tion theme—male expression in totemic cattle ritual—war and hunting—
fertility goddess showing Mesopotamian influence—rain ceremony.

THE CULT of cattle plays an important role throughout north-eastern Africa. So far we have indicated its presence in Egypt and among predominantly Negroid peoples. There is, however, a group of Caucasoid peoples in Ethiopia who arrived from the north in the late Neolithic period, displaced the Bushman, checked the advance of the Negroes, and probably brought with them Egyptian influences. Among these the Galla, who inhabit the high plateaus and maintain a pastoral economy and exhibit an archaic psychology, are particularly interesting, for they seem to have retained early types of religion in arrested form.

Occupying areas which have been called the African Switzerland with snow-capped mountains as high as 16,000 feet and gorges through which cataracts drain toward the Nile, they adopted the horse in the sixteenth century and gained a reputation as fierce warriors. Indeed, in the eighteenth century the ruler of Abyssinia married a Galla queen, and her kinsmen became the palace guard and played an important role in succeeding regimes.

The Galla are reddish- to brown-skinned, their features Caucasoid, with thin noses, their hair more or less frizzy according to the amount of Negro mixture. The men wear a short kilt and a toga or fringed mantle, the women a leather or cotton skirt. They wander in nomadic bands, their temporary dwellings consisting of bent poles set in the ground, fastened together at the top and covered with mats, brush, or hides. This is, of course, the type of house used by the Pygmies and other early hunting peoples. The Galla place these huts around a central cattle corral surrounded by an outer enclosure of thorns.

Social organization is unique. This people is divided into ten clanlike *gada* groups, each of which is composed of five age grades in which individuals remain for eight years. Circumcision takes place from third grade to fifth, depending on the tribe, generally after marriage.

Curiously enough, tribal government is rotating, each Gada group's elected chief, or Hayu, being in power for eight years. Each Gada is supposed to possess a particular character which individualizes the regime: one, man or reason; two, running water or progress; three, sheep or quietude; four, lion or force, five, vulture or war; etc.

The most important religious expression of this people takes place during initiations into new age groups. A supreme god by the name of Waqa, who has no image or temples but to whom bulls are sacrificed, rules over a group of minor spirits, some of which are animals such as snakes. It is clear, however, that male expression is embodied in the relation to cattle, hunting and war. Murder or killing in battle is a social necessity. Among the Arusi a man cannot hold tribal office until he has killed a large animal or a man. The men of this group are accustomed to drink blood which is supposed to drive them to a frenzy; whereupon they hide and kill unsuspecting travelers, remove their genitals and bring them home as trophies (this is also practiced by the Jívaro of Ecuador). They are then allowed to marry and wear a copper ring in one ear. The taking of enemy genitals seems to be equivalent in its sadomagical significance to the taking of heads among other peoples. An equivalent scale of values between killing of men and animals states that one buffalo equals one man, one leopard three men, one elephant ten mounted men, one mounted man two men.

The cattle ceremonies during initiation into the third age grade are particularly elaborate. A heap of dung is spread out in front of the house of the sacrificer to make a platform. A calf is tied to the nearest olive tree. Five men, ritually clean, each offer a vessel of milk; the last one unties the calf. The milk vessels are set in a row on the edge of the platform. The sacrificer, his head shaven, bears a wooden wand. Members of the age grade place twelve sticks across the dung platform, over which an ox is then thrown and killed by a spear thrust. The meat is ritually distributed. The men of the age grade bend down while the five officiants pour milk over their shaven heads. A piece of meat cut from the thigh of the ox is tied under the chin of the Hayu, or chief. The bystanders then dance on the platform of dung. After this the Hayu and the age grade move toward the center of the village while the women run after them carrying jars of milk which they throw over the men, crying, "Are you not returning to the hut?" The group stops at the hut of the Hayu's ritual sister where he boasts of his deeds in war and she of her erotic exploits. She brings a wooden stool for him to sit upon and the meat is cut loose from his chin.

Still another ceremony of initiation involves the building of the platform of dung, the killing of the ox by the sacrificer using an ax. He then cuts out the peritoneum and hangs it around his neck. The ox gut is used in divination, mythologically rationalized. It is said that the Galla once possessed a sacred book but it was eaten by a cow and thus their only way of knowing the will of their deities is by examining the insides of cattle. The sacrificer covers his face with blood as the ox horns are placed on a stake. The sacrificer is now called "the father of the bull" and a second chief is designated "the father of the cow." Both put on masks made from the face skin of sacrificed animals. They lead the age grade into running water, stirring up the mud as cattle do. They then drape grass and fresh leaves over their heads and shoulders and return to the village, singing. Since they have now entered a new age grade, the elders of the village meet them at the entrance of the village and place a jar of milk on the ground. The two cattle fathers shake their muzzles over the jar, upset the milk, and bellow like cattle. The onlookers sing a song in praise of the age grade. Barren women come with wooden bowls of milk. The cattle fathers put their muzzles in the milk and bless the women. The group goes to the drinking hole of the village cattle and the leaders bless it. The next step is to proceed to the hut of an elder, the father of vulture feathers, a renowned warrior, who is wearing vulture plumes. Here the group boasts of the animals or men they have killed.

Several elements appear to be blended in these bizarre activities. The mimicking of cattle in masks certainly shows a transition from the masked hunting ceremony to pastoral rites. Furthermore, the killing of animals or men and male virility is related to the whole complex. Interestingly enough, age grade number four, in which the young men are able to marry, is called *luba,* which is the word for phallus. Castration of enemies or rival males has been exemplified before in African groups and in Egyptian tradition. It appears that the pre-agricultural mentality has been fossilized among the Galla. Although hunting is no longer economically important, the killing of animals has retained its status value and has been blended with the pastoral bull virility image.

The Galla have a strong poetic tradition. The song which accompanies the boasting ceremony mentioned above goes in part as follows. The first victims mentioned are all ignoble or low-caste individuals.

> O thou with the vulture's feathers,
> I have killed a blacksmith,
> A Mussulman who was keeping fast.
> I have killed a Muslim missionary on the tree,
> A monkey who looks like thee I have killed.

O thou with the vulture's feathers,
I have killed a big baboon
Farting in his den . . .

.   .   .

I have killed a foot soldier,
A strong warrior who wore a leopard's skin,
A foot soldier who looks like me I have killed.

One or two taboos, such as not killing the viper because it is called grand-mother or that of not eating deer because the deer were created on the same day as men, have a faintly totemic sound. On the whole, since there is an evil spirit called Saitan, and both Muslim and Christian influence has been brought to bear on the Galla, it appears that Waqa may be a late de-velopment due to foreign influence. There is one detail which relates Galla pastoral rites to pastoralism in Egypt and among the Shilluk. At Galla burials the body is buried in a toga; honey and milk are put into the grave. An ox is killed, the meat given to the poor and strangers, while upon the burial mound, which is covered with stones, a post is set up on which are hung the dead man's weapons and the skull and horns of the ox. As will be remembered, horns are placed on a Shilluk grave and bulls' horns were found at the base of the tomb of the Egyptian monarch Uadji.

Another major element in Galla religion which links it to Egypt or Mesopotamia is worship of a fertility goddess, named Atete, which means fortune or wealth. Friday is sacred to her, and also a great yearly festival, part of which is taboo to men. It begins with a four-day feast at which the chief sits down before two great leather bags, one filled with hydromel, the other with beer. The women sing a song invoking the goddess which begins:

> The wood of the enclosure is fragrant,
> When shall we meet?
> Tomorrow at midnight
> By stealth we shall meet.
> A handful of barley
> The concubine has toasted.
> What the sterile woman has hoarded
> The fertile woman has gained!

The chief rises and sings a liturgy, with choral interjections, asking the festival to protect the people. He then spits into the two vessels, takes up the wooden wand lying across them and hands it to the head of the family at whose house the festival is taking place. The wand remains hanging from the ceiling of the house until the next festival and is regarded as a sacred object. Glass necklaces and amulets are hung on it. (Probably this object has a phallic significance.)

The women wear a necklace dedicated to the goddess. After the feast they go in a group armed with long sticks to collect sacred herbs which they place at the foot of a sacred tree. Here they dance, invoking the deity. After this they go to the house of a woman who has had many children. There they burn certain of the herbs as incense and perform mysteries which R. Chambard says "they refuse to disclose." Father de Salviac (who seems to have peeked) writes: "Christian modesty proscribes certain details of the festival of Atete." We therefore assume that something erotic takes place. The necklace sacred to the goddess reminds us of the eye goddess of Europe and Asia Minor, and the worship at the tree has echoes of Crete. Atete is certainly the earth mother of the Near East in her fertility aspect, yet strangely enough she appears to be completely divorced from her male consort, the bull of virility.

The religious traditions of the Galla, therefore, constitute a strange medley of archaic and more sophisticated developments. Since their own agriculture is rudimentary, Atete must certainly have been taken over bodily from the Fertile Crescent. It may be this is why she has not been associated with the cattle cult and bull image. The Galla rain cult consists of eating barley pudding, after which women and children go in a solemn procession to gather grass with which they weave wreaths. A line of the accompanying song speaks of the magician beating the drum to obtain rain. This archaic and shamanistic ritual indicates that rain and fertility never coalesced with the fertility goddess or a bull-thunder god. The rites of this people, though modified by outside influences at various times, seem to reflect something of that particular stage of historical development of which we know so little, the beginning of pastoralism. They may possibly suggest something of the situation which existed in the Nile valley in predynastic times when the hunters were just beginning to acquire agriculture and the cattle complex was filtering in from the Semitic civilizations. Yet to these ancient elements the course of Galla history has added a special character, in particular the lyrical songs with which nearly all of their ceremonies are accompanied. Indeed the following liturgy to Waqa is in curious contrast to the barbarity of ritual murder and martial boasting.

> PRIEST The wonders are six:
> The hornbill complains without being ill;
> The hidden lily flourishes without food;
> The water runs without being urged;
> The earth is fixed without pegs;
> The heavens hold themselves up without supports;

In the firmament Waqa has sown the chickpeas.
These things fill me with wonder.
Let us all pray to Waqa.
O Waqa who caused me to pass the day,
Cause me to pass the night well.

CHORUS Cause me to pass the night well.

CHAPTER 28

Souls in Stools

Dahomeans, Yoruba and Ashanti of West Africa—ancient kingdoms and well-developed social organization—importance of cities—elaboration of pantheon with trickster—ancestor cult as status expenditure—god cults and social groups—police function of men's societies—stoic philosophy expressed in ritual chants.

THE WESTERN world has, in the twentieth century, become aware of African culture through an appreciation of fabulously carved and painted masks, impressively formalized wooden sculpture of the human figure, and technically and aesthetically expert bronze and brass casting, the latter embodying a tradition beginning as far back as the late Middle Ages. This great African art all stems from West Africa. Here urban Negro kingdoms arose as early as the fourteenth century. Here the grim annals of the slave trade constitute a chapter of shame in the history of the European powers, yet this same traffic in human lives was a source of wealth to the warrior monarchs of Africa. Here, although such brutal traits as ritual homicide, funeral butchery and despotic exploitation of conquered territories persisted, enforced political unity did guarantee a certain stability of life to the dominant populations, specialized craftsmen were attracted to the feudal capitals, a true priesthood arose, and, though the surplus of advanced agriculture was not attained, trade and markets flourished. The Bambara, as we have seen, arrived at a unified mythology, but they did not attain the elaboration of cult and observance and the further development of pantheon which arose in the kingdoms of Yoruba, Dahomey, and Ashanti of the Slave and Gold coasts. In this area Negro barbaric spiritual culture achieved its most complex manifestations.

In most of Nigeria the familiar conical hut gives way before a rectangular house with walls made of mats or twigs and mud, the gable roof thatched with palm (now often with tin). These are situated along regular streets or around a rectangular compound in villages, towns and cities. The compounds are united in precincts which make up the five wards of a city. Each Yoruba compound consists of a family, including the wives of the children and perhaps a few unrelated persons. A number of compounds may be inhabited by the same clan. In each compound there is a special room for meetings and ceremonies. Nine of the largest cities in Africa are Yoruban, all of them having a population of over 45,000. Today Ibadan, the capital of the Yoruba nation, is the largest Negro city in Africa, with a population of about 400,000.

The Yorubans developed a great style of bronze casting and stone carving. Tradition always maintains that at a certain point the god turned to stone. This accounts for the stone heads and busts. For instance, the head of an Ife warrior of antiquity who converted himself into stone is shown to children and they are told that the bust still breathes faintly and if they look sharply it will just perceptibly wink its eyes! The German anthropologist Leo Frobenius first unearthed this type of sculpture, and also the bronze portrait heads and figures from Ife, and brought them to the attention of Europeans who had refused to believe that African art could reach such a peak of idealized style, rivaling that of the Greeks.

The Fon of Dahomey conquered the petty coastal states, became masters of the gateway to West Africa in the early eighteenth century, and for a hundred and fifty years monopolized the slave trade with Europe. Their rulers established an elaborate court in which the queen mother had her own retinue and outranked the king. The crown prince, not always the eldest son, also had an important position. Commoners who approached the ruler had to throw dust on their heads. Princes and princesses constituted a leisure-class aristocracy who were granted unlimited sexual freedom and who led lives of sophistication and luxury. Court officials included a commander in chief of the army who was also a sort of prime minister and head executioner. The chief of protocol was also collector of taxes and guardian of the royal children. The governor of the port of Ouidah was equivalent to foreign minister in charge of dealings with the Europeans. The head of espionage and the security police also assumed the duties of supervisors of the palace. The minister of the interior controlled markets and agriculture, while the royal treasurer was head of the palace commissary. Finally there was a grand eunuch in charge of the harem. The organization of this kingdom probably reflects Western influence.

Dahomean art includes excellently carved gourds, some crude wooden idols and cult figures and posterlike wall decorations in shrines and palaces. Similar figures of men and animals are appliquéd upon textiles. The Dahomeans excel, however, in bronze casting, producing small figures, expertly stylized yet full of life and movement.

The Ashanti are notable for their indomitable struggles to preserve their independence. Their leopard-skin-clad warriors fought the British fiercely throughout the nineteenth century and inflicted some severe defeats on the

Westerners. Rather than surrender, Ashanti chiefs sometimes seated themselves on kegs of gunpowder and blew themselves up. They still constitute the least westernized population of Ghana.

Of the three groups they are the most advanced architecturally; the palace of the king is decorated with elaborate reliefs. Because of the belief that the souls of men inhabit sacred stools, the Ashanti specialize in the carving of this ceremonial object. In addition they cast small bronze gold weights (as a result of trading gold with the Westerners) which range from portrayal of the human figure to symbolical designs.

Since the British possessions in Nigeria have now, as in Ghana, become independent, the ancient barbaric cultures of West Africa are in the process of adapting to the modern technical world. It will be interesting to see how much of the indigenous spiritual development can be reshaped under the impact of modern science.

The Dahomeans are diligent smiths and agriculturists. The men cut the trees, supervise the burning of the ground and hoe it, using the short-handled, broad-bladed hoe which forces the laborer to bend double. Before planting, sacrifice is made to the earth, which is molded into the form of a human head with cowry shells for eyes. The offering consists of maize, blood of a chicken, flour and water. The whole family plants the seed, while the women do the weeding and drive off the birds. This people has taken a step ahead in agricultural technique in that it practices rotation of crops. Palm trees are cultivated because they produce both palm wine, oil from the nuts, and material for weaving and thatching. A few cattle are raised, but not milked, and many sheep, goats, fowl and pigs.

Despite the basically urban character of the Dahomeans, hunting still plays a minor economic and a major ceremonial role (perhaps because cattle have not come to play a role in male ego expression). Each village has its group of hunters organized under a chief. Hunters are thought to be particularly versed in magic, taught them by the forest spirits. Their supernatural experiences are as important to them as the animals killed and they are accustomed to gather under a special tree to recite their exploits. The coastal Dahomeans dance in a raffia costume, wearing a stylized human mask and horns on top of their heads. A survival of totemism appears in the belief that members of the Dahomean royal family are human leopards. They are forbidden to kill leopards or even the spotted antelope. The myth states that a certain king's wife was made pregnant by a leopard. There are also clans which claim descent from the horse, pig, toad and peanut. Since there are also animal taboos, all this is evidence of an archaic strata of magico-religious belief.

The aristocratic society of the Dahomeans rests on slave labor. Among the commoners, however, there are cooperative societies for carrying out such activities as thatching roofs or building walls. The existence of many religious societies is also evidence of a high degree of cooperation and specialization, for a full-time priesthood is supported by contributions from the families of its members and by the foodstuff offered in sacrifice at cult shrines.

In general the basic outlines of West Coast religion are similar to those in other parts of Africa. A creator god or force, who is called in Ashanti Nyame, receives worship in the shape of a forked stick holding a brass or earthenware bowl or pot containing magical materials. (Geoffrey Parrinder suspects him of being originally a thunder god.) Olorun or Olodumare is the Yoruba equivalent. In Dahomey the world was created by an androgynous god Nana-Buluku who gave birth to twins, Mawu (male) and Lisa (female). The former is the moon, living in the west and in charge of the night, while the latter is the sun in the east in charge of the day. This entity has three shrines.

On the whole, the Yoruba concentrate on an elaborate system of divining, among the Ashanti ancestor worship predominates, while the Dahomeans have the most elaborate priesthood and theology. Interestingly enough, all three use a word which means the gods but also has a more general significance of magical essence, the host of semi-anthropomorphized spirits which permeate trees, rivers, stones and various objects. *Vodu* of Dahomey is carried over in the new world as voodoo in Haiti. *Orisha* of the Yoruba is also a word which appears in Afro-Cuban folklore, while the equivalent term in Ashanti is *obosom*. All three terms are close to the mana concept.

Royal ancestor worship among these West African kingdoms, as elsewhere, involved the death of human beings. The Dahomeans killed a score of war captives at the funeral of the king. Ashanti court officials requested the relatives to kill them so that they could continue to serve their master in the other world. The Yoruba not only killed war captives but made a new gate by which the royal heir entered the palace.

Ashanti ancestor worship takes the peculiar form of the stool symbol. The spirits of ordinary forebears enter elaborately carved wooden stools made from certain trees whose obosom must be propitiated by offerings of broken eggs. The stools are then placed on low platforms in shrines and fed with mashed plantain. Since ancestor rites are celebrated twice every forty-three days, the stools are always wet with the blood of sacrificial animals. Historically important was the golden stool which, with rumbling of thunder, sank down from a black cloud floating in the sky until it rested upon the king's knees. It contained the spirit of the king's ancestors and was responsible for the power, wealth, and honor of the Ashanti nation. It was never sat upon, but once a year was carried in a solemn procession, under its own umbrella, followed by more attendants than there were in the king's train. When a naïve English colonial administrator demanded that the stool be brought to him for a throne he provoked a bloody war.

Ancestor rites in Dahomey are characterized by elaborate funeral customs, involving a kind of secondary burial. At first a wake is held with much wailing by the women mourners. The body is rolled in a cloth for the "partial" burial and the young men dance, holding it in turn. The grave is dug in the compound or under the floor of the house from outside. The body is placed in it and the hole half-filled. In former times it was entirely filled and the corpse dug up later for the second part of the rite. A period during which condolences are offered to the family now takes place. Then for the final burial each son-in-law furnishes a drummer. The whole battery of percussion plays together deafeningly, accompanied by singing, while the dead man is supposed to be dancing upside down behind the compound. The family and the mourners eat together as payments are made to those who officiate at the funeral. Presents are also given to the dead by the children of the official best friend. Some of the mourners wrap themselves in funeral cloths (although most Dahomeans now wear commercial fabrics, ceremonial cloth is still hand-woven). At this point (about ten at night) the body used to be dug up; now it is represented by a roll of cloth which is wrapped in matting. This is placed in the house while elaborate songs are sung, one of which begins:

> Behold what death has done!
> What death has done to a family!
> Friend and friend are united;
> The death of one leaves the other grief-stricken.
> The song itself cries out and says:
> Behold what death has done,
> What death has done to a friend!

Now the pallbearers (who belong to a cult society) seize the effigy of the body and run off with it. The mourners pursue them through the village, begging for its return. Meanwhile the spectators throw money to the pallbearers. Finally a message is sent to the family stating that the dead will not return without more gifts of money and cloth, which are forthcoming, and the corpse is returned. At this time the dead man's household goods are destroyed by a diviner, who also receives presents from the family. The drumming and ceremony described have taken all night; at eight o'clock in the morning the corpse effigy is taken to the grave where it is interred with more ceremonial grave fabrics. Those who accompany it to the grave also put in ceremonial fabric as a gift to their own dead. More singing and drumming take place as the earth is stamped down over the grave. There is an endless amount of detail and gift giving. Food is placed on the grave and then divided among the mourners for another funeral feast. The wives of the dead man's sons give presents to the pallbearers. Two days later there is another wake and another feast and the heads of all the members of the family are shaved as a part of the purification to rid them of the harmful mana of death. Two months later there are more sacrifices and ceremonies with drumming, dancing and gaiety, at which the older ancestors are asked to accept the recent dead as a deity. Since Dahomean society is fairly well-to-do, the whole affair involves conspicuous expenditure without which it is felt that the deceased will not be assured of status and acceptance in the other world. This region is not localized; in general it is believed that the spirit of the dead must cross a river, climb a mountain, and then cross another river. If the final burial ceremonies are not carried out properly, the dead cannot perform this journey or be welcomed by his ancestors. The short shadow, voice, or vital soul dies with the body and becomes deified. A second spiritual part is a bit of Mawu, an ancestral soul which the sky entity takes back. A third spiritual principle, the *se,* undergoes sixteen incarnations and finally enters a tree.

The chief Dahomean gods, Mawu and Lisa, are twins, or sometimes Mawu is an androgynous figure. (Twins in West Africa create the usual ambivalence; among the Yoruba there is a twin cult, while the Ashanti destroy royal twins as offensive to the stool.) Mawu is cool, gentle, forgiving; Lisa hot, angry and ruthless. They are supposed to copulate at night during eclipses. Most of the gods are their children, including the gods of the bush and of animals, or earth, thunder and sea. More or less on a par with them, however, is Gu, god of iron and war, who is the cutting power of iron anthropomorphized (rather like fire in Aryan theology). Youngest of the sons is Legba (Eshu among the Yorubans) who is particularly interesting because here we have a phallic trickster who is actually worshiped. Legba is in some respects a sort of Mercury or messenger because he is the word of Masu, *fa* or fate, ascertained by divination. Among Legba's escapades are a quarrel which he provoked between the earth god, Sagpata, and one of his brothers over rain, and a method of stealing from Mawu in which he wore her sandals and accused her of robbing herself. His phallic aspect is dramatized in a myth which anthropomorphizes fa as a woman. Legba has sexual relations with both her and her daughter. A quarrel ensues during which Legba is brought before Mawu and stripped, whereupon his penis is revealed as erect. Mawu ordains that as a punishment for deceiving his sister his penis shall always be erect. As a result, in dances he is represented as trying to possess every woman. At the end of the initiation into the Mawu cult, a comic Legba dance takes place in which a girl impersonates the trickster, wearing a wooden phallus.

The cults of the various gods tend to rise and fall and assimilations take place. The Dahomean temples are built with polished molded pillars of unbaked clay. Bright murals depicting snakes, chameleons or leopards are painted on the walls in red, white, blue or black. The vodu of the particular cult is described by one of Herskovits's informants as follows: "The vodu itself is in the ground. One does not know what it is. It is not secret. The vodu has a jar next to it but the vodu is not in the jar which is in the cult house. It is the power, the force that goes about in the temple."

Each cult group has a house and is presided over by a hereditary high priest. Cult membership is sometimes inherited; at other times new members go through elaborate initiation rites. One individual may be a member of several cults, just as a Westerner belongs to several lodges. Possession occurs during ceremonies but it is not so marked as among the Ashanti. In certain cases the novices go into a "convent," subscribe to sexual taboos and undergo a death-and-resurrection symbolic routine in which their hair is shaved and they learn the secret language of the cult. After seven months of initiation they are "redeemed" by relatives with gifts. They then beg ritually in raffia costume, discard this, and wear white for three months. According to Herskovits, some cult members feel a sense of mystery and spiritual participation but to many the whole affair is merely a social activity.

In P. Mercier's view, the complexity of myth and pantheon, which involves contradictions and doubling of myths, arises from conquest. The Dahomeans imposed their own cults but also "bought" those of the conquered. Marriages of kings with foreign queens also brought in new cults. The result is a multiplicity of observance but no state religion, although the king exercised control over the building of temples.

According to Bolaji Idonu, professor of religion in Ibadan University, Olodumare is the correct term for the creator god of the Yoruba (Olorun is a vulgarization). In the beginning he inhabited the sky with several other divinities while below there was a watery waste. The hunting god came down on a spider's thread to engage in his profession. Olodumare sent Orishanla down below with a package of loose earth in a snail shell. He was accompanied by a five-toed hen and a pigeon. (In certain ceremonies the five-toed hen is dramatized in costume.) Orishanla threw down the earth, letting loose the birds, who scratched it in all directions, and then returned to the sky. After a time his master sent down a chameleon to see what progress was being made. (Curiously enough, the chameleon also appears as a divine messenger among the Pygmies and the Bantu.) The lizard returned with the news that the earth was not dry enough. On a second visit he decided that it was dry and wide enough. The two birds propagated. Orishanla returned on a second visit during which he planted the palm and several other trees. He then sculptured human beings from dust (he is the god of sculpture). The images were put into a hut whither Olodumare repaired and breathed the breath of life into them. In this early period the earth and the sky were fairly near together, allowing for unrestricted travel. Various explanations, including one in which a woman soiled the face of heaven with her dirty hands, account for the fact that they were now far apart.

It seems likely that Olodumare is simply the creative principle that we have encountered elsewhere, that he pervades the orishas, or minor spirits, just as mana pervades everything, and that any anthropomorphic worship paid him may very well be due to the impact of Islam and Christianity.

Idonu, in his discussion of the orishas, says there is a myth in which Orishanla was crushed by a stone, rolled upon him by an evil slave, and suggests that they are a fragmentation of an archdivinity. They are also said to be Olodumare's children. "Ori" etymologically means in the general sense "that essence which derives from the head source."

The pantheon of orishas is variously estimated from four hundred to twelve hundred. Multiplication has taken place by fusion of clans which adopted each other's gods with new names. The same divinity has different names in different areas. Ancestors, elevated to hero and eventually divinity status, also add to the number. In short, the situation is rather similar to that in ancient Mesopotamia. The chief orishas are similar to the Dahomean vodus. Eshu has already been equated to Legba. Ogun is Gu the hunter, also god of iron and war. When he came down on his spider thread to hunt on earth he alone was able to cut through the jungle with his iron machete; the other gods had weapons of lead. He is in charge of circumcision, tribal markings, tattooing and surgery (parallel to the blacksmith deity of the Bambara), and since all iron and steel belong to him, he is now the patron of engines and machines, including the automobile!

Shango is unique in that he is supposed to be the fourth king of Oyo who ascended to heaven. He is also the wrath of Olodumare manifested in thunder and lightning. Interestingly enough, in Cuba, according to Lydia Cabrera, he is Changó, the most popular of the orishas, equated with Santa Barbara, and the royal palm is his throne. He is still remembered as a man and a king and continues as a thunder god.

The Dahomean earth god, Shagpata, becomes Yoruban Shangpana. In both cases great care must be taken not to offend this deity because he strikes back by causing smallpox. In Yoruba medicine it is the *hot* earth which causes fever, hence the identification of disease with the earth god. The priests of this god were said to attack their enemies by throwing powdered smallpox scabs into their houses.

The worship of orishas on sacred days is preceded by purification, including abstinence from sex the night before. The worshiper stands before the shrine which may house, as in the case of Orishanla, a stone image. Orishanla's temple is whitewashed and contains white ornaments. Pure water is brought to it every day. His priests dress in white. Part of his liturgy describes him as:

> Immense in white robes!
> He sleeps in white clothes.
> He works in white clothes.
> He rises in white clothes.

The worshiper calls the orisha by his praise names and begs that he will listen to his child. A kola nut which divides into four quarters, two male and two female, is cast to learn if the orisha will listen. On a second day, offerings of food and drink are brought and whatever has been promised in payment of vows. The priest intercedes as the worshiper's request is stated. Kola nuts are cast again as the suppliant kneels facing the shrine. The priest stands facing it, his back to the worshiper. If the divination is favorable he turns, blesses the worshiper, completing the ceremony. Annual festivals follow the same pattern with more pomp and display. Festival meals are eaten and there is much chanting of liturgies to the accompaniment of sticks of bamboo or metal struck together, gongs, drums, or all three. Acceptable offerings include chickens, rams, dogs; all the orishas accept kola nuts and Orishanla is particularly fond of snails cooked in butter.

In times of stress, human sacrifice was resorted to. Ashes and chalk were thrown on the head and face of the victim to hide his identity. The crowd pushed near to lay hands on him, for by so doing guilt, trouble, and evil were transferred to him as a scapegoat. He was then taken to a sacred hut of palm branches which only the priest and his assistant might enter. Here the victim started his last song, and it was taken up by a great assemblage outside. At the last word his head was cut off, whereupon there was a beating of drums, dancing and general joy because the divine wrath was now appeased.

As among the Dahomeans, worship of a specific deity may descend along the maternal or paternal line or the worshiper may be called, either in dreams or by the prophecy of a diviner. Ifa or divination consists of 256 patterns, each with a name, arrived at by casting eight seeds or palm kernels. Each pattern has a number of verses associated with it. The diviner casts and recites the appropriate lines (which he memorizes as a part of his training). The client listens and selects the statement which applies to his problem. This is really another example of the absence of the Western idea of chance.

William R. Bascom has discussed the nature of the so-called secret societies, which he feels are not particularly secret. He maintains that they tend to arise out of groups who are living near together, often out of an age group. He is inclined to feel that there is an orisha-like spirit patron. The Egungun and Oro societies of the Yoruba definitely represent spirits of the dead; in the case of the first, its members dramatize them as returning to earth in masks and white robes.

There are several types of Egungun activities. One set, wearing elegant costumes, goes about town singing and dancing simply in the hope of arousing admiration. A second wears costumes of dirty rags. They carry on their heads bulky wooden masks or lumps of clay smeared with the blood and oil of sacrifice. They also carry whips of death, practice magic, and exercise punitive powers. A third group consists of tricksters in elaborate masks of animals. Their dancing is dramatic and entertaining and they are adept at quick changes. They go from village to village receiving gifts; in short, they are a primitive theatrical troupe.

The Oro group is not masked. Oro, whose voice is heard in the sound of a bullroarer, cuts off a piece of his flesh, probably his penis, which becomes the bullroarer. It is death for women to see the bullroarer. Although Oro is thought of as a generalized ancestor spirit, it appears that orisha and ancestor are not sharply differentiated in these particular cult groups. Sacred groves are dedicated to them in which they put on their regalia, costumes which are often inherited.

Members of a third society, the Ogboni, which does not mask, form the cabinet of the king. They also lay out the corpse at funerals. The Egungun function at spring festivals and funerals while the Oro observe special funeral rites in their sacred grove at the death of one of their members.

Since the Egungun and the Oro both executed witches (like the societies of the Bambara) this punitive function apparently developed a role halfway between a terrorist organization and a police force. Dennet reports that the Oro cut off the heads of criminals and nailed them to trees. In Bascom's view, although these groups do have political and social functions, they are not joined because of political ambition but always for religious reasons.

The Dahomeans possess similar organizations, some of them borrowed from the Yorubans. In other parts of West Africa, notably in the case of the Poro human leopard society of Sierra Leone, this type of group degenerates into a terrorist organization.

As elsewhere in Africa, Dahomean, Ashanti and Yoruban groups practice elaborate forms of magic. The Dahomeans, for instance, use magic leaves, powders (externally and internally), things wrapped or tied around the body or limbs, bits of cloth wrapped around wood, rings of iron or brass. A favorite object is the dried body of a small frog with a needle and a stick projecting from its mouth. This is carried in a sock. The stick is taken from the frog's mouth and placed in cold water. If the water is used to wash the body of a smallpox patient, a cure results. The same object can be used for black magic. The frog is bathed in pox fluid from a patient suffering from the disease. It is then stuck with the needle, and while this is done, if a person's name is mentioned four times he will contract the disease.

Like most divinatory religions, that of West Africa expresses the basic ambivalence of the human spirit. Although there is no room for chance and the future is predestined, yet hope and free will can never be quite ruled out. The belief exists that in specific detail destiny can be altered by the right kind of sacrifice. West African gods are not particularly ethical, directing their anger chiefly against the breaking of taboos or imperfection of ritual; yet oral literature is not without philosophy. The Yoruban conception of the good life is exemplified by the following liturgy:

> Let us not run the world hastily;
> Let us not grasp at the rope of wealth impatiently;
> What should be treated with mature judgment,
> Let us not treat in a fit of temper;
> Whenever we arrive at a cool place,
> Let us rest sufficiently well.
> Let us give prolonged attention to the future,
> And let us give due regard to the consequence of things,
> And that is on account of our last sleep.

The Pacific

CHAPTER **29**

"I Am Throwing Up
My Headdress..."

Negritos—hunting culture similar to that of Pygmies of Africa—sky entities as ancestors or nature spirits—odd initiation ceremonies involving food taboos—shaman and familiar spirits—trickster—mimetic animal dances.

T HE MALAYSIAN jungle consists of "huge grayish trees (in some species with enormous buttresses), masses of rather sad-colored foliage meeting overhead and making the light in the forest somewhat dim but giving grateful coolness, and an undergrowth of bushes with occasional rattan or other palms. This undergrowth is usually fairly dense, but rarely so dense that it is necessary to chop a way through when traveling. Patches of bamboo jungle occur in some districts and the usual sage green foliage of the forest when viewed on a hillside is sometimes relieved by trees whose leaves are of an arsenical green hue. On the trunks of the trees, especially on those which are dead and dying, are all sort of epiphytes, while lianas dangle like ropes here and there. Flowers are seldom seen. Those that are there are usually at the tops of trees where sunlight reaches them." Ivor Evans also points out that the larger animals such as elephant, rhinoceros or tapir are scarce. Leopards and monkeys are found and the call of the argus pheasant accompanies the mist of early morning, while in the river valleys the hornbills fly up with strange hollow cries and creaking wings.

The Malay Peninsula, Java, Sumatra, Borneo, the Andaman Islands, the Celebes and the Philippines form a chain of land masses which have been inhabited from very early times. The Java man belongs on one of the apelike branches of the hominoid tree but he is probably not in the direct line of human evolution. The present population shows that later wandering of peoples have made the area something of a melting pot in which Caucasoid, Mongoloid and Negroid-Pygmy strains have met and mingled. Since in Paleolithic times the islands were not separated from the mainland, it was easy for all these peoples to spread through the area. The Caucasoids of Asia were probably somewhat like the present Ainu of

Japan. Little trace of them exists in the present population though their ethnic strain is noticeable in the Polynesian peoples who pushed on to the islands of the Pacific.

The present population of Indonesia therefore consists of Negritos, Malays who are predominantly Mongoloid and comparative latecomers, and some intermediate groups. The Negritos, a Pygmy group not unlike the Pygmies of Africa in appearance and culture, seem to represent the oldest continuous occupation and the most archaic way of life. They are found chiefly on the Malay Peninsula, the Andaman Islands and in the Philippines.

The three groups differ somewhat in the details of their culture but are sufficiently related to be treated together. Like the African Pygmies, the men are generally under five feet high, their noses tending to be very broad; some exhibit the long arms and slender limbs that we have encountered in Africa and in some cases they are rather dependent upon the Malays for articles which they do not make themselves. The Philippine Negritos practice some agriculture, the Malays and Andaman Islanders are nomadic, the latter adding fishing to their hunting activities. All use the bow and arrow, though the peninsula group has tended to discard it for the blowpipe borrowed from the Malays.

The men originally wore a bark-cloth breechclout, the women a sort of kilt of dried fungus with a loincloth under it or a few leaves. The young men of the peninsula are particularly fond of decorating their heads with wreaths of purple, white or yellow blossoms.

The Andaman Islanders do not use dressed stone tools and none of the Negritos are pottery makers. The peninsula group cooks by placing meat in a cleft stick and leaning it over the fire. Some groups, particularly those in the Philippines, use nets for hunting like the little people of Africa.

The Negritos have no chiefs or clans. Authority rests with the old men or with those whose particular skill in hunting or war gives them prestige. Although private property exists it is tempered by communal sanctions. For instance, an animal killed belongs to the hunter but he has a social responsibility to distribute the meat among the rest of the band. A canoe belongs to the man who selects the tree for its manufacture but a group helps him make it.

The band consists of a group of families who make their huts in a circle around a central clearing used for dancing. The individual hut consists of a crosspiece set on two forked sticks in front and a second lower one in the rear, connected by sloping roofpoles covered with woven palm mats. In the Andamans, in the past, large communal dwellings were built by setting two circles of poles in the ground and bringing the roofpoles to the center in the shape of a beehive.

Like other hunting and gathering people, in good weather the women go out to gather tubers, fruit or small objects such as cicadas and beetle larvae. The men hunt, chiefly wild pigs. At night the game is cooked and distributed and then each family recooks its share. The evening is given over to dancing or storytelling.

Since the Negritos are a vanishing minority, in some areas in the process of being absorbed, their spiritual culture is also subject to influences by the dominant peoples of the area. It is possible that some echoes of Islam or Christianity may have reached them via the Malays and this perhaps accounts for the difference in religious development between the peninsula people and those of the Andaman Islands. The latter are noteworthy for their rather odd puberty ceremonies. Both boys and girls are compelled to sit in constricted positions, three days in the case of the girls. The girls bathe each day in the sea and are then given a flower name from the plant or tree in blossom at the time. The boys' ceremony is more complicated. It begins by the initiant being rubbed with turtle fat while his relatives weep. Such weeping is not an expression of sadness but of religious emotion; it takes place on all important occasions. (It is perhaps not unlike the weeping of female relatives in Western society when a child graduates or gets married.) The boys dance all night, bathe in the sea and have their backs scarified. Both boys and girls undergo a period of food taboo in which they do not eat turtle meat. Finally the initiation is completed by the official turtle-eating ceremony. The boy is fed a little turtle meat, massaged, then spattered all over with white clay. For forty-eight hours he must sit with his arms folded and his legs outstretched, speaking to no one. He is then washed, repainted red and white, and a dance takes place. For a week he does not touch a bow and arrow.

Both Andamaners and peninsula people desert the camp after a burial. The Andamaners place ornaments and water in and on the grave and light a fire which is supposed to keep the dangerous spirits of the dead under control. They also avoid mentioning the name of the dead man. Apparently the danger evaporates with the decay of the flesh, for Radcliffe-Brown states that the islanders wear the skulls of relatives suspended from their necks and hanging between their shoulders.

In view of the importance of red paint in Paleolithic burials, the Andaman attitude toward it is revealing. It is identified with the warmth of the body, blood and fire. It symbolizes vitality and force. Since sick people need strength, they are daubed with red. White paint apparently has a connection with the supernatural and probably signifies purification, as it does all over Africa when used in initiation ceremonies. In the Andamans, a murderer is purified by being painted both red and white.

While none of the Negrito groups is totemistic, their mythology does exhibit a proto-totemic mentality; that is, an identification with animals.

Both the groups under discussion have myths stressing the relationship. The peninsula people maintain that animals were once men but the creator spirit changed them into animals because they did not perform the proper sacrifices. The Andaman myth states that in the days of the ancestors the monitor lizard went to a big meeting at which there was a dance. He began to get wild and danced so madly that the others present were afraid of his strength. Some caught hold of his arms. He became angry and shook them off. Some fell in the sea and became fish and turtles while others became birds and animals on islands. The monitor lizard is also credited with creating men. There are two versions of this. In one he went hunting, climbed a tree, and got stuck in it. A civet cat came along and got him down. After she became the lizard's wife, the two were the ancestors of men. In the other version there were only men and no women. The lizard caught one of them, cut off his genitals, and made him into a woman who became his wife and the ancestor of men. (This castration story is of course a remarkable example of the basic human sexual fear emphasized by depth psychology.)

Andaman mythology is conflicting and far from organized. The most powerful supernaturals are connected with the weather. Bitiku is the northeast wind (also sometimes a spider and sometimes identified with the monitor lizard). Tarei is the southwest wind. Sometimes they are man and wife, sometimes the sexes are reversed, sometimes they are both male. They can cause storms, mostly in retaliation for the breaking of taboos such as annoying cicadas or burning wax. (The anger of the peninsula sky gods is caused by indulging in sexual intercourse in the daytime or laughing at butterflies.) Storms may be stopped by placing magical leaves and twigs under a rock in the sea.

In the Andamans there are also a host of minor spirits, called *lau,* either nature spirits or the ghosts of ancestors. At death the double leaves the body, becomes a lau and either goes underground, goes up to the sky or wanders in the jungle until the flesh rots from the bones. There is no general agreement as to just what happens.

Among the Malay Peninsula Negritos, shamanism, which has died out in the Andamans, is well represented. Again the most important supernaturals seem to be connected with weather. Tak Pern is a deified tribal ancestor who climbed into heaven to escape a tribal war. He has a brother, Kari (who is sometimes female and his wife), who is responsible for the thunder. There are also three grandmothers under the earth who can cause floods when Tak Pern is angry. There are various creation stories. In one version the dung beetle brings up a little soil out of the waste of water. The earth increases until Tak Pern and his wife are able to create a man and a woman out of clay. (This sounds suspiciously like Malay mythology and Mohammedanism.) Apparently the female of this couple dreamed of a girl. She picked a flower in which was a crystal. This became a girl child. She repeated the process with the shoot of a plant and obtained a boy. After this children were created by sexual intercourse. Since Tak Pern and Kari are thought of as having long white hair like a monkey, there are also traces of animal origin. They are considered to be magicians. The peninsula Negritos have devised an odd picture of the heavenly residence of these two. A stone rather like a pillar supports another stone which is loose but is anchored by four cords which extend toward the base of the pillar. There are four boards, apparently extending from the base of the pillar to the four points of the compass, along which Kari rolls the thunderstone to which is attached a cord. As the cord unwinds, the lightning flashes. Since storms are a punishment for broken taboos (making fun of turtles and watching dogs copulate are forbidden activities), methods to vanquish thunder have been devised which differ from those in the Andamans. Blood is drawn from the right leg near the shin and thrown toward the sky. This is supposed to make the thunder go back to the roots of the waters.

A lunar eclipse is caused when the sun, jealous of the moon because the latter has so many star children, sends a butterfly to attack it. An eclipse is called a "butterfly swallow."

Aside from the sky deities, who are propitiated rather than worshiped, there are a host of minor spirits which seem to correspond to the Andaman lau but which, according to Evans, are not ancestors but nature entities. They are said to inhabit animals such as hornbills or vultures or certain plants but they are able to leave these corporeal shapes. These *chinoi* originate in water which collects in the stem of a wild ginger plant. The water gives rise to a crystal which becomes a chinoi. Since the chinoi nourish themselves by sucking flowers or fruits in the sky and send out long retractile threads from their fingernails up which they climb to the sky, we might almost expect Peter Pan to turn up in the Negrito fantasy world. Rain comes from a stone flower in the sky guarded by chinoi. When it turns downward, water falls.

The chinoi are fairly interchangeable with the shaman or *halak*. He is inspired by them and is also able to turn into a chinoi or a tiger. This last is a belief shared with the Malays but the sorcerer-into-animal concept is so universal that it may well be indigenous to the Negritos as well. Halaks also practice a lethal *sending*. A sliver of bamboo two inches long is laid on the right palm and told to go and kill the intended victim. It flies straight through the air and pierces his heart.

The halak carries out a public trance ceremony to invoke the chinoi and diagnose illness. First a hut is made which the shaman enters. Outside, the women and children gather to sing choral responses, characterized by Evans as musical and sweet. The halak gives evidence of possession by first grunting, whistling, wailing, slapping his body and slapping the walls of the hut. Then, as he is possessed by male and female chinoi, he sings in various voices.

A female cries out and demands her flower wreath.
"How shall we hold a magical ceremony, if I have no headdress?"
Then she sings:
"Plaiting a girdle, spinning, I hang at the end of the speaking stone."
The halak sings:
"I am throwing up my headdress."
A tiger spirit sings:
"Spinning, spinning in the sunset glow on the shore of the Sengak River!"
A spirit of the middle air:
"Father, father, I have climbed the bridge of the rising sun."
An Argus pheasant:
"I laugh loudly on the hilltops. I, a virgin, fly fluttering by moonlight."
A chinoi guards the bridge of the dead:
"I shake the bridge up and down and I wreathe my head with ferns."
A leaf monkey:
"I, I am ashamed as I leap on every crossbeam."

These curiously lyrical outbursts with choral interludes continue for a long time during the *panoh* ceremony. When it is over and the halak has obtained his diagnosis, he comes out of the hut. After the ceremony Evans witnessed, he said, "Very long is my tiredness."

Interestingly enough, the Negritos also have created a cycle about a trickster being. Tak Chemempes is rather more hostile than the Bushman Mantis. He, too, is a shape changer, becoming a rhinoceros, a bee tree, a crocodile and a lizard. As a lizard he sat in a tree near a Negrito camp. When he saw food he liked, he came down from the tree and obtained his share by saying he was a traveler. Finally he abducted a girl and ran away from the camp. He is characterized as greedy and erotic but he is also said to have invented the rattan saw for fire making, to have discovered iron, and to have been the first blacksmith. His death occurred when he overreached himself. He heard a whistling noise made by two crossed tree trunks. When he put his hand between them to take hold of whatever had made the noise, he was caught and held until he died.

The Philippine Island Pygmies have been only superficially studied. They are said to cut a small part of the entrails of an animal killed while hunting, cut them up fine and scatter them about, saying, "Spirits, we thank you for this successful hunt. Here is your share of the spoils." Mabel Cole also describes them as leaving offerings by a great rock in which ancestral entities were supposed to reside. Kilton Stewart, who carried out psychological tests among them, also indicates that their religious practices resemble those of the Malay Peninsula. Their shamans possessed familiar spirits, went into trances in connection with diagnosing disease and also officiated in animal dances. When they planned to kill a certain animal, an image of the beast came into their minds which demanded expression. The dance which followed expressed thanksgiving to the animal, the skill and valor of the hunter, and the speed and grace of the pig, deer or bird. A shellfish dance was half an apology to the fish and half a charm to ensure a good catch. Before and after gathering honey there was a bee dance, first requiring permission to eat the honey and afterward giving thanks. The shaman expressed the bee image in a special rhythm and song in which the bee's voice used human words. The shaman went into a trance allowing the grandfather of all the bees to speak through him. The latter was a great doctor who taught the shaman how to cure cuts and burns with honey, and aching joints with the poison of the bee sting.

The Philippine Negritos also propitiated a thunder spirit, Tolandrian, in almost exactly the same way as those of the peninsula. Stewart describes a fierce cloudburst during which the natives cried, "I have insulted your earthworms and laughed at your monkeys," gashed their thighs and threw the blood up into the air. (Geza Roheim concludes that this peculiar sort of taboo which prohibits annoying animals is a kind of totemic restriction.)

Pygmies, with their age-old hunting culture, seem in every case to have been early settlers who have been driven into remote areas by later peoples. A few still exist in the heart of New Guinea in almost unexplored areas, and in consequence little is known about them. Like the Bushmen, they cannot or do not wish to adapt to modern civilization and thus, as the bulldozer creeps inevitably onward, they are doomed to perish as the primeval forest gives way before the machine.

CHAPTER 30

Rice Spirits and Severed Heads

Malays—lack of unified mythology—ancestor cult—multiplicity of spirits called up by shamans—multiple souls—harvesting of the rice child—head-hunting as castration.

THE MALAY *panang* or shaman, like that of the Pygmies, is able to transform himself into a tiger. W. W. Skeat describes a therapeutic session at Selangur in which the panang and his wife began by chanting and dispelling hostile spirits. The patient was stretched before the physician. The latter stroked the sick man with a sheaf of palm blossoms, gradually working himself up into a state of intense excitement. He then sank down to the floor on his face, his head enveloped in a sarong. "A long interval now ensued but at length, after many convulsive twitchings, the shrouded figure arose amid the intense excitement of the entire company, and went upon its hands and feet. The tiger spirit had taken possession of the panang's body, and presently a low but strikingly lifelike growl—the unmistakable growl of the dreaded Lord of the Forest—seemed to issue from somewhere under our feet, as the weird shrouded figure began scratching furiously at the mat upon which it had been quietly lying and then, with occasional pauses for the emission of growls, which had previously startled us, and the performance of wonderful catlike leaps, rapidly licked up the handfuls of rice which had been thrown upon the floor in front of it. This part of the performance lasted, however, but a few minutes, and then the evident excitement of the onlookers was raised to a fever pitch as the bizarre and, as it seemed to our fascinated senses, strangely brute-like form stooped suddenly forward and slowly licked over, as a tigress would its cub, the all but naked body of the patient."

Later the panang with his dagger drew blood from his arm and fought with the invisible disease spirit. He then crooned charms, stroked the patient with his headcloth, and lay down exhausted. After ten minutes, with con-

356

vulsions and twitchings, he came to life and presently had a severe attack of nausea.

Such shamanistic possession is typical of the Mongoloid peoples who are distributed throughout Malaysia and the Philippines and include a group in southern India. Their numbers are estimated at about 60,000,000 and it is believed that various migrations from southern Asia to the island areas took place between 2500 and 1500 B.C. The earliest waves (called proto-Malay) carried with them such archaic Asian traits as the small reaping knife (designed so as not to frighten the rice spirit), headhunting, the sacrifice of the cock, pottery, the domestication of the pig. Possession by the tiger spirit is a very early Mongol trait. In ancient times none of these peoples buried their shamans; the bodies were left in a tree in the forest or on a platform so that its spirit might easily escape.

The seance tends to be a dramatic performance, highly entertaining and exciting to the spectators, as evidenced from Skeat's description. Among the Tinguian of the Philippines the medium is more often a woman. Here the session goes on for hours; one spirit after another takes possession of the priestess, causing her to speak in different voices. Some are tricksters who play bawdy jokes, some are jeered and mocked by the audience, some threaten and boast of their lethal powers, some give constructive advice.

Today Hindu influence dominates the major portions of Java and Sumatra and Bali, and some Mohammedan conversion has also taken place in Sumatra. We are here concerned, therefore, with the pagan Malay groups who practice slash-and-burn agriculture, do a certain amount of hunting and, in coastal areas, also fish.

The typical Malay dwelling is raised on piles and reached by a bamboo ladder. It consists of a thatched gable and side walls covered with flattened bamboo or leaves. The furnishings include woven mats, pottery jars, bamboo water tubes, coconut-shell dishes and a hearth near the entrance made of clay and ashes and defined by three stones set in a triangle. The family's livestock includes pigs and chickens. Iron knives are now usually obtained by trading but some smiths still practice their trade. The men possess bows and arrows in some areas though the blowgun is more generally used for hunting.

Villages are generally situated near watercourses (on which dugout canoes are used since there are few jungle trails) and are administered by a chief. Although most Malay groups observe incest taboos of various sorts, there are no clans or totems.

Agriculture is, in jungle areas, of the slash-and-burn variety; rice culture takes two forms, either dry or wet. The most primitive groups still use the digging-stick, while in the Philippines the iron plow is employed and terraced fields on hillsides permit the control of water in the paddies.

As has been indicated, the Malays are a Mongoloid-looking people. Some have the Oriental eye fold; others show some Negro mixture evidenced in the broad nose; still others are nearer to the Polynesian type with its greater percentage of Caucasian blood. The skin color varies from reddish to copper brown. Well-fleshed, their skins rather free from body hair, these people are handsome by European standards.

The spirit world of Malaysia is characterized by multiplicity. In some cases there are thousands of supernatural entities. Among the Tinguians, they can be divided into ancestor spirits and nature spirits for whom ritual with sacrifices and special formulas is carried out. Kadaklan is a powerful male entity who lives in the sky, having created earth, the sun and the moon (which are stones) and the stars (which are lights). Sometimes he sends his dog Kimat (the lightning) to bite a tree, a field, or a house. He amuses himself by playing his thunder drum. He has a wife about whom not much is known except that she bore two sons who are servants of their father. Kaboniyan is even more important than (and sometimes identified with) Kadaklan. This spirit is a culture hero, who lives either in a cave or in the sky. He taught his people to plant and reap rice and sugarcane. With a spear as big as a tree and a head ax as big as a house he keeps off evil spirits. Sometimes he appears as a red rooster or a white dog.

A somewhat more coherent creation story appears in the folklore of the Tempasuk Dusun, a proto-Malay group of north Borneo. Kinorolungan and Yumun were a first couple who lived above in the sky. They said, "Our place is not heavy if there are no people below." Yumun took his shield and a round tray, turned them upside down, and let down the first for the earth, the second for the sky. The pair came down to earth but said, "It is not heavy enough." Yumun got a boulder and made Mount Kinabalu. Since the creation was still not heavy enough, he got another boulder and made the Montanani Islands. He was still not satisfied because there was no sea. With their hands the two dug a hole which became full of sea. Then they walked around the earth but it was still soft and shook. They said, "Our country will not be heavy enough until there are people on it." The wife made a man and woman out of wood and told them to walk and talk. Unfortunately they could not. Yumun said, "This will not do. You had better make them out of this." He pointed to a termite nest. The wife tried again. The man and woman manufactured from the termite nest were able to walk and talk. Yumun then buried his wife and told the newly created pair to look at her grave—all good things to eat, sweet potatoes, coconuts, onions, buffalo, fowls, pigs, were there. Yumun went back to heaven where he was joined by Kinorolungan.

There is, however, no general mythology shared by all the Malayan

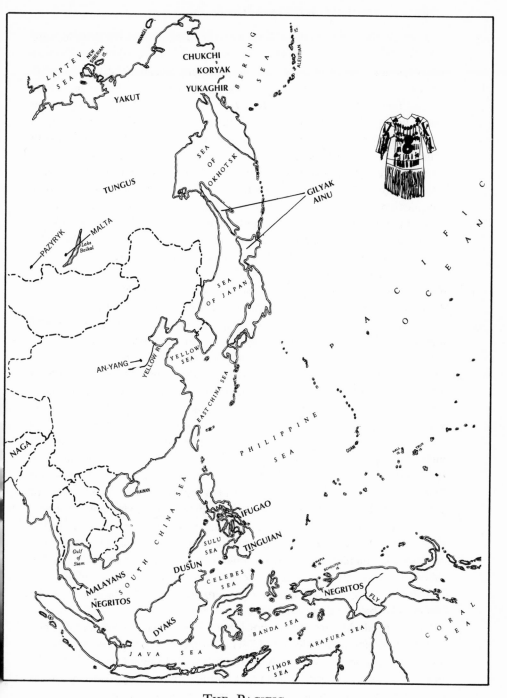

THE PACIFIC

peoples. A few scattered beliefs, such as the explanation for the tides, are archaic and widespread. The tides, it seems, are in flood when a giant crab sits in his hole. When he goes out, the tides ebb because the water is able to flow down through his hole into the underworld. Another widespread culture trait is the belief in a number of souls or spiritual entities in the human being. The Jakun of the peninsula say that those of the right hand go to the afterworld while those of the left wander on earth as unfriendly demons. The Dusun, whose folklore is permeated with the number seven, say there are seven souls which leave the body at death in the form of a butterfly either through the big toe or a cowlick on the head. Soul number one rides on a buffalo, crosses a river, bathes to purify itself, and then returns to the haunts of men. Other souls take the form of moths or swallows. Peninsula Malay souls can wander at night and must be enticed back by the shaman. Dusun souls are at the mercy of minor mischievous spirits who catch them and turn them into fish.

There are a host of grotesque and dangerous spirits in the lower hierarchies of the Malayan supernatural world. The Tinguians conceive of one with a head, long slimy arms and legs, and no body. The *alan* are half human, half birds, rather batlike creatures. Both the Sea Dyaks of Borneo and the Ifugao of the Philippines have elevated one of their spirits to the position of war god in connection with headhunting. The Dyak deity is called Singalong Burong and is identified with the rhinoceros hornbill whose carved image represents him in war ceremonies. The Ifugao call the equivalent god Ifu.

The animistic attitude is a characteristic of the Malays: not only do animals and trees possess indwelling spirits but domestic utensils and the roofbeams of a house as well. As a result there are elaborate ceremonies before taking possession of a house and when household objects are put into a grave they are broken so that their spirits can accompany the dead.

Most important is the complex of belief and ceremony concerning the souls or spirits of the rice. A small crescent-shaped knife, set crosswise on a short wooden handle, is held by the fingers of one hand while the stalks are pulled against it. Its small size is supposed to prevent the spirit of the rice from taking fright. A whole series of ceremonies takes place among the Dusun, who believe there are seven rice spirits.

The peninsula Malays at Selangor intensify this harvest ceremonial. They call it the "taking of the rice child." The priestess sits with trays and bowls about her containing various kinds of cooked and uncooked rice, incense, nuts, a hen's egg, a stone, an iron nail and a reaping knife. An oval basket fourteen inches long, bound with a creeper, serves as a cradle for the baby. This contains a piece of white cloth, colored threads, a hen's egg, a candle, a nut, a cockleshell, an iron nail and a piece of red cloth. Before placing the basket on the ground near the mother sheaf, the priestess chants:

> Herons from all this region
> Roost upon the shaft of my bow.
> Away O spectral reapers
> That we may place our baskets on the ground.

She covers her head with a white cloth, faces the sheaf and waves the ends of the cloth three times to the right and three times to the left. She places a stem of sugarcane in the center of the sheaf and sprinkles it with a paste of rice and water. The cane is left for the rice to lean against when its baby is taken away. The waist of the sheaf is then bound about with rice straw, the shell, candle and nut are taken from a tray and the iron nail is planted near the foot of the sugarcane. Cooked rice is tossed over the sheaf and the bystanders. Then a cord of tree bark is drawn around and up the sheaf. Repeating ten prayers, the priestess digs a lump of soil with her left great toe and puts it in the center of the sheaf. After anointing the rice cutter with frankincense, she presses her right thumb in her mouth, cuts the first seven heads, puts them together, kisses them, turns up the whites of her eyes three times, and three times swallows her own saliva.

The seven ears are placed on the white cloth from the basket, anointed with oil, tied with the colored thread, fumigated with incense, cooked and uncooked rice is scattered over them, they are folded in the cloth, put in the basket, and once more the officiant throws rice over her head and over the bystanders.

The bearer slings the basket around her neck and shields it with an umbrella. The priestess cuts another seven heads, puts them into one of the rice baskets, and sets two reapers reaping the field in parallel lines. The wife of the family meets the rice child at the foot of the house ladder, saying, "What news?" The priestess replies, "All is well."

The rice child, with the special objects in the basket which keep evil spirits away, is laid on a new sleeping mat with pillows at its head. The three first baskets reaped are brought in and placed on a mat at the foot of the cradle. The wife of the household then has taboos imposed upon her, some of which were identical with those observed for three days after the birth of a child.

The implications of this ceremony are most interesting, for it is the first time that we have encountered a symbolical identification between human procreation and vegetable fertility among modern preliterates with a simple agricultural economy. It is noticeable, however, that, although women officiate, no female fertility goddess has crystallized. It is possible that a line of development could occur in which the priestess might take over this role. The sheaf is thought of as the mother of the grain spirit and this concept is similar to the last-sheaf ceremony, or the bringing in of the corn mother, which occurs in peasant tradition in Europe. Also the flinging of rice with a fertility significance is still with us, in Western society, at weddings.

If rice culture has given rise to characteristic ceremonies, the basic reason for headhunting, which is also indigenous to Indonesia, is more difficult to unravel. Although it results in a paranoid and diseased cultural situation, it is so widely distributed that it more deservedly merits the term archetype (at a certain cultural stage) than does the well-publicized "great mother." A glance at its distribution shows, as we have already seen, that most Indo-European and Aryan peoples practiced it. We also find it in Siberia, South Asia, the Torres Straits, New Guinea, New Caledonia, and Polynesia. It also turns up in Dahomey (heads of slain enemies were exhibited) and on the northwest coast of North America; the Aztecs preserved severed heads, and numerous tribes of South America practice headhunting in elaborate form. Scalping, which took place in North America, may or may not be symbolically related. Even the Bible provides us with the story of David and Goliath. We have also seen evidence that headhunting may have begun in the early Stone Age. Headhunting covers some of the same areas as those in which skulls of ancestors are preserved but the latter custom is not as widely distributed and, though in a sense overlapping, the motivation is not precisely the same.

In Indonesia where headhunting is a religion and a duty, we discover, as is often the case, that it is connected with cannibalism. The Tinguians, in the past, after displaying the captured heads on bamboo spikes, carried them to the center of the village where the praises of the victors were sung. The skulls were then split open, the brains taken out and handed to the young girls, who stirred them up in jars of fermented sugarcane juice. They were then served to the warriors. The joints of little fingers and the lobes of the ears of the slain men were also added. Now we have seen that cutting off finger joints is symbolical of castration so that in this case brain cannibalism is strongly associated with assimilation of sexual powers. Further evidence of this can be found in the Borneo Sea Dyak custom that a chief could not be married unless he had taken a head. This is rationalized in a myth. A young man, desirous of marrying, killed a deer and brought it to his girl who refused him. He then killed an orangutan (considered a greater feat) and brought it to her, but she still rejected him. In desperation he rushed out and decapitated the first man he met and threw the head at her feet. She then accepted him. It might be added that the Sea Dyaks also practiced brain cannibalism. The Naga of South Bengal require that a warrior bring home a head before he marries.

The basic concept of mana here applies, since both the head and the sex organs (or symbols for them) are particularly endowed with supernatural power. By depriving the slain enemy either of his head or genitals the victor acquires his mana (his courage and sexual potency which are also equated). If he eats the amputated members, this is in accordance with the science of magic. This is of course the preliterate rationalization. The orthodox Freudian would dig deeper and see the death or castration of the father in order to identify with him and absorb his qualities. However, psychologically the impulse at work here is broader than the oedipal situation. Puberty ceremonies, with their sadism and castration attacks, show that male rivalry works both ways. If the son desires to castrate the father, the father, fearing his own sexual degeneration and the triumph of potent youth, also wishes to eliminate this threat or contain it. A third element is the sadomasochism of war which has homosexual erotic overtones. Male groups which band together for hunting and war and eliminate intercourse with the opposite sex, contain their erotic impulses in the group activities. In warfare they set out to give pain and to have pain inflicted upon them. Warlike frenzy, as the chapters dealing with the Indo-Europeans have shown, is basically the same as erotic excitement and can be accompanied by it. The victors in this homosexual encounter, without loss of semen, then absorb the sexual mana of their victims and turn it to the use and enjoyment of their womenfolk.

H. S. Darlington describes the Naga of Assam as placing the captured heads upon a huge slotted drum in the middle of the village (which he interprets as a symbolical village vulva). The drum is then beaten with (phallic) drumsticks and the heads dance upon it while the women are supposed to look on with extreme enjoyment. In addition, in the center of the village stands the head tree which is obviously phallic and against which the heads lean for five days. Is it going too far to see them as symbolically additional testicles? Among the Sea Dyaks, the only time when women dance is when heads arrive.

If male virility and acquired mana is the basic idea in the headhunting complex, with the development of the concept of detachable spirits of the dead another element is added. Mana is ambivalent, and if its virtues can be acquired from the dead its destructive powers must also be dealt with. Hence the notion that the spirits of the heads may have a dangerous side and must be placated. The Dusun call them *tandalou*. They look like fowls, follow the heads and remain in the head house. If not fed with scattered rice, they enter the heads of the hunters, who cease to be able to walk and soon die. They are also given rice before a new headhunting expedition. The Sea Dyaks, the Naga, the Tinguian and the peninsula Malays all believe that the spirits of the dead become the slaves of their captors. From this rationalization of acquired mana on a personal level comes the custom of capturing a head before an ancestor rite or before building a new house. The peninsula Jakun take a head before a funeral. The Tinguians wear old clothes before a funeral, a taboo which must be removed by taking a head. The same is true of the Sea Dyaks, who also stuff food into the mouths of the heads in a feast in honor of the war god. Since the spirits of the heads become the property of their owners, still another element is added to the complex in that they are sometimes connected with rice culture. Whether this is an association of male virility with fertility, or the heads in a sense become acquired ancestors and thus able to bestow fertility and good harvests, is not clear. The trophies are cleaned and hung upon the wall of the owner's house and when the rice begins to ripen, each house-holder grinds some of the new grain into flour and smears it on the head. The head basket is sometimes placed in Tinguian rice fields; it appears that the Ifugao, also of the Philippines, likewise connect the heads with fertility of the fields.

Headhunting occurs only among isolated self-sufficient groups and produces a situation of justified paranoia since the taking of a head starts a feud, with the result that both groups raid each other continually. In some cases actual war is not involved; a headhunter merely waylays a stray individual. The psychological situation is clearly described in Mabel Cole's book *Savage Gentlemen*. When her anthropologist husband prepared to move on to the next village, he was always told that the neighbors were bad people who would take his head. When he reached the new group he was always received courteously and promptly warned against the *next* village which contained bad people and headhunters. The phenomenon of headhunting seems to show that the worst of aggressive customs are fundamentally associated with deep-seated and unbalanced sexual compulsions which arise in the evolution of human culture. In the Philippines the custom eliminated itself when better roads were built and social intercourse between isolated groups began to take place. Perhaps social and cultural intercourse is the only cure for the vicious and elaborately rationalized paranoias of contemporary civilization.

The Magic of the Arrow

Veddas—ancient ethnic strain related to Australian aborigines—spiritual poverty—shamanism—ancestor worship—trance dances.

I N NORTH-CENTRAL Ceylon a small, vanishing group of people crouches under overhanging rocks and pursues a hunting and gathering existence so spiritually poverty-stricken that the Pygmies and Bushmen seem highly cultivated in comparison. C. G. Seligman, who carried out the only systematic study, found no decoration except a few beads worn at the men's waists and sometimes earplugs in the women's ears. The wild Veddas make scarcely any basketry, they do no carving, they have no folklore, the only artistic expression is a little finger painting done by the women on the walls of rock shelters. The Veddas, who count by saying one and one, have forgotten their own language. They build no temples, make no idols, and their young people are not put through any initiation ceremony.

When Richard Spittel visited them thirteen years after Seligman, in 1924, they were dirtier, more diseased, customs were vanishing, and the small remnant which was not yet assimilated or intermarrying with the dominant Singhalese was obviously dying out.

The jungles in which they live are not unfriendly. In the valleys there are thickets and small trees scattered about as in a young orchard, their trunks protected by coarse grass that grows four or five feet high. There are many clear, rocky streams whose banks are hidden by deep green leaves splashed with bright red flowers. Scattered outcropping masses of rock form the shelters under which the Veddas build their small fires and roast the deer and wild boar upon which they subsist. Generally under five feet in height, with wavy hair which hangs down to their shoulders, they are a Caucasoid-looking people, although the brow ridges are heavy, the noses moderately broad and the skin black to bronze.

We know that the wild Veddas, from descriptions of early travelers, were pursuing the same existence in the sixteenth century as they do now. They then wore bark-cloth loincloths, now they barter for commercial cloth and wear dirty rags.

The only significance of this people derives from the fact that physical anthropology has pronounced them proto-Australoid. It should be remembered that this human type is one of the earliest to be identified by archaeology in Africa, that it crops up in the Indus Valley as a probably subservient element in the population. In addition, the Veddas are similar physically to other contemporary jungle tribes in southern India and to the natives of Australia. They may also be related to the first peoples who entered America. The proto-Australoid is therefore a very early ethnic strain (earlier than the Negroid, Mongoloid and Caucasian) which was, from all indications, the original population of India and Ceylon, and from there migrated to Australia. Attempts have also been made to relate the Sakei of the Malay Peninsula to it but some authorities regard these groups as a Negrito-Malay mixture.

At any rate, the wild Veddas of Ceylon are a survival of a once much more widely distributed archaic group. Whether they have degenerated culturally is an open question. Although the Singhalese have a legend that they were once more civilized, with chiefs and temples, it is more likely that they have never advanced beyond their present cultural level. Only one fact relates them to their far more elaborately organized relatives in Australia: they do possess exogamous clans, though the clans are not distinguished by any trace of totemism.

Indeed, the Vedda relationship to animals is exceptional. Although they are dependent upon hunting they make no masks, never impersonate animals in their dances, and exhibit no trace of animal folklore. Seligman says they are poor in magic, having no verbal charms or amulets for success in hunting. Although eating fowl is taboo before a ceremony and shamans do not eat pork, in the case of the large animals the Veddas are so unenterprising that they never attempt to kill them and for this reason refrain from eating them. They fear the elephant, the leopard, the buffalo, and the bear. They do not call the bear by name if it is nearby but shout a charm naming it "the enemy" which is guaranteed to drive it away. They also possess a charm to drive away elephants. When we remember that the tiny African Pygmies are elephant hunters, the behavior of the Veddas seems curiously lacking in initiative.

A faint echo of ritual cannibalism lingers in the old custom of carrying a bit of dried human liver in the pouch which ordinarily contains betel nuts. The owner was supposed to chew this in moments of crisis. This would result in making him strong and drive him to a frenzy in which he would kill "the one who had insulted him."

Vedda religion centers around shamanism and ancestor worship. Fear of the dead is evidenced by the fact that there is no burial. The body is left stretched out in the shelter, covered with leaves and branches or perhaps with a stone on its chest. The group then leaves the spot for a long time. Years later they may come back, throw out the bones and occupy the habitation again. In spite of this kind of avoidance which we have already encountered among Bushmen and Negritos, there is no discarding of the property of the dead and no purification ceremony. The danger to be avoided is hostility on the part of the spirits of the dead, who cause stones to fall on any who linger near the body.

On the whole, the ancestor spirits are considered kind and helpful. The shaman dances around the offering which used to be meat and yam and now includes rice (which they obtain by barter). The possessing spirit speaks in a harsh guttural voice through the mouth of the shaman saying he approves the offering. He generally promises success in hunting. The shaman then collapses. When he comes to, all present eat the offering; even the dogs which are used in hunting get their share. There is a strong feeling of communion with the friendly dead in the shared meal.

The spirits of the ancestors have a certain tendency to assimilate the name of the hill they inhabit and thus, under Singhalese influence, turn into evil nature spirits. The only hierarchies which occur in the pure Vedda religion consist of ordinary *yaka* and a certain great hunter, or Kande Yaka, who is a culture hero, his brother, Bilindi (whom he killed in a fit of temper when the latter was a baby), and a certain Panikki Yaka. Kande Yaka, among some of the Veddas, is thought of as having some authority; the ordinary ancestor spirits must report to him before they are allowed to receive offerings. This is the extent of Vedda theology.

The ritual arrow or *aude,* which is an eight-inch blade with a three- or four-inch handle, is used in rituals, generally held in the hand of the shaman. Arrows are also stuck in the ground in certain dances while the officiants dance around them. In dances invoking the hunter Kande the performers move spasmodically in a circle around the arrow, jerking backward with each step, making trembling movements, and executing half turns. After every half turn they slap their bodies, which serve as drums because they have no musical instruments, and gasp out a monotonous song to which they keep time. Their heads are flung up and down after every turn, tossing their tangled mops of hair. One after another (there are sometimes three officiants), howling between gasps and trembling more violently, they work themselves into a seizure in which they are possessed by the yaka and

finally fall to the ground. Seligman found the procedure only partially voli-
tional. When the shaman came to he did not know what he had been doing.

The Veddas also dance a deer dance, mimicking the call of dogs, the
tracking of the deer and the killing of the animal. A similar dance of boar
hunting included a bundle of leaves hanging from a platform of saplings
which a small boy, squealing like a boar, manipulated with a string. Still
another dance was performed to make delivery for a pregnant woman easy,
in which the patient was wiped over with a bunch of bast. Finally there was
a collecting honey dance in which the performers mimicked the driving away
of bees.

When the Veddas are in a good mood they are inclined to parody their
own dances. Their songs consist of tunes with three or four intervals, the
words being unimaginative. The women and sometimes men paint on the
rock shelters with a finger dipped in ashes mixed with saliva. The subjects
are men and women, animals, including the leopard and the hide container
for honey, seen from above, a circle with rays which could easily be mistaken for a sun symbol. The Veddas deny that the drawings have any magical or symbolical meaning. They are done merely to pass the time. The
stylization of the human body by a straight line and two curving lines and
the comblike treatment of dogs is similar to the Mesolithic and early Neolithic drawings on rock shelters which have been discovered in Spain. In the
light of the Veddas' denial of any special significance to their art, perhaps
the interpretation of the Spanish rock pictures has been overelaborate.

After much inquiry, Seligman was able to record one folk tale which
seems to exemplify the limits of Vedda imagination. It runs as follows:
"There was a man who had fire; he distributed this to animals, trees and
stones but a little remained to him at the end and this he swallowed. His
name was Wasa Watiya. We cannot say whether he was a Vedda. Because
he swallowed this fire we all get hungry, for we all have fire within us. There
were men below before Wasa Watiya but they could not talk; otherwise
they were as ourselves. Wasa Watiya made and sent the first dog to these
people, and the dog barked at them so that these people feared greatly and
stammering and stuttering began to talk and the first words were 'Battakai,
battakai! Dog will bite!' "

CHAPTER 32

The Eternal Dream Time

*Australia—single ethnic strain and homogeneity of culture—conservatism of
Stone Age society—the flowering of totemism—ancestor worship as socially
cohesive mythology—theory of spirit children—lack of acceptance of sexual
intercourse as necessary to procreation—types of totemism—ritual dramatizing of myths—castration theme and aggressive circumcision ritual—trickster
—sexuality and seasonal symbolism—rainbow python and great mother
possibly influenced by Indonesia.*

SINCE there is a trough in the ocean bed between Borneo and
Celebes which was at least thirty miles wide even when sea
levels were at their lowest in glacial times, this portion of Indonesia and also
Australia were settled relatively late in prehistory, from 20,000 to 10,000
B.C. Yet the continent of Australia preserves the oldest types of mammals,
the duck-billed platypus and the kangaroo, and one of the oldest types of
living ethnic strains. The Australoids, with long wavy hair and beards, low
foreheads and prominent brow ridges, noses with low, broad roots, and
dark brown skins, are related to the Veddas. Hence it is believed that the
route of migration may have been from south India through Ceylon, Indonesia to Australia, while some pushed on to Melanesia and colonized the
Bismarck Archipelago and New Caledonia.

The natives of Australia numbered about 300,000 when they were first
encountered by the whites in 1788. The varied ecology of the country has
affected their culture but all groups share a great many basic traits. Coastal
regions and some river valleys and the southern forested areas provide a
better living than the central deserts, but even here the Arunta, who have
been particularly well studied, have managed to eke out a difficult existence
among a succession of sand hills and low mountains whose only foliage in
the dry season is pincushion-like porcupine grass and belts of desert oaks,
scrubby mulga trees and acacias. A short rainy season, however, causes a
hectic growth from dormant seeds. Although a hot sun beats down during
the day, at night the temperature falls below freezing and the Australians,
who wear no clothes whatsoever (except a tassel on the penis to indicate

369

initiate status), curl around small slow fires when they sleep. Indeed many of them are scarred by burns from this bedroom habit.

Houses are generally mere lean-tos of branches, although in some areas a dome-shaped hut of saplings covered with grass or mud is constructed. The women's only household utensil is a *pitchi,* a three-foot shallow wooden trough which is used to carry objects on the head, as a mixing bowl, and sometimes as a cradle, rocked by the mother's foot while she performs other household tasks. Her other tool is the digging-stick, used to unearth wild yams, lily bulbs and other edible tubers.

String is made from spun opossum fur, and kangaroo tendons are used for lashing of tools. Men's equipment includes wooden spears and spear-throwers, wooden shields and in some areas boomerangs. In the north the technique of pressure-flaking flints for knives is still known. A sharp flint is fixed in the end of the spear-thrower to serve as a knife.

The women are of course gatherers and their province includes such game as snakes, small lizards, opossums, the collecting of goose or emu eggs and witchetty grubs (the larvae of a large moth) which are cooked in hot ashes and taste like slightly sweetened scrambled eggs.

The chief game animals are kangaroos, wallabies, lizards and emus. The technique of hunting the latter is particularly significant in relation to totemistic ceremonies. The hunters first rubbed the crevices of the body with ochreous clay to kill their scent. The birds which they planned to stalk were feeding on some berries. Herbert Basedow, the observer, continues, "I now observed two objects emerging from the thicket surrounding the plain. The objects had the appearance of shrubs carried by a pair of human legs. They moved stealthily forward, stopping now and then to give the scene an air of peace and repose. . . . The birds were aware of the unnatural intrusion. They ruffled their feathers, ran short distances and ran back. I could now hear the hunters imitating the calls of the birds—some the deep guttural grunt of the adult cock, others the shrill whistling shriek of the chick. The birds seemed bewildered. . . ." Now the hunters extended their hands above the bush and waved a plume of feathers, which piqued the curiosity of the birds so they actually moved toward them. The hunters then dropped the foliage, snatched up their spears, which they had been dragging between their toes, and killed two birds as the flock panicked. In hunting kangaroos, sometimes a group beat the bushes while the hunters lay in wait and leaped up to spear them. Lizards were knocked over with sticks.

Since the Australians manage without benefit of pottery, the bow and arrow in most areas, or any agriculture whatever, we might expect them to be as spiritually poverty-stricken as the Veddas, but instead they have developed one of the most complex theologies, based on totemism, in the preliterate world. The early anthropological notion that they are living fossils has had to be drastically modified. They have not remained static (diffusion of certain rites is still going on) and they have not remained as they are merely because of isolation but because, like the African Pygmies, they are a basically conservative people. There has been contact with Indonesia through the north which has resulted in the borrowing of the dugout canoe and, for a time, pottery; but even these have fallen into disuse. Ceremonial practices, in which the Australians were more interested, have definitely been introduced from the north and also certain mythological elements.

Australian totemism, therefore, does not reflect the earliest type of psychic relationship to animals but is rather a final flowering of an archaic concept which has developed through the millennia just as the complex symbolism of the Bambara has undoubtedly had a long history.

Although much of the Australian habitat is not favorable to agriculture, the complex dogma of the religion itself would be an obstacle in the way of economic change. It is difficult for technical-minded Western man to realize that lack of material progress does not necessarily mean low intelligence. Some efforts have been made to use intelligence tests to measure the abilities of Australian and Negrito children. On the whole, the results indicate that they are just as bright as young Americans. As adults their adaptation and skills differ so much from those of literate men that an accurate comparison is impossible. It must be admitted, however, that they show just as much ingenuity in adapting to their environment and rationalizing their relationship to it as literate man has shown in modifying it and distorting it.

Australian totemism is a system of belief which unites social organization, attitudes toward the means of subsistence, ancestor cults, art, mythology and ceremonial life. It is a remarkable achievement of social cohesion in that the ceremonial life teaches mythology, traditional history, social custom, acts as a focus of emotional exaltation, and at the same time provides drama and entertainment.

Universal is the belief in the "eternal dream time" of the ancient past when the world was peopled with ancestral spirits who created it, shaped the landscape, the moon, sun, the flora and fauna, and were a source of life and magical power. These entities were gigantic humans or animals, the source of the original stock of spirits which return to create new life. On earth they lived like the natives of today. After traveling about and hunting, sometimes indulging in cannibal acts and sex acts which come straight out of the unconscious, establishing customs, social divisions and animal or plant totems, they died, were transformed into landmarks, or departed. In the southeast they tended to go into the sky; in Arnhem Land to the north, their apotheosis took place in water holes, rivers and lakes; in the central area they became trees and rocks. In the south individualized hero cults predominate, all-father figures with wives and children; in the north snakes and women play important roles; in the central area ancestors tend to be local and less individualized. Myths are composed of repetitive and random episodes without literary form, serving as a basis for and a rationalization of custom.

The cohesion of myth, poetry and crude dramatic action is exemplified by Ankotaringa, an Arunta myth. The story recounts that a man without father or mother who had sprung from the earth lived at Ankota. He had been lying on the earth and the white ants had eaten his body hollow. Finally he rose up from the soft soil of a little watercourse. He saw churingas (magic strips of wood) waving all about him. These belonged to other people who had originated the same way that he had. He wondered where he should go, and finally went to a swamp, sat down at the edge of the water and decorated himself with red eagle's down. A great churinga arose from his head. He breathed the four winds, a warm breeze from the west invigorated him. The churinga fell from his head. He left it lying and traveled west— underground. He encountered some men and women and ate them. A man from the west cut off his head. The men he had swallowed came out and climbed the rocky hills swinging bullroarers. The head rolled back to Ankota and went underground.

In the actual ceremony, observed by T. G. H. Strehlow, while the red down was stuck on the actor's body and a churinga fixed to his head, the first verses of the chant were repeated over and over.

> Red is the down which is covering me;
> Red I am as though burning in a fire,
> Red I am as though burning in a fire.
> Bright red gleams the ochre with which I have
>   rubbed my body.
> Red I am as though burning in a fire.
> Red, too, is the hollow in which I am lying.
> Red I am like the heart of a flame of fire.
> Red, too, is the hollow in which I am lying.
> The red churinga is resting upon my head.
> Red, too, is the hollow in which I am lying.

The churinga attached to his head had bullroarers hanging from it. A hollow in the ground was scraped out with a boomerang into which the actor crept. Meanwhile he was singing of the tall churinga.

> Like a whirlwind it is towering to the sky.
> Like a pillar of red sand it is towering to the sky . . .

He scratched away the sands with a handful of gum leaves, imitating a dog because this ceremony was connected with the dog totem. Then he sang:

> A mass of red pebbles covers the plains.
> Little white sandhills cover the plains.
> Lines of red pebbles streak the plains.
> Lines of white sandhills streak the plains.
> An underground pathway lies open before me.
> Leading straight west it lies open before me.

The chorus sang:

> He is sucking his beard into his mouth in anger,
> Like a dog he follows the trail by scent . . .

The churinga was taken off, he had now completed his journey and like a dog he scratched furiously to show his cannibal rage. The chorus sang:

> Irresistible and foaming with rage,
> Like a whirlwind he rakes them together.
> He devours the Chilpa men at Parr Erultcha.

The actor then scratched the ground very slowly to show he was gorged after his cannibal feast. Then he sang:

> Out yonder, not far from me is Ankota.
> The underground hollow is gaping open before me.
> A straight track is gaping open before me.
> An underground hollow is gaping before me.
> A cavernous pathway is gaping before me.
> An underground pathway is gaping before me.
> Red I am like the heart of a flame of fire.
> Red, too, is the hollow in which I am resting.

Although the action was rudimentary, the effect on the audience was that of a sacred and inspiring mystery play by which they were transfigured and exalted.

While there seem to be no Australian myths describing the shaping of the world, the making of men occurs in various ways. Baiami, the hero of New South Wales, created men out of clay; his brother or servant, Daramulan, brought women up out of the water to be their wives. The Arunta myth, which is widespread, describes two self-created beings, the Numbakulla who found larvalike creatures on earth (neither animal nor human) with no distinct organs or limbs. They did not eat and looked something like human beings doubled up foetus-fashion. The Numbakulla cut loose their limbs with stone knives and shaped them into human beings. Later the creators turned into little lizards. In the northeast there are numerous creator spirits called the Mura Mura. They made men out of lizards, created landmarks and totem centers.

Geza Roheim, as a result of his fieldwork, maintained that the hero or sky gods were more nearly related to demons and medicine men than to the people of the ancestor cults. Demons called *eruncha* abound. Some cause menstruation by clawing women's vaginas, others may destroy individuals who venture out of the camp at night into the dark. They are either anthropomorphic or animal in form and are likely to bite or mutilate human bodies. The sky gods, Roheim pointed out, are the product of ambivalence. They are called beautiful, helpful, wicked, deformed, and the same entity can have various aspects. The hero deity of the Arunta, Alchira Ilinka, looks like a big strong man but he has emu feet. He wears a white forehead band, a hair string around his waist and a pubic tassel. He has a wife who bore him emu-footed sons and dog-footed daughters. He is said to have originated in an emu's nest and he stands for the emu totem. He kills people he does not like, drives men crazy, and initiates them as medicine men. Writes Roheim, "One thing is absolutely certain—the origin of supernatural beings from infantile anxiety." In his view the child's anxieties are in part oedipal (erotic attraction toward the mother and hostility toward the father) and in part created by witnessing the "primal scene," the sexual act between the father and the mother. Since primitive children do witness parental coitus early in life, this psychoanalytical tenet may well apply. Good and bad supernaturals, good and bad medicine men, and finally the ambivalence of mana, the good and bad aspects of the unusual, may be rooted in the child's basic emotional patterns, shaped as they are by an ambivalent reaction to sex. In the analyst's view, coitus is fascinating and terrifying to the young child because of the size of those who perform it, his own feeling of sex stimulation and the apprehension that his own small organ will be inadequate. Analysis has also revealed that children frequently interpret the primal scene as an aggressive attack of the male on the female, which also shrouds it in fear. Australian children, however, indulge in sex play, without incurring any parental sanctions before they reach puberty, which shows that their interpretation of the act is not wholly traumatic. Indeed Roheim adds, "But as supernaturals are nothing else than magnified parents, the protective aspect of the latter is subsequently mirrored in the spectres created by our anxieties and imagination." In all probability love and hostility are inextricably mingled, with the result that all interpersonal emotions are ambivalent. "It is because our infancy lasts longer than that of other animals that we need supernatural beings. If we had developed harmoniously, if there were not a fatal discrepancy between what we desire and what we can bear, between the id and the ego, we should not have become human. Mankind spells disharmony."

Primitive peoples, far from embodying Rousseau's idyllic image, mirror the eternal disharmonies. The terms in which they dramatize their compulsions are different from those of modern Western man but the fascination which primitive life holds for all of us lies in the fact that the real meaning of our rationalizations is often revealed by the doings of our naked brothers of the desert and forest. We are all children of the eternal dream time.

To return to the over-all picture of Australian totemism, the Alchira, or ancestors of the dream time, are the source of new life in both animal and human because they are responsible for the production of spirit children. The mother conceives when she happens to be near a totem center (or she or her husband dreams of an animal, or an animal is associated with perception of the first stirrings of life in the womb). The spirit child is thought of as entering the mother through the loins and not through the vulva. These spirit children are often, in part at least, reincarnations of ancestors; sometimes they return to the totem center at death, sometimes they go to an unspecified otherworld. As a result of this dogma of conception, throughout all of Australia there is a denial that coitus is necessary or essential for the production of new life. It is considered merely a stretching of the vulva or "opening" of the woman so that the child may have a home. This doctrine has aroused considerable controversy among anthropologists, some feeling that the role of male semen is understood and the knowledge repressed or disregarded for theological reasons. Ashley Montagu, who has studied the problem exhaustively, concludes that relating the sex act to pregnancy and birth requires considerable scientific acumen, since a great amount of premarital activity takes place among primitives without conception and likewise the time lapse between the act and the perception of life in the womb is so long as to make the connection unclear. It is also true that preliterate notion of cause and effect generally depends on special or temporal juxtaposition. He therefore concludes, "Amongst every people of whom we have any knowledge, where an awareness of the relationship between intercourse and childbirth exists, that awareness is unexceptionally accompanied by beliefs and practices which in the first place prove that intercourse is not regarded as solely the cause of childbirth, and in the second place would, at least, strongly suggest that this limited awareness was once preceded by a still more limited awareness, in which intercourse played no part in the production of children." He is inclined to believe that this was the case with primeval man.

As regards the Australians, among whom sex and phallicism play an important role, it is a fact that, with the exception of the northern area, such practices have nothing to do with fertility or the desire for children. Basedow describes a ceremony with phallic dances performed by the men to renew their potency. Montagu points out that, "since the phallus is a great source of pleasure to the savage it is of small wonder that he performs ceremonies in celebration of it and with the object of preserving its pleasure-giving benefits."

As we have seen, the phenomenon of erection and ejaculation is full of mana and also an expression of male ego, and in some cases women are avoided before warlike or hunting activities lest the male power be weakened. Mana, of course, can be either dangerous or beneficial. Among the Australians the positive side of sex comes to the fore. The psychologist Porteus records that a group of Central Australians at the end of a war dance imitated the movements of intercourse. He adds, "It is interesting also from the psychological viewpoint to see that the aborigines do not differentiate between certain forms of excitement, that induced by sexual images and practices being held so closely akin to the excitement occasioned by shedding blood that one is deemed a preparation for the other." Roheim states that, "Before setting out on a blood avenging expedition the Pitjantjara excite themselves by mutual masturbation."

Among the Arunta, blood to cement birds down to the naked body for ceremonial purposes is often obtained by puncturing the erect phallus. During preparation for rituals, women are kept in readiness so that the officiants may have intercourse with them, as a kind of magical charm so that their headdresses will not come loose.

The magical functions of sex, therefore, are quite apart from the ancestor theology which explains the increase of life. Connected with the latter are the wooden objects called churingas. These are slats from six inches to nine feet long decorated with symbolic patterns. A set of rings may mean a hill, a water hole, a tree, or a spider's web. Wavy lines can stand for grubs, snakes, rivers, or the wandering of tribal ancestors. Two half circles within each other mean men or women sitting down, or a camp. These patterns record the wandering and acts of the spirit ancestors. Churingas themselves represent the transformed bodies of the totem ancestors. One is assigned to each newborn child when his totem animal is determined. Churingas are brought out for ceremonies and often become a part of the elaborate down headdresses worn by the officiants, as in the Ankotaringa drama. Their most important role is that of concretizing mythological history, a kind of symbolic script which helps a preliterate people preserve tradition. They are extremely sacred, a focus of emotion equivalent to the role of the host in Christian theology. When not in use they are rubbed with grease and red ochre (blood of the Alchira). Friends of a dead man often weep when his churinga is displayed. They are, of course, completely taboo to women (a woman never sees her own). These objects are kept in storehouses, sometimes in hollow trees or rock shelters. Such spots are holy; a criminal is safe in their vicinity and no animals may be killed near them. Dust scraped from a churinga is drunk in water to cure illness. Possession of these objects acts like a magical amulet.

Mention has been made of totems, but so far their role has not been elaborated. As we have seen, ancestors are identified with animals and these animal (or plant) men traveled about in the dream time performing ritual acts and sanctifying various spots. These travels represent early migrations; they justify the native's relationship to a certain territory and affirm his unity with the natural world. In addition, it is probable that the association of certain animals with certain spots originally meant that they were plentiful in these areas. Aside from the identification with animals because of hunting activities and their central economic importance, animals have become badges of social groups and thus the word totem has various implications. There are four kinds of animal totems: an individual totem in which one person is connected with one natural species; a sex totem in which the men and the women of the tribe are all under the protection of separate specific animals; moiety totems in which the tribe is divided in half and then subdivided once or twice, each group being given a totem; and finally clan totems in which a kinship group is related to a locality.

In practice more than one kind of totemism may be present and the chief functions are: (1) to set off marriage groups, and (2) to record mythology and to stimulate increase in the food supply.

In marriage-group totemism or social totemism the members of the group are all supposedly descended from a common ancestress. All members of the clan are brothers and sisters. A man's flesh is therefore kangaroo or emu (if one of these is the totem) and, as a result, he must not eat it, kill it, or marry a person of the same flesh. He therefore marries out of the clan. Very often he is supposed to marry his cross-cousin, the child of his mother's brother or father's sister. Marriage regulations of this sort become endlessly complicated because (since blood relationship through intercourse is not significant) incest prohibitions are worked out on a formal basis. They confused early anthropologists and require elaborate charts for clarity, yet the preliterate inhabitants of Australia seem to have kept them in mind for centuries. Disregard of marriage taboos is, however, considered as close to sin as anything in aboriginal philosophy. In the past at least, sanctions against it were supposedly as severe as the death penalty.

Ceremonial totemism, being local, and male-dominated, tends to mean that a man is associated with the same animal as his father. (He may be of a different totem if conceived by a spirit child outside of the locality, but in that case he cannot play a leading part in the rites.) Such groups are composed of initiated male members who have certain mythological tasks to perform. One type of ceremony is historical and commemorates the travels and deeds of the ancestors. Different groups of the same totem may be in charge of separate chapters in a myth. Elaborate preparations are undertaken such as manufacturing symbols, disguising the officiants with eagle down and towering headdresses, and "singing" the ground before dancing upon it. Each act, which may take only a couple of minutes of singing, dancing or mimicry (like the Ankotaringa ceremony), is explained to the newly initiated by the old men. Sometimes these pageants are enacted in connection with circumcision and subincision. They are always taboo to women, who are sometimes ceremonially chased away. They produce in spectators and performers high states of tension and emotion; in fact the old men sometimes require that their stomachs be rubbed with churingas in order to quiet their agitation.

The animal-increase rites are particularly interesting since they are probably the oldest layer in the Australian totemic complex, being connected with the basic problem of the food supply. In some cases it is easy to see the connection between hunting practice and dance mimicry. The method of stalking emus, described by Basedow, by disguising the upper part of the body with shrubbery is reproduced in the Kimberlys where there is a dance performed in similar disguise. Spencer and Gillen describe an Arunta emu ceremony in which a number of men gashed their arms and allowed the blood to drip upon the ground in an area three feet square. When the spot was sufficiently covered, it was allowed to dry hard and used as a background upon which to paint sacred emu designs. Round yellow spots represented areas of fat in the emu's body; various colored circles stood for the eggs in several stages of development. Several churingas were decorated with emu and cockatoo feathers and stuck in the ground near the picture. Three old men were chosen to act as clan ancestors while a group of young men represented their descendants. Their chests were decorated with emu totem pictures. The three churingas were then taken up and extended with feathers and other material in a drooping curve, a tuft at the end representing the emu's head and neck. These were attached to the heads of the old men while the young ones sat about the pictures and sang songs. In the actual performance, which was repeated twice on one day and three times on the next, the women and children were herded by the young men to the edge of the theater. The performers swayed their heads in imitation of the emu gazing about. They glided toward the women who cried out in alarm, stopped, bobbed their heads, then ran toward the women again, whereupon the latter ran to their camp. At the end of the last performance the decorations were removed from the churingas and the pictures destroyed. One of the interesting elements in this ceremony is the use of symbolic pictures which is reminiscent of Paleolithic cave art.

In a third emu ceremony of a Luritcha group recorded by Porteus, one man stabbed his arm and another his subincised penis to obtain blood to decorate a ball of fur string with pink and white feathers. This was hung around the neck of the old man who was custodian of the ceremony. A little space was cleared for a nest in which three round stones spattered with blood and down were placed to represent the eggs. The old man entered the consecrated area bent over, his hands behind his back to represent the bird's tail. He peered about him and imitated the grunt of the adult bird. The young men bent over the same way and followed him in a line, emitting cries like emu chicks. They knelt in a group around the nest, the old man standing above them, the emu "heart" swinging over the nest. The young men swung their shoulders from side to side while the leader contracted his stomach rhythmically to indicate the emotional effect the ceremony was having upon him. Here the sacred picture is replaced by stones, but it is notable that the sounds made by emus were imitated precisely as in the process of stalking the birds.

In other cases, increase rites are merely symbolical, consisting of rubbing, painting or striking the stone or tree which marks the animal totem center. In general, animal increase is believed to occur in the same way as human reproduction: spirit children have to be encouraged to come forth and be incarnated. In eastern Australia, according to the Worora tribe, giant human beings called Wandjinas came out of the sea. Several of these belong to each clan. They created the world, spirit children and animals. They are painted in caves as large figures with no mouths because the heads are skulls which cannot speak. The bodies are striped and dotted red, yellow, black and pale blue. Groups of these entities are depicted, husbands with wives and children, and along with them totem animals. The increase ceremony consists of repainting the Wandjinas. The fact that these beings came from the sea indicates that this is an alien ritual, probably diffused from Melanesia.

Circumcision, which also came in from the north relatively late, exists all through the central areas of the continent. Added to it is subincision, slitting open of the urethra from the glans, either for a short distance, or all the way to the root. This painful and curious custom does not interfere with intercourse because it is practiced with the woman lying on her back, her legs around the man's thighs. Basedow's description emphasizes the aggressive character of circumcision. The old men came on the dance ground dressed in ochre and pipe clay, rustling leafy branches on their legs. One carried a waninga, a kite-like rectangle which is a grid of fur string on a frame borne on a spear. This was inhabited temporarily by the totem deity. The men stamped and a chorus sang as the waninga was planted in the ground. The atmosphere grew tense, the onlookers breathed hard, then: "As out of the mouth of a legion of demons the space surrounding the waninga was suddenly vibrant with a tumult of massed bullroarers. The effect was deafening. Some were buzzing and droning, others seemed to be shrieking. I imagined, too, I heard some terror-stricken feminine voices adding to the discord from afar." The bullroarers (oval slats swung on a cord) were the voices of Alchira from the dream time. The initiates were brought in blindfolded and painted red. The bandages were taken off and they were told to hug the waninga as a precaution against the pain of the operation. The chorus sang and beat on wooden shields. Then the waninga bearer did a terrific dance. "His stamping knees nearly touched his chin as they were alternately raised, arms swaying gracefully outward." He finally flung himself to the ground, went into convulsions and produced the stone knife from his body. (It was carried concealed in the hair.) He poked his long black beard into his mouth and made awful grimaces. The others on hands and knees made a living table. The initiate was backed up to it, his foreskin pulled out as far as possible, and cut off.

A myth from southeast Australia also strengthens the aggressive theme behind these operations on the sex organ. One of two young men flung a boomerang which fell into a lake and in its passage through the air became sharpened and pointed. One of the boys dove for the weapon, landed upon its point and was circumcised. The other did the same. They were highly satisfied to have become men and immediately thought of their father who, being uncircumcised, had remained a mere boy. They sneaked up on him and circumcised him with a piece of flint. Though weakened by loss of blood he continued to have relations with his wife and soon died. Since circumcision appears to be a rite which has entered Australia relatively recently, it may well have been transmitted from Islamic areas of Indonesia.

The group of cults found in the north which involve women and the great snake are also probably influenced by recent intrusions from Indonesia. The form found in east Arnhem Land and studied by William Lloyd Warner seems to be the most elaborate and most highly synthesized. Here the myth of the two sisters and Yurlungur, the great python, underlies all the major ceremonies.

In the dream time there were Wongan men, and animals were like men. The two sisters made a long journey from the interior toward the coast (on the way they had intercourse with two men). One carried a child and one was pregnant. During the journey they killed various animals. Eventually the baby was born to the second woman. As they continued their journey they named clan territories, assigning totem names. They came to a water hole with a python in it. When they cooked the animals they had killed over the fire, the animals jumped off the fire and ran into the water hole. This was meant to indicate that the well was sacred. One of the women went to draw water and let some of her menstrual blood fall into the spring, profaning it. The python was aroused by this act. He spat out some of the water and lunged out of the well. This caused a flood from the totem well and torrential rains from the sky. The two sisters sang and danced rituals to prevent the flood and to keep the snake from swallowing them. Presently they were surrounded by all the snakes in the country. Feeling that their magic was not strong enough, they sang taboo menstrual songs. Yurlungur was only more violently aroused and swallowed the women and their children. The water then receded and he sang various ceremonies. At the same time a number of clan snakes told their names, totems, kinship relationships and what they ate. Yurlungur then spewed up the women and children, who fell into an ants' nest. The snake went back to his well, at which point his trumpet came out of the well and began to play. It blew over the women and children and brought them to life. Yurlungur swallowed them a second time. Since the snake had risen up and fallen down several times, each time he fell he created dance grounds. He finally spat the women out again, whereupon they turned to stone. As a kind of afterthought it is said that the women intended to circumcise their sons. After the main events took place, two Wongan men followed the tracks of the sisters. They also found the spoor of the snake and, noticing that the totem well shone like a rainbow, they realized that the snake was inside. Some blood had fallen from the heads of the boys and women. This they gathered up. They then dreamed of what the women had sung and danced. They were told by the women to circumcise boys, to paint with blood and feathers, and to sing and dance the things the women had named and seen on their travels. This they did and it is still done to this day.

This story pervades all the ceremonies of the group, being treated thematically rather than as a narrative. In the circumcision ceremony, bull-roarers, a drum, and a wooden trumpet are used. The trumpet is manufactured from a small tree, the core of which has been hollowed by termites. It is cleaned and shaped into a trumpet which will be later painted to become the totemic emblem of Yurlungur. The boys who are of age for circumcision are told the snake smells their foreskins. Hearing the great snake begin to bellow for them through the trumpet, they run to their mothers. When the men come for them the women defend them with spears in mock fight. They often shed tears. The boys are sent on their travels for a month (apparently a reflection of the travel theme in the myth). Upon their return, a ceremonial pole is erected and two dance grounds are prepared, one for the women and the uncircumcised which plays a minor role, and a triangular one which represents Yurlungur's body with the women and children inside. At the apex there is a heap of branches which stands for the totemic well. Two poles with a bush at the top are carried about. They symbolize the boys who are to be cut, the bushes being pubic hair. The women wail for the boys who are lost to them. Dancing takes place at night as various animal totems are dramatized. Yurlungur's song is sung and the trumpet is blown over the initiates, who hide their heads under women's mats. The usual bloodletting takes place in order to gum on the down costumes. Although the blood is supposed to symbolize the menstrual blood of the sisters it is highly taboo to women; the sight of it would make them ill. Totemic designs are painted on the boys' chests and abdomens. They are threatened with spears as if about to be killed. Animal dances take place for many nights. Finally the men come out of the well in a line, painted like iguanas and carrying the trumpet. This symbolizes the emergence of the snake, for the iguanas are his children. When the circumcision takes place it means that the snake and the flood have returned. Afterward the boys are steamed over a fire of wet leaves and the trumpet is buried.

Several other important ceremonies are tied to the same myth. In one, tribal brothers exchange wives and ritual copulation takes place which "makes their bodies clean." If they do not do this, the snake will make them ill.

The amount of synthesis that has taken place in this ritual complex seems surprising when it is remembered that there is no professional priesthood among the Murngin. Aside from the geographical and historical mythology encountered everywhere in Australia and the usual totemic basis, Warner pointed out that the whole has been welded into a nature cycle. In eastern Arnhem Land there is a heavy rainfall bringing floods for five months and also high and dangerous tides. During the wet period hunting is poor. As in so much pre-agricultural mythology, women have come to play the role of the enemy. The profanation of menstrual blood started the rain cycle and human copulation. The ceremonies are supposed to keep the balance of nature and restrain the floods. The snakes and the men's group are thought of as pure. The male snake group swalllows the unclean initiates into the ritually pure masculine group.

The way in which disparate elements are joined can be seen in the statement that the two sisters had intended to circumcise their sons. Circumcision is never carried out by women; it is a male sex mystery. The fact that in the actual ceremony the women wail and try to protect their sons proves that circumcision has been grafted onto the two-sister-and-python flood symbol. Furthermore the essential castration impulse in circumcision is here clearly enlarged into the ritual killing of the initiates when they are threatened by the spears of the men. Psychoanalytical theory indicates that coitus and death are emotionally connected. The castration impulse of the mature man is also a sadistic sexual attack upon the boys. After being assaulted sexually, symbolically castrated, and in various ways equated with women, they are then allowed to become reborn as men and join the "pure" antifemale group.

Significantly enough, a trickster cycle is present in the folklore of the group. Bamampana breaks all taboos, is sometimes stupid, acts crazily, fights with dogs as if they were human beings, and, above all, is blatantly phallic. He uses his penis as an aggressive weapon and equates it with a spear. In one case his penis is so large that in coitus he breaks a girl's legs and pierces her heart. Again, when women reject him, he drives his spear right through them. There is even a phallic dance of the trickster in which he uses a spear to symbolize the male organ and mimics intercourse with a man dancing the part of a woman. In the light of this male sadism, the attack upon the circumcision candidates with spears certainly reflects the unconscious impulses behind the ceremony.

Two other areas of Arnhem Land show foreign influence even more strongly. While the Murngin still adhere to the spirit theory of children and the males are dominant as represented by the snake, a great mother among the Ynkalla is responsible for the fertility of human beings and natural species and the cycle of the seasons. Significantly Kunapipi, the great mother, originally emerged from the mouth of a tidal river.

In western Arnhem Land among the Oenpelli the two-sisters myth is also copulatory. Here the rituals were brought by a whale-man who came from the east with his belly full of people. This would appear to symbolize a canoe. In this western area, rainfall is less plentiful and as a result the practical purpose of the rites is different, for here they are supposed to bring on the rainy season. The basic theory of spirit children persists but frequent copulation is considered essential to build up the *body* of the child in the womb before the spirit can enter.

Elkin suggests that the emphasis on the fertility mother and the changed attitude toward coitus may be due to the Macassar Malays who are known to have visited the north Australian coast. The mother theme would thus be an alien idea (the product of an agricultural culture) resulting from the influence of Indonesian Hinduism. Since the northern cults are far more unified and elaborated than the basic Australian ancestor worship, it appears that a stimulus from a more sophisticated religion can help to create a new structure on an archaic base.

The creation of the Australian shaman is also placed on a metaphysical basis. Very often it is thought of as a kind of death or transformation. In South Australia a snake swallows him and ejects him as a baby. It requires the singing of other doctors to restore him to normal size. In other cases supernatural agencies remove his entrails and replace them with magical substances. It is believed that shamans can transmit their thoughts to persons at a distance and that they can kill by pointing a bone in the direction of the intended victim.

The rituals of the Australians with their fantastic decorations, dance, and drama go on for days, weeks, even months. The balance of this elaborate psychic life has, however, been destroyed in recent times by the missions. Since these institutions distribute food, the younger members of the tribes tend to become hangers-on. They lose respect for the old men with whom the esoteric mysteries die. The new generation attends rote Christian services which they do not understand and, at the same time, since they have rejected the ritual heritage, loses the ethics of the traditional way of life and the dignity of its integration with nature.

CHAPTER 33

The Power of Mana

Polynesia—colonization of Polynesian Islands from Indonesia and Asia— organized mythology and nature gods—poetic chants preserve tradition—the trickster Maui—theory of mana—stratified society reflected in religious belief—sacred chiefs and priesthood—multiple afterworld—multiple souls— phallic magic—cannibalism and head taking—influences from advanced societies and possible contacts with South America.

NOWHERE is the colonizing adventure of early man more striking than in Oceania where peoples with a Stone Age equipment sailed for hundreds of miles in open double canoes or outriggers to plant their settlements on tiny coral atolls or in the shadow of volcanoes on lush islands which, on rediscovery thousands of years later by the Europeans, gave rise to myths of an earthly paradise.

The coral reefs, built on the submerged tops of ancient mountains, are no more than stony rings over one side of which the surf pours, supporting on part of their surfaces a growth of coco palms, the pandanus or screw pine which bears a tough but edible fruit and yields useful fibers, and a coarse sort of taro, a plant with a starchy root equivalent to the potato. On the smallest of these atolls the only indigenous animal is the flying fox fruit bat and a smaller insectivorous bat. Within the calm lagoon and about the reef, however, there is an abundance of fish, sea turtles and shellfish. To add to these resources the voyagers brought with them the dog, the pig, and the jungle fowl.

On the large volcanic islands, in addition to the flora and fauna just mentioned, the breadfruit, giant ferns, some bamboo and other useful palms flourish. Yams and sweet potatoes were introduced early in island history. The mournful sobbing note of the rose-crowned fruit dove echoes in the forest where giant banyan trees probe the earth with their aerial roots. In the upland volcanic region, trees disappear to be replaced by fields of tall sharp-edged sword grass. Along the harbors, where the shore tends to be muddy and the water brackish, grow the convolvulus with pinkish purple flowers, the beach plum, and the custard apple.

It was probably the pressure of the expanding Shang empire early in the second millennium B.C. which set off waves of movement among the peoples of South Asia and, being transmitted to those already moving into Indonesia, resulted in the continuous voyaging which went on into the Christian era and did not cease until Easter Island, which today belongs to Chile, received its quota of inhabitants.

Two groups of peoples took part in these migrations, one predominantly Negroid and one predominantly Caucasoid, the Melanesians and the Polynesians. As we have already seen, the melting pot of the South Asian area had been blending ethnic strains. The Melanesians and Polynesians shared some cultural traits and their languages can be traced back to the same family. As human types, however, they diverged most likely on the mainland and the Polynesians, in particular, retained a unity in their psychic and material way of life which can be identified throughout the great triangle which extends from New Zealand to Hawaii and to Easter Island. Polynesian culture continued to develop into a highly organized barbarism with a stratified society, central authority, an organized priesthood and a body of myth and poetry which is one of the outstanding achievements of the preliterate world.

Though less Mongoloid than the Malays and with sometimes a slight indication of Negro blood, the Polynesians are not unlike some groups in the Philippines. Golden-skinned, tall, and well built, they have inspired a good many rhapsodic descriptions by early European explorers, and everyone is familiar with Paul Gauguin's brilliant tapestried canvases in which the bodies of Tahitian women glow in a world of dreamlike magnificence.

The canoes in which these daring sailors crossed the Pacific were shaped with chanting and invocation of the artisan god, Tane. The outrigger type could be fifty to sixty feet long, with carvings or skulls fixed on the stern, the prow being shaped like the head of a bird. When the wind blew from the outrigger side the skipper sat far out on the platform to balance his craft. The largest vessels of all, the double canoes used for the long colonizing voyages on which domestic animals, food and water had to be carried in considerable quantities, could run over a hundred feet in length with a depth and width of about six feet. On a platform built catamaran-fashion across the two decked-over hulls, a hut was constructed which functioned as a cabin. Since no metal was used, all parts were lashed together, a flexible design which permitted a good deal of play and made the ship highly seaworthy. A great sail, rigged lateen-style, manufactured from woven pandanus mats was fastened to a mast stepped in one hull. Since there was a long steering paddle at each end of the ship, it could be brought about by simply changing ends. In these vessels the brown-skinned pioneers successively sailed from New Guinea and the Philippines to the Marianas, Samoa, Tonga, the Cook Islands, the Society Islands, Hawaii, the Marquesas and New Zealand.

That a unity of imagery and myth must have been present from the very beginning is proved by the concept of Hawaiki, an island source of culture and wisdom, the ancient home and origin of the Polynesians. In native tradition this is identified with Raiatea in the Society group but in actuality Hawaiki was probably a changing region, the homeland left behind whenever a large fleet set out toward the sunrise.

In general the Polynesian economy in the past was one without metal and without pottery or the bow and arrow. That pottery had originally been known is proved by archaeology but in areas where no clay was available this skill was lost. Shell and bone are admirably shaped into fishhooks, and bones of slain enemies were often used since they were full of valuable mana. Agriculture extends only to yam, sweet potato, taro and banana culture. Palm and pandanus fiber are used to lash the bamboo framework of rectangular thatched houses. Coconuts serve as receptacles, and the meat of the nut is ground into a paste and sometimes fermented. Most important and basic as a food is the breadfruit. This large round fruit, when baked in hot ashes, tastes rather like potato.

Kava, a drink made from the root of the pepper plant, has a narcotic effect. Old men drank it in connection with ritual cannibalism and sometimes as an aid to bring about shamanistic possession. It produced a fit of trembling, considered to be possession by the god Papaiea, which had to be exorcised by means of the man's wife sitting naked on his chest. Actually the vulva was also thought to have medicinal value in cases of sickness because, possessing maleficent mana associated with female processes, it could be used as a sort of sponge to remove the evil spirit.

The spirit world of the Polynesians consisted of a hierarchy of great gods, only a few of whom were worshiped, and a host of minor spirits and demons. Although, as will be discussed later, influences from various cultures went into its shaping, this world is characterized by a mixture of subtle, abstract concepts, and a number of archaic features expressed with considerable narrative skill. Since it has now been destroyed by the missions, it is necessary to reconstruct it from accounts by early explorers and observers who were able to question the old men who still remembered their pagan traditions.

In those areas which had the best-organized priesthoods, the philosophy of creation was developed in terms of a creator entity (not conceived in human form), Io in New Zealand, Taaroa in Tahiti, which was self-created existing-in-nothingness.

> He existed, Taaroa was his name,
> In the immensity.
> There was no earth; there was no sky;
> There was no sea; there was no man.
> Above Taaroa calls.
> Existing alone he became the universe.
> Taaroa is the origin, the rocks,
> Taaroa is the sands.
> It was thus that he is named.

It is interesting to note the similarity between this view and that of the Africans whose creator entity, likewise abstract, is an emanation of omnipresent force, actually more contemporary and more in line with modern scientific thinking than the naïve, anthropomorphic ideas of the Christian missionaries.

> Taaroa is the light,
> Taaroa is within,
> Taaroa is the germ,
> Taaroa is beneath,
> Taaroa is firm,
> Taaroa is wise.
> He created the land of Hawaii,
> Hawaii the great and sacred
> As a body and shell for Taaroa.

Following the initial creative activity of Taaroa there are sixteen to eighteen other eras of creation, all pervaded by an evolutionary image in which there is a suggestion of a tree whose root becomes development, sound, chaos and night, etc. In New Zealand the whole metaphysical first chapter was an esoteric body of knowledge preserved by the organized priesthood, while the population in general was concerned with the doings of the gods in human form.

Eventually, to follow the New Zealand version, earth and sky, the former a female, Papa, the latter a male, Rangi, came into being in close embrace. They produced five brothers who debated as to whether the two elementals should be separated. Tane-mahuto, a sky and forest god, was in favor of the separation. Tawhiri-ma-tea, god of the winds and storm, was against it. Nevertheless, Bongo-ma-tane, the god of cultivated food, tried to push them apart unsuccessfully. Tangaroa (lord of sea and marine life) tried in vain as did Houmia-tikitiki (god of wild food) and Tu-matauenga, the war god. Finally as they shrieked with pain, Tane tore them apart and pushed the sky upward while pressing down

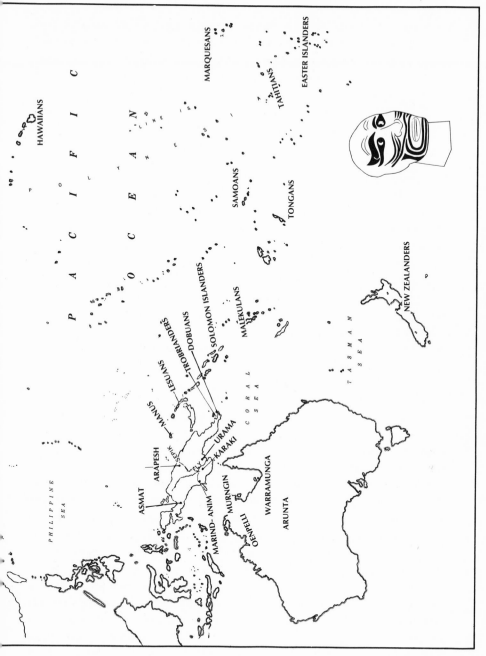

OCEANIA

the earth. (In some versions pillars were set up to keep them apart.) A multitude of minor gods concealed between their bodies came into being. The wind god, aroused by the complaints of the sky and the earth, made war upon the other brothers. The gods of the sea and wild and cultivated food fled but Tane made spears from his trees with the aid of the war god and successfully resisted the winds and storm. Since Tane was angry at the cowardice of his other brothers, who had fled to their various habitats, he used his artisan techniques to make the digging-stick, nets and fishhooks to catch and eat their progeny, wild food, domesticated food, and marine life.

The life force behind all of this dynamism is really mana, which in Polynesia is an articulate concept. Mana, as well as being the force behind the universe, is also the luck, skill, or individual energy. Gods, animals or people are conductors of this force which can be generated by ritual. Bad luck or failure can indicate loss of mana either from breaking a taboo or from being bewitched. It will be seen that this attitude is very close to that of the Indo-Europeans, particularly the Teutons. Similarly, tools and weapons possess mana, as does the craftsman. The beneficent side of mana is associated with male sexuality, power and light. Tane, who made man from the mount of Venus of mother earth, then impregnated the woman he had thus created, whose name was Hina or Hine-aha. Tane, being phallic power and light, is associated with the sun. Temples were often faced toward the sunrise. Consequently the sunset is associated with the female, the dark earth principle which possesses maleficent mana. Although the Polynesians understood the role of coitus in procreation, they nevertheless believed that the female made no contribution; like the Australians, they considered her merely an inferior being, a receptacle for the child.

The role of the major gods varies somewhat from island group to island group but they are on the whole ancestral nature gods individualized by priest poets. Tangaroa embodies the rage of the sea; epic chants describe the vengeance he takes upon those who displease him. Tane, as well as being phallic (his penis is personified as Tiki, which becomes the name for an image since most images were phallic), is also the god of the forests and by association of the artisans who work in wood. Hence he presides over canoe making. Rongo, whose name is associated with sound and with singing functions, is chiefly a rain god and patron of cultivated foods. Oro, who takes over his role elsewhere, is a war god in the Society Islands. In Hawaii, Lono plays the role of Rongo. A myth exists which states that in a fit of jealousy he killed his wife, fought with everyone, and left in a boat promising to return in another ship. When Captain Cook first discovered Hawaii he was worshiped as Lono. Tu, whose name means to strike, is the basic war god. Elaborately carved wooden clubs were used by the Maoris, who dedicated their first victim in battle to him. Ritual cannibalism is also associated with this god. Hina, the only female in the upper hierarchy, aside from being the first woman, is also a moon goddess. Although these high gods are not considered to have been men, they are nevertheless listed in the sacred genealogies as the ancestors of divine chiefs. Since there are also images of ancestors, ancestor worship, and divinized chiefs who become tutelary gods, it seems clear that the nature gods arose by associating ancestral heroes with natural phenomena as sometimes took place in Africa.

In the role of demigod or divine hero is Maui, a trickster about whom a cycle of tales is woven. Maui's parentage is not entirely clear although he is sometimes said to be the son of Tu and his mother at times appears to be Hina. Since he was an abortive birth, he was thrown into the sea by his mother. Miraculously reared by the sea deities, he returned and hid among his five brothers during a festival. His mother disowned him but he told his story and asserted his parentage. Maui was a skilled magician who caught the sun in a net and beat him with the jawbone of an ancestress until, weak and exhausted, the source of light moved more slowly. When Maui wished to go fishing with his brothers, they refused to take him along. He hid under the bottom boards, taking the magic jawbone to serve as a fishhook. When the brothers refused him bait, he bloodied his own nose and smeared the hook. The others caught a great number of fish but Maui pulled up a mass of earth which became an island. Maui left the brothers aground, telling them not to touch any of the fish until he had taken some to the gods. When they disobeyed his orders, the fish, which was also Tangaroa, the sea god, thrashed about angrily. This is why the surface of New Zealand is rough and uneven.

The myths and hero legends were, in the past, preserved by the priests, who maintained regular schools in which neophytes learned their duties and memorized the sacred lore. It was necessary to repeat the chants without a single mistake; if anything went wrong the whole ceremony had to be abandoned. In this respect Polynesian practice resembles that of the Aryan Brahmins. Since there is such a body of poetry reflecting elaborate ceremonials, it is quite possible that much more of a primitive theater existed than was recorded by the Europeans.

Maui fished up other islands in various areas, and in Samoa is replaced by the phallic Tiki. According to one version, his death was inevitable because his father made an error in his initiation ceremony. This detail is typical of the formalistic attitude prevalent in Polynesian society, whose class structure is reflected in the character of its religion.

The concept of aristocrat and commoner is clearly shown in the extreme development of taboo. In Polynesia there were three types of leaders: the shaman, the ritual priest and the divine chief. In Samoa, the most democratic of these societies, all three were combined. In other areas there were various combinations but the divine chiefs of Haita, Tahiti, Tonga and the Society Islands were so hedged about with taboo that it became a liability. At the sight of the Hawaiian chief or king: "The crowd began to shout, admiring his beauty. Even the ants were heard to sing his praises, the birds sang, the pebbles rumbled, the shells cried out, the grass withered, the smoke hung low, the rainbow appeared, the thunder was heard, the dead came to life, hairless dogs were seen and countless spirits of all kinds." The taboo emanating from this miraculous being was so intense that if a commoner's shadow fell upon the king's house, he was doomed. The mana of a Marquesan chief was so dangerous that his house was burned after his death. In Tonga a commoner who accidentally touched a chief could not feed himself with his hands lest he become ill. Head taboo was so acute that touching the head of a social superior was reckoned a major sin. A chief or a priest was also able to impose taboos. A piece of white bark cloth in the shape of a lizard or a shark would give notice that the property near it must not be disturbed. Thus private ownership could almost always be abrogated since anything touched by a social superior could no longer be used by the commoner.

In New Zealand the mana which emanated from a priest could be transmitted at his death to a pupil by the pupil's closing his teeth on the dying man's ear in symbolic cannibalism.

Class distinctions were also clear in matters of death and burial. The head of a hereditary chief was often preserved or his body was mummified or certain bones kept because of the mana they contained. The otherworld was as segregated as this one, for, in some cases, it was felt that only aristocrats had souls. The soul at death was thought to leap into the otherworld, either from certain rocks, or trees, or into caves. At the time of a Maori chief's death, because of his supreme mana, his subjects were obliged to show a perfect frenzy of grief, wailing, lacerating their flesh, cutting off finger joints or knocking out teeth.

In the Marquesas where the otherworld was equated with Hawaiki, the ancestral home, the spirit left the body at death through the mouth in the form of a dragonfly. A dog was hung up near the dead body to chase away evil spirits and a pig was put under its legs to furnish food for demons. This otherworld had three classes like a European railway. In the lowest lived the great chiefs to whom many pigs had been sacrificed. The next floor offered less luxury, for fewer pigs had been killed at the inhabitants' funerals. Third-class denizens, who rated only one pig's head, lived on disgusting food. Those who had no pig sacrifice at all lay in eternal mud.

Although the Maori did not practice the type of dancing known to the Western world as hula, it is from their culture that we get glimpses of magical attitudes toward the phallus. If a man thought he was being bewitched, he would take his penis in his hand and say, "Let the evil be averted, let my penis be the object of your destructive power!" Theoretically the male organ was so filled with mana that the spell would rebound from it and kill the sorcerer. Also, as sometimes happened before a battle, if a warrior lost his nerve (he was naturally bewitched), the cure was to crawl between the legs of a great chief whose penis would thus shed its strength upon the victim of battle fatigue.

There were several vital elements in the body of man, according to the Polynesian view, but the most important was the *waira* which might leave the body during sleep, act as a medium of clairvoyance, and which survived after death. The waira could sometimes be seen reflected in the kava drink of the priest or in the form of a shadow. After death it might be gradually purified as deified ancestors scraped it with shells until it, too, was ready for deification. The waira in some cases of sickness remained outside the body, refusing to return. A delectable feast was then prepared and placed in a hut. The priest waited outside until the wandering spirit was attracted by the food and then rushed in and caught it in the form of a caterpillar. He would point to scratches on the food to show that it had been eating. He then forced the caterpillar-waira to re-enter the patient's body through the ear.

Inanimate things had a nonmaterial *ata*. It was this which was eaten by the gods when sacrifices were presented. In the case of the gods themselves, however, their ata were animals. There was a boar of Oro, a seagull of Tane, a turtle of Tangaroa. Since some taboos concerning eating animals are reported and also ancestors incarnated as lizards, it is probable that these concepts represent survivals of an archaic totemic period.

As Polynesian religion was elaborated by an organized priesthood and could count on government support, it is not surprising that temple building, one of the favorite status activities of a divine aristocracy, flourished. In Tahiti, Hawaii, the Marquesas and Cook Islands, the actual structure varied from a stone-walled enclosure with a raised platform at one end, around or within which stone slabs with stone back rests for dignitaries were placed, to a still more ambitious stage in which the platform became a stepped oblong structure something like a pyramid. The temple was a votive offering in Hawaii, a status symbol in the Society Islands, and in the Marquesas both.

The men's house and the chief's house were generally constructed near the temple, while in the Marquesas a special edifice for the shaman was built before each festival. About eighteen feet wide at the bottom and sixty feet high, it resembled an obelisk. Images of red birds were placed on the roof. Temples were sometimes adorned with figures of gods or ancestors in stone or wood. On Easter Island the great busts of stone with long upper lips and arrogant expressions were originally placed within the enclosure and later on the platform itself. On the actual occasion of festivals, during which there was much drumming, blowing of conch shells, dancing, and chanting, the temple area was also gay with offerings. Calabashes of food were placed in the area, and bamboo containers of liquids. The chiefs and priests wore long robes over the usual bark-cloth loincloth, and turbaned headdresses or feathers. The odor of roast pork was wafted from countless ovens filled with red-hot stones.

On Tonga and Samoa, temples were simply large huts. Although the Maori of New Zealand developed no temple architecture, the supporting pole and gables of the house fronts and storehouses were beautifully carved with double masks and sinuous lines which remind us strikingly of the decorative style of the Shang empire.

Polynesia, in the minds of most Western literates, is associated with cannibalism and human sacrifice. The two are, of course, closely connected. Human sacrifice took place before battle, before building a temple, even before constructing a canoe. In general it was thought that the mana of the slain would reinforce the material object like a guardian spirit. Brain cannibalism is also reported and in some ceremonies the eye of the living or recent dead was supposed to be a focus of mana. Since the eyes and also the heart of victims were sometimes torn out and eaten by the priest, mana was of course absorbed through cannibalism. The emphasis on the eye also has overtones of castration. There was a conscious intent to subjugate the spirit of the slain enemy. Although the basis of cannibalism was religious, Polynesia seems to be one area where this custom assumed a more secular character. Some chiefs acquired a depraved taste for human flesh. The Maori, according to Ralph Linton, cut up the bodies of slain enemies, boned the meat, and packed it in baskets.

An interesting indication that ancient Polynesian culture once exhibited more advanced elements which are now lost is the famous *rongorongo* script, a system of signs which was handed down by the priests of the sacred college of Easter Island. The existing examples are few in number and carved on pieces of wood. Thomas Bartels has shown that the signs are ideograms capable of expressing fairly complicated ideas. Although not fully translated, it is known they deal with historical and ritual matters.

Since the Shang empire was literate, the survival of rongorongo script strengthens the presupposition of Asian origins. Various elements, woven together, form the basis for Polynesian culture. An Aryan element in the mythology is similar to the early Vedic concepts, while a strand of Indonesian custom would account for trophy head taking. The metaphysical element might have been a reflection of Hinduism, and secondary burial and cherishing of ancestral relics might result from Melanesian influence.

One more conjecture ties Polynesia with the New World. The practice of tearing out the hearts of sacrificial victims and eating them may point to contacts with Middle America. The stone architecture with the somewhat pyramidal temple platform looks like an Aztec or Mayan borrowing from Polynesia or vice versa. Since Polynesia also acquired the sweet potato, which is an American food plant, the chances are that the Polynesian explorers may well have preceded the Europeans in making contact with the independent cultures of the Americas.

CHAPTER 34

Status Ritual and Ancestor Skulls

Melanesia—settled by Pygmy-Negroid strain—skull and ancestor cult—magic and spirit world—types of ancestor worship—harmful magic—status rituals in connection with men's clubs—initiation assault and sodomy—myth of the brothers and trickster—headhunting—Polynesian and Australian influence or similarities.

W HILE the Polynesians pushed on intrepidly to colonize the islands of the far Pacific, the outriggers of the dark-skinned Negroid peoples of Oceania cruised the groups of atolls and volcanic archipelagos which lie nearer to Asia and Australia. The great land mass of New Guinea (so called because a Spanish explorer in 1546 thought the natives looked like those of West Africa) was also populated by Melanesian ethnic groups.

In recent decades, exhibitions in museums of art and ethnology have familiarized Westerners with the crude and powerful art of Melanesia. Tall shields with baroque red and white designs, wooden masks with staring eyes and jutting noses, dark figures carved from tree ferns, bristling cloaks of palm leaf or raffia topped by woven helmets, paddles, spears and canoes ornamented with intricate abstract or animal patterns, have all played a role in modifying contemporary taste and influencing modern art. These elaborate ceremonial objects created with the simplest stone, shell or bone tools derived their strength from an intense psychic life which has developed and proliferated in astonishing variety in remote jungles and arid islets of the Pacific.

Here the accident of history has preserved many of these cultures almost undisturbed until today. In some cases there was nothing on the islands which the Westerners cared to exploit and, except for a little trading and kidnapping of native labor, contact with the inhabitants was brief. Other groups were headhunters and cannibals who repelled colonial contacts with vigor. In New Caledonia early French missionaries were killed and eaten. Much of New Guinea is such difficult terrain that it still remains unexplored. The second largest island in the world (1,500 miles long), its rugged contour rises in the central area to snow-capped peaks and temperatures vary from tropical to below freezing.

All these obstacles in the way of social change have been of great benefit to anthropology. In the first decades of the twentieth century, some of the best field technique was developed recording the precious data embalmed in Melanesian cultures, cultures more isolated from the technical world than those anywhere else on the earth.

World War II, however, during which Western technology erupted into the Pacific, brought about abrupt changes in the areas where men of the Stone Age came suddenly into contact with the bulldozer, the tank and the airplane. After the war, messianic cults arose in which revolutionary and magical ideas were mingled as peoples who had vegetated for centuries with the simplest economic base suddenly coveted the luxuries of the West and attempted to find a psychic synthesis which would mediate between the fossilized past and the present. Margaret Mead, returning to the Manus, whose traditional civilization will be discussed later, found them attempting to run town meetings on the North American pattern after having thrown their dancing costumes into the sea.

Other areas, however, such as uncharted central New Guinea and the interiors of some other islands, still continue as the last outposts of the unknown and for some decades will still be the resort of the fieldworker in search of societies relatively uncontaminated by mechanization and preserving a vital connection with nature.

Unlike Polynesia, which presents a remarkably cohesive picture, the melting pot of Melanesia is broken up into areas in which small groups have developed special configurations of culture often so dominated by a single complex as to seem parodies of social evolution. On the whole, there is no well-developed central political organization; authority rests either upon prestige or nonhereditary chieftainship. There is also a lack of an organized priesthood and as a result a great variety in mythology, with borrowing from group to group resulting in mixtures which at times resemble the Australian complex, at times recall Indonesia and at times show the influence of Polynesia.

A few basic elements which have already appeared in many preliterate societies, such as ancestor cults, men's clubs, totemism, headhunting, and magic, pervade the whole region. The limitation of natural resources, including a lack of large animals, an absence of metal ore, and a terrain unfavorable to advanced large-scale agriculture, has helped to mold Melanesian cultural forms. In particular what might be called status ritual is everywhere important. This runs the whole gamut from genuinely religious expression in connection with ancestors, to semireligious economic exchange, to purely secular giving of gifts.

Both here and in Australia, it seems clear that the rejection of or inability to develop a rich material culture is compensated for by elaboration of ceremonial behavior. In other words, man makes his life interesting by complicating his relationships with nature and with his fellows. This elaboration is often, to the Western observer, responsible for remarkable aesthetic achievement, yet this same achievement often rests upon hostility rather than cooperation and upon practices which seem irrationally nonconstructive.

Since it is impossible in a limited space to cover completely the wide variety of religious expression in Melanesia, a few specific groups will be cited to show what forms the major cults have taken. The skull cult, for example, is among the Manus an integrating type of ancestor worship which has been exhaustively studied by Reo Fortune.

This people of the Admiralty Islands east of Australia lives by fishing. Houses are built on stilts in sea lagoons. The Manus' status ritual is concerned with complicated marriage payments. This puts a heavy burden on the average head of a family. As a result the villagers are hard-working, aggressive, and, because of the pressures and exigencies of their elaborate economic life, rather quarrelsome. They are also prudish sexually, exhibiting an ethos close to New England Puritanism.

Psychic life and social ethics revolve around the skull of the father of the head of the house. The skull is cleaned and placed in a carved wooden bowl hung high above and just inside the front of the house. Offerings of herbs are put in the bowl. At festivals food is thrown up at it. This guardian (who may also have been an older brother) is called Sir Ghost and is intimately connected with the family. "The spiritual presence of which the skull is the material relic guards the house and supervises the morals of its people." Since the skull is merely a symbol, if it should be lost or destroyed a coconut takes its place. When illness or misfortune strikes, or fishing is poor, this is evidence that the ghost is angry and an oracle must be consulted to find out who has sinned. Sin consists of adultery, seduction, failure to pay debts, stealing, failure to carry out festivals, inadvertently seeing the exposed sex of a male or female, or using obscene language to other than joking cousins. The Manus are fairly unique among preliterates in this sense of sin, Sir Ghost being as hard on sexual offenses as Cotton Mather.

Among the Manus, magic is relatively unimportant and there seems to be no belief in an afterworld. When the head of the father of the family is elevated to the post of censor, the skull of the grandfather is thrown out. It was his duty to protect his son from death and, having failed, he has lost his value.

Such evicted ghosts wander for a time in the middle spaces of the ocean and finally turn into sea slugs. Other people's ghosts are harmful; shamans must be used against them. Indeed, even the family ghost is not without ambivalence, for at funerals he is given shell money to buy a ghost wife so that he will not bother the women of his kin.

The shamans or diviners who interpret the will of Sir Ghost are either men or women. Sometimes they gain their power through a trance but this is not essential. Their skill comes from their own Sir Ghost. They are consecrated by another diviner who throws two bones from the left lower arm of an old woman who was afraid of ghosts, tied by a string, over his shoulder so that one hangs down in front and one behind. If his back itches on the left side the answer is no, if on the right, yes. Women mediums are those who have lost a male child. They first whistle, then translate the utterances of the spirit. The method used is a sort of third degree in which the sinner is finally browbeaten into confessing and making payments for his sins.

Those Manus who threw out their old religion after World War II and tried to modernize themselves, adapting a kind of modified Protestantism led by a native prophet, confided to Margaret Mead that the transition was difficult. "One thing we have not yet learned from the West," they said, "that is how to commit adultery successfully."

As has been said, magic plays a very limited role among the Manus. Another culture, that of the Trobriand Islanders studied by Bronislaw Malinowski, combines ancestor cult with magic woven throughout all daily activities. The Trobrianders who live north of New Guinea are excellent sailors and set out on ritual trading voyages on which they exchange shell necklaces with their neighbors. These Kula voyages have little practical value; the exchange of heirloom necklaces and bracelets is preceded by spells to make the traders beautiful and acceptable to their trading partners, and spells to obtain favorable winds. The objects are passed on from island to island, sometimes making a complete circuit. The whole enterprise is one type of status ritual. Since the Trobriand economy is based largely on taro and yam gardens, here too magical practice is important. The gardens are of the slash-and-burn variety, and planting is done with the digging-stick. Although the gardeners know about the properties of soil and the need for cultivation, magic takes care of the unusual situation, exceptionally good or bad luck being the result of success or error in magic. The village headman is generally the magician. Spells are recited at each step, before cutting scrub, before burning, before planting and weeding, and to ensure a good harvest. Food presents are also made to ancestors, who emerge from the ground bringing the magic with them. On the whole, magic accompanies every activity from love-making to building a canoe.

When death takes place, the dead man is mourned ritually and his body is adorned with all his wealth so that he may carry the spiritual essence of it with him. Two spirits are released, the *baloma* which goes to a nearby island,

and the *kos* which may linger about the village or knock at the doors of friends' houses. This entity is mildly malicious but not particularly feared, since it does no more than laugh eerily and throw stones or gravel. The only real fear at burials is lest female sorcerers, who love to feed on corpses, be present. After such ghoulish behavior they are particularly dangerous to the living. Magic must be used to ward them off.

The baloma or, more nearly, the soul, sits down on the beach of his island and wails. His deceased friends and kinsmen join him and sing or mourn with him. The spirit then washes his eyes, an act which makes him invisible, and proceeds toward Tuma, the underworld. The headman of this place must be paid off with the spirit valuables of the deceased before the latter is allowed to enter. If a spirit arrives destitute, he does not get in, but turns into a fish, half shark, half sting ray. In Tuma, chiefs retain their rank; in general the newly dead are made comfortable by their relatives while spirit women go out of their way to make the otherworld pleasant.

During this period the baloma continue to visit their old home on earth where they are sometimes helpful in magical spells and sometimes rather critical. They are seen in dreams or communicated with by possessed persons, but above all they return in a body at the annual *milamila,* a festival which is held after the yam crop has been harvested but which does not appear to be an increase ceremony but rather an expression of satisfaction on completion of the harvesting.

The milamila is a period of from one to two or three months at which dancing, feasting and sexual activity take place and the yam crops are piled up for all to admire and then stored in the decorated yam houses.

Next the drums are consecrated and ritual exchange of gifts of yams takes place while the men dress in white halo-shaped headdresses of cockatoo feathers topped with a plume of red-tipped feathers. In some of the dances the men wear women's grass skirts and dance slowly in a circle. Young people pay visits to other villages in search of amorous experience; in this society there is complete sexual freedom before marriage. Official visiting from village to village also goes on, and dances are bought and sold.

Meanwhile the baloma have arrived and either camp on the beach or live in the houses of maternal relatives. On small platforms valuables are displayed such as shell disks, strings, armlets of shell and circular pig tusks. When the spirits have had enough of viewing these they are able to feast on the spiritual essence of food offerings placed on special scaffoldings which surround the dance ground. Cooked food is also available in the houses; after being feasted upon by the baloma, it is exchanged with that of friends or relatives. The baloma are also likely to knock down a great many coconuts which then become public property and may be drained of their milk by anyone. If the spirits are not pleased by the milamila, they can cause a bad harvest next year; thus no pains are spared to make the festival a success.

On a particular date a ritual chasing out of the baloma takes place. An hour before sunrise the drums intone a special beat while the young men sing, "Baloma, go away, we'll stay behind." The following day a procession carries out the same rite, passing through the village to make sure it is swept clean of all supernaturals. This is the end of the milamila and the villagers have taken care of their responsibilities toward their ancestors. The latter also play an important role in all magical spells.

Back in Tuma the baloma grow old, bathe in salt water, shed their skins, and become embryos. Old baloma women pick them up, put them in baskets, carry them back to the earthly village, and insert them into the vaginas of Trobriand women who thus become pregnant, for in the Trobriands, as in Australia, sexual intercourse is not the cause of procreation.

A report by R. H. Codrington provides an example of how an individual cult comes about in the Solomon Islands. On Florida Island, Ganindo, a famous warrior, was killed in battle. His body was brought home and the head removed. After a basket was woven for it, a special house was built in which it was placed. Ganindo had now become a *tindalo,* the local word for ghost or spirit. On a subsequent headhunting expedition his friends practiced canoe divination. All the crew ceased paddling and waited until the canoe rocked of itself. They then began to call out the names of various tindalos. When Ganindo's name was mentioned, the canoe rocked again. This meant that his spirit was looking after them. Continuing the divination, they also learned what village to attack. Since in this case the war party was successful, Ganindo was given the credit. A new house was built and his image placed within it. Eight men ceremonially carried his bones, a shell trumpet and betel nuts to the shrine and placed them on a bamboo platform. Offerings of food were made. A pig was killed and its blood poured on a fire made on a stone within the shrine. The pig was then eaten. Ganindo's power was attributed to his special mana. (The concept of mana and taboo occurs throughout Melanesia, borrowed, some authorities believe, from the Polynesians.) In the case of a great man such as Ganindo, his worship continues as long as he is remembered or his descendants survive.

Though magic is important to the relatively mild Trobrianders, their neighbors, the Dobu, are a classic example of a society centered on magic—and in most cases harmful magic. The habitat of this people is the gloomy Amplett Islands dominated by high dark mountains. The inhabitants are cannibals, organized in totemic groups whose patron animals are always birds such as the white pigeon, the green parrot, the crow or the brown eagle. This bird people pays tribute to no real deities; the supernaturals have secret names which when pronounced can command their magical power. There is, for instance, a superturtle and a certain bird which embodies the spirit of the woman who first grew yams. Different clans have their own magic. For instance, a woman of the time of the first ancestors of the green parrots, whose name was Anabuyueta, bore a many-armed son who was an octopus. She put him in fresh water where he curled up and nearly died. She put him in salt water, whereupon he swam away and made himself a home in a rock cave on the deep sea floor. The woman went down to visit him taking seed yams with her. She planted them on the sea floor and charmed them till they grew. Descendants of these yams are planted by the green parrots today, which is why salt water is poured over them and a charm said, retelling the story. The green parrots are convinced that yams will not grow if not treated by magic.

Charms are also owned individually and used competitively, for the culture as a whole is characterized by suspicion and a hostility which to the average outsider seems paranoid. Particularly malevolent use is made of disease charms. They are placed upon private property to contaminate possible thieves. On the other hand, a good crop is proof that magical theft has taken place. It will also cause envy and more disease sanctions used by jealous rivals. As among most preliterates, sickness and death are believed to be the result of hostile magic. Husband and wife even suspect each other, while a funeral is a time of tension and hostility between the two families because the relatives of the dead person blame the magical activities of the other group and try to trap the sorcerer who is responsible. One of the most unpleasant disease magics is that used to cause gangosa, a kind of syphilis which attacks the nose. The spirit of a woman named Nebagieta wore a rough, jagged nose and gave birth to an archetypal hornbill. This monstrous being uses his great beak to hack out tree hollows. The boom of his voice is compared to the nasal utterance of the victim whose nose is being eaten away. The spell runs in part:

> Hornbill dweller of Koyatabu
> In the Iowana treetop,
> He slices up,
> He booms, crying, droning,
> He cuts, he cuts,
> He rends open,
> He rends flying.
> He crouches bent [the victim],
> He crouches hand over kidneys.

From the root of the tongue,
From the throat,
From the kidneys,
From the entrails,
He rends open,
He rends flying.

In contrast to the Trobrianders who are well organized with paramount chiefs, the Dobu have no real chieftains. The fragmenting effect of their magical practice results in a society which seethes with treachery and secret conflict. The Dobu psychic attitude is proof that religion cannot be divorced from magic, for this people does not propitiate supernaturals nor use sacrifice to achieve their cooperation. Dobu activities are entirely coercive and the power they believe they possess over their spirits is entirely derived from knowing their names, a power obtained by inheritance or purchase.

Status ceremonies of a more or less religious nature vary tremendously both as to ritual, masks, and sacred objects, and are carried out independently or at funerals or initiations. For example, the institution of *Malanggans,* described by Hortense Powdermaker among the Lesu on the east coast of New Ireland, is central to this culture. This group of people fishes, hunts wild pigs, grows yams and bananas and once a year feasts on a marine worm which rises to the surface of the water to reproduce.

The malanggans are long wooden objects which look something like a shield lying on its side. The carving, said to represent ancestors, is cut through the wood. Animal, human and baroque shapes painted red and yellow can be made out. The village is divided into hawk and eagle moieties. The right to make malanggans belongs to old men of the clan. It can, however, be acquired by purchase. Each citizen of Lesu has a kind of familiar spirit or *gas*. In a dream the spirit comes to the owner of the ceremony and reveals the pattern of the malanggan and the appropriate dances. The prospective owner of the object then goes to a professional carver to whom he imparts the pattern and whom he pays to execute it.

Malanggans are made at circumcision rites. Here the women weep, dance, and stone the men who come to take their boys for the operation. The dances take place, the objects are displayed, a great feast ensues, and the malanggans are finally destroyed. Malanggans are sometimes made after a death but often it takes a year to collect the supplies for the feast. The amount of conspicuous expenditure that goes into the ceremonial is stressed, and if they are not made for a relative a loss of status ensues. Although malanggan making is clearly derived from an ancestor cult, this element has been obscured and the status theme predominates.

Pigs, the chief source of meat on the Oceanic Islands, where they have run wild since their introduction by either the first settlers or the Spaniards, acquire a bizarre status role in Malekula, of the New Hebrides.

Here, as in many Melanesian areas, great ten-foot wooden slit gongs stand or lie in the middle of the dancing ground. The Malekulans have a totemic clan system with each clan confined to a village. The slit gongs, as well as being used for ceremonials, also serve as a means of communication between villages, each clan having a specific rhythm signature. The spirit world of this people, aside from a population of ancestors, consists of demons, deformed monsters with long hair or lacking a leg or arm. There are also beings associated with sacred clan spots, and here animal increase rites are carried out. There are no true chiefs but special clan magicians own totem rituals and certain men acquire power by buying the services of skilled magicians.

In this culture the men's society with grades of initiation is extremely important, combining ancestor cult with status. It is in these ceremonies, which become more and more elaborate from grade to grade, that certain boars stand for conspicuous wealth. The upper tusks of the animals are knocked out so that the lower ones will continue to grow in a circle. Sometimes they return, pierce the lower jaw, and grow into a second circle. The value of these status boars depends upon the development of the tusks which, after the animals are killed, are used as bracelets.

When a man is to pass from one grade to another, certain carved images called *temes,* made from tree fern, must be commissioned and paid for with ritual pigs. These are considered the temporary habitation for a deceased member of the grade. When the man himself dies his spirit is likely to go into one of his temes. A small symbolic clubhouse is constructed of several short poles with a door which can be opened to let the candidate into his new grade. Dancing and singing takes place, then the new member pays for his acceptance with a curve-tusked boar. Part of the dancing goes on around the slit gongs while the tree-fern image is set up on the edge of the dancing ground. The new member is given a pig-tusk bracelet and the boar offering is killed, cooked, and eaten.

For some of the higher grades, the teme becomes a pole carved with a number of faces and bodies, painted red, white and black. With each grade the initiate gains the right to special patterns of body painting. Fantastic masks appear at different age grade ceremonies. In one case a mythical old man who lives underground is represented by a hollow wooden figure eight feet high (ithyphallic and with a long nose) which reaches to the mid-thigh of the dancer and can only be worn for a few minutes. Another mask costume which includes a cloak of tree-fern bark is named after a giant ogress; still another is a tunic completely covering the dancer, made of spider web and provided with artificial arms and hands. The higher grades of the society are particularly sacred. Like men's societies in Africa, this one assumes certain punitive powers toward individuals who have offended its members. An elaborate and fantastic account is given of how the victim is killed by drawing his intestines out through his anus.

Men's secret societies in Melanesia generally possess clubhouses of their own which are distinct from clan houses or large men's houses built in the villages near the dance ground. Such secret houses are generally in the depths of the forest at some distance from the settlement. The Dukduk society of the Bismarck Archipelago northeast of New Guinea and the Tamate of the Banks Islands of the west Solomon group both appear to have almost lost their ancestor cult character. The Tamate have no grades but initiation involves fasting, offering of a pig, and terrorizing of the new member. The Dukduks float in on a raft on six canoes six times a year. They wear conical masks of woven fiber five feet high with great eyes painted on them, and palm-leaf cloaks, and approach the beach dancing and shrieking. For three weeks they live in their secret clubhouse in the woods and frequent the village where they beat the young men of the tribe and collect food offerings.

It has already been suggested that Australian initiation ceremonies exhibit traces of homosexuality as well as castration assault. In the Melanesian area the former becomes overt. The New Guinea Iatmul are a group which shows strong tensions between the men and the women. The men are headhunters who indulge in emotional boasting in the men's house. The initiation ceremony involves scarification which is performed roughly. After the first bout is over, the novices are threatened with a second operation on their backs, which sets them screaming almost hysterically. They are also ritually splashed with icy water. A crocodile bone is also stuck into their mouths with such violence as to make their jaws bleed. Finally the novices are called wives of the initiators and made to handle their penises. "The end of all this is the adoption of the novices of the masculine ethos, but it seems the first step in inducing this process is to compel the novices to behave as women. . . ." Successful headhunters in the past could wear a flying fox pubic apron. The enemy's body was brought back and ritually killed by a man wearing a hawk mask. Heads were placed on phallic stones which represented ancestral spirits. Gregory Bateson states that masculinity is equated with violence and pride. Headhunting is the main source of the pride of the village, "associated with prosperity, fertility and the male sexual act." In other words, we have here the same warrior complex we have encountered often before, of sadism, head taking, male sexuality and the desire to reduce other males to the status of women.

Pursuing this element further, on Malekula we find the voice of the bullroarers is that of a great fighter of the past who has returned to "kill" the novices. A series of hazing hoaxes follow. One consists of the initiators putting on immense penises which, as they lie on the ground, reach from one body to another. John Layard interprets this as a symbol of continuous male line united by homosexual acts to the ancestral ghosts. The novices are made to go up and pull the false penises. Another hoax consists of a man attaching huge rolls of leaves to his scrotum to simulate giant testicles. He dances to frighten the boys, who are made to touch these objects. In the Big Namba area of Malekula, where circumcision is practiced, homosexuality is ritualized and takes precedence over heterosexual eroticism. Each "guardian" who acts as initiator acquires a boy "wife" and becomes his husband. He has sexual access to the novice up until the operation. During the seclusion period sex activity ceases but continues again for a certain time. Then the boy acquires a bark belt and himself is free to take a male lover. In the Small Islands nearby, the novices and initiators are also called wives and husbands and, although homosexuality is not practiced, the boys are threatened with sexual aggression by initiators, representing ancestral ghosts. In all this area there were originally incessant wars with head taking and excessive cannibalism.

In southwest Papua of New Guinea among the Karaki tribes, where no circumcision is practiced, a sexual aura hangs over the bullroarer. An ancestor creator-being, Kambel, made his wife pregnant with the primal bullroarer which was eventually snatched from her vagina by a bird. At that point it was covered with hair. When a head raider struck his victim dead he was supposed to say, "The primal bullroarer is copulating with you." At the ceremony of initiation the novices are paraded through the streets. They are beaten and handed over to the initiators who practice sodomy. For about a year the boys are at the service of the opposite moiety of the tribe; thus marriage regulations are adhered to in the homosexual situation. In addition the boys are made to drink a blistering solution of lime to prevent pregnancy. Obviously the bullroarer (which is treated with awe rather like an Australian churinga) is equated with the penis and the novices are feminized even to the point of the myth of possible pregnancy. Cannibalism here is only ritual, a bit of the cheek being eaten after the women have cooked the heads.

The whole Melanesian spirit world reflects the variety of cultural elements which we have just been discussing. In some cases the supernaturals, other than ancestor spirits, appear not to be organized into any system. The Koita of southeast New Guinea associate supernaturals, most of whom are thought of as malicious, with certain spots. These are identified as haunted if sickness or death occurs after tribesmen have camped, sat, eaten, or urinated there. Margaret Mead reports that the Arapesh of the

Sepik River area, in the north, associate spirits called *marsalai* with certain localities. They can cause misfortune or death if not neutralized. When a man enters his own district he must take care to announce his name and his right to be there. An interesting similarity with northern Australia arises from the fact that these creatures are often two-headed striped snakes. Their harmful powers include the ability to cause rain or floods. Sometimes they are linked with ancestral ghosts and are thought of as protectors of the clan lands. Menstruating women must be careful not to trespass on an area inhabited by one of these serpents. It will be seen that enough elements are present to suggest that these beliefs and the python theology of northern Australia may have emanated from a common source.

Creator entities with local characteristics are reported from various areas. Kambel of the Trans-Fly region of New Guinea has already been mentioned. He is one of the *gaunjan,* archetypal beings who lived in ancient times among whom there is a great snake and a great crocodile. Kambel has a wife and a son, though the son is often confused with the father. He is said to have split open a tree from which the Karaki tribes emerged. This same entity can cause sickness or floods of rain when angered. According to the people of Bougainville in the Solomons, at a time when the world was incomplete, manlike beings called *kapunas* came from islands to the south. They moved about clearing land, cutting river beds, inventing food plants, marrying, procreating and giving birth to the first Sivai natives. Most important of these were Maker and Orphan. Maker created food plants. He told his children to put him in a pot. He defecated in it and secretly escaped. When the children removed the cover they found it full of taro, yams, and bananas. Orphan is a trickster who fights with his brother and commits adultery with his brother's wife, thus inventing sexual intercourse (his brother had used his wife's armpit). Orphan causes his enemies to be stung, bitten, or defecated upon.

The trickster described elsewhere in the Solomons (Banks Islands) as Quat is more of a culture hero. He has nine brothers, some of them trees and plants. He is credited with making men, pigs, trees and rocks and to have brought night from the Torres Islands. When night had gone on long enough, he cut it open with a stone knife and let the light out. His brothers tried to destroy him but each time he was saved by a powerful spider spirit. Quat sounds somewhat like Maui and since elsewhere he is called Tagaro, the latter name is no doubt a corruption of Tagaroa and a proof of Polynesian borrowing.

A more highly organized symbolic theology is described by Jan van Baal as developed by the Marind-Anim of south New Guinea. This group lives in a tropic area with distinct dry and rainy seasons. The climate is cool from May to December. The staple foods come from the sago and coconut palms and are augmented by pork and fish. The Marind-Anim are organized into clans and practice headhunting.

The themes which underlie the tribal theology suggest a synthesis of various elements which pervade the Pacific region. In the first place, the shapers of the cosmos are the people of the ancient time. A group of these is attached to each clan and embodied in rivers, hills, stones and forest. They are the *dema* and possess cosmic mana. They are primarily male and cause the spirit to go in during procreation. Local myths concerning these entities are associated with clan groups. It is clear that here we have the familiar dream time of Australia and that the alchira of the continent are closely paralleled by the dema and also, indeed, by the marsalai of the Sepik River and the kapuna of the Fly River.

Since in the mythology of this people the southeast is day and is associated with youth and male sexuality and the southwest is night, age, and female sex, we here have echoes of certain Polynesian ideas, and indeed, as in Polynesia, the sky is male and the earth female.

It seems probable that during the migration period there must have been a good deal of give and take culturally between different groups, but because of our fragmentary investigations and the rapid decay of native institutions after contact with the Westerners we shall never know exactly how they came about. After the various regions acquired settled isolated populations, microevolution probably took place (that is, local change and adaptation to specific surroundings), producing the fascinating and bizarre types of human behavior encountered when the South Seas were rediscovered by the Europeans.

CHAPTER 35

Journey to the Otherworld

Siberian tribes—reindeer hunters and breeders turned fishermen and sea hunters—hunting magic related to bear cult of Ainu—Big Raven, the trickster, here a deity—masters and guardian spirits—multiple otherworlds—performance of ecstatic shamans—male and female shamans and change of sex—Yakut horse cult.

IN THE far north, the two continents of North America and Asia approach each other so closely that there is every reason to believe that in Paleolithic times there was a connection between Alaska and eastern Siberia, a bridge over which ancient hunters poured into the New World in various migratory waves. When and how this took place will be discussed in connection with the North American peoples. In Siberian culture, however, there are elements which will reappear in America.

Although the Siberian nomads differ ethnically among themselves and do not all pursue the same way of life, they are all united by a peculiar type of elaborate, ecstatic shamanism which involves a journey to the spirit world. This particular practice extends over the central region, inhabited by the Tungus, is found in the northeast, the abode of the Yakut, and along the extreme northeast coast peopled by the Koryak and the Chukchi. The same custom is also found among the Gilyak of Sakhalin Island and the Ainu, who were the original inhabitants of the Japanese Islands.

The tribes just mentioned subsist from three types of economy. The Yakut, mixed Mongol and Scythian stock, who came from the central steppes, were driven up to the northeast by the pressure of the Tungus. The former are essentially horse breeders who have now acquired some cattle; the latter of Caucasian stock, but influenced by Mongol culture, are hunters and reindeer breeders. The Koryak, Yukaghir and Chukchi were originally reindeer hunters or breeders but where they have settled on the east Siberian coast they have adapted their hunting technique to marine animals, acquired the skin boat and taken to fishing. The Ainu and Gilyak continued to be hunters.

It has been suggested by Waldemar Jochelson that some of the Upper

Paleolithic reindeer hunters, who followed the herds north as the climate changed, crossed over to North America and later moved back to the Siberian coast. He finds possible parallels in the movement of wild sheep between the two continents. In any case, the presence of archaic hunting ceremonies does suggest that there is a survival of very ancient layers of religion in Siberia.

We have already cited the bear ceremony of the Ainu in Chapter 1. Exactly parallel with it is the Koryak treatment of the captured whale. Carried out in October after a successful hunt, this festival is supposed to ensure future good hunting and keep the village in good health and free from evil spirits during the winter. The whale is treated as an honored guest who will stay some time and go home to tell its relatives how respectfully it has been entertained. The man who kills the whale invites all his neighbors to the festivity, which is held in the largest house in the village. (The houses are octagonal, framed with poles, roofed and sided with split logs, the crevices stuffed with dry grass. Earth is piled up along the sides and a funnel-shaped opening is left in the roof for a winter entrance. A ladder leads down into the building.) When the whale is first brought to the beach, the women come to meet it in dancing costumes carrying firebrands from the hearth in their hands. These firebrands symbolize an invitation to the dwelling. The women dance, shaking their shoulders, squatting and rising. They then put sacrificial grass in the mouth of the animal as a token meal. Its head is covered so that it shall not see how it is flensed. An invocation used at this time runs as follows: "Big Raven [the creator] said, 'I shall go get a white whale for my children as food.' He went and got it. Then he said, 'I shall go for an alder branch.' He went and brought the branch. He brought this branch for the whale. Later he again procured the same white whale; again he brought a branch. Thus he always did and thus he always hunted." A dog is then slaughtered as a sacrifice to the Master of the Sea. When the festival starts, all the women gather to cut up and cook blubber. Certain guardian images are placed at the left of the door. With them is put a small wooden carving of the whale, a cup of clear water, changed every day, and choice bits of nostril, lips and fins are boiled and placed in a bag as an offering. A big fire roars on the hearth as the work goes on silently, talk being carried on in respectful whispers. Puddings are made from whale oil, salmon spawn and berries for the whale to take on his journey. The head of the whale is brought in and hung on a crossbeam at one side of the hearth while gifts are exchanged. "There are cries of 'The dear guests have come! Visit us often! When you go back to sea, tell your friends to call on us, too. We will prepare just as nice food for them as for you.' " And with this they point to the puddings in which the whale's substance is being offered to the whale. Some of the whale fat is burned in the fire; the latter represents the sea. Then they divine (to learn if the whale will go back to sea) by heating a seal shoulder blade in the fire. Feasting, singing and drumming go on for days, sometimes rising to a frenzied pitch as the villagers sing the praises of their revered guest. On the fifth day the puddings are put in plaited grass bags and, with the head of the whale, set on an altar by the hearth. Women put on plaited grass masks (it is death to look at the whale spirit) and make an offering of pudding. Some scratches found on the food show that the whale has accepted it. If the whale should refuse to go home, dire calamities might take place. Cords are finally let down from the roof, and the head of the whale and the provisions are pulled up to symbolize that the spirit of the animal has gone on its journey home.

Interestingly enough, when a bear is killed and brought to the house, the women also come to meet it, dancing with firebrands in their hands. The skin and head are taken off, one of the women puts it on, dances in it, and entreats the bear not to be angry but to be kind to its captors. Some of its meat is put on a wooden platter and the villagers say, "Eat, friend." After the bear is given puddings in plaited bags for its home journey, the stuffed bearskin is carried around outside the house and sent toward the sunrise. Some of the Koryak who are reindeer breeders greet the returning reindeer herds with firebrands from the hearth in the same way. The Chukchi carry out very similar whale and bear ceremonies.

It is interesting to note that the dog sacrifice on the beach is probably a Mongolian element, for we have already encountered it in the Shang culture. Dog sacrifice is also practiced by the Yukaghir and Chukchi.

In the invocation to the whale, Big Raven was invoked. Most important in Koryak religion, he appears in that of the Yukaghir and the Chukchi, and will also be encountered in North America. Big Raven is both a transformer kind of creator and a trickster. Here for the first time the trickster, whom we have encountered hovering on the outskirts of various religions, becomes a leading deity.

At times he is thought of as self-created, at times another shadowy deity hovers behind him who, in part, appears to be the do-nothing type of sky god, a Master of the Sky approaching an abstract concept because he is sometimes called "universe." On the other hand, in a crudely sexual myth the Master of the Sky has a wife and causes rain by attaching his wife's vulva to a drum and beating it with his penis until the water squirts out. Big Raven, to stop the rain, puts them both to sleep and dries their sex organs at the fire, whereupon the sky clears.

Big Raven is the first man and ancestor of the Koryak. He finds the earth in darkness, brings light, creates animals, is a great shaman, and is supposed to be present at all shamanistic séances; a raven is even believed to fly into the house. Although Big Raven is both creator and trickster among the Koryak, the Chukchi divide his activities into two persons.

Big Raven has a wife, Miti, whom he fools and who fools him. Characteristic is the motif of detachable organs. They both remove their sexual organs, turn them into people and use them as messengers. Big Raven pounds up his penis in a pudding and feeds it to his wife; she does the equivalent. He enters her anus as if it were a house (a return to the womb fantasy) or they both turn their sexes into dogs. In the light of depth psychology, the myth in which Big Raven turns his excrement into a woman is a curious parallel to child fantasies of anal births. Big Raven's feud with the mouse people closely resembles in theme some of the adventures of Kagan, the Mantis, on the other side of the world. The mouse people find a dead seal which Big Raven is determined to have. He invites the mice to delouse his hair. While they are creeping about in it, he shakes it violently and flings them away. With the aid of some enchanted grass they bewitch him in his own house and steal back the seal meat, at the same time putting sharp stones in Big Raven's and Miti's boots. Our hero takes his big club and goes to kill all the mice but they offer him cloudberry pudding which he cannot resist. After eating greedily he falls asleep. They sew a seal bladder over his anus. As a result when he defecates he cannot find his feces. When his wife solves the problem, he rushes back again with his big club to take vengeance, only to fall victim to the pudding once more.

In the mythological period any animal could turn into a man and a man could turn into an animal by putting on a skin. A Chukchi shaman said, "All that exists lives. The lamp walks around. The walls of the house have voices of their own. Even the chamberpot has a separate land and a house. The skins in the sleeping bags talk at night. The antlers lying on the tombs arise at night and walk in a procession around the mounds while the dead get up and visit the living." His own relation to this living world is consistent. "On the steep bank of the river life exists. A voice is there and speaks aloud. I saw the master of the voice and spoke with him. He subjected himself to me and sacrificed to me. He came yesterday and answered my questions. The small gray bird with the blue breast sings shaman songs in the hollow of the bough, calls her spirits and practices shamanism. The woodpecker strikes his drum in the tree with his drumming nose. Under the ax the tree wails as a drum under the drumstick. All these come at my call."

The Koryak spirit world contains, in addition to Big Raven, his family and the sky entity, *kalau,* harmful cannibals or soul eaters. Big Raven carries on hostilities against them to protect human beings. In one ceremony the Koryak put on flat wooden anthropomorphic masks and impersonate

Big Raven and his family destroying the kalau. For the Yukaghir these beings are *kukul,* the Chukchi call them *kelet.* They often assume animal shape. The Yukaghir highest being is called Pon and is so abstract that it is thought of as controlling natural phenomena. Actually the word means "something." No prayers or sacrifices are offered to this entity. The Chukchi call all good spirits *vairgin* and divide the "directions" (positions of the sun from sunrise to sunset) into twenty-two parts, each controlled by a vairgin, that at the zenith being the most important. In Chukchi mythological tales a vague creator is occasionally mentioned.

It is clear that the Siberian world of spirits includes many components, some of them the result of strata of influence. Jochelson feels that the kalau may be of Mongolian origin. The concept of masters or "owners" may also be a late idea blended to the general animistic base. The Koryak recognize a master of heaven, a master of the sea, and a master of wild deer. The Chinese also revere a master of deer. Among the Yukaghir and Chukchi the master idea goes further. The former feel that the master of the sea has beneath him in authority a "keeper" of each marine species, and similarly the master of the earth delegates authority to keepers of various animal groups. Individual animals, in turn, have protective guardian spirits. There is evidently a blending here, for a hunter cannot kill an animal unless the guardian permits it but the animal itself must also consent. The Yukaghir also treat the slaughtered animal as a dear friend and cover its head. They assemble the bones of deer or elk and place them on a platform out of reach of marauders in the belief that in some way the beast will come to life again.

A Chukchi lake spirit was a seal with human hands. The master of the reindeer was considered to be very small, leaving footprints like a mouse. Clearly all these concepts have much in common, for the spirits which appeared at Chukchi séances witnessed by Bogoras buzzed like mosquitoes and sometimes the tapping of their tiny feet could be heard running across the shaman's drum.

Objects animated by spirits become "guardians" of the house or individual. For instance, the board used in making fire, the family drum, even the skin boat, is consecrated and becomes a guardian. A post outside the Koryak house is smeared with blood and sacrificed dogs hung near it. The Chukchi carve rude figures of men and animals and carry them as amulets. Koryak guardians are kept in the house on the left side of the entrance. The Tungus use small, crude anthropomorphic figures in groups of nine in certain ceremonies. These S. M. Shirokogorov feels are definitely Mongolian and derived from ancestor worship.

All these spirits are controlled and invoked by magicians who have been given the name of shaman by the Russians, and it is thus the term

has come to be used in anthropology for the ecstatic sorcerer. Almost anyone may function as a shaman on a domestic basis among the Chukchi by
drumming and attempting to call up spirits. The Koryak family officiant
merely carries out rituals in connection with the guardians, while the professional has familiar spirits. He is generally a young man given to severe
fits alternating with exhaustion, who acquires a familiar spirit which tends
to be a wolf, bear, raven, seagull or eagle. He wears no special equipment
and uses the family drum.

Both the Yakut and the Tungus shaman use an extraordinary coat made
of calfskin, in itself a musical instrument and covered with iron or copper
pendants. The Yakut coat has a chain on the back which the assistant holds
in order to prevent the spirits from carrying the shaman away. The shaman
carries a triple willow branch with horsehair tied to it which symbolizes a
steed to take him to the underworld. (Sometimes the drum is considered
to be a horse.)

Among the Tungus two magic coats are carefully distinguished; one, the
duck coat, for flying to the upper world, the other the reindeer, for subterranean traveling. The first has a tail and chamois fringes on the arms
to symbolize wings. The pendants are fairly light and include bird symbols,
iron straps to represent their bones, boats, sun and moon symbols. The
headdress used is of soft skin. The lower world coat carries symbols for
all of the bones of the reindeer and can weigh as much as eighty pounds.
With it goes a headdress of deer horns set in an iron crown or on a skin
cap. Added to both outfits is an apron of skin with a brass mirror attached
to it which is used as an aid in self-hypnosis. A staff with a hooked head
also symbolizes a horse used in traveling.

Among the reindeer Tungus, the ceremony of healing the sick starts
with a reindeer being led around the shaman's tipi (this people and the
Yakut use skin or bark tipis in summer) and sacrificed. The antlers, hooves
and skull are kept together. A sort of raft of four wooden fish tied together
with reindeer skin is made, on it the sacrifice is placed, and the whole
brought into the tipi. The shaman sings and drums to get help from his
animal spirits, smoking and drinking vodka to work himself up to ecstasy.
Four times he falls down upon the sacrifice. He cuts off two legs from the
deerskin and throws them to the west. By drumming and dancing he
reaches a peak of ecstasy, at which he throws himself on the deerskin
and lies motionless. In this first act the spirits are accepting the sacrifice,
then when the shaman falls and lies in a trance he is making his journey,
going down a mountain range where he may have trouble with hostile
shamans and also passing through a small hole where spirits might capture his soul. He has sung a description of his journey which may involve
fights in which he uses his drum as a shield. He finally crosses three rivers

and, after a fight or negotiation with spirits of the lower world, he brings back the soul of the sick person. In this he must be aided by his assistant, who strikes a spark with flint and steel to light his way and sprinkles him with sacrificial blood. If his spirit did not return he would die. When all this has been performed satisfactorily, the shaman revives, to the delight of the audience. All drink tea and eat meat. The third act, in which the shaman thanks the spirits for their help, takes place at daybreak or next day.

The trip is difficult and dangerous and requires much help from the assistant who repeats refrains, talks to spirits, plays the drum when the shaman cannot, and in general helps to maintain ecstasy.

The number of otherworlds varies with the different groups. The Yakut distinguish three, with a sky-spirit creator-being in the upper world, masters and hostile eaters or cannibal spirits and people in the middle world, a horrible monster in the underworld. The Chukchi worlds vary from five to nine. The Koryak settle for about five regions, three above and two below. Those above contain the sky entity and the cloud people, those below the kalau and the dead. In the mythical time Big Raven could visit any of them. In this period there used to be a crack through which people could enter the lower worlds and return, but this exists no longer and only shamans can make the trip.

The character of the shaman has been much discussed, especially from the point of view of pathology. Jochelson speaks of "arctic hysteria," which has also been noted among the Eskimo. It is suggested that the rigorous habitat and, especially near the Arctic Circle, the long dark winter disturb the human psyche until ordinary individuals are subject to sudden seizures during which they do not know what they are doing. This could result in a predisposition to shamanistic behavior.

Jochelson admits that the indescribable screams, animal voices, leaping, grinding of teeth and whistling which a Yukaghir shaman kept up for hours unnerved him so that he could do no more work that evening. This particular practitioner was so possessed that his wife had to hit him over the head with a board several times in order to make the spirits leave him. He was finally calmed by placing one of his children astride his shoulders. The sincerity and impressive quality of the séance is attested by all Western observers. Although the apparent ventriloquism is no doubt a technique for using the voice, the strange psychic state of the performer is related to that of mystics in general. In this connection the testimony of Owen Lattimore concerning a Tungus shaman is interesting. The expression on the shaman's face was something like that of a wild animal mixed with inexpressible yearning. "He was not altogether released from something—I do not know what—he was man, not animal. He was man on another plane than that of intellect and reason. The whole thing was magnificent. It went down below the darkest, most groping, formless thoughts; it was the struggling of a blind soul and a leashed will in a world of forces apprehended but not comprehended."

The sex of the shaman poses some curious problems. Although both men and women enter the profession, men command most prestige except for the fact that certain men change their sex and are considered to be the most powerful shamans of all. This inversion runs from mild transvestism, the assumption of a female hairdo or a female coat while the man remains normal, marries and has children, to real inversion in which the homosexual magician actually marries and assumes the passive role in sodomy with his husband. On the mythical plane there is even a belief, among the Koryak, Yukaghir and Chukchi that his organs finally turn into those of a woman. In the Big Raven cycle the trickster and his wife also exchange sex and then change back again.

On the whole, among nonagricultural peoples women play no role in religion, hence the Siberian situation is unusual. Siberian shamans are of three kinds: members of the family who carry out guardian rituals in the household (in the case of the Yukaghir and Chukchi generally women), male clan shamans who operate in behalf of the group, and the individual practitioners who can be of either sex.

The Chukchi sacred household objects are in the care of women, who are the hearth keepers. Among the Koryak, women also take part in the whale ceremony. It is interesting to speculate as to whether this role played by women has any relation to the clan mother whose presence is deduced from the female images of the Upper Paleolithic which were especially prevalent in Russia.

On the other hand, in the past, the male clan shaman of the Yukaghir was actually revered in a cult after death. The flesh was removed from his bones and made into amulets worn for good luck. The bones and skull were dried, assembled and dressed, and the skull was covered with a mask and cap. The whole was placed in the corner of the house and offered food at meals by the man's children, who in a sense became priests of an ancestral cult. Wooden images were also made of deceased shamans and hung up out of doors. Yukaghir shaman skulls were asked where the hunters should go in order to obtain game and the clan shaman went through his séance and prayed to the various guardians of animal groups to obtain the spirits of the animals. When the spirits were turned over to the shaman, the hunters were able to go out and kill the actual animals. There is also evidence of phallicism in connection with male shamans. Bogoras reports that Chukchi magicians in the past went out naked and exhibited their genitals to the moon, asking for help in destroying an enemy. They also mimicked chewing and eating the victim. In some séances they stripped and invoked the power of their genitals in calling up the spirits. He also reports that one shaman said his penis was a familiar spirit. All this is reminiscent of the phallic magic of the Maori.

Along with ambivalence of sexual emphasis in Siberian magic, there are also strong menstrual taboos. In the twenties, when Jochelson and Bogoras were writing, there were very few female shamans. Somewhere in cultural history there may have been shifts from male to female dominance in religious practice. We would expect the male hunting shaman to develop with the earliest hunting rites. Among the Yukaghir there is a special clan hunter who leads his men in search of game. It is quite possible that at some point the clan hunter and clan shaman were one.

The reindeer horns worn by the Tungus shaman relate to one of the deepest layers of a Siberian culture. It will be remembered that in Altai Scythian burials, horses were discovered with antler headdresses, and further back in prehistory the reindeer hunters of the Upper Paleolithic probably sacrificed reindeer by throwing the carcasses into a lake and also mounted antlers on a pole. Even the famous sorcerer painted on the wall of the cave of Les Trois Frères, in France, wears antlers. The Yukaghir pile up antlers as an offering to the spirit of a mountain. The Chukchi place antlers on a pole and dedicate them to the vairgin of the zenith. A wealthy man also collects the shed antlers of his herd, piles them up, and covers them with branches, guardian fireboards are leaned against them, and charms hung on their tips. Then meat and tallow are offered and finally tossed in all directions, some being buried in the ground. When a reindeer is sacrificed, it is held by two ropes, speared, and watched to see on which side it will fall, the unwounded side signifying luck. Finally, among the Tungus, a reindeer is killed at a burial and the skin hung on a bar between two trees in the belief that the soul will ride the animal down to the underworld. The Yukaghir kill the reindeer for the same reason but, now that they have changed from platform exposure of the dead to inhumation, give the skin and legs to the gravediggers. The Chukchi mark the graves of the dead with reindeer antlers.

The Yakut culture, since it was originally developed on the central steppes, retains religious rites which differ from those of the neighboring tribes in the eastern peninsula and, centering around the horse, may well be related to ancient Scythian custom. Festivals are divided into spring rites in honor of good spirits of the East and autumn celebrations to propitiate the evil beings of the West. In the spring an altar, consisting of two poles with a crossbeam against which three young birch trees lean, is set up in a meadow. The crossbar is decorated with tufts of horsehair. Kumiss is poured into decorated birch-bark goblets. At a large clan gathering, libations are poured to the sky god and horses are consecrated by being driven in an easterly direction. Nine young girls and nine young men also consecrate goblets of kumiss to the sky god. A steward then prays for all types of increase and the health of the group. When libations are again poured, the ladle is thrown toward the sky. If it comes down bowl upward, good luck is sure to follow. The young people then pass goblets of kumiss to the elders. A feast of horsemeat and beef is finally served. The day passes with songs, dances, games and horse races. There is also a winter and spring conflict between a son of the sky god dressed in white and a man in black who is an "eater" or cannibal spirit.

The autumn festival takes place at night and involves nine female and nine male officiants. At this ceremony horses and cattle are sacrificed to the eaters and monsters of the underworld. Curiously enough, despite the steppe horse culture and ethnological relation to the Scythians, Yakut decorative art shows no trace of the ancient animal style; it consists merely of geometrical patterns.

Siberian religion exhibits some of the oldest elements in Asian history. The most eastern peoples have borrowed some techniques and concepts from the Eskimo. Today the Siberian Eskimo have been absorbed by the Chukchi but the Eskimo of the New World form one of the links between two continents, and the Siberian heritage is important for an understanding of psychic life in primitive America.

The Americas

CHAPTER 36

The Realm of Sedna

*Eskimo—culture related to that of Siberia—lack of true mythology—creator
entity as mana—the initiation of ecstatic shaman—use of masks in Alaska—
social nature of religious ceremony.*

THE coming of man to the Americas is one of the most controversial topics in physical anthropology and archaelogy.
Conservatives for a long time would not grant him more than two or three
thousand years of prehistory, thus making him no more than a transient.
Then in 1926 came the discovery of the Folsom point imbedded in the ribs
of an extinct bison. In later finds Folsom points were associated with material suitable for carbon dating indicating that the points were about ten
thousand years old. Since then a steady series of discoveries has pushed
the date of early man further back for other areas and even on the very
tip of South America a date for human artifacts has been set as early as
8000 B.C. Furthermore, beneath the carefully fluted Folsom point, exquisite
long, flaked spear blades were found associated with extinct elephants and
named Clovis points, and below them still older points. It is now unde-
niable that Stone Age elephant hunters frequented the southwest plains well
before 10,000 B.C. and that their stone blades gave rise to those of the
bison hunters as the elephant, camel and horse began to die out. At the
same time nomadic gatherers and hunters were developing the Cochise culture around 7500 B.C. in Arizona. In the last few years the traces of early
man in California go still further back to 27,000 B.C and even 43,000 B.C.,
though these dates are still under discussion. Diehard conservatives point
out that few skeletons have been found to match the oldest artifacts and
likewise we have no way of knowing just when extinct animals became
extinct.

Nearly all experts are agreed that the highroad which early humanity
traveled from Asia to North America is across the Bering Strait. Those
who would see the ancient pioneers moving throughout the Americas before

the last glaciation would have to set the date as early as 40,000 B.C. because, after that, the traversable corridor to the south was blocked off by sheets of ice in Canada. Between 25,000 and 20,000 B.C. the corridor once more opened up as the glacier retreated for the last time.

But what sort of people were these oldest inhabitants and what relation is there between them and the historical ethnic strains found in America by the European invaders?

Here again opinion is divided into that of the conservatives who will scarcely hazard a guess because there are too many gaps in the record and the way-out theorists who posit all sorts of migrations. The furthest out of these is Harold Gladwin who suggests that the first invaders may have been of Pygmy stock. Paul Rivet, scrutinizing ancient Middle and South American sculpture, finds Negroid or Papuan traits. There are also a whole series of stylistic resemblances between East Asian civilizations and the high cultures of Middle and South America which suggest possible voyages across the Pacific in the first millennium B.C.

The problem is complicated and in a state of flux. The earliest skulls found in the Americas are long-headed with heavy brow ridges. This leads Gladwyn, José Imbelloni and Paul Rivet to see them as belonging to people related to the Australians; and the picture of the earliest American emerges as dark-skinned, wavy-haired and beetle-browed. The Veddas and spear-throwers, bullroarers and a sort of boomerang (artifacts found in the southwest states) are thrown in to prove the theory. Joseph Birdsell saves the day for white supremacy by pointing out that the ancient whites of Asia, represented by the Ainu of Japan, were also long-headed and beetle-browed. He reproduces photographs of California Indians who could be mistaken for Ainu.

Everyone agrees that a short-headed, truly Mongolian type entered America somewhat later. Since the American Indians, or Amerinds proper, vary from Mongoloids with the Asian eye fold to hawk-nosed Caucasian-looking types, Birdsell would therefore see varying amalgamations with the early archaic whites.

The sequences from the very early hunting cultures up to the Woodland or historic Indian culture have not yet been worked out. Some Folsom and Clovis points have been found in New England. In the same area and elsewhere, nomadic hunters and gatherers with a different type of chipped stone points and no pottery were in evidence as early as 7000 B.C. Their culture is called the Archaic and transitions are being established between it and the pottery makers and bow-and-arrow users who created the Woodland culture which was extant when the Europeans arrived.

Another curious fact is that the cord-marked pottery of the North American Woodland people is very much like that made by the beaker people of the second millennium in Europe! At any rate, most authorities agree that the Eskimo were latecomers, perhaps arriving only a few hundred years B.C.

Psychic history of the New World can therefore only begin with pure speculation. For all we know, the ancient whites or Australoids may have performed totemic rites and smeared themselves with blood and feathers. Arguing from the Veddas, the chances are that among them were ecstatic shamans who practiced hunting magic.

Although the Eskimo are latecomers, since we are proceeding geographically, it will be convenient to start with them and move downward through the Americas in our scrutiny of the religions of the aboriginal peoples.

In the first place, we have mentioned Jochelson's guess that the coastal Siberian tribes were reindeer hunters who crossed to the North American continent before the last glaciation, developed marine hunting technique, and backtracked when the ice expanded. It has, however, been suggested that the Upper Paleolithic hunters first reached the Arctic Circle in Europe and developed a substantially Eskimo way of life (which is attested by artifacts in Norway). Other tundra hunters developed the same way of life in northern Siberia but did not cross the Bering highroad to the Americas. Because of this conservatism they lagged behind white reindeer hunters, who moved north, passed them, and entered America about 7000 B.C. to become the creators of Amerind culture. The tundra-hunters-turned-Eskimo then followed them about 1000 B.C.

All these theories bridge large gaps in the evidence with speculation. Whenever and wherever the Eskimo may have come north and learned how to hunt seals, walruses and whales, we do know that their religion relates to those we have just encountered in Siberia and that, as a whole, they are a rather Mongolian-looking group.

Why do people choose to gain a difficult living in austere and forbidding areas of the earth? This is another of those questions which social science has never tried to answer. The Eskimo is obliged to swathe himself in furs against the cold, to sit for hours waiting for the seal to show himself at the breathing hole, to pursue whales in fragile skin boats easily capsized by the great water mammal and finally, when the ice breaks up, to venture out, harpoon in hand, in his tiny kayak which tides and winds can sweep out to sea. And yet these pioneers of the north are a happy, humorous people who continually express themselves in song with a true poetic gift. Any Eskimo can compose songs. One of them told Knud Rasmussen, "How many songs I own I cannot say. I have not kept count of them. I only know I have many, and that everything in me is song. I sing as I draw breath."

Here is a lyric which expresses the tensions of the seal hunter's life.

And again I thought over
My small adventure
As with a shore wind I drifted out
In my kayak
And I thought I was in danger.

My fears were those small ones
I thought so big
For all the means of life
I had to get and to reach.

And yet there is only one great thing.
The only thing:
To live to see, in huts and on journeys,
The great day that dawns,
The light that fills the world.

The Eskimo country, when not snow-covered, consists of endless moss-
and lichen-covered tundras, barren rocky plains, heather moors and low
willow thickets. In the short, cool summers the temperature seldom climbs
above fifty degrees Fahrenheit. From the Bering Strait and the Aleutian
Islands through Alaska, the Hudson Bay area to Labrador, and eventually,
by the first millennium A.D., in Greenland, we find dome-shaped huts or
tipis recalling the Asian pattern, made of willow, moss or skins and sod
covering the framework; the snowhouse of the extreme north being an
adaptation of the same pattern. In Greenland there are benches or platforms raised from the floor under windows covered with transparent skin.

Interestingly enough, there is curious taboo existent among the Caribou
hunters and the Alaskan Eskimo, who also combine caribou hunting with
fishing and sealing. Caribou meat must not be eaten with that of sea animals; the two types of food cannot even be placed next to each other when
they are stored. Evidently some sort of religious barrier dividing one way
of life from another survives in this custom.

On the whole, a spirit world, reached and interpreted by shamans, which
is common to all the northern groups, presents many similarities to Asian
religion. Behind everything is an unseen power, *silua* or *sila,* which is vague
and remote but corresponds pretty closely to mana. Sometimes it is thought
to speak through the snowstorm and the waves and breakers of the sea.
Birket-Smith says, "Everything outside the everyday is caused by a special
power, an impersonal magical force which permeates existence." The "master" concept is personified in a supernatural woman called by the Alaskan
Eskimo Nulijajuk, and by the central tribes Sedna. In Greenland she is the

mistress of the sea; seals and narwhals come to shore when she combs her hair. In Alaska she is mistress of animals on land and sea and also ruler of the sky. She set up taboos—the meat taboo, death and childbirth avoidances—and ordained that no sewing be done in summer. The dead are supposed to be reborn in her realm and brought back to earth as animals by the moon when it is not shining. The central Eskimo have the most to say about her. In their myth she is the daughter of an Eskimo who marries a bird of the petrel family. Since the bird refuses to support her in the style to which she has been accustomed, her father takes her back but is pursued by the birds who create a magical storm. Her father decides to sacrifice her to the birds and manages to fling her overboard but she clings to the side of the boat. He cuts off the first joints of her fingers which turn into whales. As she still clings, he cuts off the second joints which become seals. In one version she gets back in the boat, nursing her revenge which she obtains by inciting her dogs to gnaw off his hands and feet while he is asleep. The earth then opens and they enter the underworld. In a second version her father puts out one eye and kills her, hence when she is visited by the shaman or *angakok,* she is described as one-eyed and very tall. Amaquaksak of Greenland lives in the depths of the ocean and sits in front of her lamp beneath which a pot catches the oil flowing down from it. From this vessel and from the dark of the house she sends out animals which furnish food to man. Sometimes she withholds them because of parasites in her hair which must be extracted by the angakok. To reach her he is obliged to cross an abyss, evade dog or seal guardians, and pass over a bridge as narrow as a knife.

The central Eskimo shamans feel Sedna to be dangerous and in a winter ceremony dramatize a conflict in which she is mastered. Boas described how the angakok sat in darkness in the back of the hut. Presently he began to scream and throw his arms about. At last his familiar spirit was induced to respond. While he lay in a trance, two assistants coiled a rope on the floor of the hut to represent a seal hole. One held a seal spear, the other the harpoon rope. The angakok in the back of the hut now began to lure Sedna with his song. Up she came through the hard earth. They could hear her heavy breathing which was the sound of the wind and the sea. As she came nearer and nearer the sound grew louder. At last she broke through but the harpoon was ready. They struck without mercy. Back went Sedna into the underworld. The two shamans clung to the rope, but after a struggle in which she tore loose they proudly exhibited a blood-stained harpoon. The village knew the wounded Sedna was angry, and all during the festival on the following day everyone wore an amulet on top of his hood to protect himself.

The Chukchi, who have borrowed this deity from the Eskimo, describe her as having tusks of a walrus, one of which is broken off. Because of this she is angry and sometimes withholds the sea animals.

It has sometimes been said that preliterates do not distinguish between the real world and their worlds of supernatural fantasy. To this generalization there are exceptions but it does seem that the Eskimo are particularly prone to inhabit a dream region where anything can happen. In their case, as well as among the Siberian tribes, arctic hysteria is a recognized phenomenon. It takes the form of trance or seizure, sometimes compared to epilepsy. According to Dr. Wayne Barker, the epileptic attack includes a great variety of symptoms. It runs from complete loss of consciousness with convulsive movement to a momentary seizure. The content of the fit may be only intense auditory, visual or olfactory hallucinations. In some cases the whole life history of the patient flashes through his mind. Although the classic explanation of epilepsy is that it is caused by brain damage, Barker suggests that tension generally precedes an epileptic fit. He adds, "Freud's statement that the 'neurosis' may use the convulsive mechanism for discharge of masses of energy which it cannot handle psychically is not entirely unacceptable to the experienced clinician who is usually willing to admit that emotional turmoil may 'precipitate' fits." Whether the basic predisposition to epilepsy is brain damage or not, a spasm or seizure does appear to be one way in which a sensitive individual's body handles the problem of extreme stress. It seems clear enough that the shaman is a human type whose body functions in this way. Since such strange behavior easily acquires a religious significance from the mana point of view, it is easy to see how the phenomenon could be socialized and techniques used to produce it. Mystical significance is then, of course, added.

The visions of a woman endeavoring to become an angakok in Greenland are curiously literary. At first she sank down in sleep and reached the interior of the earth where she was met by two guardian spirits. They set off chanting: "We reached the boundary of the ocean and the boundary of the earth. I said 'Which way shall we go?' My companion answered me 'This way shall you go. Along the boundary of the soft sea.' He put his hand along his hip and drew forth a thing as long as my forearm, a quite black thing with which he began to make a boundary. Whereupon the softness was diminished. Then I followed eastward. We set off down to the deep sea, we wandered, we wandered, we wandered. My younger and elder brother who had died earlier—I should see them! I ceased to weep. I then ascended through the interior of the ocean, there I saw a great many tents of the dead." The meeting with her elder brother reminds us of the underworld journey of Aeneas. "How was it you stayed away? 'I capsized,' he said, 'alas!' I stuck my arm down in the neck opening of his parka, I touched his upper arm amulets. . . . While I wept my elder brother descended. I, myself, ascended, weeping from grief, and crawled up to the boundary of the world."

Even as in Australia, there is a conception that the body of the angakok must be destroyed. It is then reshaped and the eater becomes a familiar spirit. Often the destroyer is a huge bear. A Greenland Eskimo describes the experience as follows: "He had a very great black snout and, swimming ashore, he rested his chin upon the land and when he then laid one of his paws upon the beach the land gave way under his weight. He went up on land and circled around me, bit me in the loins, and then ate me. At first it hurt but afterwards feeling passed from me. I retained consciousness but when it bit me in the heart I fainted and then I was dead. When I came to again the bear was away and I lay wearied out and stark naked at the same place by the lake. I went down to the sea and having walked a little, I heard someone come running after me. It was my breeches and boots that came running after me and when they had got past me, they fell down on the ground and I drew them on. I heard something come running; it was my frock and when it had got past me it fell down—that, too, I put on. Peering down the river, I saw two little folk as big as a hand. One of them had a fur pouch in which there was a little child. Both the bear and the three little folk became my spirits."

The amulets which have been mentioned are worn tied around the body or in the hair or on the fur hood. Owls' claws, for instance, make the handgrasp powerful, caribou ears quicken the sense of hearing, while fish-skin may be used to ensure luck in fishing. Among the Mackenzie Eskimo there is a connection between the animal amulet and the individual which contains the germ of totemism. A legend also states that all Eskimo once had invisible guardians who would make snowhouses for them and were, in general, helpful. A thoughtless person once said, "What do we want with these people?" and waved his knife. Immediately after this the invisible companions left and went to live in volcanoes which still smoke from the cooking fires roaring inside them.

Apparently the concept that all things have a master spirit passes over into the shaman's familiar, which is sometimes called a *tornak,* and is variously described. To the Greenland people it is as long as a seal with red arms and a red mouth. Another species of spirit is half man and half dog. This spirit originated when a woman married a dog and gave birth to a litter of creatures which include the progenitors of the various kinds of men (among them the Europeans). Still another specialized spirit is the *amortortok* which is large and black, whose touch turns the victim black and causes death. G. Holm was present when this creature materialized at a séance. After a long wait in which the shaman prepared himself, he walked into the room as if in a trance. He sat down and arranged a flat stone, the drum and drumstick in front of him on the floor. His arms were then bound behind his back, wound with rawhide from hands to elbows. All the lamps were put out while the spectators cried, "Goi, goi!" to help summon the apparition. The shaman puffed and sighed while the skin covering the door rattled as if in a strong wind. The drum then began to dance of itself, accelerating in speed and mounting up to the ceiling. After this, a chorus of weird sounds began, a clattering and puffing like that of steam engines and a flapping as of great winged creatures while the platforms and windowsills vibrated. Meanwhile the angakok began to succumb to unearthly powers, groaning, wailing, shrieking, whining. All sorts of spirits' voices, from grumblings to whispers, seemed to come from underground, all over the house, and even from outside it. All this ended with a crash as the drum fell to the floor and the amortortok stamped in heavily. The spectators fled to the walls of the room so as not to be touched. The amortortok roared, "Amo! Amo!" and tugged at the skin upon which Holm sat, holding his ground. It tore off a piece of the skin and left without turning the anthropologist black. It was followed by a spirit crying like a fox. The lamps were then lighted, revealing the shaman sitting in the same spot, bathed in sweat. "His hands were tied behind him in the same way, but not nearly so well as before," Holm writes and goes on to say that many Eskimo could do the voice and sleight-of-hand tricks but nevertheless believed that they were produced by the spirits in the séance. As elsewhere, the shaman combined clever showmanship with genuine trance experience.

It is only in southern Alaska and on the Bering Sea where the northwest Indian influence is strong that extensive use is made of masks. Here the shaman's tornak is induced to take up residence in him when he puts on the appropriate disguise. He first makes a journey to the land of spirits where he gains an impression of the mask to be made and learns the appropriate song. He then either carves the mask himself or shows a sculptor how to make it. Some masks are used inside the festival house and after the performance either left there or given away. Others are made for outdoor use, the usual pattern being that of an animal with human features. A wolverine carrying an arm and leg in its mouth is insurance against the hostile practices of rival shamans (they are being eaten by it). A walrus mask is used to promote successful walrus hunting. In order to affect the weather an eagle mask is necessary to fly to the distant home of the spirit who controls the elements. In these ceremonies a group sings chorally while the shaman executes solo dances. Rasmussen stresses the mana concept. The magicians' power does not come directly from the animal but from something "in the air, in the land, in the sea, far away and around them."

The number of taboos surrounding death is evidence of fear of the departed spirits. As soon as a death takes place, all skins are taken out of the house, apparently to avoid contamination. No work, no dog driving, no washing, hair combing or delousing is allowed, and no meat can be brought into the house as the mourning chant goes on for three days. If all these customs are not observed, the soul of the dead will turn into an evil spirit, according to the Mackenzie Eskimo. The body is either left in the house or exposed and ringed with stones. The whole settlement then moves away. The Greenland tribes believe that man consists of body, soul, and name. The soul is as small as a finger and can be stolen by a malicious angakok, causing sickness or death. After death the soul comes to life again below the sea or in the sky in the form of an animal. The name is buried with the body. This part of the individual returns, however, when the name is given to a baby.

On the whole, Eskimo mythology does not deal with origins or with gods. The South Alaskans have taken over the Big Raven cycle and given the tales an Eskimo touch, but the most common type of myth is a hero tale of shamanistic exploits or a folk story involving shape changing.

Like the Siberians, the Eskimo are ruled by no chiefs and a picture emerges of a rather democratic people whose society is shaped by group opinion and whose emotional life is infused with communal feeling. The Mackenzie Eskimo open their autumn festival of the bearded seal with days spent in darkness in the ceremonial house meditating and preparing new songs. When all the rites have been completed, the group meditates again, "in the silence of good wishes and good intentions." Then the hunting season begins. The Greenlander then uses specific hunting magic. As he sets out alone in his kayak he sings:

> You, who are the common seal,
> You are always compliant.
> You, who are the Greenland seal,
> You are always compliant.
> You, who are the bearded seal,
> You are always compliant.

CHAPTER 37

The Cannibal at the
North End of the World

*Northwest Indian tribes—stratified society showing Siberian influences—
mythology in support of aristocracy—elaborate masked ritual of totemic
origin—ecstatic shamans—significance of dreams—potlatch as symbolic warfare—cannibal society—war and head taking—supernatural world.*

DURING the winter season on the northwest coast of Alaska
and Canada, the Indian tribes gave themselves up to dramatic and vivid ceremonial which lasted for weeks or months. An early
explorer describes a great number of Tlingit Indians grouped around the
central fire in the great cedar-plank ceremonial house. They were
naked and carried stone daggers in their right hands. Other clothed spectators sat in a circle outside the group. The participants sang and circled
the group of drummers slowly. Then suddenly a curtain rose in the back
of the hall and the shaman, in a richly decorated cloak, came flying out and
circled the fire, sometimes on all fours. He was wearing a deer helmet or
mask placed on the top of his head. As he ran and leaped, the men with
daggers menaced him. Finally he was caught in a net and dragged behind the curtain. Other costume regalia was lowered through the smoke
hole at the top of the building. The shaman repeated his dance, in various
disguises; the capture was also repeated. Finally from behind the curtain
he prophesied.

Music, poetry, carved and painted masks, the most vivid art style on
the North American continent, all contributed to the wild dramas enacted
in halls and villages of the northwest Indians. The great staring eyes, jutting
beaks, eagles' wings, bearskins and shaggy cedar-bark costumes, the mad,
ecstatic behavior of the dancers, reflected a turbulent spirit world, richly
mythological and shaped to substantiate ancestral pride and aristocratic
pretensions.

430

This group was never very numerous and is now reduced to a few thousand rapidly dying out in reservations, thanks to the Canadian government which prohibited and the missionaries who discredited its ceremonial life. Nevertheless it achieved perhaps the highest cultural expression among the aborigines of North America.

Like so many barbaric achievements, this one was based to some extent on slavery. The Kwakiutl, Tlingit, Tsimshian, and Haida raided each other and traded in slaves; their aristocrats accumulated wealth by slave labor and unhesitatingly sacrificed slaves on important occasions such as the death of a chief or the building of a house or a canoe. Indeed, it is estimated that one third of the Tlingit population consisted of slaves.

Not slaves alone but a favorable environment with thick woods full of game, coast and island seashores and rivers teeming with marine life made possible the accumulation of surplus which precedes barbaric ostentation and stratification of society. There was hunting of mountain goat, bear, otter, fox, marten, and small game as well as sealing and whaling in certain areas, with fishing as a staple, especially the netting of salmon on their way up the rivers to spawn.

As a result the northwest Indians created a stable life, building their great wooden gabled halls which accommodated several families (as many as thirty persons) along the shores of rivers and the sea. These houses were ornamented with carved posts, painted designs, and in front of them rose twenty- to thirty-foot totem poles, carved from a whole log, on which figures of animals and men and composites recounted mythological episodes belonging to individual lineages, episodes which bestowed special magical powers, good fortune, wealth, and the right to certain heraldic crests.

Within the house was a large front room with a smoke hole above it, and along the walls were cubicles in which members of the families slept. The walls were often decorated with heraldic paintings or carvings. For everyday wear the inhabitants possessed blankets woven from cedar bark or fur cloaks. They also possessed elaborate goat-hair blankets decorated in the characteristic style, cedar chests and boxes, mats, and wooden eating utensils.

Dugout canoes were built with gracefully curved high prows and held as many as fifty men. Sometimes when a groom's party came for the bride they would contain dancers in full eagle or bear regalia who with drums beating would dance up from the shore to the bride's house. War parties set out in them wearing wooden armor and terrifying masks, accompanied by the shaman.

Through all of the culture of these tribes runs a strain of excessive pride or violence and shame; the giving of gifts at the great feasts called potlatches was a mixture of high finance, since guests had to accept gifts and return them later doubled, conspicuous expenditure, since wealthy chiefs went so far as to destroy property surpluses as a form of male exhibitionism, and a positively paranoid boasting and exchange of insults. To be shamed by a rival was the greatest grief. From this wars could result. The aristocratic sense was so highly developed that all acts considered socially undesirable were called by the Tlingit "low-caste."

The potlatch was given in connection with regular religious secret society ceremonies (these were strongest among the Kwakiutl and borrowed by the Haida and Tsimshian), at stages of initiation in a man's career, at weddings or at funerals. In the case of the Tlingit, the institution was generally related to the dead, for when food was burned in the fire or a blanket given to a member of the opposite clan group, one of the dead was named who was supposed to receive its essence. In the Kwakiutl society potlatches reached an apex of competitiveness and conspicuous waste.

In all cases songs were sung by the chief distributing gifts which were calculated to shame the recipient. A Tsimshian boast goes as follows:

> He is uttering lies! A lie it is!
> He is lying! Lies!
> Now the words—
> Who is afraid of you,
> Snow-on-the-leaves!
> Where is your wealth?
> You are only boasting.
> Sing louder! These are lies!

Kwakiutl rivalry involved "putting out the fire" by heaping goods on it. In one of these contests a chief poured candlefish oil on the fire saying, "Now, spirit of fire, open your mouth, son, so that you get enough to eat." Meanwhile, he sent for blankets. "Then those who went to get the blankets came in and the members of the Numaym of the rival chief each take hold of an end of the blanket and spread them over the fire of the host. . . . Nolis, who died some time ago, at Aleut Bay tried to put out the fire with four canoes and he had oil poured on his face by the great host of the Lawetses. Besides he put on four hundred blankets. The house nearly burned. And this is the most real attempt at putting out the fire of a feast I have ever seen. The feastgiver of the Lawetses had two hundred blankets and five canoes. And also small coppers." The coppers mentioned by the informant were flat pieces of metal with hammered decorations. They were provided by the Tlingit, who often traded them with other groups for slaves, and they more or less played the role of bills of large denominations.

Three types of organization comprised the northwest Indian system of nobility. In the first place, the lineages varied from the matrilineal Haida,

Tlingit and Tsimshian to the system of the Kwakiutl, Bellacoola and Nootka who recognized both descent lines. Lineage heads possessed both material and spiritual wealth. Riches consisted not only of blankets, coppers and canoes but also songs, myths, names, the right to bring in tallow for the dancers to rub on their faces, or the right to tie a dancer to a post, animal crests, the right to be bitten by a cannibal dancer; all these things had value in the effort to rise in status and, in turn, carried weight in the potlatch. The secret societies functioned parallel to the lineages and their members acquired the same tokens of value. Finally, among the Tsimshian, lineal chiefs became village chiefs and some of these were elevated to tribal chiefs, a sort of royalty which had advisory authority but had to listen to a council of the lineal chiefs.

Although outside the clan or family all was tension and competition, within the group the members cooperated, for the only way persons of low caste achieved anything was through the reflected glory of the head of the group. Thus the minor members of the family worked and saved to heap up a surplus for the potlatch.

How was this elaborate status structure related to religion? In the first place, most of the nonmaterial values were religious; the wealthy and important were supposed to have gained their eminence through some religious experience and, as a result, they also played the most important roles in religious ceremonies.

Essentially, the northwest coast religion was based upon two institutions that were well developed in northeast Asia, that of the familiar or guardian spirit and the ecstatic experience achieved either by shamans or by individual initiates. These supernormal experiences, which often involved mythical animals, gave rise to mimetic dances and songs. They could be inherited, traded for, and a warrior always took over the name, myth, and crest of his victim.

For instance, a group of Blackfish Tsimshians in a canoe happened to anchor over the house of the spirit Nakgunake. He, hearing the noise, sent a blue cod slave to investigate. One of the Tsimshians was annoyed by the splashing of the cod. He caught it and broke its fins. The group went to sleep. When they awoke they were under the sea. Nakgunake invited them and many sea people to a great feast. He told the Indians not to harm the sea people wantonly and he also made the sea monsters promise not to harm the Indians. Before they returned home the Blackfish tribesmen were given a magical copper canoe and paddles. When they got back to their village they had been gone four years. The steersman became a great hunter and very wealthy.

In another caste a Kwakiutl hunter had a quarrel with his wife and went in search of bear. He disappeared. Since one leg was found he was believed to have been killed by bears. A year later, "The howling of many wolves was coming near behind the village that night. In the morning when day came one of the men went out of the house and he saw many wolves on the bank at the upper end of the village, walking along the bank. And a great wolf stalked out of the woods and back of his head a man was sitting." The man had a baton. He got off the wolf and destroyed a mountain by pointing at it. Something had to be done to socialize him again, for he was the missing hunter. Since menstrual blood is one of the strongest profanations in this area, it was decided to use it against him. The women burned their menstrual napkins in a ring around the man. This made him human once more. He came into the house and explained how his body had been torn into four parts and scattered by four bears, after which the wolves had put him together again. He came to in a ceremonial house where dances took place carried out by beings in wolf masks. The man was then given a new name, possessed special magic, and the episode was dramatized in the winter festival.

Still another way of obtaining magic and a crest was by a mixed marriage. Curiously enough, these often occurred because the animal partner had been offended. While a Tlingit chief's daughter was berry picking she made fun of bears. Immediately a number of bears came and killed all of her tribe except the girl. The leader of the bears married her. She bore a daughter who was a bear with a human face and became the ancestor of the bear clan.

Animal identification of a totemic sort runs all through these tales. A Tsimshian man puts on a frog blanket to catch fish and seal for his family. It becomes harder and harder for him to get the blanket off. Finally he turns into a frog. Likewise two Haida youths put on the dorsal fin of a killer whale and go down to the whale's house. The elder stays there but the younger comes back and becomes a great hunter. He finally destroys a killer whale who turns out to be his brother. The brother is ceremonially buried in a grave house and the killer whale becomes a family crest.

The most elaborate mythological cycles deal with the trickster-transformer type of culture hero who may be Raven or Mink or a personage called Great Inventor among the Kwakiutl. One of the recurrent themes in these cycles is the hostile father-in-law or uncle, exemplified by the early part of the Tlingit Raven story. In this a certain chief had a young wife of whom he was very jealous. He killed all of his sister's sons so that they should not inherit his wife after his death (which was the Tlingit custom). His sister, in despair, went into the woods to kill herself but here she met an old man who gave her good advice. He told her to go back to the beach at low tide to find a round pebble, heat it in a fire and swallow it. She did as she

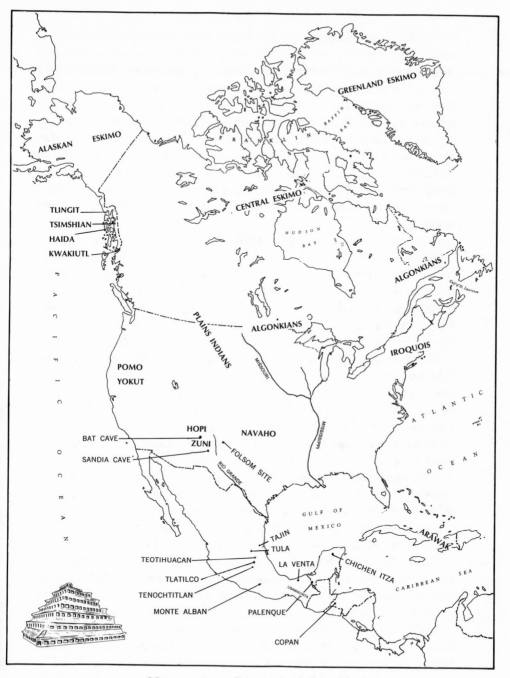

GREENLAND ESKIMO

ALASKAN ESKIMO

CENTRAL ESKIMO

BAFFIN BAY

FRANKLIN

HUDSON BAY

ALGONKIANS

Gulf of St. Lawrence

TLINGIT
TSIMSHIAN
HAIDA
KWAKIUTL

PLAINS INDIANS

ALGONKIANS

IROQUOIS

P A C I F I C   O C E A N

POMO
YOKUT

MISSOURI

MISSISSIPPI

A T L A N T I C

O C E A N

HOPI
BAT CAVE
ZUNI
SANDIA CAVE

NAVAHO

FOLSOM SITE

RIO GRANDE

GULF OF

MEXICO

ARAWAK

TAJIN
TULA
TEOTIHUACAN
TLATILCO
TENOCHTITLAN
MONTE ALBAN
LA VENTA
CHICHEN ITZA

CARIBBEAN   SEA

USAMACINTA

PALENQUE

COPAN

NORTH AND CENTRAL AMERICA

was told and became pregnant. She built a shelter near the spot where the conception took place and was delivered of a beautiful boy who was Raven. After Raven's uncle attempted to kill him in various ways, Raven caused a flood. He and his mother put on bird skins and flew up to the sky. Here Raven got his beak stuck. He hung for ten days, after which the waters receded, and he pulled loose and fell on a heap of seaweed. Now there was no water at all in the world. Raven by trickery stole some from Old Man Petrel and spewed it out to make oceans and lakes. He also stole three boxes containing the sun, moon, and stars, which belonged to a certain chief, and dumped them out. Finally he got fire from an island and dropped the brand on a piece of wood and a stone, which is why fire can be made from flint and wood.

Along with these culture hero traits, Raven is also a stupid trickster. Putting on a bearskin, he tries to steal food from some hunters and gets beaten. His parallel, Mink, among the Kwakiutl plays a number of erotic tricks on women in which the detachable organ element appears. For instance, he sees Sawbill Duck Woman take off her vulva and put it in a box. He goes to the box, takes it out, and has intercourse with it. Again he kills his younger brother, Seal, and eats him because he is greedy.

Raven occurs in Haida, Tlingit and Tsimshian mythology. Viola Garfield sees some indication of a gradual growth into a responsible being. In some versions the wicked uncle, after being overcome, gives him special powers and as the cycle progresses, his more beneficial qualities emerge until, in the last episode, he invites dangerous sea monsters to a feast and turns them into stone so that they can no longer harm human beings. He and his carved house then turn into a stone likewise.

Northwest Indian shamans tended to derive their powers through individual exercise of purification, fasting and purging and with the aid of the ministrations of older shamans. An older Kwakiutl shaman claimed to have put a crystal into a younger man's body to make him a practitioner. The young man also dreamed that a wolf put foam from his mouth all over the dreamer's body and then licked it off, turned into a man, and said, "Now take care, friend, now the shaman-maker has come into you. Now you will cure the sick and you will catch the souls of the sick and you will throw sickness into anyone among your tribe whom you wish to die."

The method of treatment was to dance around the fire while the song leaders led the music and drumming. The shaman then went to the sick man and, in the case reported by Boas's informant, "He was sucking for a long time and when he lifted his head he took out of his mouth the blood in his right hand and he squeezed the blood so that it dripped into the water dish, the receptacle for wetting the mouth. When the blood was all out, he stood up and sang his sacred song, going around the fire in the middle of the house. Then he stretched out his left hand, opening his fingers and something stuck like a worm in the middle of the palm of his hand. That was referred to as the illness." The same informant explained that a bit of eagle down was held between the upper lip and the gum to be produced as the "worm." Tlingit performers used many masks and had many spirits to help them, symbolized by smaller figures surrounding the features; those near the nose strengthened the sense of smell, those around the eye improved the doctor's eyesight, etc.

Northwest Indian attitudes toward animals were very similar to those of the hunters of Asia. After a Kwakiutl had shot a bear he said, "Welcome friend, you have come, trying to come to me that I may get you, for this is the reason why you came, made by the one who created you also. Now, welcome, friend, I welcome you heartily that you have come and walked in front of me. Now take care, friend, and call your parents and your elder brothers and your younger brothers and also your wife that they may all come and try to come to me, friend." The hunter then answered for the bear, saying, "Wa, that is indeed what I will do." The Tlingit were even respectful toward soft-shelled clams. While digging them they said, "Do not go down so fast or you will hit your mother-in-law in the face." This was, of course, assuming that the clams practiced mother-in-law avoidance and would not wish to disregard the taboo.

Still more interesting as an example of basic hunting mimicry was the Tsimshian goat hunting dance. A symbolic mountain was built in the festival hall after which a performer in a goat costume entered and climbed the mountain while a song was sung.

> That is why
> The large mountain was moved.
> The large goat spirit of the sky
> Will go there.

The goat dancer was killed in pantomime with bows and arrows and the hunters pretended to cut its head off and roast it, still singing the song. Since the head was a spirit, the goat mask fell open revealing a thunderbird. By means of strings it was closed again. Meanwhile a real goat, killed in the mountains, was being roasted.

The highest point of tension and drama was reached in the initiation ceremonies of the secret societies, the Cannibals, the Dog-Eaters, the Fire-Throwers, and the Destroyers. All these are believed to have originated among the Kwakiutl but were enthusiastically adopted by the Tsimshian and the Haida and less generally by the Tlingit. Among the Kwakiutl, initiation involved invocation of the Cannibal-at-the-North-End-of-the-World. When the novice first felt twinges of possession, spirit whistles were sounded and he ran out of the house singing. He disappeared for several months, generally living in a cave in the woods. Meanwhile male and female anthropomorphic masks were carved. When he returned he was surrounded by attendants. (In all groups the cannibals were surrounded by attendants who continually restrained their excesses.) As the possessed person gave his cry of "Hap! Hap!" (eat, eat) he was ushered into the festival house where he was shown the male and female mask. These caused him to faint because they were incorrect and did not correspond to his spirits. He was brought out, supposedly dead, while the shaman and four women chanted and danced around the fire, shaking rattles. The initiate showed signs of life and was tied up and taken back into one of the rooms or cubicles. Later he ran away and the same procedure was repeated. After four days a potlatch was given for cannibal initiates. By this time the frenzied novice was getting wilder. Clouds of eagle down were blown into the hall as, in his madness, he leaped out over the wall of his cubicle. He now rushed about and bit his attendants. A corpse was then brought in to appease him. All the other cannibals at this point became excited and all ate pieces of the corpse. After this, the novice danced more peaceably. A name was mentioned which turned out to be taboo and made him faint. After three winters of dancing he was able to reach high rank.

According to Helen Codere, the whole violent ethos was connected with an earlier head-taking type of warfare. Kwakiutl warriors were trained to disregard taboos and all proper social behavior. They were hardened by bathing and fasting. Warriors were supposed to be terrible beings. War was carried out to avenge insult and to gain prestige yet bravery was not stressed. In true headhunting style, actual hostilities consisted of surreptitious raids. Heads were brought home and tied to poles in front of the village of the victors. Ritual shows the origin of much of the violent ceremonial in war. A cannibal song runs:

> Everybody is afraid of the cannibal mask . . .
> His hooked beak mask makes the heart flutter . . .
> I was a little too late to see the blood of his
>   victims,
> To see the putrid heap of those whom he had killed . . .
> I went all around the world to find food.
> I went all around the world to find human flesh.

Then a gradual shift took place, from gory raids to fighting with property in the potlatch, as a potlatch song indicates by its mixed imagery.

Food will be given to me, food will be given to me
  because I obtained this magic treasure.
I am swallowing food alive, I eat living men;
I swallow wealth, I swallow the wealth my father
  is giving away.

To balance this picture of a psychic world of violent and destructive spirits expressed in possession which approaches temporary madness, a Kwakiutl bear ceremony was conceived in a pure spirit of comedy. The bear was first seen on the beach where he chased the villagers. Attendants surrounded him, prodded him with spears and drove him into the dance hall and into a cubicle. While the song leaders led the dancing and singing, the bear roared and tried to break out. The spectators pretended intense fear. Sometimes blankets were held up through which the bear charged, upset things, and ran through the village again. Back in his cubicle, he again roared and threatened. Finally, in real music-hall style, instead of a bear a decrepit old man hobbled out.

What sort of world view is expressed by all of this elaborate theatricality? Most scholars believe there was no real synthesis. On the whole, the tribes distinguished between a mythological time when creating and transforming went on, as exemplified by the Raven cycle, and a historical one in which also, however, magical episodes took place.

John Swanton points out: "Supernatural power impresses them as a vast immensity, one in kind and impersonal, inscrutable as to its nature but wherever manifesting itself to men taking a personal and it might be said human personal form in whatever object it displays itself." In other words, this is once more the familiar concept of mana. The earth was flat, the sky a solid vault between which numberless spirits lived. There was Old-Woman-Underneath-the-World who had charge of a post made from a beaver's foreleg on which the world rested. When Raven tried to drive her away from it, the earth quaked. Thunder was caused by the thunderbird flapping its wings or even moving a single quill. When it winked its eye, lightning flashed. Upon its back was a large lake which accounted for the rain during a thundershower. The bird, which looked something like an eagle, sometimes caught whales and carried them up to the mountains where their bones could be seen. It once almost carried off a Russian ship because the sailors made fun of it. Those whom the bird spoke to became rich.

Without a true priesthood, northwest supernatural beliefs had scarcely achieved a real synthesis. What is most striking is the echo of oceanic traits such as headhunting, human sacrifice on important occasions, elaborate masking and status rituals, trickster cycle, and stratified society. Indeed the

carved house posts of the Maori remind us not a little of northwest architecture. On the whole, northwest Indian culture once reached a point far
more elaborate than that attained by most of the hunting and gathering
bands of America but socially less cohesive than the peak of Middle and
South American civilizations.

CHAPTER 38

The Trickster and Dictates
of the Dream

Plains and hunting tribes—trickster ubiquitous as creator or associated with creator—role of unconscious in mythology—toothed vagina and flood myth —lack of organized pantheons—prevalence of hunting magic—guardian spirit acquired through dream—shaman and guardian spirit—plains Indian sun dance—Iroquois false-face society and white dog sacrifice.

"ON THE Trickster proceeded. As he walked along he came to a lovely piece of land. There he sat down and fell asleep. After a while he woke up and found himself lying on his back without a blanket. He looked up above him and saw to his astonishment something floating there. 'Ah, Aha! The chiefs have unfurled their banner! The people must be having a great feast, for this is always the case when the chief's banner is unfurled.' With this he sat up and first realized that his blanket was gone. It was his blanket he saw floating above. His penis had become stiff and the blanket was floating above. 'That's always happening to me,' he said. 'My younger brother, you will lose the blanket, so bring it back.' Thus he spoke to his penis. Then he took hold of it and, as he handled it, it got softer and the blanket finally fell down. Then he coiled up his penis and put it in a box. And only when he came to the end of his penis did he find his blanket. The box with his penis he carried on his back." This trickster episode comes from the Winnebago cycle in which, instead of Raven, the hero is Coyote. Like Raven he is wildly priapic and his organs are detachable. He sends his penis under water to copulate with a chief's daughter and it is only at the end of his history that he ceases to carry it on his back in a box and finally affixes it where it belongs. He is also a butt for various animals and even punishes himself. In one episode, he sets his anus to guard his dinner and when the duck is stolen by some foxes, burns it with a hot coal and then cries out in pain. There are heroically excremental episodes in which he creates mounds of filth. He also turns himself into a woman, allows himself to be impregnated by a fox, and gives birth to a boy. On the one hand the trickster's behavior arises from the depths of the unconscious and on the other, as we have seen in the northwest, he combines creator and transformer qualities and often sets the moon, sun and stars in their places and provides fire. In north and northeastern Algonkian mythology he becomes anthropomorphic; as Nanabozho he is his usual erotic and scatological self, as Tschapis he plays a few tricks but on the whole is an altruistic culture hero. In California among the central Yuki, a true creator, Takiomal, is opposed to the trickster Coyote, while to the south, among the Pomo, he is again a creator. In Paul Radin's view the culture hero traits are a shamanistic addition, probably a blending of another character or characters. On the whole, Radin feels that such shamanistic shaping accounts for the roles and behavior of spirits in North America. The trickster as an erotic rascal, however, "is admittedly the oldest of all figures in American Indian mythology, probably in all mythologies." Apparently theological shaping could go in two directions; either an attempt was made to keep him out of the rank of true deities, more or less opposed to the actual creator, or else he was gradually transformed, and in some cycles he gradually lost his stupidity and his tendency to break every taboo and finally became a fully conscious man aware of social responsibilities. Thus his history becomes a kind of parable of the socializing of man, a fable in which the wildest drives of the unconscious are tamed by the necessities of group life.

Still another motif in American folklore which ties up with basic psychological attitudes is that of the toothed vagina which was noted by Boas as early as 1910. No less than twenty-two versions have been discovered ranging from northwest and Eskimo tradition through Canada, the central plains area of the United States and the Iroquois mythology of the east. It also occurs as far south as the Gran Chaco, is widespread in the northeast Siberian tribes, and has also been noted in India. Robert Gessaim, himself a psychoanalyst, points out that this fantasy is symbolical of the fear of castration and ties up with the reveries of modern patients. A typical version, that of the Wichita Indians, makes it an episode in the exploits of the hero (from a non-Indian point of view not too happily named), Child of a Dog. The hero meets two women, a good witch and a bad witch, the latter inviting him home to marry her two daughters. The good witch privately informs him to beware, for they have teeth in their vaginas which will bite off his penis. He is told not to sleep, not to have intercourse with them, and to watch the old woman carefully. The good witch also tells him to shove a log of firewood in at the door before he enters his future mother-in-law's house. This is a wise precaution, for it overturns the old woman who was about to brain him with a war club. Nothing daunted, the hero goes to sleep between the two girls and rebuffs all their efforts at seduction. By keeping awake he is also able to avoid the old woman, named Little Spider, who is awake and hovering about with lethal intention. The next night he is armed by the good witch, Buzzard Woman, with two long whetstones. She tells him to choose one of the girls for his wife and cautions him what to do, also giving him a charm to put Little Spider Woman to sleep. During the night he picks the sister who pleases him most and files off the teeth with his whetstone, "thus rendering her harmless and fit for a man to copulate with." The other he kills by ramming a whetstone up her vagina. He then flies with his bride, hotly pursued by Little Spider Woman. Buzzard Woman takes a hand, however, carries the bad witch up in the sky and drops her, thus saving the hero and his girl.

An interesting variation, reported by B. W. and E. G. Aginsky, as formerly current in the mythology of the Pomo Indians of California, is the episode in which Wood Rat courts the daughters of Morning-Star. One of them admits, " 'Well, Wood Rat, if you like me all right, I will marry you, but you must know that my father has placed thorns all about my vagina.' " Rat then took a stone, broke off all the thorns and married the girl. This same people interjects its xenophobia into the male-female relationship. Women of other tribes are thought of as potential poisoners, while certain supernatural Sun girls entice lonely hunters, who are killed in intercourse because the vaginas of these spirits contain live rattlesnakes.

Clearly enough in the motif of the toothed vagina with its menace of castration we have a symbol of the whole primitive attitude toward the dangers of female sexuality, in ritual so often expressed by menstrual taboos and by the exclusion of women from important activities.

The ubiquity of the trickster—we have noted his appearance in other parts of the world—and the distribution of the toothed vagina story support most clearly the suggestion that many elements in early religion are shaped by the deepest drives of the unconscious. Other mythological elements are widespread but their basis cannot be so clearly discerned. In North America there is in particular the idea of an ancient time in which there was no distinction between men and animals, followed by the period of transformation in which animals lost their power to assume human shape. In a sense, this seems analogous to the dream time of the Australians and perhaps can be equated with the early layers of hunting magic in which identification between man and animal was close. On the other hand, there is a flood story in which the earth is drowned and generally four animals survive on a raft with a culture hero who orders them to dive down to secure earth to make a new world. After several failures one of them brings up a little soil and the world is saved. In the case of the Algonkian, the muskrat is the hero; among the Crow it is the hell-diver. This myth is widespread in the northern, central, and northeastern areas of North America. It also appears in Middle and South America. Although there is a superficial re-semblance to the deluge of the Near East, it would be difficult to assign them a common psychological origin. More likely they both arose from environmental factors.

When we come to examine the character of North American deities in general, with the exception of the southwest area, which will be discussed separately, the concept of mana once more arises. Robert Lowie says of the plains Crow that "Divine power is not crystallized in a few major personali-ties, let alone a single supreme ruler, but diffused over the universe and likely to crop up in unexpected places." In general he feels the Dakota term *wakan* means the unusual or the mysterious. The *manitu* of the Naskapi Algonkian is a spirit force or supreme power, "everything not understood is implied in it," which is a standard definition of mana. Among the Nebraska Omaha Indians, *wakanda* stands for the mysterious life power embodied in all natural forces and creatures as well as in man.

Supreme deities are, on the whole, lacking, with a few local exceptions such as the Shawnee who put an Old Grandmother in charge of the spirit world. The thunderbird is a widespread entity who is prayed to by the plains Indians. Among the Crow, the Sun at times assumes creative powers but is not clearly distinguished from Coyote who is the creator and is never in-voked. Concerning the Sun, Lowie writes, "From an ethical point of view he is sometimes benignant but also turns malevolent towards the whole tribe when his mistress is seduced by a boy hero and is even represented as boiling and eating the flesh of brave warriors!"

It is not possible, therefore, to find really consistent North American gods or developed pantheons. On the whole, social ethics are quite divorced from them. The attitude toward them is a magical one; they are not, except per-haps among the Iroquois, thanked or venerated. The familiar bargaining relation exists. When the Winnebagos of the plains, for instance, make offer-ings of tobacco to thunderbirds, the smell is so tempting that the birds suc-cumb. Once they have accepted the gift they automatically serve man.

The Aginskys' presentation of the life of the Pomo Indians of California exemplifies very well the unity in the psychic life of an American aboriginal people whose two preoccupations were the desire for health and prosperity and the fear of sickness and misfortune. The preservation of one and the avoidance of the other were based on power obtained in various ways from the supernaturals. This power is clearly mana since it can be used to obtain success or to heal or it can poison and destroy. A rather anxiety-ridden people, the Pomo channelized their fears into the belief that any outgroup was dangerous and liable to practice poisoning either with physical sub-stances or by magic. Hence the average Pomo Indian went about aware of the intricacies of the mana power and constantly taking precautions. Even the great communal festivals had a basic health-giving function. Like the Azande of West Africa and the Dobu of Melanesia, the Pomo exaggerated the world of magic, particularly that of black magic. A comparable situation would be a modern literate who made a religion of the germ theory of disease and the danger of contagion.

The most widespread form of expression of North American aboriginal religion is the dream or trance and the concept of the guardian spirit. This complex, which we have already encountered in Siberia and the northwest and through the arctic Eskimo area, appears everywhere throughout the continent. It varies considerably as it is combined with other traits. Most socialized among the northwest group, elsewhere it was an individual experience, sometimes enjoyed only by shamans, sometimes participated in by everyone. Sometimes it was attached to puberty ritual with training for manhood, sometimes it was sought at every crisis in life. Sometimes it was incorporated into a totemic system, in which the guardian was a totemic animal, sometimes the spirit was anthropomorphic. Although, on the whole, the psychic experience and the spirit were individualistic, and everyone was free to experience anything he liked, visions always fell into cultural patterns; Shasta shamans of California, for instance, always saw their spirit in terms of a tiny man with a bow and arrow. The basis of this religious practice was the need for a genuine emotional experience, a psychic thrill which might be either a dream or a trance and might come without warning or be sought by various techniques varying from narcotics, fasting, purging, and isolation to self-torture.

For instance, among the Naskapi Algonkian (considered to be the most primitive tribe of this group) where every man is both hunter and conjurer, the guardian seems to be the individual's own soul called the Great Man. In dreams and by introspection the hunter gains greater knowledge of his Great Man and listens to his promptings. Not only does every hunter use a drum but he sometimes drinks and smokes to produce ecstasy. By these techniques he passes into a stupor and consults the Great Man.

In contrast, the plains Crow experience was a fully developed guardian complex. This tribe had no puberty initiation, no divination and no sacrifice; the dream experience was everything. The individual in search of guidance went up to a lonely mountain, stripped, fasted, went without water, laid his left forefinger on a stick and cut off one joint, holding it toward the sun and saying, "Uncle, you see me. I am pitiable. Here is part of my body, I give it to you to eat. Give me something good. Let me live to old age, may I own a horse, may I capture a gun, may I strike a coup. Make me a chief. Let me get good fortune without trouble."

Thanks to physical mortification, most individuals succeeded in having visions, although some were temperamentally unlucky. The hallucination could be of various kinds. Sometimes animal spirits or human supernatural messengers appeared and prophesied good fortunes or gave instructions; sometimes the visionary was given medicine and became a shaman or he was told to join some society. Visions concerning war were common. To one warrior a horseman appeared and said, "If you want to fight all the people on earth, do as I do, and you will be able to fight for three or four days and still not be shot." Then the horseman began to ride east. Enemies attacked him but he knocked them down with a spear. A storm came up and hailstones as big as fists knocked down the enemies. As a result Scratchface, the visionary in this case, killed an enemy without being wounded, obtained horses and married a highly satisfactory wife.

The Ojibway, an Algonkian group, who inhabit an area from the Dakotas along both north and south shores of the Great Lakes, treated the dream as property. All members of the tribe, even children, were encouraged to dream. In particular, dreams gave rise to new dances. Both dance and dream could be bought and sold. Theoretically the contents of the dream were never revealed. Dreams among these people bestowed the power to cure illness. The shaman entered the tent in which the sweat bath was prepared (red-hot stones were placed in it and a little water poured over them). He then communed with a guardian turtle who summoned other supernaturals. The people outside could hear the different voices; the turtle's was shrill, the eagle's gentle. There were bells at the top of the lodge which jangled as the spirits entered. Shamans had themselves bound before entering the tent to show that it was the spirits who rang the bells and shook the sides of the tent. Among this people the bear spirit was the most powerful, next to him the thunderbird. We are strongly reminded of Negrito shamans on the other side of the world.

Among the woodland Indians, archaic hunting practices are recorded. The Naskapi of Labrador regard hunting as a holy activity and retain practices and ideas similar to those of Siberia. Shamans, addressing animals, said, "You and I have the same covering, the same mind and spiritual strength." The master concept prevails. The Master of the Caribou, for instance, is thought of as an Indian who has intercourse with female caribou or as a great caribou. He must be placated before killing the animal. Strangely enough, the Master of the Fish is a moose fly which hovers about dead fish to see that nothing is wasted. Bear ceremony is pre-eminent. Before hunting, the Indian takes a ritual sweat bath. When he corners the bear in its den, he says, "Come out, grandfather, I will light your pipe." The bear is called "short-tail" to avoid using his name. Only married women are allowed to skin the bear and only men can cut it up. A piece of its fat is thrown in the fire. The skull is picked very clean, carried all winter, then hung on a peeled fir tree and tobacco put in its nose. In the case of famous hunters, after burial, bear skulls and beaver skulls are hung on poles near the grave.

Plains ceremonial, since the economic base of the plains Indian life was the buffalo, naturally involved rites connected with this animal. Although the familiar stereotype of the American Indian is based on the mounted plains hunter, the rapid modification produced by the European introduction of the horse did not take place until the eighteenth century. Before that there were many thousands of years of buffalo hunting on foot with the aid of the dog, as is proved by the Folsom point. Ancient techniques of capturing this game animal included stalking in wolfskins, collective hunting, using grass fires to drive the buffalo in the desired direction, driving them over a cliff, and fences and beaters that channeled the herd into a corral.

The plains Indians occupied themselves little with weaving, basketry or woodwork; buffalo skin was their basic material, supplemented by some deer, antelope and elkskin. Skin was used for moccasins, leggings, and for the fore and aft aprons which preceded the breechclout and was decorated by painting or embroidering with dyed porcupine quills.

Hide was used for the tipi. The plains Indians also built earth lodges. Ten-foot stockades were driven into the ground in a circle and pegged or tied together. There were from four to eight central posts. Willow branches were used for rafters, thatched with grass and covered with sod. Earth was also heaped up against the sides. A third type of house, the grass lodge, consisted of poles bent inward overlaid with grass, looking something like a haystack.

Before the arrival of the horse, dogs were used to carry loads or pull the travois. The latter consisted of a couple of poles joined together at one end with a sort of flat basket of laced hide in the middle on which a load could be lashed. The joined poles were then fastened to the dog's neck in such a way that he could drag them. A large dog could manage about sixty pounds.

The North American Indian ethos was a warlike one, particularly among the plains tribes where the killing or touching of an enemy (counting coup) was the basis of prestige and scalps were brought home to be carried in a ceremonial dance by the women. This is particularly evident in the buffalo dances whose primary purpose, to secure increase of the animal or to bring the herds within reach, was overlaid with bellicose elements. A dance of the buffalo bulls is found in almost all plains tribes. The Fox dance, as cited in Chapter 3, stressed the increase idea but the Mandans danced with spears and shields and the Hidatsa wore, in addition to buffalo-head masks, tails tied above their buttocks so that they stood upright to show that the bulls were angry and ready to charge upon the enemy. All these dances were supposed to originate in dreams.

Although the plains Indians were organized into exogamic totemic clans (either matrilineal or patrilineal), dance societies were independent groups not connected with age grades or puberty rituals (which were lacking) and a man could belong to more than one. Membership was bought, special gifts being given to a man's clan father who sponsored him. Such societies were parallel to men's societies in other parts of the preliterate world but differed from them in that they were unrelated to ancestor worship. True ancestor cults existed nowhere in North America. Another continental characteristic was the fact that women possessed dance societies of their own and took part in various ceremonies.

Tobacco was revered in a particular ceremony and was, in general, used as incense, puffing on the pipe being ritually regulated. Among the Lakota there was a sacred pipe ceremony in which the object was unwrapped with great reverence.

The most important group ceremonial was the sun dance. Although the sun was invoked, the dance as a whole was not in honor of any one deity but was definitely a composite of a number of elements. In fact, since the individual dream was the basis of all new rites, and an individual of strong personality could thus leave his imprint on the ceremonial life of the group, it is surprising that the basic form of so many institutions remained constant over such a wide area. Group conservatism, however, tends to halt change and the individual contribution seems to have been in the addition, elimination or modification of detail.

The Crow sun dance took place as a prayer for vengeance because a man's kinsman had been killed by an enemy. Elsewhere it was initiated as a result of a vow taken in times of distress and in general was a technique of acquiring power, a search for the vision embodied in an elaborate communal rite. Its performance generally coincided with the summer buffalo hunt which was organized when scattered hunting groups came together. The opening of many medicine bundles also took place at this time. These were collections of sacred objects such as dried birds, animal skins, herbs, etc., which symbolized the owner's vision and were opened with certain ceremonies to freshen the power of the guardian spirit.

In the Crow dance, there was an initiator who was called the Whistler and a shaman who possessed medicine dolls, crude anthropomorphic images made of skin. The Whistler announced the dance, took sweat baths, and began to fast. To the doll owner he said, "Sing for me and I will dance for you." Meanwhile the chief of the group was notified that everyone should save buffalo tongues, which were the most important provision used in the feast.

Various preliminary dances took place in the Whistler's tipi, there was ritual smoking and passes were made over the doll. Then came the building

Above: Copulating couple, possibly a sun god and an earth goddess, from Chimú pot, 1000–1400 A.D. *Below:* Chimú pot showing bird-headed deity holding trophy head while severed heads of llamas indicate llama sacrifice.

Photo by the author

In South America the pyramid once more becomes the base of a temple. Adobe pyramid of the sun at Moche, north Peruvian coast, Mochica culture, 500–300 B.C.

The Mochica god still retaining feline teeth and snake decoration. Stirrup-spouted grave pot with painted decoration.

The Museum of Primitive Art

The feline motif appears on the southern coast, a textile from Ica (influenced by Tiahuanaco culture of Bolivia) 500–1000 A.D.

The Museum of Primitive Art

Photo by the author

Sculptured figure from San Augustín, Colombia, showing feline teeth and trophy head hung around the neck, 850–500 B.C.

Sculptured figure from San Augustín of a warrior, one of a pair at entrance to a temple. Above the head the "alter ego" can be seen.

Photo by the author

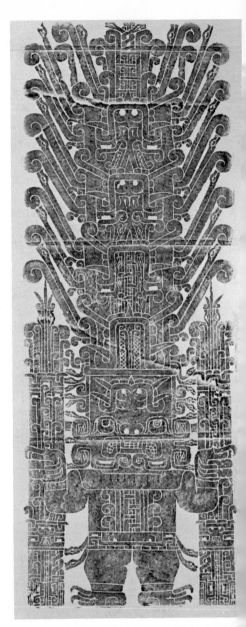

The Museum of Primitive Art

Rubbing of the stela Raimundi, Chavín culture, 850–500 B.C., Peru, showing monster with feline and human attributes adorned with snake-headed rays.

Photo by the author

Relief from Tula showing vultures eating human hearts flanking the rain god and above felines and coyotes. Militaristic Toltec culture, late first millennium A.D.

The warrior Atlantides, probably supporting a temple on the top of the large pyramid at Tula.

Photo by the author

Mural showing Quetzalcoatl from pyramid at Xochicalco, near Cuernavaca, Mexico, Theocratic period.

The pyramid again becomes the base of a temple. Pyramid of the sun at Teotihuacán, Theocratic period.

Museo Nacionál de Antropología, Mexico

Rain god from mural in the palace of Tepantitla at Teotihuacán, Theocratic period, 300–900 A.D.

Detail from Tepantitla mural showing the dead disporting in the rain god's paradise.

Museo Nacionál de Antropología, Mexico

Colossal Olmec head from the Veracruz region of Mexic
Note curiously Oriental features.

Typical jaguar-faced cherub, Olmec culture 800–400 B.C
Mexico.

Clay female figurine, possibly an early fertility godde
Tlatilco, Valley of Mexico, same period.

An offering of six jade celts and six figurines, Olmec cultur
From a burial mound at La Venta, Tabasco, Mexico.

Photo E. S. Curtis

Hopi snake dancers entering the dance plaza.

Iroquois false-face society equipped to fight disease.

The American Museum of Natural History

A sun dancer faces the sun and dances for hours in one spot in order to obtain game, success in war, or other benefits.

Assiniboin plains Indian performs a ceremony to placate the spirit of an eagle he has killed.

Photo E. S. Curtis

Photo E. S. Curtis

Photo E. S. Curtis

Arikara plains Indians perform black-tailed dance around a sacred tree.

Teton Dakota plains Indian sun dance torture. Splints are inserted through his breast muscles so that the body of the worshiper hangs from the pole.

After Catlin, The Smithsonian Institution

Masked Kwakiutl dancers in a winter ceremony, British Columbia. The figure at the left with staff and bark ring around his neck is the wealthy chief who is paying for the affair.

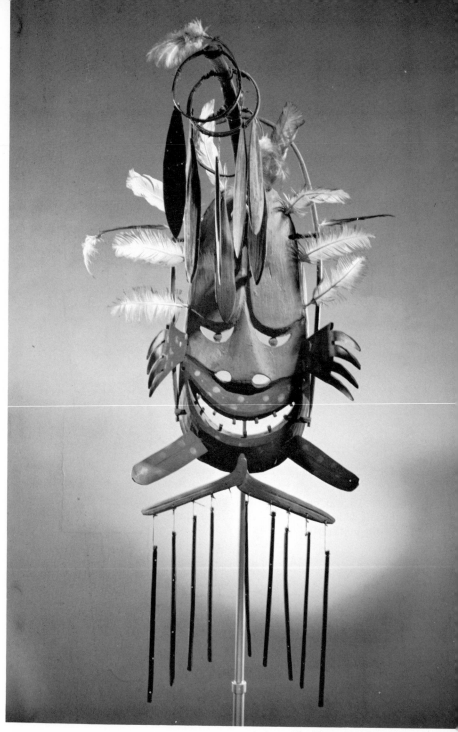

Alaskan Eskimo mask.

The American Museum of Natural History

Two dancers of the Camayura tribe of the Xingu River. This group is related to the Tupi-Guarani. The long woodwinds symbolize male ancestor spirits, as do trumpets in other parts of the South American forest area.

Photo Gusinde

Ona tribesman from Tierra del Fuego, costumed as a nature spirit which appears in ceremonies intended to frighten the Ona women.

Photo Paul Fejos, Wenner-Gren Foundation

Group of Witoto women, Río Negro area of the South American forest, painted in preparation for a dance.

Photo by the author

A folklore survival from the central Peruvian Highlands near Jauja. Children dressed as a fertility couple garlanded with fruit, bread and streamers for a ceremony at which sheep are symbolically sacrificed (probably a survival of llama offering). Behind them a woman sings and beats a drum.

The ceremonial center of Machu Picchu, a late Inca town situated above the Urubamba River, second millennium A.D. A fine example of the fitted stonework employed in temple architecture.

Photo by the author

Yakut shaman of Siberia inducing his trance by beating the hand drum.
The American Museum of Natural History

The American Museum of Natural History

Yakut shaman's coat used for traveling to the underworld. Note deer bones simulated by iron strips on sleeves.

Offering of antlers on a Chukchi grave, Siberia.
The American Museum of Natural History

Koryak of Siberia about to sacrifice a dog.

Sacrificed dogs hung on poles outside of Koryak dwelling which is entered from the roof. Dogs are offered up every year to the "Owners" of wild animals to improve the game supply.

of the sun dance lodge which was erected about three miles from the village. Most important was the cutting of the tree for the center pole. For this cere- mony three people were needed, a woman with a record of sexual purity, a captive from the tribe which had killed the Whistler's relative, and a *berdache,* a homosexual transvestite. The chaste woman had to be very sure of herself, for if her record was not clean any paramour could challenge her. The one chosen reflected great honor on her husband. Among the Canadian Dakota, chaste men had to cut the tree, men who had not even toyed erotically with their sisters-in-law, a privilege granted by their kinship structure. The duty of the Crow woman was to touch the tree with the prongs of an elk antler. The captive painted a black ring around it, the berdache cut it down. (The latter seems to be an echo of the homosexual shaman.) The tree lay where it fell and the young men counted coup, for it represented an enemy to be killed. Other tribes used the actual tree as a center post of the lodge. In the light of Omaha rites, the sacred tree seems to have been a separate religious development. For the Omaha a sacred tree was a symbol of tribal unity connected with a vision of a cedar tree shining with light, four paths leading to it, along which animals came and rubbed it smooth. The Omaha tied a twig basket to the middle and a scalp lock to the top "to give it hair." It leaned in a crotched stick and, like the Crow tree, symbolized a man, probably in phallic form. Songs were sung to it and it was anointed with grease and red paint after the summer and winter hunt. It also had its own medicine bundle.

The Crow ceremony continued with the erection of the lodge. While the lodge was still half finished, groups of warriors, one after another, danced in it in the hope of obtaining a vision. Then a chaste man made a clay bed for the Whistler within the lodge and two buffalo skulls were placed beside a cedar pole behind it.

Meanwhile buffalo tongues were being cooked for the feast and war pantomimes were carried out. Finally the Whistler and shaman went into the lodge carrying the doll. The doll was suspended from a pole so that the Whistler could concentrate on it to help him reach a trance as he danced on his clay bed. The shaman also danced and put a whistle in the Whistler's mouth. The attainment of the vision sometimes took more than one day, although by now the Whistler was weak from fasting. Meanwhile other men, who sought visions by self-torture, had also been fasting and now martyrized themselves in two ways. Some pinched the flesh of the breast muscle to- gether, slit it, put a wooden peg through and tied the peg to the lodge pole. They danced leaning back and hoping to tear the flesh. Others put skewers through the muscles of their backs, tied a number of buffalo skulls to them and dragged them about the camp. The Whistler danced on and on while famous warriors recounted their exploits. When his vision came, in which he saw himself revenging his kinsmen by killing an enemy, everyone in the lodge received a buffalo tongue, the self-torturers were freed, and a feast of buffalo tongues took place.

The tree ceremony, the use of buffalo skulls, which suggests buffalo increase rites, and the self-torture all represent accretions to the central element of attaining a vision by concentrating on a medicine doll. The buffalo skull was rationalized as contributing wakan, because it belonged to a powerful animal. In some areas the principal dancer himself underwent the torture. The dancers always remained in one place, rising on their toes with a springing motion; in some cases they took care to face the sun.

A well-known example of the vision is that obtained by Sitting Bull, himself a shaman, when he initiated a sun dance before the encounter with General Custer. In his vision he saw men with hats on falling off their horses, a symbol of victory which proved to be a true prophecy and greatly enhanced Sitting Bull's prestige.

Ceremonialism was also well developed in the eastern woodland area occupied by the tribes of the Iroquois federation. Although this group was well organized politically, practiced rather more maize, squash and corn agriculture than the Indians of the plains, and seems to have achieved a well-integrated culture, contacts between them and the Europeans began very early with the result that their customs were somewhat modified. Longhouse ceremonies were still being kept up by the Senecas, however, when William Fenton discussed them in 1936.

Iroquois festivals are all agricultural except for that at New Year, in midwinter. There was a maple sugar festival, a corn planting in May, a strawberry festival with jam made of berries and maple sugar, a green corn festival and harvest rites in October.

An archaic and interesting detail of the winter festival is the sacrifice of the white dog. This was a time of renewing visions and general purification. The ceremony was announced by the Bigheads who dressed in bear or buffalo skins with braided corn husks around their arms and legs and carried red-striped wooden pestles. (Fenton suggests that this costume unites agriculture and hunting.) The Bigheads told the householders to clean away old rubbish, not to mourn the dead but to prepare for the new year. On the first day a white dog was strangled. It was decorated with paint and wampum and hung from a pole for the next five days. On the second day the Keepers of the Faith (in a sense priests) in warrior costume visited all the houses and stirred the ashes of the hearths, giving thanks that the inmates had lived to witness the new year. On the third and fourth day dancing groups moved from house to house. Boys in false faces went about begging, preceded by an old woman with a basket. If they were refused, they had a right to steal what they could. The objects were then taken to the longhouse and if anyone wanted to redeem a particularly prized possession, he could do so by paying for it.

It should be said here that longhouses were used as dwellings as well as ceremonial centers. Somewhat like those of the northwest, they were gabled, constructed of bark laid on a frame of upright poles, and often a hundred feet long, having tiers of bunks along the sides and fireplaces down the center for different family groups.

False faces have been mentioned in connection with the second day of the New Year's celebration. Actual False-Face Societies wore masks with twisted faces. In origin they represented evil spirits to be propitiated, but had come to be medical groups. In the spring and fall they went about whisking disease spirits from under beds. Anyone in bed they routed out. The unmasked headman then collected tobacco to be used in the invocation which followed. All then went to the longhouse where the headman sang the False-Faces' song to the winds and to spirits called the thunderers.

The fourth day of the New Year ceremony was the point at which dreams were announced and people were asked to guess them. If they guessed correctly, they were asked to give an interpretation. The famous chief Cornplanter resigned his office as a result of a dream.

On the fifth day the white dog was laid on a bench in the longhouse along with baskets of offerings containing tobacco, beans, etc. A keeper walked around it chanting. The people told it their wishes and it was sent as a messenger to the creator. (The creator had an evil brother, a counterpart of the culture hero and a trickster.) The dog was laid on a bark litter, carried three times around the outside of the longhouse and ritually burned. Then there was a feast, speeches of thanksgiving were made, and the feather dance took place. In the dance headdresses with a single backward-pointing feather were worn with embroidered kilts and deer-hoof rattles around the knees. Fifteen to thirty men danced in an elliptical line around the longhouse with an intricate step, involving multiple heeltaps, accompanied by two singers with turtle-shell rattles.

The Iroquois appear to have socialized the dream experience, as is to be expected of a people with a rather highly developed political organization. Remarkably enough, even on reservations, their ancient tradition has outlasted that of Indian groups in most other areas. In the southwest of the United States, however, lives a group of tribes with a relatively long history and they, too, have preserved much of their custom and belief in spite of white men's schools and the well-meaning efforts of missionaries.

CHAPTER **39**

Dancing Gods

Pueblo Indians—agricultural tradition can be traced far back in prehistory—sedentary village life and controlled, well-organized ceremonial—golden mean and lack of ruling group—emergence myth and multiple supernaturals—masked dances and rainmaking—ceremonial buffoon as dramatic trickster—lack of emphasis on funeral rites.

IN THE southwest area of the United States an Indian people is notable for achieving a highly integrated communal way of life and indeed, in the classic Pueblo period, for having invented the apartment house. Nestling up against the walls of canyons, complicated structures of adobe and stone, with great beams supporting the roofs, consisted of hundreds of small dwelling rooms entered from the top. Most of the daily activity took place on flat roofs and open plazas, the superimposed tiers being reached by ladders. One of these apartments, it has been estimated, sheltered as many as twelve hundred people, a record not surpassed in the canyons of New York until the 1880's.

More historic continuity is glimpsed in this area than has been established elsewhere. The ancient hunters with their fluted points came first, twenty to twenty-five thousand years ago, and after them the Cochise culture around seven thousand B.C. The appearance of grinding stones and a scarcity of chipped points indicate that this people depended on gathering and grinding grain, roots, and nuts. Whether the same people developed into the Basket Makers whose earliest established date is about 217 A.D. is not definitely established but the inference is that a continuous tradition of agriculture was developing. Points similar to those few found in the Cochise culture have been recovered in Bat Cave near Magdalena, New Mexico, and with them the ears of maize which presumably was first developed in Middle America. Although the dating is uncertain, the material is probably at least as old as three or four thousand B.C., suggesting that the corn culture which is the economic base of later developments had already begun in Cochise times.

With the Basket Makers, who were great weavers, we arrive at identifiable modern Indians, for their dead, buried in blankets woven of strips of fur and yucca fiber, have been semimummified in the dry cool atmosphere of the high plateaus. This people used the spear-thrower, went on grinding corn, and made sandals of yucca fiber, a new pair of which was always placed in the grave, suggesting an idea of a journey after death. Their baskets were so tightly constructed that they could hold liquids, and no doubt could be used for cooking by putting hot stones in them.

Pottery did not appear until 700 A.D., the beginning of the Pueblo period. Influx of a new ethnic group may or may not have stimulated this important step forward. At any rate, it has been shown that the elegant geometric designs of Pueblo pottery were derived from various types of basket weave. Cotton also began to be grown. The classic Pueblo culture of the apartment houses developed about 1050 A.D. from the villages of their predecessors. Such cooperative living stimulated the growth of a highly formalized culture and a ceremonial religion which has held its ground even in the face of American technical civilization. As far back as Basket Maker times a ceremonial room (often partly underground and entered from the top) used by religious groups for meetings and rituals, and as a men's clubhouse (now called the kiva) has been found, and in the cliff dwellings it was an important architectual element. We know, therefore, that a priesthood was developing, but, judging from modern times, it never crystallized into an autocracy but was integrated into a democratic political structure.

Around 1400 A.D. the cliff dwellings were all abandoned. Although defense may have been one reason for the building of the apartment houses, it does not seem to have been the chief reason. Attacks by Navahos or Apaches are not an adequate explanation for their evacuation. Lack of water or the need to move to more fertile areas is a possible reason for the change to the adobe villages of modern times.

Ruth Benedict in her book *Patterns of Culture* has used the Pueblo area as a type of an Apollonian pattern, contrasting it to the wild Dionysian rites of the northwest. "The Zuñi are a ceremonious people who value sobriety and inoffensiveness above all other virtues. Their interest is centered upon their rich and complex ceremonial life. The cult of the masked gods, of healing, of the sun, of the sacred fetiches, of war, of the dead, are formal and established bodies of ritual with priestly officials and calendric observances. No field of activity competes with ritual for foremost place in their attention."

Status depends upon ritual possessions, and endless pains are lavished upon letter perfection of detail in magico-religious observances. In addition, the ethos of moderation and self-control is tied in with the ceremonial life, for no one who is hot-tempered, drunken, or sexually promiscuous merits a place as an official. Indeed a Pueblo officiant at a ceremony must take care to show no anger shortly before it takes place.

Modern Pueblo houses are arranged around courts which contain kivas and also are used for outdoor dances. The older houses are two-story, the more recent only one. In relation to the outside world there is considerable privacy, for there is little visiting back and forth except between related families.

Looking in through the windows is particularly frowned upon and likely to cause accusations of witchcraft. Anyone who behaves differently from the norm—a nonconformist, in short—may be accused of being a witch. This sort of accusation is obviously a release from the tensions of the ordered life and thus the community projects its concealed hostilities upon the competitive, ambitious individual, and in the past, torture was used to make him confess his evil magical practices.

The Pueblo village functions as a unit but there are also matrilineal clans. Authority is mainly vested in the heads of religious societies and priests. The latter have no civil power, however, and only the war chiefs have some executive and policing duties. On the whole, the ethos of moderation dictates that no one shall demonstrate excess individualism and hence political domination by any individual or group is ruled out.

What is the Pueblo notion of the supernatural? Curiously enough, the basic myth starts with an emergence and with no real creation of the world. Emergence from the ground is, of course, an idea which occurs in various places: we have encountered it in Africa; Malinowski records it for the Trobriand Islanders. The Hopi and Zuñi versions differ in detail. In the case of the Hopi, it all starts with a sex war. At first people lived underground as ants; and then migrated and turned into people with tails. Since the women decided they would do without the men, they went and lived on the other side of a river. The women, however, did not make a go of it. Each year they planted less and less crops. Finally when the underworld was menaced by a flood they built a tower to reach the sky which was unsuccessful. The men planted seeds which grew into plants that actually pierced the sky. In this reversed flood story they send the badger up to look around. All is dark, he can see nothing and returns. A second scout is the shrike, who has better luck. The bird encounters Masuauwu, a supernatural character, who has put aside his mask and made a fire to cook green corn. Shrike explains that people are busy killing, raping, and getting sick. Masuauwu says that if he had had his mask on he would not have let them emerge but since he is caught without it they are free to come up, which they do just in time, since the flood is reaching the underworld village. Once aboveground, various matters need arranging. Coyote is assigned the job of helping put up the stars. Some of them are put in constellations, but finally he grows lazy and merely scatters the rest all over. Coyote also decides that death shall be permanent, promptly overeats and dies—for good.

The Zuñi myth starts with an empty world in which the sun makes his journey every day but there is no one to offer him prayer sticks or sacred meal. He therefore sends his two children down below to bring up the people. In all of the emergence myths there is a subsequent elaboration involving movement of groups and episodes which rationalize ceremonies and clan matters, accretions of detail no doubt invented by priests to justify the Pueblo way of life.

The spirit world is likewise tremendously elaborate; the Zuñi distinguish over a hundred different masked gods alone. The cloud beings, residing on four sacred mountains, are identified with the cardinal points and specific colors. The northern one has attributes of yellow mask, yellow corn and yellow butterflies; the western attributes are blue, the south red, the east white. Above is the black chief with black attributes; below, the variegated one with many-colored birds, speckled corn, melons, squash and beans. The masked gods are *kachinas,* supernatural ancestors, who live in the bottom of a lake or river and come back to dance for the people. Impersonating them by putting on masks gives them pleasure, while for a time the impersonator becomes the god. There are also kachina priests who do not dance.

One function of the priests is to scare boys at initiation time by whipping them with yucca-fiber whips. On the whole such ordeals are mild, and in a second ceremony, in which slightly older boys (about fourteen) are whipped, the masks are lifted from the kachinas, placed on the boys and they are given the whips to use on the initiators. They are now told a myth of punishment in which a boy who revealed the secret was beheaded. With this they become members of the cult.

Other supernaturals are the Shalaka war chiefs who live on a mountain, the benevolent Koyemshi family, the sun, moon, stars, dawn youth, dawn girls, and corn maidens. The sun must be helped on his journey, particularly at the solstices, and sacred meal is sprinkled for him at dawn and dusk.

The war brothers of the morning star are, in one myth, told to bring the heads of seven enemies to the corn girls. Significantly enough, in all mythology headhunting is a part of warfare but in historic times the Pueblo Indians took scalps. This might indicate a line of development or the influence of the plains culture.

Animism indeed pervades the Pueblo view of life. The scalp, the ear of corn, fire stick, anything fantastic or unusual, clouds, trees, houses, pots, clothing, are endowed with life. A chief phrased it as follows: "The universe is endowed with the same breath, rocks, trees, grass, earth, all animals, all men," which is a clear formulation of mana.

In general the attitude toward the spirits is the familiar one of payment for favors such as good weather, fertility, health, longevity. Mimetic magic is much used to influence the supernaturals. Rituals are carried out by the many groups of societies which pervade the social structure. The masked gods, the war and hunting societies, the medicine groups and the clowns comprise the main divisions of ritual organization.

When a man is married and in possession of some property he undergoes the initiation of the mask. He is ritually whipped again and gives a feast for the men of his kiva. The mask becomes his and is painted to represent any kachina he chooses, being refurbished for different ceremonies. Most masks are helmet-shaped, fitting over the entire head, painted in bright colors and topped with superstructures of feathers, cotton wool, flowers, horns and the like. Masks may have ears, snouts, stuffed cotton-wool bulging eyes, or tongues. Beheaders are spotted red from their victims; warrior masks have a bear paw painted on the face. A Zuñi's mask is buried with him. Masks of kachina priests are inherited by family lines from the beginning of the world. Much ritual is associated with them. Some dances, however, are performed without masks.

In general, all groups dance quietly in a line about the open plaza or in the kiva, now and then facing about. Sometimes two groups alternate while the clowns burlesque the dance patterns. Pueblo dancing, in keeping with their ethos, is not ecstatic. Sometimes they dance for success in hunting but most often they are calling for rain or helping the corn to sprout. Even the snake dance in which rattlesnakes are held in the mouth is a sober affair (the reptile's poison sacs have been first removed).

Medicine cults are conducted by priests who are maintainers of ritual and not shamans. They do not derive their power from dreams or ecstatic experience, neither of which enters into the Pueblo ethos. They do impersonate animal spirits, however, for healing ability comes from them, among the Zuñi the bear in particular.

In hunting dances, animal masks or antlers are worn. The Hopi attitude toward eagles, which they capture young and raise for their feathers, much used in ceremonial dress, resembles hunting magic elsewhere. Animals are not destroyed or wantonly exploited just for the excitement of the chase. They are protected, entreated humbly not to become angry if killed and urged to give themselves or their young for the use of their human kinsmen. When the nests are robbed, the eagles are given gifts in exchange for their young who are then adopted into the clan. A ritual dance takes place when they are killed. The eagle's head is covered as it is strangled. After the feathers are removed, the body is taken to the eagle cemetery with prayers that it may fly home and be born again.

Ceremonies are supposed to be carried out in letter-perfect fashion and involve chants of considerable poetic interest. A rain rite involves the creation of a cornmeal picture on the floor, a cloud terrace design and eight disks. An altar is also set up. Altars are of wood, painted in designs which represent the supernaturals or symbols for rain. Sometimes figures are also painted on the wall near the altar. In the case of the rain ceremony, the rain society priest takes seed symbols from a bowl and puts them on the cloud terrace. A powdered root is whipped into suds to symbolize clouds and a bullroarer is swung to imitate thunder while an assistant plays the flute. The chant that accompanies this describes the action. It begins:

> This day
> With the flesh of white corn,
> Prayer meal commissioned with our prayer,
> This day with prayer meal
> Four times we shall spread the mist blanket.
> We shall fashion a house of massed clouds,
> We shall fashion the life-giving road.
> Four times we shall fashion your spring . . .

When the morning star rises, a bundle of prayer sticks is carried to the field of the officiant. The sticks are willow wands adorned with feathers and often tied in bundles. An assistant also goes to the field with the bullroarer. As meal is sprinkled, the prayer sticks are laid on the ground facing east.

Meanwhile singing continues in the house and offerings are laid on the altar. The suds maker gives a bowl of suds to the women present, who rub the suds on their bodies. All the other participants do the same and take a drink from the medicine bowl. Finally the altar is dismantled, everything is put away and food is served, bits of which are thrown into the fire as an offering.

Interestingly enough, the one area in which a safety valve is furnished in a carefully moderated culture of the golden mean is that of the clown dance societies. As has been said, these characters sometimes burlesque the kachinas, the most important of which ignore them; some of the more frivolous masks, however, engage in rough-and-tumble with them. In a typical performance the group came singing and drumming into the kiva wearing knobbed masks, old black dresses draped around their middles and carrying rattles. At first they burlesqued a ball game, failing to catch the ball and falling down when hit by it. Then Chevaiya entered wearing a great conical black mask which had great teeth, gray horsehair plumes, his body pink with white blotches, his legs black with white spots. He carried a handsaw with which he beat the other clowns, demanding offerings. Various things were refused, only venison was accepted. Horseplay continued in which his meat was stolen and recovered. Finally he made his exit. The clowns were then given a pot of hot food which they tried to eat through their masks, finally ending by smearing it on each other's penises and anuses. In the end the chief of the clown society got ashes from the hearth and, pulling aside their breechclouts, poured them on their penises.

In other clown dances they pretended to stick feathers up each other's anuses, denuded each other's privates or came on wearing enormous false penises.

The distribution of the ceremonial buffoon indicates that it spread either from Mexico or the Pueblo area and that the institution is typically American. The clown is always a breaker of taboos and a defiler of sacred things and blatantly phallic. The Zuñi clown may sprinkle with sand, burlesquing the sprinkling of sacred meal. The clown in the Navaho Night Chant dances out of step. The plains Indian fool speaks backward and the Maidu clown of California parodies the speeches of the shaman. It is quite obvious that the Pueblo clown dramatizes the eruption of the drives of the unconscious, held in check by a highly organized culture. As such he seems very much like a survival of the trickster, particularly in his excremental and phallic humor and in his defiance of taboo. The Aginskys record clown dances among the Pomo and, interestingly enough, in this culture which combines a moderate and controlled daily ideal with a good deal of formalization of sexual behavior, great communal ceremonies took on a wild and ecstatic character, as ghost dancers tossed hot coals about and frightened the women. The ghost dancers used reverse language like the plains clowns.

The influence of the Pueblo culture is apparent upon the Navahos, their traditional enemies and neighbors. The Navahos are an Athapascan group which at some time must have moved down from Canada, perhaps as early as 1000 A.D. They have absorbed some plains Indian traits but have chiefly borrowed from the Pueblo peoples whom their myths clearly show they regarded as wealthy and sophisticated. Originally hunters, they took up agriculture by the sixteenth century and sheep and goat herding by the eighteenth. Colors for the cardinal points, sand painting, the bullroarer and chanting all appear to be of Pueblo origin, but the Navahos concentrate their ceremonial on the chant as a part of a curative ceremony. The chants are long, poetic and repetitive, accompanied by rattles and carried out by a singer and a group of assistants; except for the Night Chant they do not involve public dancing. Thus the Navahos have adapted Pueblo practice to a less socialized way of life.

The repetitive character of Indian chants parallels the monotonous beat of the dance. Both a semitrancelike state, which takes the participant out of the everyday world, and a reassuring sense of stability, created by patterned recurrence, are evidently basic psychic solaces which religion has employed through the ages and still does today.

The Pueblo attitude toward death is consistent with the over-all structure of orderliness and decorum. Since sex and death are disturbing experiences, there is a tendency to control or avoid emotional emphasis upon them. In Pueblo mythology there is an avoidance of sex symbolism or sex as a creative power; only in the release of the clown dances does this drive break out in rampant exhibitionism. Similarly there is no orgy of grief as in some cultures. Food is taken to the grave for four days, during which time the spirit lingers. The mourner isolates himself for four days, does not speak to anyone, and takes an emetic every morning for purification. He also casts black cornmeal about him outside the village to rid himself of the destructive mana. After the four days are over, the chiefs take the personal possessions of the dead out of the village, destroy them and bury them. They return at a run, not looking behind them. The chief then tells the people not to remember the departed any more because he has been dead for four years and thus, with this deliberate falsification of time, the dangers of death are put far behind them, immediate ancestor cult is clearly ruled out, and the community returns to its golden mean.

CHAPTER 40

Butterflies and Skulls

Mexico and Guatemala—growth of agricultural tradition parallels prehistory of Pueblo area—village life and clay female figures—rise of cities and theo- cratic culture—pyramids and the early rain god—ritual ball game and human sacrifice—multiple creation myths—the figure of Quetzalcoatl—gods and the calendar—Tula and the coming of militarism—mystique of war and death— headhunting base—religion at the service of imperialism—elaborate pantheon unified by mana—sadness of life theme.

TLALOC was sometimes an individual and sometimes a class of gods. The Aztecs considered him responsible for scattering rain or hail like seed and causing vegetation to sprout and bloom. He could also produce floods and fling thunderbolts. His image or representative appeared with face painted with black rubber and spotted with amaranth seeds. He wore a cloud jacket of quilted feathers, a crown of heron feathers, a neck- lace of green stones and carried a rattle and a banner made of woven reeds.

His feast took place in the first month of the year at the temple in the great plaza of Tenochtitlán. The Tlaloc temple shared the top of the pyramid with that of Huitzilopochtli (god of war) and faced the sunset. The most important part of the festival was the mass sacrifice of children, who were brought to the temple, richly dressed, in litters adorned with feathers and flowers. They were then encouraged to dance and play before the altar of the god. Finally the priests dragged them to the sacrificial stone where their hearts were ripped out. If they wept a great deal, it was a sign there would be plenty of rain.

This aspect of Aztec life cannot be glossed over or prettified, for in Middle America where a high barbarism achieved a great style in art, litera- ture and poetry, where the science of astronomy produced a calendar, where a fairly advanced social organization made widespread commerce possible, where a spartan ethos of stoicism and self-control flourished, religion, in its later phase, was ferociously dedicated to blood and death.

The Aztecs, however, represent a late and brief flowering of a long tradi- tion of human culture and their civilization rested upon the ruins of many other great achievements. Indeed, the history of the rise of agriculture and the growth of cities is fairly complicated though recent archaeology has made great strides in piecing the story together.

As has been pointed out before, maize is the key to New World agriculture. We have already seen how it played an important role in the life of the aboriginal peoples in the southwest of the United States. The little cobs, about the size of a strawberry, found in Bat Cave, New Mexico, dating to between four and three thousand B.C., are thought to have been derived from a Middle American source. Where then did corn originate?

In the northeastern Mexican state of Tamaulipas a series of deposits has been excavated containing material from the culture of the early hunters of 10,000 B.C., topped by grinders and grinding stones, with, just above these, basketry and tiny ears of corn not unlike those of Bat Cave. These date to about 2500 B.C. Pumpkin seeds were present but evidence of beans, the third member of the basic American triad, was not found although they turned up in an equivalent stratum farther south. Still farther south, in a cave in the state of Puebla, squash seeds were found along with six tiny ears of corn which have been identified as wild maize or corn in the very first stage of domestication. These date to approximately 4000 B.C. Thus, although the precise birthplace of maize has not been pinpointed, it seems safe to say that it was somewhere in central Mexico. These early maize cultivators are believed to be very similar to the North American Basket Makers.

From the domestication of maize and the appearance of basketry, social and material evolution ran its customary course. In 1500 B.C. in southern Mexico, pottery was being made, although whether it was a local invention or introduced from elsewhere has not been established. By the first millennium B.C. little villages of adobe houses with thatched roofs were springing up in the Valley of Mexico and elsewhere. In these sites thousands of small clay figures of nude women have been found. The bare bodies are painted in black, red and white designs and the heads are adorned with modish turbans. The thighs are rather heavy but the breasts are not particularly emphasized. No other representations of gods or goddesses have been recovered from these villages and therefore the speculation arises as to whether these little figures (which remind us of the Near East and Indus Valley pre-urban days) are the remains of a household cult involving the worship of an earth mother. As we have seen, a goddess associated with vegetable fertility did arise in the Middle East. We have also seen in the rice child and rice mother of the Malays, one case among contemporary preliterates in which vegetable fertility was feminized. We have also seen that it is dangerous to attribute much abstract thinking to early cultures. In later eras of Mexican religion there was a young maize mother who may or may not be a survival of the early cult. In any case, this type of goddess never became dominant, as in the Near East and the Mediterranean, but was merely one spirit among many. In fact, male corn gods are common in later cultures.

Even in this early formative period there are indications of a surplus. Shells, jade, turquoise and pots are exported. From one of the villages of Mexico Valley, Tlatilco, come figures of men with masks over their faces. They are dressed in cloaks and hats and wear anklets and bracelets. In all probability they are priests, and thus usher in a period which has been conveniently named the Theocratic by Eric Wolf.

The rise of organized religion and priest rulers in about 900 B.C. is most clearly indicated by a style, called the Olmec, which spread from sites in the southeast coast as far north as the Valley of Mexico and as far south as Costa Rica.

The great Olmec centers are at La Venta in Tabasco on the southern gulf coast and at Tres Zapotes near Veracruz. La Venta contained a large clay pyramid, oblong and circular mounts, walls of adobe brick marking out a plaza in which were various stone monuments. Different colored clays were used in these constructions which were also painted red, yellow and purple. Especially remarkable are eight-and-a-half-foot stone heads with curiously fleshy features and stelae with carved reliefs. The hallmark of Olmec religious art is carved jade and a strange Oriental-looking baby whose face is half that of a jaguar, the mouth being built out into that of a carnivore's, the lips drawn back in a snarl from the great canine teeth. This marks the beginning of the jaguar symbol which appears so frequently in both Middle and South American cultures. The Olmec artists carved the jaguar on ceremonial axes and altars; teeth, spots and claws are found on pottery, earplugs and masks; jaguar skins were worn and jaguar designs tattooed on faces.

What was the significance of the jaguar religion? On the basis of a relief showing a jaguar copulating with a woman, there must have been an archaic (and probably totemistic) myth in which baby half-human jaguars were born from this union. They may have been heavenly rain spirits, since later on in history they become associated with the various manifestations of Tlaloc, the Aztec rain god. The child sacrifice, mentioned in the beginning of the chapter, might have some remote connection with the rain-cherub jaguar. On the other hand, Eric Wolf points out that Tlaloc possesses the heart of the land. Thus he would see the jaguar-cherub as a symbol of domination over the orifices of the earth. It is possible that the Olmecs spoke a Mayan language. The jaguar is also an important ceremonial symbol among the Mayas and in the Chavín culture of the Peruvian highlands.

In connection with Chavín, there is also a tie-up with the most important early town in the Valley of Mexico, Tlatilco. Here there are evidences of a stratified society around 800 B.C. Olmec artifacts are common and also pottery with stirrup-shaped spouts and such decorative techniques as rocker stamping. Since the latter traits appear in Chavín, along with an improved variety of maize, there is a strong supposition that Mexicans spread elements of this culture to South America.

Because there is relatively little indication of warfare or coercion in the art of the Theocratic period, it is believed that the sanctions of religion were strong enough to unite the labor force for the building of huge pyramids and cathedral cities which now began to rise toward the sky. The leading figure in all representation was the religious specialist, the full-time servant of the gods who mediated between the supernatural powers and ordinary men. Although slash-and-burn agriculture predominated and cooperative techniques of irrigation do not appear until later, somehow the priests were able to unite a scattered population for ceremonial observances. There is, of course, a strong parallel with early Sumeria, but the inhabitants of the cathedral cities of the Near East were organized both for warfare and for irrigation projects. It is also pointed out that the residential areas near the American centers were relatively small, housing only the religious elite with their retainers, while the peasant farmers who made up the bulk of the population were scattered in small hamlets throughout the countryside. The great markets, however, were undoubtedly held in the plazas of the temple complexes and thus when the populace was united for both religious and commercial activities, administrative control could have been exercised and tithes exacted. Eventually, too, it was the religious calendar worked out by the priest which combined mythology with the proper dates for harvesting and planting.

The Olmec culture spread, perhaps through missionary effort (some warriors are shown fighting with clubs but no war on a large scale), not only to the south where it stimulated early Mayan civilization but also westward to the state of Oaxaca where the earliest monuments of Monte Alban reflect Olmec style. Number symbols found on La Venta monuments may well be the basis of Mayan dating. On Monte Alban stelae, numbers also appear and what are probably the oldest symbols for phonetic elements. It is quite possible that the interest in measuring time, which dominated all American cultures, originated in the Olmec heartland.

From 300 to 900 A.D. occurs the real flowering of the Theocratic period in which the cathedral cities flourished all over Middle America. On the gulf coast at Tajín, at Cholula, Monte Alban, in the rain forests of Guatemala, at Tikal and Uaxactún, pottery styles, murals, pyramids, all testify to the sophistication of an elite. Greatest of all and a dominant influence upon the areas near it was Teotihuacán, twenty-five miles north of Mexico City. Probably the largest settlement in Middle America, by 650 A.D. it covered two thousand acres.

The largest pyramid, that of the Sun, is 689 feet square and 210 feet high. This, together with the slightly smaller Pyramid of the Moon, dominated a long avenue, flanked by a grid of streets along which were built temples and civic buildings. An underground drainage system led from the main avenue to the nearby river. There were numerous plazas, large and small, which indicate that the city was divided into districts, each with its market and religious center. The discovery of a complex of 176 rooms with many forecourts and five courtyards shows that this was a true city with living quarters for traders, artisans and other nonagricultural specialists. In the porticoes and on the interior walls were elaborate frescoes. Feathered serpents, shells, and abstract symbols of divinity were sculptured in stone on cornices and façades.

The Teotihuacán influence was dominant in Cholula, in the early art of Tajín near Veracruz, in Kaminaljuyú in Guatemala, and to a lesser degree in Monte Alban. Pyramids were broad and massive, the temple at the top an impermanent thatched hut. In contrast, the Mayan pyramids were tall, narrow and topped with a stone hut with a dark, mysterious interior surmounted by an elaborate comblike decoration on the roof. Teotihuacán decoration tended toward formalized sculpture with reliefs in the space between the areas. The painted reliefs, however, like the sculptured and painted murals of the Mayans, were focused on figures whose outlines were blurred by an excessive exaggeration of symbolic attire. Mayan relief often becomes a snakelike riot of sinuous curves made up of headdress, scepter, breechclout, sandals and necklace. Mayan frescoes and carvings, however, often achieved amazingly flexible use of foreshortening and expressive gesture, while the Mexican style tended to be stiffer and more primitive in feeling.

A series of gods had crystallized along with this artistic and social development. Most important in Teotihuacán was the rain god eventually called, in Nahuatl, Tlaloc, among the Zapotecs, Cocijo, and in the Mayan area, Chac. The extravagant interest in symbolic detail which runs through Middle American art is here well exemplified in the shifting elements which appear in the likeness of this god. A broad band for an upper lip and sometimes the wide cheek and teeth connect him to the jaguar and perhaps to the Olmec animal rain-cherub. His left hand, too, sometimes appears as a jaguar claw. A long cleft tongue lolls from his mouth; a serpent helmet is worn by his priests who march in a procession on the friezes of Teotihuacán; a plumed serpent appears among his servants and a serpent borders the great mural in the palace of Tepantitla. The wide circle around the eye which sometimes appears and the use of an owl as a pectoral decoration, also connect the rain god with this animal. Finally the god's face sometimes acquires the wings of a butterfly and formalized antennae. This, in turn, ties up with the butterflies with whom the spirits of the dead play in a Teotihuacán palace mural representing a joyous land of the dead equivalent to the Aztec Tlalocan. A dry bough was placed at burial on the tomb of one who had been chosen by the rain god or who had died of certain diseases, or by accident in water, or struck by lightning. On reaching the otherworld the dry bough became green, indicating that in the place of abundance he acquired new life. After intoning a long song of thanks to the god above, indicated by two speech plumes at the mouth of the figure in the mural, he joined his companions to enjoy a life of eternal happiness spent reposing beneath the trees heavy with fruit on the banks of the rivers of Paradise or he submerged in the waters of the lagoons far beyond death and passed the time singing with his companions and sharing their games.

The Theocratic rain god was a far more important figure than his descendant. At Teotihuacán, by association with the jaguar, he represented the lord of the earth. He stood for vegetation and general abundance. He also wore a headdress of quetzal feathers which seem to connect him with the plumed serpent, Quetzalcoatl. It is probable, however, that Quetzalcoatl, the culture-hero-creator god, had not yet crystallized as a separate entity. The ancient rain serpent is an image of the clouds full of water, an image which exists among the Huichols of Nayarit to this day. The Mexican landscape indeed drives home the importance of rain rituals. Fields of dry yellow grass, empty dusty streambeds, arid stony hills, all show clearly that need for water shaped some of the basic tensions of the Middle Americans.

A fire god, however, has definitely been identified. His image is that of a naked old man upholding a brazier. A similar image has even been found in the Olmec sites and continued to be worshiped by the Aztecs, who called him Huehueteotl. He, too, has survived among the Huichols.

There is evidence of sacrifice of children to the Teotihuacán rain god and also skeletons have been found buried under the cornerstones of buildings in this site. This appears to be the extent of human sacrifice at Teotihuacán. As we shall see, it was not absent elsewhere in the Theocratic period but it never assumed the proportions it did among the later Militaristic peoples.

A maize god of the Theocratic period at Monte Alban was called Pitao Cosobi. He was incarnated in the largest and finest maize ear of the harvest. The ear was finally buried in the field on a small altar in order to promote the next harvest.

The Zapotecs of Monte Alban were accustomed to bury clay urns ornamented with figures of deities, surmounted with their characteristic headdresses, in tombs. Cosobi is identified by ears of corn in his headdress; the feathered serpent also appears, as well as a bat god and the ancient fire god.

In the Veracruz area certain other elements strike a grimmer note in Theocratic religion. At Tajín (which is the local name for the rain god) very extensive ruins, including a niched pyramid, palaces, and other structures, are scattered over thousands of acres. Here, judging from the elaborate reliefs in stone, there was a preoccupation with the death god, human sacrifice, and the ritual ball game. There were no less than seven courts where the game was played, and on their walls are portrayed ceremonies which were connected with it.

We have fragmentary testimony from Spanish chroniclers, Mayan, and Aztec documents which tell us something about this sport and show clearly how every department of life was infused with theological ideas. The rules appear to have differed in various regions, but basically the game was a sort of cross between soccer and basketball, played with a heavy solid rubber ball. The court was H-shaped, the bar of the H being the playing area, flanked top and bottom by two slanting mortar buffers, while the corners of the upstrokes of the letter were foul areas. In some cases scoring was a matter of driving the ball over a center line, in other courts there were stone rings on the walls through which the ball was bounced. The ball could only be struck with the elbow, hip, or knee. Since it was heavy, the players wore a stuffed leather glove on the left hand (on which they supported themselves when they crouched to receive the ball) and also a stuffed leather girdle and projecting loin guard, and a kneepad. These may be clearly seen in the Tajín reliefs. It was a violent game, producing such bruises on the hips of the players that the skin had to be lanced to release the blood. The ball court was really a temple, the ball symbolizing the course of the sun, moon, or firmament. Ballplayers were warriors. One panel of a ball court frieze shows a young warrior-player facing priests as if in an initiation ceremony. In another, however, a ballplayer is having his heart cut out by other figures in athletic dress. Above, the death god, with a skull head, is descending like a rocket, while at the side another skulled figure is arising from an urn. A Spanish chronicler wrote: "The ball courts were enclosed with splendid walls well-fashioned and with the ground smoothly cemented and with many paintings of the figures of idols and demons to whom the game was dedicated and whom the players considered to be the judges of this exercise." We also know that in later times the players prayed before a ball game; the glove and hip guards were hung up on a pole and the ball placed on a plate before the altar. Stakes ran high; precious stones and ornamental feathers and human lives were wagered, and tradition speaks of a Militaristic king who even put up his kingdom. Aztec custom demanded a human sacrifice at the ball court during the New Fire ceremony. The Tajín sacrificial scene might mean the losing captain was offered up to the god-referees. In the Quiche-Mayan myth of the heroic twins, one of them is magically beheaded in the underworld and his head is hung up on the ball court. It is quite possible that in early times the head of a victim in trophy headhunting may have been replaced by a symbolic ball and the ideas of sexual potency derived from it transformed into other concepts, such as that of a sun symbol, to fit later theology elaborations. If the two teams were thought of as opposing armies, the death of the defeated leader re-affirmed the original triumphant headhunting concept. At any rate, sacrifice by removing the victim's heart had already begun in Mexican Theocratic culture.

Along the Usamacinta River in the rain forests of Guatemala, and in southern Mexico, Theocratic culture among the Mayan-speaking peoples reached a high point in the calendric and mathematical achievements embodied in great stone stelae, or time markers, set up with solemn ceremonies in the plazas of the religious centers. The Maya had reached the point of making books of folded bark paper in which they recorded their sacred astronomical and mathematical sciences (they were unique in developing the concept of zero), history, and mythology in hieroglyphic signs. Although the un-anthropologically minded Bishop Diego Landa burned most of these, a few documents written in Spanish characters after the conquest provided glimpses of a rich mythology.

The Quiche, whose account of creation has been preserved in a post-conquest document, were a conquering group of militarists but there is no doubt that their mythology includes much of the ideology of the Theocratic heritage. It begins with a majesty which parallels the poetry of the Near East.

> This is the story of how all was in suspension, all was calm, silent, motionless, hushed and the spread of the sky was empty. . . .
> There was nothing nearby which made a sound, not a thing that moved, nor shook, nor any noise in the sky.
> There was nothing that stood up, only the sleeping water, the peaceful sea, lonely and tranquil. Nothing was endowed with existence.

Then follows an account of multiple creation, a concept widespread in Middle America. Two gods, Tepeu and Gucumatz (the Quiche form of Quetzalcoatl), began the work.

> Let it be so! Let space be filled. Let the water retire and empty out, let the earth arise and establish itself. So they spoke. Let there be light, let there be dawn in the sky and on the earth. There will be no glory or greatness in our creation, and our shaping until human beings exist, man fully formed.

Animals were at first created but they could only shriek and screech. The creators said to each other that it was not well, for the animals could not speak the name of their creators. The first men were then made of earth but they could not move or speak and understood nothing. They melted away in water. After a consultation among all the gods (we are now aware that there are many more than two) the shapers made a second type of man out of wood. These wandered about on all fours and had no understanding. This failure was destroyed by a flood of black rain day and night and by a revolt of the rest of the world, wild animals, domestic dogs, pots and even grinding stones. The dogs accused men of ill-treating them and fattening them for food, and the pots complained of being burned over the fire. Only a few of these men escaped to become monkeys. After a new consultation a third creation took place.

> And they went on discussing the creation and shaping of our first mother and father; of yellow maize and of white maize they made his flesh, of maize dough they made the arms and legs of man. Only maize entered into the flesh of our first fathers.

With unerring lyrical acumen the ancient Mayan poets selected the basis of their civilization as the proper stuff of which to make the human race.

Another concept which is basic in Theocratic religion is that of the group god. Chac, the rain god who is portrayed as long-nosed with a serpent upper lip and sometimes the body of a snake, is both one god and four, one for each cardinal point, each assigned to a color, north—white, south—yellow, east—red, north—black. (Although the colors are not the same, the concept is similar to that of the Pueblo Indians and, also, as will be remembered, to Shang rain mythology.) Nearly as important as the Chacs were the four-in-one-person Itzamnas who were the sons of the creator and seem to have been the rain gods of the priestly elite while the Chacs were firmly embedded in peasant belief.

The maize god was represented as an idealized youth with a corn-plant headdress. He was at the mercy of Mayan dualism; Chac was favorable to him while Ah Puch, the skull-headed death god, was his enemy. One of the strangest members of the pantheon was a goddess of suicide represented as a woman hanging by a rope around her neck. Suicide was respectable among the Maya; those who killed themselves went straight to bliss.

Theological elaboration had a paradoxical effect, according to Eric Thompson. "The creator god was assigned so many names and attributes that definite confusion ensued and there seems little doubt that the layman who worshiped him under one name failed to realize that he was also worshiped under a different name. . . . Therefore, whereas the rank and file had still a firm belief in a large and possibly increasing number of deities, the religious thinker may have progressed forward toward the goal of monotheism." There is a strong parallel here with the Egyptian situation and in the case of the Aztec religion, which we shall discuss later, the parallel is even stronger.

Of course, as elsewhere, a multitude of gods and a calendar go hand in hand, for the calendar was used to appoint the time for the many festivals, and reciprocally, specific gods presided over months and days, and their heads were even used as numerals in one method of counting. In fact, the nine gods of the underworlds, whose name symbols stood for days, were also a single collective god, and similarly the thirteen gods of the upper worlds, who were the patrons and names of twenty-year periods, were also thought of as a collective entity. At the same time the basic accuracy of the calendar, so necessary in order that agricultural undertakings should occur at the right time, was taken care of by correcting the 365-day count with a second system of counting more accurate than our own addition of one day to February every four years.

Copán, in Honduras, was the center of the Mayan scientific world toward the end of the seventh century A.D. when this correction was worked out. Two altars commemorate a meeting of the priestly academy of sciences. Since one of the figures wears the ceremonial headdress of the Bat People of Chiapas, Eric Thompson suggests that the assembled calendric priests may have gathered in a kind of National Congress of Astronomers from all of the Mayan region.

The religion which stimulated this mathematical scholarship also demanded the pain and cruelty of human sacrifice and self-torture. The excision-of-the-heart ceremony began with the stripping of the victim who was painted blue. Four Chac priests, also painted blue, wounded him in the sexual parts and smeared the blood on the face of the idol to whom the victim was being offered. The four then stretched him backward over a special altar stone while the *nacom* ripped open his breast with a flint knife, reached in and pulled out the throbbing heart and handed it to another priest who smeared its blood on the idol. The body was then skinned by priests of lower rank; the head priest stripped, dressed in the bloody skin, and danced with the spectators. If the victim had been a brave warrior, his body was divided and eaten by important persons present. It was this fate which overtook the first Spaniards who went ashore at Yucatán and were captured by the Maya. Another form of sacrifice, imported from central Mexico, consisted of tying the victim to a stake while the priests, after having first danced with him, then danced around him shooting arrows into a bull's-eye marked on his chest. Fasting and sexual taboos were observed by priests before festivals. Individual penance also consisted of such self-torture as pulling a cord studded with thorn through the tongue. When frightened by illness, the Mayan penitent also confessed his transgressions.

The culture of the Theocratic period was therefore a remarkably rich synthesis in which early science went hand in hand with theology regulating an agricultural civilization, the symbols of this synthesis finding expression in stone, paint, and poetry. It must be remembered, however, that the magical point of view survived; the people of this world were convinced that the universal order which they had detected was preserved by the human mind and will, by use of the correct formulas, by the propitiation and coercion of supernatural powers. To what excesses this led we shall presently see.

There may have been an inherent weakness in Theocratic control which accounted for the sudden, swift and unexplained revolution which came about toward the end of the first millennium A.D. We know that the Mayan forest religious centers were abandoned, although peasants continued to live in their vicinity. Teotihuacán was burned around 800 A.D.; the tombs and temples of Monte Alban were deserted about the same time. Tajín died around 1200 A.D. In some cases, such as that of Copán, Honduras, the priests seem to have simply packed up and left. In other Mayan sites there are some signs of violence. The theory of peasant revolt against the privileged theocratic elite has been suggested but nowhere else in the world do we find evidence of ancient revolt against supernatural authority. Scarcity of water or exhaustion of the soil by slash-and-burn agriculture is another suggestion but, again in the case of Copán, this city was located in an inexhaustibly fertile valley.

If the transition period poses unresolved problems, we do know that a shift in emphasis took place from the priest to the warrior or warrior-priest, supernatural power was superseded or reinforced by violent military domination. And, as so often in history, change in cultural development was accompanied by the movements of peoples.

Two peoples are associated with the rise of Militarist civilization, the Toltecs and the Aztecs. Much of the traditional material which has been preserved from Aztec sources is basically Toltec and indeed efforts were made by many groups to identify themselves with the Toltecs as the most cultured and important people of the period.

Concerning the Toltecs there has, until recent decades, been a basic confusion in archaeological thinking; they were said to come from a paradisal Tollan which was thought to be Teotihuacán. More accurate dating and further excavation has revealed that Tollan was probably Tula, fifty miles north of Mexico, where pyramids, temples and ball courts exemplify a different style and a different mentality from that of the Theocratic era.

In the north, stelae carved bleakly in the form of grim warriors, with spear-throwers and swords, adorn the top of the great Tulan pyramid, and around the sides are friezes of jaguars, coyotes, and eagles consuming the hearts of men. Fortified cities appeared in the north and spread to other parts of Mexico, and eventually many bands of Toltecs and pseudo-Toltecs (who used the name to legitimate their claim to power) founded new towns in the Valley of Mexico.

Apparently the northern people, originally nomads, took to irrigation, which may have helped create a tighter political organization. At the same time border fighting was carried on with the less civilized hunting people who, in turn, were at times absorbed into the more urban culture, just as the Germans fell under Roman influence.

The Toltec warrior ethos was not forged without a struggle, however; apparently the priest and kingly warrior were at odds when a certain priest of Quetzalcoatl who sought the throne of Tula was driven out about 987 A.D., because he opposed human sacrifice. Beautiful and fantastic mythology records the magical exploits of this priest-leader who himself was eventually identified with the feathered-serpent supernatural culture hero and, in one version of the story, set fire to himself, rose from his ashes as a bird, and became the morning star. In another version (the one which disturbed Moctezuma when the Spaniards arrived) he set off with his followers on a raft of serpents toward the east, from whence he was one day to return.

That this leader was a historical personage is indicated by Mayan accounts of the arrival of a Mexican conqueror named Feathered Serpent in 987 A.D., and by the spread of Mexican traits and feathered serpent worship in Yucatán.

At any rate, a couple of hundred years after the triumph of the military and the intensification of mass human sacrifice among the Toltecs, the border barbarians (whom they called Chichemecs) became too much for them. Tula fell and the last legitimate king migrated to the Valley of Mexico where he set up a new capital.

Other bands of northern immigrants settled on Cholula, and some even penetrated to Nicaragua. One lowly band of marauders, who were called the Mexica, arrived in the Valley of Mexico only to be driven into a miserable swamp. At their lowest ebb they were reduced to serfs by other peoples and lived on snakes and vermin. By a series of raids, clever alliances and finally all-out conquest, in a few hundred years they managed to consolidate all the small aggressive military kingdoms in the vicinity until, in the fifteenth century, under an able king with an intellectual prime minister, they manufactured a divine mission of conquest, a mystical military ethos, which carried them to power over the major area of Middle America. These people were the Aztecs of history. Not Toltecs themselves, although they spoke the same language (they probably came from an undistinguished northwestern region), they admired Toltec culture and appropriated it rather as the Romans absorbed the heritage of the Greeks. Tenochtitlán, the metropolis which was to succeed Teotihuacán, was founded in 1325 A.D. in the Valley of Mexico; today it is Mexico City.

One of the first Franciscan friars to arrive after the conquest in 1529 was Bernardino de Sahagún. A member of the liberal group which had felt the breath of the Reformation, unlike Bishop Landa, he was an anthropologist hundreds of years ahead of his time. A fine linguist, he learned Nahuatl and set up a school for the children of the Aztec nobility. He also realized that in order to decide how best to adapt the natives to Christian society it was first necessary to know all that could be found out about their culture. Sahagún set his pupils to copying out Aztec books and also interviewed educated members of the native community, taking down their statements in their own tongue. So advanced was his critical sense that he recorded different accounts of the same matters from various areas. All this material was sent home to Spain, the whole being pulled together in his Spanish résumé of the history of the Indies.

Thanks to Sahagún, therefore, we have a good deal of Nahuatl literature as well as firsthand accounts of how ancient Mexican civilization functioned. It must be remembered that the Aztecs had absorbed remnants of the Theocratic heritage as well as the achievements of the Toltecs and added to this their own, especially violent, contribution.

We have seen that the concept of multiple creation already existed in the Theocratic era. According to the Nahuatl version, there were a series of ages each with a sun. The men of the first sun, which was a water sun, were made of ashes, and with the destruction of the sun turned into fish. The second sun was a tiger sun and with its destruction tigers ate men. The sign of the third was fire. Consequently it rained fire and the people of that decade were burned up. The sign of the fourth sun was wind; everything was carried away by great winds and the people of this creation turned into monkeys. In the era of the fifth sun, whose sign was movement (its destruction would be through earthquakes) Quetzalcoatl went into the underworld to rescue the precious bones of the dead for a fifth creation aided by his guardian spirit, or nahual. When the lord of the dead learned what the hero wished, he said:

> Very well, you must sound my shell-trumpet.
> And walk four times around my precious circle.
> But there were no holes in his shell-trumpet.
> Then he [Quetzalcoatl] called the worms
> And they made holes for him
> And then the drones and the bees entered
> And made it sound.

Other magical trials were overcome until finally Quetzalcoatl obtained the bones, ground them to powder and sprinkled them with blood from his phallus, another example of phallic magic. (Causing the male member, the tongue, or the ears to bleed by wounding them with thorns was also the Aztec form of penance.) Thus the men who were last created were called those-who-merit-by-penance. The fifth sun and moon did not move, however. All the gods gathered and took counsel.

> How shall we live if the sun does not move?
> How indeed shall we keep people alive?
> So that, by means of us, the sun shall be
>   strengthened
> We must sacrifice ourselves; we must all die.

The sacrifice took place at Teotihuacán, which shows that the ancient city was considered a sacred spot by the Aztecs. In actual practice the rationale of penance and sacrifice was extended to mean that human beings must be offered up to all the gods continually to keep the sun moving. (Curiously enough the Hopi creation myth also stated that the sun would not move until death came to mankind.)

The ethos of sacrifice was basic in the warlike Aztec culture. The mystical notion that magic and coercion practiced by men was necessary to maintain the rhythm of the universe was expressed in poetic form, in which the field of battle was compared to a field of flowers. The warrior called his captive "beloved son" while the captive referred to the victor as "my venerated father." Either side was prepared to die without protest because most of the Militaristic people subscribed to the same religious ideals.

Festivals which required human victims took place every month. The toll rose to thousands yearly. Twenty thousand were offered up when the great Tenochtitlán temples were founded. In many barbaric groups we have seen that human sacrifice and sati burial were occasionally practiced, but no people has been so obsessed with death as the Aztecs. No doubt a national insecurity was fostered by their humble origins and an ethos which raised voluntary death to the plane of martyrdom was consistent and necessary for an imperialist way of life. Poetry and practicality go hand in hand. The basis of the theological edifice is clearly revealed by the head rack, a structure on which the severed heads of captives were set up and displayed, hundreds of them, in the great square of Tenochtitlán. Thus, although among the Aztecs ideals of sexual purity and continence were stressed with truly Spartan insistence, the fundamentally disturbed sexual drive of head-hunting was elaborated into a monstrous social cancer. Along with noble ideals, philosophical dignity, a lyrical delight in flowers and butterflies, went a bondage to grotesque ideas of the supernatural which seem horrifying to the modern sensibility.

Yet the humane impulses were not wholly lacking in Mexican civilization. The myth of the founding of Tenochtitlán states that Aztecs were told by a prophecy to choose the spot where an eagle was seen devouring a serpent. Now the eagle is the symbol of the sun, shown eating human hearts on the Tula pyramid, and was also to become an order of dedicated warriors, while the serpent was associated with the ancient rain and soil worship. The serpent wears feathers and is called Quetzalcoatl. Around this concept center the most enlightened ideas of Middle America.

The history of Quetzalcoatl reveals that this deity is a complex of different elements. We have already encountered him as a creator in the Aztec mythology. He was also revered by them as a culture hero, the inventor of maize, the calendar, and other arts of civilization, and is associated with Venus, the morning and evening star. The Jaliscans conceived of a fire serpent who, when he put on the feathers of the quetzal bird, symbolized the drought of the land being overcome by reviving vegetation. This visual concept appears to have existed in the rain and vegetation religion throughout the Theocratic period; the feathered serpent is found all over Middle America. Where, then, does the humane inventor and creator come from? Using the analogy of another culture hero in Peru, Viracocha, Pedro Armillas suggests that a historical individual was raised to hero status and finally to the rank of deity. In his opinion, a priest of the Teotihuacán rain god might have played this role. It would be easy for him to thus assume the visual symbol of the older god.

Still another element remains to be accounted for, the historical leader who stemmed from Tula. A fresco on the rocks facing the city shows an elaborately dressed individual accompanied by a feathered serpent. Glyphs identify him as Topiltzin Quetzalcoatl. Apparently the priesthood of the culture hero took his name and real individuals therefore played a part in history carrying with them his humane religion and opposing human sacrifice. That the feathered serpent god contained perhaps the germs of monotheism is suggested by the song:

> They were concerned with the affairs of the gods
> They had only one god;
> They invoked him,
> They supplicated him.
> His name was Quetzalcoatl....
>
> This single god,
> Quetzalcoatl is his name,
> Asks for nothing

Save serpents, save butterflies
Which you must offer him,
Which you must sacrifice to him.

It was certainly the influence of this cult which inspired the Toltec poet-king of Texcoco, Hungry Coyote, to set up his own monotheistic god and disavow human sacrifice. Allied with the Aztecs, his state was eventually dominated by them; the eagle devoured the serpent; the skull replaced the butterfly.

The Aztecs were hospitable to a multitudinous pantheon which contained Tezcatlipoca, a warrior god of Tula (the mythical enemy of Quetzalcoatl), a lady of the waters, a corn goddess, Tlaloc, a Filth Eater earth goddess, a wind god who was often blended with Quetzalcoatl, a god of flowers and love. Their own contribution was eventually gods for almost everything. Their national deity was Hummingbird-on-the-Left, Huitzilopochtli, the sun god who lived upon the blood of the victims whose hearts were torn out in his honor.

Attempts were evidently made by the theologians to bring some order into this crowd of supernaturals. At the head of the pantheon were a Lord and Lady of Two symbolizing an abstract sense of origin or creation and not actively worshiped, though their dual creative power was associated with Quetzalcoatl in terms of Venus as both morning and evening star. The warlike Tezcatlipoca was turned into a group god; in his own person he was the black god of the north; as Huitzilopochtli he was the blue god of the south and as red god of the west he was merged with Xipe Totec, the deity who symbolized the rebirth of vegetation by putting on the flayed skin of a captive.

The term *teotl* seems to apply to the supernatural in general and has pretty much the significance of mana. The group god concept strengthens this theory. Thus, as in Egypt, the sense of general supernatural power no doubt made possible the permutations and combinations by which the priests were able to equate one god with another and thus create a kind of continuity in multiplicity.

Interestingly enough, we have survivals of ancient hunting magic but translated into the typical Aztec forms. In the ceremony to promote deer hunting, the usual captives were the victims. "They cut their ears, squeezed out their blood, smeared their forehead with it. They said, 'They deer-blood tap themselves; they fasted for the deer in order that they might be hunted.' " At the end of the rite four captives were taken to the foot of the pyramid. Their hands and feet were then tied and four priests carried each up, face upward, head hanging down toward the ground. At the sacrificial stone they were killed in the usual manner with the rationale: " 'In this way they die like deer. They imitate deer as they die.' "

Most official holidays were celebrated with dancing and solemn processions ending with the same grim rite at the top of the pyramid. Priests, who let their hair hang long and clotted with blood, were trained in special schools which required fasting and sexual abstinence. Warriors were educated in their own institutions and the social structure was sufficiently democratic so that gifted members of the lower classes were also allowed to attend these schools which were compulsory for the nobility. Thus the warrior-priest elite carried on a tradition of mythology, art, poetry, and the science of astronomy upon which the Aztec calendar was based.

Aside from the rulers, this stratified society included heads of lineages which had developed out of clans, the order of Eagle Knights of Huitzilopochtli, and Ocelot Knights of Tezcatlipoca, and a merchant class with its own aristocracy and religious observances which seem to indicate that it was of a different ethnic group. It was the merchants who carried on the trade which filled the markets with luxuries such as precious stones, goldwork, fine ceramics and feather-embroidered garments.

At the bottom of the pyramid were the slaves, largely people so poor they were obliged to sell themselves into service, or criminals who had to serve those whom they had injured, plus a few female servants captured in war. Such slavery was not hereditary and the slaves themselves could hold property and maintain their families. They were, of course, condemned to do the menial labor.

A festival, described by Sahagún, the Eating of Tamales, was carried on by just such people and is a refreshing contrast to the official calendric shedding of blood.

Tamales stuffed with green vegetables were made by the women everywhere and were offered by them in the local tribal temple. Then the whole family sat down to eat after having offered five in a wooden vessel to the fire, perhaps the ancient god of earlier ages. A few more were offered to their dead. Then they ate the hot tamales, "sweating, burning themselves with the hot food, enveloped in steam, sucking and gulping the food and smearing it upon their lips."

At the opposite end of the scale there were some thinkers who were overcome by the sadness of life, as happens in all sophisticated civilizations. They doubted, and for them the mystique of self-immolation was not the answer to everything.

> We only came to sleep,
> We only came to dream,
> It is not true, not, it is not true
> That we came to live upon earth.

We are changed into the spring grass;
Our hearts will grow green again
And they will open their petals,
But our body is like a rose tree,
It puts forth flowers and then withers.

True believers could rely on some promise of continued existence. The majority of the people passed to the underworld where they had to overcome many dangers. The dead man was buried with amulets and valuable objects to appease the death god and to pass through the nine hells, including mountains which could crush the journeying dead, snakes and alligators that ate hearts, wind that hurled stones and obsidian knives; and sometimes a little red dog buried with him carried him on the last part of the journey. Life in Mictlan was a shadowy one like that of the Greek Hades. There were also twelve heavens above, presided over by various gods, to which more privileged persons went. Most poetic of all was the equating of the now legendary Teotihuacán with a promise of eternal life, perhaps a memory of the paradise of the rain god.

And they called it Teotihuacán
Because it was the place
Where the lords were buried
And they used to say
"When we die
We shall not truly die
Because we live, we are resurrected.
This makes us happy...."

In this legendary place the gods said to them:

"Awake, the sky is already reddening,
Already it is dawn
And pheasants the color of flame are singing,
And swallows the color of fire,
And already butterflies are soaring."

CHAPTER 41

Jaguar in the Sky

The Andes—discovery of ancient hunting culture in the Andes—growth of villages on the coast—Theocratic culture with animal symbolism in the Andes and coast—temples, rain gods and pyramids—spread of feline god throughout Peru—sculpture of San Augustín and trophy heads—pyramids and feline god in coastal kingdom of the north—fish god in south and funeral cults—sexuality and fertility religion in Chimú empire—the Tiahuanaco deity spreads to coast—Inca empire and sun worship—religion at the service of imperialist power—Viracocha, culture hero similar to Quetzalcoatl—worship of local spirits, by the masses, and mana.

THE NORTHWESTERN area of South America, the site of the other great ancient civilization in the New World, is a region of extraordinary contrasts. From Peru to well down the coast of Chile a strip of desert lies between the coast and the Andes in which nothing can survive except in the occasional valleys of rivers supplied by the sierra rains and ice caps. In the north every seven years or so a change in the warm Humboldt Current causes an exceptional rain, a destructive torrent which produces a temporary increase in vegetation, but to the south there has not been a drop of rain for thousands of years and the hot, steely sand supports nothing but a faint sprinkling of tiny grasses. Here a footprint made centuries B.C. can remain undisturbed until today. On the intercontinental highway which traverses this desert the traveler can drive for hours or days without meeting a soul except in the oases of the river valleys. And everywhere there is dust.

A few miles up into the cordilleras there are fertile valleys and wooded *faldas* (small plateaus) which support agriculture since there is a winter rainy season. Here the temperature ranges from hot to chilly, all in one day. At 10,000 feet the great plateaus of the altiplano of Peru and Bolivia which surround Lake Titicaca are cool, dry, treeless, the plains covered with dry, spiny ichu grass. And everywhere there is dust.

Once over the often snow-covered crest of the Andes, the western slopes rapidly become thick with verdure and increasingly tropical. There the forest-outpost city of the Incas, Machu Picchu, hangs over a steamy ravine through which flows the Riobamba whose waters eventually reach the Amazon.

Unlike the plateaus and less steep mountains of Mexico which permitted a good deal of communication among the ancient civilizations, the greater ruggedness of the terrain seems to have hindered unification in early prehistory, with the result that ancient centers of culture, each with a specific style, abound, particularly along the coast.

The real obstacle in gaining a clear picture of the past is the state of South American archaeology which, if it is not in its infancy, is certainly no more than adolescent. In many cases sequences are lacking, the relation between contemporary isolated cultures is not clear, and vast areas have simply not been touched by the investigator's spade. A beginning has been made in Peru and Bolivia but Ecuador, Colombia and Venezuela have yielded only sporadic data.

The realm of the Incas has been well publicized, but the activities of this energetic people took place during no more than a century, while during the two and a half millennia which preceded them a series of elaborate and sophisticated population centers flourished with religions as fascinating as any in similar stages of development elsewhere.

Just to make it harder, there is a divergence of point of view between South American and North American archaeologists. In the apt phrase of Hannah Wormington, scientists tend to be either lumpers or splitters. In this case the Peruvians, following the lead of Julio C. Tello, who almost single-handed carried on what there was of archaeology in Peru for decades, are lumpers. With a romantic enthusiasm he traced what he believed were broad cultural unities. North Americans are splitters, impressed by differences in art styles, and conservatively loath to interpret the meaning of artifacts until all the missing pieces of the puzzle are filled in. Of this we shall see some examples presently.

As it is, things are in a state of flux. Americanists are not even in accord on the names which are to be given to various periods. In consequence the writer intends to ignore orthodox terminology and simplify matters by applying the terms used by Eric Wolf for Middle America, since they are sensibly descriptive, and the prehistory of South America, in its broad outlines, roughly parallels that of Middle America.

As recently as 1957 (although, as we have seen, there is evidence of man in the southernmost tip of South America around 8000 B.C.) J. Alden Mason could write that the earliest known date in Peru was about 4300 B.C., that of a pre-pottery, pre-maize, fishing community on the northern coast at the mouth of the Chicama River valley. This people did grow, however, beans, squash and cotton. Nothing was then known of the very early history of the sierras. In 1959 Augusto Cardich presented a paper to a congress of Peruvian archaeologists reporting an excavation at Lauricocha in the central Andes dated by carbon 14 to 9500 B.C. The lowest level contained the bones of an extinct vicuña, crude scrapers, and points and tools made from bones. This therefore indicates the presence of ancient hunters in the Andes. The second level, which Cardich estimates as enduring from 6000 to 3000 B.C., contains technically better points. Llama, guanaco, and vicuña bones appear and the early variety becomes scarce. The third level, which is estimated as lasting another two millennia, is characterized by more bone tools and smaller points, fewer in number in comparison to the bone tools. Finally there is a fourth level which begins to contain pottery. The points of Lauricocha resemble some found in Argentina more closely than any found in coastal Peruvian sites. Skeletons were also recovered which dated to 9500 B.C. If this is accepted generally, it will be the oldest date for the presence of man in South America.

Although this discovery does not establish a series from hunting economy into the formative and village stage, it does push back the dating of human culture in the sierras and tends to support the point of view that the movement of peoples and cultural influences was from the mountains in two directions, toward the coast and the Amazonian forests. At the same conference Federico Engel announced the excavation of tombs on the south coast near Paracas dated at 5000 B.C. The bodies were buried in wrappings of decorated reed mats, while farther to the south cemeteries dated at 3800 B.C. contained cotton, gourds and lima beans.

For more details concerning the Early Formative we must return to the fishermen of the north coast. Houses were small, single-roomed and subterranean, walls sometimes lined with cobblestones, and where the latter were scarce, rectangular adobe bricks were the building material. The roofs were of timber and whalebones resting on posts. Graves were small chambers dug in ground, eventually lined with stones. These fishermen carved shell fishhooks, made no stone tools, and used gourds for everything from crockery to floats for fish nets. Some of these gourds were crudely decorated. Along with twined cotton cloth and rush and twig weaving, beaten bark cloth was found. Since this is a typical tropical forest trait, it suggests that their ancestors might have lived on the other side of the Andes.

Chicama Valley does not carry the story further. Next we move a little south to the Viru Valley where around 1250 B.C. crude, plain black and red pottery appears. In this and in similar sites in neighboring valleys weaving improved, the dead were buried with funerary offerings, and still farther down the coast at Supe a structure of stones and mud plaster, consisting of one large and two small rooms with a platform in the middle of the large room, is believed to be a temple. Here were found llama bones and maize, probably imported from the highlands. If so, who in the highlands was

SOUTH AMERICA

planting maize and how was it obtained from Middle America? This is one of the unsolved problems.

Then almost as abruptly as Olmec culture introduced an organized religion into the Mexican scene, something oddly similar took place in Peru. In the northern highland on a tributary of the Marañon River we find an advanced architectural complex built of stone, highly sophisticated stone carving, and a distinctively decorated pottery. Thus begins a Theocratic period around 850 B.C. at almost the same date as in Middle America.

The Peruvian archaeologists find evidences of the style from this site, Chavín de Huantar, all up and down the coast, and even in a site in the central highlands. The North Americans, more impressed by differences in the various population centers, tend to deny that sites show Chavín influence and call Chavín style a "tradition" rather than a culture.

When is style a culture? Actually a culture is generally spread by political domination during which not only aesthetic forms but the forms of material and spiritual life in general are continuous over a whole area; power monopoly and a power elite go hand in hand.

The minimum basic elements of Chavín are an interlaced ribbonlike decoration incised on pottery and the omnipresence of a feline figure or parts of the feline figure and other animal forms blended with it. The stirrup-spouted pot is characteristic of the coast, as is beaten goldwork.

Architecturally Chavín de Huantar in the highlands is a complex of platforms and buildings with stone reliefs, stelae and sculpture in the round. Coastal sites include masonry temples or terraced pyramids with clay reliefs painted in several colors, more or less reminiscent of Chavín style. Finally, in the extreme northern sierra, stone platform complexes were recently found at Kuntur Wasi and Pacopampa with temples, reliefs and stone statues.

Kuntur Wasi introduces a new complication, for, although reliefs in classical Chavín style are present, some sculptures are vaguely similar to those of a mysterious architectural site in Colombia at the headwaters of the Magdalena River. Here among grassy fields and wooded hills a series of shrines and temples is scattered over an area of several acres. Unlike anything in Peru, the architecture is megalithic, curiously reminiscent of the gallery graves of Europe. Temples as large as ten by fourteen feet are walled with stone slabs and roofed by a single thick slab. Some of the stones are dressed but most are merely split or selected. Often a pair of caryatid guardians stand at the entrance to the half underground galleries, in one case lizard men, in others a pair of warriors with clubs and a kind of alter-ego spirit perched on their heads. The stone idol is situated in the middle of the underground gallery, for the whole temple is heaped over with earth like the European megalithic graves. One idol holds a small human figure like a doll. Countless large and small sculptured images have been found in the area; the largest, about fifteen feet high, holding a little figure upside down. The style of carving varies from almost abstract, with square incised eyes and mouth, to a stylized naturalism of great power. Some images were used as grave markers or tomb covers. Simple, abstractly decorated ceramics and indications of weaving have been found, but no dwelling sites. Possibly they were thatched huts which would leave no trace. Stone beds of streams were also worked in a ceremonial way. Lavapatas is a mere brook; the stone slabs over which it flows are incised with snakes and lizards which seem to be drinking from canals which lead the water into three pools. Human figures, a monkey, and a sort of footstool are also carved in the rock.

How does all this tie up with Kuntur Wasi? Although the sculptures in the two sites are never identical, there is a certain simplicity of mass in both which differs from the Chavín treatment. The nose is broad and Negroid in certain San Augustín statues, a trait repeated in those of Kuntur Wasi. Some statues of the former site wear trophy heads around their necks and one of these appears on a figure in Kuntur Wasi. The mouth treatment, with crossed upper and lower canines, a basic decorative element in Chavín, appears in sculpture in the other two sites. On the other hand, at San Augustín there is no real feline representation as there is at Kuntur Wasi and Chavín. One more unifying trait is the serpent motif found in all sites under discussion.

Noticeable in some of the San Augustín figures is the absence of breech-clout, the penis being tied up by a string around the waist, a custom which still exists among the Amazonian tribes (and also in New Guinea). This suggests that the San Augustinians were of forest origin.

Rebeca Carrión would see San Augustín as the northern boundary of a Chavín "empire." There is, however, little specific support for the concept of an empire. Although here and there warriors are depicted, there is no indication of military domination and there are no fortifications in this period. Likewise variations in material culture indicate that the various highland and valley populations were rather self-sufficient. If Chavín was neither an empire nor a culture, all Americanists do agree on the spread of some basic religious concept, centering around the feline, over all the Andean and west coastal region of South America; a religious tradition which, as we shall see, was to persist for a long time.

What was the Chavín religion? In the absence of written documents, all that can be used as a key to the sculpture is tradition and analogical material. In the first place, the predominance of animal form suggests a totemic base. Many forest Indians are totemic and some decorate themselves with jaguar spots. Totemism has been found among the Araucanians of Chile including birds, fish and plants. The Indians of Tumbez adored tigers. The

Chibcha Indians of Colombia used animals as heraldic badges and wore masks and skins in their dances, and artisan groups also had animal symbols—messengers the tiger, weavers the bird. The Aymara of Bolivia spoke of their ancestors as coming out of a river and hence they were blood brothers of the fish. From lists of mine workers, and old documents we learn that such animal names as condor, falcon, hawk, crow, mountain lion and deer were common among them.

Granted there is a totemic background for animal symbols, it appears that certain of these animals became identified with natural phenomena. The Chibcha regarded a bird as a symbol of the sun, while the mountain lion stood for the god Nemacatacoa. Myths from the forest tribes show that they associate the jaguar with thunder and lightning. According to W. La Barre, the chief Aymara god was one of thunder and lightning, although what form it took is obscure. The modern Quechua believe in a Ccoa which brings lightning and hail. He is a striped gray cat with a big head. Hail runs out of his eyes. Sorcerers propitiate him with offerings of wine, incense, gold and silver tinsel, llama fat and other vegetable offerings which are burned on high ground.

It is with these traditional ideas in mind that interpretation of the monuments of Chavín is attempted. In the first place, the Chavín complex is 490 feet in length and is based on three or four superimposed platforms on which are placed two large building units. The *castillo* which faces on a large sunken plaza is a three-story affair with flat slabs roofing it, a dressed stone exterior with a row of tenoned heads and a cornice of felines surrounding it. The interior rooms, connected by ramps and staircases, were provided with air by a series of ventilating shafts. The whole is an amazing feat of engineering, especially since few habitation sites have been found nearby and the surrounding terrain would not support a large population. The labor used to construct this elaborate stonework must therefore have been drawn from a distance. It has been suggested that crowds may have been assembled at festival time to collect the materials, while the actual building could have been done by skilled priestly masons who resided near the site.

In the center of the plaza stood an obelisk with an intricate figure carved on each side. Inside one of the chapels a prism-shaped stone carving called the *lanson* was also decorated with the characteristic feline. The stela Raimundi, found near Chavín, is another important monument of this culture.

When we examine drawings and photographs of the Chavín monuments we are struck by a curvilinear, florid style, on the one hand vaguely reminiscent of Middle American Tajín, particularly because of the interlaced ribbon effect, and on the other somewhat like that of the late Chou empire of the Bronze Age in China. Robert Heine-Geldern has compared a Chou bronze tiger with the stone one found at Chavín. The same scholar also finds similarities between Tajín and Teotihuacán and Asian cultures. He points out that the late Chou and Chavín both date to about the seventh century B.C. The theory of Pacific contacts is still controversial, but it adds one more problem to the puzzle of the origin of the Chavín style.

To return to the actual monuments, the most elaborate is the obelisk on which twin monsters half-serpentine but with four-clawed appendages are formed of a glyphlike pattern of jaguar heads, serpent heads and the crossed-fang motif. Fruit is held in these creatures' claws; in one case the sex turns into a jaguar head whose tongue becomes a plant. Around one animal's head are placed a jaguar, a condor and a fish. The Raimundi stela is an upright figure, basically human but with a feline head and multiple headdress of stylized feline heads upside down, snake appendages sprouting from the sides. Scepters or arrows and spears grasped by the hands end in snake and feline heads. The lanson is a feline head with a collar of feline heads. The condor appears on Chavín stelae and friezes with a semi-jaguar head and a feline head, the crossed fangs prominent; elsewhere it is blended with the lower part of a winged human figure. The serpent head appears among the thirty-five heads which surrounded the castillo in various stages of amalgamation with the face of an old man. Serpent heads as a detail appear all over. Finally, at another site at Yauya, there is a representation of a fish with four legs and feline detail. A similar fish in Punkuri is adorned with felines and feline-headed fish.

In all this sculpture, skillfully made by pecking with stone tools, there is a kind of writhing life and an interest in symbolic detail which reflects a most sophisticated theological system.

The probability is that totemic animals have blended with the worship of natural forces and that the feline (and/or dragon) is a rain and sky deity. The fruit associated with the dragon suggests fertility. Snakes and lizards at San Augustín are geographically associated with water. Arguing from this, and the analogy of snakes in Middle America, they would be lightning or rain cloud symbols in Chavín. In fact, pushing the analogy further, the Chavín god could be a sort of parallel to the Middle America rain god to whom serpent, jaguar and bird attributes were blended. Certainly the fact that, overlaid upon the major Chavín sculptural forms, we find the other animal forms serving as decorative detail or attributes suggests that feline, bird, serpent and fish were manifestations of the same power and that the basic mana principle united them.

We would expect a condor religion to arise in the highlands, enriched perhaps by forest beliefs concerning the jaguar, since these animals belong in the habitats just mentioned. There is no way of identifying the fish, which could be a river or sea species. We would expect a fish deity on the coast but, with the usual human disregard of logic, the coastal populations adopted the feline and condor which are not coastal animals. Since the coastal populations obviously were not conquered, a more advanced highland theology may have spread through trade and assimilated local beliefs to it. Below Lima all that survives is the pottery style and the feline motif.

Paracas, the ultimate limit of the style on the southern coast below Lima, consists of two types of sites. The first is a series of bottle-shaped graves excavated in rock containing as many as fifty-five bodies with artificially flattened heads, wrapped in textiles and accompanied by offerings such as pottery, fairly elaborate brocade and painted cloth, and small gold ornaments. The stirrup-spouted jar of the north coast has been replaced by a two-spouted jar, now decorated with polychrome. Not far from these tombs a necropolis consisting of burials in the sand, probably contemporary in date with the rock tombs, furnishes evidence of a special religious cult. In the pottery, Chavín influence disappears, but it is the textiles which distinguish this particular people. Their dead, dried and eviscerated, were seated nude in a basket and wrapped in layers and layers of magnificent weaving while between the layers were tucked fans, gold ornaments, small pottery vessels, corn, beans, yucca, and sweet potatoes. Dress consisted of cloak or mantle, cape, skirt and headband but there were also kilts, turbans, veils and slings, mostly of llama or vicuña wool. As many as one hundred and fifty articles of clothing were placed in one bundle which might be five feet high, roughly shaped like an onion and topped with a mask. Paracas textiles have never been surpassed; from gauze to embroidered brocade they are masterpieces. The rainless southern desert has preserved many of them in as perfect a state as when they were made. The great mantles are four and a half by eight feet, generally with a dark reddish woolen background on which were embroidered repeat figures in four to six colors, bright reds, soft yellows, deep blues. And all this exquisite craftsmanship seems to have been exerted strictly for funeral purposes; most of the burials being those of elderly men, probably priests or chiefs.

Obviously great stress was placed on either afterlife or continuance of life in the tomb, or there may have been a special ancestor cult. On the textiles a feline appears, triangular or square-headed and sometimes at either end of a snake body. Was this an echo of the deity of the north? We have no way of knowing. So far no habitations connected with the Paracas burials have been found and thus we have no other evidence to go by.

A study of the figures in the textiles reveals an anthropomorphized species of shark playing an important role in the Paracas spirit world. It is shown seated surrounded by smaller fish as attributes, holding a sacrificial knife, and offerings are made to it. Also significant are birds, most of which are falcons or condors. Many of the human figures carry trophy heads.

By now various cultures with specific pottery styles were appearing in coastal valleys, all with the same village-agricultural type of economy. The next great step in Theocratic development and in social organization takes us up north again to the region near the present city of Trujillo.

Today two great blunt forms arise from the plain outside the city near the village of Moche (which gives its name to the culture). One is the temple of the sun, the other of the moon; these temples are called locally, *huacas*. Partly washed away by the occasional rains, scarred by random digging and surrounded by a sea of potsherds, these monuments are 750 and 260 feet long respectively, by 450 and 195 feet. The huaca of the sun has a stepped pyramid on the fifth terrace. The other monument has traces of rooms with frescoes in black, white, red, yellow, blue, pink and brown. It has been estimated that 130 million adobe bricks went into the construction of the huaca of the sun.

The Mochica kingdom, for now we are in a period where military domination begins, extended over all the northern valleys from Pacasmayo to Casma. Other pyramids with ruins of temples exist and a few structures with walls, entered by narrow steep stairs, which were probably forts.

Temples, villages and cemeteries were situated in the desert on the edge of the fertile land. In the villages, which were not large and rather unplanned, houses consisted of several rectangular rooms, on terraces or with patios, gabled and thatched with straw. The walls were of adobe on stone bases.

Evidence of political organization appears in the remains of irrigation ditches which extended the fertility of the river valleys farther than today, as well as in temple building. Fishing was carried on in the seas by means of *balsa* boats, solid bundles of reeds upturned at the bow and stern. One-man balsas can be seen on the beaches near Trujillo today. Large ones are, of course, still rigged with matting sails on Lake Titicaca. Road building was also well developed.

Although no written documents exist, we know a good deal about the Mochicans from their extraordinary development of the stirrup-spout jar into a sculptured and painted picture book on which they recorded their lives in great detail. We see stocky little men with big noses, often wearing conical caps, frenetically active warriors, messengers, servants, always on the double as they pursue each other in single file around the jars. The warriors, sometimes leading nude captives with ropes around their necks, look oddly like archaic Greeks. Wearing a crested helmet, a round shield, kilts and sleeveless shirts with actual Greek key designs, and brandishing clubs, their legs apparently painted black, these ferocious little men sacrificed captives by hurling them down a cliff. They also dismembered the bodies, for scenes of amputated legs, arms or genitals seem to imply that such fragments were taken home as trophies.

The Mochicas had developed a unique means of communication—they wrote on lima beans! Larco Hoyle has produced many scenes of messengers running with bags, persons handing each other beans, scrutinizing them and obviously interpreting them, while the beans themselves float above the scene. The range of symbols included various numbers of dots, wavy lines, some portion or portions of the beans being painted black, and combinations of these markings. Very often the individuals engaged in these pursuits are drawn with bird, deer, fox, or feline heads.

Larco Hoyle interprets these as symbolical of swiftness or sagacity. It is far more likely that they stand for totemic lineages. Often a deer is shown communicating by beans with a feline, or a bird with a feline, and thus this would signify that clan groups from different villages were in contact. There are also scenes of animal-headed persons squatting before a fully human dignitary, which might indicate domination of several clan groups by a chief. The fact that servants are sometimes shown as lizards need not be symbolical of subserviency; it might merely show that these belonged to a conquered clan group.

The Mochica culture does not directly follow that of Chavín. Another stratum called the Salinar intervenes in which all Chavín traits are lost. In the Salinar culture, however, an unusual element appears. We have so far seen that sex in the Americas seldom plays a ceremonial or important public role; on the whole, restraint or even puritanism is the social ideal and the destructive side of female sexuality is stressed. With the Salinar people a blatant sexuality begins which is to continue on the north Peruvian coast. In Salinar pottery, for the first time human copulation is depicted. Mochica pictorial pottery also delights in depicting copulation, animal or human; llamas, monkeys, even mice appearing in the sexual act. In the Larco Herrera Museum at Chiclín a whole room houses a collection of pottery illustrating practically every known human perversion. That this attitude toward sex may have had something to do with religion, we shall see when we discuss the culture of the Chimús, the inheritors of the Mochicans.

According to Larco Hoyle, religion among the Mochicans was centered around feline symbolism: "And it seems reasonable to believe that in this period we have, with a new elaboration and sophistication of animal worship, a continuation of the old feline deity of the North Coast." He was anthropomorphized into a man with crossed fangs and catlike whiskers. He received the sacrifice of humans thrown from the cliff and accepted their blood as an offering. He was also shown as an agriculturist, a fisherman, a sailor, a musician and a hunter. He fought demons and was often attended by anthropomorphized eagles, lizards, dogs or owls.

The great political chiefs were probably also priests and always sat at a higher level than their guests. They were carried about on litters. The portrait effigy of the high chief or priest can be found all over the Mochica area but portraits of regional governors were recovered only within their own territories.

Mutilations such as cutting off lips, nose, or feet seem to have been common punishments, with public stoning the method of execution.

Aside from the priest-rulers, in Mochica art we have evidence of shaman physicians. They are attired as chiefs with feline attributes. While the patient lay on his back, the shaman prayed, and shook rattles. He is also depicted as listening to and manipulating the sick man's body.

Religious festivals involved animal costume and dances to the music of drums, silver and copper bells, flutes, panpipes, conch trumpets and gourd rattles. Some of the ceremonies appear to be dramatic scenes; but the nature of the Mochica mythology which, judging from the variety of fantastic monsters, must have been elaborate, can only be guessed at from the silent cinema of the documentary art of this people.

That the concept of diminished life in the tomb existed is proven by graves with hollow canes which led from the mouth to the surface of the ground so that the deceased might be fed. Graves were sometimes lined with stone, cane, or adobe, and in niches were food and, in particular, the pictorial pots which, like the funeral art of the Egyptians, carried images of gods, animals, scenes from life, and various foods. It is rather hard to fathom why the pots showing sexual perversions also were a part of the pottery offering. In the mouths of the dead, according to status, were placed sheets of gold, silver or copper wrapped in a piece of cloth. Since the Mexicans placed a piece of jade in the mouth of an aristocrat and a green stone in that of a commoner, to serve as amulets on the journey to the underworld, we can assume that the Mochicans had developed a similar idea.

The Mochica period runs roughly from 400 B.C. to 1000 A.D. Meanwhile, in the south coastal region a new Theocratic culture developed out of the Paracas civilization and lasted a couple of hundred years longer. There are no great temples although some adobe houses were built and grouped in small villages. Since there was also no extensive irrigation, it is clear that social organization had not reached the centralization of power evident in the north. Fine weaving continued and hammered gold objects were made, but the Nasca culture was pre-eminent for its superb pottery. Round-bottomed bowls, beakers, and double-spouts are decorated with animals, mythological monsters, human figures and human heads or faces, some of the latter having a chic sophisticated air that is curiously modern. A sharp elegance of draftsmanship and a fine sense of space relationships give this ceramic art its distinction. A square-faced, whiskered feline appears which may be an echo of the Chavín tradition. Unlike the pictorial art of the

Mochicas, Nasca style is formalized and tends to make use of repeat figures like the textiles. There are subtle color combinations of dull red, white, cream, gray, black, buff, yellow, and violet.

Trophy heads are prominent in Nasca art both in textiles and in ceramics; figures carry them hung from a rod. J. Tello points out that the Mundurucú Indians of the Amazon enlarge the foramen to remove the brains, then dry the head and pierce the forehead so that a string can be passed through it and the foramen for carrying. Such heads have been found in Nasca burials. (Both the Paracans and Nascans elongated their skulls by squeezing those of infants between boards so that the head was practically pointed. The Maya did the same.) Tello also believed he found the Jívaro type of shrunken trophy head depicted on some pots. He wrote, "The mummied head is the continual companion of the gods of Nasca as it is of most of the divinities of the aboriginal pantheon of Peru." A figure carrying one is carved on a Chavín frieze; we have already noted their presence at Kuntur Wasi and San Augustín and in the weavings of Paracas. In the Tiahuanaco sites of Bolivia, too, they are carried by stylized human figures. We know that Jívaro head taking was connected with symbolic brain cannibalism. Accounts of the revolt of the Aymara Indians of Bolivia in 1899 prove that there brain cannibalism was practiced. In addition, one historian states that eyes and testicles of their white enemies were cut off and eaten to absorb the valor of the victims. It is also noteworthy that among the severed trophies depicted by the Mochica pots, circumcised male sex organs are prominent.

The Nasca people are remarkable for still another achievement which indicates an advance in theological science. In the late forties, airplane photographs revealed strange markings and lines in the desert which were subsequently studied on the terrain. Millennia of dew and desert heat on the south coast have oxidized the surface pebbles, which contain a good deal of iron, to a depth of two or three inches. By removing the blackened surface, lines, shapes and drawings have been created in the paler sand. The stones were carefully piled at the edges of cleared spaces in a forty-mile section of the desert near the foothills of the Andes to create lines as long as 595 feet. Lines radiate in all directions and sometimes great cleared triangles and trapezoids are drawn on the blackboard of the ground. The straightness of these markings is amazing. Maria Reiche feels they were made with the aid of long ropes and careful sighting. She points out that some of her native helpers who were professional furrow tracers in cotton fields could see a stake two thirds of a mile away, which indicates that their ancestors must have developed the same ability. It has been proved that several of these lines mark the solstices and equinoctial points, which tends to verify the theory that the whole was a giant farmer's almanac or calendar marking the seasons. Bits of Nasca pottery have been found at this site as well as drawings representing human figures, a bird with outstretched claws, a fish, a spider and various mazelike tracings. This evidence indicates that these people, like Middle American groups, were in possession of considerable astronomical science.

Parallel with the Nasca development, a new region began to play an important role in South American prehistory. In the altiplano, at a height of 13,000 feet near Lake Titicaca, in the midst of the chilly desolate tundra is located the great architectural site of Tiahuanaco. Here megalithic structures rival those of Carnac in Brittany. There is a terraced pyramid faced with stone and the remains of a large reservoir with an overflow canal, a square area, about 400 feet on a side, lined with monoliths and enclosing a sunken court entered by a stone staircase. The greatest monolithic gateway, decorated with figures in low relief, is carved from a single block ten by twelve and a half feet, estimated to weigh about ten tons. Some stones are held together by copper clamps. Stone statuary also occurs. The tallest, a figure holding two scepters or clubs, is twenty-four feet high, stiffly angular in style, and done in low relief in the round. Since all these great blocks of basalt and sandstone were brought from a quarry three miles away, once more we are astounded at the achievements of a people whose technical equipment did not include the wheel or metal tools.

There is no doubt that this site was a great ceremonial center but, since little systematic investigation has been done, we know little of the people who created it. The area, now occupied by a few Aymara Indians pasturing their llama, is not suited to intensive agriculture and could not have supported a large population. Nevertheless there must have been a civilization with a strong central power to produce such results. That it may have extended its influence by force is suggested by the fact that typical Tiahuanaco textiles, pottery and goldwork appear all along the coast and indeed practically everywhere in Peru. The Nasca style was completely overwhelmed, while at Moche the influence was only slight. Huari, a site four miles square in the central sierra, in the province of Ayacucho, consists of mud and stone houses, public buildings and walled enclosures. This appears to have been a truly residential city. Stone statues resemble those of Tiahuanaco and the pottery is very similar to the Tiahuanaco style as it appears on the coast.

The chief motifs in the decorative art of this people are the puma, the condor, the fish and front-view warriors. On the whole, the designs are stiff, graceless and cluttered. The squarishness of the stone carving suggests that the influence of textile weave had not been shaken off.

Interpretations of Tiahuanaco religion remain highly conjectural. The central figure on the gate of the sun is flanked by three rows of eight run-

ning figures on each side, some of which have condor heads. A highly romantic archaeologist, Arthur Posnansky, considers the main figure to be a
sun god and works out an elaborate calendric meaning for the forty-eight
units surrounding him. This interpretation is not generally accepted. A
coastal pot with a standing figure, which holds two feline-headed scepters,
depicts the same entity as the main figure on the gate. The belt from which
hang three trophy heads is adorned with condor heads. Around the figure's
head protrude rays or hair ending in condor heads, feline heads and ears of
maize. Two more trophy heads hang from the eyes. The arrangement of the
zoomorphic rays is parallel to the headdress treatment of the Raimundi
stela, as are the feline-headed scepters. Although snakes are not present,
the familiar elements of the feline and condor are here brought into conjunction with the maize. It appears as if traditional symbols were therefore
blended with some type of vegetation fertility god, and the trophy heads
point to ceremonies of human sacrifice. Felines and feline heads with crossed
fangs are common forms of Tiahuanaco pottery. Curiously enough, there
seems to be a meeting of Chavín and Tiahuanaco in small sites in the northern highlands.

The Tiahuanaco influence lasted for about a thousand years, ending in
the neighborhood of 1000 A.D. We have the feeling this was a civilization
perhaps parallel to that of the Toltecs. There is something similar in the
grim stone figures produced by both, and the wide distribution of the culture marks the beginning of Militarist expansion.

Other petty, socially stratified states were developing and, on the northern coast, the inheritor of Mochica civilization was the Chimú kingdom or
empire which extended from Piura in the north to Paramonga, not far from
Lima, in the south. The Chimú went on building pyramids and adobe forts
but they also moved into a true urban phase with their capital at Chanchan.
It covered over eight square miles and was considerably larger than the
modern city of Trujillo near it. Chanchan is carefully planned on the grid
system, surrounded by walls and divided into ten wards, probably clan
groups, also walled. There are pyramids, temples, gardens, remains of water-
works. Although the occasional northern rains have blunted and washed
away the tops of the walls, what is left is still imposing. Extensive irrigation
allowed for gardens in the city between the wards and the streets may have
been adorned with trees. Today all is dust and desolation as the desert has
once more taken over.

On some of the walls, protected by dust and sand, friezes with repeat
patterns have been uncovered in which birds and fish occur looking as if
incised in adobe with a cookie cutter. Other walls were adorned with colored
murals of a similar type.

There is no doubt that the Chimú possessed a central authority, district governors, a high degree of specialization, and a highly stratified society. Indeed the latter is recorded in reports of the Spanish chroniclers (the culture lasted until the conquest) who describe an aristocratic and autocratic court. Artistically this people was inferior to their forebears, the Mochicas, whose pottery they copied, turning out cruder stirrup jars in molds in a polished black ware. They gave up pictorial painted scenes entirely.

There is a curious ceramic series from the Chimú period in which a mythological couple is seated under a tree; the couple is then depicted in the act of intercourse surrounded by calendric signs, carnivores and monkeys, and finally the pair is surrounded by monkeys. The same copulation scene appears again and again with more and more rays emanating from the pair. There is certainly an idea of symbolic fertility portrayed here connected with animals, a fruit-laden tree, and monkeys. Whether the rays indicate solar and lunar gods is not absolutely certain. The rays are depicted with ears and are, if anything, weakly executed felines. What is interesting is the similarity in treatment to the headgear of the figure on the Tiahuanaco pot.

The representations of copulation between a human pair also may relate to the earlier Mochica emphasis on scenes of intercourse between animals. It would appear that in this particular area the sex act assumed a special religious significance.

The other most important deity represented in Chimú pottery and in related cultures is a maize god. Curiously enough, this concept appears rather late in Peruvian prehistory. His image assumes a multiplicity of forms. A link with the past are the crossed feline fangs in the human face, while the body is composed of ears of corn. Other representations include maize emanating from the god's head and scepters in rays, or a headdress of maize ears. Sometimes this entity is associated with felines. Other scenes show the sacrifice of llamas and decapitated human heads.

Contemporary with the Chimú empire, other valleys show urban civilizations. The stage was now set for unification. The imperialist power which was to accomplish this feat was a small Militarist group in the southern highlands somewhere near Cusco who called themselves Incas and, as they became a ruling aristocracy, their emperor The Inca.

Under various leaders, of whom we have in some cases only mythological accounts, this group, like the Aztecs, fought its way to dominance of the southern highland and Bolivian area, conquering the Colla or Aymara, expanded to the coast, defeating the tough Chimú after a hard struggle, and finally by the arrival of the Spaniards in the sixteenth century dominated the northwestern area of South America from Ecuador to upper Chile. Less bloodthirsty than the Aztecs, although they, too, took trophy heads and sacrificed captives, they were far better organizers. They moved hostile population groups from one area to another to neutralize them and brought conquered leaders to the capital at Cusco to indoctrinate them with the Inca way of life. Indeed as their empire developed they worked out a kind of autocratic state socialism which provided security for every citizen, based on a careful yearly census, government planning and controlled distribution of the land. The ruling group was privileged but if Garcilaso de la Vega is to be believed (he was half Inca and inclined to idealize his mother's people), they subscribed to a feeling of *noblesse oblige* and dedicated themselves faithfully to efficient government. Laws and maxims corroborate this attitude.

Artistically the Incas were less imaginative than earlier groups. Functionalists, they made technically superb pottery in simple classic shapes with formalized decorative patterns, but they produced no stone sculpture or reliefs. Their textile industry carried on and equaled the Paracas tradition and their gold and silver work was excellent. It is by their great public works that the Incas impress us most, however; the roads and bridges spanning the highlands dotted with stone forts and lookouts, the terraced and irrigated agricultural areas which can still be seen in the highlands today, the great fitted monoliths of the fortress of Sachsuahuamán and the superb little city of Machu Picchu. Perched on the jungle side of the Andes with its stone houses, countless stairways, water system, and ceremonial center of beautifully dressed stone, it is a legacy from a smooth-working, integrated and vital society which was in many ways in advance of that of the Spanish bandits who destroyed it.

Inca official religion, as in all well-organized barbaric states, reflects the efforts of a priesthood to develop a rationale for the dominant ethos. Like the Egyptian monarch, The Inca was descended from the sun and, being divine, was worshiped. Since his health was correlated with that of the sun, antisocial actions committed by his people affected the well-being of both. From this stemmed the institution of penitence and confession. The most serious sins were murder by poison or witchcraft, carelessness in worship, neglect of festivals and cursing or disobeying the emperor. Fornication and seduction were secondary but forbidden by the ruler. Confession was made to priests of both sexes; the royal family confessed directly to the sun. Divination was used to learn whether the penitent had come clean. The divination procedures were many: counting a pile of stones or pebbles to learn if they were odd or even; consulting the viscera of a sacrificed llama; observing the movements of animals. If the penitent was holding something back he could be grilled or beaten. Absolution was granted after fasting or prayer. The Spanish chroniclers, who were experts in such matters, reported that those who were able to pay the confessors well got lighter penances. Washing in running water was the final purification. Another political aspect of the sun religion was the dogma that it was the purest and highest form of worship and consequently The Inca's duty was to spread it throughout the world by conquest. One of the ironies of history is the fact that the Spaniards rationalized their behavior in exactly the same terms.

The sun god, who must have originally been connected with the royal house, perhaps as a clan god, was male and sometimes represented by a gold disk with rays and a human face upon it. Sanctuaries and fields set aside to support religious officials and the convents of the Chosen Women, or nuns who dedicated their life to religious chastity, were all said to belong to the sun. The fact that the sanctuaries contained images of all the sky gods, which were served by the Chosen Women and supported by the fields of the sun, shows that the sun religion was a late political device. In fact another tradition, that of Viracocha, was equally important and seems to have been a cult of the intellectuals.

Viracocha, combining the attributes of creator and culture hero, strongly parallels Quetzalcoatl. In Inca myth, Viracocha made a world of earth and sky but neglected to light it. At first he carved giant statues of stone and gave them life. When they displeased him, he turned some back to stone at Tiahuanaco and elsewhere and destroyed the rest in a flood, except two whom he saved to be his helpers. He gave the world light by making the sun and moon emerge from the Island of Titicaca. In a second creation he made a race of his own size. Finally at Tiahuanaco he modeled animals and men out of clay. He gave men food, languages, songs and customs and called tribes out of the earth in the regions where they were to live. After other adventures on the coast and at Cusco he said good-by to his peoples and set out from Ecuador across the Pacific, walking on the water. Pizarro was at first identified with the returning culture hero.

A very important god was the thunder and rain deity called Ilyapa who held a war club in one hand, a sling in the other and wore shining garments. The thunder was the crack of his sling, the lightning the flash of his garments, the lightning bolt his slingstone. Wendell Bennett suggests that he might be the same person as the figure on the great Tiahuanaco gate, since the Aymara of that region worshiped the sky god as their chief deity. Indeed it is perfectly possible that he was the ultimate anthropomorphization of the old fertility and rain god who has appeared in so many early Peruvian religions identified with various animals. Since he had a wife, the moon, who was important in regulating the calendar, there could have been some connection with the copulating gods of Chimú. On the other hand, there was a separate earth goddess, Pacamama, worshiped by farmers, and a sea goddess, Mamacocha, who was the patroness of the fishermen of the coast. Since the Inca pantheon was obviously synthesized, the latter might have been a descendant of the fish deity of Paracas.

Inca temples were made of beautifully dressed stone. The base of one is still a part of the convent in Cusco, and another small one in Machu Picchu is in perfect condition. They housed the gods and were only entered by the priests and Inca officials. Sometimes they consisted of several one-room buildings containing various shrines or serving as dwelling places for the religious officials. Ceremonies took place in the large square near them, to which images, cult objects and mummies of kings were brought.

Most ceremonies were agricultural, regulated by a lunar calendar. How it was adjusted to the agricultural seasons we do not know. This people was not as advanced as the Middle Americans in astronomical science. The monthly festivals were celebrated with dances, prayers and offerings of food, and coca leaves. The latter came from the cocaine plant and are still used in mountain ceremonies today. The leaves are also chewed by the contemporary Indians to dull hunger and thirst. Little gold and silver figures were also given to the gods and the really indigent offered up a few eyelash or eyebrow hairs. Guinea pigs, a favorite food animal in ancient times and today, were sacrificed by the hundreds. Llamas, being expensive, were sacrificed by wealthy individuals and by the state from its own herds. White were for the sun, brown for Viracocha, and mottled ones belonged to the thunder god. The priest led the llama around the image and made it face it, recited the proper prayer, and cut the animal's throat, smearing the image with its blood.

Every great festival included llama sacrifice. Human beings were immolated only on most important occasions or in times of crisis. The gods required physically perfect boys and girls about ten years old. When these and prisoners of war were offered up, hearts were sometimes ripped out in Aztec style.

Public prayers were literary, carefully memorized by the priests in verse form. An invocation to Viracocha runs as follows:

> O Viracocha, unequaled,
> From one end of the world to the other,
> Who proclaimed the being and the worth of man,
> Who proclaimed that man should be man
> And woman, woman,
> And thus saying, made them, shaped them,
> And gave them being.
> Keep those whom you have made safe and well,
> Living in peace, unendangered.
> Where art thou?
> In the height of the sky
> Or below in the clouds and thunders
> Of the tempests?

Hear me,
Respond, grant what I ask,
And give us eternal life,
For you hold us forever in your hand.
And receive this offering
Wherever thou beest,
O Viracocha!

The official priesthood was stratified, the high priest being a close relative of the emperor and the upper ranks all of imperial Inca blood. These offices were combined in a council of nine, each member in charge of a large area, paralleling the efficient secular administration. Important priests lived ascetic lives, complying with many taboos. The priesthood was subject to inspection, as was the secular administrative hierarchy.

The relation between the government priest and the shamanistic healer is not altogether clear. Those who attended the royal family must have been priests but the chances are that some medical practitioners were laymen. Power was acquired in a vision or dream as in archaic cultures and, as in other parts of America, medical theory included the idea of a foreign body such as a worm, a toad or a bit of straw which had to be sucked from the abdomen of the patient. A man's ancestors or the gods might become angry because of neglect of worship and cause disease. When this type of diagnosis was determined by divination, the patient was obliged to pray and make offerings. Washing in a river, if the sick man could walk, was also a part of healing.

The Incas buried their dead with grave goods in stone tombs or in caves. The bodies were flexed and wrapped in mats or sewed into a skin, which resulted in a sort of mummification. Sometimes wives and servants of an aristocrat were killed (supposedly they were willing) and buried with him. A double conception of life after death prevailed. The nobility went to live with the sun, regardless of their behavior on earth. The good were supposed to join them but sinners went to an underworld where they suffered from cold and had no food but stones. At the same time there was a belief that the dead lingered near their old homes. It was for this reason that the desiccated dead were brought out on festal occasions and offered food and chicha (maize) beer.

The religious practices which have been described above were a development of the empire. Behind them there was a whole area of local belief and rite which was probably much older and links the ancient population with the Quechua of today. We have already mentioned the fact that coastal pyramids are called huacas. This was the word for shrine but it is clear that its meaning was very general. John Mason writes, "Almost anything strange or unusual was considered sacred and a waca: twins, persons with supernumerary digits, plants of peculiar forms. Corpses of course." In addition, dangerous or important places in the road were in this category, and also springs, stones, caves, boundary markers, mountains, springs and lakes. There is a strong parallel with the Roman numena which is, of course, a basic mana concept. The contemporary Quechua believe in *aukis* or mountain spirits. Although their fiestas are regulated by saints' days, very often, as at Copacabana in Bolivia, they take place at an ancient sacred spot. In this particular place the local virgin is confused with Pacamama the earth goddess. Ritual drinking of chicha occurs and masked dances.

Although some authorities deny that the *ayllu,* or ancient kinship unit, is a totemic clan, it preserves certain communal characteristics of the clan, such as joint ownership of land, even today. Many Inca dances were carried out in masks and animal skins. Although modern dances often involve European elements and devil masks in medieval style, introduced by Spanish priests, some very archaic traits are also present. The writer witnessed a dance at Pisac which dramatized hunters and animals. The hunters were dressed in curious knitted helmet masks and carried staves, while the animals were attired in dark llama skins. After considerable confused scuffling, one of the animals was killed symbolically and carried about in triumph on a litter created by the crossed staves. Whether or not the Incas were an exception and did not develop or lost their totemic clans, there is certainly evidence of a very ancient layer of religion involving animal identification and hunting magic.

In comparison with other high barbaric cultures, the Inca empire comes off as relatively humane and, for its time, socially progressive. It did succeed in unifying the highland peoples, chiefly by spreading Quechua as a common language. Several hundred years have passed since the Spanish conquest swept away the benefits of Inca administration and during this period the people as a whole have been left very much as they were after the conquest. Imprisoned in their own language and their simple, poverty-stricken tilling of the soil, their Indianism is an ancient and cohesive way of life which so far has received nothing from, and been offered nothing by, modern technology.

CHAPTER 42

The Golden Crocodile

The Caribbean—influences from both Middle and South America found in Central America—links between Colombia and ancient Panamanian cultures —traces of Andean animal symbolism—the ubiquitous jaguar—Arawak migration to Caribbean—Arawak priesthood and myth—migration to Amazonian forest.

THE STORY of the peopling of the great forest areas of South America and the development of the cultures that exist there today is only partially clear. We do know that a role was played by the region bordering the Caribbean, particularly the southern portion of Central America and Colombia. Although the narrow highroad of mountain and forest which joins the two continents must have been traversed by the very ancient long-headed hunters millennia before Christ, we have no material survivals to tell us of their wanderings. Later the high civilizations of Middle America and the Andes became important in this region. In Honduras and El Salvador settlements have been found with stone temples, ball courts, ceramics and artifacts which show a dominance of Mexican and Mayan styles. From Panamá toward Costa Rica and Nicaragua, however, the current flows from south to north. Here some strikingly original achievements have been unearthed.

Although archaeology has not yet established connections between the Andes and Panamá in detail, the region of western Colombia provides some significant clues. The first of these takes us back to the statues of San Augustín. It will be remembered that Chavín influences were seen in this site. A particular characteristic of the stone figures was the "alter ego," a face and arms surmounting the head which seemed to be a symbol rather than a headdress. In Costa Rica and Nicaragua, stone statues have been found with a similar creature above the head, although in Central America the second entity is generally an animal. Sometimes the statue's head is enclosed in an animal's jaws. These figures have been found placed near rough mounds of stone blocks. Although recognition of stylistic similarities is always subjective, these figures do have a simplified monumental quality which is akin to those of San Augustín though less technically skillful in execution. Samuel Lothrop calls them the work of Chorotegans whom he identifies as pre-Mayan. If this is true, then they would date to several hundred years B.C., which accords well with the suggested age of the San Augustín site and indicates that already the earliest Theocratic Andean religion had spread to Central America.

Two other important links with Colombia are the Chibcha language which is spoken by tribes from Panamá to Costa Rica and Nicaragua and the technique of making gold ornaments which was practiced by the Chibcha, Quimbaya and Sinú of Colombia and equaled or surpassed by their pupils in Central America.

Unfortunately the only documentary record concerning the Colombia tribes exists in the Spanish reports on the Chibcha sixteenth-century society. Living near Bogotá, this people had reached the stage of a sedentary village life, cultivating maize and potatoes like the Peruvians, but lacking domestic animals since their highlands were beyond the range of the llama and alpaca. A stratified society existed which was beginning to be organized under one leader. Although there were no cities, there was an organized priesthood which tended idols, performed human sacrifices and tended trophy skulls. Goldworking technique included casting by the lost wax process figurines, pendants, heads of staves, and pins. The Quimbaya, who are only known from burials in the Cauca Valley near Medellín, carried metalwork further, creating hammered masks, nose ornaments, collars, vases, and beautiful pendants. This goldwork is the best in the Andes. Anthropomorphized animal figures are in evidence with the frog pendant particularly common. Indeed, although Chavín and Chimú sites yield beaten goldwork and the Chimú people got as far as welding, it has been suggested that the Quimbaya invented the lost wax process of casting (a mold made over a wax model; when the mold was heated, the wax ran out leaving space for the metal).

Quimbaya pottery includes effigies which have an archaic look, incised ware, and a few types of vessels such as the stirrup and double-spout which show Peruvian influence. Another site at Sinú, near the coast, of which little is known, has produced excellent goldwork as well as high relief modeling of human figures on pots in a different style from that of the Quimbaya.

These last two cultures have not been dated. Little is known of the antecedents of the Chibcha, but the chances are that they came later than San Augustín, perhaps contemporary with early coastal Peruvian society, around 200 A.D.

What is the relation between the goldsmiths of Colombia and those of Panamá? The Coclé people who, with the Veraguas, their neighbors, were the finest metalworkers and ceramists of the isthmus, may have been a western Amazon group (there are traces of Amazon design in their pottery) who moved north and passed into Colombia at about the time of the San Augustín sculptors. On their passage through Colombia they learned the technique of goldworking, eventually moved into Panamá and here developed their own way of life which exhibits highly individual characteristics. Since they traded with the Chibcha and Quimbaya, they must have moved in hundreds of years before the conquest. Although they did not produce stone architecture or live in cities, we may be sure from the rich grave goods that they had powerful chiefs and perhaps about the same type of society as the Chibcha (which included slaves).

The Veraguas people, who may or may not have been of the same stock as the Coclé, also achieved an individual style but share with them certain motifs which seem to tie up with the oldest strata of Andean religion, specifically a rich animal symbolism blended with or accompanying anthropomorphic representation.

Most important in this are the images of the jaguar and the crocodile. The jaguar head with crossed fangs is found carved on stone metates (grinding stones) from Nicaragua to Panamá. Nicaraguan and Costa Rican pottery often takes the form of a jaguar, decorated in polychrome, and on some vessels painted scenes of a man fighting a jaguar and stylized jaguar elements as a design element occur. The crossed fang motif persists in Coclé ceramic representations of human faces, and figures depicted on the rather elegant polychrome pots include a bird, bird-animals, a monkey-crocodile, and specific crocodile and turtle images which Lothrop calls gods.

The Veraguas people, as well as carving jaguar metates, also produced an elaborate grinding-stone base which consisted of a standing crocodile god holding a snake by the tail in its mouth. It is flanked by four monkeys standing on the rumps of jaguars who balance with their forepaws on human heads. Lothrop believes all this must have a mythological significance. Veraguas gold pendants, which were the finest jewelry of this type in the Americas, are also almost a picture book in themselves. The beasts represented include the jaguar, frog, fish, crocodile and a bird which has been called an eagle but which might even be related to the Andean condor. Since many elaborations occur in the treatment of this bird, we can assume that it was a significant symbol. Sometimes it is surmounted by a jaguar head or it carries a fish, a human figure, or a snake in its beak. Circles which resemble earplugs adorn the sides of the head or the head is surmounted by earlike appendages. The crocodile often becomes a composite which resembles a dragon. Human figures of deities can have animal attributes such as bird, crocodile, or jaguar heads.

It is significant that all the Chavín animals—the crocodile, bird, jaguar, fish, and snake—appear in this jewelry as well as the animal-headed human figure. The inference is that a symbolical religion similar to that of the Andes existed in Panamá. Since the jaguar occurs all through Middle America, and it has been established that the Panamá people traded with Peru, it is a moot question whether this symbol came from the north or the south. In Central America the crossed fangs are treated like the letter N, a style which appears in San Augustín and Tiahuanaco.

At the time of the conquest the religion of the Nicaragua-Costa Rican area was thoroughly Middle American. According to the chronicler Fernandez de Oviedo, there were wooden temples with idols, a priesthood which removed hearts of sacrificial victims, and maintained the institutions of confession and self-torture by gashing the tongue. He also mentions the flaying of a victim as in the cult of Xipe and describes the volador game which consisted of whirling around a pole at the end of a rope, also a Mexican custom.

The Caribbean area was therefore a meeting ground for religious currents from the northern and southern high civilizations. Then, before the conquest, a new group of people appeared on the scene who were destined to play an important role in both the Caribbean and the jungles of the southern continent. These were the Arawak whom Paul Radin describes as taking the long road from northwest Canada across the Rockies to the southeast coast of the United States. Radin believes they may have arrived as nomadic hunters in the east about 600 A.D., some five hundred years before maize appeared on the southeast North American coast, as a result of Mexican influence. The voyaging newcomers, who evidently had the dugout and/or bark canoe, then submitted to Mexican and Central American influence which increased the sophistication of their culture.

They must have been excellent seamen, for they managed to reach Cuba and Haiti and overwhelmed some still simpler people who were there before them. They were described by an early priest-anthropologist, Ramon Pané, whom Columbus deposited as a missionary in Haiti. The friar took down some mythology including a curious story of culture heroes who had no women and wished very much to have some. In the trees one day, they discovered certain creatures which were neither sex, having, like angels, no sex organs. The resourceful culture heroes bound them and tied woodpeckers to them, whereupon the birds went to work and pecked out the desired orifices.

The Arawak at this time had priests, temples, and stone idols called *cemi* which represented sky gods. The shaman-priests drank tobacco powder which threw them into a frenzy from which they learned secret wisdom. They then sucked out stones or other objects from the bodies of their patients. The cemi granted good harvests and were consulted by the king, after taking snuff, concerning the outcome of warfare. Apparently among the idols were animal gods; one was supposed to climb down from the roof of the palace and eat human flesh when he was displeased and another sometimes ran on all fours into the woods and had to be coaxed back into his chapel. The friar also reported that there was a female who produced clouds, wind and rain through her assistants. She and all the other cemi were supposed to prevent flooding by controlling the mountain streams.

Other myths, collected by Pané, can be traced to both North and South America. However, the nobility, temples and idols and a professional priesthood all related to Mexico and Central America.

The chief enemies of the Arawak were the Caribs, who gave their name to the sea between the northern and southern continent, and who were such fierce fighters and cannibals that Pané tells us the poor Arawak at times gave up all hope of opposing them and simply took to the woods. Despite the fact that the Caribs came from South America, probably from the northern Amazonian region, fear of them did not dampen the colonizing impulse of the Arawak, who continued their voyages until they reached the mouth of the Orinoco, believed to be their port of entry into the forest which they still inhabit.

CHAPTER 43

"I, Your Food, Have Come!"

Amazonian forest tribes—slash-and-burn agriculture—level of culture similar to Africa and Oceania—twin myth and trickster—ancestor cult associated with snake and trumpet—sadistic initiation ceremonies—ritual murder— head taking and cannibalism—Andean influences.

IN 1549 a German by the name of Hans Staden was taken prisoner by a tribe of Indians in eastern Brazil. Immediately his captors disputed as to who had touched him first. When they had settled this, they eventually brought him to their village where he was made to cry out, "I, your food, have come!" He knew by now the fate that probably awaited him. The women went before and behind him singing and dancing. Some hit him with their fists or pulled his red beard, saying "With this blow I avenge my friend, the one killed by the people you were with." Hans had been in the service of the Portuguese, who were disliked by his captors (with good reason). The unfortunate prisoner desperately kept insisting he was French, for he knew that the French maintained trading relations with his captors. Finally a Frenchman was unearthed who came and spoke to Hans in French. Since the poor German could not answer in this language, the calloused trader told the natives that their prisoner was Portuguese and they might as well eat him.

Hans was not eaten and lived to write the first account of the customs of the Tupi-Guarani. This group of tribes, together with the Arawak and Caribs, constitute the majority of the tropical forest people who practice slash-and-burn maize culture. They also share mythological themes and shamanistic practices and a good many other culture traits.

The Orinoco and the Amazon, two of the world's greatest rivers, are the highroads along which early peoples traveled and eventually settled. To anyone who has flown above the jungle it becomes abundantly clear why, for far below a thick, impenetrable green velvet is threaded with brown ribbons, the only pathways for a human vehicle. The vehicle is, of course, the dugout or bark canoe. In the rainy season the rivers rise and are most easily navigable. When they are low, all sorts of fallen trees, shoals and islands emerge, around which channels must be carefully traced.

The three groups of Indians mentioned above may all have been of North American stock. The Arawak have left traces of pottery, better than that which they now make, which indicate that they progressed up the Orinoco, the Río Negro, to the Amazon. The earliest evidences of the Caribs are in the Amazon region but the basic twin-creator culture-hero myth connects them with North America.

The Tupi-Guarani seem to have moved about a great deal so that nothing is certain concerning their origin. In general the Arawak and Caribs are now found largely on the northwest bank of the Amazon and on its tributaries, some of the Arawak stock (or at least its culture) even penetrating as far as the Ucayali in the Montaña of Peru. The Tupis range mostly from the east bank of the Amazon and its tributaries to the eastern area of Brazil. Westward and south their territory extends to the farther bank of the Madeira River.

In order to clear ground for planting, the larger jungle trees must be killed. Since good stone for axes is scarce it was often traded over long distances. The larger trees have their bark ringed by the axes, which kills them. They are afterward burned to get rid of the dried brush and left standing. The underbrush can then be cleared and burned. All this is done by the men, whereas the women do the planting and tending of the crop.

In addition to maize, the manioc, an edible root of two kinds, provides a basic starch in the forest diet. One kind of manioc is harmless, another must be crushed and squeezed in a woven basket to rid it of the sap which contains prussic acid. The sap is first exposed to the sun to evaporate the acid, then it is mixed with pepper for a sauce in pepper-pot stews.

The South American forest is poor in game in comparison to that of Africa but some hunting of peccary, deer, and monkeys is done with either the bow and arrow, the spear (using a spear-thrower) or the blowgun. Stupefying poisons are used in fishing, while larger fish are secured with the bow and arrow.

The typical forest house is a large round or oval structure with a central post and a ring of side posts joined by rafters and heavily thatched, either left open-walled, with thatched sides, or sometimes the roof thatch is brought all the way to the ground. Such structures can house a whole clan, each family cooking over an individual fire. Since there is no smoke hole, the interior is murky but this atmosphere, which Europeans find hard to breathe, has the virtue of discouraging mosquitoes. Indeed houses on piles found north of the Amazon are probably built in this way to avoid the same tormenting insect pests, for mosquitoes do not fly above the level of the grass. A great many forests tribes go absolutely naked; in other cases the women wear an apron and the men nothing, or vice versa.

Ceremonial dress and painted masks remind us of Africa, and indeed the variety of ritual behavior is far more Melanesian or African in character than anything in North America. Feathered headdresses are used a great deal, as are labrets (decorations inserted in lips or cheeks), and bodies are painted with red, black and white, or decorated with areas of down, glued to the skin in Australian fashion. Other customs reminiscent of the other side of the world are men's houses containing masks and sacred musical instruments as well as conical consultation houses of shamans.

The three most indigenous traits, aside from the use of manioc, are the religious use of tobacco, the weaving of hammocks, an invention gratefully accepted by the rest of the world, and the discovery that rubber can be used for balls and to make syringes for giving enemas.

Social organization tends to be matrilineal and matrilocal and chiefs are seldom hereditary, their prestige depending upon their personal energy and wealth. Since these peoples live in isolated village groups, the usual primitive xenophobia and suspicion of sorcery results in a general state of hostility and many feuds.

When we come to scrutinize the supernatural ideas most widespread among these three groups, we find a vague first cause or creator god among the Caribs. The Tupis have a creator-transformer, Monan, who destroys the world by fire to punish the ingratitude of its first inhabitants and, later, there is a second destruction by water. This takes place when one of the creator's sons, Tamendonare, gets angry with his brother and strikes the ground so hard that a tremendous spring gushes forth which floods the earth. Tamendonare and his brother take to the trees with their wives, to return later and repeople the earth. Paul Radin connects the flood idea with the widespread North American myth and thinks the fire destruction is Middle American. In his view the forest mythology is late, which contradicts Tello's thesis that the ancient Andean animal religion might have been influenced by the jaguar tales of the Amazon.

At any rate, the two brothers are the basic culture heroes of this area. The myth as told by the Caribs goes as follows. An unidentified woman (possibly an earth or moon symbol) was made pregnant by the sun. On a journey in search of her husband she lost her way and was taken into the house of the Rain Frog whose son was the Jaguar. Although the Rain Frog tried to protect her, Jaguar killed the woman. The twins, however, were saved and, protected by the Rain Frog, grew up with miraculous speed. Learning the manner of their mother's death, they finally killed the Jaguar and his mother. This is in fundamental outline the myth of the Children of the Sun which is found in various parts of North America. The twins or brothers are probably related to the split figure of the trickster and culture hero, as is shown by the trickster characteristics of one or other of the two. Makunaima is sometimes the strong one who continually deludes his older brother. For instance, both create miraculous trees with fruit. Pia complains that his fruit has no taste. Makunaima takes the fruit, rubs it on his penis, and hands it back, saying "Try it now." Yet the same character is obtuse enough to make fishhooks out of wax. Under another name the trickster-creator betrays his brother (who has slept with his wife) to the bush spirits, who extract all the victim's bones. The trickster then saves him, puts the bones back, and goes through a number of adventures in which he defeats many bush spirits. On the whole, one brother is intelligent and a magician while the other is continually eaten or torn to pieces. Many stories are told to explain how they created mosquitoes, fish, and various sorts of birds.

Although it is true that the twin myth is characteristic of North America, there is also a very strong parallel between Makunaima and Pia and Maker and Orphan of the Kiraki tribes of New Guinea; there is the same resolved antagonism between the two and even the same adultery motif. This is one of the tantalizing similarities, which keep cropping up, between Melanesia and South America.

In another version, in which Pia is the creative hero and not Makunaima, Pia teaches the Indians the arts of civilization. As a result of his teaching, the *piai* or shamans were created who were the benefactors of the Carib tribes. Thus an explicit connection is made between trickster, culture hero and magician.

A different mythological cycle dealing with the parentage of the twins takes us back to a theme recorded by the Friar Pané. In this story the father of the twins seeks a wife who is provided for him by the Alligator. Alligator, however, has no real daughter; he has carved one from the plum tree. Unfortunately he omits the very necessary matter of genitalia. This is remedied, as in Pané's tale, by letting the woodpecker create the female organ. It will be remembered that we have encountered castration stories, in Oceania and Indonesia, in which there were no women and a man had to be turned into a woman. That we have here the same basic concept arising from the unconscious, is indicated by a variant in which the father-in-law is obliged to remove a snake from the girl's vagina before his son can consummate the marriage. The snake of course stands for the male organ which has to be amputated. Other stories make the snake symbol even clearer. The great water snake is an entity which is widespread in South America. Women are not supposed to bathe in ponds or watercourses lest snakes become their lovers. Once a man was warned by his sister to stay away from a certain pond while she was menstruating. She bathed, however, was caught by a large snake and made pregnant. She used to go every day to gather the

seeds of a certain tree and, although she never took an ax, always returned with her bag full. Her brother followed her and saw a snake come out
of her vagina, climb the tree, turn into a man, and shake down the seeds.
It then turned back into a snake and returned to its domicile. The brother
next day brought his friends, who attacked the snake just as it came down
from the tree and cut it into small pieces. The woman buried them under
some leaves and earth mold and each one grew into a Carib.

Remembering the snake and trumpet symbolism of north Australia, it is
curious to find a similar sort of complex, which has not been studied in any
detail, in South America. In connection with an ancestor cult on the Río
Negro, artificial snakes thirty to forty feet long and a foot in diameter are
made of bundles of twigs. These are carried on the shoulders of tribesmen in
dances. Both the Caribs and the Tupis of this region possess the institution
of the sacred trumpets which may be even fourteen feet long and are
strictly taboo to women and uninitiates. The Tucanoan boy is whipped and
initiated into a lineage group when he is shown these trumpets. They are
later sounded at ceremonies. A related tribe, the Cubeo, who also carry out
elaborate mourning ceremonies in masks, possess the same sort of ancestral
trumpets. Ancestor sagas are narrated at festivals and most of the religious
life of the tribe centers around the mythical founders of the lineages. They
are considered protectors and imparters of strength to their descendants.
Every morning the men of the tribe bathe to the sound of the trumpets to
obtain strength and courage. That the trumpets are phallic symbols representing the potency of the ancestors seems clear. Theodor Reik's discussion
of the Hebrew shofar as a phallic symbol is an interesting parallel.

The Witoto, of the same area but of a different ethnic stock, also possess
sacred instruments. Thomas Whiffen describes Witoto trumpets as "lengthy
affairs, made from the hollow stem of a palm and fitted with a trumpet
mouthpiece. The note is akin to that of a bassoon." They are kept concealed in a hut with other initiation paraphernalia including tapir-hide whips
used on the boys. They are as taboo as the Australian bullroarer. The
women are brought up in the belief that the music of the trumpets is an
essential element in the exorcism of the spirits from the bodies of the
initiates. Interference would result in the continual residence of the ancestor spirit in the novice. When the music of the trumpets is heard, women
and uninitiated run to the bush and stay there until the instruments are put
away. The ceremony is a profound secret. Whiffen adds that a connection
is reported between the great water snake and the trumpet music. Some relation, both as a visual symbol and as a representation of potency, between
snake and trumpet emerges. Still another bit of evidence appears in the
sounding of sacred trumpets under palm trees on the Orinoco so that the
trees may bear fruit.

In this connection, it will be recalled that the Caribs were created from bits of the phallic snake. Others claim to be descended from jaguars. On the whole, in all of the mythology under discussion the animal-human identification is strong. Just as in North America transformations can be brought about by putting on or taking off skins, the Caribs narrate a story of a woman who was a monkey but, by taking off her skin, became human and married an Indian. When he ill-treated her, she went back to the tree-tops, taking her child with her. The man pursued, on the ground, but she crossed a river when her relatives magically moved the opposite bank nearer so she could leap from branch to branch, and he never saw her again.

The region of the northwest Amazon and some parts of the eastern bank are notable for elaborate dances, with and without masks, carried on by the men's societies. The Witoto, mentioned in connection with the sacred trumpets, carry out one dance, the okima, in which ancestors are invoked at the time of the new moon, involving a multiple symbolism. The songs indicate that the forefathers are represented by animals. The growth of the moon is mimicked by the evolutions of the dancers, accompanied by two flutes, and along with the waxing moon, manioc, maize and peanuts are renewed. Thus the festival, with the aid of the power of the forefathers, maintains the cycle of nature.

Witoto dancing is vividly described by Thomas Whiffen, who was less impressed by symbolism than by the tendency for all the songs to be laden with sexual humor. Both sexes prepare elaborately for a dance. "The most vain of English beauties probably spends less time over her adornment for any function than do these young women as they squat in chattering crowds over the calabashes of vegetable dye, white, scarlet, black or purple, with which they trace upon each other the ceremonial patterns that make their only dress." Meanwhile the men are painting and putting on feather tiaras, necklaces, armlets and sounding garters of polished nuts. "Great bonfires are set ablaze and the interior of the tribal lodge, where the chief has a place in the center, flares ruddy with the light of the torches. The men make loud clangor with their instruments, flutes, panpipes, or drums, and out in the clearing they form a line, clutching their jingling dance poles while the women form up facing them. . . . Forward two steps—*thud!* Backward two steps—*thud!* Clattering and fluttering with the pipes shrieking high above all other sounds, as the drums growl deep below, the procession slowly encircles the maloka [communal house] and then enters. In a frenzied flutter of feathers and leaves the performers move round the chief, to a jangle of seed pods and rattles, till the company is completed and the tribal lodge is packed with dancers, when he signals for silence. The dance stops. The instruments cease their outcry and in the sudden contrast of silence the chief sings a line which is the keynote of the occasion, the explanation, the reason for the assembly. The dance and song begin, while those who are not taking active part squat round upon their haunches and ejaculate hoarse cries of approval and encouragement at intervals."

Although the Arawak, in the time of Friar Pané, had achieved idols and a priesthood, in their migrations they lost their organized religion and reverted to the shamanistic forms which are also characteristic of the Tupi-Guarani and the Caribs. The typical shaman undergoes long and difficult periods of initiation. The Carib magician may spend as much as two years in the woods fasting and drinking tobacco water, so that he comes home looking like a skeleton. The tobacco liquid, which is supposed to send the initiate into the land of the spirits in a tranced state, is drunk so often that it no longer acts as an emetic. Often the candidate becomes very sick from this and other concoctions so that he almost dies. There is also the ordeal of passing through a bonfire. The instructor goes on all fours imitating a jaguar, growling and clenching his fingers. He then leads his pupils through the blaze. After more tobacco water, the tormented candidates are sent to bathe in the river where the women pelt them with balls of clay and insult them. If they survive all of this, they are then allowed to participate in the festival which marks their graduation.

Tupi-Guarani shamans depend on talent and inspiration rather than on teaching for their power. They prove themselves by successful rain-making, cures, and divination. Their prestige is so great that there are even cults of their bones after death which remind us of practices in Siberia. The skeleton of the dead magician is placed in a hammock, covered with feather cloth, offerings are made to it, and advice asked. There is a belief that such shamans can sometimes return to earth.

Methods of cure generally consist of the familiar technique of sucking and producing some object from the body of the patient. He is also sometimes smoked at. Divination procedures are interesting, for they center about the rattle known as a maracca which is currently familiar as a percussion instrument in Latin-American dance bands. The Carib maracca is surrounded by ritual. The stone or seeds which clatter within the gourd are supposed to have been extracted from the stomach of the teacher who initiated the shaman. The rattle must be decorated with the feathers of a particular parrot. Sometimes a string of iridescent beetle wings is added. Shaking the rattle evokes the spirits while a little doll or crudely carved image does the actual divining. If it stands during the incantation the patient will get well, if it falls he is doomed to die. Sometimes the doll may be beaten to drive off the evil disease spirit. Among the Tupis the rattle itself attracts a spirit. From Hans Staden's description, all the men possessed maraccas, but it was the shaman's task to call up the spirits and make them prophesy. He spoke to them and by changing his voice made them answer him. The maraccas were kept in special houses and addressed as "my dear son." Tupi shamans also paint faces on gourds which are the abode of spirits.

With the exception of a thunder god, Tupan, among the Tupis identified with a thunderbird, the supernatural world of the forest tribes generally consists of a horde of "bush" spirits. The Caribs conceive of them in many shapes and forms, generally as somewhat hostile and always defeated by the trickery of the culture hero twin. They play a similar role among the Tupis.

Sadistic impulses expressed in various ritual forms are an unattractive characteristic of the forest tribes. The Caribs are noteworthy for the savagery of their initiation practices at puberty during which, in contrast to most groups, the girls suffer as much as the boys. The Arawak, who possess the same institution, may have adopted it from the Caribs. Ants are secured by their middles in the interstices of plaited frames. The side with the heads protruding is applied to the chests of the unfortunate children. Sometimes wasps, treated in the same way, are allowed to sting their bodies. Some Caribs wound the boys' bodies with a boar tusk or a toucan's beak. The girls may be scarified and pepper rubbed into their wounds. This they are supposed to endure, along with flogging, without a murmur, supported by the rationalization that it will make them industrious and clever. Afterward there is a festival with drinking of maize beer at which the initiates all eat a bit of dried hummingbird. The girls may have white down stuck on their legs, arms and head, or receive a coat of red paint.

The infliction of pain even extends to hunting magic among the Caribs. They put pepper in their eyes in order to make their sight more acute. This of course ties up with initiation procedure and is obviously based on the idea that whatever hurts is good for you. Although in crude form this appears savage, we should not forget that it contains the germ of the Christian concept of martyrizing the flesh and the final rationalizations of more philosophical theology in which human suffering is supposed to possess spiritual value.

A highly neurotic expression of fear and xenophobia is embodied in the institution of *kanaima*. This results from the usual preliterate belief that sickness, misfortune or death is caused by sorcery. If an individual has suffered some such disaster and feels quite desperate, he dedicates himself to magical revenge and becomes an outcast. It is a method of revenge more terrible than violence, poisoning or simple magical rites. When a shaman has diagnosed a death caused by a kanaima, a relative of the dead person assumes the responsibility of himself becoming a kanaima. Thus a vicious circle results. He disappears from his social groups, practices abstinence and subscribes to food taboos in order to become possessed with the spirit which carries out the ritual assassination. The individual dedicated to the rite sometimes puts on a jaguar skin, and turns into this animal. (We are reminded of the leopard men of Sierra Leone.) While occupied with his activity, a kanaima can be killed by anyone if he is encountered in the woods. The reason for this is clear since, once he has killed the proper victim, he is likely to destroy innocent persons. Thus the whole rite becomes a kind of social running-amok. The method of killing is magical, for the victim must not die immediately. A spider web anointed with certain juices must be stretched across the victim's path. When he touches it, he falls in a trance. When he is discovered and taken home he soon dies. He must not die immediately, however, for the ritual murderer must have time to resocialize himself so that he can once more join his group. When the murdered man is buried, his destroyer must pay a visit to the grave, drive a stake through the body, remove it and lick the blood. With this he is purified and once more normal.

The ultimate in sadism, rationalized by ritual, is of course head taking and cannibalism, both of which are widespread among the forest tribes. The trophy heads of the Mundurucú, a Tupi tribe, have already been mentioned. The tribes of the Peruvian Montaña, who may be of Arawak extraction also, in the past took heads and the elaborate procedures of the Jívaro of Ecuador have been touched on in Chapter 1.

The cannibalism of the Tupis is accompanied by an elaboration of ritual which makes it unique and indeed suggests that several elements have coalesced. To return to the imperiled Hans Staden once more, he was surprised to find that his captors shaved his eyebrows and beard with a crystal, put a feather headdress on his head and rattles on his legs, and made him dance at what appeared to be his own funeral. As Paul Radin points out, all this was to make him into a Tupi warrior, for, after the victor "counted coup," a defeated warrior was the slave of his captor yet in a sense adopted into the tribe. He might remain in this state for some time but he was always eaten in the end. One of the rites which took place was the parading of the prisoner before the graves of the captors' ancestors. The prisoner was given the dress and ornaments of the dead person for whom he had been captured and for whom he was to be killed in revenge. During the waiting period he was treated well and allowed to sleep with any of the unmarried girls of the tribe who would have him. The actual execution rites took five days. The cord with which he was to be bound was plaited ceremonially. Meanwhile the women danced around him and insulted him. A special hut was built of cane in which the cooking fire was to be made. Particularly elaborate was the consecration of the club which was to kill him. As Staden describes it, crushed eggshells were glued to it, and one of the women traced lines on it. It was decked out with feather tassels, hung in an empty hut on a pole around which the women danced and sang all night. The prisoner, ritually painted, drank and danced with them. On the day of the execution, after the fire was lit, the prisoner was brought forth, painted and decorated with a red diadem of feathers, and also fastened to his rump was a great wheel of feathers similar to that worn by some of the plains Indians of North America. The executioner then came and danced around the prisoner, making terrible faces. An old man brought the club and passed it between the legs of the executioner. The prisoner was menaced and in turn boasted that his relative would avenge him. The executioner then attacked the victim, who was given some liberty of movement during which he tried to evade the death blow. Sometimes he was even allowed a small club with which to defend himself. When he was killed, a great cry of joy went up from the audience.

What are the various elements which went into this curiously elaborate death ceremony? Hans Staden, who was always in a state of peril, but who finally escaped because he made a couple of lucky medical suggestions and gained the reputation of a shaman, records one curious fact. "And this Kongan Bebe had a large basket full of human flesh before him, ate off a leg and held it before my mouth and asked if I would eat it. I replied, 'Unreasoning animals hardly devour their kind, ought one man, therefore, to devour another?' He took a bite, saying, 'Jauware sch; I am a jaguar. It tastes well.' "

From this, it seems that some notion of animal identification might have been associated with the rite. Although the revenge motif was loudly proclaimed, the fact that the prisoners were paraded before ancestors' graves suggests actual sacrifice, which is strengthened by the fact that one group said they offered the victims to the gods. Paul Radin points out the similarities to Aztec practice. A prisoner, who was a representative of the god Tezcatlipoca, was well treated for a year, given four young women as temporary wives, and received worship as if he were the god himself. He was taught aristocratic behavior and walked about playing the flute. He finally led a procession, which was accompanied with jubilation and feasting, to the pyramid upon which he was sacrificed. Sagahún describes a kind of gladiatorial sacrifice at Temolacatl in which the officiating priest was a wolf-man who stationed the captive near the sacrificial altar. "And when he had put the captive in his place he offered him the pine club and he gave him a feathered staff. And then went one arrayed as an eagle or an ocelot to belabor him. He then struck down the captive as if he warred against him." It is interesting that an ocelot knight was the executioner and that Staden's cannibal chief called himself a jaguar.

The matter of passing the club between the executioner's legs suggests that it was to gain power from contact with his genitals, a parallel with

Polynesia. No doubt the eating of the flesh was to acquire the captive's qualities; but a second kind of cannibalism was also practiced by the Tupis and even the Shipibo of the Montaña. This was the eating of deceased relatives. From the central Australians, who did the same, we can interpret it as a desire to acquire the qualities of the departed, a curious method of strengthening the bonds of the clan group.

CHAPTER 44

Big Fox and the War of the Sexes

Marginal tribes—simple hunting economy suggests these groups an earlier migration to South America—trickster as Big Fox—jaguar and sun myth—multiple afterworld—secularization of ritual among Ge tribes—parallels with Oceania—men's societies and nature spirits.

THE REGIONS outside the rain forests include eastern grassy plains, the southern pampas, the windswept beaches of Tierra del Fuego and that central area, the Gran Chaco, the cause of a brutal jungle war between Bolivia and Paraguay from 1928 to 1935 in which innocent Indians were slaughtered by both sides. Between the Amazon and the Argentine pampas this region consists of monotonous, unattractive "flat lands of an alluvial nature created by flooding waters, with a dry vegetation of spiny bushes, brambles and cactus. Forest alternates with savannas, marshes and desert areas containing salt pans. Groves of palms near the rivers are the only bright and pleasing note in the heart of this sad and surly landscape." So writes Alfred Métraux. There was, however, more game in the past and this region was always able to support hunters and gatherers.

The Indians who inhabit this region of South America have been, for convenience, grouped under the head of the marginal tribes. While they differ in specific ritual expression and in adjustments to these environments, they all exhibit a less elaborate material civilization than that of the agricultural forest tribes. The marginals either do not carry on agriculture or have acquired it late. On the whole, pottery is crude and weaving often absent. Houses may be mere lean-tos or small beehive huts, and bodies of the dead are often disposed of by exposure or cremation. Numerous traits link them with tribes in North America and certain others are reminiscent of Melanesia or Australia.

There has been some tendency to regard them as the Australians were once regarded, as remnants of primeval man. Like the Australians, however, despite their material poverty they often display surprising elaborations of social organization and ceremonial culture. In consequence we must remember that, even if they do represent an older migration than do the Caribs, Arawak and Tupis, they have not stood still. Also from the point of view of physical anthropology, though a few long-headed types appear, on the whole most of them appear to belong to the same Mongolian ethnic stock as their Amazonian neighbors.

A sample of a pure hunting and gathering culture are the Botocudo as they were in 1915. Unfortunately this tribe had already suffered persecution by the Brazilians; the methods of extermination included poisoning, contamination with contagious diseases, and enslavement of their women and children. What remained of them then lived on a rocky, partially forested plateau near the northeast coast of Brazil. Here, during the dry season the rivers disappear and the trees lose their leaves. In the rainy season lilies and other flowers abound, and cottonwoods, acacia and bamboos put forth their foliage. Houses were small, dome-shaped affairs, lower than a man's height, made of saplings stuck in the ground and joined together in the center, or small bark tipis. Each day the men went out to hunt tapirs, peccary, and monkeys while the old and young women gathered. Both sexes were naked, the men tucking the penis under a waistcord. They rubbed their bodies with *urucú,* a red dye from the fruit of the annatto tree which they felt protected them against the cold and the bites of insects. Since the climate was hot during the day and cold at night, fever was prevalent. This people used the bow and arrow and made knives from sharpened bamboo. A man's hunting equipment was placed with him when he died, and his body was left in the hut in which he lived or abandoned in the forest.

In general the life of the Botocudo appears to parallel rather closely that of the African Pygmies. Unlike the latter, however, they were always hungry and inclined to beg from the whites. The details reported of their religious life are scanty, either because their beliefs were simple or because they had begun to decay. There was one supernatural being, Maret-Khmak-mam, who appeared to have been a legendary ancestor (Maret means old). He was taller than a man, his head white, his face all covered with red hair. His most striking characteristic was a penis so long that when he had intercourse with an ordinary woman it would reach to her throat and strangle her. He copulated with his own wife from a distance. He was said to live in the sky and to have many children. He could walk on the clouds and on the water, invisible to men. Nothing in nature could harm him but when he was angered he could kill with an invisible arrow. There was some belief that if the Botocudo danced and sang, Khmakmam would bestow benefits on them. Their attitudes toward this entity seem to make him half a demon and half a trickster hero.

Another report indicates that *marets* were about the size of men or smaller. Shamans were individuals especially privileged by being able to see and communicate with them. Since the marets were always kind and helpful to men, this was why the Botocudo never needed hunting magic. The marets sent game, left a fine heap of food in the forest, or even planted maize like industrious European brownies. Once a man was caught by some of them and tossed about between them like a shuttlecock. He was told they did this to bestow certain powers on him. He came home in a daze, then began to sing, and finally received a present of pineapples. Marets were able to change people into animals and to cure sickness. Father Whitehead, the oldest maret, lived in the sky and had nothing to do with the earth. A ceremony took place in which a post was carved, terminating in a human head with stumps for arms and legs. The face, when it was set up, was turned to the east and painted with lines of urucú. The image represented a maret and indicated the site in the village where these spirits were to descend. When a certain shaman sang before the statue, all the villagers would put on a coat of red paint and assemble around him. Ten to twelve marets would descend after he sang all afternoon. As he sang to the statue, the spirits did not enter it but stood about it, seen only by him. His chants made them watch over the village and preserve it from harm.

The Botocudo believed that men had five or six souls, acquiring the first at the age of four, the others as time went on. They could wander in sleep and cause dreams; loss of a soul was connected with sickness. At death one soul died with the body, the rest went to the sky. Father Whitehead was accustomed to imprison the souls of murderers in the sky, which caused the bodies of the criminals to go into a decline. Dangerous ghosts were also supposed to arise from the dead; when met in the woods they must be attacked and killed.

Other supernaturals included the sun who was a male and the moon who was a male, when full, but female when only a crescent. A great snake was lord of the water and caused floods. It signaled for the rain to descend by means of the rainbow.

Thus, when all these details are assembled, it appears that the Botocudo probably shared some myths with their neighbors (great snake and sun and moon) and had even achieved a kind of germinal idolatry.

Moving southward to the Chaco which is populated along the rivers and deserted in other areas, except where a few lakes provide water, we have detailed reports of religious belief from the Mataco, the Toba and Pilagá tribes. It should be remembered that to the west are tribes mediating between the Andean and hunting cultures, including the Diaguita who created a pottery tradition on a high level and built villages defended by stone fortifications. Some of the Chaco tribes borrowed the horse from the Spaniards and became accomplished horsemen rather like the western plains Indians of the United States. Their cavalry tactics enabled them to defend themselves fiercely against the Spaniards well up into the nineteenth century, as did the Araucanians of southwestern Chile, who also adopted the horse.

The three most primitive groups of the Chaco do a little farming but depend a good deal on hunting and still more on fishing, in the latter pursuit using bows and arrows and nets. They gather wild beans, squash and tubers and make a beer from the pods of the algorroba tree. Game includes deer, peccary and small rodents. Rheas, the small American ostriches, are not much esteemed but are sometimes hunted by covering the head and shoulders with grass or leaves, a technique similar to that used by the Australians. Houses are either small dome-shaped structures like those of the Botocudo or a group of them are put together without interior partitions to make a communal dwelling. Men dress in a cloth wound around the waist and a skin cloak, the women wear a shorter skin skirt. Weaving is a late acquisition, as is the simple pottery made by these people.

The fact that these tribes were accustomed to scalp their enemies is a surprisingly North American trait but when we examine their psychic life the number of parallels with the north is still more striking. Métraux finds no supreme being, but various kinds of animals have masters who prevent wanton destruction by the hunters. Soñidi gets particularly angry if fish are caught and left to rot. This, of course, is exactly like the beliefs of the Algonkians. Métraux states that the word *payak* means spirit but "the same word is applied as an adjective to all kinds of phenomena and animals which appear strange, mysterious, or uncanny." Another trait is the belief that disease can be caused by spirits which enter the body and possess it, also subscribed to by North American hunting and gathering tribes. Great importance is attached to dreams. Dreams being the dictates of the soul, they are accepted as guides to living. Even the shaman who operates by sucking, as is common, is said to have a familiar or guardian spirit.

Some of the mythological concepts, however, carry us back to Asia and the northwest coast of America—particularly the conception of three or more worlds, all of which are populated. When sickness is caused by loss of souls, the shamans travel across the underworld to seek them, for they have been kidnapped by spirits and put in cages. To free them the shamans must cross swamps over which they fly in the form of birds. Even in this shape some shamans get stuck and perish. Another tribe, the Chamamcoca, goes as far as five worlds. In one above lives Jaguar, in the next higher Big Fox the trickster, down below there is a world which used to be peopled but is now vacant, and below that the residence of the sun from which it rises every day.

Strangely enough, the flood myth begins to sound Australian. It was caused by a menstruating woman who was not supposed to enter the river because the Rainbow Python would resent it. She broke the taboo, where-upon Rainbow caused the flood. The basic elements here are the same as those found in northern Australia.

To add to the mingling of themes, there is also a destruction by fire (which is Middle American) and a great darkness in which objects revolt against men as in the Quiche Popol Vuh.

More typically South American is the sun, moon and jaguar tradition. The sun is a fat woman, at the winter solstice young and able to walk across the sky fast, hence the days are short; in summer she grows old and walks more slowly. The moon is a fat-bellied man whose bluish intestines can be seen through the skin. When eclipses take place his enemy, the celestial jaguar, springs up to devour him. The moon strives to defend himself but his club breaks. As the jaguar tears at his body, pieces break off to fall on the earth as meteors. When the moon is in danger of being completely devoured the Chaco people beat drums, strike their dogs, and shout to drive him off. This particular belief is almost universal among South American groups, being found among the Quechua as well as the forest tribes.

A final element in this potpourri of themes is the twin motif, here divided into Carancho, the benevolent hero, and Fox, who is a trickster almost identical with Coyote of the north. Carancho has "master" aspects in that he saw to it that the forest animals became wild because men were killing them wantonly. He taught men how to make weapons but his chief role is a kind of knight-errant killing of monsters. He is also supposed to be the first shaman. When Fox tries to play his evil tricks he is often unmasked, sometimes magically, by Carancho. Fox is phallic, greedy, on the whole stupid and deceitful, but endowed with some magical attributes himself. Fox attempts unsuccessfully to seduce the woodpecker's wife but succeeds with the wife of the jaguar who is depicted as dangerous but stupid. He destroys the jaguar by crawling into his body and cutting out his heart. He is then tricked by a bird who suggests they dive into a pool while the meat cooks. The bird leaves some feathers on the water to deceive him, slips out and eats the meat.

In a myth explaining the origin of women, Fox also plays a role. He goes on a hunting expedition with a number of animal-humans including Hawk. While the latter is alone he sees a number of women climb down from the sky on ropes. Hawk announces that he has procured wives for the men but warns them not to approach the women sexually because he has perceived that they have toothed vaginas. Fox typically cannot control himself. As soon as he starts to make love to his woman she cuts off his penis and testicles with the teeth in her vagina. Fox dies of his wound. Later, rain falls on him and brings him back to life. He makes a new phallus from a piece of wood and supplies testicles by using two black fruit. When he penetrates his wife again she tries her best to bite off his male organ but can only dent it. Next day Hawk breaks off all the teeth in the vaginas of the other women, except one which remains as the clitoris. Fox is destroyed appropriately trying to rape a wooden mortar with a crack in it. His penis gets stuck in the crack with the result that he dries up and dies. Among the Mataco the same incidents are told with a human trickster, Tawkxwax, in the leading role.

Turning from the mythology of the Chaco to the Ge tribes, who occupy an area from Xingu, a tributary of the Amazon, to the southwest corner of Brazil, we find a social and ceremonial structure unlike anything else in the Americas and only matched by the elaborate activities of the Australians.

A tribe of the Ge group, the Timbira, lives in the steppe area bordering on dry forest. They practice some agriculture, some gathering, hunt with the bow, kill anteaters and armadillos with clubs and stalk the rhea. Falcons they kill for their meat and also for the white down which they stick to their bodies with resin on ceremonial occasions.

Their houses are dome-shaped, thirty or so being arranged in a circle about a central circular street which has paths like spokes of a wheel connecting it to the central dance plaza.

This tribe wears no clothes at all and considers nakedness the only socially acceptable condition. When a neighboring group, invited to join them in a ceremony, appeared wearing breechclouts and shorts, they were politely asked to disrobe before taking part in the proposed dancing. They embarrassedly refused. The anthropologist, himself naked and painted, was amused to discover that his hosts considered their neighbors indecently dressed. In the end, the joint ceremony had to be given up. Some of the Timbira women now and then wore pubic aprons but the chief made them remove them before dancing and complained of their obscene behavior.

A complete dualism runs through Timbira theory and practice. Half the world is red and white, the other black. The first, or Ka, division includes the east, sun, day, dry season, fire, earth, red animals and plants, maize and manioc. Atuk contains the west, the moon, night, rainy season, firewood, water, black animals and plants, gourds, the sweet potato.

The whole group of people is also divided into Ka and Atuk depending on the name given at birth. The first paints with red, the second with black, and each has its own war cry. These groups are important during the rainy season in which they hunt separately and indulge in the peculiar sport of log racing in opposing teams. There is also a moiety division of the men into two exogamous marrying groups. Finally there are groups with animal badges and ceremonial houses who gather in certain parts of the plaza, whom Kurt Nimündajú feels might once have been totemic clans. Still another division is into age classes which coincide with the exogamous divisions. The age classes, however, mark the initiation groups who go through ceremonies which take ten years before they graduate!

The lives of the Timbira are wholly taken up with ceremonial activity. The young girls dance in the plaza three times a day. When they go on gathering expeditions they take a dance director (an older man who knows the rules) with them and keep up their daily exercise.

In addition to the social groupings already mentioned there are six men's societies: Jaguars, Agoutis, Ducks, Falcons, Water Monsters, and Aquatic Birds. They also carry out dances. Besides these clubs there is an order of King Vultures who are a sort of aristocracy of honorary chiefs who wear a special down and red paint costume, and are buried with certain honors. One more organizational element is a system of paired friendships, which may be of the same or opposite sexes, in which the friends have certain obligations and privileges toward each other; they come to each other's aid in case of a fight and confide in each other.

The initiation ceremonies among the Canalla, a related tribe, go on for ten years and include periods of seclusion in a hut in the woods during which the boys' ears and lower lips are pierced and their hair is ceremonially cut. The boys march to the village to be fed at their homes in groups in a certain order led by a preceptor. They have meetings, sing songs and are instructed by their leaders. In their camp they make the insignias of their groups. They organize relay races with logs which they carry at top speed, ending the race at the plaza. The Timbira rites also include three days of afternoon dancing in the plaza which is supposed to put them in communication with their dead ancestors. A rationalizing myth speaks of some boys once entering a village where the dead were dancing. They returned with the tale, whereupon a brave man went to the assembly of the dead and learned the chants and ceremonies. Apparently the boys are possessed by the ancestors, for there are various token whippings as water is poured over them to drive the spirits out of their bodies (as among the Witoto). A bull-roarer is also swung during some of these rites.

An example of the men's society activities is the dance of the masqueraders of the Water Monster society. The costume consists of a stick resting on the dancer's head from which hang two mats with heavy fringes which envelop him. On one side are painted two large red and black eyes. From either side of the head protrudes a pointed horn. The masqueraders danced in the plaza, stamping and gesturing, humming instead of singing. They were joined by the clowns of the Aquatic Bird society. The latter made fun of the mummers, giving them names which referred to peculiarities of their sex organs. One clown put on a burlesque of a woman's little apron, another wore a long false penis. They also did a riotous travesty of Timbira family life in which the members of the group fought and beat each other, and finally they simulated adultery with the mother of the family. Still another pretended to be a skunk engaged in a scuffle with two girls, who barked like dogs, and splashed them with water which was supposed to be the skunk's effluvium.

Two interesting points emerge from the description of this culture. Although, as can be seen, an enormous amount of ceremonial detail goes on, Nimündajú insists that it is practically all of a secular nature. Except for the connection between the initiates and the ancestors there is no integration with a body of religious belief, no sense of awe. The moiety division is purely formal and the rites are carried out in the spirit of good clean fun. This could not always have been the case; Nimündajú himself points out the exogamous restrictions are rarely adhered to, which shows that there has been a progressive loss of meaning. There is no doubt that clans and ancestor cult must have once had an elaborate significance, since everything else similar to the Australian situation is present. Apparently, just as among literate churchgoing groups, true religious emotion and experience have given way to gregarious social activity. The only really significant religious rite described took place on a late afternoon when a man stood in the center of the plaza with his back to the sun and said, "May the grandfather sun protect all beasts so they grow up and can be eaten by man." Ge mythology concerns the trickster twins in which the sun is the trickster and the moon, thought of as masculine, is the butt. The sun is also occasionally asked for rain. Ancestors are supposed to live in a village near where they are buried. On the whole they tend to accompany and protect living relatives. Although the Timbira have shamans who suck out disease, sometimes people who are sick try to dream of their ancestors in order to learn the appropriate remedy for their own illnesses.

Despite the loss of religious emotion, the whole ceremonial structure does support a tribal ethos and this ethos reminds us strongly of the Pueblo Indians. The bad citizen is the quarrelsome man who refuses to yield personal privilege, who is not ready to compromise. The ideal person never fails to take part in the group activities. Even after the curious log races, in which opposing relay teams run themselves to exhaustion, carrying heavy blocks of wood, there are no prizes and no praise for the victors; strenuous participation is all that counts. In their loyalty to group ideals the Timbira appear to have moved from religious to secular communism.

Just as in the case of the Pueblo Indians, the clowns are a safety valve and a defiance of the orderly behavior which is the norm or ideal. Their sexuality and wild burlesque of family life (ordinarily so well-mannered) exactly parallels the antics of the buffoons of North America.

At the farthest tip of South America, the Island of Tierra del Fuego is the habitat of three tribes, the Alakaluf, the Yahgan and the Ona, who, on the theory that the oldest groups of humanity in America would be those who have progressed farthest from the port of entry, have been considered remnants of an archaic type of man. The fact that some of the Ona are long-headed has been used to support the suggestion that they represent a survival of the oldest hunting culture. The material which has been gathered on this people indicates that, although their material poverty is extreme, their psychic life is far from simple and probably represents a mixture of traits. The Ona are far from being all of one type and, although they are tall and some do have Caucasoid features, others are fairly Mongolian. The Yahgan are wholly Mongolian in type as are the Alakaluf.

The history of these people also has a bearing on the reliability of ethnological investigation. Missionary work began in 1856. Then in the seventies sheepherders arrived. The Ona, who could not understand why their land was being taken from them and who were guanaco hunters, simply treated the sheep as guanaco. The same situation resulted as with the Bushmen of Africa. The ranchers hired professional killers to get rid of the Indians, offering a pound a head for men, women or children. The killers shot them on sight or poisoned a sheep carcass with arsenic and left it for the unsuspecting Indians to find, a system which had already proven efficacious against the natives of Australia.

When this became a scandal and was stopped, Catholic missionaries arrived and destroyed the natives with uninformed kindness. The Ona wore no clothes but a guanaco cloak which they took off when it rained. Although the temperature of the island is chilly, seldom above 50 degrees in summer and hovering around 30 degrees or lower in winter, these people were so hardened that they could endure cold, and when they got wet, as often happened, their skins soon dried at the fire. The missionaries huddled them into wooden huts and dressed them in modern clothes. As a result the Ona lost their resistance and, from going about in wet clothes, succumbed to pneumonia and tuberculosis. One group was entirely disposed of in twenty years. It is therefore well to remember that contact with the whites had been going on from the middle of the nineteenth century. (In 1932 there were scarcely any Ona, about fifty Yahgan and a hundred Alakaluf.)

The Ona, as has been said, were hunters. Tierra del Fuego consists of rolling plains covered with short grass to the north and east. Because of the low temperatures grain does not ripen. The southern area consists of cold, damp, misty forests and peat bogs. On the trees are many fungi which were an article of diet with these Indians, who also hunted foxes for their skins and did not scorn small rodents. Guanaco skins were their only shelter; they hung them over slanted saplings to make a windbreak.

All the Fuegians lacked the fishhook, spear-thrower, drill and pottery or weaving. The Ona used skin containers; the Yahgan made baskets. They all entered the chilly water to obtain shellfish and the giant spider crab, important items in their diet. The Yahgan and Alakaluf used canoes, keeping a small fire going on a clay hearth in the bow, and in consequence they were able to visit the mainland. Since the Ona had no boats at all, it is rather a mystery how they reached Tierra del Fuego unless they persuaded their neighbors to ferry them over the strait.

As the Yahgan were coast dwellers, they concentrated on capturing seals, porpoises, netting fish and feasting on whales whenever they were washed ashore. Uncured sealskin, much stiffer than guanaco hide, furnished them with cloaks and coverings for their shelters. Like the Ona, they possessed the bow and arrow.

None of the Fuegians, when they were studied, showed evidence of clans or totemism. They did, however, practice exogamy as far as prohibiting marriage between second cousins. Organized in family groups, they had no chiefs, their only officials being shamans.

The Ona believed in a creator god, who was not personalized, who had something to do with forming the earth and sky, who never came to earth, and to whom the spirits of the dead ascended. He was also referred to as the first man who created plants and animals. Most important in tribal life were the complicated initiation ceremony and the isolation rites, in all probability borrowed by the Yahgan.

Initiation lodges were tipi-like structures of poles piled part way up with sods. The novices underwent trials for two years, living in solitude on lean guanaco meat. Now and then they were taken to the lodge, each pole of which had a name and was assigned to one of the initiates. The boys were treated sadistically. Burning splinters were thrust into their arms. They were also supposed to sit for long periods without moving, talking or laughing. Then a masked figure flung himself upon them and a struggle ensued. When the novice was exhausted and terrified, the spirit unmasked. The young men then became a part of the secret society. The spirits represented by the masks were connected with nature. One with crooked legs lived underground and appeared completely covered with feathers stuck on with grease. A woman spirit of mist and the clouds was all white with a large head made of twigs. Still another had a claw on each forefinger. He gathered firewood but never made a fire and seemed to personify the fear engendered by the sudden snappings of twigs in the forest. The tall conical masks of bark were sometimes striped in red and white as were the nude bodies of the masqueraders. Although these spirits were not supposed to represent ancestors, there was something oddly Australian-looking about the regalia.

The *kloketen* ceremony itself took place when the masked figures sallied forth to terrorize the women, children and uninitiated. The myth behind the rite stated that at one time women were the original maskers who terrified the men. A man one day caught them making their preparations. The men were disabused of their fear and in revenge attacked the women. One, who was thrown into the fire, ran and flung herself in the sea and afterward became the moon; the scars can still be seen on her face. Some of the others turned into water birds. Since then the men wear the masks and frighten the women.

The Yahgan possessed the same myth and carried out a similar ceremony. Their initiation rites were extended to girls. Both sexes were made to sit in constricted positions in seclusion. During this period they were taught useful arts and frightened by a masked man. The Alakaluf initiation was a weaker imitation of that of the other two tribes.

The Yahgan are ambivalent toward a supernatural called Watauineiwa, for they publicly curse him for bringing early death and killing children. The name itself is the word used for ancestors and mythical heroes. Truly revealing, however, is the fact that Watauineiwa is the owner of wild things, all animals and birds belong to him. He watches carefully that animals are not killed needlessly and that meat is not wantonly wasted. Here we have, of course, the familiar master of animals who has already appeared among the Algonkians, in the Gran Chaco, and originally in Siberia. The fact that simple requests for benefits are addressed to him (in archaic language which proves they are old) scarcely makes him a supreme being as Gusinde claims. There had been plenty of time for missionary influence to affect an old Mongolian supernatural. Sedna of the Eskimo is probably an example of the original concept. Indeed, Diamond Jenness speaks of finding similarities between the Yahgan and Eskimo languages.

These are not the only parallels with other regions. The men's society, possessing tall conical masks and ceremonial lodges from which women are excluded, is also found in east Brazil. Even a similar myth is told describing the original masking of women and the rebellion of the men. We can push the parallel even further if we recall northern Australia where elaborate rites in connection with the great snake are carried out. In one area it is maintained that the women originally possessed all the rituals which were eventually taken over by the men.

The peoples of the tip of South America therefore, far from being the most archaic in the New World (some natives of central California are even more primitive), show the same curious mixture of North American mythology and tantalizing Australo-Melanesian-like traits in their ceremonial life which appear elsewhere in the forest and the steppes. Considerable development must have gone on since early times. That the Ona culture has not always been the same is proved by archaeologists who have discovered, in their habitat, five strata of early occupation, beginning with the small arrow points used by the Ona and leading back to spearheads and bones of horses eaten by the primeval hunters. A truer understanding of how the non-Andean cultures came about and their relation to other areas will therefore have to wait upon the archaeology and anthropology of the future.

CHAPTER 45

What Happened in Early Religion

*Summary and conclusions—hunting magic—animal identification—trickster
and shaman develop into earliest deity—shaman and creator god—head
taking, warrior ethos—fertility goddess and bull as male potency symbol—
sacral king and blood sacrifices—priesthoods and political power—growth
of pantheons—religion and the unconscious.*

THE STUDY of early religion involves the investigation of all of
man's psychic life. In our journey around the world it has become abundantly clear that the shape of his dreams molds his behavior, and
his beliefs about himself and his world are continually played out in the
drama of social existence. This does not mean that the effect of environment can be ignored. In some cases quite explicitly he creates a lyricism
from some essential element in his economy. The Egyptians unified their
faith in the symbol of the sun whose heat quickened vegetation in the Nile
mud. The Middle Americans created a rain god in fantastic and multiple
forms. On the other hand, what is the explanation for the omnipresence of
the jaguar throughout the New World, especially in areas where jaguars are
not particularly prevalent? This animal is neither a source of food nor is it
connected in any logical way with the weather. We can only conclude that
the beauty, power, or ferocity of the beast somehow stimulated the imagination of the peoples, who molded it on their pots, carved it on the stones of
their temples, wove it into their textiles, and wore its spotted hide in their
ceremonies. Man is, of course, the only animal which manipulates symbols
but the case of the jaguar shows that the choice and elaboration of these
symbols is not always determined by practicality or profit.

The jaguar should serve as a warning against too broad and easy types
of generalization in the field of human culture, especially too great an
emphasis on environmental or economic determinism. To balance it, another case in point is the suggestion that the Mesopotamians built pyramids
because they were nostalgic for the mountains from which they had
migrated. The Egyptians may have borrowed the form but in the New
World we find pyramids constructed in highlands and lowlands, on plateaus

527

and in jungles. Here perhaps a purely functional explanation is the answer. When a culture achieves a priesthood and important communal ceremonies, a simple way to lend importance to these rites is to raise them on a platform above the crowd. As the platform becomes higher and the pomp and circumstance increase, steps are necessary for the dignitaries to reach the top. At the same time, in order to preserve sight lines so that the crowd below may have an unobstructed view, the superimposed platforms would need to be narrower—and thus automatically we have the pyramid form.

It cannot be denied that certain determinants of man's symbolic behavior derive from his inherent biological nature. All human beings dream. Almost universally the dream plays some role in religion, ranging from the experience of the Crow warrior who meets his familiar spirit to Joseph's successful divination in the Old Testament. Time and time again the dream is considered a method of communicating with supernatural powers. When it comes to the actual content of the dream, however, as Ruth Benedict has shown, the established pattern of the culture comes into play and the spirits or communications which come to the dreamer may be shaped by his environment and his economy.

Although the variables which affect human behavior are so multiple that, as Boas felt, chance enters into the picture, perhaps a tentative formulation might be made. In the elaboration of man's psychic life, on the one hand, the pressure of environment and economic necessity is a molding process, and on the other, certain compulsions below the level of consciousness, which are always present as long as two or more human beings attempt to live in close association, continually rebel against the inhibiting effects of group living. The interplay of these two forces is capable of creating amazingly complex structures of belief and activity.

After having surveyed the major areas of the world, past and present, in which archaic forms of religion have been, and are, practiced, what sort of a picture can we form of the early history of human belief?

Since we know for certain from archaeology that hunting cultures are the oldest in the world, we would expect that animals would play an important role in man's first symbolic achievements. This is amply exemplified by the evidence. The ritually treated bear skulls found in Paleolithic caves in the Alps have already been related to Siberian behavior toward animals, and the Ainu bear festival is very suggestive. Indeed we have found that most of the hunting groups of North America feel that animals must be treated with respect, apologized to and persuaded willingly to become the food of man. This line of development is also exemplified by the report of the dances of the Philippine Negritos who both dramatized, apologized to, and thanked the animals they were about to kill. Among the same people the shaman spoke with the voice of the grandfather of the bees. Here, therefore, we find another very early trait which as a survival is universal, that of human-animal identification. The famous Upper Paleolithic sorcerer from the cave of the Trois Frères with horns on his head, horse tail, and mask is clearly a shaman closely identified with several animals.

This, of course, brings up the subject of possession or epilepsoid seizure through which the shaman gains his power. Judging from the universal distribution of this type of medicine man, there is every reason to believe that he is the oldest religious specialist in the world. It will be remembered that even the Veddas, otherwise so spiritually poverty-stricken, concentrated their religious life in the person of this individual. We have found him among both Bushmen and Pygmies as well as among all the other more advanced hunting peoples and persisting among the simple agriculturalists of both Africa and South America. The ability to dream or to see visions, to foam at the mouth and fall in a fit, to visit a world outside the ordinary one, must have coalesced in the very beginning of human society; we may safely assume that such shamans existed among the Neanderthals. It appears that the further development of the shaman can go in more than one direction and before attempting to sketch these directions out, it is necessary to pause and discuss one other archaic religious phenomenon, ancestor cults.

It will be remembered that along with ritual treatment of bear skulls, evidence of some rites in connection with human skulls was also found in the Paleolithic. If animal cults are the result of economic determinism, the attitude toward ancestors springs, as we have before suggested, from the deepest layers of the unconscious, the ambivalence of fear and love. The taking of trophy heads with or without accompanying cannibalism and the preservation of the skulls of relatives relate directly to this ambivalence. Both activities have been interpreted from the deposits of severed skulls. Judging from the modern preliterates, however, ancestor worship is not so universal as involvement with animals and the phenomenon of the shaman. It is completely absent from eastern Siberia and from nearly all North American hunting cultures and a good part of those of the Amazon forest.

The figure of the ancestor can take several forms. Either immediate relatives are thought of as helpful (and in this case their skulls or other bones may be preserved) or, in other cases, a supernatural is thought of as a vague first man or mythical forefather. The latter figure shows that considerable speculation has already taken place. Besides, because of the deep ambivalence present in the parent-child relationship and also the dangerous mana aspect of death, the attitude toward the ancestor may be entirely one of fear, as is evidenced by the behavior of the Bushmen who sometimes put stones on their dead to keep them in the grave and immediately abandon the area. The Pygmies, the Eskimo and the Veddas also desert their burials. In the Upper Paleolithic, stones were also placed on the dead for probably the same reason, which suggests that fear was the dominant emotion. Grave goods which appear in the Upper Paleolithic do not necessarly mean a cult. They are sometimes given to the dead to keep them satisfied so that they will not annoy the living.

All in all, it seems likely that a true ancestor cult does not develop very early; rather, some magical precautions would be taken to nullify the harmful potentialities of the dead. Severed skulls in the Paleolithic would therefore more likely be trophies since, like the shaman, head taking survives throughout the world. And indeed, as has been suggested, the beheading or dismembering of the enemy is probably the result of a primal urge to castrate and effeminize male rivals.

To return to the shaman, a very early crystallization about this figure ties up both with the trickster and with animal identification. The trickster, on the one hand, is a breaker of taboos, he represents the anarchistic individual protest against the inhibitions of good behavior and formalized sex expression which must exist in the simplest of social groupings. On the other hand, the shaman, too, is an outlaw who makes use of the dire power of mana to brave the supernatural world and make use of it. Selfish individualism and the individualism of the unusually gifted, the sensitive, epilepsoid, primitive intellectual here coincide, as indeed they have, to an extent, throughout history. The artist and visionary has always tapped the power of the unconscious and has always broken through the norms of conformity.

In primitive terms, Kaggen the Mantis, although he is not worshiped, is a good example of the shaman who can also turn into or is an animal. Since one of the functions of this religious specialist is the promotion of successful hunting, the shaman is the leader in dances involving animal mimicry. He wears the costume of the beast, no doubt sometimes evolved from the method of stalking it. Because of the emotional empathy involved in hunting, he often feels himself to be the beast and thus his image coalesces, in tales of trickery and transformation, with a supernatural entity. The richness and color of his personality and his ubiquity are derived from the fact that the forces of environmental determinism and the drives of the unconscious here coincide.

Of course there is no straight and single path of evolution. The trickster may remain a fairly secular phenomenon apart from the shaman. He may, however, achieve greater prestige and socialization and become an actual deity; we have encountered him in the form of Big Raven, or Old Man Coyote, creator and transformer and primal medicine man. As Pia of South America he is both culture hero and shaman. Again venturing into the realm of speculation, it seems likely that the trickster-shaman-creator cycles represent the first ventures into fiction which survive from prehistory.

Coyote's unabashed phallicism, his excremental humor, his complete irresponsibility, belong to the most artless layer of the human fancy. Man has slowly made himself something more than an animal. The gradual molding of the trickster cycles into satire and narration with ethical meaning illustrates the very beginning of literary artistry.

Another type of tale which is at times purely secular and at times attains religious significance is the just-so story which explains the origin of some natural phenomenon. That it is probably a very old as well as a continuing process of the human imagination is suggested by the fact that it continually crops up as an ending tacked onto a longer myth or becomes an element in a creative process. Very often, just as Kaggen made the moon out of his shoe, some magical episode explains why the heavenly bodies got where they are or why animals or birds obtained certain markings. It is probably from such a store of brief, popular, random fancies that shamanistic speculation drew episodes which were finally elaborated into lunar, stellar and creation myths, all of which developed during the hunting stage. In other words, instead of sky mythology evolving from the worship of sky gods, a semisecular nature mythology was already extant which, when a priesthood created heavenly deities in connection with astronomy and the calendar, could be reshaped in literary form.

Returning to ancestor worship, it is clear that it becomes a cult with the development of clan or lineage structure. In Bronze Age China and in Africa and in South America it coincides with at least sedentary village life and with simple agriculture. The sense of clan unity which continues beyond the grave evidently tips the scale against fear of the dead. Likewise the force of privilege and obligation which enters into the very grain of clan structure makes it unthinkable that the dead relative can remain wholly indifferent to his duty. Even so, as we have seen in Africa, some ambivalence does creep in for, if the dead feel neglected, they can cause sickness. Ancestor worship is certainly the least mystical of religions. The dead are invited to parties; they accept and eat and drink their share. In return for good treatment they influence the weather and protect their relatives. And when they behave badly they are scolded. Since there is no room for the ecstatic element in this matter-of-fact operation, it is not surprising that the possessed shaman continues to flourish along with the ancestors and takes over the function of interpreting their wishes through dreams or divination techniques.

The theme of animal identification enters a new phase with clan development. Previously what we might call a pre-totemic mentality has existed in which the relationship to animals has not been codified. In certain cases, with the new interest in lineages and marriage regulations, whole families, perhaps because they were specialists in hunting a particular animal, or in other cases arbitrarily, decide that they are descended from an animal. This is generally connected with taboos concerning eating the beast-relative. Although this development in some areas becomes very complex and takes on a geographical character, it is a stage which some human groups have probably omitted altogether. The complex—animal-symbol, ancestor-spirit and social grouping—also crops up in the phenomenon of men's clubs found in Africa, Oceania and South America. Since men's clubs can exist at the same time as the clan, they seem to be an independent social form. The magical, social, and at times guardian activities of men's clubs, however, also connect them with religious life.

The moiety system in which a tribe is divided into two exogamous halves (sometimes with subdivisions) with animal badges also ties in with animal identification. This appears to be a late phenomenon in Australia. The case of the Ge in South America is less clear. If they once had clans, it, too, may be a recent addition. Totemic clans can weaken and disappear, leaving only remnants of animal symbols or bits of folklore connecting them with lineages.

The presence of animal masks and animal dances, which linger in so many cultures which are far from the hunting stage, shows that the old identification with beasts is a trait which leaves a deep impression upon the human psyche long after the economic motivation has lost its validity. It appears that the drives of the unconscious also seize upon these symbols and manipulate them into indirect forms of expression. The use of the snake as a phallic symbol is the most obvious example. It may be, too, that the constant use of carnivores and birds of prey is derived from deep layers of unconscious hostility. A suggestion of this occurs in the widespread belief that shamans or hostile magicians can turn into leopards or jaguars, and the folklore of werewolves. Some memories of totemism may also be involved.

Still another direction in which animal identification developed is that of animal gods. The path from clan animal to regional animal god in Egypt is reasonably clear. Something similar seems to be engraved upon the rocks of Camonica Valley. The shadow of the animal lingers over the Greek pantheon, crystallized sometimes into an emblem, just as it does in Mesopotamia in the bull-man and the various demons depicted upon the seals.

In the transitional stages from hunting and gathering to simple agriculture and village life, the basic philosophy of preliterate life, which is mana, at times reaches articulate expression. The feeling that everything unusual is imbued with a supernatural electricity which may be either harmful or helpful has been encountered throughout the world. We have suggested that once more the insights of depth psychology throw some light on its origin. The basic ambivalence of human emotion is intimately connected with the child-parent relationship. The world of the unreasoning young creature consists of the protective and sexually attractive parent and the rejecting sexually competitive parent; security and fear are the two poles which coincide with love and hatred. When the child and the primitive is faced with the unknown, the disturbing, anything which disrupts the comfortingly routine, a sense of unseen power, helpful or hurtful, is born. When the added drives of economic necessity and the need for social stability reinforce this emotion, it follows that something must be done to nullify or enlist the aid of the supernatural. From a sense of mana and the force of the human will, magic arises. Animism is, of course, no more than the objectification of mana in terms of natural phenomena, animals, or objects. Whether a spirit resides in a tree like a double, or whether the tree itself is the supernatural entity (a question which has so concerned the theologically minded) is purely academic. The feeling toward the object is the same, as are the techniques of propitiation or control. Articulately or inarticulately, the manipulation of mana is an eternal preoccupation: the African anoints his magic bundle, the American Indian pours cornmeal in sacred designs, the Aztec smears the faces of his gods with the blood of sacrificial victims, the Polynesian chieftain refrains from touching his own head because of its contagious power.

The question of supreme beings is tied up with a lingering misapplication of evolutionary thinking which presupposes that all of mankind must pass through certain stages. There is no indication of true monotheism, the worship of a single, exclusive, jealous god, anywhere among very early peoples, or peoples still in an early stage of culture. A creator entity of various sorts does appear sporadically; sometimes he is abstract as among the Bantu or Eskimo, no more than mana with a name, sometimes he is a sort of master of animals as among the Yahgan, again he is obviously a glorified mythical ancestor, or a thunder god, or he has clearly evolved from the trickster. In most cases he is not worshiped and often, after the creative effort, he has withdrawn from the world. To understand this phenomenon it is well to remember Paul Radin's distinction between the religious intellectual and the average man which holds good even in fairly simple hunting tribes. No doubt the speculation of the shaman intellectual has at times resulted in various types of creator concepts. The fact that such beings are not worshiped tends to show that they were a matter of indifference to the average tribesman. The shaman evidently made no effort to endow them with a cult. Various other characters who have no cult appear in early mythologies. Certainly, judging from the evidence throughout the world, early peoples did not pass through any stage in which their religion consisted of belief in a supreme being. When priesthoods became educated intellectual groups, their poetic thinking moved toward an epic form. The time was then ripe for individuals, with more or less success, to evolve true monotheistic supreme beings. Some early Hebrew prophet and Zoroaster succeeded, Hungry Coyote and Ikhnaton failed.

It must be repeated again and again that the elaboration of human culture follows no single path and takes the form of broad regional variations. We have been discussing the transitional stage from hunting to simple agriculture which, in the New World, is a fairly continuous process. In some regions, however, the domestication of animals, either before or concomitant with the practice of simple agriculture, prolongs the nomadic or pastoral stage and has its effect on psychic life. In most hunting and early transitional cultures males are dominant and, along with early social development, some sort of raiding takes place which may involve headhunting. In accordance with the instinctive mana principle, anything alien is suspect, hence the small nomad groups or village groups exhibit intense xenophobia, accuse their neighbors of witchcraft, and consider them fair game (indeed among cannibal peoples there is not much distinction between enemies and game animals). With the domestication of the horse, a kind of stasis takes place. The step forward into urbanism does not occur and, particularly among the Indo-European peoples, the headhunting, warrior ethos becomes intensified into cult proportions. The male sexual hostilities are exaggerated into berserkir phenomena (with its curious parallel of the kanaima in South America and running amok among the Malayans). Butchery, symbolic castration, and the warrior-sexual spasm assume the proportions of a psychic social disease.

The development of a ritual priesthood, whose duty is to carry out traditional group ceremonials, rationalized by myth, does not preclude the activities of the archaic shaman, as is exemplified by the two sorts of religious specialists among the Polynesians. Religion has now become a business and has room for various kinds of professionals. With the rise of a self-perpetuating body of this sort comes blood sacrifice.

The offering of game or vegetable products to spirits in terms of payment for services rendered, or to be rendered, occurs among the simplest groups; it has been mentioned as a Pygmy practice. There seems to be no case of blood sacrifice among predominantly hunting peoples. Food is not too plentiful and capturing it is an arduous task. Often, as we have seen, a special master spirit sees to it that game is not slaughtered wantonly or meat wasted. Head taking and cannibalism sometimes border on the idea of sacrifice but the flowering of the institution involves a new level of symbol manipulation which is the handiwork of any intellectual priesthood. Since both animals and humans are the victims in blood sacrifice, the concept seems to include killing of the god in both forms or in one form as a substitute for the other.

The killing of the god so that he may be reborn or so that his blood may bring benefits and fertility to the social group is, of course, a metaphysical idea which lives on in Christianity. Can we find a germ of the concept in the archaic attitude toward the animal who is persuaded to die willingly so that the hunter may eat? The animal is called dear friend, guest, and benefactor among the Siberians. Since the transition from wild to domestic animal sacrifice is clearly automatic with domestication, the attitude toward the noble Aryan steed who is praised, addressed as beloved and friend, and apologized to for any mistreatment he has received in life, is remarkably parallel. Then, too, in many cases where the totem is ritually eaten so that the clan may achieve communion with itself, the totem animal is also apologized to and expected to acquiesce in its own death.

The divine king of Africa, as we have seen, is a direct development from the shaman who, in the simplest groups, is the only individual wielding any authority. His death, too, is supposed to be a willing sacrifice and in the interests of fertility. Whether he was at some point a totem animal, as Straube believes, is not too fully substantiated. Human sacrifice in Middle America is clearly a reflection of god killing for, as in the case of Tezcatlipoca, the victim is worshiped as the god's representative. In Aztec mythology, too, the gods themselves willingly leap into the fire to cause the sun to move. There does not, however, in this region seem to be any earlier totem-sacrifice or animal identification on record. Rather, the institution of the head frame shows that primitive trophy headhunting had developed directly through clerical theologizing into the mass sacrifice of supposedly willing prisoners, not only for the benefit of the tribe, but to maintain the rhythm of the universe.

In the over-all picture of the development of early religion the female fertility goddess does not seem so important as classical scholars and upholders of the archetype theory have attempted to make her. If the Venuses of the Upper Paleolithic were clan mothers, there are certainly very few, if any, real parallels among contemporary hunting peoples. The nearest is perhaps the Siberian female shaman who may be, from early times, a kind of household priestess. If this was the case in the Paleolithic, no direct transition to a fertility goddess is likely. The little clay figures of the transitional period in the Near East, the Mediterranean, and India are only paralleled by the brief appearance of a similar artifact in Middle America. We can trace no significant development from the latter discoveries in Mexico. In the Near East the earth mother is of local importance and probably by diffusion she spread to India and the Mediterranean. Although she is the earliest deity to be dated, the probability is that the omnipresent trickster preceded her.

The contemporary of the earth mother, the bearded bull, is also a local phenomenon which seems to have been disseminated over a similar area.

Since there were no cattle in Indonesia, Australia, Oceania or the Americas, environmental determinism effectually prevented him from becoming an archetype. A convincing pedigree can be made out for him as an animal spirit in his wild state who, with domestication, became an overlord of cattle, a male potency symbol and, with theological shaping, was assimilated to the more or less divine king, rain god, and mate of the earth goddess. From then on the two have a long career in sophisticated theology and myth.

The final developments in barbaric religion, once it has become a business carried on by a state-supported class of specialists, take place in the urban stage of culture. Theology now goes into politics and rationalizes the power of structure of the society. In this case the king and priesthood co-operate, with either high priest and king upholding each other's divine authority, or the two functions combined in one. In the Near East the master-slave ethos was reinforced by myth turned into artistic form by priest-poets. At the same time the growth of advanced agriculture stimulated the study of astronomy, which was of practical use in measuring time and marking the season for planting and harvesting. As a result sun gods, moon gods, and stellar divinities add to the complexities of a true pantheon. In Middle America and the Andes, where dedication to conquest was the ethos of an imperialist state, religion supported the divine right of the authoritarian clan to rule over other peoples. The Aztec poet-priests created a mystique of death and dedication to the ideal of warfare. Here, too, astronomy elaborated the pantheon with sky deities.

Other stratified societies without astronomical science, such as those of Polynesia, West Africa, or India, show in the nature of their pantheons that sophisticated myth making in general tends to elevate the forces of nature, patrons of the arts of civilization, and even important substances such as fire, iron, or fermented liquor to divinity status.

It has been said that history as a source of instruction is a failure. In a world threatened with power struggles and violence, however, we look longingly for examples of religious syntheses which promote peace and bloodless ceremonies of worship and praise. The list is not a long one. A thousand years of peace on the small island of Malta, according to the archaeological evidence, is one bright spot. We do not know what sort of rites were practiced. An era of peace of similar duration seems to have occurred in the Indus Valley, and again we are ignorant of the actual religious ceremonies. The inhabitants of Crete and the Danube peasants are pictured as peaceful. The Eskimo have a good record as a nonviolent friendly folk. The Pueblo Indians, on the whole, have upheld a peaceful ethos and their latter-day rites are devoid of cruelty and bloodshed. A few other tribes of Oceania perhaps, including Margaret Mead's mountain Arapesh, and one or two of the marginal South American groups exhaust the roster.

On the whole, the gods behave badly. Even Jehovah, who inspires so much enthusiasm among monotheists, when stripped of modern interpreting is found to be ruthlessly intolerant and as bloody as any Aztec war god. The gods behave precisely as they do because they are gods. They are immune to the price that ordinary men must pay for living in a social situation. They are therefore at liberty to be heroically priapic, cannibalistic, castrators and castrated; anarchists of sex, they commit incest gaily and do not shrink from sodomy, bestiality or coprophilia. Indeed blood and sex often seem to be the stuff from which ritual is made.

If early religion is the inspiration for schools of great art and much noble poetry, it just as often reflects man's darkest drives. Thanks to the inexhaustible resources of rationalization of which man is capable, as he builds his social institutions, almost any human activity can be exalted into a respectable religious practice.

We cannot shrug off the destructive elements in ancient religion as mere youthful aberrations of the human psyche. If the Aztecs could be persuaded that thousands of human beings must be immolated to keep the sun moving, in our own time the followers of another mystical quasi-religious creed were also willing to destroy men wholesale and to die themselves in support of their theory of racial superiority. Let us not forget that most conquests have been justified on religious grounds whether they were those of Inca sun worshipers or those of Spanish Roman Catholics. Let us also remember that the unconscious desire for father domination was reinforced by a religion in the Near East which upheld the slave ethos and that all loyalties in Egypt were concentrated in a divine king, which resulted in a cultural stasis. This should be a sobering reminder when we find ourselves caught up in the mystique of leadership and are asked to give up our hard-won right to dissent.

Man cannot live without his myths, without ceremonies which sustain group emotions, without the consolations of a poetic vision of the world. At the same time he is still at the mercy of compulsions within his nature which give rise to conflicts as he struggles to find a way of living with his fellows. The past is a kind of distorting mirror in which his best and worst features are exaggerated. It is well to look into it and ponder deeply.

Bibliography

CHAPTER 1

Campbell, Joseph, *The Masks of God: Primitive Mythology,* New York, 1959.
Cazeneuve, Jean, *Les rites et la condition humaine,* Paris, 1957.
Durkheim, Emile, *Les formes élémentaires de la vie religieuse,* Paris, 1912.
Fahrenfort, Johannes J., and Van de Graft, C. C., *Dodenbezorging en Cultuur,* 2 vols., Amsterdam, 1947.
Goode, William, *Religion Among the Primitives,* Glencoe, 1951.
Kluckhohn, Clyde, "Myths and Ritual, a General Theory," *Harvard Theological Review,* XXXV, Cambridge, 1942.
Malinowski, Bronislaw, *Magic, Science and Religion* (Doubleday Anchor), New York, 1948.
Marett, Robert Ranulph, *The Threshold of Religion,* New York, 1914.
Radin, Paul, *Primitive Man as Philosopher,* New York, 1927.
———, *Primitive Religion,* New York, 1937.
Schmidt, William, *Der Ursprung der Gottesidee,* 11 vols., Münster, 1912–1954.
Tylor, Sir Edward Burnett, *The Origins of Culture,* 2 vols. (Harper Torchbooks), New York, 1958.
Webster, Hutton, *Magic,* Stanford, 1948.
———, *Taboo,* Stanford, 1942.

CHAPTER 2

Batchelor, J., *The Ainu and Their Folklore,* London, 1901.
Breuil, Henri, and Lantier, Raymond, *Les hommes de la pierre ancienne,* Paris, 1959.
Burkitt, M. C., *The Old Stone Age,* Grantchester, 1955.
Clemen, Carl, *Urgeschichtliche Religion,* Bonn, 1932.
Hallowell, A. Irving, "Bear Ceremonialism in the Northern Hemisphere," *American Anthropologist,* 1926, Menasha.
Landtman, Gunnar, *The Kiwai Papuans of British New Guinea,* London, 1927.
Leenhardt, Maurice, "Les canaques," in *Histoire générale des religions,* Vol. I, ed. M. Gorce and R. Mortier, Paris, 1948.
Maringer, Johannes, *The Gods of Prehistoric Man,* New York, 1960.
Wernert, Paul, "L'anthropophagie rituelle et la chasse aux têtes aux époques actuelles et paléolithique," *L'Anthropologie,* Paris, 1936.
———, "Le culte des Crânes," in *Histoire générale des religions,* Vol. I, ed. M. Gorce and R. Mortier, Paris, 1948.

CHAPTER 3

Breuil, Henri, and Lantier, Raymond, *Les hommes de la pierre ancienne,* Paris, 1959.
Burkitt, M. C., *The Old Stone Age,* Grantchester, 1955.
Clemen, Carl, *Urgeschichtliche Religion,* Bonn, 1932.

Golomshtok, E. A., *The Old Stone Age in European Russia,* American Philosophical Society N.S., XXIX, Philadelphia, 1938.

Hančar, Franz, "Zum Problem der Venusstatuetten im Eurasischen Jungpaleolithikum," *Prähistorische Zeitschrift,* Berlin, 1939.

Maringer, Johannes, *The Gods of Prehistoric Man,* New York, 1960.

Michelson, Truman, *The Buffalo Head Dance of the Thunder Gens of the Fox Indians,* Bureau of American Ethnology, Bulletin No. 87, Washington, 1928.

Obermaier, Hugo, *Fossil Man in Spain,* New Haven, 1924.

Wissler, Clark, ed., *Societies of the Plains Indians,* Anthropological Papers of the American Museum of Natural History, Vol. 11, New York, 1916.

CHAPTER 4

Boas, Franz, *Primitive Art,* Oslo, 1927.

Childe, V. Gordon, *The Dawn of European Civilization,* London, 1957.

Obermaier, Hugo, *Fossil Man in Spain,* New Haven, 1924.

Spencer, Sir Baldwin, and Gillen, F. J., *The Native Tribes of Central Australia,* London, 1899.

Wernert, Paul; *Representaciones de antepasados en el arte Paleolítico,* Comisión de Investigaciónes Paleontológicas y Prehistóricas, Memorial 16, Madrid, 1916.

CHAPTER 5

Chiera, Edward, *Sumerian Epics and Myths,* Oriental Institute Publications, XV, Chicago, 1934.

Childe, V. Gordon, *New Light on the Most Ancient East* (Evergreen), New York, 1956.

Kramer, Samuel Noah, *History Begins at Sumer* (Anchor), New York, 1959.

———, *Mythologies of the Ancient World* (Anchor), New York, 1961.

———, *Sumerian Mythology,* revised (Torchbooks), New York, 1961.

Marsh, O. T., *The Origins of Invention,* London, 1895.

Roheim, Geza, *Animism, Magic, and the Divine King,* London, 1950.

Woolley, Sir Leonard C., *Excavations at Ur,* London, 1954.

———, *The Sumerians,* Oxford, 1929.

CHAPTER 6

Contenau, Georges, *Daily Life in Babylon and Assyria,* New York, 1954.

Cottrel, Leonard, *The Anvil of Civilization* (Mentor), 1957.

Dhorme, Edward, *Les religions de Babylon et Assyrie.*

———, *Les religions des Hittites et des Hourites.*

Frankfort, Henri, *Cylinder Seals,* London, 1939.

———, *Kingship and the Gods,* Chicago, 1948.

Frazer, Sir James George, *The Golden Bough,* New York, 1940.

Furlani, Giuseppe, *La religione Babilonese e Assire,* 2 vols., Bologna, 1928–1929.

———, "The Basic Aspects of Hittite Religion," *The Harvard Theological Review,* XXXI, Cambridge, 1958.

Gadd, C. J., "Babylonian Ritual," in *Myth and Ritual,* ed. S. H. Hooke, Oxford, 1933.

Garstang, John, *The Hittite Empire,* New York, 1930.

Gaster, Theodor, *Thespis,* revised (Anchor), New York, 1961.

Gurney, O. R., *The Hittites,* London, 1954.

Güterbock, Hans Gustav, "Hittite Religion," in *Forgotten Religions,* ed. Virgilius Ferm, New York, 1960.

——, "The Hittite Version of the Kumarbi Myth," *American Journal of Archaeology,* Vol. 52, Norwood, 1948.

Heidel, Alexander, *The Babylonian Genesis,* Chicago, 1942.

——, *The Gilgamesh Epic and Old Testament Parallels,* Chicago, 1946.

Hooke, Samuel H., *Babylonian and Assyrian Religion,* London, 1953.

James, E. O., *The Ancient Gods,* New York, 1960.

——, *The Cult of the Mother Goddess,* London, 1959.

Langdon, Stephen, "Semitic Religion," *The Mythology of all Races,* Vol. II, Boston, 1931.

——, *Tammuz and Ishtar,* London, 1914.

Oppenheim, Leo, "Assyro-Babylonian Religion," in *Forgotten Religions,* ed. Virgilius Ferm, New York, 1960.

Pallis, Svend Aage, *The Babylonian Akitu festival,* Det Kongelige Danske Videnskabernes Selskab, Historisk-filologiske Meddelelser, XII, 1. Copenhagen, 1926.

Van Gennep, Arnold, *L'état actuel du problème totémique,* Paris, 1920.

CHAPTER 7

Albright, W. F., *The Archaeology of Palestine* (Pelican), Harmondsworth, 1961.

Cooke, Samuel H., *The Origin of Early Semitic Ritual,* London, 1938.

Driver, G. R., *Canaanite Myths and Legends,* Edinburgh, 1956.

Gaster, Theodor, "The Canaanites," in *Forgotten Religions,* ed. Virgilius Ferm, New York, 1950.

——, *Thespis* (Anchor), New York, 1961.

Haldar, Alfred, *Associations of Cultic Prophets among the Ancient Semites,* Upsala, 1945.

Heidel, Alexander, *The Babylonian Genesis,* Chicago, 1942.

——, *The Gilgamesh Epic and Old Testament Parallels,* Chicago, 1946.

Hooke, Samuel H., *Origins of Early Semitic Ritual,* London, 1938.

——, ed., *Myth and Ritual: Essays on the Myth and Ritual of the Hebrews in Relation to the Cultural Pattern of the Ancient East* (by A. M. Blackman, C. J. Gadd, J. Hollis, S. H. Hooke, W. O. E. Oesterley, and E. O. James), Oxford, 1933.

James, E. O., *The Ancient Gods,* New York, 1960.

Kenyon, Kathleen, *Archaeology in the Holy Land,* New York, 1960.

Kapelrud, A. A., *Baal in the Ras Shamra Texts,* Copenhagen, 1952.

Pope, Marvin H., *El in the Ugaritic Texts,* Leiden, 1955.

Schaefer, C. F. A., *The Cuneiform Texts of Ras Shamra-Ugarit,* London, 1939.

CHAPTER 8

Evans, Arthur, "Pillar and Tree Cult," *Journal of Hellenic Studies,* London, 1901.

——, *The Earlier Religion of Greece,* London, 1931.

——, *The Palace of Minos,* 4 vols., London, 1921–1936.

Glotz, Gustav, *The Aegean Civilization,* New York, 1925.

Malten, Ludolf, "Der Stier in Kult und mythischer Bild," *Archäologischer Anzeiger* (Jahrbuch des Deutschen Archäologischen Instituts), Berlin, XLIII, 1928.

Nilsson, Martin P., *The Minoan-Mycenaean Religion* (revised ed.), Lund, 1950.

Pendlebury, John S., *The Archaeology of Crete,* London, 1939.

Persson, Axel W., *The Religion of Greece in Prehistoric Times*, Berkeley, 1942.
——, *The Royal tombs at Dendra*, Kungliga Humanistiska Vetenskapssamfundet, Skrifter, 15, Lund, 1931.
Picard, Charles, "Les religions préhelléniques," *Mana*, II, Pt. 1, Paris, 1948.
"Scholar of Minoan Crete, Cyrus Herzl Gordon," *The New York Times*, April 4, 1962.
Ventris, Michael, and Chadwick, John, *Documents in Mycenaean Greek*, Cambridge, 1956.
Webster, T. B. L., *From Homer to Mycenae*, London, 1958.

CHAPTER 9

Cook, A. B., *Zeus*, 3 vols., Cambridge, 1914–1940.
Dumézil, Georges, *Le festin d'immortalité*, Musée Guimet, Annales, Bibliothèque d'Études, No. 34, Paris, 1924.
——, *Le problème des centaures*, Musée Guimet, Annales, Bibliothèque d'Études, No. 41, Paris, 1929.
Farnell, L. R., *The Greek Hero Cults*, Oxford, 1921.
Guthrie, W. K. C., *The Greeks and Their Gods* (Beacon), Boston, 1961.
Harrison, Jane, *Prolegomena to the Study of Greek Religion*, Cambridge, 1903.
——, *Themis*, Cambridge, 1912.
Hesiod, *Collected Works* (Carmina, recensuit Aloisius Rzach), Stuttgart, 1958.
Lawson, John Cuthbert, *Modern Greek Folklore and Ancient Greek Religion*, Cambridge, 1910.
Nilsson, Martin P., *Greek Folk Religion* (Torchbooks), New York, 1961.
——, *The History of Greek Religion* (revised ed.), Oxford, 1956.
——, *The Mycenaean Origin of Greek Mythology*, Cambridge, 1932.
Rohde, Erwin, *Psyche*, London, 1926.
Rose, H. J., *Primitive Culture in Greece*, London, 1925.
Wilamowitz-Möllendorff, Ulrich von, *Der Glaube der Hellenen*, Basel, 1956.

CHAPTER 10

Evans, J. D., *Malta*, New York, 1959.
——, "The Prehistoric Culture-Sequence in the Maltese Archipelago," *Proceedings of the Prehistoric Society*, Vol. XIX, London, 1953.
Zammit, Sir Themistocles, *Prehistoric Malta*, Oxford, 1930.
——, *The Neolithic Hypogeum at Hal-Saflieni*, Malta, 1928.
——, *The Neolithic Temples at Hajar Kim*, Valetta, 1927.
——, and Singer, "Neolithic Representations of the Human Form from the Islands of Malta and Gozo," *Journal of the Royal Anthropological Institute of Great Britain and Ireland*, Vol. LIV, London, 1924.

CHAPTER 11

Atkinson, R. J. C., *Stonehenge* (Pelican), Harmondsworth, 1956.
Bibby, Geoffrey, *Testimony of the Spade*, New York, 1956.
Childe, V. Gordon, *The Dawn of European Civilization*, London, 1950.
——, *What Happened in History* (Pelican), Harmondsworth, 1960.
Crawford, O. G. S., *The Eye Goddess*, London, 1957.
Daniel, Glyn, *The Megalith Builders of Europe*, London, 1956.

Hawkes, C. F. C., *The Prehistoric Foundation of Europe to the Mycenaean Age,* London, 1940.

Hawkes, Jacquetta and Christopher, *Prehistoric Britain* (Pelican), Harmondsworth, 1958.

Kirchner, Horst, *Die Menhir in Mitteleuropa und der Menhirgedanke,* Akademie der Wissenschaft und der Literatur, Geistes und Socialwissenschaften Abhandlungen, Heft 9–12, Mainz, 1955.

Nordmann, C. A., "The Megalithic Culture of Northern Europe," Suomen Muinaismuistoyhdistys, Helsingfors, Aikakauskirja, XXXIX, 3, Helsinki, 1935.

Röder, Joseph, *Pfahl und Menhir,* Neuwied, 1947.

CHAPTER 12

Almgren, Oscar, *Nordische Felszeichnungen als Religiöse Urkunde,* Frankfurt, 1934.

Anati, Emmanuel, *Camonica Valley,* New York, 1961.

Bing, Just, *Die Felszeichnungen von Fossum, ein Deutungs-versuch,* Ipek, 1936–1937.

———, *Die Götter der Sudskandinavischen Felszeichnungen,* Manno, 1922.

Breuil, Henri, *Les peintures rupestres schématiques de la péninsule Ibérique,* Lagny, 1933.

———, and Burkitt, M. C., *Rock Painting of Southern Andalusia,* Oxford, 1929.

Crawley, A. E., *The Mystic Rose,* New York, 1902.

de Manteyer, Georges, "Les dieux des alpes de Ligurie," *Bulletin des Hautes-Alpes,* Gap, 1945.

Kühn, Herbert, *Die Felsbilder Europas,* Stuttgart, 1952.

Maurice, Louis, *Les gravures préhistoriques de Monte Bego,* Tende, 1950.

Njoberg, Eric, *Vom Phalluskult in Nordaustralien,* Archiv für Anthropologie, Bd. 46–47, Braunschweig, 1920–1933.

Obermaier, Hugo, *Las pinturas rupestres,* Madrid, 1919.

Pacheco, Hernández, *Las figuras humanas antropomorfas en el arte Paleolítico y su significación,* Appendix, Comisión de Investigaciónes Paleontológicas y Prehistóricas, Memoria 16, Madrid, 1916.

Raudonikas, W. J., *La gravure préhistorique des bords du lac Onega et de la mer blanche,* 2 vol., Moscow, 1936–38.

Roheim, Geza, *Animism, Magic and the Divine Kingship,* London, 1930.

———, *Eternal Ones of the Dream,* New York, 1945.

———, "Psychology of Primitive Cultural Types," *International Journal of Psychoanalysis,* Vol. 13, London, 1932.

Schneider, Hermann, *Germanische Religion vor dreitausend Jahren,* Leipzig, 1934.

Schoolcraft, Henry Rowe, *Narrative Journal of Travels Through the Northwestern Regions of the United States, 1821,* East Lansing, 1953.

CHAPTER 13

Best, Elsdon, "Notes on the Art of War Among the Maoris," *Journal of the Polynesian Society,* XIII.

Dottin, G., *L'épopée irlandaise,* Paris, 1926.

Gudgeon, W. E., "A Phallic Emblem from Aliu Island," *Journal of the Polynesian Society,* XIII.

Hubert, Henri, *Les Celtes et l'expansion celtique jusque l'époque de la Tène.*

———, *Les Celtes depuis l'époque de la Tène,* rev. ed., Paris, 1950.

Hull, Eleanor, ed., *The Cuchulainn Saga in Irish Literature,* London, 1898.
Kendrick, T. D., *The Druids,* London, 1928.
MacCulloch, John Arnott, *Celtic Mythology (Mythology of All Races,* Vol. III), Boston, 1918.
Powell, T. G. E., *The Celts,* New York, 1958.
Roheim, Geza, *Animism, Magic and the Divine King,* London, 1930.
Sjoestedt-Jonval, Marie Louise, *Gods and Heroes of the Celts,* London, 1949.
van Hamel, Anton Gerardus, "Aspects of Celtic Mythology," *Proceedings of the British Academy,* Vol. XX, London, 1935.
Vendryes, Joseph, "La religion des Celtes," *Mana,* II, No. 3, Paris, 1948.

CHAPTER 14

de Vries, Jan, "The Problem of Loki," *Folklore Fellows Communications,* 110, Helsinki, 1933.
Dumézil, Georges, *Aspects de la fonction guerrière,* Paris, 1956.
———, *Loki,* Paris, 1948.
———, *Mythes et dieux des Germains,* Paris, 1939.
Grönbech, Vilhelm, *The Culture of the Teutons,* 2 vols., London, 1931.
Höfler, Otto, *Kultische Geheimbünde der Germanen,* Frankfurt, 1934.
Hollander, Lee M., trans., *The Poetic Edda,* Dallas, 1928.
MacCulloch, John Arnott, *Eddic Mythology (Mythology of All Races,* Vol. II), Boston, 1930.
Owen, Francis, *The Germanic People,* New York, 1960.
Radin, Paul, *The Trickster,* London, 1956.
Schneider, Hermann, *Die Götter der Germanen,* ed. Germanische Altertumskunde, München, 1931.
Tacitus, *Germania,* tr. and ed. by Rodney Potter Robinson, Middletown, 1935.
Tonnelat, Ernest, "La religion des Germains," *Mana,* II, Pt. 3, Paris, 1948.

CHAPTER 15

Bloch, Raymond, *The Etruscans,* New York, 1958.
Clemen, Carl, *Die Religion der Etrusker (Untersuchung zur allgemeinen Religionsgeschichte,* Heft 7) Bonn, 1936.
Grenier, A., "La religion étrusque et romaine," *Mana,* II, Pt. 3, Paris, 1948.
Hadas, Moses, "The Etruscan Enigma," *Columbia University Forum,* Vol. LV, No. 4, New York, 1961.
Hus, Alain, *The Etruscans* (Evergreen), New York, 1961.
Pallotino, M., *The Etruscans* (Pelican), Harmondsworth, 1955.
Randall-MacIver, D., *The Etruscans,* Oxford, 1927.

CHAPTER 16

Bailey, Cyril, *Phases in the Religion of Ancient Rome,* Berkeley, 1932.
Bloch, Raymond, *Origins of Rome,* New York, 1960.
Dumézil, Georges, *Aspects de la fonction guerrière,* Paris, 1956.
———, *Jupiter, Mars, Quirinus,* Paris, 1941.
———, *L'heritage Indo-européen à Rome,* Paris, 1949.
Fowler, Warde, *The Religious Experience of the Roman People from the Earliest Times to the Age of Augustus,* London, 1911.

Grenier, Albert, "La religion étrusque et romaine," *Mana,* II, Pt. 3, Paris, 1948.

Otto, J. Karl, *Römische Sondergötter,* Rheinische Museum für Philologie, Bd. 64, Frankfurt, 1909.

Rose, Herbert J., *Primitive Culture in Italy,* London, 1925.

CHAPTER 17

Childe, V. Gordon, *New Light on the Most Ancient East* (Evergreen), New York, 1957.

———, *The Aryans,* London, 1926.

Daniélou, Alain, *Polythéisme hindou,* Paris, 1960.

Ghirshman, R., *Iran* (Pelican), Harmondsworth, 1954.

La Vallée-Poussin, Louis de, *Indo-Européens et Indo-Iraniens* (*Histoire du monde,* Tome 3), Paris, 1924.

Mackay, E., *Early Indus Civilization* (revised ed.), London, 1948.

———, *Further Excavations at Mohenjo Daro,* New Delhi, 1938.

Marshall, Sir John, *Mohenjo Daro and the Indus Valley Civilization,* London, 1931.

O'Malley, Lewis S. S., *Popular Hinduism,* Cambridge, 1935.

Piggott, Stuart, *Prehistoric India* (Pelican), Harmondsworth, 1961.

Rice, Stanley, *Hindu Customs and Their Origins,* London, 1937.

Weber, Max, *The Religion of India,* tr. Hans H. Gerth and Dan Martingale, Glencoe, 1958.

Wheeler, Sir Mortimer, "Harappa, 1946, the Defense and Cemetery," *Ancient India,* No. 3, New Delhi, 1947.

———, *The Indus Valley Civilization* (*The Cambridge History of India,* Suppl. Volume), Cambridge, 1953.

CHAPTER 18

Cazeneuve, Jean, *Les rites et la condition humaine,* Paris, 1957.

Childe, V. Gordon, *The Aryans,* London, 1926.

Dumézil, Georges, *Les dieux des Indo-européens,* Paris, 1952.

Hubert, H., and Mauss, Marcel, "Essai sur le sacrifice," *Année Sociale* II, 81–82, Paris.

Keith, Arthur B., *The Religion and the Philosophy of the Veda and the Upanishads* (*Harvard Oriental Series,* Vol. 31–32), Cambridge, 1925.

La Vallée-Poussin, Louis de, *Indo-Européens et Indo-Iraniens* (*Histoire du monde,* Tome 3), Paris, 1924.

Piggott, Stuart, *Prehistoric India* (Pelican), Harmondsworth, 1961.

Straube, Helmut, *Die Tierverkleidungen der afrikanischen Naturvölker,* Wiesbaden, 1955.

The Hymns of the Rigveda, tr. by Rolfe T. H. Griffeths, Benares, 1889.

CHAPTER 19

Alföldi, A., "Theriomorphische Weltbetrachtung in den hochasiatischen Kulturen," *Archäologischer Anzeiger* (Jahrbuch des Deutschen Archäologischen Instituts), XLVI, 1931.

Andersson, J. G., *Hunting Magic in the Animal Style,* Ostasiatiska Museet Bulletin No. 4, 1931, Helsinki.

Auboyer, Jeannine, "Les Scythes, Sarmates, les Altaiques," in *Histoire générale des religions,* Paris, 1948.

Minns, Ellis H., *Scythians and Greeks,* Cambridge, 1913.

———, *The Art of the Northern Nomads,* Cambridge, 1942.

Mongait, A. L., *Archaeology in the U.S.S.R.* (Pelican), Harmondsworth, 1961.

Rice, Tamara Talbot, *The Scythians,* New York, 1957.

Rostovtzev, Mikhail, *Iranians and Greeks in Southern Russia,* Oxford, 1922.

———, *The Animal Style in Southern Russia and China* (Monographs in Art and Architecture, XIV), Princeton, 1929.

Salmony, A., *Antler and Tongue (Artibus Asiae,* Supplementum XIII), Basel, 1954.

———, "An Unknown Scythian Find in Novocherkask, *Eurasia Septentrionalis Antiqua,* No. X, Helsinki, 1935.

CHAPTER 20

Creel, Herrlee Glessner, *The Birth of China,* London, 1936.

Cheng, Te K'un, *Archaeology in China,* 2 vols., Cambridge, 1960.

Chi, Li, *The Beginning of Chinese Civilization,* Seattle, 1957.

Karlgren, Bernard, *Legends and Cults in Ancient China,* Ostasiatiska Museet (The Museum of Far Eastern Antiquities), No. 18, Stockholm, 1946.

Shun-Shen, Ling, "Dog Sacrifice in Ancient China and the Pacific Area," Bulletin of the Institute of Ethnology of the Academica Sinica, No. 3, Taipei, 1957.

The She King, or *The Book of Poetry,* translated by James Legge, Hong Kong, 1960.

Wing-Sou, Lòu, *Rain-worship Among the Ancient Chinese and the Nahua-Maya Indians,* Bulletin of the Institute of Ethnology of the Academica Sinica, No. 4, Taipei, 1957.

CHAPTER 21

Childe, V. Gordon, *New Light on the Most Ancient East* (Evergreen), New York, 1957.

———, *What Happened in History* (Pelican), Harmondsworth, 1960.

Derry, E. D., "The Dynastic Race in Egypt," *Journal of Egyptian Archaeology,* Vol. 41–43, London, 1955–1957.

Emery, W. B., *Archaic Egypt* (Pelican), Harmondsworth, 1961.

Erdman, Adolf, *Die Religion der Ägypter,* Berlin and Leipzig, 1934.

Faulkner, R. O., "The Man Who Was Tired of Life," *Journal of Egyptian Archaeology,* Vol. 41–43, 1955–1957, London.

Frankfort, Henri, *Ancient Egyptian Religion,* New York, 1948.

———, *Kingship and the Gods,* Chicago, 1948.

Frankfort, H. and H. A., ed., John A. Wilson, Thorkild Jacobsen, William A. Irwin, *The Intellectual Adventure of Ancient Man,* Chicago, 1946.

Gauthier, Henri, *Les fêtes du dieu Min (Recherches d'archéologie, philologie et d'histoire,* Tome 2), Cairo, 1931.

Hall, H. R., *Excavation at Ur (Al Ubaid),* Vol. I, Oxford, 1926.

Hodgson, A. G. O., "Some Notes on the Wahehe of the Mahenge District of Tanganyika," *Journal of the Royal African Institute,* Vol. 56, London, 1926.

Hopfner, Theodor, *Der Tierkult der alten Ägypter,* Kaiserliche Akademie der Wissenschaften, Denkschriften Philosophisch-historische Klasse, Bd. 57, Abhandlung 2, Vienna, 1913.

Hornblower, G. D., "A Further Note on Phallicisms in Egypt," *Man,* No. 97, London, 1927.

———, "Predynastic Figures of Women and Their Successors," *Journal of Egyptian Archaeology,* Vol. XV, London, 1929.

James, E. O., *Prehistoric Religion,* London, 1957.

———, *The Ancient Gods,* New York, 1960.

Jensen, Adolf S., *The Sacred Animal of the God Set,* Det Kongelige Danske Videns-kabernes Selskab, Biologiske Meddelelser, 11, No. 5, Copenhagen, 1934.

Kees, Hermann, *Der Götterglaube im alten Ägypten,* Leipzig, 1941.

Mercer, Samuel A. B., *Literary Criticism of the Pyramid Texts,* London, 1956.

Moret, Alexandre, and Davy, G., *From Tribe to Empire,* New York, 1926.

Murray, M. A., "Burial Customs and Belief in the Hereafter in Predynastic Egypt," *Journal of Egyptian Archaeology,* Vol. 41–43, London, 1955–1957.

Newberry, Percy E., *The Set Rebellion of the Second Dynasty, Ancient Egypt,* London, 1922.

Reisner, George Andrew, *Excavations at Kerma,* Peabody Museum of Archaeology and Ethnology, Harvard African Studies, Vols. 5–6, Cambridge, 1923.

———, *The Development of the Egyptian Tomb,* Cambridge, 1936.

Seligman, Charles G., *Egypt and Negro Africa,* London, 1934.

Smyth, E. W., and Dale, A. M., *The Ila Speaking Peoples of Northern Rhodesia,* London, 1931.

Vandier, Jacques, "La religion Egyptienne," *Mana,* I, Pt. 1, Paris, 1944.

CHAPTER 22

Bleek, Dorothea, *Cave Artists of South Africa,* Cape Town, 1953.

———, "The Bushmen of Central Angola," *Bantu Studies,* Vol. III, No. 2, Cape Town, 1928.

———, *The Mantis and His Friends,* Cape Town, 1923.

———, *The Naron,* Cambridge, 1928.

Bleek, Wilhelm Immanuel, and Lloyd, Lucy C., *Specimens of Bushman Folklore,* London, 1911.

Breuil, Henri, *Rock Paintings of Southern Africa,* Vol. I, *The White Lady of the Brandberg,* London, 1955.

———, *Ibid.,* Vol. III, *The Tsisab Ravine and Other Brandberg Sites,* Paris, 1959.

———, *Ibid.,* Vol. IV, *Anibib and Omandumba and Other Erongo Sites,* Clairvaux, 1960.

Burkitt, Miles Crawford, *South Africa in Stone and Paint,* Cambridge, 1928.

Dornan, Samuel Shaw, *Pigmies and Bushmen of the Kalahari,* London, 1925.

Ellenberger, Victor, *La fin tragique des Bushmen,* Paris, 1962.

Englebrecht, J. A., *The Korana,* Cape Town, 1936.

Leakey, Louis Seymour Bazett, *Stone Age Africa,* London, 1936.

Lebzelter, Victor, "Die Religiöse Vorstellungen der Kun Buschmänner," *Festschrift für P. W. Schmidt,* ed. W. Koppers, Vienna, 1928.

Obermaier, Hugo, *Bushman Art,* London, 1930.

Pasarge, Siegfried, *Die Buschmänner der Kalahari,* Berlin, 1907.

Schapera, Isaac, *The Khoisan People of South Africa,* London, 1930.

Schoeman, Pieter J., *Hunters of the Desert Land,* Cape Town, 1956.

Seligman, Charles G., *Races of Africa,* London, 1959.

Stow, George W., *Rock Paintings of South Africa* (Intro. and Notes by Dorothea Bleek), London, 1930.

———, *The Native Races of South Africa,* London, 1905.

Summers, Roger, *Prehistoric Rock Art of the Federation of Rhodesia and Nyasaland,* Nat. Publications Trust, Rhodesia and Nyasaland, 1959.

Thomas, Elizabeth Marshall, *The Harmless People,* New York, 1959.

Thomas, E. W., *Bushman Stories,* London, 1950.

CHAPTER 23

Ballif, Noël, *Les danseurs de dieu*, Paris, 1954.
Czekanowski, J., *Forschungen im Nil-Kongo-Zwischengebiet*, Vol. 2, Leipzig, 1924.
Fahrenfort, J. J., *Het hoogste Wezen der Primitieven*, Den Haag, 1927.
Immenroth, Wilhelm, *Kultur und Umwelt der Kleinwuchsigen in Africa*, Leipzig, 1933.
Murdoch, George Peter, *Africa, Its People and Their Cultural History*, New York, 1959.
Putnam, Anne Eisner, *Madami*, New York, 1954.
Schebesta, Paul, *Les Pygmées du Congo Belge*, Bruxelles, 1952.
———, *Revisiting My Pygmy Hosts*, London, 1936.
Schumacher, Peter, "Gottesglaube und Weltanschauung der Central Afrikanischen Kivu Pygmäen," *Festschrift für W. Schmidt*, ed. W. Koppers, Vienna, 1928.
Trilles, H., *L'âme du Pygmée d'Afrique*, Paris, 1945.
———, *Les Pygmées de la forêt ecuatoriale*, Paris, 1932.
Turnbull, Colin, "Initiation Among the Bambuti," in *Cultures and Societies of Africa*, ed. by Simon and Phoebe Ottenberg, New York, 1960.
———, *The Forest People*, New York, 1961.
Vanden Bergh, Leonard J., *On the Trail of the Pygmies*, New York, 1921.

CHAPTER 24

Dieterlen, Germaine, *Essai sur la religion bambare*, Paris, 1957.
Griaule, Marcel, *Les âmes des Dogon*, Paris, 1941.
———, "The Idea of Person Among the Dogon," in *Cultures and Societies of Africa*, ed. by Simon and Phoebe Ottenberg, New York, 1960.
———, "The Mande Creation Myth," *Africa*, Vol. 27, London, 1957.
———, and Germaine Dieterlen, *Signes graphiques Soudanis*, Paris, 1951.
de Ganay, Solange, "Aspects de mythologie et de symbolisme bambare," *Journal de Psychologie normale et pathologique*, Paris, 1949.
Henry, Joseph, *Lâme d'un peuple africain, le Bambara*, Münster, 1910.
Monteil, Charles, *Les Bambara*, Paris, 1924.
Paques, Viviane, *Les Bambara*, Paris, 1954.
Tauxier, L., *La religion bambare*, Paris, 1927.

CHAPTER 25

Ankerman, Bernhard, "Verbreitung und Formen des Totēmismus in Africa," *Zeitschrift für Ethnologie*, Bd. 47, Berlin, 1915.
Ardener, Edwin, *The Coastal Bantu of the Cameroons*, London, 1956.
Burton, W. F. P., "The Country of the Baluba," *The Geographical Journal*, Vol. LXX, No. 4, London, 1927.
Callaway, Henry, *The Religious System of the Amazulu*, London, 1870.
Driberg, J. H., "The Secular Aspect of Ancestor Worship in Africa," *Journal of Royal African Society*, Supplement Vol. 35, No. 38, London, 1936.
Forde, Daryl, *African Worlds*, Oxford, 1954.
Hambly, Wilfred D., *Source Book for African Anthropology*, Field Museum of Anthropology Series, Vol. XXVI, Chicago, 1937.
Junod, Henri A., *The Life of a South African Tribe*, London, 1927.
Laubscher, B. J. F., *Sex, Custom and Psychopathology*, London, 1937.

Mair, Lucy P., "Totemism among the Baganda," *Man,* 71, London, 1935.

Murdoch, George P., *Africa,* New York, 1959.

Ottenberg, Simon and Phoebe, editors, *The Cultures and Societies of Africa,* New York, 1960.

Ritter, E. A., *Shaka Zulu,* New York, 1955.

Schapera, Isaac, *The Bantu Speaking Tribes of South Africa,* London, 1937.

Seligman, Charles G., "The Unconscious in Relation to Anthropology," *British Journal of Psychology,* Vol. XVIII, Cambridge, 1928.

Tempels, Placide, *Bantu Philosophy,* tr. Colin King, Paris, 1959.

Verhulpen, Edmond, *Baluba et Balubaises du Katanga,* Anvers, 1936.

Wagner, Günter, *The Bantu of North Kavirondo,* 2 vols., New York, 1949.

Willoughby, W. C., *Nature Worship and Taboo,* Hartford, 1932.

———, *The Soul of the Bantu,* London, 1928.

CHAPTER 26

Evans-Pritchard, E. E., *The Divine Kingship of the Shilluk,* London, 1948.

Hofmayr, W., *Die Schilluk,* Vienna, 1925.

Howells, P. G., and Thompson, W. P. G., "Death of a Reth of Shilluk and the Installation of His Successor," *Sudan Notes and Records,* Vol. XXVII, 1946.

———, "The Shilluk Settlement," *Sudan Notes and Records,* Vol. XXIV, London, 1941.

Lienhardt, Godfrey, "The Shilluk," in *African Worlds,* ed. by Daryll Forde, Oxford, 1954.

Nadel, S. F., "A Shaman Cult in the Nuba Mountains," *Sudan Notes and Records,* Vol. XXVIII, London, 1947.

Pumphrey, M. E. C., "The Shilluk Tribe," *Sudan Notes and Records,* Vol. XXIV, London, 1941.

Seligman, Charles G., *Egypt and Negro Africa,* London, 1934.

Thompson, W. P. G., "Further Notes on the Installation of a Reth," *Sudan Notes and Records,* Vol. XXVIII, London, 1948.

Van Gennep, Arnold, *Les rites de passage,* Paris, 1909.

Westermann, Diedrich, *The Shilluk People,* Berlin, 1912.

CHAPTER 27

Azais, F., "Étude sur la religion du peuple Galla," *Revue d'Ethnographie et des Traditions populaires,* Tome VII, No. 25, Paris, 1926.

Cerulli, E., "The Folk Literature of the Galla of Southern Abyssinia," Harvard African Studies, Vol. 3, Cambridge, 1922.

Chambard, R., "Notes sur quelque croyances religieuses des Galla," *Revue d'Ethnographie,* Tome VII, No. 25, Paris, 1926.

Huntingford, G. W. B., *The Galla of Ethiopia (Ethnographic Survey of Africa,* ed. Daryll Forde, *North-eastern Africa),* London, 1955.

Salviac, Martial de, *Un peuple antique au pays de Menelik,* Paris, 1901.

CHAPTER 28

Bascom, William R., *The Sociological Role of the Yoruba Cult Group,* The American Anthropological Association Memoirs, No. 63, Menasha, 1944.

Bascom, William R., "The West African Complex of Primitive Cultures," *American Anthropologist,* Vol. 50, No. 1, Menasha, 1948.

Dennet, R. E., *Nigerian Studies,* London, 1910.

Farrow, Stephen S., *Fact, Fancies and Fetish,* London, 1926.

Forde, Daryll, *The Yoruba-Speaking Peoples of South-western Nigeria (Ethnographic Survey of Africa, Western Africa,* Pt. 4), London, 1951.

Herskovits, Melville, *Dahomey,* 2 vols., New York, 1938.

Idonu, E. Bolaji, *Olodumare, God in Yoruba Belief,* London, 1962.

Lucas, Olumide J., *The Religion of the Yorubas,* Lagos, 1948.

Mercier, P., "The Fon," in *African Worlds,* ed. by Daryll Forde, Oxford, 1954.

Parrinder, Geoffrey, *West African Religion,* London, 1949.

Rattray, R. S., *Ashanti,* Oxford, 1923.

———, *Religion and Art in Ashanti,* London, 1927.

Real, M. Daniel, "Note sur l'art Dahoméen," *Anthropologie,* Tome 30, Paris, 1920.

Talbot, P. A., *Some Nigerian Fertility Cults,* London, 1927.

———, *The People of Southern Nigeria,* London, 1921.

CHAPTER 29

Cole, Fay Cooper, *Peoples of Malaysia,* New York, 1945.

Cole, Mabel, *Savage Gentlemen,* New York, 1929.

Evans, Ivor H. H., "Negrito Belief," *Journal of the Federated Malayan States,* Vol. VI, pt. 4, 1916; Vol. IX, pt. 1, Kuala Lumpur, 1920.

———, *The Negritos of Malaya,* Cambridge, 1927.

Radcliffe-Brown, Alfred, *The Andaman Islanders,* Cambridge, 1932.

Reed, William Allen, *The Negritos of Zambales (Philippine Islands Publications, Ethnological Survey,* Vol. I, No. 1), Manila, 1905.

Schebesta, Paul, *Among the Forest Dwarfs,* London, 1927.

Stewart, Kilton, *Pygmies and Dream Giants,* New York, 1954.

Wollaston, A. F. R., *Pygmies and Papuans,* New York, 1912.

CHAPTER 30

Ackerknecht, Erwin, *Origin and Distribution of Skull Cults, Ciba Symposia,* Vol. 5, Summit, 1944.

Barton, R. F., *The Religion of the Ifugaos,* The American Anthropological Association Memoirs, No. 64, Menasha, 1946.

Cole, Fay Cooper, *Peoples of Malaysia,* New York, 1945.

———, *The Tinguian,* Field Museum of Natural History Publications No. 209, Anthropological Series, Vol. XIV, No. 2, Chicago, 1922.

Cole, Mabel, *Savage Gentlemen,* New York, 1929.

Darlington, H. S., "The Meaning of Head Hunting," *The Psychoanalytic Review,* Vol. XXVI, No. 1, Albany, 1931.

Duyvendak, J., *Inleiding tot de ethnologie van de Indische Archipel,* Groningen, Batavia, 1935.

Evans, I. H. S., *The Religion of the Tempasuk Dusun,* Cambridge, 1953.

Geddes, W. R., *Nine Dyak Nights,* Oxford, 1957.

Gomez, Edwin H., *The Sea Dyaks of Borneo,* London, 1911.

Skeat, W. W., *Malay Magic,* London, 1900.

Winstead, Richard, *The Malay, a Cultural History,* New York, 1950.

CHAPTER 31

Seligman, Charles G., *The Veddas,* Cambridge, 1911.
Spittel, Richard L., *Wild Ceylon,* Colombo, 1924.

CHAPTER 32

Ashley Montagu, M. F., *Coming Into Being Among the Australian Aborigines,* London, 1937.
Basedow, Herbert, *Knights of the Boomerang,* Sydney, 1935.
———, *The Australian Aboriginal,* Adelaide, 1925.
Berndt, Ronald M., *Kunapipi,* New York, 1951.
———, and Catherine H., *Sexual Behavior in West Arnhem Land,* Viking Fund for Anthropology, No. 16, New York, 1951.
Dixon, Roland B., *Oceanic Myth* (*Mythology of All Races,* Vol. IX), Boston, 1916.
Elkin, Adolphus P., *Australian Men of High Degree,* Sydney, 1945.
———, *The Australian Aborigine,* London, 1938.
McCarthy, Frederick D., *Australian Aborigines,* Melbourne, 1957.
———, "The Oceanic and Indonesian Affiliations of Australian Aboriginal Culture," *Journal of the Polynesian Society,* Vol. 62, No. 3, Wellington, 1953.
Matthews, John, *Eagle Hawk and Crow,* London, 1899.
Porteus, Stanley B., *The Psychology of a Primitive People,* New York, 1931.
Roheim, Geza, *Australian Totemism,* London, 1925.
———, "Primitive High Gods," *Psychoanalytic Quarterly,* Vol. 3, No. 1, Pt. 1, New York, 1934.
———, "The Psychology of Primitive Cultural Types," *International Journal of Psychoanalysis,* Vol. XIII, 1932.
———, "Women and Their Life in Central Australia," *Journal of the Royal Anthropological Institute of Great Britain and Ireland,* Vol. 63, No. 1, London, 1933.
Spencer, Sir Baldwin, and Gillen, F. J., *The Native Tribes of Central Australia,* London, 1899.
Strehlow, T. G. H., "Ankotarinja, an Aranda Myth," *Oceania,* Vol. IV, No. 2, Melbourne, 1933.
Warner, William Lloyd, *A Black Civilization* (revised ed.), New York, 1958.

CHAPTER 33

Best, Elsdon, *The Maori,* Memoirs of the Polynesian Society, Vol. 5, Wellington, 1924.
Buck, Sir Peter, *Vikings of the Sunrise,* New York, 1938.
Duff, R., *The Moa-Hunter Period of Maori Culture,* Canterbury Museum Bulletin No. 1, Canterbury, 1950.
Firth, Raymond, *The Work of the Gods in Tikopia,* 2 vols., Monographs on Social Anthropology No. 1 and No. 2, London School of Economics and Political Science, London, 1940.
Gifford, E. W., "Tongan Society," Bernice P. Bishop Museum Bulletin No. 61, Honolulu, 1929.
Grey, Sir George, *Polynesian Mythology,* London, 1956.
Handy, E. S. Craighill, "Polynesian Religion," Bernice P. Bishop Museum Bulletin No. 34, Honolulu, 1927.
———, "The Native Culture in the Marquesas," Bernice P. Bishop Museum Bulletin No. 9, Honolulu, 1923.

Handy, E. S. Craighill, "The Society Islands," Bernice P. Bishop Museum Bulletin No. 79, Honolulu, 1923.

Linton, Ralph, *The Ethnology of Polynesia and Micronesia,* Memoirs of the Polynesian Society, Vol. 5, Wellington, 1924.

Lowie, Robert, *Primitive Religion,* New York, 1924.

Métraux, Alfred, "The Ethnology of Easter Island," Bernice P. Bishop Museum Bulletin No. 160, Honolulu, 1940.

Suggs, Robert C., *The Island Civilization of Polynesia* (Mentor), New York, 1960.

Williamson, Robert W., *Religion and Social Organization in Central Polynesia,* Cambridge, 1937.

———, *Religions and Cosmic Beliefs of Central Polynesia,* 2 vols., Cambridge, 1933.

CHAPTER 34

Bateson, Gregory, *Naven,* Cambridge, 1936.

Codrington, R. H., *The Melanesians,* New Haven, 1957.

Deacon, Arthur B., *Malekula,* London, 1934.

Fortune, Reo F., *Manus Religion,* Memoirs of the American Philosophical Society, Vol. III, Philadelphia, 1935.

———, *Sorcerers of Dobu,* London, 1932.

Haddon, Alfred C., "The Kabiri of the Girara District, Fly River, Papua," *Journal of the Royal Anthropological Institute of Great Britain and Ireland,* Vol. 46, London, 1916.

Krieger, Herbert W., *Island Peoples of the Western Pacific,* Smithsonian Institution War Background Studies, No. 16, Washington, 1943.

Landtman, Gunnar, *The Kiwai Papuans of British New Guinea,* London, 1927.

Layard, John, *Stone Men of Malekula,* London, 1942.

Lewis, Albert B., *Ethnology of Melanesia,* Field Museum of Natural History, Department of Anthropology, *Guide,* Pt. 5, Chicago, 1932.

Malinowski, Bronislaw, *Magic, Science and Religion* (Anchor), New York, 1948.

Mead, Margaret, *New Lives for Old,* New York, 1955.

———, "The Marsalai Cult," *Oceania,* Vol. IV, Melbourne, 1933.

———, *The Mountain Arapesh,* American Museum of Natural History Anthropological Papers, Vol. XXXVI, New York, 1938.

Oliver, Douglas, *A Solomon Island Society,* Cambridge, 1955.

Peekel, P. G., *Religion und Zauberei auf dem mittleren Neu-Mecklenburg, Bismarck Archipel, Südsee,* Münster, 1910.

Powdermaker, Hortense, *Life in Lesu,* New York, 1933.

Seligman, Charles G., *The Melanesian of British New Guinea,* Cambridge, 1910.

Van Baal, Jan, *Godsdienst en Zamenleving in Nederlansch Zuid-Zee-Nieuw-Guinea,* Amsterdam, 1934.

Williams, F. E., *Papuans of the Trans Fly,* Oxford, 1936.

Williamson, Robert W., *The Mafula Mountain People of British New Guinea,* London, 1912.

CHAPTER 35

Bogoras, Waldemar, *The Chukchee,* Memoirs of the American Museum of Natural History, Vol. XI, New York, 1904–1911.

Eliade, Mircea, *Schamanismus und archäische Ekstasietechnik,* Zurich, 1957.

Jochelson, Waldemar, *Peoples of Arctic Russia,* New York, 1928.

———, *The Koryak,* Memoirs of the American Museum of Natural History, Vol. X, New York, 1905–1908.

———, *The Yakut,* Anthropological Papers of the American Museum of Natural History, Vol. XXXIII, Pt. 2, New York, 1933.

———, *The Yukhagir,* Memoirs of the American Museum of Natural History, Vol. IX, New York, 1924–1926.

Lattimore, Owen, *The Gold Tribe "Fishskin Tatars" of the Lower Sungan,* The American Anthropological Association Memoirs, Vol. 40, Menasha, 1933.

Nioradze, Georg, *Der Schamanismus bei den Sibirischen Völkern,* Stuttgart, 1925.

Shirokogorov, S. M., *The Psychomental Complex of the Tungus,* London, 1935.

CHAPTER 36

Barker, Wayne, "Epilepsy" (unpublished paper).

Birdsell, Joseph C.,"The Problem of the Early Peopling of the Americas as Viewed from Asia," William Laughlin, ed., *Papers on the Physical Anthropology of the American Indian,* Viking Fund, New York, 1951.

Birket-Smith, Kaj, "The Caribou Eskimo," *Fifth Thule Expedition Report,* Vol. 5, Copenhagen, 1920.

———, *The Eskimos* (revised ed.), London, 1959.

Boas, Franz, "The Central Eskimo" (Extract from the 6th Annual Report of the American Bureau of Ethnology), Washington, 1888.

———, *The Eskimo of Baffin Land and Hudson's Bay,* American Museum of Natural History Anthropological Papers, Vol. XV, New York, 1901.

Bogoras, Waldemar, "Early Migrations of the Eskimo Between Asia and North America," *Twenty-first International Congress of Americanists, Report,* Göteborg, 1925.

Chard, Chester, "Old World Sources for Early Lithic Cultures," *Thirty-third International Congress of Americanists, Actas,* San José, 1959.

Freuchen, Peter, *Arctic Adventure,* New York, 1935.

Gjessing, Gutorm, "The Circumpolar Stone Age," *Acta Arctica,* II, Copenhagen, 1944.

Gladwin, Harold S., *Men Out of Asia,* New York, 1947.

Holm, G.,"Ethnographical Sketch of the Angmagsalik Eskimo," *The Ammassalik Eskimo,* ed. by William Thalbitzer, Part 1, No. I, Copenhagen, 1914.

Imbelloni, José, *La segunda esfinge indiana,* Buenos Aires, 1955.

Jenness, Diamond, *People of the Twilight (Copper Eskimo),* New York, 1959.

Kroeber, Alfred L., "The Eskimo of Smith Sound," Bulletin of the American Museum of Natural History, No. XII, Art. 21, New York, 1899.

Macgowan, Kenneth, *Early Man in America,* New York, 1950.

Rasmussen, Knud, "The Intellectual Culture of the Igulik Eskimo," *Fifth Thule Expedition Report,* Vol. VII, Copenhagen, 1929.

———, "The Mackensie Eskimo," *Fifth Thule Expedition Report,* Vol. X, Copenhagen, 1942.

Rivet, Paul, *Les origines de l'homme américain,* Paris, 1957.

Stephanson, Vilhjalmar, *Hunters of the Great North,* New York, 1922.

Thalbitzer, William, *The Ammassalik Eskimo,* Part 2, No. III and IV, Copenhagen, 1923.

Wormington, Hannah, *Ancient Man in America,* Denver, 1957.

CHAPTER 37

Barbeau, Marius, *Tsimshian Songs,* University of Washington Publications in Anthropology, Vol. 7, No. 3, Seattle, 1939.

Boas, Franz, *Ethnology of the Kwakiutl,* Bureau of American Ethnology, 35th Annual Report, Washington, 1913–1914.

Boas, Franz, *Kwakiutl Tales,* Columbia University Contributions to Anthropology, Vol. II, New York, 1910.

————, *Kwakiutl Texts,* Memoirs of the American Museum of Natural History, No. 10, New York, 1905.

————, *The Religion of the Kwakiutl Indians,* Columbia University Contributions to Anthropology, Vol. X, No. 2, New York, 1930.

————, *The Social Organization and Secret Societies of the Kwakiutl Indians,* Report of the United States National Museum, Washington, 1897.

————, *Tsimshian Texts,* Bureau of American Ethnology, Bulletin No. 27, Washington, 1902.

Bogoras, Waldemar, *The Folklore of Northeastern Asia as Compared with That of Northeastern America,* reprint from *The American Anthropologist,* Vol. 4, New York, 1902.

Codere, Helen, *Fighting with Property,* Monographs of the American Ethnological Society, XVIII, New York, 1950.

Drucker, Phillip, *Kwakiutl Dancing Societies,* University of California Publications in Anthropological Records, Vol. 2, No. 6, Berkeley, 1940.

————, *The Northern and Central Nootkan Tribes,* Bureau of American Ethnology, Bulletin No. 144, Washington, 1951.

Garfield, Viola, *The Tsimshian and Their Neighbors,* American Ethnological Society Publications, XVIII, New York, 1951.

————, *Tsimshian Clan and Society,* University of Washington Publications in Anthropology, Vol. 7, No. 3, Seattle, 1939.

Jenness, Diamond, *Indians of Canada,* National Museum of Canada Bulletin No. 65, Anthropological Series No. 15, Ottawa, 1960.

Krause, Aurel, *The Tlingit Indians,* tr. Erna Gunther (original edition, Jena, 1885), Seattle, 1956.

Müller, Werner, *Weltbild in Kult der Kwakiutl-Indianer,* Wiesbaden, 1955.

Olsen, Ronald, "Notes on the Bella Bella Kwakiutl," University of California Publications in Anthropological Records, No. 14, Part 5, Berkeley, 1955.

Swanton, John R., *Haida Texts,* Memoirs of the American Museum of Natural History, Vol. X, New York, 1905.

————, *Social Condition, Beliefs, and Linguistic of the Tlingit Indian,* Bureau of American Ethnology, 26th Annual Report, Washington, 1904–1905.

CHAPTER 38

Aginsky, Burt W. and Ethel G., *Deep Valley, a Presentation of the Pomo Indians,* University Microfilms Inc., Ann Arbor, 1958.

Benedict, Ruth, *The Concept of the Guardian Spirit in North America,* The American Anthropological Association Memoirs, No. 29, Menasha, 1923.

Boas, Franz, "The Mythology of Folk-tales of the North American Indians," *Journal of American Folklore,* Vol. XXVII, New York, 1914.

Dorsey, George, *The Mythology of the Wichita,* Washington, 1904.

Fenton, William, *An Outline of Seneca Ceremonies at Coldspring Longhouse,* Yale University Publications in Anthropology, No. 9, New Haven, 1936.

Fisher, Margaret, "Mythology of Northern and Northeastern Algonkians in Reference to Algonkian Mythology as a Whole," Robert Peabody Foundation for Archaeology, Papers, Vol. III, Andover, 1946.

Fletcher, Alice C., and LaFlesche, Francis, *The Omaha Tribe,* Bureau of American Ethnology, Annual Report No. 27, Washington, 1911.

Gessaim, Robert, "Le motif vagina dentata," *3rd Int. Congress Americanists, Proceedings,* Copenhagen, 1958.

Kroeber, Alfred L., "The Religion of the Indians of California," University of California Publications in American Archaeology and Ethnology, Vol. IV, No. 6, Berkeley, 1907.

Lowie, Robert H., *Indians of the Plains,* Handbook No. 1, American Museum of Natural History, New York, 1954.

———, "Societies of the Hidatsa and Mandan Indians," American Museum of Natural History Anthropological Papers, Vol. XI, Part 2, New York, 1913.

———, *The Crow Indians,* New York, 1925.

Morgan, Lewis, The League of the Iroquois, New York, 1901.

Müller, Werner, *Die Religionen der Waldlandindianer Nordamerikas,* Berlin, 1956.

Radin, Paul, "The Religion of the North American Indians," *Journal of American Folklore,* Vol. XXVII, New York, 1914.

———, *The Trickster,* London, 1956.

Skinner, Alanson, "Societies and Dances of the Blackfeet," American Museum of Natural History Anthropological Papers, Vol. XVI, Part 2, New York, 1921.

Speck, Frank, *Naskapi,* Norman, 1934.

Spier, Leslie, "The Sun Dance of the Plains Indians, Its Development and Diffusion," American Museum of Natural History Anthropological Papers, Vol. XVI, New York, 1921.

Wallis, W. D., "The Sun Dance of the Canadian Dakota," *ibid.,* Vol. XVI, New York, 1921.

Wissler, Clark, "Societies and Dances of the Blackfeet," *ibid.,* Vol. XI, Part 2, New York, 1913.

CHAPTER 39

Beaglehole, Ernest, "Hopi Hunting and Hunting Ritual," Yale Publications in Anthropology, No. 4, New Haven, 1936.

Benedict, Ruth, *Patterns of Culture* (Mentor), New York, 1948.

———, *Zuñi Mythology* (two vols.), Columbia University Contributions to Anthropology, Vol. XXI, New York, 1934.

Bunzel, Ruth, *An Introduction to Zuñi Ceremonialism,* Smithsonian Institution, Bureau of American Ethnology Annual Report No. 47, Washington, 1932.

Kluckhohn, Clyde, and Leighton, Dorothy, "An Introduction to Navaho Chant," The American Anthropological Association Memoirs, No. 53, Menasha, 1940.

———, *Navaho,* Cambridge, 1946.

Parsons, Elsie Clews, *Pueblo Indian Religion* (two vols.), Chicago, 1939.

Steward, Julian H., "The Ceremonial Buffoon of the American Indian," Michigan Academy of Sciences, Arts and Letters, *Journal,* Vol. XIV, Ann Arbor, 1931.

Schumaker, Wayne, *Literature and the Irrational,* New York, 1960.

Wormington, Hannah, *Prehistoric Indians of the Southwest,* Denver, 1951.

CHAPTER 40

Armillas, Pedro, "La serpiente emplumada," *Cuadernos Americanos,* VI, No. 1, Mexico, 1947.

———, "Los dioses de Teotihuacán," *Universidad Nacional de Cuyo, Anales del Instituto de etnología Americana,* Tomo VI, Mendoza, 1945.

———, "Teotihuacán, Tula y los toltecas," *Runa,* III, Buenos Aires, 1950.

Caso, Alfonso, *The Aztecs, People of the Sun,* Norman, 1958.

Coe, Michael, *Mexico,* New York, 1962.

Hvidtfeldt, Arild, *Teotl and Ixiptlatli,* Copenhagen, 1958.

Leon-Portilla, Miguel, *Los antiguos Mexicanos a través de sus cronicas y cantares,* Mexico, 1961.

Krickeberg, Walter, *Altmexikanische Kulturen,* Berlin, 1956.

Morley, Sylvanus, *The Ancient Maya,* 3rd ed., Stanford, 1936.

Popol Vuh, tr. Adrián Recinos, Mexico, 1947.

Peterson, Frederick, *Ancient Mexico,* New York, 1959.

Sahagún, Fray Bernardino de, *General History of the Things of New Spain,* tr. by Arthur J. O. Anderson and Charles E. Dibble, Santa Fe, 1950–1955.

Soustelle, Jacques, *La vie quotidienne des Aztèques,* Paris, 1955.

Spinden, Ellen, "The Place of Tajín in Totonac Archaeology and Anthropology," *American Anthropologist,* XXV, No. 2, Menasha, 1933.

Thompson, J. Eric S., *The Civilization of the Mayas,* Chicago, 1958.

——, *The Rise and Fall of the Maya Civilization,* Norman, 1954.

Valliant, G. C., *The Aztecs of Mexico* (Pelican), Harmondsworth, 1956.

CHAPTER 41

Bennett, Wendell C., "The Andean Highlands," Smithsonian Institution, Bureau of American Ethnology, Bulletin 143 (*Handbook of South American Indians*), Vol. II, Washington, 1947.

——, "The Archaeology of Colombia," *ibid.*

Cardich, Augusto, "Investigaciones prehistóricas en los Andes Peruanos," *Espacio y Tiempo,* Trabajados presentados a la semana de arqueología Peruana, 9–11 noviembre, 1959, Lima, 1960.

Carrión Cachot de Guirard, Rebeca, *La Cultura Chavín,* Lima, 1959.

——, *La religion en el antiguo Perú,* Lima, 1959.

——, "Revision del problema Chavín," *Twenty-ninth International Congress of Americanists, Selected Papers,* edited by Sol Tax, Chicago, 1957.

Collier, Donald, "The Archaeology of Ecuador," Smithsonian Institution, American Bureau of Ethnology, Bulletin 143, Vol. II, Washington, 1947.

Engel, Federico, "Datos con referencia al estudio de sitios prehistóricos en su texto morfológico y climato-lógico," *Espacio y Tiempo,* Lima, 1960.

Garcilaso de la Vega (el Inca), *Los comentarios reales,* etc., Lima, 1959.

Heine-Geldern, Robert, "Chinese Influences on Mexico and Central America," *Thirty-third International Congress of Americanists, Actas,* San José, 1959.

Hernández de Alba, Gregorio, "The Archaeology of San Augustín and Tierradentro, Colombia," Smithsonian Institution, Bureau of American Ethnology, Bulletin 143, Vol. II, Washington, 1947.

Jiménez Múñoz, Edith, "La representación símbolo del dios Sua; el dios sol entre los Chibcha," *Twenty-ninth International Congress of Americanists, Selected Papers,* edited by Sol Tax, Chicago, 1957.

Kroeber, Alfred L., "The Paracas Cavernas and Chavín," University of California Publications in Archaeology and Anthropology, Vol. 40, No. 8, Berkeley, 1953.

La Barre, Weston, *The Aymara,* The American Anthropological Association Memoirs, No. 68, Menasha, 1948.

Larco Hoyle, Rafael, *Los Mochicas* (two vols.), Lima, 1938.

——, "A Cultural Sequence for the North Coast of Peru," Smithsonian Institution, Bureau of American Ethnology, Bulletin No. 143, Vol. II, Washington, 1947.

Latcham, Richard E., "The Totemism of the Ancient Andean Peoples," *Journal of the Royal Anthropological Institute of Great Britain and Ireland,* Vol. 57, London, 1927.

Mason, J. Alden, *The Ancient Civilizations of Peru* (Pelican), Harmondsworth, 1957.

Métraux, Alfred, *Les Incas,* Paris, 1961.

Mishkin, Bernard, "The Aymara," Smithsonian Institution, Bureau of American Ethnology, Bulletin No. 143, Vol. II, Washington, 1947.

Molina de Cusco, Cristóbal de, *Relación de los fabulos yoritos de las Incas,* Lima, 1916.

Posnansky, Arthur, *Tiahuanaco, the Cradle of American Man* (2 vols.), New York, 1946.

Reiche, Maria, *Mystery in the Desert,* Lima, 1949.

Rowe, John Howland, "Inca Culture in the Time of the Spanish Conquest," Smithsonian Institution, Bureau of American Ethnology, Bulletin No. 143, Vol. II, Washington, 1947.

Tello, Julio C., *Chavín,* Vol. I, Lima, 1949.

———, *El uso de las cabezas artificialmente momificadas y sus representaciónes en el antiguo arte Peruana,* Lima, 1918.

———, "Vira Cocha," *Inca,* Vol. I, No. 1, Lima, 1923.

Willey, Gordon R., "The Chavín Problem," *Southwestern Journal of Anthropology,* Vol. 7, No. 2, Albuquerque, 1951.

CHAPTER 42

Longyear, John M., *The Archaeological Investigations in El Salvador,* The Peabody Museum of Archaeology and Ethnology, Harvard University, Memoirs, Vol. IX, No. 2, Cambridge, 1944.

Lothrop, Samuel K., *The Archaeology of Central Panamá,* The Peabody Museum of Archaeology and Ethnology, Harvard University, Memoirs, Vol. VII, Cambridge, 1937.

———, *The Archaeology of the Southern Veraguas, ibid.,* Vol. IX, No. 3, Cambridge, 1950.

———, *The Coclé,* Pt. II, The Peabody Museum of Archaeology and Ethnology, Harvard University, Memoirs, Vol. VIII, Cambridge, 1942.

———, *The Pottery of Costa Rica and Nicaragua,* Contributions of the Museum of the American Indian, Heye Foundation, Vol. VIII, New York, 1926.

Radin, Paul, *The Indians of South America,* New York, 1942.

Steward, Julian H., "The Circumcaribbean Tribes," Smithsonian Institution, Bureau of American Ethnology, Bulletin No. 143, Vol. IV, Washington.

CHAPTER 43

Gillen, John, "The Barima River Caribs," The Peabody Museum of Archaeology and Ethnology, Harvard University Papers, Vol. 14, No. 2, Cambridge, 1936.

Goldman, Irving, "Tribes of the Uaupe-Caqueta Region," Smithsonian Institution, Bureau of American Ethnology, Bulletin No. 143, Vol. III, Washington, 1948.

Koch-Grünberg, Theodor, *Vom Roima zum Amazon,* Vol. II, Berlin, 1916; Vol. III, Stuttgart, 1923.

Métraux, Alfred, *La religion des Tupinamba,* Paris, 1928.

———, *Les peaux-rouges de l'Amérique du Sud,* Paris, 1950.

Preuss, Konrad T., *Religion und Mythologie der Uitoto,* Leipzig, 1921.

Roth, Walter, *The Caribs,* Smithsonian Institution, Bureau of American Ethnology, 30th Annual Report, Washington, 1915.

Radin, Paul, *The Indians of South America,* New York, 1942.

Reik, Theodor, *Ritual: Psycho-analytic Studies,* tr. by Douglas Bryan, New York, 1958.

Staden, Hans, *The True History of His Captivity,* tr. Malcolm Letts, New York, 1929.

Steward, Julian H., "Culture Areas of the Tropical Forest," Smithsonian Institution, Bureau of American Ethnology, Bulletin No. 143, Vol. III, Washington, 1948.

Whiffen, Thomas, *The Northwest Amazon,* London, 1915.

CHAPTER 44

Bird, Junius, "The Alakaluf," Smithsonian Institution, Bureau of American Ethnology, Bulletin No. 143, Vol. I, Washington, 1946.

Cooper, John, "The South American Marginal Tribes," *8th American Scientific Congress, Proceedings,* Vol. II, Washington, 1942.

Gusinde, Martin, *Die Feuerland Indianer,* Vol. I, *Die Selk'nam,* Vienna, 1931; Vol. II, *Die Yamana,* Vienna, 1937.

Lothrop, Samuel K., *The Indians of Tierra del Fuego,* Contributions of the Museum of the American Indian, Heye Foundation, Vols. 10–11, New York, 1908.

Manizer, Henri H., "Les Botocudos d'après les observations receuillées pendant un séjour chez eux en 1915," *Museo do Rio do Janeiro, Archivos,* Vol. XXII, Rio, 1919.

Métraux, Alfred, *Les peaux-rouges de l'Amérique du Sud,* Paris, 1950.

———, "Myths of the Toba and Pilagá Indians of the Gran Chaco," American Folklore Society Memoirs, Vol. 40, Philadelphia, 1946.

Nimündajú, Kurt, "Social Organizations and Beliefs of the Botocudo of Eastern Brazil," *Southwestern Journal of Anthropology,* Vol. II, No. 2, University of New Mexico, Albuquerque, 1946.

———, *The Eastern Timbira,* University of California Publications in Archaeology and Ethnology, No. 41, Berkeley, 1946.

Radin, Paul, *The Indians of South America,* New York, 1942.

Index